SOMETHING ABOUT THE AUTHOR

SOMETHING ABOUT THE AUTHOR

Facts and Pictures about Authors
and Illustrators of Books for Young People

ANNE COMMIRE

VOLUME 22

GALE RESEARCH COMPANY
BOOK TOWER
DETROIT, MICHIGAN
48226

Editor: Anne Commire

Associate Editors: Agnes Garrett, Helga P. McCue

Assistant Editors: Dianne H. Anderson, Susette A. Balogh, Kathryn T. Floch,
Mary F. Glahn, D. Jayne Higo, Linda Shedd,
Susan L. Stetler, Victoria H. Welling

Sketchwriters: Deborah A. Beckwith, Rosemary DeAngelis Bridges,
Mark Eisman, Barbara G. Farnan

Research Assistant: Kathleen Betsko

Editorial Assistants: Lisa Bryon, Susan Pfanner, Elisa Ann Sawchuk

Production Supervisor: Nancy Nagy

Cover Design: Arthur Chartow

Special acknowledgment is due to the members of the *Contemporary Authors* staff
who assisted in the preparation of this volume.

Also Published by Gale

CONTEMPORARY AUTHORS

*A Bio-Bibliographical Guide to Current Writers in
Fiction, General Nonfiction, Poetry, Journalism,
Drama, Motion Pictures, Television,
and Other Fields*

(Now Covers More Than 60,000 Authors)

Table of Contents

Introduction

Beginning with Volume 15, the time span covered by *Something about the Author* was broadened to include major children's writers who died before 1961, which was the former cut-off point for writers covered in this series. This change will make *SATA* even more helpful to its many thousands of student and professional users.

Authors who did not come within the scope of *SATA* have formerly been included in *Yesterday's Authors of Books for Children,* of which Gale has published two volumes.

It has been pointed out by users, however, that it is inconvenient to have a body of related materials broken up by an arbitrary criterion such as the date of a person's death. Also, some libraries are not able to afford both series, and are therefore denied access to material on some of the most important writers in the juvenile field.

It has been decided, therefore, to discontinue the *YABC* series, and to include in *SATA* at least the most outstanding among the older writers who had been selected for listing in *YABC*. Volumes 1 and 2 of *YABC* will be kept in print, and the listings in those two volumes will be included in the cumulative *SATA* index.

A Partial List of Authors and Illustrators
Who Will Appear in Forthcoming Volumes of
Something about the Author

Adrian, Mary
Ahlberg, Allan
Ahlberg, Janet
Ainsworth, William H.
Allard, Harry
Allen, Agnes B.
Allen, Jack
Ashley, Bernard
Atwater, Richard
Ault, Phil
Ayme, Marcel
Bach, Alice H.
Baldwin, James
Ballantyne, Robert M.
Baskin, Leonard
Becker, May Lamberton
Bennett, Jay
Beim, Jerrold
Beim, Lorraine
Bell, Robert S. W.
Bernheim, Evelyne
Binzen, Bill
Blyton, Enid
Blos, Joan W.
Boegehold, Betty
Bolognese, Don
Boning, Richard A.
Bonsall, Crosby Barbara
Bowden, Joan C.
Bowman, James C.
Boylston, Helen
Branscum, Robbie
Brewton, Sara W.
Briggs, Raymond
Bright, Robert
Broger, Achim
Bronin, Andrew
Bronson, Wilfrid
Brookins, Dana
Brooks, Charlotte K.
Bruna, Dick
Brunhoff, Jean de
Brunhoff, Laurent de
Burchard, Marshall
Burgess, Gelett
Burkert, Nancy Ekholm
Burstein, Chaya
Butler, Hal
Carey, M. V.

Carigiet, Alois
Carrick, Malcolm
Carroll, Ruth R.
Chandler, Caroline Augusta
Chesterton, G. K.
Christopher, John
Clarke, Joan B.
Cleaver, Elizabeth
Clements, Bruce
Cohen, Joel H.
Cohen, Miriam
Colby, Jean Poindexter
Cole, Joanna
Collodi, Carlo
Cooper, Elizabeth Keyser
Cox, Palmer
Craik, Dinah M.
Crews, Donald
Dabcovich, Lydia
Danziger, Paula
Dasent, Sir George Webbe
Dauer, Rosamund
D'Aulnoy, Marie-Catherine
DeGoscinny, Rene
Delessert, Etienne
Disney, Walt
Ditmars, Raymond
Donovan, John
Doty, Jean Slaughter
Dumas, Philippe
Eaton, Jeanette
Eckert, Allan W.
Elwood, Roger
Erickson, Russell E.
Ernst, Kathryn F.
Erwin, Betty K.
Etter, Les
Everett-Green, Evelyn
Falkner, John Meade
Falls, C. B.
Farber, Norma
Farmer, Penelope
Fischer, Hans Erich
Forest, Antonia
Foster, Marian Curtis
Freeman, Barbara C.
Freschet, Berniece
Fujikawa, Gyo
Gackenbach, Dick

Gans, Roma
Gardam, Jane
Gardner, John C.
Gatty, Margaret
Gauch, Patricia L.
Gault, Clare
Gault, Frank
Gelman, Rita G.
Gemme, Leila Boyle
Giovanni, Nikki
Goble, Dorothy
Goble, Paul
Gorey, Edward St. John
Gould, Chester
Grabianski, Janusz
Greene, Ellin
Gregor, Arthur S.
Gridley, Marion E.
Gross, Ruth B.
Gruelle, Johnny
Gutman, Bill
Gwynne, Fred
Halacy, Daniel S., Jr.
Haley, Gail E.
Hale, Lucretia P.
Hayes, Geoffrey R.
Hazen, Barbara S.
Heide, Florence Parry
Hentoff, Nat
Henty, George Alfred
Hicks, Clifford B.
Highwater, Jamake
Hirshberg, Albert S.
Hood, Thomas
Housman, Laurence
Hughes, Ted
Hunt, Clara Whitehill
Ingelow, Jean
Isadora, Rachel
Jacobs, Joseph
Jacques, Robin
Jameson, Cynthia
Jeschke, Susan
Jewell, Nancy
Johnston, Norma
Jones, Hettie
Judson, Clara Ingram
Kahl, Virginia
Kahn, Joan

Kalan, Robert
Kantrowitz, Mildred
Keith, Eros
Kemp, Gene
Kent, Jack
Kerr, Judith
Kessler, Ethel
Ketcham, Hank
Klein, Aaron E.
Knotts, Howard
Koehn, Ilse
Kotzwinkle, William
Kraske, Robert
Leach, Maria
Leckie, Robert
Levoy, Myron
Levy, Elizabeth
Lewis, Naomi
Lines, Kathleen
Livermore, Elaine
Lowry, Lois
Lubin, Leonard
Macaulay, David
MacDonald, George
MacGregor, Ellen
MacKinstry, Elizabeth A.
Marryat, Frederick
Mazer, Norma Fox
McKee, David
McKillip, Patricia A.
McNaught, Harry
McPhail, David
Mendoza, George
Milgrom, Harry
Miller, Edna
Molesworth, Maria L.
Molly, Anne S.
Momaday, N. Scott
Moore, Lilian
Moore, Patrick
Morgenroth, Barbara
Moskin, Marietta
Murphy, Shirley Rousseau
Myers, Elisabeth P.
Myers, Walter Dean
Nordhoff, Charles
Oakley, Graham
O'Brien, Robert C.
O'Hanlon, Jacklyn
Orr, Frank
Orton, Helen Fuller
Overbeck, Cynthia

Packard, Edward
Peake, Mervyn
Pearson, Susan
Perkins, Lucy Fitch
Perrault, Charles
Plotz, Helen
Pogany, Willy
Pope, Elizabeth M.
Porter, Eleanor Hodgman
Poulsson, Emilie
Prather, Ray
Pursell, Margaret S.
Pursell, Thomas F.
Pyle, Katharine
Rae, Gwynedd
Raphael, Elaine
Rees, David
Reid, Mayne
Reynolds, Marjorie
Ribbons, Ian
Richler, Mordecai
Roberts, Elizabeth Madox
Rock, Gail
Rockwell, Anne
Rockwell, Harlow
Rockwell, Norman
Rose, Elizabeth
Rose, Gerald
Ross, Diana
Ross, Frank, Jr.
Ross, Wilda
Roy, Cal
Ruskin, John
Sabin, Francene
Sabin, Louis
Salten, Felix
Schick, Alice
Schneider, Leo
Schoonover, Frank
Seaman, Augusta
Sendak, Jack
Sewall, Marcia
Sewell, Anna
Sewell, Helen
Shapiro, Milton J.
Shearer, John
Silverstein, Shel
Simon, Hilda
Smith, Doris Buchanan
Steiner, Charlotte
Stevens, Leonard A.
Stevenson, James

Stong, Phil
Sutton, Felix
Tallon, Robert
Taylor, Ann
Taylor, Jane
Taylor, Mark
Tenniel, Sir John
Todd, Ruthven
Tomalin, Ruth
Tomes, Margot
Tripp, Wallace
Tunis, John R.
Turska, Krystyna
Van Iterson, S. R.
Varga, Judy
Villiard, Paul
Waber, Bernard
Wagner, Jenny
Walters, Hugh
Watson, Nancy D.
Watts, Franklin
Welber, Robert
Welles, Winifred
Wellman, Alice
Westall, Robert
Wild, Jocelyn
Wild, Robin
Wilde, Oscar
Willard, Nancy
William-Ellis, Amabel
Wilson, Gahan
Windsor, Patricia
Winn, Marie
Winterfeld, Henry
Wolde, Gunilla
Wolf, Bernard
Wolitzer, Hilma
Wong, Herbert H.
Wood, Phyllis Anderson
Wyss, Johann David
Yeoman, John
Yonge, Charlotte M.
Zei, Alki
Zollinger, Gulielma

In the interest of making *Something about the Author* as responsive as possible to the needs of its readers, the editor welcomes your suggestions for additional authors and illustrators to be included in the series.

GRATEFUL ACKNOWLEDGMENT

is made to the following publishers, authors, and artists, for their kind permission to reproduce copyrighted material.

ADDISON-WESLEY PUBLISHING CO., INC. Illustration by Jim Arnosky from *Nathaniel* by Jim Arnosky. Text copyright © 1978 by James Arnosky. Illustrations copyright © 1978 by James Arnosky. Reprinted by permission of Addison-Wesley Publishing Co., Inc.

ATHENEUM PUBLISHERS. Jacket illustration by Allen Davis from *A String in the Harp* by Nancy Bond. Copyright © 1976 by Nancy Bond./ Illustration by Margery Gill from *Requiem for a Princess* by Ruth M. Arthur. Illustrations copyright © by Margery Gill./ Illustration by Paul Sagsoorian from *The Monstrous Leathern Man* by Lou Hartman. Copyright © 1970 by Louis E. Hartman./ Illustration by Mary Rayner from *Mr. and Mrs. Pig's Evening Out* by Mary Rayner. Copyright © 1976 by Mary Rayner. All reprinted by permission of Atheneum Publishers.

AUGSBURG PUBLISHING HOUSE. Illustration by Jim Roberts from *Aaron's Christmas Donkey* by Lois Walfrid Johnson. Copyright © 1974 by Augsburg Publishing House./ Sidelight excerpts from *Either Way, I Win* by Lois Walfrid Johnson. Copyright © 1979 by Augsburg Publishing House. Both reprinted by permission of Augsburg Publishing House.

AVENEL BOOKS. Illustration by Walter Crane from *Household Stories* from the collection of the Brothers Grimm by Lucy Crane. Copyright © 1973 by Crown Publishers. Reprinted by permission of Avenel Books.

THE BODLEY HEAD. Illustration by Errol Lloyd from *Shawn's Red Bike* by Petronella Breinburg. Text copyright © 1975 by Petronella Breinburg. Illustrations copyright © 1975 by Errol Lloyd. Reprinted by permission of The Bodley Head.

BRADBURY PRESS, INC. Jacket illustration by George Thompson from *Secret Selves* by Judie Angell. Copyright © 1979 by Judie Angell Gaberman./ Illustration by Bernard Brett from *The Bushman's Dream: African Tales of the Creation* by Jenny Seed. Copyright © 1974 by Jenny Seed. Illustrations copyright © 1974 Bernard Brett./ Illustration by Errol le Cain from *Thorn Rose* by the Brothers Grimm. Text and illustrations copyright © 1975 by Errol le Cain. All reprinted by permission of Bradbury Press, Inc.

JONATHAN CAPE LTD. Sidelight excerpts and photographs from *The Autobiography of Arthur Ransome,* edited by Rupert Hart Davis./ Illustration by Arthur Ransome from *Peter Duck* by Arthur Ransome. All reprinted by permission of Jonathan Cape Ltd.

COLLECTORS EDITIONS LTD. Photograph from *George Cruikshank: A Catalogue Raisonné* by Albert M. Cohn. Reprinted by permission of Collectors Editions Ltd.

WILLIAM COLLINS PUBLISHERS, INC. Illustration by Jean O'Neill from *Fairy Tales* by the Brothers Grimm. Copyright 1947 by The World Publishing Co. Reprinted by permission of William Collins Publishers, Inc.

COLLIER-MACMILLAN PUBLISHERS (London). Illustration by Susan Wells from *Understanding Your Body* by Lawrence G. Blochman. Copyright © 1968 by Lawrence G. Blochman. Copyright © 1968 by the Macmillan Co. Reprinted by permission of Collier-Macmillan Publishers (London).

COWARD, McCANN & GEOGHEGAN, INC. Illustration by Joel Schick from *Farley, Are You for Real?* by Marjorie N. Allen and Carl Allen. Text copyright © 1976 by Marjorie and Carl Allen. Illustrations copyright © 1976 by Pongid Productions./ Illustration by Don Almquist from *Getting to Know New York State* by William B. Fink. Text copyright © 1971 by William B. Fink. Illustrations copyright © 1971 by Don Almquist./ Photograph from *Women*

by Margaret Gles. Copyright © 1975 by Margaret Gles. Reprinted by permission of Garrard Publishing Co.

DAVID R. GODINE PUBLISHER, INC. Sidelight excerpts from *The Caricature of George Cruikshank* by John Wardroper. Copyright © 1977 by John Wardroper. Reprinted by permission of David R. Godine Publisher, Inc.

GREENWILLOW BOOKS. Illustration by Lillian Hoban from *Stick-in-the-Mud Turtle* by Lillian Hoban. Copyright © 1977 by Lillian Hoban./ Photograph by Tana Hoban from *Big Ones, Little Ones* by Tana Hoban. Copyright © 1976 by Tana Hoban./ Photograph by Bruce McMillan from *The Alphabet Symphony: An ABC Book* by Bruce McMillan. Copyright © 1977 by Bruce A. McMillan./ Illustration by Marylin Hafner from *It's Halloween* by Jack Prelutsky. Text copyright © 1977 by Jack Prelutsky. Illustrations copyright © 1977 by Marylin Hafner./ Illustration by Marylin Hafner from *Jenny and the Tennis Nut* by Janet Schulman. Text copyright © 1978 by Janet Schulman. Illustrations copyright © 1978 by Marylin Hafner. All reprinted by permission of Greenwillow Books, division of William Morrow & Co., Inc.

GROSSET & DUNLAP, INC. Illustration by Fritz Kredel from *Grimm's Fairy Tales* by the Brothers Grimm. Copyright 1945 by Grosset & Dunlap, Inc. Reprinted by permission of Grosset & Dunlap, Inc.

GYLDENDAL PUBLISHERS. Illustration by Svend Otto from *Tom Thumb* by the Brothers Grimm, translated by Anthea Bell. Illustrations copyright © 1976 by Svend Otto. Reprinted by permission of Gyldendal Publishers.

HAMISH HAMILTON LTD. Illustration by Jim Spanfeller from *Where the Lilies Bloom* by Vera and Bill Cleaver. Copyright © 1969 by Vera and William J. Cleaver./ Picture by Uri Shulevitz from *The Fool of the World and the Flying Ship*, retold by Arthur Ransome. Pictures copyright © 1968 by Uri Shulevitz./ Illustration by Trevor Stubley from *Angry River* by Ruskin Bond. Copyright © 1972 by Ruskin Bond. Illustrations copyright © 1972 by Trevor Stubley. All reprinted by permission of Hamish Hamilton Ltd.

HAMLYN PUBLISHING GROUP LTD. Illustration by Jiří Trnka from "The Three Spinners" in *Grimm's Fairy Tales* by the Brothers Grimm. Copyright © 1961 by Artia. Reprinted by permission of Hamlyn Publishing Group Ltd.

HARCOURT BRACE JOVANOVICH, INC. Illustration by Harriet Pincus from *Little Red Riding Hood* by the Brothers Grimm. Copyright © 1968 by Harriet Pincus. Reprinted by permission of Harcourt Brace Jovanovich, Inc.

HARPER & ROW, PUBLISHERS, INC. Illustration by Fred Brenner from *Rutgers and the Water-Snouts* by Barbara Dana. Text copyright © 1969 by Barbara Dana. Illustrations copyright © 1969 by Fred Brenner./ Jacket illustration by Frank Schoonover from *Robinson Crusoe* by Daniel Defoe./ Illustration by Frank Schoonover from *Grimm's Fairy Tales* by the Brothers Grimm./ Illustration by Lillian Hoban from *A Birthday for Frances* by Russell Hoban. Illustrations copyright © 1968 by Lillian Hoban./ Jacket illustration by Charles Mikolaycak from *The Empty Chair* by Bess Kaplan. Copyright © 1975 by Queenston House./ Illustration by Marcia Sewall from *Come Again in the Spring* by Richard Kennedy. Text copyright © 1976 by Richard Kennedy. Illustrations copyright © 1976 by Marcia Sewall. All reprinted by permission of Harper & Row, Publishers, Inc.

GEORGE G. HARRAP & CO. LTD. Illustration by Joyce L. Brisley from *Peter Perkin's Puppets* by H. Waddingham Seers./ Illustration by Stephen Reid from *The Children's Robinson Crusoe* by Edith L. Elias. Both reprinted by permission of George G. Harrap & Co. Ltd.

HARVEY HOUSE, PUBLISHERS. Photograph from *Skateboards: How to Make Them, How to Ride Them* by Glenn and Eve Bunting. Copyright © 1977 by Harvey House, Publishers. Reprinted by permission of Harvey House, Publishers.

HASTINGS HOUSE, PUBLISHERS, INC. Illustration by Floyd James Torbert from *Fifth Inning Fade-Out* by C. Paul Jackson. Copyright © 1972 by Cook-Jackson, Inc. Reprinted by permission of Hastings House, Publishers, Inc.

HEARTLAND HOUSEBOOK. Illustration by Jim Baker from *Trains of Yesteryear* by Jim Baker. Copyright © 1973, 1975 by Jim Baker. Reprinted by permission of Heartland Housebook.

HERALD PRESS. Illustration by Ivan Moon from *The Outside World* by Lucy Ellen Bender. Copyright © 1969 by Herald Press. Reprinted by permission of Herald Press.

THE HERITAGE PRESS. Illustrations by Reginald Marsh from *The Fortunes and Misfortunes of the Famous Moll Flanders* by Daniel Defoe. Copyright 1942 by The Heritage Press. Reprinted by permission of The Heritage Press.

HOLIDAY HOUSE, INC. Illustration by Matthew Kalmenoff from *Weasels, Otters, Skunks and Their Family* by Dorothy Hinshaw Patent. Text copyright © 1973 by Dorothy Hinshaw Patent. Illustrations copyright © 1973 by Holiday House, Inc. Reprinted by permission of Holiday House, Inc.

HOLT, RINEHART & WINSTON. Illustration by James Heugh from *Rockets Through Space* by Lester del Rey. Copyright © 1957 by Lester del Rey. Reprinted by permission of Holt, Rinehart & Winston.

HOUGHTON MIFFLIN CO. Illustration by E. Boyd Smith from *The Life and Strange Surprising Adventures of Robinson Crusoe* by Daniel Defoe./ Illustration by Jane Flory from *It Was a Pretty Good Year* by Jane Flory. Copyright © 1977 by Jane Flory. Both reprinted by permission of Houghton Mifflin Co.

INDEPENDENCE PRESS. Illustration by Carolyn Ewing Bowser from *Happy Apple Told Me* by Audrey Penn Zellan. Copyright © 1975 by Audrey Penn Zellan./ Illustration by Alta Adkins from *Hannah's House* by Rhoda Wooldridge. Copyright © 1972 by Rhoda Wooldridge. Both reprinted by permission of Independence Press.

JALMAR PRESS, INC. Illustration by Regina Faul-Jansen from *T.A. for Teens (And Other Important People)* by Alvyn M. Freed. Copyright © 1976 by Alvyn M. Freed. Reprinted by permission of Jalmar Press, Inc.

LAROUSSE & CO., INC. Illustration by Svend Otto from *The Musicians of Bremen.* English translation copyright © 1974 by Anne Rogers. Illustrations copyright © 1974 by Svend Otto. Reprinted by permission of Larousse & Co., Inc.

CHARLES E. LAURIAT CO. Illustration by Sir John E. Millais from *The Small House at Allington* by Anthony Trollope./ Illustration by F. C. Tilney from *The Warden* by Anthony Trollope. Both reprinted by permission of Charles E. Lauriat Co.

LERNER PUBLICATIONS CO. Illustration by Sharon Lerner from *Butterflies are Beautiful* by Ruth F. Brin. Copyright © 1974 by Lerner Publications Co./ Illustration by L'Enc Matte from *The Girl Who Owned a City* by O. T. Nelson. Both reprinted by permission of Lerner Publications Co.

THE LIMITED EDITIONS CLUB. Illustration by Edward A. Wilson from *The Life and Strange Surprising Adventures of Robinson Crusoe* by Daniel Defoe. Reprinted by permission of The Limited Editions Club.

J. B. LIPPINCOTT CO. Illustration by Alan Baker from *Benjamin Bounces Back* by Alan Baker. Copyright © 1978 by Alan Baker./ Illustration by Jim Spanfeller from *Where the Lilies Bloom* by Vera and Bill Cleaver. Copyright © 1969 by Vera and William J. Cleaver./ Illustration by Ellen Raskin from *Lady Ellen Grae* by Vera and Bill Cleaver. Copyright © 1968 by Vera and William J. Cleaver./ Sidelight excerpts from *Defoe* by James Sutherland. Copyright 1938 by J. B. Lippincott Co./ Illustration by Arthur Ransome and Helene Carter from *Coot Club* by Arthur Ransome. Copyright 1935 by J. B. Lippincott Co./ Illustration by Mary E. Shepard from *Pigeon Post* by Arthur Ransome. Copyright 1937 by J. B. Lippincott Co./ Illustration by Helene Carter from *Swallowdale* by Arthur Ransome. Copyright 1932 by J. B. Lippincott./ Sidelight excerpts from *P. G. Wodehouse: A Portrait of a Master* by David A. Jasen. All reprinted by permission of J. B. Lippincott Co.

LIPPINCOTT & CROWELL, PUBLISHERS. Drawing by Romare Bearden from *Poems from Africa* by Samuel Allen. Copyright © 1973 by Samuel Allen. Illustrations copyright © 1973 by Romare Bearden./ Jacket illustration by Gail Owens from *Does Anybody Care About Lou Emma Miller?* by Alberta Wilson Constant. Copyright © 1979 by Alberta Wilson Constant./ Illustration by Ati Forberg from *Jeanne D'Arc* by Aileen Fisher. Copyright © 1970 by Aileen Fisher. Illustrations copyright © 1970 by Ati Forberg./ Illustration by Errol Lloyd from *Shawn's Red Bike* by Petronella Breinburg. Text copyright © 1975 by Petronella Breinburg. Illustrations © 1975 by Errol Lloyd./ Jacket illustration by Kinuko Craft from *The Ennead* by Jan Mark. Copyright © 1978 by Jan Mark./ Illustration by Earl Thollander from *Cesar Chavez* by Ruth Franchere. Copyright © 1970 by Ruth Franchere. Illustrations copyright © 1970 by Earl Thollander./ Illustration by John Wilson from *Becky* by Julia Wilson. Copyright © 1966 by Julia Wilson. Illustrations copyright © 1966 by John Wilson. All reprinted by permission of Lippincott & Crowell, Publishers.

LITTLE, BROWN AND CO. Illustration by Trina Schart Hyman from *Snow White* by the Brothers Grimm. Translation copyright © 1974 by Paul Heins. Illustrations copyright © 1974 by Trina Schart Hyman. Reprinted by permission of Little, Brown and Co.

MACMILLAN, INC. Etching by Nonny Hogrogian from *About Wise Men and Simpletons* by the Brothers Grimm. Translations copyright © 1971 by Elizabeth Shub. Copyright © 1971 Nonny Hogrogian./ Illustration by Lisl Weil from *Mindy* by Vicky Shiefman. Copyright © 1974 by Vicky Shiefman. Copyright © 1974 by Macmillan Publishing Co., Inc. Both reprinted by permission of Macmillan, Inc.

McGRAW-HILL, INC. Jacket illustration by Steve Daniels from *Investigating Science in the Swimming Pool and Ocean* by Norman D. Anderson. Copyright © 1978 by Norman D. Anderson./ Illustration by Paul Galdone from *The Frog Prince* by the Brothers Grimm. Illustrations copyright © 1975 by Paul Galdone. Both reprinted by permission of McGraw-Hill, Inc.

DAVID McKAY CO., INC. Decorations by Allan Thomas from *The Silver Wolf* by Merritt Parmelee Allen. Copyright 1951 by David McKay Co., Inc./ Illustration by N. C. Wyeth from *Robinson Crusoe* by Daniel Defoe. Both reprinted by permission of David McKay Co., Inc.

JULIAN MESSNER. Cartoon by Kevin Callahan from *Exploring with Metrics* by Gary G. Bitter and Thomas H. Metos. Text copyright © 1975 by Gary G. Bitter and Thomas H. Metos. Cartoon copyright © 1975 by Kevin Callahan./ Photograph by David Pickens from *Circle of Life: The Miccosukee Indian Way* by Nancy Henderson and Jane Dewey. Text copyright © 1974 by Nancy Henderson and Jane Dewey. Photographs copyright © 1974 by David Pickens. Both reprinted by permission of Julian Messner.

WILLIAM MORROW & CO., INC. Illustration by Lydia Rosier from *Lakes* by Delia Goetz. Text copyright © 1973 by Delia Goetz. Illustrations copyright © 1973 by Lydia Rosier./ Illustration by Miriam Schottland from *Maggie Flying Bird* by Marion Lawson. Copyright © 1974 by Marion Lawson./ Illustration by Gustav Schrotter from *Avalanche!* by A. Rutgers van der Loeff. Copyright © 1957 by A. Rutgers van der Loeff-Basenau. All reprinted by permission of William Morrow & Co., Inc.

W. W. NORTON & CO., INC. Photograph from *Hello Brazil* by David Bowen. Copyright © 1967 by David Bowen. Reprinted by permission of W. W. Norton & Co., Inc.

OXFORD UNIVERSITY PRESS, INC. Illustration by Clare Bice from *Thunder in the Mountains: Legends of Canada* by Hilda Mary Hooke./ Illustration by Charles Mozley from *The Duke's Children* by Anthony Trollope. Copyright © 1973 by Oxford University Press, Inc. Both reprinted by permission of Oxford University Press, Inc.

PANTHEON BOOKS, INC. Illustration by Josef Scharl from "The Devil's Sooty Brother" in *The Complete Grimm's Fairy Tales* by the Brothers Grimm. Copyright © 1972 by Random House. Reprinted by permission of Pantheon Books, Inc.

PELICAN PUBLISHING CO., INC. Illustration by James Rice from *Cajun Alphabet* by James Rice. Copyright © 1976 by James Rice. Reprinted by permission of Pelican Publishing Co., Inc.

PENGUIN PUBLISHING CO., INC. Illustration from *The Collecting Book* by Ellen and Lewis Liman. Reprinted by permission of Penguin Books.

PRAEGER PUBLISHERS. Sidelight excerpts from *The Brothers Grimm* by Ruth Michaelis-Jena. Copyright © 1970 by Ruth Michaelis-Jena. Reprinted by permission of Praeger Publishers.

PRENTICE-HALL, INC. Sidelight excerpts from *Fabre, Poet of Science* by Dr. G. V. Legros./ Illustration by John Kaufmann from *Old Abe: The Eagle Hero* by Patrick Young. Copyright © 1965 by Prentice-Hall, Inc. Both reprinted by permission of Prentice-Hall, Inc.

PRIME PRESS. Sidelight excerpts from introduction to *". . .And Some Were Human* by Lester del Rey. Reprinted by permission of Prime Press.

PUFFIN BOOKS. Illustrations by George Cruikshank from *Grimm's Fairy Tales* by the Brothers Grimm. Reprinted by permission of Puffin Books, division of Penguin Books, Inc.

G. P. PUTNAM'S SONS. Illustration by Charles Howes from *Knights and Daze* by F. Emerson Andrews. Copyright © 1966 by F. Emerson Andrews./ Illustration by George Cruikshank from *The Cruikshank Fairy-Book.*/ Illustration by Lee J. Ames from *Emma Edmonds: Nurse and Spy* by Marian Talmadge and Iris Gilmore. Copyright © 1970 by Marian Talmadge and Iris Gilmore./ Illustration by Ruth Kirschner from *Biography of a River Otter* by

Lorle Harris. Text copyright © 1978 by Lorle Harris. Illustrations copyright © 1978 by Ruth Kirschner./ Illustration by W. B. Park from *Jonathan's Friends* by W. B. Park. Copyright © 1977 by W. B. Park. All reprinted by permission of G. P Putnam's Sons.

RAINTREE PUBLISHERS GROUP. Illustration from *Let's Play Cards* by John Belton and Joella Cramblit. Copyright © 1975 by Advanced Learning Concepts, Inc. Reprinted by permission of Raintree Publishers Group.

RANDOM HOUSE, INC. Drawing by Daniel Carter Beard from *200 Years of American Illustration* by Henry C. Pitz. Copyright © 1977 by Edward Booth-Clibborn./ Illustration by Susan Swan from *The Pop-Up Book of Trains,* paper engineering by Ib Penick. Copyright © 1976 under the International Union for the Protection of Literary and Artistic Works. Both reprinted by permission of Random House, Inc.

REGENSTEINER PUBLISHING ENTERPRISES, INC. Photographs from *Algonquin Indians at Summer Camp* by June Behrens and Pauline Brower. Copyright © 1977 by Regensteiner Publishing Enterprises, Inc. Reprinted by permission of Regensteiner Publishing Enterprises, Inc.

REILLY & LEE CO. Woodcut by Robert Borja from *Siege Hero* by Dorothy Rossen Greenberg. Copyright © 1965 by Reilly & Lee Co. Reprinted by permission of Reilly & Lee Co., division of Henry Regnery Co.

SCHOCKEN BOOKS, INC. Illustration by Mervyn Peake from *Household Tales* by the Brothers Grimm. Text adaptation copyright © 1973 by Methuen Children's Books Ltd. Illustrations copyright 1946 under the Berne Convention by Mervyn Peake. Copyright © 1973 by Maeve Peake. Reprinted by permission of Schocken Books, Inc.

SCHOLASTIC BOOK SERVICES. Illustration by Tom Eaton from *The Organized Week* by Tom Eaton. Copyright © 1976 by Scholastic Magazine, Inc./ Illustration by Lisl Weil from *The Little Store on the Corner* by Alice P. Miller. Text copyright © 1961, 1973 by Alice P. Miller. Illustrations copyright © 1973 by Lisl Weil./ Illustration by Stan Tusan from *Giggly-Wiggly, Snickety-Snick* by Robyn Supraner. Text copyright © 1978 by Robyn Supraner. Illustrations copyright © 1978 by Stan Tusan. All reprinted by permission of Scholastic Book Services.

CHARLES SCRIBNER'S SONS. Illustration by D. C. Beard from *Shelters, Shacks and Shanties* by D. C. Beard. Copyright 1914, © 1922 by Charles Scribner's Sons./ Illustration by Adrienne Adams from *Hansel and Gretel* by the Brothers Grimm. Text copyright © 1975 by Charles Scribner's Sons. Illustrations copyright © 1975 by Adrienne Adams. Both reprinted by permission of Charles Scribner's Sons.

THE SEABURY PRESS, INC. Illustration by Nancy Winslow Parker from *Warm as Wool, Cool as Cotton* by Carter Houck. Text copyright © 1975 by Carter Houck. Illustrations copyright © 1975 by Nancy Winslow Parker. Reprinted by permission of The Seabury Press, Inc.

SIMON & SCHUSTER, INC. Sidelight excerpts from *Author! Author!* by P. G. Wodehouse. Copyright 1953 by P. G. Wodehouse. Reprinted by permission of Simon & Schuster, Inc.

UNIVERSITY OF CHICAGO PRESS. Sidelight excerpts from *Daniel Defoe, Citizen of the Modern World* by John Robert Moore. Reprinted by permission of the University of Chicago Press.

VANGUARD PRESS, INC. Illustration by Lino S. Lipinsky from *The Ghost of Peg-Leg Peter, and Other Stories of Old New York* by M. A. Jagendorf. Copyright © 1965 by M. A. Jagendorf. Reprinted by permission of the Vanguard Press, Inc.

DAVID WHITE, INC. Illustration by Harold Berson from *Folktales of the Irish Countryside* by Kevin Danaher. Text copyright © 1970 by Kevin Danaher. Illustrations copyright © 1970 by Harold Berson. Reprinted by permission of David White, Inc.

ALBERT WHITMAN & CO. Illustration by Lois Axeman from *Mine, Yours, Ours* by Burton Albert, Jr. Text copyright © 1977 by Burton Albert, Jr. Illustrations copyright © 1977 by Lois Axeman. Reprinted by permission of Albert Whitman & Co.

WHITTLESEY HOUSE. Illustration by Wesley Dennis from *Mighty Mo: The Story of an African Elephant* by Jocelyn Arundel. Copyright © 1961 by Jocelyn Arundel and Wesley Dennis./ Illustration by W. N. Wilson from *The War Between the States* by Eric Wollencott Barnes. Copyright © 1959 by Eric Wollencott Barnes and W. N. Wilson. Both reprinted by permission of Whittlesey House.

WORLD'S WORK LTD. Illustration by Ferelith Eccles Williams from *The Oxford Ox's*

Alphabet by Ferelith Eccles Williams. Text and illustrations copyright © 1977 by Ferelith Eccles Williams. Reprinted by permission of World's Work Ltd., division of William Heinemann Ltd.

THE WRITER, INC. Sidelight excerpts from an article "Fiction Techniques in Nonfiction Writing," December, 1971, in *The Writer*. Copyright © 1971 by The Writer, Inc. Reprinted by permission of The Writer, Inc.

YOUNG SCOTT BOOKS. Illustration by Honoré Guilbeau from *Who Goes There In My Garden?* by Ethel Collier. Copyright © 1963 by Ethel Collier. Illustrations copyright © 1963 by Honoré Guilbeau. Reprinted by permission of Young Scott Books.

Illustration by Joseph M. Sedacca from *The Story of Cosmic Rays* by Germaine and Arthur Beiser. Copyright © 1962 by Germaine and Arthur Beiser. Reprinted by permission of Georges Borchardt, Inc./ Photograph from *The Story of Oceanography* by Robert E. Boyer. Copyright © 1975 by Robert E. Boyer. Reprinted by permission of Mr. Robert Boyer./ Illustration by Margery Gill from *Requiem for a Princess* by Ruth M. Arthur. Illustrations copyright by Margery Gill. Reprinted by permission of Curtis Brown Ltd./ Photograph from *George Cruikshank: A Catalogue Raisonné* by Albert M. Cohn. Reprinted by permission of Collectors Editions Ltd./ Illustration by Arthur Ransome from *Peter Duck* by Arthur Ransome. Reprinted by permission of The Arthur Ransome Estate./ Illustration by Arthur Rackham from "Rapunzel" in *Grimm's Fairy Tales*, translated by Mrs. Edgar Lucas. Reprinted by the kind permission of Mrs. Barbara Edwards./ Illustrations by Arthur Rackham from "Snow-drop" and "The Seven Ravens" in *Fairy Tales of the Brothers Grimm*, translated by Mrs. Edgar Lucas. Reprinted by the kind permission of Mrs. Barbara Edwards./ Sidelight excerpts from an article "Jacob Abbott: A Goodly Heritage" in *The Hewing Lectures, 1947-1962* by Lysla I. Abbott. Copyright © 1963 by The Horn Book, Inc. Reprinted by permission of Mrs. Robert W. Hellum./ Sidelight excerpts from an article "Introducing Illustrators: Margery Gill" by Judy Taylor, October, 1966, in *Junior Bookshelf*. Copyright © 1966. Reprinted by permission of the *Junior Bookshelf*./ Illustration by Mervyn Peake from "The Nose-Tree" in *Household Tales* by the Brothers Grimm. Illustration copyright 1946 under the Berne Convention by Mervyn Peake. Copyright © 1973 by Maeve Peake. Text adaptation copyright © 1973 by Methuen Children's Books Ltd. Reprinted by permission of Maurice Michael. Theatre still from an early theatre production of "Snow White and the Seven Dwarfs." Reprinted by permission of the Performing Arts Research Center of the New York Public Library at Lincoln Center. Illustration by Paul Galdone from *Full Moon* by P. G. Wodehouse. Reprinted by permission of Scott Meredith Literary Agency./ Illustration by Leonard Kessler from *The Sukkah and the Big Wind* by Lily Edelman. Copyright 1956 by United Synagogue of America. Reprinted by permission of United Synagogue Commission on Jewish Education.

PHOTOGRAPH CREDITS

Marjorie Allen: Olan Mills; Mildred Ames: Wiener; F. Emerson Andrews: Fabian Bachrach; Eric W. Barnes: Van Vliet Studio; Bernard Brett: Colin G. Futcher; Joseph Cottler: Vogue Studios; Noel B. Gerson: James Brennan; Tana Hoban: Edward Gallob; Joseph M. Joseph: Lewis Studio; Bess Kaplan: Towne Studios, Ltd.; Irene Lieblich: Alexander Archer; Errol Lloyd: Vanessa Stamford; Guy L. Luttrell: Alan Forrest; Helen MacInnes: Gilbert Highet; Alice P. Miller: Rappoport Studios; Wilson Rawls: Bacon (Idaho); Virginia Schone: Dan Levin; Trevor Stubley: Ken Dawson; P. G. Wodehouse: Jill Krementz; Rhoda Wooldridge: Universal Studio..

SOMETHING ABOUT THE AUTHOR

JACOB ABBOTT

ABBOTT, Jacob 1803-1879

PERSONAL: Surname originally spelled Abbot; Jacob and brother John, the biographer and historian, added the extra "t" while in college; born November 14, 1803, in Hallowell, Maine; died October 31, 1879, in Farmington, Maine; son of Jacob II and Betsey (Abbot) Abbot; married Harriet Vaughan, 1828 (died, 1843); married Mary (Dana) Woodbury, 1853 (died, 1866); children: (first marriage) six children, including Lyman Abbott, theologian and editor of *Outlook. Education:* Attended Bowdoin College, graduated at age 17; studied for the Congregational ministry at Andover Theological Seminary. *Religion:* Puritan. *Home:* Farmington, Maine.

CAREER: Author of books for children, educator, and clergyman. Taught for a year at Portland Academy (where Henry Wadsworth Longfellow was one of his pupils); appointed tutor, and at age 21, professor of mathematics and natural philosophy at Amherst College, Amherst, Mass.; organized and conducted the Mt. Vernon School for Girls in Boston, where he experimented with his own theories of education, 1829-33; with his three brothers, he started the Abbott School for Girls in New York (where Helen Hunt Jackson was among the pupils), and served as its president, 1843-51. Minister and co-founder of the Eliot Congregational Church, Roxbury, Mass., beginning 1833.

WRITINGS—Fiction; "Rollo" series, 36 books, published by Sheldon, beginning 1834: *Rollo Learning to Talk; . . . Learning to Read; . . . at Work; . . . at Play; . . . at School; . . . on the Atlantic,* circa 1858; *. . . in Paris; . . . in Switzerland; . . . in London; . . . on the Rhine; . . . in Scotland;*

Phonny had no knife to cut the cord, and he was obliged to gnaw it off with his teeth. This took some time. ■ (From *Caroline* by Jacob Abbott. Illustrated by W. Roberts.)

. . . in Geneva; . . . in Holland; . . . in Naples; . . . in Rome; . . . in the Woods; Rollo's Vacation, reissued, 1969; *. . . Experiments; . . . Museum; . . . Travels; . . . Correspondence; . . . Philosophy: Air; . . . Philosophy: Water; . . . Philosophy: Fire; . . . Philosophy: Sky; . . . Garden; Trouble on the Mountain; Causey Building; Apple Gathering; Two Wheel-Barrows; Blueberrying; The Freshet; Georgie; The Steeple Trip; Labor Lost; Lucy's Visit.*

"Jonas" series, six books, published by Clark & Maynard, 1839: *Jonas Stories; Jonas, a Judge; Jonas on a Farm, Winter; Jonas on a Farm in Summer; Caleb in Town; Caleb in the Country.*

"Cousin Lucy" series, six books, published by Clark & Maynard, circa 1841: *Cousin Lucy's Stories; . . . Conversations; . . . Studies; Cousin Lucy at Play; . . . on the Seashore; . . . among the Mountains.*

Marco Paul's Voyages and Travels in Pursuit of Knowledge, Harper, circa 1843, Volume I: *Marco Paul in New York*, Volume II: *. . . on the Erie Canal*, Volume III: *. . . in Maine*, Volume IV: *. . . in Vermont*, Volume V: *. . . in Boston*, Volume VI: *. . . at the Springfield Armory.*

The Franconia Stories, Harper, Volume I: *Malleville*, 1850, Volume II: *Wallace*, 1850, Volume III: *Mary Erskine*, 1850, Volume IV: *Mary Bell*, 1850, Volume V: *Beechnut*, 1850, Volume VI: *Rodolphus*, 1852, Volume VII: *Ellen Linn*, 1852, Volume VIII: *Stuyvesant*, 1881, Volume IX: *Caroline*, 1853, Volume X: *Agnes*, 1881.

"Harper's Story Books" series, published by Harper, beginning 1855-56: *Bruno; or, Lessons of Fidelity, Patience, and Self-Denial Taught by a Dog; Willie and the Mortgage, Showing How Much May be Accomplished by a Boy; The Strait Gate; or, The Rule of Exclusion from Heaven; The Little Louvre; or, The Boys' and Girls' Gallery of Pictures; Prank; Emma; or, The Three Misfortunes of a Belle; Virginia;*

or, A Little Light on a Very Dark Saying; Timboo and Joliba; or, The Art of Being Useful; Timboo and Fanny; or, The Art of Self-Instruction; The Harper Establishment; or, How the Story Books Are Made, reprinted, Shoe String Press, 1956; *Franklin, the Apprentice Boy; The Studio; or, Illustrations of the Theory and Practice of Drawing, for Young Artists at Home; The Story of Ancient History, from the Earliest Periods to the Fall of the Roman Empire; The Story of English History; The Story of American History, from the Earliest Settlement of the Country to the Establishment of the Federal Constitution; John True; or, The Christian Experience of an Honest Boy; Elfred; or, The Blind Boy and His Pictures; The Museum; or, Curiosities Explained; The Engineer; or, How to Travel in the Woods; Rambles among the Alps; Three Gold Dollars; or, An Account of the Adventures of Robin Green; The Gibraltar Gallery: Being an Account of Various Things Both Curious and Useful; The Alcove; Containing Some Further Account of Timboo, Mark, and Fanny; Dialogues for the Amusement and Instruction of Young Persons; The Great Elm; or, Robin Green and Josiah Lane at School; Aunt Margaret; or, How John Kept His Resolutions; Vernon; Carl and Jocko; or, The Adventures of the Little Italian Boy and His Monkey; Lapstone; or, The Sailor Turned Shoemaker; Orkney the Peacemaker; or, The Various Ways of Settling Disputes; Judge Justin; or, The Little Court of Morningdale; Minigo; or, The Fairy of Cairnstone Abbey; Jasper; or, The Spoiled Child Recovered; Congo; or, Jasper's Experience in Command; Viola and Her Little Brother Arno; Little Paul; or, How to be Patient in Sickness and Pain.*

The Florence Stories, Sheldon, Volume I: *Florence and John*, 1859(?), Volume II: *Grimkie*, 1860, Volume III: *The Orkney Islands*, 1861, Volume IV: *The English Channel*, 1863, Volume V: *The Isle of Wight*, 1864; *Harlie Stories*, Sheldon, 1863, Volume I: *The New Shoes; or, Productive Work by Little Hands*, Volume II: *The French Flower; or, Be Kind and Obliging to Your Teacher*, Volume III: *Harlie's Letter; or, How to Learn with Little Teaching*, Volume IV: *Wild Peggie; or, Charity with Discretion*, Volume V: *The Seashore; or, How to Plan Picnics and Excursions*, Volume VI: *Friskie, the Pony; or, Do No Harm to Harmless Animals.*

"The Gay Family" series, 12 books, published by Hurd & Houghton, circa 1865: *John Gay; or, Work for Boys, Autumn; . . . Spring; . . . Summer; . . . Winter; William Gay; or, Play for Boys, Autumn; . . . Spring; . . . Summer*, 1869; *. . . Winter*, 1869; *Mary Gay; or Work for Girls, Autumn; . . . Spring; . . . Summer*, 1866; *. . . Winter; Juno Stories*, Dodd, Volume I: *Juno and Georgie*, 1870, Volume II: *Mary Osborne*, 1870, Volume III: *Juno on a Journey*, 1870, Volume IV: *Hubert*, 1870; *August Stories*, Dodd, 1871-72, Volume I: *August and Elvie*, Volume II: *Hunter and Tom*, Volume III: *Schooner Mary Ann*, Volume IV: *Grandville Valley; Stories of Rainbow and Lucky*, Harper, 1887-88, Volume I: *Handie*, Volume II: *Rainbow's Journey;* Volume III: *The Three Pines*, Volume IV: *Selling Lucky*, Volume V: *Up the River.*

Nonfiction: *Lecture on Moral Education* (delivered in Boston before the American Institute of Instruction, August 26, 1831), Hilliard, Gray, 1831; "Young Christian" series, four books, published by Harper, beginning 1832: *The Young Christian; or, A Familiar Illustration of the Principles of Christian Duty, The Cornerstone; or, A Familiar Illustration of the Principles of Christian Truth, The Way to Do Good; or, The Christian Character Mature, Hoaryhead and M'Donner; The Teacher; or, Moral Influences Employed in the Instruction and Government of the Young*, Peirce & Parker, 1833; *The Duties of Parents in Regard to the Schools Where Their Children Are Instructed* (lecture delivered before the American Institute of Instruction), Tuttle & Weeks, 1834; *Fireside Piety; or, The Duties and Enjoyments of Family Religion*, Leavitt, Lord, 1834; *The Way for a Child to Be Saved*, Leavitt, Lord, 1835; *China and the English; or, The Character and Manners of the Chinese*, Leavitt, Lord, 1835; *New England and Her Institutions*, J. Allan, 1835; (compiler, with brother, Charles Edward Abbott) *The Mount Vernon Reader: A Course of Lessons Designed for Junior Classes*, T. H. Carter, 1838; (compiler, with C. E. Abbott) *The Mount Vernon Reader: A Course of Lessons Designed for Senior Classes*, W. Crosby, 1840; *The Rollo Code of Morals; or, The Rules of Duty for Children*, Crocker & Brewster, 1841; (with C. E. Abbott) *The Mount Vernon Arithmetic*, Saxton & Miles, 1846-47; *A Summer in Scotland*, Harper, 1848; *An Alphabet of Quadrupeds*, Grambo & Co., 1852.

Biographical Histories, Harper, circa 1849, Volume I: *History of Cyrus the Great*, Volume II: *. . . Darius the Great*, Volume III: *. . . Xerxes the Great*, Volume IV: *. . . Alexander the Great*, Volume V: *. . . Romulus*, Volume VI: *. . . Hannibal the Carthaginian*, 1876, Volume VII: *. . . Pyrrhus*, Volume VIII: *. . . Julius Caesar*, Volume IX: *. . . Cleopatra, Queen of Egypt*, Volume X: *. . . Nero*, Volume XI: *. . . King Alfred of England*, Volume XII: *. . . William the Conqueror*, Volume XIII: *. . . King Richard the First of England*, Volume XIV: *. . . King Richard the Second of England*, Volume XV: *. . . King Richard the Third of England*, Volume XVI: *. . . Margaret of Anjou, Queen of Henry VI of England*, Volume XVII: *. . . Mary, Queen of Scots*, Volume XVIII: *. . . Queen Elizabeth*, reprinted, Scholarly Press, 1976, Volume XIX: *. . . King Charles the First of England*, Volume XX: *. . . King Charles the Second of England*, Volume XXI: *. . . Hernando Cortez*, Volume XXII: *. . . Henry IV of England*, Volume XXIII: *. . . Louis XIV of France*, Volume XXIV: *. . . Marie Antoinette*, Volume XXV: *. . . Madam Roland*, Volume XXVI: *. . . Josephine*, Volume XXVII: *. . . Joseph Bonaparte*, Volume XXVIII: *. . . Hortense*, Volume XXIX: *. . . Louis Philippe*, Volume XXX: *. . . Genghis Khan*, Volume XXXI: *. . . Peter the Great, Emperor of Russia*, reprinted, Scholarly Press, 1976, Volume XXXII: *. . . King Philip*.

(With brother, John Abbott) *Abbott's First Reader: A Course of Reading Lessons Designed for Junior Classes*, T. Allman, 1853; (with John Abbott) *Abbott's Second Reader: A Course of Reading Lessons Designed for Middle Classes*, T. Allman, 1853; "Little Learner" series, five books, published by Harper, circa 1855: *Learning to Talk; or, Entertaining and Instructive Lessons in the Use of Language; . . . To Think; or, Easy and Entertaining Lessons Designed to Assist the Unfolding of Reflective and Reasoning Powers of Children; . . . To Read; or, Easy and Entertaining Lessons Designed to Interest and Assist Young Children in Studying the Forms of the Letters and in Beginning to Read; . . . About Common Things; or, Familiar Instructions for Children in Respect to the Objects around Them; . . . About Right and Wrong; or, Entertaining and Instructive Lessons for Young Children in Respect to Their Duty.*

"American History" series, eight books, published by Sheldon, circa 1860: *Discovery of America; The Northern Colonies; Revolt of the Colonies; The Southern Colonies; Visit to the Mountains; War of the Revolution; Wars of the Colonies; Washington;* "Science for the Young" series, four books, published by Harper: *Heat*, 1871; *Light*, 1871; *Water and Land*, 1872; *Force*, 1873; *Gentle Measures in the Management and Training of the Young*, Harper, 1872; *A Primer of Ethics*, edited by Benjamin B. Comegys, Ginn, 1891.

MARY BELL AND THE FLOWERS.

Mary Bell looked at Wallace and smiled, and then said to the children, "Come, the boat has gone by, let us walk along." ■ (From *Wallace* by Jacob Abbott. Illustrated by W. Roberts.)

Poetry; "Rollo and Lucy Books of Poetry," published by Dodd, circa 1863: *The Rollo and Lucy First Book of Poetry; Carlo; or, The Rollo and Lucy Second Book of Poetry; The Canary Bird; or, The Rollo and Lucy Third Book of Poetry.*

SIDELIGHTS: **November 14, 1803.** Born in Hallowell, Maine into a religious and conservative Puritan family. Years later brother, John Abbott, described his father's training in his memoir: "My parents and grandparents belonged to the strictest class of Christians. My father never omitted morning and evening prayers, or to ask a blessing and return thanks at each meal. We knew that our mother had a season each day in which she retired to her closet and shut the door that she might 'in secret pray for each child by name. . . .' Sabbath evening mother gathered us seven children around her knee. We then recited to her the Catechism, and each one repeated a hymn from Watts or some other poet, which she had selected for us in the morning. . . . We children all knew that both father and mother would rather we would struggle all our days with adversity, and be Christians, than to have all the honors of genius, and all the wealth of millionaires lavished upon us, without piety. . . . We loved those Puritan parents with a fervor that could hardly be surpassed." [Lysla I. Abbot, "Jacob Abbott: A Goodly Heritage," *The Hewing Lectures 1947-1962*, Horn Book, 1963.[1]]

1817. Entered Bowdoin College. While in college he and his brother, John, added an extra "t" to their family name, Abbott. "Besides the distinction of having my name take precedence of all my classmates, on the next catalogue that was printed, I gained by my admission to college another distinction, namely, that of becoming entitled to a traditional nickname. . . . It had been the custom in college, for many classes previous to mine, to give the youngest student the ridiculous name of Putt."[1]

If there were any people in the street of the village when we went through, they had to back up against the wall when we passed them, to prevent being knocked down. ■ (From *Rollo in Geneva* by Jacob Abbott. Illustrated by John Andrew.)

1820. Graduated from Bowdoin at the age of seventeen.

1820-1824. Taught at Portland, Maine Academy and Beverly, Massachusetts while continuing his study of theology at Andover Seminary. Among his Portland students was Henry Wadsworth Longfellow who later wrote of his teacher: "He was very amiable and indulgent and much beloved by his pupils. This is an evidence, if any were wanting, of his sympathy for the young, which seems to have been through life so marked a trait in his character."[1]

March, 1826. Engaged to Harriet Vaughan whom he married two years later.

May, 1826. Entered the ministry of the Congregational Church.

1829. Invited to organize a school for young ladies in Boston. "I was called upon . . . to remove to Boston and take the charge of a sort of high-school, which some gentlemen are disposed to establish there. Two are contemplated, one for girls, and another for boys. It was expected that both would be supported by substantially the same persons; but two different committees were appointed to take measures to establish them, each of which, separately and without the knowledge of the other, voted to make application to me. When this interference was subsequently discovered, it was determined to send a delegation from each committee to me, to lay both plans before me, that I might decide to favor of either or neither. . . ."[1]

June, 1829. Mount Vernon School opened with Abbott as its administrator. "*Teaching* a pupil is not all that is necessary to be done for her in school. There are many other things, such as supplying her with the various articles necessary for her use, seeing that her desk is convenient, that her time is well arranged, that she has not too much to do, nor too little, and that no difficulty which can be removed obstructs her progress in study or her happiness in school. . . .

"The exertion by the principal of a decided moral and religious influence over the hearts of the pupils is one of the prime objects of school. The means employed to this end are: first, general religious exercises with the school as a whole, in connection with its regular work; secondly, a special religious meeting on Saturday afternoons, attendance at which is of course voluntary; and, thirdly, personal religious instruction, usually by means of notes, which, however, must always be begun by the pupil."[1]

1833. Resigned from Mount Vernon School and became minister of the Eliot Congregational Church in Roxbury, Massachusetts. Began a lifelong affiliation with Harper who published his "Rollo Books" and other juvenile series. "I have been engaged during the dog days in writing some more Rollo books. I write these occasionally because, 1st, they seem to be approved and are perhaps, in their humble way, useful. 2. They are very easy to write. 3. The(y) go some way towards furnishing me with an income, and 4 as the publisher is willing to have them appear anonymously, I get along with them without obtruding my name before the public, which I wish to avoid as much as possible.

"I have, however, been intending all summer to take hold of something more serious as soon as the season for cold and storms and study should fairly arrive. [Perhaps] . . . my plan for a 'Vindication of an Evangelical Faith.' That will probably not be the title, but that will be the object of the book. I should design to take up in it, the subject of *the way of salvation through Jesus Christ as an atoning sacrifice for sin,* and the other doctrines of grace connected with it, as they have been held by the most devoted Christians in all ages, in contrast with the views secretly or openly maintained by Unitarians and others, of salvation through the general forgiveness of God, bestowed on those whose lives are serious and exemplary. I should endeavor to take up the subject not at all in a controversial form; but with something of the air and manner I should assume by the fireside, with a serious-minded and thoughtful Unitarian who should wish me to tell him frankly what I thought was the real difference between the two systems, and why I embraced the evangelical one. If I do not mistake there are a great many enquiring and doubtful minds, all over New England, upon whom such a discussion might exert some influence.

"I have been revolving this plan for some time, & talking with John [his brother] about it and I am rather inclined to take it up next. . . ."[1]

1837. Built a cottage, "Little Blue," in Farmington, Maine. ". . . [I] built a small cottage home with a view to doing some literary work near farm occupied by my father—lived here about five years and wrote most of the *Rollo* books."[1]

1843. Wife died during the birth of their sixth child. Left his children with his parents in Maine and joined three of his brothers who were organizing a school for girls in New York.

Late 1843. Travelled to Europe, where he visited Dr. John Newman (who later became the famous Roman Catholic cardinal) at Littlemore, Oxford.

Summer, 1847. Made a trip to Scotland which resulted in an informal travel book. "Having spent a month or two . . . in rambling among the Highlands of Scotland, I have written the . . . account of my adventures for the amusement of my pupils, and of such other readers as may honor these pages with a perusal." [Jacob Abbott, *A Summer in Scotland*, Harper & Brothers, 1848.[2]]

1851. Retired from his presidential post at the Abbott School for Girls in New York. Abbott's principles of governing children were based on the belief in a child's goodness.

> "When you consent, consent cordially.
> "When you refuse, refuse finally.
> "When you punish, punish good-naturedly.
> "Commend often; never scold."

[Lyman Abbott, *Silhouettes of My Contemporaries*, Doubleday, 1921.[3]]

1853. Married Mary Dana Woodbury. The couple traveled a great deal during their marriage.

1866. Second wife died. Abbott continued to write his juveniles—he was loved by a large family and especially by his grandchildren. His influence over their futures was described by a granddaughter: "My father's father, Jacob Abbott, was very much interested in the education of the young, especially, we children felt, in the Christianizing of us, but always there was a considerable amount of history, geography, and even a little bit of French tucked in on the side.

"For a few years, in frequent association with him either in Cambridge or at the chosen home of his later years in Farmington, Maine, he wielded a very significant influence over us. Not alone as the only one of our 'ancestors' whom we had never really seen, but as a majestic personality in his own right we loved him dearly but were also, I think, considerably in awe of him. To me especially he always loomed as a beloved but rather alarmingly grave and ponderous person moving indomitably to 'noble ends.' Even if you, yourself, didn't happen to be the 'noble end' towards which he was moving at the moment, but were only standing beside the same, it made your knees knock a little, though he came smiling."[1]

1870. Spent his declining years gardening and writing in the countryside of Farmington, Maine. Abbott was a natural landscape gardener, but took no interest in raising flowers, fruits or vegetables. "There is no objection to a fruit tree, if you can be sure that it will bear no fruit. But if you plant a fruit tree for the fruit, the winter will kill it, or the frosts will kill the buds, or blight will attack the leaves, or worms will burrow in the trunk, or summer drought will shrivel the fruit, or, if it survives all these dangers, the boys will pick the fruit for you some night and you will find an empty tree in the morning." [Lyman Abbott, *Reminiscences*, Houghton, 1915.[4]]

October 31, 1879. Died peacefully at his home in Farmington, Maine. Two sons were at his bedside—one of them, Lyman,

described his father's last hours: "My brother, who was stronger than I, lifted my father up during a paroxysm of pain and then laid him down again upon the pillow, saying to him, 'Are you more comfortable now, Father?,' and received the whispered answer, 'Too comfortable. I hoped that I was going.' These were, I think, his last words."[3]

Abbott's manuscripts are included in Hubbard Hall, Bowdoin College.

FOR MORE INFORMATION SEE: Lyman Abbott, *Reminiscences*, Houghton, 1915; L. Abbott, "Jacob Abbott: Friend of Children," in his *Silhouettes of My Contemporaries*, Doubleday, 1921; Stanley Kunitz & Howard Haycraft, editors, *Junior Book of Authors*, H. W. Wilson, 1934; *Horn Book* Magazine, Jan.–Dec., 1948; Carl Jefferson Weber, *Bibliography of Jacob Abbott*, Colby College Press, 1948; John Mason Brown, "Prigs Is Prigs," in his *Seeing More Things*, McGraw-Hill, 1948; Alice Mabel Jordan, *From Rollo to Tom Sawyer, and Other Papers*, Horn Book, 1948; L. Abbott, "Jacob Abbott: A Goodly Heritage," *Horn Book*, April, 1954; L. Abbott, "Jacob Abbott: A Goodly Heritage," *The Hewing Lectures 1947–1962*, Horn Book, 1963.

ADAMSON, Joy (Friederike Victoria) 1910-1980

OBITUARY NOTICE—See sketch in SATA Volume 11: Born January 20, 1910, in Troppau, Silesia (now Opava, Czechoslovakia); died January 3, 1980, in Kenya. Painter, conservationist, and writer. While on a vacation trip to Kenya, Austrian-born Joy Adamson fell in love with that East African nation, and moved there permanently in 1937. For several years she devoted herself to painting pictures of the native flowers, animals, and people, many of which are displayed in Kenya's National Museum in Nairobi. In 1956, she and her husband, game warden George Adamson, adopted a motherless lion cub named Elsa. Their efforts to train Elsa to fend for herself in the wild are chronicled in Adamson's *Born Free*, a best-selling book that spawned a movie and television series. Two subsequent books, *Living Free* and *Forever Free*, continue Elsa's story. Among Adamson's other works are *The Spotted Sphinx*, *Pippa's Challenge*, and an autobiography, *The Searching Spirit*. Proceeds from her books and movies are turned over to the Elsa Wild Animal Appeal, an organization that Adamson founded to preserve threatened wildlife species. During the last five years of her life she was working on a study of leopards at a camp near the Samburu game preserve. When her body was discovered near that camp, officials at first speculated that Adamson had been mauled to death by a lion. But later reports said that she had been murdered. *For More Information See:* Roy Newquist, *Counterpoint*, Simon & Schuster, 1964; *Horn Book*, December, 1969; *Current Biography*, Wilson, 1972; *People*, October 4, 1976; *Contemporary Authors*, Volume 69-72, Gale, 1978; *Fourth Book of Junior Authors and Illustrators*, Wilson, 1978; *Who's Who in America*, 40th edition, Marquis, 1978; Joy Adamson, *The Searching Spirit*, Harcourt, 1979. *Obituaries: New York Times*, January 5, 1980; *Washington Post*. January 5, 1980; *Publishers Weekly*, January 18, 1980; *Time*, January 21, 1980; *Contemporary Authors*, Volume 93-96, Gale, 1980.

WENDY WRISTON ADAMSON

ADAMSON, Wendy Wriston 1942-

PERSONAL: Born June 25, 1942, in Glen Falls, N.Y.; daughter of George W. (a stockbroker) and Gladys (Micks) Wriston; married William De Lancey Adamson (a teacher), 1965; children: Edward De Lancey, April Elizabeth. *Education:* Syracuse University, B.A., 1964; Simmons College, M.L.S., 1971. *Home:* 3616 40th Ave. S., Minneapolis, Minn. 55406. *Office:* Environmental Library of Minnesota, Minneapolis, Minn.

CAREER: Brown University, Providence, R.I., government documents assistant in library, 1967-68; Macalester College, St. Paul, Minn., assistant reference librarian, 1969-71; Minneapolis Public Library, Minneapolis, Minn., librarian in Environmental Conservation Library, 1971-72; Environmental Library of Minnesota, Minneapolis, librarian, 1972—.

WRITINGS—Juveniles: *Saving Lake Superior: A Story of Environmental Action,* Dillon, 1974, 1976; *Who Owns a River?, A Story of Environmental Action,* Dillon, 1977; *Sun Power: Facts About Solar Energy,* Lerner, 1978.

SIDELIGHTS: "My first book on Lake Superior was an experiment for me because I had never done professional writing of any sort. I found I enjoyed meeting people and talking to them about the environment. For example, I made several trips to Duluth and the North Shore of Lake Superior for my first book. Sitting down at the typewriter was the hardest part, but I found if you have the basic outline of the book, the rest is not too difficult.

"I am the kind of writer who tries to get substance on paper first and worries about style later, so I type furiously a first draft, disregarding punctuation and sentence structure. Then I put it away for awhile and write my revisions later.

"I write books because I believe that the hope of the world is with young people. If at an early age they can be made sensitive to certain ethical and moral dilemmas on this planet, then they can make intelligent choices which will, I like to think, insure the future of the world as we know it. Since I have two children of my own, I think a lot about that future!"

ADLER, Peggy

PERSONAL: Daughter of Irving (an author) and Ruth (an author-illustrator) Adler; married Jeremy A. Walsh. *Home:* New Haven, Conn.

CAREER: Author and illustrator. Began illustrating books by her father, Irving Adler, as an adolescent.

WRITINGS: (With father, Irving Adler) *Adler Book of Puzzles and Riddles,* John Day, 1962; *The Second Adler Book of Puzzles and Riddles,* John Day, 1963.

Illustrator; all published by John Day: Irving Adler, *Hot and Cold,* 1959, revised edition, 1975; (with mother, Ruth Adler) I. Adler, *Weather in Your Life,* 1959; I. and R. Adler, *Sets and Numbers for the Very Young,* 1969; (with R. Adler) I. Adler, *The Changing Tools of Science: From Yardstick to Synchrotron,* 1973; (with R. Adler) I. Adler, *Magic House of Numbers,* 1974; I. Adler, *Petroleum: Gas, Oil and Asphalt,* 1975; I. Adler, *The Environment,* 1976.

HIDDEN GEOGRAPHY: I like the tree in the garden very much, but I liked the one in the field much better. ■ (From *The Second Adler Book of Puzzles and Riddles* by Peggy Adler. Illustrated by the author.)

SIDELIGHTS: At the age of sixteen, Adler illustrated *Hot and Cold,* a science text written by her father, Irving Adler. Many of the author-illustrator's later works have also been family efforts. *Weather in Your Life* was written by Adler's father and co-illustrated with her mother, Ruth Adler. A *Horn Book* critic found the book written with clarity and commented, "I was particularly intrigued by a diagrammatic illustration. . .explaining why Death Valley is what it is. The accompanying text makes the reasons clear enough but the illustration does it even more sharply, and in capsule form."

ALBERT, Burton, Jr. 1936-
(Brooks Healey)

PERSONAL: Born September 25, 1936, in Pittsfield, Mass.; son of Burton and Isabel (Deming) Albert; married Lois Bent, June 27, 1963; children: Heather Leigh, Kelley Lynn. *Education:* North Adams State College, B.S. (magna cum laude), 1958; Duke University, M.A., 1962. *Home:* 3 Narrow Brook Rd., Weston, Conn. 06883. *Agent:* McIntosh and Otis, Inc., 475 Fifth Ave., New York, N.Y. 10017.

CAREER: Elementary school teacher in Greenwich, Conn., 1958-60, 1962-63, high school teacher of English in Greenwich, Conn., 1963-64; Harcourt Brace Jovanovich, Inc., New York, N.Y., assistant editor in language arts, 1964-66; *Reader's Digest,* educational division, Pleasantville, N.Y., senior editor and product developer, 1966-76, editorial director, 1976-77; educational consultant and writer, 1977—. *Member:* International Reading Association, National Council of Teachers of English, International Platform Association. *Awards, honors:* Article, "Are You Giving Writing Its Due?," was nominated for the Educational Press Award, 1977.

WRITINGS: (Ghostwriter) *Language for Daily Use Workbook,* Grade 5, Harcourt, 1965; (ghostwriter) *Language for Daily Use,* Grade 8, Teacher's edition, Harcourt, 1966; (with Donald M. Murray) *Write to Communicate: The Language Arts in Process,* Levels 3-6, Reader's Digest Services, Inc., 1973-74; *Codes for Kids,* A. Whitman, 1976; *Monster Riddles,* Firefly Book Club, 1976; *More Monster Riddles,* Firefly Book Club, 1976; *Puzzle Fun,* Firefly Book Club, 1976; *Mine, Yours, Ours,* A. Whitman, 1977; (under pseudonym Brooks Healey) *The Giggles and Game Puzzle Book,* Firefly Book Club, 1977; *Holiday Party Panels,* Sets 1-3, Instructor Curriculum Materials, 1978; (under pseudonym Brooks Healey) *It's True, By George!,* Firefly Book Club, 1978; (under pseudonym Brooks Healey) *Star Words,* Firefly Book Club, 1978; (under pseudonym Brooks Healey) *The Stranger and the Scarecrow,* Firefly Book Club, 1978; *Sharks and Whales,* Platt & Munk, 1979; *More Codes for Kids,* A. Whitman, 1979; (under pseudonym Brooks Healey) *Maze Daze,* Firefly Book Club, 1979; *Teacher Time Savers,* Random House, 1980; *Sure Steps to a New Job,* The Learning Pyramid, Inc., 1980; (contributor) *Houghton Mifflin Reading Series,* Houghton, 1980; (contributor) *Scholastic Social Studies Program,* Grade 5, Scholastic Book Services, 1980. Author of "Reader's Digest Reading Skill Practice Pads," Level 3 and Advanced, Reader's Digest Services, Inc., 1967. Developmental editor of "Reader's Digest Reading Skill Builders," silver edition, Reader's Digest Services, Inc., 1977. Contributor of articles and poems to educational and literary journals, to newspapers, and to children's magazines.

BURTON ALBERT, JR.

WORK IN PROGRESS: Carlo: Ship's Boy on the Santa Maria; Celebrity Riddles; Clubs for Kids; Dad's Crumb Catcher, Foolish Ghoulish Monster Jokes; Skeeter's Big Tiny Surprise; Whee! A Cartwheel Spree; Willie's Wink-on-the-Brink; Hark'n Mark Reading Games; Shing-Shang, Fing-Fang and Foo; What Makes My Daddy Cry?.

SIDELIGHTS: "Writing is a thinking process, a voyage of self-discovery. A writer isn't a specially gifted person who retreats to a library of leather-bound volumes, pours a goblet of wine, lounges in a silk robe, courts the muse, and finally pens an inspired text. That misconception thrives, however, because we seldom see or hear evidence of a writer's struggles—the cross-outs, the inserts, the mutterings, the vagueness, the curlicues, the elliptical leaps, the paste-ons, the typos, the pacing back-and-forth, the awkward constructions, the groans, and so on.

"Most often students view and analyze finished products frozen on a page. But a practicing writer rarely produces polished copy on the first draft. In fact, many writers would be horrified to have anyone see their initial blunderings. . . .

"When writers confront the blank page, they may be cramped by conflicting emotions—compulsion, emptiness, fullness, excitement, ignorance, apprehension. Nevertheless, they push off into the uncharted, not quite knowing what to expect." [Burton Albert, Jr., "Are You Giving Writing Its Due?," *Instructor,* October, 1977.[1]]

"I get my ideas from the world around me—whenever I can people-watch and wonder 'What if . . .?' Like a giant sponge, my senses soak up all they can. Then suddenly they surprise me.

(From *Mine, Yours, Ours* by Burton Albert, Jr. Illustrated by Lois Axeman.)

"I like to start with a neat desk. But gradually it becomes a traffic jam of discarded drafts and pencils, sheets of Ko-Rec-Type, books and felt-tipped pens, staples, rubber cement, 12-inch shears, file folders, and anything else I happen upon or need during the flurry of creation.

"I also whisper and mumble a lot, because I like to test the sound and rhythm of each word, phrase, and sentence.

"The best part of writing is mailing the manuscript! It's a tremendous relief. Next to that I prefer rewriting. I love chiseling a blob of clay and seeing it take shape."

When asked how he creates his various codes, Albert responded: "You might call it thinking backwards. I might see a popsicle stick, a paper clip, or a caterpillar crawling up the screen on our back porch. Then I wonder how I might use the object in a tricky way to reveal secret letters. With most codes, however, an idea comes to me in a flash. It's something that can't be explained. Like an unbroken code, the source of the idea is even a mystery to me!"

FOR MORE INFORMATION SEE: Burton Albert, Jr., "Are You Giving Writing Its Due?" *Instructor,* October, 1977.

ALEXANDER, Jocelyn (Anne) Arundel 1930-
(Jocelyn Arundel)

PERSONAL: Born June 16, 1930, in Washington, D.C.; daughter of Russell Moore and Marjorie (Sale) Arundel; married David Ord Alexander (an engineer), May 10, 1958; children: Anne Cresap, Russell Ord, Jocelyn Lee. *Education:* Smith College, B.A., 1952; studied at Sorbonne, University of Paris, 1951. *Religion:* Episcopalian. *Home and office:* 2323 Porter St., N.W., Washington, D.C.

CAREER: Washington Daily News, Washington, D.C., writer, 1952-53; International Union for Conservation of Nature and Natural Resources, Brussels, Belgium, and Washington, D.C., U.S. liaison and public relations chief, 1955-57; National Geographic Society, Washington, D.C., writer, *School Service Bulletin,* 1957-58. *Member:* Authors Guild of America, Washington Children's Book Guild, National Parks Association, Wilderness Society, Nature Conservancy (chairman, Wildcat Mountain Natural Area), Defenders of Wildlife (president). *Awards, honors:* Boys' Clubs of America award, 1958, for *Simba of the White Mane.*

WRITINGS: Simba of the White Mane, McGraw, 1958; *Jingo, Wild Horse of Abaco,* Whittlesey House, 1959; *Dugan and the Hobo,* Whittlesey House, 1960; *Mighty Mo: Story of an African Elephant,* Whittlesey House, 1961; *Whitecaps Song,* Whittlesey House, 1962; *Shoes for Punch,* McGraw, 1964; *The Wildlife of Africa* (Junior Literary Guild selection), Hastings, 1965; *Little Stripe,* Hastings, 1967; *Land of the Zebra,* National Wildlife Federation, 1974; *Lions and Tigers,* National Wildlife Federation, 1974.

WORK IN PROGRESS: Two juvenile books.

Mighty Mo would be ripping bark from a tree. Jay could almost hear the sound of it, smell the pungence of wood beneath, hear the flap of elephant ears. ■ (From *Mighty Mo: Story of an African Elephant* by Jocelyn Arundel. Illustrated by Wesley Dennis.)

JOCELYN ARUNDEL ALEXANDER

SIDELIGHTS: "My love of wildlife is inherited from my parents as well as from those early contacts with the out-of-doors. My father's idea of a vacation when I was tiny was to join an expedition into the remote jungles of Dutch Guiana to look for a single strange species of bird. In more recent years he and my brother helped secure gorillas for the National Zoological Park in Washington."

After receiving her B.A. degree from Smith College, Arundel studied at the Sorbonne in Paris for a year and then did newspaper and public relations work. "An important turning point was my acceptance of a position in Brussels, Belgium, working with an organization then called the International Union for the Protection of Nature. Today it is the growingly influential International Union for Conservation of Nature which, along with such groups as the World Wildlife Fund, is struggling to save wildlife species around the world from extermination. I worked hard and learned a sobering lesson or two about the ways in which mankind is draining the natural wealth from our planet.

"I worked with IUCN in the United States after leaving Brussels. Also, I had the unforgettable experience of going to Africa on a photographic and study safari. I needed no further spur to start serious writing. I had come to realize that our children, and children all over the world, growing up amid swelling populations and vanishing natural frontiers, will have both a desperate need to find renewed contacts with nature and yet a harder time fulfilling that need. The toughest conservation problems will be their responsibilities."

HOBBIES AND OTHER INTERESTS: Wildlife, natural history, conservation.

ALEXANDER, Raymond Pace 1898-1974 (Rae Pace Alexander)

PERSONAL: Born October 13, 1898, in Philadelphia, Pa.; died November 23, 1974, in Philadelphia, Pa.; son of Hilliard Boone and Virginia Margaret (Pace) Alexander; married Sadie Tanner Mossell (a lawyer), November 26, 1923; children: Mary Elizabeth (Mrs. Melvin Frank Brown) and Rae Pace (Mrs. Thomas K. Minter). *Education:* University of Pennsylvania, B.S. (magna cum laude), 1920; graduate study, Columbia University, summer, 1921-22; Harvard University, LL.B., 1923. *Religion:* Baptist. *Home:* 700 Westview St., Philadelphia, Pa. 19119. *Office:* 1004 One East Penn Square, Philadelphia, Pa. 19107.

CAREER: Admitted to the Bar of Pennsylvania, 1923; member of the law firm of Raymond Pace Alexander, Philadelphia, 1923-58; elected to Philadelphia City Council, 1951, 1955; appointed to the bench, 1959; Philadelphia Court of Common Pleas, judge, 1959-70, senior judge, 1970-74. Served as counsel for the National Medical Association, the Philadelphia and Pennsylvania chapters of the NAACP, and the American Civil Liberties Union; held a number of civic, professional, and political positions, including chairman of the Council for Job Opportunities of the Fellowship Commission, chairman of the international legal education section of the World Peace through Law Center, national chairman of the Young Republicans, 1923, associate chairman of the Young Democrats, 1932-36, counsellor of the Haitian embassy, Washington, 1946-49, special advisor to the Secretary of Defense, 1949; Crime Prevention Association of Philadelphia, director, 1960, president, 1967, chairman of the executive committee, 1970; member of the national board of directors, Association for the Study of Negro Life and History; national director of the March of Dimes and the Free Europe Committee; served with the National Baptist Convention, Pennsylvania Baptist Convention, A.M.E. Church, board of bishops, and the Philadelphia Council of Churches.

MEMBER: American Judicature Society, the National, the American, the Pennsylvania, and the Philadelphia Bar Associations (past president of National Bar Association), Barristers Library of the High Court of India, American-Turkish Bar Association of Ankara, Turkey, Brandeis Law Society, Alpha Phi Alpha, Phi Beta Kappa, Beta Gamma Sigma, honorary member of Lambda Sigma Kappa. *Awards, honors:* LL.D., Shaw University and Virginia State College, 1940; Litt.D., Western University, 1947, and Campbell College, 1948; outstanding service awards from Alpha Phi Alpha, Phi Beta Sigma, Pyramid Club, Barristers Club, 1951, African Methodist Episcopal Church of New York City, 1955, and the Baptist Ministers Conference, Philadelphia, 1959; honored for outstanding achievement in civil liberties by the American Jewish Congress, 1950; C. Francis Stradford award from the National Bar Association, 1967; Carter G. Woodson award from the Association for the Study of Negro Life and History, 1968; personal portrait given in honor to the Raymond Pace Alexander Gallery, Jenkins Memorial Library by the Philadelphia Bar Association, 1970; and others.

WRITINGS: (Compiler) *Young and Black in America,* Random House, 1970. Contributor of articles to periodicals, including *Interracial Digest, Negro History Bulletin, Ebony,* and *Nation.* Co-founder and editor of the *National Bar Journal,* 1940.

Raymond Pace Alexander viewing his portrait.

SIDELIGHTS: Alexander was a nationally known civil rights lawyer and activist. He was the first black Common Pleas judge in Pennsylvania. After graduating magna cum laude from the University of Pennsylvania in only three years, Alexander went to Harvard Law School on a scholarship. He also received the honor of induction into Phi Beta Kappa.

Upon receiving his degree in 1923, Alexander opened his own law firm in Philadelphia. His wife, whom he married the same year, was also a lawyer. Together they worked to build the practice, eventually establishing themselves as an influential legal team among the Philadelphia black community.

In 1933 to 1935, Alexander won a case for desegregation of the public school system of suburban Berwyn. A report which Alexander wrote in 1951 was influential in the desegregation of the U.S. armed forces. He was instrumental in opening a formerly all-white school to fatherless black boys. In addition, Alexander was active in crime prevention in the Philadelphia area.

Alexander was honored in 1950 by the American Jewish Congress, which cited him for "25 years of outstanding achievements in the field of civil liberties for all people. Very active in civic, professional, and political groups, Alexander continued his campaign for civil rights until his death at the age of 76.

Alexander remained on the Philadelphia bench until he died of an apparent heart attack in 1974. As reported in the *Phil-*

adelphia Bulletin, a fellow Common Pleas Court jurist called Alexander's death a great loss in terms of the Philadelphia judiciary.

FOR MORE INFORMATION SEE: Ebony Magazine, February, 1964; *Negro History Bulletin,* October, 1964, January, 1965, October, 1965, January, 1968, January, 1969, April, 1970; *Time* Magazine, August 5, 1966; *New Republic,* December 26, 1970. *Obituaries: New York Times,* November 25, 1974; *Philadelphia Bulletin,* November 25, 1974; *Biography News,* January/February, 1975.

ALLEN, Marjorie 1931-

PERSONAL: Born December 8, 1931, in Manchester, N.H.; daughter of Andre (a salesman) and Lauretta (an executive secretary; maiden name, Elliott) Nicholson; married David Allen (a florist), July 6, 1957; children: John, Carl, Dena. *Education:* Attended on a part-time basis SUNY [State University of New York] at Plattsburgh, SUNY at Oswego, and the University of Massachusetts. *Religion:* Methodist. *Home:* 39 Montgomery Ave., Pittsfield, Mass. 01201.

CAREER: Berkshire Medical Center, Pittsfield, Mass., personnel clerk, 1974-76, unit co-ordinator, emergency room, 1974—. Continuing education instructor in writing for children, Berkshire Community College, 1976; Berkshire Athenaeum, Pittsfield, Mass., director of workship in writing for children, 1979—. Lecturer, author of children's books and children's book reviewer. *Member:* Society of Children's Book Writers, Massachusetts Reading Council.

WRITINGS—Juveniles: (With Alice Schick) *The Remarkable Ride of Israel Bissell as Related by Molly the Crow,* Lippincott, 1976; (with Carl Allen) *Farley, Are You for Real?,* Coward, 1976; (with Carl Allen) *The Marble Cake Cat,* Coward, 1977; *One, Two, Three-Ahchoo!,* Coward, 1980. Contributor to *Humpty Dumpty, Happy Times, Grit, Denver Post,* and other periodicals.

Marjorie Allen and family.

As he stood in the cold night air, Archie began to notice that he was not alone. ■ (From *Farley, Are You for Real?* by Marjorie N. Allen and Carl Allen. Illustrated by Joel Schick.)

WORK IN PROGRESS: The Purple Martin Pyramid; Lavender and Listerine; Voices from the Sea; The Strange Disappearance of Patty Ann Decker.

SIDELIGHTS: "Books have always been magic to me. When I was very young, I couldn't get enough of them. But when I was twelve, I thought I had to start reading adult books. It wasn't until I started writing for children about ten years ago that I rediscovered children's books. Now, because I'm a children's book reviewer, I get many books in the mail and can read to my heart's content. And because I'm so familiar with what is being published, I know what still needs to be published. When I write my books, I try to fill that need.

"When I get an idea for a new book, I think about it for two or three months before I write anything at all. It is often necessary to do some research, even on a picture book. In one of my books, there are frogs, snakes and hermit crabs. The research I did helped me develop the story. The boy in the story has allergies, and I had to research that as well. When I'm ready to write the story, it only takes me a day. I have three teenagers, and I usually have to tune out the television, the stereo, the radio and the telephone in order to write. I don't like to shut myself away physically in a room all alone. When the children were younger, my husband used to take them out for a ride so that I could write; and I never accomplished a thing until they returned and resumed normal activity. I like to be in the middle of everything and shut myself away mentally.

"After my story is written, I seek the advice of friends who are also writers. There are always changes to be made, and I might rewrite the story four or five times. When I finally decide it's as good as I can make it, I send it to my editor. The editor contacts an illustrator, sends me a contract and suggests minor changes in the manuscript—that is, if the story is accepted. Even published authors get rejection slips.

"All my books are for children. I want to encourage children to discover the joys of reading as I did. Every day is a new adventure for me; and my ability to appreciate life comes in large part from the books I have read."

HOBBIES AND OTHER INTERESTS: Reading, summer theatre, woman's barbershop chorus.

ALLEN, Merritt Parmelee   1892-1954

PERSONAL Born July 2, 1892, in Bristol, Vermont; died December 26, 1954; son of Rolla E. and Gertrude (Parmelee) Allen. *Education:* Attended public schools in Bristol, Vermont. *Home:* Bristol, Vermont.

CAREER: Author of historical novels, juvenile fiction, biography, and numerous short stories.

WRITINGS: In Greenbrook (illustrated by James H. Mather), L. C. Page, 1923; *The Ghost of the Glimmerglass* (illustrated by Victor Hall), Harper, 1928; *Tied in the Ninth* (illustrated by Charles Lassell), Century, 1930; *The Hermit of Honey Hill: A Mystery Story for Boys* (illustrated by Manning De Villeneuve Lee), Century, 1931; *Sir Henry Morgan, Buccaneer* (illustrated by M. De V. Lee), Century, 1931; *Joaquin Miller, Frontier Poet,* Harper, 1932; *Wilderness Diamonds* (illustrated by M. De V. Lee), Century, 1932; *William Walker, Filibuster,* Harper, 1932; *Drake's Sword* (illustrated by Henry C. Pitz), Appleton-Century, 1934; *Raiders' Hoard,* Longmans, Green, 1936; *Out of a Clear Sky,* Longmans, Green, 1938; *Black Rain* (illustrated by James MacDonald), Longmans, Green, 1939.

Western Star: A Story of Jim Bridger, Longmans, Green, 1941; *The Green Cockade* (illustrated by Henry S. Gillette), Longmans, Green, 1942; *The Sun Trail,* Longmans, Green, 1943; *The White Feather,* Longmans, Green, 1944; *The Mudhen,* Longmans, Green, 1945; *Red Heritage,* Longmans, Green, 1946; *The Spirit of the Eagle,* Longmans, Green, 1947; *Battle Lanterns,* Longmans, Green, 1949; *Make Way for the Brave: The Oregon Quest,* Longmans, Green, 1950; *The Mudhen and the Walrus,* Longmans, Green, 1950; *Johnny*

"Then you will understand that this trail is my province. I shall report this incident to the authorities in Santa Fe and the States."

"A lot of good it will do to report a Comanche raid!" ■ (From *The Silver Wolf* by Merritt Parmelee Allen. Decorations by Allen Thomas.)

Reb, Longmans, Green, 1952; *The Silver Wolf,* Longmans, Green, 1951; *The Flicker's Feather,* Longmans, Green, 1953; *The Wilderness Way,* Longmans, Green, 1954; *The Mudhen Acts Naturally,* Longmans, Green, 1955; *East of Astoria* (illustrated by Millard McGee), Longmans, Green, 1956; *Blow Bugles Blow,* Longmans, Green, 1956.

Also author of several sketches which have been used by the National Broadcasting Company. Contributor to numerous magazines, including *Youth Companion, St. Nicholas, Outdoor America, Boy's Life,* and *Forest and Stream.*

FOR MORE INFORMATION SEE: Horn Book, January-December, 1947; (for children) Stanley J. Kunitz, editor, *Junior Book of Authors,* 2nd edition, revised, H. W. Wilson, 1951. Obituaries—*Publishers Weekly,* February 12, 1955; *Wilson Library Bulletin,* April, 1955.

Blessings on thee, little man,
Barefoot boy, with cheek of tan!
With thy turned-up pantaloons,
And thy merry whistled tunes.
                                            —John Greenleaf Whittier

ALLEN, Nina (Strömgren) 1935-

PERSONAL: Born September 17, 1935, in Copenhagen, Denmark; daughter of Bengt G. D. (an astrophysicist) and Sigrid (Hartz) Strömgren; married Robert Williams, July 18, 1958 (divorced); married second husband Robert Day Allen (a biologist), September 11, 1970; children: (first marriage) Erik, Harriet; (second marriage) Barbara; (stepchildren) Wayne, Elizabeth. *Education:* University of Wisconsin, B.S., 1957; University of Maryland, M.S., 1970, Ph.D., 1973. *Politics:* Democrat. *Religion:* Unitarian. *Home:* 37 School St., Hanover, N.H. 03755. *Office:* Department of Biological Sciences, Dartmouth College, Hanover, N.H. 03755.

CAREER: Free-lance illustrator. University of Wisconsin, teaching assistant, 1957-58; University of Maryland, teaching assistant, 1964-67; State University of New York at Albany, research assistant, 1970-73, research associate, 1973-75; Woods Hole Children's School of Science, science chairman, 1974-76; Dartmouth College, visiting assistant professor and research associate, 1975-76, assistant professor, 1976—. Marine Biological Lab, Woods Hole, Mass., trustee; Children's School of Science, Woods Hole, Mass., board of directors. *Member:* Society of Plant Physiologists, Corporation of Marine Biological Lab, American Society of Cell Biology, Phycological Society of America, Society for Evolutionary Protistology, American Women in Science. *Awards, honors:* Phi Beta Kappa, 1957; NIH Predoctoral Fellow, University of Maryland, 1967-70; Sigma Xi, 1972.

ILLUSTRATOR: Sean Morrison, *The Amoeba,* Coward, 1970. Contributor to scientific journals.

NINA ALLEN

SIDELIGHTS: "I have an interest in science education for children. My work deals with photomicrography and I make movies of many motile plant and animal cells. I have a very full life with many children and a busy teaching schedule. I would enjoy illustrating and even writing more books. As I teach plant systematics and phycology at Dartmouth I have compiled an extensive collection of photographs of plants and algae."

AMES, Mildred 1919-

PERSONAL: Born November 2, 1919, in Bridgeport, Conn.; daughter of Edward John and Amelia (Miller) Walsh; married William Ames (a technical writer), April 19, 1945. *Education:* Attended secondary school in Bridgeport, Conn. *Residence:* Palos Verdes Estates, Calif. *Agent:* Marilyn Marlow, Curtis Brown, Ltd., 575 Madison Ave., New York, N.Y. 10022.

CAREER: Writer, 1965—. *Member:* Society of Children's Book Writers, Surfwriters Club (president, 1978-79), Southern California Council on Literature for Children and Young People.

WRITINGS: Shadows of Summers Past (teen and adult), Bouregy, 1973; *The House of the Haunted Child* (teen and adult), Bouregy, 1974; *Is There Life on a Plastic Planet?* (juvenile), Dutton, 1975; *Without Hats, Who Can Tell the Good Guys?* (juvenile), Dutton, 1976; *The Wonderful Box* (juvenile), Dutton, 1977; *What Are Friends For?* (juvenile), Scribner, 1978; *Nicky and the Joyous Noise* (juvenile), Scribner, 1980. Contributor to *Young Miss* and *Cricket.*

ADAPTATIONS: "What Are Friends For?" was an ABC-TV Afterschool Special, March, 1980.

WORK IN PROGRESS: A young adult novel, *The Dancing Madness,* for Delacorte; a science-fiction novel tentatively titled, *Anna to the Infinite Power.*

SIDELIGHTS: "My first feeling for a story came from the ballads my mother used to sing. They were from her day, and the stories they told were always sad and melodramatic. Often, they made me cry. But children like to cry over stories as much as they like to laugh. It followed that my first story, at the age of eight or nine, was a melodrama about an 'ophran' who lived in an 'ophranage.' (I still can't spell).

"Those were Depression years. Although we were poor, we lived across the street from a branch library that held priceless

Anthony Lang, Jr. sat on the edge of the bed, feeling much younger than his eleven years.
■ (From *Without Hats, Who Can Tell the Good Guys?* by Mildred Ames. Jacket illustrated by Richard Cuffari.)

MILDRED AMES

riches. The people there even let you borrow their treasures, all of three books at a time. There was one other restriction. You could not return a book on the day you checked it out. It was always a sad moment when I realized I'd finished my three books by noon.

"My growing-up years were spent keeping diaries, writing poetry, and working on my school newspaper. When I left school I stopped writing about life and started living it. More than twenty years passed before I again began putting words on paper.

"I have worked in a magic factory and in a 'five and ten,' and learned that while there may be magic in a 'five and ten,' there is none in a magic factory. I have sold hats, run an elevator, worked as a telephone operator, travelled for a chain of photography studios, and, as a clerical worker, worked for two aircraft plants, an air base, and an automobile dealer.

"I write for children because I share so many of their beliefs. Like them, I believe that there *can* be happy endings, that people *can* live happily ever after, and that if you wish hard enough and work hard enough, a dream can come true.

"My husband and I live in Southern California, and we share the house with two cats—a very cross-eyed Siamese, and an orange Tom—who like to sign all my work with paw prints."

ANDERSON, Norman D(ean) 1928-

PERSONAL: Born January 29, 1928, in Dickens, Iowa; son of Eddie (a farmer) and Effie Anderson; married Martha Breuer, November 23, 1952; children: Brent, Beth, Jeffrey, Todd, Jonathan, Julie. *Education:* University of Iowa, B.A., 1951, M.A., 1956; Ohio State University, Ph.D., 1965. *Religion:* Presbyterian. *Home:* 1000 Lake Boone Trail, Raleigh, N.C. 27607. *Office:* Department of Science Education, 326 Poe Hall, North Carolina State University, Raleigh, N.C. 27650.

CAREER: High school science teacher in Burlington, Iowa, 1952-57, 1958-59, in Bettendorf, Iowa, 1959-61; Ohio State University, Columbus, instructor in science education, 1961-63; North Carolina State University, Raleigh, assistant professor, 1963-66, associate professor, 1966-71, professor of science education, 1971—. Harvard University, Cambridge, Mass., master teacher in science, summer, 1964; director of National Science Foundation summer institutes in earth science, 1966, 1967, 1968, in marine environments, 1971. North Carolina State Advisory Council on Elementary and Secondary Education, chairman, 1968-70; Peace College, trustee, 1970-75. *Military service:* U.S. Army, Engineers, 1946-47.

MEMBER: American Association for the Advancement of Science (fellow), National Education Association (life member), National Science Teachers Association (life member), National Association for Research in Science Teaching, Association for Education of Teachers of Science, National Association of Geology Teachers, Central Association of

NORMAN D. ANDERSON

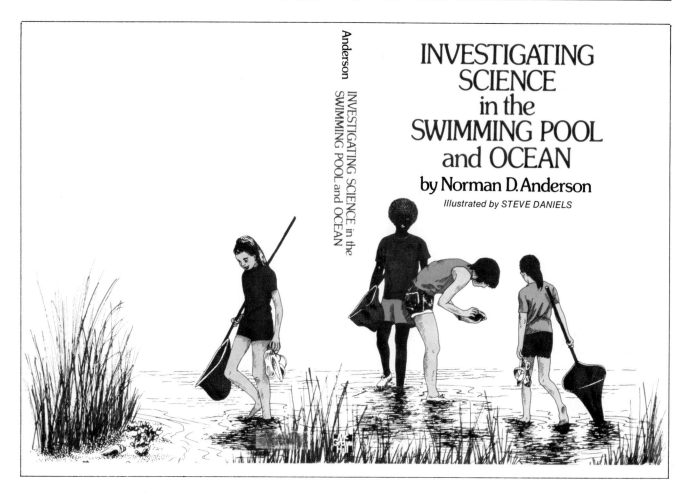

(From *Investigating Science in the Swimming Pool and Ocean* by Norman D. Anderson. Jacket illustrated by Steve Daniels.)

Science and Mathematics Teachers, North Carolina Academy of Science, Phi Delta Kappa, Phi Kappa Phi. *Awards, honors:* North Carolina State University Outstanding Teaching Awards, 1965, 1969; Alumni distinguished professorship, 1973.

WRITINGS—Young adult: (With J. Allen Hynek) *Challenge of the Universe,* Scholastic Book Services, 1962; (contributing editor in astronomy) *Compton's Illustrated Science Dictionary,* David-Steward, 1963; (with Walter R. Brown) *Life Science: A Search for Understanding,* 1971, 1977; (with Walter Brown) *Physical Science: A Search for Understanding,* Lippincott, 1972, 1977; (with Walter Brown) *Earth Science: A Search for Understanding,* Lippincott, 1973, 1977; *Investigating Science Using Your Whole Body,* McGraw, 1975; (with Walter Brown) *Historical Catastrophes: Famines,* Addison-Wesley, 1976; (with Walter Brown) *Historical Catastrophes: Snowstorms and Avalanches,* Addison-Wesley, 1976; (with Walter Brown) *Historical Catastrophes: Fires,* Addison-Wesley, 1976; *Investigating Science in the Swimming Pool and Ocean,* McGraw, 1978. Contributor to journals of science education.

SIDELIGHTS: "As a former junior high science teacher, as a father of six, and as a university professor of science education, my continuous contacts with young people and science provide more ideas than I can write about in a lifetime.

And as I read and do research for a book, more ideas for writing projects are generated. There are many motivations for writing these books—to share the excitement of science with adolescents, to create new ways of presenting ideas and activities that can be performed as part of the learning process, and perhaps most important, to organize my own thoughts and to learn myself about the many fascinating aspects of science.

"The profit motive plays a bigger part in writing textbooks than it does in doing trade books. I doubt if I could write purely for money—writing is hard work and the satisfaction that comes with creating something has to be the most important reward. In spite of these noble thoughts, royalty checks are especially welcome when they arrive at the same time as next year's college tuition bills are due."

O for one hour of youthful joy!
Give back my twentieth spring!
I'd rather laugh, a bright-haired boy,
Than reign, a gray-beard King.

—Oliver Wendell Holmes

ANDREWS, F(rank) Emerson   1902-1978

PERSONAL: Born January 26, 1902, in Lancaster, Pa.; died August 7, 1978; son of Harry and Ellen (Wiggins) Andrews; married Edith Lilian Severance, July 5, 1932; children: Frank M., Peter Bruce, Bryant. *Education:* Franklin and Marshall College, B.A., 1923, L.H.D., 1952. *Religion:* Protestant. *Home:* 34 Oak St., Tenafly, N.J. 07670.

CAREER: Macmillan Co., publishers, New York, N.Y., manager of advertising printing, 1923-26, direct mail service department, 1926-28; Russell Sage Foundation, New York, N.Y., director of publications, 1928-56, director of philanthropic research, 1944-56; Foundation Center, New York, N.Y., president, 1956-67, consultant, 1967-78. Consultant on publications to Twentieth Century Fund, 1940-55, and to National Science Foundation. Member and sometime chairman of Tenafly Planning Board. *Member:* Duodecimal Society of America (president, 1944-50, chairman of board, 1950-64), American Institute of Graphic Arts, Phi Beta Kappa, Shell Companies Foundation, Authors League of America, National Conference on Social Welfare. *Awards, honors:* First annual award, Duodecimal Society.

*WRITINGS—*For children: *The Gingerbread House,* Oxford University Press, 1943; *I Find Out,* Essential Books, 1946; *For Charlemagne,* Harper, 1949; *Upside-Down Town,* Little, Brown, 1958; *Numbers, Please,* Little, Brown, 1961, Teachers College Press, 1977; *Knights and Daze,* Putnam, 1966; *Nobody Comes to Dinner,* Little, Brown, 1977.

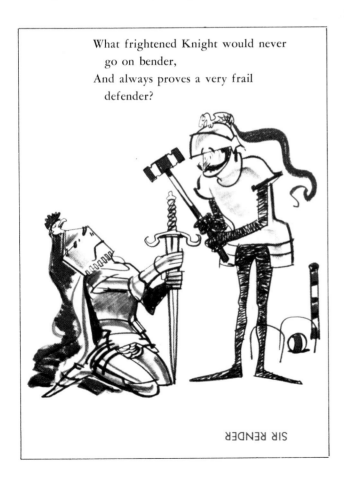

What frightened Knight would never
go on bender,
And always proves a very frail
defender?

SIR RENDER

(From *Knights and Daze* by F. Emerson Andrews. Illustrated by Charles Howes.)

F. EMERSON ANDREWS

Other writings: *New Numbers,* Harcourt, 1935; (with Shelby M. Harrison) *American Foundations for Social Welfare,* Russell Sage, 1946; (with Lilian Brandt and J. M. Glenn) *Russell Sage Foundation: 1907-1946,* Russell Sage, 1947; *Philanthropic Giving,* Russell Sage, 1950; *Corporation Giving,* Russell Sage, 1952; *Attitudes Toward Giving,* Russell Sage, 1953; *Grugan's God,* Muhlenberg, 1955; *Philanthropic Foundations,* Russell Sage, 1956; *Legal Instruments of Foundations,* Russell Sage, 1958; (with Ann Walton) *The Foundation Directory,* Russell Sage, 1960; *Foundations: Twenty Viewpoints,* Russell Sage, 1965; *Patman and Foundations,* Foundation Center, 1968; *The Tenafly Public Library, A History, 1891-1970,* The Tenafly Library, 1970; *Foundation Watcher,* Franklin and Marshall College, 1973.

Contributor to some sixty-odd national magazines, including *Atlantic Monthly, Harper's, New Yorker, Ladies' Home Journal.*

HOBBIES AND OTHER INTERESTS: Mountain climbing, tennis, mathematics.

FOR MORE INFORMATION SEE: "Man in the News," *New York Times,* July 11, 1960.

ANGELL, Judie 1937-

PERSONAL: Born July 10, 1937, in New York, N.Y.; daughter of David Gordon (an attorney) and Mildred (a teacher; maiden name, Rogoff) Angell; married Philip Gaberman (a pop and jazz music teacher and arranger), December 20, 1964; children: Mark David, Alexander. *Education:* Syracuse University, B.S., 1959. *Religion:* "Yes." *Residence:* South Salem, N.Y.

CAREER: Elementary school teacher in Brooklyn, N.Y., 1959-62; *TV Guide,* Radnor, Pa., associate editor of New York City metropolitan edition, 1962-63; WNDT-TV (now WNET-TV), New York City, continuity writer, 1963-68; writer, 1968—.

WRITINGS—For children: *In Summertime, It's Tuffy,* Bradbury, 1977; *Ronnie and Rosey,* Bradbury, 1977; *Tina Gogo,* Bradbury, 1978; *A Word from Our Sponsor, or My Friend Alfred,* Bradbury, 1979; *Secret Selves,* Bradbury, 1979; *Dear Lola, or How to Build Your Own Family,* Bradbury, 1980.

SIDELIGHTS: "My background is incredibly useful to me in writing fiction for children: the childhood imaginings, the diaries, summers at camp, teaching school, some techniques and discipline, and always the music for the mood. But most important to me are the feelings I recall so well.

"I think growing up heads the list of The Hardest Things To Do In Life. It's so hard, in fact, that some of us never get there. But even if the world changes as rapidly as it does,

(From *Secret Selves* by Judie Angell. Jacket illustrated by George Thompson.)

the feelings that we have while we're coping with those changes don't. I take a lot of those feelings, hug them, wrap them carefully in some words, and present them in a book with an invisible card that says, maybe this'll help a little— make you laugh—make you feel you're not alone."

HOBBIES AND OTHER INTERESTS: Singing, painting, cats, listening to music.

FOR MORE INFORMATION SEE: Publishers Weekly, February 28, 1977; *Horn Book,* April, 1978; February, 1980.

JUDIE ANGELL

AREHART-TREICHEL, Joan 1942-

PERSONAL: Born May 19, 1942, in Louisville, Ky.; daughter of Oscar M. (an engineer) and Isabelle (a businesswoman; maiden name, Turner) Arehart; married Horst Klaus Treichel (a shipping owner), May 13, 1972; children: Tamara. *Education:* Attended Institute of European Studies, Sorbonne, University of Paris, 1962, and Oxford University, summer, 1962; Indiana University, A.B., 1964; graduate study at New York University, 1970, and Georgetown University, 1971. *Politics:* "Conservative on economic issues; liberal on social issues (rights of the individual)." *Religion:* Roman Catholic. *Home:* 906 Ravenshead, Sherwood Forest, Annapolis, Md. 21405. *Office: Science News,* 1719 N St. N.W., Washington, D.C. 20036.

CAREER: McCall's, New York, N.Y., assistant to senior editor, 1965; Ayerst Laboratories, New York, N.Y., editor of magazine, 1966-67; free-lance science writer in New York, N.Y., 1968-70, and in Washington, D.C., 1971—; *Science News* Magazine, Washington, D.C., medical editor, 1971—. *Member:* National Press Club, National Association of Science Writers, Washington Independent Writers. *Awards, honors:* Third place award in American Medical Association, medical journalism awards contest, 1971, for "Coral Unexpected Boon to Pharmaceutical Research"; honorable mention in national Claude Bernard Science Journalism award's contest, 1978, for "The Science Behind the Laetrile Controversy," first place award, 1979, for "Brain Proteins: Matter Over Mind."

WRITINGS—Juveniles: *Trace Elements: How They Help and Harm Us,* Holiday House, 1974; *Immunity: How Our Bodies Resist Disease,* Holiday House, 1975; *Poisons and Toxins,* Holiday House, 1975.

Adult books: *Biotypes–The Critical Link Between Your Personality and Your Health,* Times Books, 1980. Contributor to *New York, Harper's Bazaar, Washington Post, True, Parents' Magazine, Catholic Digest, Lady's Circle, Modern Maturity, Kiwanis Magazine, Louisville Courier Journal, Human Behavior, Oceans, Sea Frontiers, Young Miss, Vogue, Glamour,* and other publications.

SIDELIGHTS: "I've written books for young people because I feel I have never lost my own childish wonder and enthusiasm for things and can thus communicate effectively with youngsters.

JOAN AREHART-TREICHEL

"I've written an adult self-help book about personality and disease partly because I believe my mother's suffering and death from rheumatoid arthritis were caused by personality factors. My book came too late to help her, but I hope it will still help many other people."

HOBBIES AND OTHER INTERESTS: Photography, belly dancing, hiking, biking, tennis, sailing.

ARNOLD, Elliott 1912-1980

OBITUARY NOTICE—See sketch in SATA Volume 5: Born September 13, 1912, in New York, N.Y.; died after a brief illness, May 13, 1980, in New York, N.Y. Journalist, screenwriter, and author of children's books, novels, and biographies. Arnold frequently fictionalized historical events in many books. His 1967 best-seller, *A Night of Watching,* is based on the true story of how the Danish underground smuggled 8,000 Jews into Sweden after the Nazi takeover of Denmark. Another novel, *Blood Brother,* dramatizes the lives of Apache Indian chief Cochise and Indian agent Thomas J. Jeffords. Arnold won a Screen Writers Guild prize for the screen version of this book, entitled "Broken Arrow," and later he wrote for a television series of the same name. His books for children include *Brave Jimmy Stone, The Spirit of Cochise,* and *White Falcon* which received the William Allen White Children's Book Award in 1958. Before his final illness, Arnold had been working with Marlon Brando on a film about the American Indian. *For More Information See: Contemporary Authors,* Volume 17-20, revised, Gale, 1976; *Who's Who in America,* 40th edition, Marquis, 1978; *The Writer's Directory, 1980-82,* St. Martin's, 1979. *Obituaries: New York Times,* May 14, 1980; *Chicago Tribune,* May 15, 1980; *Publishers Weekly,* May 30, 1980; *Contemporary Authors,* Volume 97-100, Gale, 1980.

ARNOSKY, Jim 1946-

PERSONAL: Born September 1, 1946, in New York, N.Y.; son of Edward J. (a draftsman) and Marie (Telesco) Arnosky; married Deanna L. Eshleman, August 6, 1966; children: Michelle L., Amber L. *Education:* Attended high school in Pennsylvania. *Residence:* South Ryegate, Vermont.

CAREER: Draftsman in Philadelphia, Pa., 1964; Braceland Brothers (printers), Philadelphia, Pa., art trainee, 1965-66, creative artist, 1968-72; free-lance illustrator and writer, 1972—. *Military service:* U.S. Navy, 1966-68. *Awards, honors: Crinkleroot's Animal Tracks and Wildlife Signs* and *Moose Baby* were named outstanding science books, 1979, by the American Science Teachers' Association and the Children's Book Council.

WRITINGS—Self-illustrated children's books: *I Was Born in a Tree and Raised by Bees,* Putnam, 1977; *Outdoors on Foot,* Coward, 1977; *Nathaniel,* Addison-Wesley, 1978; *Crinkleroot's Animal Tracks and Wildlife Signs,* Putnam, 1979; *A Kettle of Hawks,* Coward, 1979; *Mudtime and More Nathaniel Stories,* Addison-Wesley, 1979.

Illustrator: Melvin and Gilda Berger, *Fitting In: Animals in Their Habitats,* Coward, 1976; Miska Miles, *Swim, Little*

JIM ARNOSKY

artist/naturalist. Most of my close friends are working naturalists, teachers, writers, photographers, farmers, and woodsmen. For four and a half years my wife, my two daughters, and I lived in a tiny cabin at the base of Hawk Mountain in Pennsylvania. There I matured as a writer and illustrator of natural subjects. . . . We have made our home in the hills of northern Vermont because its natural pace of life fits our needs best as a family and mine as a writer and illustrator.

"My books are autobiographical. I have difficulty contriving a story that doesn't come from a personal experience. (I admire writers who can.) The character 'Crinkleroot' is a vehicle I use to express the teacher and father in me. He is an old grandfatherly woodsman who knows endless wonders about the natural world and teaches them to his readers through activities they can join in. The character Nathaniel is a caricature of the everyday part of me. He is a countryman. A gardener and outdoorsman.

"My other books are treatments of subjects I feel have been greatly neglected by children's authors. My book, *Freshwater Fish and Fishing,* will expose nine to fourteen-year olds to a thorough natural history of all the common freshwater fish and their environments and will give them ways to fish aside from the more destructive use of live bait. In this book I hope to introduce the first outdoor ethic regarding the catching and eating or safely returning of fish to the water.

"I feel strongly that, contrary to present feelings about the future—about wildlife, ourselves, and our environment and the popular illusion of seeing everything headed down some vast drain in a hurry; that the first part of a better tomorrow is the awakening to our problems today. Our children, and their children, are headed for an even better future—where man may have a closer, working relationship with his natural world. When I speak to children at their schools I express this positive and hopeful prediction to them. I tell them that I know from my own experience that the world is a far better place than what they are hoping it will be and that their attitude will be the necessary ingredient for a happy, productive future in it.

Duck (Junior Literary Guild selection), Atlantic Monthly Press, 1976; Miska Miles, *Chicken Forgets,* Atlantic Monthly Press, 1976; Miska Miles, *Small Rabbit,* Atlantic Monthly Press, 1977; Marcel Sislowitz, *Look! How Your Eyes See,* Coward, 1977; Berniece Freschet, *Porcupine Baby,* Putnam, 1978; Berniece Freschet, *Possum Baby,* Putnam, 1978; Kaye Starbird, *Covered Bridge House,* Four Winds, 1979; Berniece Freschet, *Moose Baby,* Putnam, 1979; Eloise Jarvis McGraw, *Joel and the Magic Merlini,* Knopf, 1979; Betty Boegehold, *Bear Underground,* Doubleday, 1980; Margaret Bartlett and Preston Bassett, *Raindrop Stories,* Four Winds, 1980.

WORK IN PROGRESS: Writing and illustrating *Freshwater Fish and Fishing by Jim Arnosky,* for children; illustrating *Up a Tall Tree* by Anne Rockwell, also for children.

SIDELIGHTS: "I had no formal art training but learned a great deal about drawing from my dad who is a skillful patent draftsman. With this training at home I began working in the art field as a trainee. . . . It wasn't until I had been on my own free-lancing in illustration for nearly five years that I was introduced to the writing end of books. . . . Like solid, well-written poetry, writing for children emphasizes structure and the need for every word to count.

"I have always had a deep connection with the natural world and find its rhythm close to my own. I think of myself as an

(From *Nathaniel* by Jim Arnosky. Illustrated by the author.)

"Like Seton did before me, I feel that I am now encouraging the future naturalists, poets, technicians, engineers, and sportsmen of the future. The role of my books is like that of a conch shell. The sea isn't really inside the conch, but the conch brings it all to you. This is what a naturalist can do in books."

HOBBIES AND OTHER INTERESTS: Leisurely walking, fishing, fly-tying, watching wildlife, small farming (raising sheep, beekeeping, raising vegetables, etc.), and training his team of Newfoundland dogs.

AYMAR, Brandt 1911-

PERSONAL: Born May 8, 1911, in New York, N.Y.; son of Edmund B. and Mabel (Rathbun) Aymar. *Education:* Yale University, A.B., 1933. *Home:* 183 Secatogue Lane, West Islip, Long Island, N.Y. *Office:* Crown Publishers, Inc., 419 Park Ave. South, New York, N.Y. 10016.

CAREER: Greenberg Co. (publishers), New York, N.Y., vice president, 1944-58; Chilton Co. (publishers), Philadelphia, Pa., director of sales, publishing manager and editor, 1958-64; Crown Publishers, Inc., New York, N.Y., editor of special projects, 1964—. *Military service:* U.S. Coast Guard Reserves, 1942-44, became lieutenant (junior grade).

*WRITINGS—*Books of interest to young people: (Editor) *The Personality of the Cat,* Crown, 1958; (editor, with Edward Sagarin) *The Personality of the Horse,* Crown, 1963; (editor,

with E. Sagarin) *The Personality of the Dog,* Crown, 1964; (editor) *The Personality of the Bird,* Crown, 1965; (with E. Sagarin) *Pictorial History of the the World's Great Trials, from Socrates to Eichmann,* Crown, 1967; (with E. Sagarin) *Laws and Trials That Created History,* Crown, 1974.

Other writings: *Deck Chair Reader,* Greenberg, 1937; *Cruising Is Fun,* Greenberg, 1941; *The Complete Cruiser,* Greenberg, 1947; *Treasury of Snake Lore,* Greenberg, 1955; *Guide to Boatmanship, Seamanship and Safe Boat Handling,* Chilton, 1960; *Cruising Guide,* Chilton, 1962; *A Pictorial Treasury of the Marine Museums of the World,* Crown, 1968; *The Young Male Figure,* Crown, 1970.

BABCOCK, Dennis Arthur 1948-

PERSONAL: Born June 16, 1948, in Berkeley, Calif.; son of Frederick (an air force career officer) and Dorothy (Vogt) Babcock; married Lorene Kay Evenson (an interior designer), March 7, 1970; children: Bri Nicole (daughter); Brooke Adam (son). *Education:* Iowa State University, B.S., 1970; University of Minnesota, M.A., 1974, currently candidate for Ph.D. *Politics:* Democrat. *Religion:* Lutheran. *Office:* Guthrie Theater, Vineland Pl., Minneapolis, Minn. 55403.

CAREER: High school director of theater in the public schools of Des Moines, Iowa, 1970-72; Guthrie Theater, Minneapolis, Minn., actor/technician, 1974-75, publications director, 1975-78. Special events producer of "Vincent," starring Leonard Nimoy; business manager, 1978—. *Member:* Theta Alpha Phi.

WRITINGS: (With Preston Boyd) *Careers in the Theater* (juvenile), Lerner, 1975.

WORK IN PROGRESS: A history of theatre-in-the-round; research on famous actors and actresses.

SIDELIGHTS: "We wrote our book, *Careers in the Theater,* because we had the perfect opportunity—both Preston Boyd and I were unemployed actors and working part-time as stock persons at Lerner Publications. We approached the president of the company with the idea [for the book] and convinced him we were qualified, and *voila!*"

HOBBIES AND OTHER INTERESTS: "I love to canoe, camp, golf, and attend plays and movies."

BRANDT AYMAR

Children pick up words as pigeons peas,
And utter them again as God shall please.

—Proverb

Learn to live, and live to learn,
Ignorance like a fire doth burn,
Little tasks make large return.

—Bayard Taylor

BAKER, Alan   1951-

PERSONAL: Born November 14, 1951, in London, England; son of Bernard Victor (a machinist) and Barbara (Weir) Baker. *Education:* Attended Croydon Technical College, 1969-71, Hull University, 1971-72, and Croydon Art College, 1972-73; Brighton Art College, B.A., 1976. *Religion:* "Agnostic." *Home and office:* Ferrings Lodge, Plumpton Lane, Plumpton, East Sussex, England.

CAREER: Author and free-lance illustrator of children's books. *Awards, honors:* First class honorary degree in art and design, 1973, and Distinction Award for art and design, 1976, from Brighton Art College.

WRITINGS—All juveniles: (Self-illustrated) *Benjamin and the Box,* Andre Deutsch, 1977; (self-illustrated) *Benjamin Bounces Back,* Lippincott, 1978; *Short Stories from Dr. Finlay's Casebook,* Longman, 1978; (self-illustrated) *Benjamin's Dreadful Dream,* Andre Deutsch, 1980.

Illustrator: *Battle of Bubble and Squeeks,* Andre Deutsch, 1978; *The History of Flowers,* Hutchinson, 1980.

ADAPTATIONS: Benjamin and the Box was read and shown by the Canadian Broadcasting Corporation on the children's program, "The Friendly Giant," Spring, 1980.

WORK IN PROGRESS: A fantasy book, as yet untitled.

SIDELIGHTS: "My free-lance work tends to be very different from the books that I do and I think of it as a separate career—this work is greatly influenced by my environment. I live in the country just outside a small village in a very quiet corner of England.

"My illustrations are mostly of plants, animals, and fantasy (pixies, dragons, etc.). I derive much inspiration from travel, which I do a lot of (living very simply, which I think is important in order to really 'see' things). As a child, I had a pet hamster—hence the 'Benjamin' books."

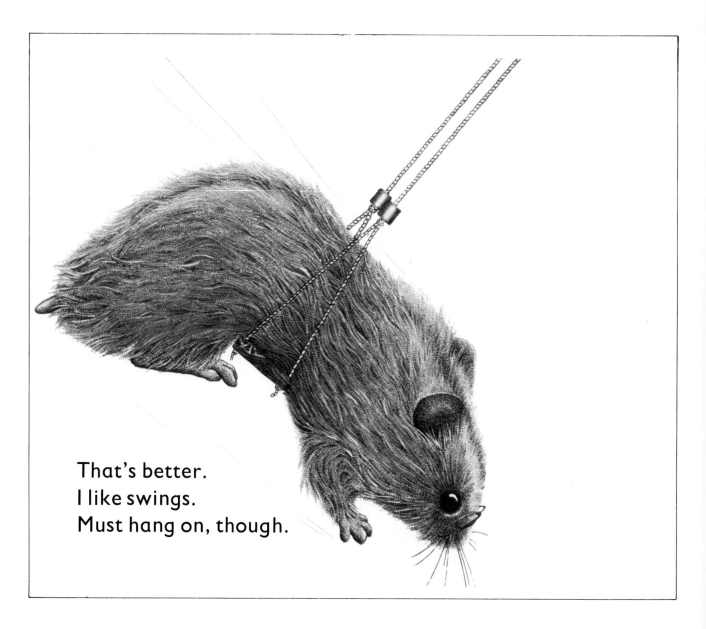

That's better.
I like swings.
Must hang on, though.

(From *Benjamin Bounces Back* by Alan Baker. Illustrated by the author.)

ALAN BAKER

"I do enjoy writing for children, but the illustration comes first; I tend to think of certain pictures I would like to create and then link them with a simple story. I like to think of the writing as adding a further dimension to the illustrations. The words hold the story line when the idea cannot be illustrated."

FOR MORE INFORMATION SEE: Times Literary Supplement, December 2, 1979.

BAKER, James W. 1924-
(Jim Baker)

PERSONAL: Born June 24, 1924, in Owensboro, Ky.; son of Roy (a salesman) and Sidney (Crutcher) Baker; married Mary Louise Swickard (a writer and editor), February 21, 1948; children: Barbara E., James N., John M., Elizabeth A. *Education:* Attended DePauw University, 1942-45. *Home:* 210 Hardy Way, Worthington, Ohio 43085. *Office:* Pioneer Press Service, Inc., P.O. Box 149, Worthington, Ohio 43085.

CAREER: Columbus Dispatch, Columbus, Ohio, cartoonist, 1947-66, creator of cartoon strip "Ben Hardy," 1952-66; author of cartoon strip "Ben Hardy," and panel "As You Were" for Pioneer Press Service, Worthington, Ohio. *Member:* Ohio Historical Society. *Awards, honors:* Ohio Governor's Award, 1948; distinguished service award from Ohioana Library, 1966.

WRITINGS—Under name Jim Baker: *From Settlement to Statehood,* Pioneer Press Service, 1965; *Cabin in the Clearing,* Pioneer Press Service, 1965, new edition, 1974; *Frontier Medicine,* Pioneer Press Service, 1965, new edition, 1974; *Ways of the Warriors,* Pioneer Press Service, 1966, new edition, 1975; *How Our Countries Got Their Names,* Pioneer Press Service, 1973; *Naming the States,* Pioneer Press Service, 1973; *Trains of Yesteryear,* Pioneer Press Service, 1973; *Get Out and Get Under,* Pioneer Press Service, 1973; *How to Be a Kid Again,* Pioneer Press Service, 1975; *Forts in the Forest,* Heartland House, 1975; *For the Ohio Country,* Heartland House, 1976; *Benjamin Franklin, Uncommon Man,* Heartland House, 1976; (with wife, Mary Louise) *Worthington, New England in the Wilderness,* Worthington, Ohio Historical Society, 1976.

SIDELIGHTS: "A lucky accident of birth made me a Kentuckian on my mother's side; growing up in history-rich Ohio and artistic and literary Indiana put me where I could do what I enjoy most: draw newspaper features about American history. One is an adventure strip whose hero, Ben Hardy, participates in events in our past; the other is a two-column panel.

"I have never felt the urge to travel beyond the United States, which has provided a gold mine of fascinating and humorous anecdotes for 'As You Were,' which is all about the scalawags and buffoons as well as the giants in our social history. A lot of the material is pure nostalgia, but that's nothing to be ashamed of. The field has been overrun lately by the fast-buck boys, but it's really here to stay. A healthy interest in

JAMES W. BAKER

WYOMING – PRETTY AS A PICTURE

THE PRETTY LITTLE EIGHT-WHEELER SHOWN HERE IS THE "WYOMING", SHOPPED OUT IN 1857. IT WAS BUILT BY THE NORRIS WORKS OF PHILADELPHIA. THE WYOMING WAS POSSIBLY THE MOST ORNATE ENGINE EVER CONSTRUCTED. MUCH OF THE DECORATION TYPICAL OF LOCOMOTIVES OF THIS ERA WAS DUE TO THE FACT THAT MANY BUILDERS HAD BEEN ARTISANS IN OTHER FIELDS BEFORE TURNING TO RAILROADING.

FOR EXAMPLE, PHILADELPHIA'S MATTHIAS BALDWIN HAD BEEN A JEWELER; THE FAMED GEORGE PULLMAN, A FINE CABINET MAKER.

(From *Trains of Yesteryear* by Jim Baker. Illustrated by the author.)

our collective family history and our own yesterdays is a sign of maturity in a nation. We've just begun to realize that newest isn't always best, and to appreciate selectively the good parts of what's gone before. Look at the strong steady undercurrent of interest in the Big Bands, my own first love.

"I'm a family man, enjoying four grown children, all different and all interesting to watch as they mature, and a wife who is the other half of our business; we call it the world's smallest conglomerate. For a while we were operating a newspaper syndicate, doing free-lance art and editorial work and publishing a string of books. Now it's simmered down to just the syndicate; the Ohio Historical Society now publishes the books, which I hope have brought a small knowledge of American and Ohio history and a few laughs to a couple of generations so far, thanks to the cooperation of the Ohio Historical Society, among others. Lately, I have returned to painting portraits and landscapes in oils, in the primitive style used by the early American painters.

"I've wanted to be a newspaper cartoonist since I was a little kid, so it doesn't bother me that I'm not rich. I just want to draw, do some wood-carving and make some furniture and muzzle-loading rifles, build a log cabin in the Ohio countryside, and take walks with our two collies through the autumn leaves."

BAKER, Janice E(dla)   1941-

PERSONAL: Born June 18, 1941, in Shreveport, La.; daughter of Glenn Jackson (a geophysicist) and Edla (Hill) Baker. *Education:* Southwestern College at Memphis, B.A. (with honors), 1963; Louisiana State University, M.A. (American history), 1967; University of Wisconsin, M.A. (comparative history), and Certificate in African Studies, 1971. *Religion:* Presbyterian. *Home:* 2122 Massachusetts Ave. N.W., Washington, D.C. 20008. *Office:* Presidential Commission on World Hunger, 734 Jackson Place, N.W., Washington, D.C. 20006.

CAREER: U.S. Peace Corps, Washington, D.C., English teacher in Guinea, West Africa, 1963-65; American Historical Association, Washington, D.C., assistant editor, 1967-69; Library of Congress, Washington, D.C., analyst for Congressional Research Service—Environmental Policy Division, 1972-79. *Member:* Phi Beta Kappa, Phi Alpha Theta, Phi Kappa Phi.

WRITINGS—"The Enchantment of Africa" series, all published by Childrens Press: (With Alan Carpenter) *Enchantment of Africa: Upper Volta,* 1974; (with Alan Carpenter) *Niger,* 1975; *Central African Republic,* 1978.

Some of Marie's relatives have gone blind from a disease called river blindness. When Marie visits them, she leads them around the village as this boy is doing. ■ (From *Enchantment of Africa: Upper Volta* by Allan Carpenter and Janice E. Baker. Photograph courtesy of the United Nations.)

WORK IN PROGRESS: Annotated bibliography on development theories.

SIDELIGHTS: In addition to Peace Corps work in Africa, Baker has spent time in Mexico, Western Europe, Yugoslavia and the Caribbean. ". . . [I am] particularly interested in cross-cultural exchanges throughout history, and in interpreting Third World cultures to American readers."

BARNES, (Frank) Eric Wollencott   1907-1962

PERSONAL: Born May 7, 1907, in Little Rock, Ark.; died December 31, 1962; son of William Gustavus and Louisa (Burnett) Barnes; married Margaret Ingalls Marvin, March 29, 1941; children: Eric Marvin, Charles Taylor. *Education:* Student at the University of California, 1925-26; received his diploma from the Ecole des Sciences Politiques, 1930; graduate of the University of Paris, 1931; obtained his doctorate from the University of Paris, 1940. *Religion:* Episcopalian.

CAREER: Actor, author, educator. American teaching fellow, Sorbonne, 1926-29; served in the U.S. Foreign Service, 1930-32; appeared in several New York productions as "Eric Wollencott," 1933-38; Russell Sage College, Troy, N.Y.,

instructor, 1938-39, assistant professor, 1939-40, department chairman, 1940, associate professor, 1940-42, professor of English, 1945; Dickinson College, Carlisle, Pa., department chairman and professor of English, 1946-53; Free University of Berlin, professor of American Literature, 1951-54; teacher at Loomis School, Windsor, Conn., 1957. Has contributed articles and short stories to several magazines. *Wartime and military service:* Civilian consultant to the Joint Chiefs of Staff, 1942; Military Intelligence officer, Air Force Headquarters, Algiers, 1942-44. *Member:* Zeta Psi. *Awards, honors:* Recipient of the Bronze Star.

*WRITINGS—*For children: *The War between the States* (illustrated by W. N. Wilson), McGraw, 1959; *Free Men Must Stand: The American War of Independence* (illustrated by W. N. Wilson), Whittlesey House, 1962, reissued as *Free Men Must Stand: The War That Made a Nation*, Popular Library, 1964.

Other writings: *L'Esthetique de Henry James,* [Paris], 1940; *The Lady of Fashion: The Life and the Theatre of Anna Cora Mowatt,* Scribner, 1954 (published in England as *Anna Cora: The Life and Theatre of Anna Cora Mowatt,* Secker & Warburg, 1954); *The Man Who Lived Twice: The Biography of Edward Sheldon,* Scribner, 1956 (published in England as *The High Room: A Biography of Edward Sheldon,* W. H. Allen, 1957).

SIDELIGHTS: Dr. Barnes's two books for juvenile readers, one an account of the Civil War and the other a chronicle of the American Revolution, have been highly praised by the critics for their broad scope, objectivity, and clarity. *Kirkus Reviews* reports that *The War Between the States* is "an

ERIC WOLLENCOTT BARNES

The "bummers" of the Union Army had a special talent for ferreting out hidden livestock.
■ (From *The War Between the States* by Eric Wollencott Barnes. Illustrated by W.N. Wilson.)

extremely cogent and explicit account" of the entire Civil War, while a critic from *New York Times Book Review* notes that this book is the first "recent account of the entire conflict for young readers, written factually, without imaginative embellishments."

Similar to *The War Between the States,* Barnes's second book for young people, *Free Men Must Stand,* is a commendable effort to clarify the issues and action of the American Revolution. *Christian Science Monitor* comments: "Dr. Barnes has done a remarkable job of presenting the entire American Revolution with clarity and balance. Boys and girls chiefly get this story in segments. Here is a whole picture, yet there is nothing encyclopedic in the telling. . . . No American school library should be without this distinguished book."

FOR MORE INFORMATION SEE: Kirkus Reviews, August 1, 1959; *New York Times Book Review,* December 13, 1959; *Christian Science Monitor,* November 15, 1962; *Who's Who in America, 1962-63.*

BEALER, Alex W(inkler III)   1921-1980

OBITUARY NOTICE—See sketch in SATA Volume 8: Born March 6, 1921, in Valdosta, Ga.; died March 17, 1980, in Atlanta, Ga. Author, blacksmith, woodworker, and advertising executive. Bealer built and operated his own blacksmith and woodworking shops, where he refused to use any power tools. In these workshops, Bealer recreated an atmosphere of excellent craftsmanship using the tools, techniques, and standards of old-time blacksmiths and woodworkers. He shared his knowledge of these crafts in such books as *The Art of Blacksmithing* and *Old Ways of Working*

Wood. For children he wrote *The Picture-Skin Story* and *Only the Names Remain.* The latter has been cited on the *Horn Book* Honor List and named an ALA Notable Book. *For More Information See: Contemporary Authors,* Volume 45-48, Gale, 1974. *Obituaries: Publishers Weekly,* April 4, 1980; *Contemporary Authors,* Volume 97-100, Gale, 1980.

BEARD, Dan(iel Carter)   1850-1941

PERSONAL: Born June 21, 1850, in Cincinnati, Ohio; died June 11, 1941, in Suffern, N.Y.; son of James Henry and Mary Caroline (Carter) Beard; married Beatrice Alice Jackson, August 15, 1894; children: Barbara, Daniel Bartlett. *Education:* Worall's Academy, graduated as a civil engineer, 1869; attended Art Student's League, New York City, 1880-84. *Religion:* Quaker. *Home:* Suffern, N.Y.

CAREER: Author, artist, naturalist. Employed in the office of the city engineer, Cincinnati, Ohio, 1869; later worked as a map-maker; book and magazine illustrator, and writer of boys' books, beginning 1882; art instructor in the Woman's School of Applied Design, 1893-1900; editor of *Recreation Magazine,* 1905-06; associate editor of *Boy's Life.* Founder of the first U.S. Boy Scout society, honorary vice-president of the Boy Scouts of America, National Scout Commissioner, chairman of the Boy Scouts National Court of Honor for thirty years; director of outdoor camp-schools. *Member:* Society of Illustrators (past-president), American Forestry Association (past vice-president), American Geological Society (fellow), Pi Gamma Mu, Alpha Phi Omega. *Awards, honors:* Received numerous awards, including the Roosevelt Distinguished Service Gold Medal, Boy Scouts Golden Eagle Badge, Masonic Grand Master Medal; Mt. Beard, next to Mt. McKinley in Alaska, was named in his honor.

WRITINGS—Nonfiction, except as noted: *What to Do, and How to Do It: The American Boy's Handy Book*, Scribner, 1882, also published as *The American Boy's Handy Book*, 1890, reprinted, C. E. Tuttle, 1966; *Moonlight and Six Feet of Romance* (novel; self-illustrated), C. L. Webster, 1892; *Outdoor Games for All Seasons: The American Boy's Book of Sport*, Scribner, 1896, also published as *Outdoor Handy Book for Playground, Field, and Forest* and as *For Playground, Field, and Forest*, Scribner, 1900; *The Jack of All Trades; or, New Ideas for American Boys*, Scribner, 1900, also published as *New Ideas for American Boys* (a portion published separately as *The Jack of All Trades: Fair Weather Ideas*, Scribner, 1904); *Field and Forest Handy Book: New Ideas for Out of Doors*, Scribner, 1906, also published as *New Ideas for Out of Doors* (portions published separately as *Handicraft for Outdoor Boys*, Grosset & Dunlap, 1906); *Dan Beard's Animal Book and Camp-Fire Stories* (self-illustrated), Moffat, Yard, 1907; *The Boy Pioneers: Sons of Daniel Boone* (self-illustrated), Scribner, 1909.

Boat-Building and Boating (self-illustrated), Scribner, 1911; *Shelters, Shacks, and Shanties* (self-illustrated), Scribner, 1914, reprinted, 1972; *The American Boys' Book of Bugs, Butterflies, and Beetles* (self-illustrated), Lippincott, 1915; *The American Boys' Book of Signs, Signals, and Symbols* (self-illustrated), Lippincott, 1918; *The American Boys' Handy Book of Camp-Lore and Woodcraft* (self-illustrated), Lippincott, 1920, also published as *The Book of Camp-Lore and Woodcraft*, Garden City Publishing, 1936; *The American Boys' Book of Wild Animals* (self-illustrated), Lippincott, 1921; *The Black Wolf Pack*, Scribner, 1922; *The American Boys' Book of Birds and Brownies of the Woods* (self-illustrated), Lippincott, 1923.

Do It Yourself: A Book of the Big Outdoors (self-illustrated), Lippincott, 1925; *The Wisdom of the Woods* (self-illustrated), Lippincott, 1926; *Buckskin Book for Buckskin Men and Boys* (self-illustrated), Lippincott, 1929; *Boy Heroes of Today: Boy Scout Gold Honor Medal Awards*, Brewer, Warren, 1932; *Hardly a Man Is Now Alive* (autobiography), Doubleday, Doran, 1939; *Dan Beard Talks to Scouts: A Talking Book Production* (illustrated by Hardie Gramatky), Garden City Publishing, 1940.

Illustrator—All written by Mark Twain (pseudonym of Samuel Langhorne Clemens): *A Yankee at the Court of King Arthur*, C. L. Webster, 1889, reissued as *A Connecticut Yankee in King Arthur's Court*, University Microfilms, 1966 [another edition under the latter title published by Penguin, 1971]; *The American Claimant*, C. L. Webster, 1892; *Tom Sawyer Abroad*, C. L. Webster, 1894.

Contributor of articles and illustrations to various periodicals, including *St. Nicholas*, *Recreation*, and *Boy's Life*.

SIDELIGHTS: **June 21, 1850.** Born in Cincinnati, Ohio. "One can hardly believe that they used candles in the dwellings in Cincinnati when I was a baby, but I have a scarred ear, a crooked finger and a fire-marked hand—the results of a lighted candle that did not fit a brass candlestick. My nurse withdrew a Shanghai match from its soft gray paper box and lighted the ill-fitting candle, then placed it on the mantelpiece facing the bed where I was peacefully sleeping. It was a big four-poster, a grand old bedstand built to order, so that there was room for all the family if they arranged themselves crossways, but the family did not sleep that way. From the red tester overhead mosquito netting was draped to protect me.

Daniel Beard as a child.

"The wind slammed the door, the shock jarred the candle from its candlestick and the vicious, evil-minded tallow dip fell from the mantel and rolled along the floor, with the flame still burning, until it struck the mosquito bar where the latter touched the floor. Instantly the whole canopy was ablaze. Fortunately a blanket covered my body. But I had good lungs, my SOS call reached my mother's alert ears, and she rescued me from the flaming pyre. I can remember that years ago there was in my mother's upper bureau drawer a dainty little golden brace with rings to fit fingers and prevent them from being drawn up by the burn. Nevertheless, the index finger of my right hand is now permanently crooked." [Daniel Beard, *Hardly a Man Is Now Alive*, Doubleday, 1939.[1]]

1859. Family moved to Painesville, Ohio. "In addition to many things that I had seldom seen in the city there were butterflies, robins, jay birds, bluebirds, purple martins, swallows, passenger pigeons and redheaded woodpeckers. My life was one of pleasant surprises. . . .

"My mother encouraged me in all these pursuits. It was she who showed me where the green-jeweled chrysalis of the monarch butterfly could be found, hanging under the top rail of the white picket fence, also where the funny brown jug-shaped chrysales with handles to them could be dug up in the garden. Everything was wonderful to the little city child, and intensely interesting. The days were all too short.

DANIEL BEARD

"The young people's life in Painesville was filled with jollity and harmless fun. The pranks they played were humorous and comical but never malicious. Even the small boys did not wantonly break windows or destroy things. The age of malevolent hoodlum destruction had not yet reached America. It was the construction age of Brother Jonathan which preceded the destructive era of Uncle Sam and the Civil War.

"Life was beginning to become complicated to an earnest and well-meaning little chap who wished to understand and to do what was right but was troubled by the difference between the teachings of his wise mother, the example of the older boys and the incomprehensible talks of the preachers. It was much easier to understand the talk of the birds and to read the message of the stars, and much less wearisome."[1]

At an early age, Beard displayed a talent for drawing which did not go unrecognized by his teachers. "On certain days we had drawing lessons; that is, the other pupils had drawing lessons and I had fun. On such occasions the girls of our grade entered our room and took the desks on one side of the room, while we occupied the other side of the aisle. The teacher was supposed to go to the blackboard and draw objects with chalk for the pupils to copy on their slates, but in place of doing that she would smile sweetly at me and say, 'Danny, you take charge of this class.' Then she would swish out of the room, her tilting hoops swinging as she went between the desks, displaying all her beautifully embroidered lingerie up to her waist, and vanish into the girls' room.

"As an art instructor I felt the dignity of my position, but I was only a small boy and often yielded to temptation, so besides the copy which was carefully drawn, I made a series of crude caricatures of Daddy Lock, Ole Man Rice, Miss Crane, Mr. Pease and the drawing teacher with her tilting hoops, all of which would send my fellow pupils off in convulsions of laughter. There would be a premonitory rustling of skirts in the next room, and with a quick sweep I would wipe the offensive pictures from the board. But when the drawing teacher appeared and told the pupils how splendid it was of Daniel to make the drawings for them and described how disgraceful it was for them to misbehave while he was doing so, I certainly felt uncomfortable. I was, however, very proud of the loyalty of my fellow pupils, whom I allowed to take the blame."[1]

The Beard family moved back to Cincinnati. "After coming from the woods and fields and lake shore of northern Ohio back to the grimy, sooty streets of Cincinnati, and moving to a house on the corner of Longworth and John streets, with no yard at all, I was utterly miserable, and I am afraid I succeeded in making everybody else unhappy. I remember time after time lying on my back on the floor moaning and yelling, 'I want to go to the country, I want to go to the country.' Finally, one day, an omnibus drove up to our house and took us to the depot. We were bound for Branch Hill, where for a short period we lived on a farm, and again I was happy."[1]

1861. "Perhaps things were too tame in Cincinnati. Perhaps father wanted to be nearer the scene of action when war came. At any rate we moved across the river to Covington, Kentucky.

"The reverberation of the cannons that fired on Fort Sumter had shaken the foundations of thousands and thousands of happy homes both North and South. The families in many of them were violently wrenched apart, never again to be reassembled. But that did not bother me. I was a boy! Things were exciting and I gloried in my position as the man of the family. I strutted around in soldier clothes, as did all the other boys. I rode the cavalry horses down to the river to water, and the soldiers all promised to take me along with them when they left. The soldiers were themselves nothing but big boys, sixteen, seventeen, eighteen years old.

"War is a terrible thing, it is an almost unbelievable thing, but one cannot help wishing that the same personal, unselfish sacrifices by men, women and children for the good of American institutions were prevalent during times of peace. A few miles to the south of us, the Confederates were making the same sacrifices for their soldier boys. Both sides were working for a principle, working for the thing which they believed to be right."[1]

1865. Application to the Annapolis Naval Academy was rejected. ". . .I received an appointment to the Annapolis Naval Academy. I had never been away from home, and while going to Annapolis was a great adventure to me, at the same time I dreaded it because I was filled with awe of the place, its traditions, the uniforms and the officers. But at Annapolis, Father introduced me to his old friend, Commodore Meade, and all through my embarrassing campaign the commodore stood by me. They first put me through a physical examination, and it was a thorough one. There was no part of my physique that they did not examine minutely. I felt as if I were pulling through with all flags flying, when the doctor said, 'Hold out your hands.' I held them out. 'Hold the fingers straight.' I held all but one straight. Then his eagle eye discovered my crooked index finger. 'Hem,' he said, and I knew what that 'Hem' meant. I was about to be turned down because of that crooked finger.

"Commodore Meade led me to Commodore Porter. He stopped this bearded sea dog as he was proudly pacing the walk on the beautiful academy grounds. Growled the commodore, 'Let me see that finger.' Then he inquired, 'How do you expect to pull the trigger with a finger like that?' I timidly explained to him what should have been self-evident—that I could pull a trigger better with that finger because of its shape and the consequent additional strength than any fellow could with a straight one. Next he grumbled, 'How would you hang onto the topmast rigging in a storm?' Again I pointed out to him that a hooked finger would then be of more service than a straight one. Still holding onto my finger, he rumbled and grumbled until a brilliant idea struck him. Then he barked triumphantly, 'How can you point with that hooked finger?'

"'Sir, when I point I use my second finger, saying, "See that man over there," but when using my crooked finger I say, "The man you want just went around the corner."'

"Commodore Meade made Father hustle me off to Washington, and Father took me in and introduced me to Gideon Welles, Abe Lincoln's Secretary of the Navy. Gideon was just the kind of a fellow you would expect Lincoln to have in his Cabinet. He began to laugh as soon as I came into the room, picked up a musket and without warning tossed it to me. I caught the gun. Then he put me through the manual of arms, at which I was an expert because the best part of my boyhood had been spent in a fortified camp. Then Gideon, like good fellow that he was, wrote an order, passing me on my physical examination.

"I went back to Annapolis, and there I learned my lesson—that perhaps it is not safe to go over the heads of those in authority. When called up before two officers for examination the heartless young fellows were amused by my embarrassment and confusion, and increased it by gruffly ordering me to put up my handkerchief, which I was nervously twisting in my hands. In place of asking me questions in a gentle and kindly manner they barked them out like hard-boiled top sergeants giving orders to a bunch of rookies, with the consequence that they had me so fussed that I actually could not tell whether the Gulf of Mexico was in the Arctic region or the desert of Sahara. I was rejected, of course. I went home feeling as though I was disgraced for life."[1]

1867. Enrolled at Worrall's Academy in Covington where he studied civil engineering. "School became a more important part of my life after the war was over. Professor Worrall at the Academy was my particular favorite, though I am fairly confident he could not have said the same of me. He was a narrow-chested, hollow-cheeked, anemic man with an intellectual brow and eyes that could flash like a short circuit. He had weak lungs and occasional hemorrhages, but there was nothing anemic about his character. He had the utmost contempt for mollycoddles or boys who did not realize the weighty importance of life and learning. Once he threw a Webster's Dictionary at his own nephew because the boy committed the sacrilege of nodding drowsily over mathematics. Professor Worrall was the liveliest of live wires, with energy to burn. He inspired us all with pep, vim and ambition, as well as with a withering contempt for idleness and shiftlessness. He was as punctilious as a duelist in his code of

Pen and ink drawing by Daniel Carter Beard, 1887.
■(From *200 Years of American Illustration* by Henry C. Pitz.)

honor, and he demanded the same punctiliousness from his pupils. Nevertheless, it would be stretching the truth if I were to intimate that all of his sixty or seventy pupils possessed the same energy, the same reverence for honesty and honor as the professor; but, with such a leader, even the weak sisters among us were not quite so sloppy and weak as we otherwise might have been."[1]

1869. "At nineteen I was graduated from Worrall's Academy as a civil engineer, and I immediately applied for a position in Earnshaw's engineering and surveying office. Earnshaw looked over my papers and signed me up on his force at nothing a week. I paid my own expenses. After graduating, with what was considered high honors, I was terribly mortified to be compelled to drive stakes in place of building Roebling suspension bridges; or to wielding an ax in place of peering through the theodolite; or to drag the chain wearily over the dusty hills and stone quarries in place of sinking coffer dams. It took all the courage I had to sit by the roadside and eat my lunch out of a basket while carriages drove by from which girls waved with whom I danced at our social gatherings."[1]

1870's. ". . .I obtained a position in R. C. Phillips' office at four dollars a week. I spent the first four dollars on neckties. I always did want more than one necktie at a time. From there I migrated to the city engineer's office and received fifty dollars a month. While working in the city employ I did other work in my free time and made drawings of the first camelback cars for the inclined railway. At night I made maps for private individuals, from which I obtained a little additional money.

"While surveying the hills surrounding Cincinnati it was our habit to seek the shade of a beech or sugar maple tree, there

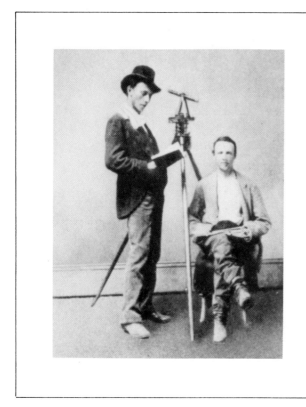

Beard with Sanborn Map Company.

eat our luncheon and rest for the noon hour. Stretching myself on my back, I watched the celestial moving pictures. I thought out plans for all the different things I wanted to do. Growing ambitious, I even planned a world in which the boys might get together and make known their wants and ambitions, not a world of gray-headed philosophers or a world of money-getting baldheads or of selfish, middle-aged people, but a world filled with men who still retained some of the urge of boyhood.

"As I grew older my dreams were not so fantastic, but fantastic enough for those prosaic days. I planned city playgrounds before any municipality had given such an idea a thought. In my playgrounds were spaces to play marbles, to spin tops, soft ground for jumping, for foot-and-a-half and leapfrog, and a wading and swimming pool, swings, teeters (see-saws), and big flying cages for birds. All these things have come true, although I cannot personally lay claim to any of them. I did write about them and talk about them in public addresses, however."[1]

1874-1878. "My opportunity to travel came at last and I left my then well-paying position in the city engineer's office to accept an appointment for a lesser amount as surveyor for the Sanborn Map and Publishing Company. While working for them I not only saw all those places I had heard about but I made maps of them, made diagrams of all the houses in each town and city I visited. I took a delight in always putting into my records mention of real occupancy, genteel or disreputable. After four or five years of this work I knew a lot about our people, saints and sinners, rich and poor.[1]

1878. "While I had been surveying, Father and our family migrated backwards from Covington to New York and at

length located themselves in the then beautiful village of Flushing, Long Island. During my spare time as a surveyor I drew and painted in water colors such natural-history objects as interested me. Once when I came home on vacation I dropped into Brother Frank's studio and showed him some of the sketches I had made. A. W. Drake of the Century Company was there. He asked if he might publish one of my sketches and a few days after that I received a check for twenty-five dollars for a picture of a fish. I was astonished. The sketch had been made for the sheer pleasure of doing it, and I decided that if they paid one so liberally for having fun, darned if I'd work any more. I journeyed around to Sanborn's and said, 'Mr. Sanborn, I won't be back for a while. I'm on a vacation. . . .' I am still on that vacation. I was never discharged; I never resigned."

Early 1880's. "After Drake of *St. Nicholas* had purchased my picture, all thought of again taking up surveying vanished, and I took easel room in my brother Frank's place where I began to draw on wood for *Forest and Stream* and similar magazines. At this time I met and worked with such sport writers as the late George Bird Grinnell and the delightful Charles Hallock. . . .

"As for myself, I was still learning to draw. I visited the department stores and made sketches of their different objects of merchandise, which I later drew on wood for their published catalogues. I drew everything. I made designs for decorated delivery carts, labels for boxes, valentines, architectural drawings, Currier and Ives pictures, designs for guns, jack lights and other poaching paraphernalia which should never have been made or published. But I was shocked by the number of people who came to us with requests for counterfeit labels of other firms. They couldn't understand why we declined to do it, when they offered good pay. Between times I haunted Wallace's taxidermist shop to sketch any fresh specimens, and also Eugene Blackford's fish stall at Fulton Market.

"Horatio Harper asked me to make some book-cover designs, which proved so successful that I was flooded with orders from all the prominent publishing houses and could have developed a lucrative profession as a book-cover designer. All this work was done for money, to enable me to become an illustrator like my brothers. In order to realize this idea I used the money that I made during the daytime to pay for my expenses at the Art Student's League night class. That meant that I left home on the half-past seven train every morning and did not reach home unitl eleven or twelve o'clock at night."[1]

About this time, Beard saw something that changed the course of his life. "One cold, raw day as I came into the city I was horror–stricken to discover newsboys sleeping on the damp stones in the enclosed space around their patron saint, Ben Franklin. They looked miserable enough to bring tears to the eyes of the bronzed statue itself. New York was a city built as if there were no such things in the world as children. Even the public school buildings were tucked away on dark streets and could not be compared with the splendid school buildings of some of the rural settlements of Illinois and Indiana. . . . It was the sight of the newsboys huddled together for warmth on the cold flagging around their patron saint, Ben Franklin, that started me on my lifelong crusade for American boyhood. I realized that I should not waste time on men, but hereafter devote all my energies to interesting boys. With this thought prompting me, I wrote and illustrated for *St. Nicholas, Harper's Round Table, Youth's*

"I SAW HE MEANT BUSINESS."

(From *A Connecticut Yankee in King Arthur's Court* by Mark Twain. Illustrated by Dan Beard.)

Companion, Wide Awake and other similar publications, while I studied art at night."[1]

1882. Beard's articles were published in *What to Do and How to Do It: The American Boy's Handy Book*. "The press was awfully kind to me and said very nice things. They called me the Gustave Doré of newspaper work, while *Public Opinion* called me the Mark Twain of art."[1]

1889. Illustrated Mark Twain's *A Connecticut Yankee in King Arthur's Court*. "In making the illustration for his book I referred to a collection of photographs of people of note. When I wanted a face or a figure to fit a character in the story I looked over this collection of photographs and made free use of them, not as caricatures or portraits of the people themselves, but for the dress, pose, or their whole figure and features as best fitted the character I was to depict. The captain of our boat club, holding a halberd in his hand, posed for one of the initial letters as a sentry dressed with a sealskin. For the Yankee himself I used George Morrison, a real Connecticut Yankee who was experimenting in a photoengraving establishment adjoining my studio. The charming actress Annie Russell appears in the pages as Sandy, the heroine. Sarah Bernhardt is there as a page. In fact no one held too lofty a position to escape my notice if I thought he or she possessed the face or figure suited to the character I wished to draw. I had more fun making the drawings for that book than any other book I ever illustrated.

"I made about four hundred illustrations in seventy working days. The first illustration was that of a knight with lance set charging on the Yankee, who was climbing a tree. This pleased Mr. Clemens very greatly. In the corner of the illustration there is a helmet as a sort of decoration with the visor partly open, of which Mark said, 'The smile on that helmet is a source of perennial joy to me.' When I finished the book he wrote: "'Dear Mr. Beard—

"'Hold me under everlasting obligations. There are a hundred artists who could have illustrated any other of my books, but only one who could illustrate this one. It was a lucky day I went netting for lightning bugs and caught a meteor. Live forever.'"[1]

1893-1900. "I taught what I am told was the pioneer class in animal drawing at the New York School of Applied Design. I also launched the pioneer class in illustration at the same art school. Previous to this, art students were taught to draw only from the antique plaster-cast figures, from the nude human figure and, in the sketch class, from costumed figures. I sent my pupils to the Wild West shows and various places of interest, and required them to make sketches. I sent them to the zoos and menageries to make drawings of animals. I made them bring butterflies, bugs and beetles into the art class and sketch them, also small mammals, snakes, toads and frogs. Then I pointed out to them the difference between the real creatures and the ordinary pictures of them. Very few, even of the famous painters, of that date made correct representations of butterflies, and as for snakes, the less said the better. The illustrations, of course, had to illustrate a story or an incident, and in them I insisted upon the costume and local color being correct."[1]

August 15, 1894. Married Beatrice Alice Jackson.

1905. "As editor of *Recreation* I got the opportunity not only to fight for conservation but to take up the cudgel for boys. My battle for the young people now began to take form and color, and my position as editor threw me in contact with such picturesque characters as Yellowstone Kelly, Buffalo Bill, John Burroughs, Bat Masterson, Buffalo Jones and Charles Russell.

"The business manager of *Recreation,* William Annis, had grown up in my study as a kind of office boy-student. He was familiar with my work for boys. One day he suggested to me that I start some organization for the juvenile sportsmen who were readers of our magazines. I already had a Boys' Department, but he wanted something more concrete. I suggested a society of scouts for boys to be identified with the greatest of all scouts, Daniel Boone, and to be known as the Sons of Daniel Boone. Each member would have to be a tenderfoot before he attained the rank of scout. Eight members would form a stockade, four stockades a fort.

"The Sons of Daniel Boone prospered. I sometimes wrote long-hand as many as fifty letters in one day to the members.

The little rascals were too impatient to wait for printed answers in the magazine"[1]

1906. "*Recreation* was sold, but I took the organization with me to the *Woman's Home Companion.* When I resigned from this last magazine I left the Sons of Daniel Boone in charge of my valued friend, Sir Robert Baden-Powell."[1]

1909. "My next work was with the *Pictorial Review.* There I started the same type of movement. This I called the Boy Pioneers and made Baden-Powell an honorary member. Don't mix my Boy Pioneers with the later-day organization by that name. There never was any connection. The Communists took our name and organized the Red youth under it.

"In both these organizations, the Sons of Daniel Boone and the Boy Pioneers, I confined myself to the United States for my inspiration. I did not summon to my aid King Arthur and his Round Table, the glistening armor of the tourney, Richard the Lionhearted, the Black Prince or Saladin of the Saracens. No, not even Robin Hood, though he was more my type of man. In place of the lance and buckler was the American long rifle and buckskin clothes, in place of the shining plumed helmet was the American coonskin cap, the tail of the 'coon its plume. I tried to put into the organization the joyousness of the blue sky with its fleeting clouds, the reliability and stability of the earth beneath our feet, and the natural democracy of Daniel Boone himself."[1]

...I built a forty-foot-front, two-story log house that is probably the pioneer among log houses erected by city men for summer houses. ■ (From *Shelters, Shacks and Shanties* by D.C. Beard. Illustrated by the author.)

Beard, at work in his studio.

1910. Beard's organization and other boys' societies were consolidated into the Boy Scouts of America. "The equipment of the Boy Scouts grew in simple fashion. We adopted the cowboy sombrero, the famous Stetson that is interwoven with the winning of the Western plains. I myself had often used it and there is nothing that is better as a shield against the weather. The world over it is now recognized as a great hat for the open spaces.

"At Culver Academy I worked with Colonel Gignilliat on the Woodcrafters, a boys' organization. Colonel Gignilliat and I together designed the uniform for these youngsters. It consisted of a short-sleeved woolen shirt open at the neck, shorts or flappers, with long woolen stockings.

"The handkerchief around the neck came from the cowboys along with the hat of which I have spoken, with its leather hat band. It was from Theodore Roosevelt's Rough Riders on their return from the Spanish-American War that I learned how to fix the backstrap or *barbiquejo,* to keep the hat on the head.

"The name Scout was of course used by Baden-Powell in his original military organization, but when I applied it in my Sons of Daniel Boone it signified to me rather those stalwart Americans, the men of the wilderness, such as Daniel Boone

himself, Simon Kent and George Rogers Clark. It had always appealed to me because of its romance and intimate connection with the history of this country. I gave it to the boys who qualified in my group. For those who had just joined I used 'tenderfoot,' which is a cowboy term originally applied to cattle shipped from the East to the West, because as they were unused to the rough country their feet became sore. The cowboys themselves used it for all greenhorns.

"My close friend, Lord Baden-Powell, in his English Scouts used the same formation of eight boys that I used in the Sons of Daniel Boone. Instead of using *stockade* and *fort,* which are American pioneer terms, he carried on the terms *patrol* and *troop* from his original military organization. He used three fingers for the salute to represent the three points of the Scout oath, instead of the two I used, which is the Indian sign for a wolf, the scouting animal of the wilderness. The latter is still used by the younger group of boys in the Scout movement, the Cubs, as we call them."[1]

June 11, 1941. Died of myocarditis at Brooklands, his estate in Suffern, N.Y., ten days before his ninety-first birthday. For many years Beard served as National Scout Commissioner, as director of outdoor camp-schools, and as an associate editor of the Boy Scout magazine, *Boy's Life.*

"Here in the United States we, the descendants of a mighty set of hardy pioneers, now find ourselves in a new age—the 'pushbutton' age. We no longer go to the well and drink from the old oaken bucket; we touch a button and a pitcher of ice water is brought to us. We no longer walk; we ride in luxurious machines. We no longer write our own speeches and reports; they are written for us and we sign them.

"We must be on our guard to see that modern conditions do not soften our fiber until, when confronted with hardships, we become as helpless as a hermit crab without a shell.

"This was a good country in the past. It is a good country today. It will be a good country tomorrow unless we fail it. As I lay down my pen I feel like saying with David, the Psalmist: 'Thou hast set my feet in a large room.' "[1]

FOR MORE INFORMATION SEE: Cyril Clemens and Edward C. Sibley, *Uncle Dan: The Life Story of Dan Beard,* Crowell, 1938; Beard, *Hardly a Man Is Now Alive* (autobiography), Doubleday, Doran, 1939; W. H. Carr, "Daniel Carter Beard, Great Scout," *Conservationist,* August, 1973.

For children: Stanley J. Kunitz and Howard Haycraft, editors, *Junior Book of Authors,* Wilson, 1934; Miriam E. Mason, *Dan Beard: Boy Scout,* Bobbs-Merrill, 1953, 2nd edition, 1962; Robert N. Webb, *The Story of Dan Beard,* Grosset & Dunlap, 1958; Jerry Seibert, *Dan Beard: Boy Scout Pioneer,* Houghton, 1963; Wyatt Blassingame, *Dan Beard, Scoutmaster of America,* Garrard, 1972.

Obituaries: *New York Times,* June 12, 1941; *Publishers Weekly,* June 21, 1941; *Newsweek,* June 23, 1941; *Times,* June 23, 1941.

BEARDEN, Romare (Howard)   1914-

PERSONAL: First name is pronounced *Rome*-ery; born September 2, 1914, in Charlotte, N.C.; son of Howard R. (some sources cite father's name as Richard Howard; an employee of the New York City Department of Health) and Bessye (a newspaper editor; maiden name Johnson) Bearden; married Nanette Rohan, September 4, 1954. *Education:* Attended Boston University; New York University, B.S., 1935; studied at the Art Students League under George Grosz, 1936-37, and at Columbia University, 1943; received certificate from the Sorbonne, Paris, 1951; also studied at the University of Pittsburgh and American Artists School. *Home:* 351 W. 114 St., New York, N.Y. 10026. *Studio:* 357 Canal St., New York, N.Y. 10013.

CAREER: Artist; early work included a position as political cartoonist for the *Baltimore Afro-American;* Department of Social Services, New York City, caseworker, 1938, 1946, 1952-66; Cinque Gallery, New York City, co-founder and director, 1969—. Art director, Harlem Cultural Council, 1964—; visiting lecturer in African and Afro-American art and culture, Williams College, 1969; Guggenheim fellow for the research of the history of Afro-American art, 1970-71; member of the board of directors, New York State council on the Arts; charter member of advisory committee, Community Gallery of the Brooklyn Museum; has exhibited his work in several one-man shows, including Kootz Gallery, New York City, 1945, 1946, 1947, Duvuloy Gallery, Paris, 1945, Barone Gallery, 1955, Michael Warren Gallery, 1960, Cordier-Ekstrom, 1964, 1967, 1973-75, all New York City,

Corcoran Gallery, Washington, D.C., 1965, Museum of Modern Art, 1971; has participated in numerous group exhibits, most notably the Harlem Art Center, 1937, 1939, Institute of Modern Art, Boston, 1943, San Francisco Museum of Art, 1969, New Jersey State Museum, 1970, Pace Gallery, New York City, 1972; collections of his work are held at the Museum of Fine Arts, Boston, Museum of Modern Art, New York City, Newark Museum, New Jersey, Albright Museum, Buffalo, and many other locations throughout the United States. *Military service:* U.S. Army, 372nd Infantry Regiment, 1942-45; became sergeant.

MEMBER: American Academy and Institute of Arts and Letters, Black Academy of Arts and Letters, Spiral Group. *Awards, honors:* National Academy of Arts and Letters (now incorporated in the American Academy and Institute of Arts and Letters), purchase award, 1970; Ford Foundation grant, 1973.

WRITINGS: (With Carl Holty) *The Painter's Mind: A Study of the Relations of Structure and Space in Painting,* Crown, 1969; (with Harry Brinton Henderson) *Six Black Masters of American Art,* Doubleday, 1972; (illustrator) Samuel Allen, *Poems from Africa,* Crowell, 1973; (author of foreword) Elton Clay Fax, *Black Artists of the New Generation,* Dodd, 1977.

Paintings: *Romare Bearden: Paintings and Projections* (exhibition catalogue; introduction by Ralph Ellison), Art Gallery, State University of New York, Albany, 1968; *Romare Bearden: The Prevalence of Ritual* (exhibition catalogue; introduction by Carroll Greene), Museum of Modern Art, New York City, 1971; *The Art of Romare Bearden* (collection of paintings; text by M. Bunch Washington), Abrams, 1973.

SIDELIGHTS: **September 1914.** Born in Charlotte, North Carolina, Bearden spent his youth in Harlem. His earliest introduction into the world of art were drawings on sheets of brown paper executed by a young boy named Eugene. "He had infantile paralysis, and he couldn't run with us—he couldn't even eat very fast—but he was always around the house.

"He'd done one drawing of a house of prostitution not far from where we lived, run by a woman named Sadie. We always liked to go there and try to sell newspapers, because the music was so interesting—that kind of rolling piano. Eugene had drawn Sadie's house with the facade cut off, so you could see in all the rooms. And somebody had shot off a pistol, and the bullet was going all through the house. Women were on top of men, and the bullet was going through them, into the next room and the next, until it came down through the ceiling into the front parlor, and Sadie had her pocketbook open, and the bullet had turned into coins and was dropping into her pocketbook. I said to Eugene, 'You did this? Can you teach me to do it?' He said, 'Sure.' So I started taking drawing lessons from Eugene.

"My grandmother set up a table in my room, and Eugene and I would go and draw every day. All his drawings were about what happened in Sadie's house, and I was just trying religiously to copy what he did. After a week or so, my grandmother came around wanting to see what we had done. She took one look, and she grabbed all those drawings and threw them into the furnace. She said, 'Eugene, where did you ever see anything like that?' Eugene said, 'My mother is a whore. She works over at Sadie's place.' My grandmother told him, 'Eugene, don't you go home tonight.'

"... Eugene never did any more drawings after he left Sadie's house. He died about a year later, and we went to his funeral. But I always thought that with his drawings he could have been another Lautrec. That was the first time I ever thought about drawing—and then for years I forgot about it." [Calvin Tomkins, "Profiles," *New Yorker,* November 28, 1977.[1]]

1936. A year after graduating from New York University with a bachelor's degree in science, he enrolled in the Art Students League to study under the German expatriate, George Grosz. "[Grosz] made me realize the artistic possibilities of American Negro subject matter."[1]

After studying with Grosz, Bearden took a job for a year with the New York City Department of Welfare as a caseworker. Shortly after taking the job, he rented a studio of his own. But, for almost a year, Bearden could do nothing with the canvas which remained on his easel. He has often told this story of how he overcame that stagnant period: "Each Saturday, a lady, who was a friend of my mother, came by to clean the studio for me, as it is a common feeling that artists are rather disorderly. This lady was very efficient, very quiet, and ... very, very homely. One Saturday she looked at the blank canvas and asked me: 'Is that that same canvas that's been there all these weeks?' I told her truthfully that it was; that I was going through a thinking process. 'Well,' she said, 'it's paint that's going to put something on that canvas. Why don't you paint me?' she asked. From the expression on my face she could see that her portrait was not the one I wished to start my career with. 'I know I'm homely,' she said, 'but, I'll tell you this: when you're able to look deep inside of me and find what is beautiful there, you will be able to begin work on the canvas.'" Bearden has commented that this lady taught him as much in those few words as did the year and a half at the Art Students League.

1940's. Bearden began exhibiting his works. Held his first one-man show at the studio of Ad Bates in Harlem. Spent three years in a Black regiment of the U.S. Army, after which Caresse Crosby gave him an exhibition in her "C" Gallery.

1943. Mother died of pneumonia.

1945-47. Samuel Kootz gave Bearden three exhibitions at his New York gallery. Bearden's paintings were based mainly on literary or Biblical themes during this time. His first Kootz exhibition featured his "Passion of Christ" series, which was sold out and served to establish some regular customers.

1946. Returned to the Department of Welfare and continued painting during his free time.

1950. Sojourned to Paris for adventure and to study philosophy at the Sorbonne.

Still unable to support himself solely with his painting, Bearden went back to the Department of Social Services upon his return to the United States. He found painting very difficult and was unable to get back into it. So, he decided to try his hand at songwriting, in hopes of making enough money to return to Paris.

Bearden was not unsuccessful as a songwriter. He recorded about twenty songs including the hit "Seabreeze."

Music, especially jazz, had always been an influence in Bearden's life. He would often listen to musicians perform with

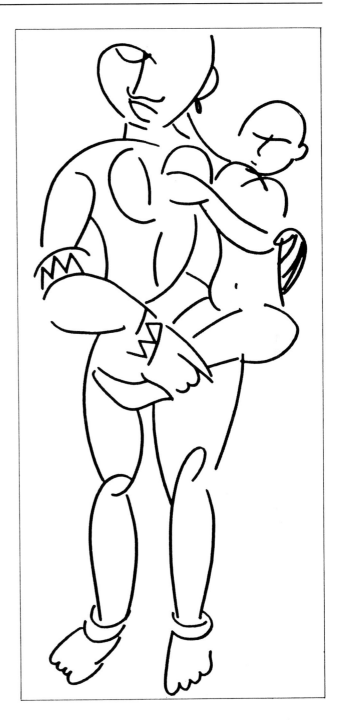

(From *Poems from Africa* by Samuel Allen. Drawing by Romare Bearden.)

paper in front of him, making lines to pick up the rhythm and the intervals of the music. He told a *Horizon* writer, "Abstract expressionism is very close to the aesthetics of jazz. That's the feeling you get from it—involvement, personality, improvisation, rhythm, color."

1952. Obliged to go back to the Department of Social Services and paint part-time. His assignment was to keep track of the gypsies moving in and out of New York. Bearden became very attached to these people and their unique culture. In his longest stint as a caseworker, Bearden worked with the gypsies for fourteen years.

Late 1950's. Began to experiment with collage. He would paste down clippings from magazines and then draw and paint over them. This experimentation led to a breakthrough in Bearden's career.

1964. Arne Ekstrom scheduled for his gallery an exhibition of Bearden's photomontages or "projections," as he and Bearden agreed to call them.

The collage paintings seemed to be the answer to all of Bearden's earlier struggles. All of his experiences seemed to culminate in the new form. The works were so fresh that some even said Bearden had reinvented collage.

Bearden's collages deal primarily with images of Negro life. Bruce Duff Hooton, writing in *Horizon,* commented that Bearden is "squarely in the tradition of American artist-reporters, and he continues to share that tradition with other living artists, including Andrew Wyeth, Jack Levine, Andy Warhol, James Rosenquist, George Segal, and the new group of photorealists." A number of critics agree that the combination of classical and modern techniques, Bearden's use of interior space, the cubist approach with rectilinear overlapping planes, and the documentary feeling summoned by the photographs, give his work tension and rhythm. Hooten observed, "With the renewed interest in figurative painting, Romare Bearden has finally gained the recognition he has justly earned."

1960's. Become a founding member of the Spiral Group whose purpose it was to help black artists.

1969. Bearden and others founded the Cinque Gallery in order to give minority artists the opportunity to exhibit their works.

The *New Yorker* quoted the Cinque's first administrative director as saying, "I think Romie's [Bearden's] success is maybe more of an influence than his work. (Younger artists) see one black man who's made it, and that makes them think they have a chance, too. Romie sees them all. When he gets home from his own studio at night, his phone never stops ringing. He spends most of his free time now helping other artists."

Bearden, who considers art to be a humanizing process, defines art as "a process that renders the things of the world about us into style," according to a *School Arts* writer. Style seems to pervade the whole of Bearden's life and his work.

FOR MORE INFORMATION SEE: Time, October 27, 1967; (exhibition catalogue; introduction by Ralph Ellison) *Romare Bearden: Paintings and Projections,* Art Gallery, State University of New York, Albany, 1968; *School Arts,* April, 1969; *Newsweek,* April 5, 1971; (slide set) *The Painting of Romare Bearden,* Educational Dimensions Corp., 1971; (exhibition catalogue; introduction by Carroll Greene) *Romare Bearden: The Prevalence of Ritual,* Museum of Modern Art, New York City, 1971; Elton Clay Fax, *Seventeen Black Artists,* Dodd, 1971; (collection of paintings; text by M. Bunch Washington; introduction by John A. Williams) *The Art of Romare Bearden,* Abrams, 1973; *Current Biography Yearbook,* 1973; *New Yorker,* November 28, 1977.

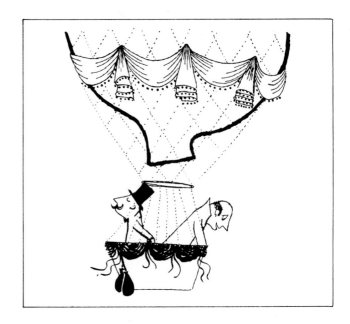

...After a preliminary test in a moored balloon, two men, Pilatre de Rozier and the Marquis d'Arlandes rose from the ground on November 21, 1783. Thus was born the Age of Flight. ■ (From *The Story of Cosmic Rays* by Germaine and Arthur Beiser. Illustrated by Joseph M. Sedacca.)

BEISER, Arthur 1931-

PERSONAL: Born in 1931; married Germaine Bousquet (a physicist; writer); children: Nadia Louise, Alexa Susan, Isabel Victoria. *Education:* New York University, Ph.D.

CAREER: Author, educator, physicist. New York University, associate professor and senior research scientist; has served as vice-president of Nuclear Research Associates, Inc.; author of several books on physics and two on sailing.

WRITINGS: Guide to the Microscope, Dutton, 1957; *Our Earth: The Properties of Our Planet, How They Were Discovered, and How They Came into Being,* Dutton, 1959.

The World of Physics: Readings in the Nature, History, and Challenge of Physics, McGraw, 1960; *Basic Concepts of Physics,* Addison-Wesley, 1961, 2nd edition, 1972; *The Earth,* Time, 1962, young reader's edition, Time-Life, 1968, reissued, 1971; *The Mainstream of Physics,* Addison-Wesley, 1962; *Concepts of Modern Physics,* McGraw, 1963, revised edition, 1967; reissued, 1973; *The Foundation of Physics,* Addison-Wesley, 1964; *The Science of Physics,* Addison-Wesley, 1964; *Modern Technical Physics,* Addison-Wesley, 1966, 2nd edition, Cummings, 1973; *The Proper Yacht,* Macmillan, 1966, International Marine Publishing Co., 1978; *Modern Physics: An Introductory Survey,* Addison-Wesley, 1968; *Essential Math for the Sciences: Algebra, Trigonometry, and Vectors,* McGraw, 1969; *Essential Math for the Sciences: Analytic Geometry and Calculus,* McGraw, 1969; *Perspectives of Modern Physics,* McGraw, 1969.

The Sailor's World (photography by Stanley Rosenfeld), Random House, 1972; *Physics,* Cummings, 1973, 2nd edition, 1978; *Schaum's Outline of Theory and Problems of Physical Science,* McGraw, 1974; *Schaum's Outline of Theory and*

Problems of Earth Sciences, McGraw, 1975; *Schaum's Outline of Theory and Problems of Applied Physics,* McGraw, 1976.

With wife, Germaine Beiser: *Physics for Everybody,* Dutton, 1956; *Study Guide for Basic Concepts of Physics,* Addison-Wesley, 1962; *Study Guide for The Mainstream of Physics,* Addison-Wesley, 1962; *The Story of Cosmic Rays* (illustrated by Joseph M. Sedacca), Dutton, 1962.

With Sidney Borowitz: *The Concepts and Principles of Physics,* Addison-Wesley, 1958; *Essentials of Physics: A Text for Students of Science and Engineering,* Addison-Wesley, 1966, 2nd edition, 1973.

With Konrad B. Krauskopf: *The Physical Universe,* McGraw, 1960, 3rd edition, 1973; *Introduction to Physics and Chemistry,* McGraw, 1964, 2nd edition, 1969; *Fundamentals of Physical Science,* McGraw, 1966, new edition, 1971; *Introduction to Earth Science,* McGraw, 1975.

SIDELIGHTS: A distinguished physicist and author of several books in the field, Beiser has been quite successful in his attempts to bring greater understanding of his subject to young people. Typical of his work, *Our Earth: The Properties of Our Planet, How They Were Discovered, and How They Came into Being* has been highly recommended by *Library Journal.* "This is a first-rate introduction to the study of earth physics. . . . It is a readable book written with infectious zest and it is amazingly comprehensive. . . . An appendix listing

properties of the earth, solar system and the moon and planets makes this an invaluable contribution, and it is especially good for the earnest beginner in earth science. Recommended for public and college collections, and for high schools."

FOR MORE INFORMATION SEE: Library Journal, January 15, 1959; Martha E. Ward and Dorothy A. Marquardt, editors, *Authors of Books for Young People,* 2nd edition, Scarecrow, 1971.

BELTON, John Raynor 1931-

PERSONAL: Born November 30, 1931, in Milwaukee, Wis.; son of Harry F. (a musician) and Neva (McLaughlin) Belton; married Jordis Lambrecht, July 17, 1953; children: Dana, Mark, Paul, Victoria, Scott, Amy. *Education:* University of Wisconsin, Milwaukee, B.S., 1957, M.S., 1959; Marquette University, Ph.D., 1968. *Politics:* Republican. *Religion:* Protestant. *Home:* W189N4978 Crest View Ter., Menomonee Falls, Wis. 53051. *Office:* Glendale Schools, 2600 Mill Rd., Glendale, Wis. 53209.

CAREER: Elementary school teacher in Brookfield, Wis., 1957-60; school psychologist in West Allis, Wis., 1960-65; supervisor of instruction for public schools in Milwaukee,

The last one to put his finger on his nose is the PIG and loses the game. ■(From *Let's Play Cards* by John Belton and Joella Cramblit.)

JOHN RAYNOR BELTON

Wis., 1965-76; Glendale Schools, Glendale, Wis., superintendent of schools, 1976—. Part-time instructor at University of Wisconsin, Milwaukee, 1957-68. *Military service:* U.S. Army, Artillery, 1952-54; became second lieutenant. *Member:* American Association of School District Administrators, American Psychological Association. *Awards, honors:* George Washington Medal from Freedoms Foundation, 1967, for filmstrip series "Robert and His Family."

WRITINGS—Juveniles: (With Joella Cramblit) *Let's Play Cards,* Raintree, 1975; (with Cramblit) *Card Games,* Raintree, 1976; (with Cramblit) *Solitaire Games,* Raintree, 1976; (with Cramblit) *Dice Games,* Raintree, 1976; (with Cramblit) *Domino Games,* Raintree, 1976.

Co-author of filmstrip series "Robert and His Family," Society for Visual Education, 1967. Editor of "Know About" series (juvenile), for Franklin Publishers, 1976—.

WORK IN PROGRESS: Developing full-color, photo-illustrated, factual books for young children; using audio-visual media to teach reading skills to young children.

SIDELIGHTS: "Children like to learn how to play card games or games using dice. When I was a child we often played many games at home. Sometimes we didn't understand the rules or we had arguments about *how* the games should be played.

"I wrote several of my books to help children learn how to play *easy,* fun games and to prevent children from arguing about how the games should be played.

"I find it interesting that almost all children everywhere play with cards and/or dice. Often they play the same basic games but with variations. Many books are written for adults but I believe children need to have books available to them, too, so that they can learn on their own without adult supervision."

Belton is interested in "developing fun-type books for young children, to motivate them to read about real-life situations they see on television and in the world around them. I would like to develop books for international distribution."

BENDER, Lucy Ellen 1942-

PERSONAL: Born June 11, 1942, in Grantsville, Md.; daughter of Melvin Williard (a carpenter) and Ruth (Beachy) Beiler; married Mark R. Bender (a farmer), August 24, 1960 (divorced, 1971); children: Stephen, Michael, Nicholas. *Religion:* Assemblies of God. *Home:* 383 Spencer Ave., Morgantown, W.Va. 26505.

CAREER: Professional secretary and author. Has been actively engaged in church-related work as Sunday school teacher, choir member, and in youth work.

WRITINGS: The Outside World (young adult novel), Herald Press, 1968. Has also written numerous short stories for adults and children.

WORK IN PROGRESS: An adult novel.

LUCY ELLEN BENDER

"...I am only one among so many." ■ (From *The Outside World* by Lucy Ellen Bender. Illustrated by Ivan Moon.)

SIDELIGHTS: "My childhood has a great deal to do with my desire to become a writer. We were always surrounded with books and magazines and literature of all kinds.

"My parents both came from farm families of avid readers and published authors. One aunt in particular, Edna Beiler, encouraged me to develop my talent in writing.

"I began keeping a journal at age ten, and from there launched into writing poetry and short stories. Throughout grade school and high school, I was always involved in creative writing and journalism activities.

"My three younger sisters and I spent many hours reading together and telling one another long, involved yarns which we invented as we shelled peas or cut up string beans. Later in life I wrote a novel which included many incidents with my sisters during our years at home together.

"After graduating from high school, I married Mark Bender (a young farmer), and we shared a great interest in reading. We read and discussed various books and took delight in

sharing little jokes or sayings from the books we had both read. I began publishing short stories soon after we married. Many of the stories included farm themes and our three little boys were character models for some of the stories. Steve, Mike, and Nick took pleasure in hearing stories about themselves.

"Later when our marriage ended in divorce, my writing lay dormant for a period of time, but emerged again with new strength after the breaking time of my life was past. I've found real joy recently in writing poetry which expresses the new life I've found in knowing God in a special way because of my great need for someone to depend upon as I raise three sons.

"Over the years I have also worked a great deal as a secretary and have been very active in church work (especially as soloist in choirs and in youth and children's work).

"My times of greatest joy and fulfillment now are when I can feel God's Spirit directing my writing. This happens usually as I write poems in praise and adoration of Jesus."

HOBBIES AND OTHER INTERESTS: "In leisure hours, I enjoy hiking and playing the piano."

BERRY, Jane Cobb 1915(?)-1979
(Jane Cobb)

OBITUARY NOTICE: Born about 1915; died March 31, 1979, in Norwalk, Conn. Columnist, critic, and author of children's books. Berry co-authored the "Sue Barton" and "Carol Page" series of novels with Helen Dore Boylston as a "silent collaborator." A columnist in the *New York Times* during the 1940's, Berry also reviewed numerous books for the same publication. In addition, she contributed stories under her maiden name to a variety of magazines. *Obituaries: New York Times,* April 2, 1979; *AB Bookman's Weekly,* April 16, 1979; *Publishers Weekly,* April 16, 1979; *Contemporary Authors,* Volume 85-88, Gale, 1980.

BICE, Clare 1909-1976

PERSONAL: Born January 24, 1909, in Durham, Ontario, Canada; died May 18, 1976; son of Archdeacon Albert Artemus and Elizabeth (McKay) Bice; married Marion Agnes Reid, 1943; children: Kevin Robert, Megan. *Education:* University of Western Ontario, B.A., 1928; studied at the Art Student's League and Grand Central School of Art, 1930-1932. *Religion:* Anglican. *Home:* 1010 Wellington St., London, Ontario, Canada.

CAREER: Curator, artist, illustrator. Curator, London Art Museum, Ontario, 1940-1972. Taught at the Doan School of Art, and summer sessions at Queen's University, Kingston, Ontario; Mount Allison University, Sackville, New Brunswick; University of British Columbia, Vancouver; and University of Western Ontario. Has had one-man shows in Montreal, and London and Hamilton, Ontario; has exhibited in major Canadian exhibitions, the New York World's Fair, 1939, Canadian Army Exhibition, 1944, the Canadian National Exhibition and the Stratford Festival, Ontario. *Military service:* Canadian Army, 1942-1945; became corporal. *Member:* Canadian Art Museum Directors' Organization (president, 1966-1968); Royal Canadian Academy of Arts (president, 1967-1970); Ontario Society of Artists; Arts and Letters Club (Toronto). *Awards, honors:* Canadian Government fellowship, 1952-1953, for study in France and England; honorary LL.D, University of Western Ontario, 1962; Canada Arts Council Senior fellowship, 1962-1963; Centennial medal, 1967; Canada Council Senior fellowship for writing, 1972-1973; Order of Canada, 1973.

WRITINGS—All for children; all self-illustrated: *Jory's Cove,* Macmillan, 1941; *Across Canada: Stories of Canadian Children,* Macmillan, 1949; *The Great Island,* Macmillan, 1954; *A Dog for Davie's Hill,* Macmillan, 1956; *The Hurricane Treasure,* Viking, 1965.

Illustrator: Lucy S. Mitchell and Margaret W. Brown, *Animals, Plants and Machines,* Heath, 1944; William S. Fox, *'T Ain't Runnin' No More,* W. Holmes, 1946; Hilda M. Hooke, *Thunder in the Mountains,* Oxford University Press,

1947; F. L. Barrett, editor, *Wide Open Windows,* Copp, 1947; David H. Russell, *The Ginn Basic Readers: Roads to Everywhere,* Ginn, 1948; Catherine A. Clark, *The Golden Pine Cone,* Macmillan (Toronto), 1950; Catherine A. Clark, *The Sun Horse,* Macmillan, 1951; William S. Fox, *The Bruce Beckons* (illustrated with Vincent Elliott), University of Toronto Press, 1953, revised and enlarged, 1962; T. Morris Longstreth, *The Force Carries On,* Macmillan (New York), 1954; William S. Fox, *Silken Lines and Silver Hooks,* Copp, 1954; Catherine A. Clark, *The One-Winged Dragon,* Macmillan (London), 1955; Mabel T. Good, *At the Dark of the Moon,* St. Martin's, 1957; William S. Fox, *'T Ain't Runnin' No More—Twenty Years After,* Oxford Book Shop (London, Ontario), 1958; Catherine A. Clark, *The Silver Man,* Macmillan, 1959; Percy Diebel and Reginald McBurney, editors, *Beckoning Trails: The Canada Book of Prose and Verse,* and teacher's guidebook, Macmillan (Toronto), 1962; Catherine A. Clark, *The Diamond Feather,* Macmillan, 1962; Adelaide Leitch, *The Great Canoe,* St. Martin's, 1963; Catherine A. Clark, *The Hunter and the Medicine Man,* Macmillan, 1966; W. J. McIntosh and J. W. Shular, *Canadian Ginn Basic*

Once upon a time (since this is the way to begin all good tales) there was a place called Baldoon.
■ (From *Thunder in the Mountains: Legends of Canada* by Hilda Mary Hooke. Illustrated by Clare Bice.)

CLARE BICE

Readers: Adventure Awaits and *New Worlds*, Ginn, 1967; William E. Corfield, *Keen for Adventure*, 1967.

Author of pamphlets and articles in his field, including the section on "Canadian Painting in the Twentieth Century," in Hugh W. Peart and John Schaffter, *The Winds of Change*, Ryerson, 1961; and a pamphlet, *Canadian Painting, 1850-1950*, National Gallery of Canada, 1967.

SIDELIGHTS: Bice achieved great renown as a painter of landscapes in the Canadian west, New England, Nova Scotia, and northern Ontario, as a portrait and figure artist, as a children's author and illustrator, and as the curator of the London Public Library and Art Museum in Ontario. He established London's Saturday morning art classes for children, an extensive educational program in cooperation with city schools, which became a regular and highly successful activity at the London Public Library and Art Museum.

Bice achieved critical success with the five children's books he wrote and illustrated. The majority of them were in the mystery-adventure vein, including his first, *Jory's Cove*. Said a *Library Journal* reviewer, "An appealing account of the unhurried, friendly, simple life of these fisherfolk. The atmosphere is enhanced by delicate wash-drawings and full-page illustrations in color. . . . Will be useful for its information as well as its story value."

Another of his mystery stories was *The Great Island*, and according to *Horn Book*, "The author, a Canadian artist, conveys the character of the Newfoundland coast in many superb drawings, as well as in his vividly written text." The *Library Journal* had a similar assessment, "Fine illustrations by this famous Canadian artist consisting of a frontispiece

in color and thirty-five wash-drawings in black and white provide the proper atmosphere and give the book distinction."

FOR MORE INFORMATION SEE: Library Journal, December 15, 1941, June 15, 1954; *Horn Book,* June, 1954; Bertha Mahony Miller and others, compilers, *Illustrators of Children's Books, 1946-1956,* Horn Book, 1958; Martha E. Ward and Dorothy A. Marquardt, *Authors of Books for Young People,* Scarecrow, 1964; E. Donnelly, "Clare Bice," *Profiles,* revised edition, Canadian Library Association, 1975; D. L. Kirkpatrick, editor, *Twentieth-Century Children's Writers,* St. Martin's, 1978.

BITTER, Gary G(len) 1940-

PERSONAL: Born February 2, 1940, in Hoisington, Kan.; son of Solomon and Elvera Bitter; married Kay Burgat (a writer), August 19, 1962; children: Steve, Mike, Matthew. Education: Kansas State University, B.S., 1962; Kansas State Teachers College, M.A., 1965; University of Michigan, further graduate study, 1965-66; University of Denver, Ph.D., 1970. *Home:* 8531 East Osborn, Scottsdale, Ariz. 85251. *Office:* College of Education, Arizona State University, Tempe, Ariz. 85281.

GARY G. BITTER

CAREER: Teacher of mathematics and science at the public high school in Derby, Kan., 1962-65, and mathematics in public schools in Ann Arbor, Mich., 1965-66; Washburn University, Topeka, Kan., instructor in mathematics education, 1966-67; Colorado College, Colorado Springs, instructor in mathematics and computer education, 1968-70; Arizona State University, Tempe, assistant professor, 1970-74, associate professor of mathematics education, 1974-77; professor of mathematics education, 1977—. Professor of mathematics education at University of Northern Colorado, summer, 1973, and at Montana State University, summer, 1975; lecturer at University of Colorado, 1968-70. Consultant to Kaman Nuclear Co. and General Cassette Corp.

MEMBER: American Association of University Professors, Association of Educational Data Processing (member of national board of directors, 1974-75), Mathematical Association of America, National Council of Teachers of Mathematics, School Science and Mathematics, Association for Computing Machinery, Arizona Association of Educational Data Systems (president, 1972-74; member of board of directors, 1974-75), Arizona Association of Elementary-Kindergarten-Nursery Education, Arizona Association of Teachers of Mathematics (member of board of directors, 1972-75), Phi Delta Kappa.

WRITINGS—For children: (With Jerald Mikesell) *Investigating Metric Measure,* McGraw, 1975; (with J. Mikesell) *Discovering Metric Measure,* McGraw, 1975; (with Tom Metos) *Exploring with Metrics,* Messner, 1975; (with J. Mikesell) *Multiplication and Division Games and Ideas,* McGraw, 1976; (with J. Mikesell) *Addition and Subtraction Games and Ideas,* McGraw, 1976; *Calculator Power* (six workbooks), EMC Corp., 1977; (with T. Metos) *Exploring with Pocket Calculators,* Messner, 1977; (with T. Metos) *Exploring with Solar Energy,* Messner, 1978; (with Jon Engelhardt and James Weibe) *One Step at a Time,* EMC Corp., 1978; *Mathematics* (basal math series for grades K through 8), McGraw, 1981.

Other writings: (With Lyle Mauland) *Limits: Computer Extended Calculus,* University of Denver Press, 1970; (with W. Y. Gateley) *Basic for Beginners,* McGraw, 1970, second

edition, 1978; (with W. S. Dorn and D. L. Hector) *Computer Applications for Calculus,* Prindle, 1972; (with Jon Knaupp) *Mathematics Activity Manual,* Addison-Wesley, 1972; (with W. Y. Gateley) *Basic Fibel,* R. V. Deckers, 1973, second edition, 1980; (with Lyle Mauland) *Functions: Computer Extended Calculus,* University of Denver Press, 1973; (contributor) N. K. Silvaroli and Lynn Searfoss, editors, *Communications, Reading, and Mathematics,* D. A. Lewis Associates, 1975; (with Charles Geer) *Materials for Metric Instruction,* ERIC, 1975; (with Jerald Mikesell) *Activities Handbook for Teaching the Metric System,* Allyn & Bacon, 1976, second edition, 1978; *Activity Handbook for Teaching with the Handheld Pocket Calculator,* Allyn & Bacon, 1980.

Contributor to mathematics and education journals. Editor of *Computer Corner;* member of the advisory board of *Teacher* Magazine and *Mathematics Journal;* editor of calculator corner of *Teacher* Magazine.

Movie: (With Tom Metos) "Using the Pocket Calculator," Centron Films, 1978.

Filmstrips—All produced by Centron Films, 1978: (With Tom Metos) "Introducing the Pocket Calculator;" (with Tom Metos) "Using the Pocket Calculator."

WORK IN PROGRESS: Exploring Computers, for Messner; *Computer Literacy,* for Holt.

SIDELIGHTS: "My writing comes from my experience with children. I like developing ideas which children can do, enjoy, and understand. Initiating exploratory activities to stimulate the children's interest in a topic, I feel, is what writing is all about!"

BLOCHMAN, Lawrence G(oldtree) 1900-1975

PERSONAL: Born February 17, 1900, in San Diego, Calif.; died January 22, 1975; son of Lucien A. and Haidee (Goldtree) Blochman; married Marguerite Maillard, February 13, 1926. *Education:* University of California, Berkeley, A.B., 1921; Armed Forces Institute of Pathology, certificate in forensic pathology, 1952. *Home:* 370 Riverside Dr., New York, N.Y. 10025. *Agent:* Anita Diamant, 51 East 42nd St., New York, N.Y. 10017.

CAREER: Worked for California newspapers in early years, as sports writer, police and courts reporter, city editor, and editor; *Japan Advertiser,* Tokyo, assistant night editor, 1921; *South China Morning Post,* Hong Kong, special writer, 1922; *Englishman,* Calcutta, India, feature writer and staff photographer, 1922-23; *Chicago Tribune,* European edition, assistant night editor, Paris, France, later editor of "Riviera" supplement, Nice, France, 1923-25; *Paris Times,* Paris, France, editorial and feature writer, 1925-27; full-time freelance writer, 1928—, with exception of stint in Hollywood as script writer for Universal Pictures, 1933-34, government service with Overseas Branch, U.S. Office of War Information, 1941-46, and six months as copy editor of *Business International,* 1960. Special correspondent, *New York Herald Tribune* in Guatemala, 1931, and for *American Weekly* in Paris, 1959. Consultant to Commission on Government Security, 1957, and U.S. Information Agency, 1962, 1964, 1967; public member, U.S. Department of State, Foreign Service Selection Boards, 1966.

King Henry's measure was not the same as Charlemagne's. So, over the years, attempts were made to find a common language of measurement. ■ (From *Exploring with Metrics* by Gary G. Bitter and Thomas H. Metos. Cartoon by Kevin Callahan.)

In the past men seemed more interested in learning about the far places of the earth than about their own bodies. ■ (From *Understanding Your Body* by Lawrence G. Blochman. Illustrated by Susan Wells.)

MEMBER: Mystery Writers of America (president, 1948-49), Overseas Press Club of America (vice-president, 1956-57; member of board of governors). *Awards, honors:* Edgar Allan Poe Award (Edgar) of Mystery Writers of America, 1950, for *Diagnosis: Homicide.*

WRITINGS—Fiction: *Bombay Mail,* Little, Brown, 1934; *Bengal Fire,* Dell, 1937; *Red Snow at Darjeeling,* Saint Mystery Library, 1938; *Midnight Sailing,* Harcourt, 1938; *Blowdown,* Harcourt, 1939; *Wives to Burn,* Harcourt, 1940; *See You at the Morgue,* Duell, Sloan & Pearce, 1941; *Death Walks in Marble Halls,* Dell, 1942; *Diagnosis: Homicide* (story collection), Lippincott, 1950; *Pursuit,* Quinn Handibooks, 1951; *Rather Cool for Mayhem,* Lippincott, 1951; *Recipe for Homicide,* Lippincott, 1952; *Clues for Doctor Coffee* (story collection), Lippincott, 1964.

General—*Here's How: Round-the-World Bar Book of the Overseas Press Club,* New American Library, 1957; *Doctor Squibb: The Life and Times of a Rugged Idealist,* Simon & Schuster, 1958; (with Evangelia Callas) *My Daughter, Maria Callas,* Fleet, 1960; (with Stanley Stein) *Alone No Longer,* Funk, 1963; (with Harlan Logan) *Are You Misunderstood?,* Wilfred Funk, 1965; (with Michael V. DiSalle) *The Power of Life or Death,* Random House, 1965; (with Michael V. DiSalle) *Second Choice,* Hawthorn, 1966; *Understanding Your Body,* (juvenile; illustrated by Susan Wells) Macmillan, 1968; *Wake Up Your Body,* McKay, 1969; (with Herbert Fensterheim) *Help Without Psychoanalysis,* Stein & Day, 1971; (with A. J. Cervantes) *Mister Mayor,* Nash Publishing, 1974.

Translator of more than fifteen novels from the French. Ghost writer of three other books, one on laboratory medicine for a doctor. Author of several motion picture scripts, and numerous radio and television programs. His several hundred short stories include the "Daniel Webster Coffee, M.D." series, which appeared in *Collier's* at intervals for ten years, and stories in *Saturday Evening Post, Argosy, American Magazine, Adventure, Ellery Queen's Mystery Magazine,* and *This Week.* Contributor to *Encyclopaedia Britannica.*

ADAPTATIONS—Movies: "Bombay Mail," Universal, 1934; "Death Walks in Marble Halls," Twentieth Century-Fox; "Pursuit," Metro-Goldwyn-Mayer, 1935; "The Secret of the Chateau," Universal, 1935; "Chinatown Squad," Universal, 1935.

SIDELIGHTS: Blochman was bilingual in French and English, had a good working knowledge of Spanish, a colloquial knowledge of Japanese and German, and a smattering of Italian, Hindustani, and Malay.

FOR MORE INFORMATION SEE: Contemporary Authors, Gale, Volume 19-20, 1968, (obituary) Volume 53-56, 1975, Permanent Series, Volume 2, 1978.

BOHDAL, Susi   1951-

PERSONAL: Born June 17, 1951, in Vienna, Austria; daughter of Bruno (an engineer) and Hermine (Nowak) Bohdal. *Education:* Attended Academy of Applied Art, Vienna, 1969-74. *Religion:* Roman Catholic. *Home and office:* Linzerstrasse 446, A-1140 Vienna Austria.

SUSI BOHDAL

There was once a special cat called Tom Cat. ■(From *Tom Cat* by Susi Bohdal. Illustrated by the author.)

CAREER: Artist and illustrator. *Member:* Der Gesellschaft bildender Künstler Österreichs Künstlerhaus. *Awards, honors:* Babbling Bookworm Award, 1977, for *Tom Cat.*

WRITINGS—Children's books; all self-illustrated: *Der schöne Vogel Adalbert,* Neugebauer Press, 1974, translation by Macdonald & Jane published as *Bird Adalbert,* Macdonald & Jane, 1975; *Kater Valentin,* Nord-Süd, 1977, translation by Alison Sage published as *Tom Cat,* Doubleday, 1977; *Jaromir komm tanz mit mir* (title means "Jaromir, Come Dance With Me"), Nord-Süd, 1979.

Illustrator: M. Damjan, *Federn nichts als Federn,* Nord-Süd, 1976, published as *Feathers Fit for a King,* Abelard, 1978; C. Morgenstern, *3 Kindergedichte,* Nord-Süd, 1977, published as *Three Nursery Poems,* translated by Ebbitt Cutler, Tundra Books, 1977; T. Simon, *Paolino geht auf Reisen,* Nord-Süd, 1978, published as *Paulino,* translated by Ebbitt Cutler, Tundra Books, 1978.

WORK IN PROGRESS: Nonsense poems about animals; a story about how to fight against fear.

SIDELIGHTS: "I was born in Vienna and lived in an old house which was built by my grandfather. A house filled with narrow corners, dark staircases, old pieces of furniture, and with a lot of secrets. Looking back I am convinced that the background of that house strongly influenced my fantasy and creativity. I started to draw at the age of four, and books fascinated me.

"I entered the Academy of Applied Art without any idea what I was going to do after I graduated. I tried all the techniques of reproduction: wood-cut, lithography, screen-print, and etching. Etching became my favorite technique. In 1973 I went to the 'Childrens Book Fair' in Bologna. There I found an editor who was interested in my work and who encouraged me to write and illustrate a book.

"I write about personal experiences or problems I had during my childhood. In *Tom Cat* I treated the problem of being different, a problem I always struggled with. My aim is to create characters. The figures and animals I draw and write about must have personality and, especially, 'soul.' Children should be able to identify with them. Throughout the entire book there should be a mood; a certain mood in the landscapes or streets which makes you want to turn the pages. On every page there should be something to discover so that the imagination of the young reader is stimulated."

BOND, Nancy (Barbara) 1945-

PERSONAL: Born January 8, 1945, in Bethesda, Md.; daughter of William H. (a librarian) and Helen L. (an elementary school teacher; maiden name, Lynch) Bond. *Education:* Mount Holyoke College, B.A., 1966; College of Librarianship, Aberystwyth, Dyfed, Wales, Dip. Lib., 1972. *Politics:* Independent. *Religion:* "Informal." *Home:* 109 Valley Road, Concord, Mass. 01742.

CAREER: Oxford University Press, London, England, member of promotional staff, 1967-68; Lincoln Public Library, Lincoln, Mass., assistant children's librarian, 1969-72; Gardner Public Library, Gardner, Mass., director, 1973-75; Massachusetts Audubon Society, Lincoln, administrative assistant, 1976-77. *Member:* Library Association (England), National Audubon Society, Jersey Wildlife Preservation Trust. *Awards, honors:* Horn Book Honor Book and Newbery Medal Honor Book award, 1976, for *A String in the Harp;* I.R.A. award; Welsh Arts Council *Tir nan 'og* award.

WRITINGS—Juveniles: *A String in the Harp,* Atheneum, 1976; *The Best of Enemies* (Junior Literary Guild selection), Atheneum, 1978; *Country of Broken Stone,* Atheneum, 1980.

(From *A String in the Harp* by Nancy Bond. Jacket illustrated by Allen Davis.)

NANCY BOND

WORK IN PROGRESS: Writing juvenile and adult fiction.

SIDELIGHTS: "Children's books are one of my greatest loves and always have been. I was much encouraged to find some fifteen years ago that I did not in fact ever have to outgrow them. But it took me rather a long time to realize I could do more than simply read them. There is a lot of very exciting fiction being written and published ostensibly for children! I wage a constant campaign to introduce it to other adults.

"My other deep interest is natural history. I am involved with organizations active in conservation, but more fundamentally, I have a real conviction that men are only a part of the natural pattern and that much of what we do to the environment is senseless, thoughtless, and tragic. Only by pausing to look and make ourselves truly aware that all the parts fit, even though we may not understand how, can we preserve and protect the balance of the whole. It is therefore essential to me that we encourage by word and deed attention to minutiae, wonder at detail, and respect for life in all forms."

FOR MORE INFORMATION SEE: Horn Book, June, 1976, June, 1978; *Bookbird,* March, 1977; *Wilson Library Bulletin,* March, 1977.

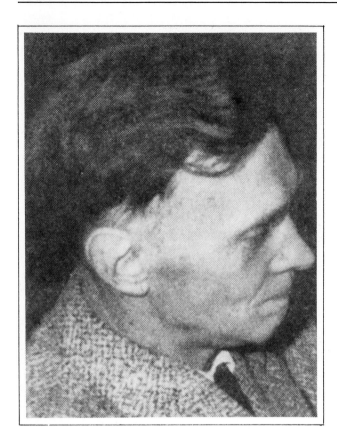

PAUL-JACQUES BONZON

BONZON, Paul-Jacques   1908-

PERSONAL: Surname is pronounced Baughn-*zauhn*; born August 31, 1908, in Sainte-Marie du Monte, France; son of Alphonse (a government administrator) and Marie (Flaux) Bonzon; married Aimee Philippon, October 26, 1949; children: Jacques and Isabelle. *Education:* Graduate of the Teachers College, Saint-Lo, Manche, 1927. *Home:* France.

CAREER: Educator, author. Chabeuil School, teacher, 1929-49; Saint-Laurent School, director, 1949-59; Academy of Letters, Sciences, and Arts, vice-president, 1960—; author of approximately one hundred books. *Awards, honors:* Prix Jeunesse, first prize, 1952; Comite National de L'Enfance, first prize, 1955; awarded grand prize by the Salon de L'Enfance de Paris for *L'Eventail de Seville,* 1958; *The Orphans of Simitra* was awarded first prize for the middle age category in the *Book World* Children's Spring Book Festival, was cited by the American Library Association as a Notable Book, and was included by the *New York Times* as one of the Year's Best Books, all in 1962; *The Runaway Flying Horse* was included in the American Institute of Graphic Arts Book Show, 1976.

WRITINGS—All for children: *Loutsi-chien et ses jeunes maitres* (illustrated by Louis Lafond), Bourrelier (Paris), 1945; *Delph, le marin; ou, l'appel de la mer,* Société Universitaire, 1947; *Le Jongleur à l'étoile* (illustrated by G. Marjollin), Hachette, 1948.

Du gui pour Christmas (illustrated by Maguy Laporte), Bourrelier, 1953; *Mamadi; ou, le petit roi d'ébène* (illustrated by

Christian Fontugne), Editions Magnard, 1953; *Les orphelins de Simitra* (illustrated by A. Chazelle), Hachette, 1955, translation by Thelma Niklaus published as *The Orphans of Simitra,* University of London Press, 1957, Criterion, 1962; *Le petit passeur du lac* (illustrated by Jacques Poirier), Hachette, 1956; *La ballerine de Majorque* (illustrated by Paul Durand), Hachette, 1956, translation from the French published as *Paquita, the Ballerina from Mallorca,* Sterling Publishing Co., 1958; *Mon vercors en feu,* [Paris], 1956, reissued, Hachette, 1975; *Tout-Fon,* [Paris], 1956; *La promesse de Primerose* (illustrated by P. Durand), Hachette, 1957; *La princesse sans nom* (illustrated by J. P. Ariel), Hachette, 1958; *Le voyageur sans visage* (illustrated by Cyril), Editions Fleurus, 1958; *L'éventail de Séville* (illustrated by Francois Batet), Hachette, 1958, translation by Anthony Cappuyns published as *The Spanish Fan,* Heinemann, 1960; *Un secret dans la nuit polaire* (illustrated by A. Chazelle), Hachette, 1959.

Contes de l'hiver (illustrated by Romain Simon), Editions Bias, 1960; *La croix d'or de Santa-Anna,* Hachette, 1960, translation by Thelma Niklaus published as *The Gold Cross of Santa Anna* (illustrated by Margery Gill), University of London Press, 1962, published in America as *Pursuit in the French Alps,* Lothrop, 1963; *Les compagnons de la Croix-Rousse* (illustrated by A. Chazelle), Hachette, 1961, translation by Godfrey Burston published as *The Friends of Croix-Rousse* (illustrated by Geraldine Spence), University of London Press, 1963; *J'irai à Nagasaki* (illustrated by A. Chazelle), Hachette, 1961; *Le cheval de verre* (illustrated by Francois Batet), Hachette, 1963, translation by G. Burston published as *The Glass Horse,* University of London Press, 1964; *Contes de mon chalet* (illustrated by R. Simon), Editions Bias, 1965; *Le jardin de paradis,* Delagrave, 1967; *La chalet du bonheur,* Delagrave, 1967; *La roulotte du bonheur,* Delagrave, 1968.

Le chateau de Pompon, Delagrave, 1970; *Pompon à la ville,* Delagrave, 1975; *Le cirque Zigoto,* Delagrave, 1975; *Diabolo pompier,* Hachette, 1975; *The Runaway Flying Horse* (translated by Susan Kotta; illustrated by William Pene du Bois), Parents' Magazine Press, 1976; *Diabolo jardinier,* Hachette, 1976; *Yani: Livre de lectures suivies,* Delagrave, 1976; *Les espions du X-35,* Hachette, 1976.

"La Famille H. L. M." series, published by Hachette; illustrated by Jacques Fromont: *Les étranges locataires,* 1966; *L'homme à la valise jaune,* 1967; *Vol au cirque,* 1967; *Luisa contre-attaque,* 1968; *Rue des Chats -sans-Queue,* 1968; *Le Perroquet et son trésor,* 1969. Other titles in the series: *Le bateau fantome; Un cheval sur un volcan; L'homme à la tourterelle; L'homme aux souris blanches; Le marchand de coquillages; Où est passé l'Ane Tulipe?; Quatre chats et le diable; La roulotte de l'aventure; Le secret de la malle arrière; Le Secret du lac rouge, Shalom sur la piste noire.*

"Les Six Compagnons" series, published by Hachette: *Les six compagnons et la disparue de Montélimar* (illustrated by Philippe Daure), 1957; . . . *Et l'homme au Gant* (illustrated by A. Chazelle), 1963; . . . *Et la pile atomique* (illustrated by A. Chazelle), 1963; . . . *Et le chateau maudit* (illustrated by A. Chazelle), 1965; . . . *Et l'émetteur pirate* (illustrated by A. Chazelle), 1968; . . . *Et les agents secrets* (illustrated by A. Chazelle), 1969; . . . *Et leurs espions du ciel* (illustrated by Maurice Paulin), 1971. Other titles in the series: *Les six compagnons à la Tour Eiffel; . . . À Scotland Yard; . . . Au gouffre Marzal; . . . Au village englouti; . . . Au Concours Hippique; . . . Dans la Citadelle; . . . Devant la Camera; . . . En Croisière; . . . Et la brigade volante; . . . Et l'ane vert; . . . Et la perruque rouge; . . . Et la princesse noire;*

...Et l'avion clandestin; ...Et le mystère du parc; ...Et le petit rat de l'opéra; ......Et le piano à queue; ...Et le secret de la calanque; ...Et les pirates du rail; ...Et les voix de la nuit; ...Et l'homme des neiges; ...Et l'oeil d'acier; ...Se jettent à l'eau.

Other titles by Paul-Jacques Bonzon: *Devant la rideau*, Amicale; *Diabolo et la fleur qui sourit*, Hachette; *Diabolo le petit chat*, Hachette; *Diabolo et le cheval de bois*, Hachette; *Le cavalier de la mer*, Hachette; *La maison aux mille bonheurs*, Delagrave; *Le relais des cigales*, Delagrave; *Le Viking au bracelet d'argent*, Editions G. P.; *Soleil de mon Espagne*, Hachette.

SIDELIGHTS: Bonzon, a prolific French author specializing in children's books, has received most of his critical attention in this country for *The Orphans of Simitra*. This is the story of Porphyras and Mina, the orphaned survivors of an earthquake which destroyed their village. The acclaim this book received in France and England has been echoed in America. *Horn Book* comments: "The story is so realistically told that one wonders how often these events may have actually happened. The characterizations are good, with even the minor characters sketched with perception." Expressing similar sentiments, the *New York Herald Tribune* adds: "This moving story does not soften for children the tragic realities of life but shows an indomitable spirit can make them bearable. Especially fine is the first third of the book when the children are in Greece. The account of the various difficulties Porphyras later encounters seems a little disconnected and involved, the ending a little pat, though it will satisfy young readers."

FOR MORE INFORMATION SEE: Horn Book, April, 1962; *New York Herald Tribune*, May 13, 1962. *Fourth Book of Junior Authors and Illustrators*, edited by Doris de Montreville and Elizabeth D. Crawford, H. W. Wilson Co., 1978.

CORINNE BORJA

BORJA, Corinne 1929-

PERSONAL: Born July 19, 1929, in Chicago, Ill.; daughter of Harold Preston (a certified public accountant) and Nora (O'Connell) Johnson; married Robert Borja (an artist), October 24, 1947. *Education:* Chicago Academy of Art, 1943-45; American Academy of Art, 1945-47; Institute of Design, Chicago, 1951-52; School of the Art Institute, Chicago, 1976-78. *Home and office:* 5136 Dorchester Ave., Chicago, Ill. 60615.

CAREER: Sculptor, author, illustrator. Borja Studio, Chicago, Ill., co-owner, 1952—; ceramic sculptor, 1972—. *Member:* Society of Typographic Arts, Hyde Park Art Center. *Awards, honors:* Award from Society of Typographic Arts, 1964; award from Chicago Book Clinic, 1965, for *Exploring the World of Fossils;* Printing Industries of America award from Chicago Society of Communicating Arts, 1972, for *Comedy of Eros;* award from Artists Guild, 1977, for a ceramic sculpture at Ft. Dearborn.

WRITINGS—All written and illustrated with husband, Robert Borja: *Making Collages*, A. Whitman, 1972; *Making Chinese Paper Cuts*, A. Whitman, 1979.

Illustrator: (With R. Borja) *Jungles and Deserts, Mountains and Plains, Big Ones, Little Ones and All Sizes in Between*

of Young Animals, Childrens Press, 1960; *Exploring the World of Fossils*, Childrens Press, 1965; (with R. Borja) Norman Richards, *Giants in the Sky*, Childrens Press, 1967; *Pacesetters Books*, seven volumes, Lyons & Carnahan, 1969; *Comedy of Eros*, University of Illinois, 1972.

WORK IN PROGRESS: Research on Chinese ceramics of the Tang and Sung dynasties.

SIDELIGHTS: "My husband and I are co-owners of the Borja Studio. We work in publishing, doing graphic design, illustration, and writing. In addition, I have a second studio where I work on ceramic sculpture (fine art). The clients there are private collectors and institutions.

"Although my husband and I retain our midwestern roots, living and working in Chicago, we have traveled extensively throughout Europe, the Mid-East, and Asia. Much inspiration has come from the Orient because of its ancient culture and fine arts and crafts. We visited mainland China, the main spring of Oriental culture, in 1978. Our experiences there have been reflected in our work.

"We hope to do more writing in the arts and crafts field because of our interest, knowledge, and personal skills in this area."

BORJA, Robert 1923-

PERSONAL: Born May 31, 1923, in Chicago, Ill.; son of Pedro Flores (a printer) and Lydia (Haarmann) Borja; married Corinne Johnson (a sculptor), October 24, 1947. *Education:* Attended University of Nebraska, University of Chicago, Art Institute of Chicago, and American Academy of Art; graduate study at Institute of Design and Columbia College. *Politics:* Independent. *Religion:* Unitarian. *Home and office:* 5136 Dorchester Ave., Chicago, Ill. 60615.

CAREER: Science Digest, Chicago, Ill., art director, 1947-52; Borja Studio, Chicago, co-owner, 1952—; free-lance illustrator, 1952—. *Exhibitions:* American Institute of Graphic Arts Learning Materials Show and Magazine Show, 1952, Chicago Book Clinic, 1960 and 1962, Society of Typographic Arts, 1964, 1968, 1972, and 1975, VOV Gallery (Chicago), 1965, Hyde Park Art Center (Chicago), 1970, 1973, 1976, and 1977, Junior Literary Guild's Chicago Show, 1972, Chicago Public Library, 1974 and 1979, KAM Art Expo (Chicago), 1977, American Bar Center (Chicago), 1978. Trustee of Unitarian Church, 1965-68. *Military service:* U.S. Army, 1943-46, served in Pacific Theatre; became corporal. *Member:* Society of Typographic Arts (director, 1966-72; president, 1973-74), Renaissance Society of University of Chicago (director, 1974-80).

WRITINGS—All written and illustrated with wife, Corinne Borja: *Making Collages,* A. Whitman, 1972; *Making Chinese Paper Cuts,* A. Whitman, 1979.

Illustrator: Illa Podendorf, *The True Book of Space,* Childrens Press, 1959; Podendorf, *101 Science Experiments,* Grosset, 1960; *Life in the Desert,* Childrens Press, 1960; (with

ROBERT BORJA

C. Borja), *Jungles and Deserts, Mountains and Plains, Big Ones, Little Ones and All Sizes in Between of Young Animals,* Childrens Press, 1960; *The Solar System,* Childrens Press, 1961; *Ross,* Childrens Press, 1961; Podendorf, *The True Book of Magnets and Electricity,* Childrens Press, 1961; Podendorf, *Discovering Science on Your Own,* Childrens Press, 1962; Dorothy Rossen Greenberg, *Siege Hero,* Reilly & Lee, 1965; (with C. Borja) Norman Richards, *Giants in the Sky,* Childrens Press, 1967; *Camouflage in Nature,* Childrens Press, 1968; *Wonders of the Pacific Shore,* Childrens Press, 1968. Also illustrator of *True Book of Weather Instruments,* and *Under the Microscope.*

SIDELIGHTS: "Woodcut is my first love. I also work in most illustrative media, including three-dimensional in clay. I do some illustrating with photography, and have designed a few hundred books. As an artist I have been strongly influenced by Brancusi, Henry Moore, and Chuang Tsu."

HOBBIES AND OTHER INTERESTS: Travel.

(From *Siege Hero* by Dorothy Rossen Greenberg. Woodcut by Robert Borja.)

Between the dark and the daylight,
  When the night is beginning to lower,
Comes a pause in the day's occupations,
  This is known as the Children's Hour.

—Henry Wadsworth Longfellow

BOULLE, Pierre (Francois Marie-Louis) 1912-

PERSONAL: Born February 20, 1912, in Avignon, France; son of Eugene and Therese (Seguin) Boulle. *Education:* Ecole superieure d'Electricite, licence es sciences, engineering diploma. *Religion:* Catholic. *Home:* 18 rue Duret, Paris 16, France.

CAREER: Engineer in France, 1933-35; rubber planter in Malaya, 1936-48; full-time writer,1949—. *Military service:* French Army, World War II; sent to Malaya, 1941, joined Free French forces there and became secret agent, using name Peter John Rule, and posing as a Mauritius-born Englishman; fought in Burma, China, and Indochina; taken prisoner and subsequently escaped in 1944; returned to France; awarded French Legion d'Honneur, Croix de Guerre, Medaille de la Resistance. *Awards, honors:* Prix Sainte-Beuve, 1952, for *Le Pont de la riviere Kwai;* Grand Prix de la Nouvelle, 1953, for *Contes de l'absurde; Grand Prix de la Société des Gens de Lettres de France, 1976,* for all of Boulle's writings.

WRITINGS—Books of interest to young people: *Le Pont de la riviere Kwai* (novel), Julliard, 1952, translation by Xan Fielding published as *The Bridge over the River Kwai,* Vanguard, 1954 (published in England as *The Bridge on the River Kwai,* Secker & Warburg, 1954), French language edition with foreword by Boulle, edited by Georges Joyaux, Scribner, 1963; "The Bridge on the River Kwai" (screenplay based on his own novel), produced by Horizon Pictures, 1958; *Walt Disney's Siam* (screenplay), Nouvelles Editions (Lausanne), 1958; *La Planete des singes* (novel), Julliard, 1963, translation by Xan Fielding published as *Planet of the Apes,* Vanguard, 1963 (published in England as *Monkey Planet,* Secker & Warburg, 1964); *Aux Sources de la riviere Kwai,* Julliard, 1966, translation by Xan Fielding published as *My Own River Kwai,* Vanguard, 1967 (published in England as *The Source of the River Kwai,* Secker & Warburg, 1967).

Other writings: *William Conrad* (novel), Julliard, 1950, translation by Xan Fielding published as *Not the Glory,* Vanguard, 1955 (published in England as *William Conrad,* Secker & Warburg, 1955, published as *Spy Converted,* Collins, 1960); *Le Sacrilege malais,* Julliard, 1951, translation by Fielding published as *S.O.P.H.I.A.,* Vanguard, 1959 (published in England as *Sacrilege in Malaya,* Secker & Warburg, 1959); *Contes de l'absurde* (stories; contains "L'Hallucination," "Une Nuit interminable," *Le Poids d'un sonnet,* "Le Regne des sages," "Le Parfait robot"), Julliard, 1953, translation by Fielding and Elizabeth Abbott published as *Time Out of Mind, and Other Stories,* Vanguard, 1966; *La Face* (novel), Julliard, 1953, translation by Fielding published as *Face of a Hero,* Vanguard, 1956 (published in England as *Saving Face,* Secker & Warburg, 1956); *Le Cas du procureur Berthier* (story), Les Oeuvres Libres, 1953; *Le Poids d'un sonnet,* Les Oeuvres Libres, 1953; *Le Proces chinois* (novel), Les Oeuvres Libres, 1954; *Le Bourreau* (novel), Julliard, 1954, translation by Fielding published as *The Executioner,* Vanguard, 1961 (published in England as *The Chinese Executioner,* Secker & Warburg, 1962); *L'Epreuve des hommes blancs* (novel), Julliard, 1955, translation by Fielding published as *Test,* Vanguard, 1957 (published in England as *White Man's Test,* Secker & Warburg, 1957); *E=MC²* (published with *Contes de l'absurde* as *Contes de l'absurde [suivi de] E=MC²*), Julliard, 1957; *Les Voies de salut* (novel), Julliard, 1958, translation by Richard Howard published as *The Other Side of the Coin,* Vanguard, 1968.

PIERRE BOULLE

Un Metier de Seigneur (novel), Julliard, 1960, translation by Fielding published as *A Noble Profession,* Vanguard, 1960 (published in England as *For a Noble Cause,* Secker & Warburg, 1961); *William Conrad* (play), Les Oeuvres Libres, 1962; *Le Jardin de Kanashima,* Julliard, 1964, translation published as *Garden on the Moon,* Vanguard, 1965; *Histoires charitables* (short stories; contains "Le Saint enigmatique," "L'Homme qui ramassait les epingles," "Histoire du bon petit ecrivain," "L'Arme diabolique," "Le Compte a rebours," "L'Homme qui haisait les machines"), Julliard, 1964; *Le Photographe* (novel), Julliard, 1967, translation by Fielding published as *The Photographer,* Vanguard, 1968 (published in England as *An Impartial Eye,* Secker & Warburg, 1968); *L'Etrange Croisade de l'empereur Frederic II,* Flammarion, 1968; *Quia absurdum (sur la terre comme au ciel),* Julliard, 1970, translation by Elizabeth Abbott published as *Because It Is Absurd (on Earth as in Heaven),* Vanguard, 1971; *Les Jeux de l'esprit* (novel), Julliard, 1971, translation by Patricia Wolf published as *Desperate Games,* Vanguard, 1973; *Les oreilles de jungle* (novel), Flammarion, 1972, translation by Michael Dobry and Linda Cole published as *Ears of the Jungle,* Vanguard, 1972; *Les Vertus de l'enfer* (novel), Flammarion, 1974, translation by Patricia Wolf published as *The Virtues of Hell,* Vanguard, 1974; *Histoires perfides* (short stories), Flammarion, 1976, translation by Margaret Giovanelli published as *The Marvelous Palace,* Vanguard, 1977; *Le bon Léviathan* (novel), Julliard, 1978, translation by Margaret Giovanelli published as *The Good Leviathan,* Vanguard, 1978; *Les coulisses du ciel* (novel), Julliard, 1979.

SIDELIGHTS: "I was born in Avignon, a small town in the south of France, on the bank of the river Rhône. There I spent the first seventeen years of my life, and probably the happiest ones. So happy in fact that I am reluctant to call up their image, and that, nowadays, when I go to the south of France, I am very careful to shun Avignon, afraid to meet again the phantoms of my youth.

"I left Avignon at the age of seventeen, went to Paris, became a student at the University, then went to a school of electronics. During these years, all the holidays saw me going back to Avignon. My father had died a few years before, but my mother and two sisters were still living there.

"I started my active life as an electrical engineer in France until 1936, at which time I left for Malaya, where a big rubber company was enlisting engineers. (I never quite understood why, because most of the job I did over there was that of a planter.) I was due to come back home for a long holiday after four years, but because of the war it was only after nine years absence that I was able to see France again. I never saw my mother—she had died during the war.

"So, I was a rubber planter for over three years in Malaya. Then I had a few strange adventures during the war. The one I remember best was the nightly descent of the Nam-Na, a torrential river flowing from China to Indochina (then under Vichy rule and partly occupied by the Japanese) in a bamboo raft I had built with my own hands, in order to establish contacts with French resistants. These adventures ended when I was taken prisoner by the Vichy French, courtmartialled and had to spend over two years in jail until the victory of the allies. This was the first period of my life and I certainly regret not a single event of it, even the long years in jail, sometimes in an isolated cell, sometimes in the cheerful company of burglars and murderers. All this I have told in *My Own River Kwai.*

"But the last and probably the greatest adventure was to come after the war when, back in Malaya, I got fed up with my job as engineer on the plantations and suddenly, in the course of a sleepless night, decided to become a writer. Was it malaria or madness? I incline towards sheer madness—I had had a scientific education. My knowledge of literature was poor. I read little. (The only two authors I really admired and whose entire works I had read were Edgar Allan Poe and Joseph Conrad.) Moreover I had not the faintest idea of the kind of books I was going to write. Yet, my mind was made up in less than an hour and I took the rather presumptuous vow to undertake nothing else. I spent the rest of the night writing a letter of resignation to the company for which I had worked, took a plane at Singapore a few days later, got back to Paris, sold everything I possessed and started writing my first novel—*William Conrad.*

"This started the second and probably the last period of my life. I have done practically nothing other than writing for nearly thirty years. . . . Sorry, I am wrong. In fact I am spending more than half of my time walking, looking about for new ideas, feverishly chasing an original theme suitable for a novel or a short story. Only when I have discovered one (or when I think I have) do I start writing. Now let no

one ask me *how* I find a new idea. No author has ever been able to answer that question. Also about my conception of literature, I am afraid I have very little to say, except that above all I value the *quality of imagination.* That is probably why my favourite authors are still Poe and Conrad."

Boulle became well-known with *The Bridge Over the River Kwai,* in which, according to Henri Peyre, the "portrayal of the muddle-headed officer was especially well-drawn." Praised not only for this main character, Boulle was also praised for his creation of "a situation that is simultaneously droll, pathetic, and appalling," C. J. Rolo stated. Boulle has been compared to Conrad and Kipling, and in this book such resemblances are evident.

William Conrad, his first novel, was also very well-received. Taliaferro Boatwright commented: "It is a penetrating, ironic, but deeply sympathetic study of the British national character." In fact, most of Boulle's novels have been about such "English" characters. *S.O.P.H.I.A.* is about "a young engineer's experiences in an exotic, faintly hostile microcosm," John Lord writes, "[The book] is actually a highly artful exposition of the character of a corporation in terms of the young man's initial infatuation with it, growing knowledge of its caprices, and final, grudgingly respectful disillusionments, as he comes to know himself better." Although the young engineer in this book is French, Boulle's concerns are really "English," encompassing the changes in the rubber industry in Malaya from management by the pioneers to the takeover by large companies, which he does not see as necessarily good.

Boulle is known to have an ironic sense of humor, which comes through in his books. This humor is chiefly philosophical, and is considered well-illustrated in *The Chinese Executioner.* Max Cosman describes Boulle's concern: "In a world where evil is the norm, a good man is a criminal when he does good. [The book] is, however, much more serious than that. Indeed, it raises an issue as ancient as history, no less than that of mankind's terrifying inability to recognize its true benefactors while they are alive." Isabel Quigley calls the book "a quirky and at times near-brilliant little piece of satire in the form of an everlasting dialogue about death, life, and Chinamen."

In some of his more recent books Boulle has been using science fiction in an allegorical manner, such as in *Planet of the Apes,* the book upon which the popular film is based. A *Time* reviewer says: "The meaning of Boulle's cheerful parable is not a mocking warning but an observation: human dignity is both precarious and precious; too often it is based on pride in achievements that can be matched by clever mimics of what has been done before. Like the Red Queen, Western man has to keep running if he is to keep his place as the lord of creation." *Garden on the Moon* is also a science fiction novel of sorts, and is considered more realistic, since it is about the moon race. P. J. Henniker-Heaton comments: "Anything that Pierre Boulle writes has several dimensions of depth. This book is a commentary on nationalism's total irrelevance in an interplanetary age—at least its almost total irrelevance."

Planet of the Apes, adapted by Rod Serling and Michael Wilson, was filmed by 20th Century–Fox, 1968; two additional films, "Beneath the Planet of the Apes," originally titled "Planet of the Apes Revisited," 1970, and "Escape from the Planet of the Apes," 1971, were released by 20th Century–Fox.

FOR MORE INFORMATION SEE: Spectator, April 9, 1954, December 11, 1959; *New Statesman & Nation,* April 10, 1954; *Chicago Sunday Tribune,* October 3, 1954, September 25, 1955; *Atlantic,* November, 1954, November, 1955; *New York Herald Tribune Book Review,* September 25, 1955, November 17, 1957, October 26, 1958, January 10, 1960; *Saturday Review,* October 8, 1955, January 7, 1960, December 3, 1960, November 18, 1967, December 7, 1968; *Times Literary Supplement,* October 12, 1956, February 9, 1962, October 21, 1965, June 8, 1967; *Manchester Guardian,* October 16, 1956; *New Yorker,* October 20, 1956, November 23, 1968; *New York Times Book Review,* October 23, 1960, March 7, 1965, October 15, 1967; *Booklist,* December 15, 1961; *Guardian,* February 2, 1962; *Time,* November 8, 1963; *Christian Science Monitor,* March 4, 1965, December 9, 1967; Henri Pevre, *French Novelists of Today,* Oxford University Press, 1967; *L'Express,* April 3-9, 1967; *Harper's,* December, 1967; *National Review,* November 19, 1968; *Critic,* April, 1969; *New York Times,* November 30, 1972.

BOWEN, Joshua David   1930-
(David Bowen)

PERSONAL: Born in 1930. *Education:* Graduated from Harvard University.

JOSHUA DAVID BOWEN

CAREER: Author, editor. Following college, worked in the theater as an actor and director; at various times in his career, has been a newspaperman in Raleigh, N.C., has served with the Foreign Political Association and has been editor of the United Fruit Company's *Middle America.* His articles have appeared in the *National Observer, New York Times* and *Reader's Digest.* Has written several books for children on South American countries, and is the author of books on labor and race relations.

WRITINGS—For children (under name David Bowen or J. David Bowen): *The Land and People of Peru,* Lippincott, 1963, revised edition, 1973; *Hello South America,* W. W. Norton, 1964; *The Struggle Within,* W. W. Norton, 1965, revised edition, Grosset, 1972; *The Land and People of Chile,* Lippincott, 1966, revised edition, 1976; *Hello Brazil,* W. W. Norton, 1967; *The Island of Puerto Rico,* Lippincott, 1968. Contributor to the ''Proceedings of the Academy of Political Science,'' 1970.

SIDELIGHTS: ''Although I am no longer writing, I am involved in every possible way with books. I have had, since 1972, an out-of-print bookstore in San Antonio and in 1977, established Corona Publishing Company which produces ''books for use'' distributed mostly in Texas. (The latest is *Digging into South Texas Pre-history: A Guide for Amateur Archaeologists,* by Dr. Thomas R. Hester, with a preface by John Graves.''

Bowen, having traveled widely in South America, wrote his books about the continent from a position of knowledge. *Hello South America,* according to the *Library Journal,* is not quite up to the quality of his books on individual South

Kite flying is fun on open beaches like Copacabana in Rio de Janeiro. ■ (From *Hello Brazil* by David Bowen. Photograph courtesy of Varig.)

American countries, though. "An author who can write interestingly and knowingly, spreads himself too thin in trying to present an informal overview of life in South America. . . . Good general maps, small maps under chapter headings, well-chosen black-and-white illustrations, attractive format. This is a useful overview and will stimulate interest, but it is inadequate in comparison with the series books on individual countries."

However, *The Struggle Within* does what it sets out to do. Says *Best Sellers,* "Bowen's book will serve as a fine introduction and general survey for young readers and will perhaps lead them to read more deeply and ponder more wisely the problem and its place in their lives." And, according to the *New York Times Book Review,* "As an example of the new view that boys and girls are intellectual beings capable of following and enjoying the direct, uncute discussion of issues, Mr. Bowen's judicious analysis of the present racial crisis and its historical antecedents is good to find. . . . It is written with painstaking lucidity, [and] there is nothing primerish or condescending about it."

FOR MORE INFORMATION SEE: Library Journal, November 15, 1964; *New York Times Book Review,* January 23, 1966; *Best Sellers,* February 1, 1966; *Horn Book,* August, 1966; *Publishers Weekly,* February 23, 1976.

BOYER, Robert E(rnst) 1929-

PERSONAL: Born August 3, 1929, in Palmerton, Pa.; son of Merritt Ernst (a civil engineer) and Lizzie (V.) Boyer; married Elizabeth Bakos, September 1, 1951; children: Robert M., Janice E., Gary K. *Education:* Colgate University, B.A., 1951; Indiana University, M.A., 1954; University of Michigan, Ph.D., 1959. *Religion:* Protestant. *Home:* 7644 Parkview Circle, Austin, Tex. 78731. *Office:* Department of Geological Sciences, University of Texas, Austin, Tex. 78712.

CAREER: University of Texas, Austin, instructor, 1957-59, assistant professor, 1959-62, associate professor, 1962-67, professor of geology, 1967, chairman of department, 1971, dean of College of Natural Sciences, 1980. *Member:* Geological Society of America (fellow), American Association of Petroleum Geologists, National Science Teachers Association, American Association for the Advancement of Science (fellow), Society of American Photogrammetry, Texas Academy of Science (honorary life fellow), Phi Kappa Phi, Sigma Xi. *Awards, honors:* National Science Foundation fellowship, 1956-57.

WRITINGS: (With Jon L. Higgins) *Activities and Demonstrations for Earth Science,* Parker Publishing, 1970; *Field*

Nekton Gamma, a two-man submersible, serves a variety of uses from inspecting offshore California petroleum production pipelines to coral reef studies along Jamaica. ■ (From *The Story of Oceanography* by Robert E. Boyer.)

ROBERT E. BOYER

Guide to Rock Weathering, Houghton, 1971; (with P. B. Snyder) *Geology Fact Book,* Hubbard Press, 1972; *The Story of Oceanography,* Harvey House, 1974; *Oceanography Fact Book,* Hubbard Press, 1974; *Solo-Learn Units in Earth Science,* Ward's Natural Science Establishment, Inc., 1974; *GEO-Logic,* Ward's Natural Science Establishment, Inc., 1975; *GEO-Vue,* Ward's Natural Science Establishment, Inc., 1979. Editor, *Texas Journal of Science,* 1962-64, and *Journal of Geological Education,* 1965-68.

WORK IN PROGRESS: (With S. P. Ellison, Jr.) *Geology and Resources of Texas.*

Children know,
Instinctive taught, the friend and foe.

—Sir Walter Scott

There was an Old Man with a beard,
Who said, 'It is just as I feared!—
  Two Owls and a Hen,
  Four Larks and a Wren,
Have all built their nests in my beard!'

—Edward Lear

BREISKY, William J(ohn) 1928-

PERSONAL: Surname is pronounced *Bry*-ski; born October 27, 1928, in Pittsburgh, Pa.; son of John V. and Laura (Baer) Breisky; married Barbara Bohl, July 4, 1960; children: John, Karen, Gretchen. *Education:* Attended University of Illinois, 1946-47; Syracuse University, B.A. (cum laude), 1950. *Religion:* Presbyterian. *Home:* 310 Pine St., West Barnstable, Mass. 02668. *Office:* Cape Cod *Times,* 319 Main St., Hyannis, Mass. 02601. *Agent:* Curtis Brown Ltd., 60 East 56th St., New York, N.Y. 10022.

CAREER: Saturday Evening Post, Philadelphia, Pa., associate editor, 1953-62; Enfield Press, Enfield, Conn., editor and publisher, 1962-67; Bermuda News Bureau, Hamilton, manager, 1968-74; *Daily Democrat,* Dover, N.H., editor, 1976-78; Cape Cod *Times,* Hyannis, Mass., editor, 1978—. Has served with organizations concerned with youth, mental health, brain-injured children, and redevelopment. *Military service:* U.S. Army, 1950-52; became captain.

WRITINGS: I Think I Can (nonfiction), Doubleday, 1974. Contributor to popular magazines, including *Smithsonian, Saturday Evening Post,* and *Good Housekeeping.*

WORK IN PROGRESS: A book on the human brain for Holt.

SIDELIGHTS: Due to complications following a viral sickness, two-year-old Karen Breisky was left blind, immobile, and aphasic. In *I Think I Can,* journalist William Breisky tells the story of his daughter's struggle to overcome her physical and mental handicaps. He traces her progress in a special rehabilitation program designed by the Institute for the Achievement of Human Potential in Philadelphia. After five years of therapy, Karen—though not fully recovered— is able to read, run, and attend school.

BRETT, Bernard 1925-

PERSONAL: Born July 18, 1925, in Birmingham, England; son of Francis Bernard and Annie (Eliza) Brett; married Daphne Joan Goodchild (a researcher), December 21, 1946; children: Bernard Anthony, Nigel Colin, Carolyn Joan, Adrian Francis. *Education:* Brighton College of Art and Design, art teacher's diploma and NDD (National Diploma of Design) in illustration and design, 1951. *Politics:* "Apolitical." *Religion:* Church of England. *Home and office:* Marlipins, Scotlands Close, Haslemere, Surrey, England.

CAREER: Wolverhampton College of Art, Wolverhampton, England, head of department of graphic design, 1948-67; West Surrey College of Art and Design, Farnham, England, vice principal, 1967-76; editorial consultant in London, England, 1976—; free-lance writer, illustrator, and designer, 1979—. Town councillor in Haslemere, 1976—. *Exhibitions:* Work has been exhibited at the Royal Academy, London, 1950-68, and at the Best 200 Children's Books of the Year exhibition. *Military service:* Royal Navy, 1943-46. *Member:* Royal Society of Industrial Artists and Designers (fellow). *Awards, honors:* First prize at Bologna Book Fair, 1973, for *Marco Polo.*

WRITINGS—Juveniles; all self-illustrated: *Captain Cook,* Collins, 1970; *Marco Polo,* Collins, 1971; *Mohammed,* Collins, 1972; (with Nicholas Ingman) *The Story of Music,* Ward, Lock, 1972, Taplinger, 1978; *Bernard Brett's Book of Ex-*

At about this time the baboons were being very troublesome. The baboons were animals. Once they had also been people. ■(From *The Bushman's Dream: African Tales of the Creation* by Jenny Seed. Illustrated by Bernard Brett.)

plorers and Exploring, Longman, 1973; *Stream of Culture,* Angus & Robertson, 1973; *Community and Leadership,* Angus & Robertson, 1974; (with Victor Sidney Griffiths) *Take-Off,* Collins, 1975; *On the Move,* New Educational Press, 1975; (with Lewis Jones) *Race to the South Pole,* Longman, 1976; *Monsters,* Firefly Press, 1977; *Submarine Disaster,* Longman, 1978; *True Adventures,* Hamlyn, 1978; *A Book of Ships,* Hamlyn, 1979; *Jumbo Jet,* Longman, 1979; *Ghosts and Ghouls,* Cavendish, 1980; *Monster or Man?,* Cavendish, 1980; *Vampires!,* Cavendish, 1980; *Werewolves,* Cavendish, 1980.

Illustrator: Ada Williams, *Between the Lights,* Dent, 1952; Julia Clark, *Crab Village,* Dent, 1954; Edward Thomas, *The Green Roads,* Bodley Head, 1965; Alan Taylor Dale, *The Message,* Oxford University Press, 1966; Alan Taylor Dale, *Paul the Explorer,* Oxford University Press, 1966; Alan Taylor Dale, *The Beginning,* Oxford University Press, 1966; Alan Taylor Dale, *From Galilee to Rome,* Oxford University Press, 1966; James McGrath, *The Poetry Makers,* Bodley Head, 1968; Eric Baxter, *Safety at Sea,* Bodley Head, 1969;

Benjamin Wigley, *From Fear to Faith,* Longmans, Green, 1969; *Child's Play,* Dent, 1969; Cowland Purton, *The Fire Service,* Bodley Head, 1969.

Arthur Catherall, *Keepers of the Cattle,* Dent, 1970; *The Crusades,* Hulton Press, 1970; Louise Foley, *A Job for Joey,* Western, 1970; Samuel Frederick Wooley, *The Romans,* University of London Press, 1972; Raymond Ward, *Tales of Lone Sailors,* Blackie & Son, 1973; Anthony Gascoigne Eyre, *The City of Gold and Lead,* Longman, 1974; Jenny Seed, *The Bushman's Dream: African Tales of the Creation,* Hamish Hamilton, 1974, Bradbury, 1975; A. G. Eyre, *The White Mountain,* Longman, 1974; A. G. Eyre, *The Pool of Fire,* Longman, 1974; Frances Wilkins, *Magna Carta, June 15, 1215,* Lutterworth, 1975; Kathleen Fidler, *Pirate and Admiral: The Story of John Paul Jones,* Lutterworth, 1975; Eilis Dillon, editor, *The Hamish Hamilton Book of Wise Animals,* Hamish Hamilton, 1975; Nicholas Ingman, *What Instrument Do You Want to Play?,* Ward, Lock, 1975, published as *What Instrument Shall I Play?,* Taplinger, 1976; Eve Sutton, *The*

Moa Hunters, Hamish Hamilton, 1978; Desmond Dunkerley, *Robin Hood and the Silver Arrow,* Ladybird Books, 1978; D. Dunkerley, *Robin Hood Outlawed,* Ladybird Books, 1978; D. Dunkerley, *Robin Hood to the Rescue,* Ladybird Books, 1978; D. Dunkerley, *Robin Hood and the King's Ransom,* Ladybird Books, 1978; Nicholas Ingman, *Gifted Children of Music,* Ward, Lock, 1978. Has also illustrated numerous brochures for private companies.

ADAPTATIONS—Filmstrips: "Captain Cook," British Broadcasting Company, 1965; "Sing Along," British Broadcasting Company, 1966.

WORK IN PROGRESS: Author, *A Book of Mysteries,* for Hamlyn; author and illustrator of *Children's Guide to Witchcraft* and *Children's Guide to Ghosts,* both for Grenada Publishing.

SIDELIGHTS: "I have always been fascinated by books—books per se, the feel of them, their design, typography and illustration, their paper and binding.

"Having joined the Royal Navy virtually straight from school, at the end of the war I found myself having to choose a career to follow. Torn between a degree in letters and one in the visual arts, I eventually plumped for the latter. Being a student in Brighton was really some experience. The town, an odd mixture of Regency charm, 'Prinney's' phantasies, vulgar cafes, tourist traps, offshore fishing fleets, and incredible Victoriana, completely captivated me. In a very short time I realized that my bent lay in the direction of illustration and typography, but toward the end of my course I became involved in teaching, having a natural inclination towards lecturing.

"So I changed direction and became a lecturer in graphics at a Midland College of Art; eventually I became head of the graphics department. It was a very happy and rewarding time—I like people. At the same time I began illustrating books and commercial brochures. Industrial scenes of the Midlands held a fascination for me. Bessemer converters belching out fierce flame and thick, acrid smoke inspired me to produce a number of lithographs based on this theme that were exhibited in many national and international exhibitions, including the Royal Academy. In fact, my work was regularly accepted at the Royal Academy for ten consecutive years, until once again I changed direction. It was during this period that I produced a number of murals—several of which were in glass applique—building up sheets of colored glass, sometimes to a depth of from six to nine inches.

"Around 1958 I moved into publicity design, becoming a partner in a design consultancy. My role in the company, apart from graphic design and illustration, was to handle the public relations aspect of the company's business. This is when I began to formulate ideas, interview people, and write. However, some time later, I was offered the post of vice principal in the south of England, and I once again found myself in teaching, but as an administrator, and when the novelty had worn off, the endless round of protracted meetings became irksome. I began to get 'itchy feet'—better to be a doer than a talker! It was about this time that a filmstrip on Captain Cook, which I was doing for the BBC, triggered a long suppressed desire to research and write nonfiction books for children, and educational material, the latter aimed to extend the pupil's knowledge and introduce multi-discipline teaching—something in which I believe very strongly—and in which I have collaborated with a number of well-

BERNARD BRETT

known educationalists. So, what else could I do but give up teaching and become a free-lance author, illustrator, designer, and editor? I have done this ever since and I love it!

"I now edit and design a national house journal and also act as an editor to a number of publishers. This enables me to devote most of my time to the things I love the most: research, writing, illustrating, and painting.

"I work very much in mixed media: acrylic color, colored inks, oil crayons, pen. I adore bright color—all mixed up with color rejection techniques—everything but the kitchen sink, and sometimes that! Basically an English romantic, I was, and for that matter still am, very influenced by Samuel Palmer, and to a lesser degree William Blake."

Fairy land,
Where all the children dine at five,
And all the playthings come alive.
—Robert Louis Stevenson

Twinkle, twinkle, little bat!
How I wonder what you're at!
Up above the world you fly!
Like a teatray in the sky.
—Lewis Carroll
(pseudonym of Charles Lutwidge Dodgson)

SUE ELLEN BRIDGERS

BRIDGERS, Sue Ellen 1942-

PERSONAL: Born September 20, 1942, in Greenville, N.C.; daughter of Wayland L. (a farmer) and Elizabeth (Abbott) Hunsucker; married Ben Oshel Bridgers (an attorney), March 17, 1963; children: Elizabeth Abbott, Jane Bennett, Sean Mackenzie. *Education:* Western Carolina University, B.A., 1976. *Home:* 64 Savannah Dr., Sylva, N.C. 28779. *Office address:* P.O. Box 248, Sylva, N.C. 28779.

CAREER: Writer, 1970—. *Awards, honors:* Christopher award, 1979, for *All Together Now.*

WRITINGS: Home Before Dark (novel), Knopf, 1976; *All Together Now,* Knopf, 1979. Contributor of stories to magazines, including *Redbook, Ingenue, Carolina Quarterly,* and *Mountain Living.*

WORK IN PROGRESS: A novel about women in one particular Southern family, and a novel about two teenagers coping with a mentally ill parent.

SIDELIGHTS: "My writing seems to find its expression in nostalgia. My personal childhood experiences and the setting of a small southern town combine with a sense of the inevitable loss of that way of life. I feel very close to my roots when I'm working, as if the writing itself, although not autobiographical, is taking me back in time and is revealing some of the complexities of what seems to be a simple agrarian way of life.

"I am also interested in family relationships, especially the tradition of the southern woman's two faces—gentility and power—as portrayed in a domestic setting."

FOR MORE INFORMATION SEE: Horn Book, April, 1977, April, 1979, October, 1979.

BRIN, Ruth F(irestone) 1921-

PERSONAL: Born May 5, 1921, in St. Paul, Minn.; daughter of Milton P. and Irma (Cain) Firestone; married Howard B. Brin (a business executive), August 6, 1941; children: Judith, Arthur, David, Deborah. *Education:* Vassar College, B.A., 1941; University of Minnesota, M.A., 1972. *Religion:* Jewish. *Home:* 2861 Burnham Blvd., Minneapolis, Minn. 55416.

CAREER: Writer. *Member:* National Council of Jewish Women, Urban League, League of Women Voters, Phi Beta Kappa.

WRITINGS: A Time to Search, Jonathan David, 1959; *Interpretations,* Lerner, 1965; *A Rag of Love,* Emmett Publishing Co. (Minneapolis), 1969; *Butterflies are Beautiful* (children's book), Lerner, 1974; *The Story of Esther,* Lerner, 1976; *David and Goliath,* Lerner, 1977; *Contributions of Women: Social Reform,* Dillon Press, 1977; *The Shabbat Catalogue,* KTAV, 1978. Contributor of articles and book reviews to *Minneapolis*

If I find a caterpillar I can identify, I put him in a box or jar with air holes, and I bring him fresh leaves every day. ■ (From *Butterflies Are Beautiful* by Ruth F. Brin. Illustrated by Sharon Lerner.)

RUTH F. BRIN

Star and Tribune, and *Reconstructionist;* also contributor of verse, articles, and fiction to Jewish and secular magazines.

SIDELIGHTS: "I have enjoyed teaching American Jewish literature at the University of Minnesota extension and at Macalester College during the last few years. I also review books for the *Minneapolis Sunday Tribune* regularly. I now have two grandsons, and they will soon be old enough to hear about my childhood summers in what was then Wisconsin wilderness. I hope to do a book on wildflowers for children soon."

Interpretations, based on the weekly Bible reading, is used as a supplement to the prayer book in a number of American synagogues.

BRISLEY, Joyce Lankester   1896-

PERSONAL: Born January 6, 1896, in Bexhill, Sussex, England; daughter of George and Constance (Oliver) Brisley. *Education:* Privately educated; art training at Lambeth Art School. *Home:* Fairlight, Bluehouse Lane, Limpsfield, Oxted, Surrey RH8 OAR, England.

CAREER: Freelance writer and illustrator. *Member:* Society of Authors.

WRITINGS—For Children; all self-illustrated: *Milly-Molly-Mandy Stories,* Harrap, 1928, reissued, McKay, 1976; *More of Milly-Molly-Mandy,* Harrap, 1929, reissued, McKay, 1976; *Lambs' Tails and Suchlike: Verses and Sketches,* McKay, 1930; *Further Doings of Milly-Molly-Mandy,* McKay, 1932,

(From *Peter Perkin's Puppets* by H. Waddingham Seers. Illustrated by Joyce L. Brisley.)

reissued, 1976; *Marigold in Godmother's House,* Harrap, 1934; *Dawn Shops and Other Stories,* McKay, 1933; *Milly-Molly-Mandy Infant Reader* (adapted by Margaret McGrea), Harrap, 1936; *Bunchy,* McKay, 1937; *Three Little Milly-Molly-Mandy Plays for Children,* Harrap, 1938; *My Bible-Book,* Harrap, 1940, McKay, 1941; *Adventures of Purl and Plain,* Harrap, 1941; *Milly-Molly-Mandy Again,* Harrap, 1948, reissued, McKay, 1977; *Another Bunchy Book,* Harrap, 1951; *Milly-Molly-Mandy & Co.,* Harrap, 1955, reissued, McKay, 1977; *Milly-Molly-Mandy and Billy Blunt,* Harrap, 1967, reissued, McKay, 1977; *Children of Bible Days ,* Harrap, 1970; *Milly-Molly-Mandy Omnibus,* Harrap, 1972; *New Testament Story,* Harrap, 1973; *The Milly-Molly-Mandy Second Omnibus,* Harrap, 1976; *The Six in One Complete Milly-Molly-Mandy Stories,* McKay, 1980.

Illustrator: Ursula Moray Williams, *Adventures of the Little Wooden Horse,* Harrap, 1938, Lippincott, 1939; (editor) Susan Warner, *Wide, Wide World,* University of London Press, 1950.

Contributor to various periodicals, including *Child Education, Teachers World,* and *Christian Science Monitor.*

SIDELIGHTS: Since Brisley began the Milly-Molly-Mandy series over fifty years ago, the stories have sold in the millions of copies in eight countries. The books are widely used as school readers in England and Scandinavia. Collections of a number of the stories, some of which were originally published in the 1920's, were reissued as late as 1980.

The author, who illustrated all of her own writings, has placed Milly-Molly-Mandy in a white cottage with a thatched roof in a provincial English village of the past. The stories relate the events in the life of this ideal little girl, her family, and her playmates. Despite the old-fashioned language Brisley used and the age of the stories, readers are still warmed by these lighthearted tales of a carefree childhood.

Brisley's Bunchy series has been placed in the same village setting, but this little girl is without playmates. To counteract the loneliness, Bunchy creates friends in her imagination. The characters in these fantasies come to life when Bunchy is all alone.

Although Brisley's writings are somewhat dated, the underlying warm tone of her work still draws readers into her little English villages.

BRONDFIELD, Jerome   1913-
(Jerry Brondfield)

PERSONAL: Born December 9, 1913, in Cleveland, Ohio; son of Nathan (a businessman) and Pauline (Solomon) Brondfield; married Ruth Weisenfeld, December 8, 1940; children: Eric S., Ellen Brondfield King. *Education:* Ohio State University, B.S., 1936. *Home:* 30 Holly Lane, Roslyn Heights, N.Y. 11577. *Office:* Scholastic Magazines, Inc., 50 West 44th St., New York, N.Y. 10036.

CAREER: Columbus Dispatch, Columbus, Ohio, sports writer, 1935-37; Newspaper Enterprise Association, Cleveland, Ohio, sports writer, 1937-40; International News Service, Cleveland, Ohio, reporter, 1940-41; Associated Press, New York, N.Y., reporter, 1942-44; RKO-PATHE, New York City, writer of film documentaries, 1944-57; Scholastic

JEROME BRONDFIELD

Magazines, Inc., New York City, staff editor, 1958—. President of local Little League, 1955, and local Booster Club, 1956.

WRITINGS: Bittersweet (juvenile), Scholastic Book Services, 1962; (under name Jerry Brondfield; with Kenneth L. Wilson) *The Big Ten,* Prentice-Hall, 1967; (under name Jerry Brondfield) *One Hundred Years of Football* (juvenile), Scholastic Book Services, 1969; (under name Jerry Brondfield) *Woody Hayes and the Hundred-Yard War,* Random House, 1974; *Great Moments in American Sports,* Random House, 1974; *Call the Cops—We've Been Robbed,* Scholastic Book Services, 1975; *Hank Aaron. . .714 and Beyond!* Scholastic Book Services, 1975; (under name Jerry Brondfield) *Rockne: A Legend Revisited,* Random House, 1976; *All-Pro Football Stars, 1977,* Scholastic Book Services, 1976; *Roberto Clemente: Pride of the Pirates,* Garrard, 1976.

Documentary films include: "This Is America," "Below the Sahara," and "Louisiana Territory."

Author of television scripts for Columbia Broadcasting System. Contributor of stories and articles to popular magazines, including *American, Collier's, Liberty, Esquire, Family Circle, Reader's Digest* and *Redbook.*

SIDELIGHTS: "I distinctly recall that when I was eleven years old, living in a small town in Ohio, I wanted to be a writer—and by the time I was fourteen I knew I wanted to start that kind of a career as a newspaperman.

"I guess I was just lucky. It worked out just that way.

"I can't think of any more enjoyable way of making a living—although there are times, when I stare at a blank piece of paper in my typewriter, two thoughts cross my mind, neither relevant to the typewriter. (1) I should have considered taking up welding or tree surgery. (2) I really ought to go out and tie up the tomato plants.

"I've never been at a loss for ideas. Deciding to go to work on these ideas is another thing. My curse, of course, is laziness. I'm not one of those writers who can bounce out of bed and be at my desk by 7:00 a.m., with my motor humming. Anyone who is at work by 7:00 is a peasant.

"But once I'm at it, I can knock out 3,000 words of polished copy in a day—my working day being four hours. I'll gladly settle for that. So would 1,000 other writers.

"Hobbies? Two. Gardening ('Don't plant it unless you can eat it!') and recruiting good student-athletes for my alma mater, Ohio State. Chief concern: constantly giving advice to my doctor son in San Francisco and college instructor daughter in Washington, and wondering why they so seldom listen to me. Hmm-mmm!

"It's been a good life and a good planet. Too bad the latter won't last much longer. BOOM!"

BROWER, Pauline (York)   1929-

PERSONAL: Born December 9, 1929, in Long Beach, Calif.; daughter of Mark H. and Aline (Stafford) York; married Edgar Brower (president of a division of a chemical company), August 27, 1958; children: Leslee, Cyndee, Kimberly, Kelley. *Education:* Attended Fullerton College, 1947-48; University of Southern California, Los Angeles, certificate, 1953. *Religion:* Protestant. *Home:* 2860 Woodford Circle, Rochester, Mich. 48063.

CAREER: Fullerton College, Fullerton, Calif., instructor in personality development, 1953-59; public lecturer and writer,

PAULINE BROWER

The leader of the war party used red paint on his face.
■(From *Algonquin Indians at Summer Camp* by June Behrens and Pauline Brower. Photographs compiled by Pauline Brower.)

1953—. Organized and conducted fashion shows for women's organizations in California and Texas, 1953-65; professional model, 1953-59; consultant to Edith Rehnborg Cosmetics. *Member:* American Historical Society, Society of Children's Book Writers.

WRITINGS—All for children; all with June Behrens: *Colonial Farm*, Childrens Press, 1976; *Algonquin Indians*, Childrens Press, 1977; *Pilgrims Plantation*, Childrens Press, 1977; *Canal Boats West*, illustrated with own photographs, Childrens Press, 1978; *Lighthouse Family*, illustrated with own photographs, Childrens Press, 1979; *Death Valley Miners*, illustrated with own photographs, Childrens Press, 1979; *Hopewell Village*, illustrated with own photographs, Childrens Press, 1980. Past associate editor for Northern Virginia Newspapers.

WORK IN PROGRESS: U.S. Senate Pages; Beauty from Head to Soul, for teenagers.

SIDELIGHTS: "I grew up in Southern California during the 1930's, the depression years. We had vegetable gardens, fruit trees and farm animals. I gathered eggs from the hen house and fed young calves milk from a bucket. The thought of writing didn't enter my mind during those early years, but I did enjoy making up stories in my mind during the hours I spent alone doing chores or going for walks with my dog, Ted. I am fascinated with people. My mental stories were more concerned with people's feelings than with an elaborate plot.

"Southern California doesn't have noticeable changes in seasons but our gardens and fruit trees changed throughout the year. The first ripe plum or tomato was a big event. I enjoyed watching nature's cycles in our trees and vegetables and soon discovered that people have cycles too. We are always changing and growing in one direction or another.

"I was young when I discovered that people in all walks of life are the same with the exception of the way they live and their exposure to different events and situations. This discovery started my interest in history. Knowing that people in history were basically the same as we are adds interest and sparks the imagination. It makes history come alive.

"The history books that I have helped write are illustrated with photographs of people living the lifestyles of the time. The stories tell of the hardships and progress we have made in this country. History also tells us that in time, man learns by his mistakes.

"I especially enjoy going to historical sites and researching old documents and papers left by the people who made the history. Each time I do I realize again that people are basically the same. I like to learn how various groups overcame their difficulties. . . .All of these groups made contributions in some way to our way of life today.

"During the last twenty years history and photography have grown to form special interests that took me into a variety of learning experiences and classrooms, to the 'Living Heritage' series I'm working on now.

"I feel privileged to have this opportunity to share the past with children and hope that I can contribute to an awareness of their heritage.

"It is difficult but necessary that our young realize the freedoms and opportunities they came into this world with, simply by being born in the United States. My travels in various countries confirm the fact that the special opportunities I was told about as a child do exist.

"I hope that the struggles, hard work, and joys found in the different lifestyles we portray in the 'Living Heritage' series will spell out what it takes to use the opportunities that exist.

"History reveals the cycles, successful and unsuccessful, that men and women repeat at different points in time. Hopefully, with an awareness of these cycles more men and women will repeat fewer unsuccessful acts in our future."

> In silence I must take my seat,...
> I must not speak a-useless word,
> For children must be seen, not heard.
>   —B.W. Bellamy

The Y. ■ (From *Skateboards: How to Make Them, How to Ride Them* by Glenn and Eve Bunting.)

BUNTING, Glenn (Davison) 1957-

PERSONAL: Born November 28, 1957, in Belfast, Ireland; son of Edward (a business administrator) and Eve (a writer; maiden name, Bolten) Bunting. *Education:* Pasadena City College, Pasadena, Calif., A.A.; currently attending San Diego State University. *Home:* 1512 Rose Villa, Pasadena, Calif. 91106.

CAREER: Cardiff Surf & Sport, Calif., assistant manager, 1978-79; Kaplan Productions, Inc., Calif., yacht refinisher, 1979—. *Member:* Environmental Design Club.

WRITINGS: (With Eve Bunting) *Skateboards: How to Make Them, How to Ride Them,* Harvey House, 1977.

WORK IN PROGRESS: A surfing handbook.

SIDELIGHTS: "I am very interested in surfing and skateboarding and became involved in competitive surfing. Many of my peers were professional skateboarders, so we combined my mother's skill with our knowledge to write *Skateboards.*"

FOR MORE INFORMATION SEE: Publishers Weekly, February 28, 1977.

Nadia's piano player played a lively "Yes, Sir, That's My Baby" as she moved gracefully through her routine. She looked like part ballerina and part cheerleader. ▪ (From *Sports Star: Nadia Comaneci* by S.H. Burchard. Photograph courtesy of United Press International.)

BURCHARD, Sue   1937-

PERSONAL: Born November 23, 1937, in Oak Park, Ill.; daughter of Louis A. (an accountant) and Candace (Mills) Huston; married Marshall Gaines Burchard (a writer), May 9, 1959, divorced; married Robert Ward Hipkens (a teacher, musician, and sea captain), March 4, 1979; children: (first marriage) Marshall Gaines, Jr., Wendy Mills; (second marriage) Sarah Elizabeth. *Education:* Vassar College, B.A., 1959. *Home:* 425 East 86th St., New York, N.Y. 10028. *Office:* Trinity School, 139 West 91st St., New York, N.Y. 10024.

CAREER: J. Walter Thompson (advertising agency), New York, N.Y., copywriting trainee and secretary, 1959-61; assistant teacher in private school in New York, N.Y., 1966-68; Trinity School, New York, N.Y., science teacher, 1968-71, librarian, 1971—.

WRITINGS—"Sports Hero" series; with Marshall Burchard; all published by Putnam: *Sports Hero: Joe Namath,* 1971; *Sports Hero: Brooks Robinson,* 1972; *Sports Hero: Kareem Abdul Jabbar,* 1972; *Sports Hero: Johnny Bench,* 1973; *Sports Hero: Roger Staubach,* 1973; *Sports Hero: Bobby Orr,* 1973; *Sports Hero: Henry Aaron,* 1974; *Sports Hero: Richard Petty,* 1974; *Sports Hero: Phil Esposito,* 1975;

Sports Hero: Larry Csonka, 1975; *Sports Hero: O. J. Simpson,* 1975; *Sports Hero: Billie Jean King,* 1975.

"Sports Star" series; all published by Harcourt: *Sports Star: Tom Seaver,* 1974; *Sports Star: Bob Griese,* 1975; *Sports Star: Walt Frazier,* 1975; *Sports Star: Brad Park,* 1975; *Sports Star: Pele,* 1976; *Sports Star: Franco Harris,* 1976; *Sports Star: Jim "Catfish" Hunter,* 1976; *Sports Star: Chris Evert,* 1976; *Sports Star: "Mean" Joe Greene,* 1976; *Sports Star: Nadia Comaneci,* 1977; *Sports Star: Mark "The Bird" Fidrych,* 1977; *Sports Star: Dorothy Hamill,* 1978; *Sports Star: Tony Dorsett,* 1978; *Sports Star: Reggie Jackson,* 1979; *Sports Star: John McEnroe,* in press.

(With Marshall Burchard) *Auto Racing Highlights,* Garrard, 1975; (with Marshall Burchard) *I Know a Baseball Player,* Putnam, 1975.

WORK IN PROGRESS: Sports Star: Elvin Hayes, for Harcourt.

HOBBIES AND OTHER INTERESTS: Spending summers in Maine and cruising aboard her ketch.

BURDICK, Eugene (Leonard)   1918-1965

PERSONAL: Born December 12, 1918, Sheldon, Iowa; died July 26, 1965 in San Diego, Calif.; son of Jack Dale (a painter) and Marie (Ellerbroek) Burdick; married Carol Warren, July 3, 1942; children: Katherine, Mary, Michael. *Education:* Stanford University, B.A., 1942; Magdalen College, Oxford University, Rhodes Scholar, Ph.D., 1950. *Politics:* Democrat. *Home:* 791 Santa Barbara Rd., Berkeley, Calif. *Agent:* Curtis Brown Ltd., 575 Madison Ave., New York, N.Y. 10022. *Office:* University of California, Berkeley, Calif.

CAREER: University of California, Berkeley, 1950-65, began as assistant professor, became professor of political theory. Naval War College, Newport, R.I., staff member, 1950-51. *Military service:* U.S. Navy, 1942-46; became lieutenant commander; awarded Navy/Marine Corps Cross. *Awards, honors:* Fellowship from the Center for the Advancement of the Study of Behavioral Sciences; O. Henry prize, 1947; Houghton-Mifflin Literary Fellowship, 1956, for *The Ninth Wave.*

WRITINGS—Books of interest to young adults: (With William J. Lederer) *The Ugly American* (Book-of-the-Month Club selection), Norton, 1958; (with Harvey Wheeler) *Fail-Safe* (Book-of-the-Month Club selection), McGraw, 1962.

Other writings: *The Ninth Wave* (Book-of-the-Month Club selection), Houghton, 1956; (editor with Arthur J. Brodbeck) *American Voting Behavior,* Free Press, 1959; *The Blue of Capricorn,* Houghton, 1961; *The 480,* McGraw-Hill, 1964; (with W. J. Lederer) *Sarkhan,* McGraw-Hill, 1965; *Nina's Book,* Houghton, 1965. Wrote television plays and motion picture scripts. Contributed to magazines and professional journals.

ADAPTATIONS—Movies: "The Ugly American," Universal, 1963; "Fail-Safe," Columbia Pictures, 1964.

SIDELIGHTS: Burdick was born in Iowa, but spent most of his life in California. "Father was an itinerant painter who married Mother when she was sixteen and took her from

EUGENE BURDICK

Iowa to Los Angeles [in 1920]. . . . There we were reared. Father promptly died from peritonitis and mother had three children all under the age of five on her hands. She did beautifully as a waitress for a year or two and then married Fritz Gaillard, a cellist in the Los Angeles Philharmonic. We three kids were raised in the odd benign mingling of Bach suites for the violin and cello and the sun and sea of Los Angeles. We came in off the beach, tanned and exhausted, and put on little white collars and black velvet pants and sat through chamber music until it poured out of our ears. To this day I cannot abide serious music. It makes me scratch all over." ["Eugene Burdick," *Wilson Library Bulletin,* April, 1961.[1]].

After earning a bachelor's degree in psychology at Stanford University, Burdick served in the U.S. Navy during World War II. He began writing in 1944. In 1950 he earned a Ph.D. in philosophy from Oxford University as a Rhodes scholar.

From 1950 until his death in 1965 he was affiliated with the University of California at Berkeley, where he was a professor of political theory. His first novel, *The Ninth Wave,* took nine years to write, saw six drafts, and at one time was 2000 manuscript pages long and weighed twenty pounds. "The theme came first, and it came right out of that hard-nosed English theorist Thomas Hobbes. Hobbes believed that people might be many things, but they were most fundamentally and continually frightened." [Judith Golwyn, "New Creative Writers," *Library Journal,* June 1, 1956.[2]]

Before his death of a heart attack at the age of forty-six, Burdick lived with his wife and three children in Berkeley, California and vacationed on the South Sea island of Moorea.

HOBBIES AND OTHER INTERESTS: Surfing, the South Pacific.

*FOR MORE INFORMATION SEE: New York Herald Tribune Book Review,*June 3, 1956; *Wilson Library Bulletin,* April, 1961; *Saturday Review,* October 20, 1962; *Newsweek,* October 22, 1962; *New Republic,* November 3, 1962; *Atlantic,* December, 1962; John Wakeman, editor, *World Authors: 1950-1970,* H.W. Wilson, 1975. Obituaries: *New York Times,* July 27, 1965; *Time,* August 6, 1965; *Publishers Weekly,* August 9, 1965; *Books Abroad,* Spring, 1966.

BURTON, Robert (Wellesley) 1941-

PERSONAL: Born June 18, 1941, in Sherbourne, Dorsetshire, England; son of Maurice (a zoologist) and Margaret (Maclean) Burton. *Education:* Attended Downing College, Cambridge, 1960-63. *Home and office:* Manor Cottage, 46 West St., Great Gransden, Sandy, Bedfordshire S9 193AU, England. *Agent:* Murray Pollinger, 4 Garrick St., London WC 2E 9BH, England.

CAREER: Author, 1967—. Meteorologist and biologist for British Antarctic Survey, 1963-66, biologist, 1971-72. *Member:* Society of Authors, Zoological Society of London, Institute of Biology.

WRITINGS: Animals of the Antarctic, Abelard-Schuman, 1970; *Animal Senses,* David & Charles, 1970; *The Life and Death of Whales,* Deutsch, 1973; (with Maurice Burton) *Life of Meat Eaters,* Western, 1974; *The Way Birds Live,* Elsevier International, 1975; *The Mating Game,* Elsevier International, 1976; *The Pond Book,* David & Charles, 1976; *The Language of Smell,* Routledge & Keegan Paul, 1976; *Introducing Hills and Moors,* Educational Publishing, 1976; *The Love of Baby Animals,* Octopus, 1976; *The Cat Family,* Macmillan, 1976; (with Maurice Burton) *Inside the Animal World,* Macmillan, 1977; *The Seashore,* Orbis, 1977; *Wildlife from the Roadside,* Educational Publishing, 1977; *First Nature Book,* St. Michael, 1977; (with Maurice Burton) *The World's Disappearing Wildlife,* Marshall Cavendish, 1978; *Carnivores of Europe,* Batsford, 1979; *Horses and Ponies,* Macmillan, 1979.

General editor with Maurice Burton, *Purnell's Encyclopedia of Animal Life,* BPC Publishing, 1968-70, published as *The International Wildlife Encyclopedia,* 1970, four volume edition, Octopus, 1974.

SIDELIGHTS: "My father was a writer who kept many kinds of wild animals in aviaries and cages in the garden, so naturally I grew up with an interest in animals. I also wanted to write and I remember the first time I tried my hand at this. I was still a schoolboy when, one evening, I made up my mind to write an article on animals and sent it to a newspaper. To my surprise, and joy, it was printed and I received a small fee. Nothing much more happened in this way until, after leaving university, I went to the Antarctic for two years. Yet I always wanted to be an author and on my return from the south polar seas I joined my father in writing an encyclopedia, Purnell's *Encyclopedia of Animal Life,* also known as the *International Encyclopedia of Animal Life.* This took us three years to finish and after that I began writing my own books."

HOBBIES AND OTHER INTERESTS: Whaling history of polar expeditions, and restoring his thatched cottage.

CALDECOTT, Moyra 1927-

PERSONAL: Born June 1, 1927, in Pretoria, South Africa; naturalized British citizen; daughter of Frederick Stanley (a receiver of revenue) and Jessy Florence (Harris) Brown; married Oliver Zerffi Stratford Caldecott (a publisher and artist), April 5, 1951; children: Stratford Stanley, Julian Oliver, Rachel Lester. *Education:* University of Natal, B.A. (honors), 1949, M.A., 1950. *Politics:* "No political affiliation." *Religion:* "Religious, but no particular affiliation." *Residence:* London, England.

CAREER: University of Cape Town, Cape Town, South Africa, junior lecturer in English, 1950; teacher at high school in London, England, 1951; Central Board for Conscientious Objectors, London, art gallery assistant and clerk, 1951-52; writer, 1953—. Has given poetry readings.

WRITINGS: The Weapons of the Wolfhound (juvenile and young adult novel), Rex Collings, 1976; *The Sacred Stones* (trilogy of young adult and adult novels), Volume I: *The Tall Stones,* Rex Collings, 1977, Hill & Wang, 1978, Volume II: *The Temple of the Sun,* Rex Collings, 1977, Hill & Wang, 1979, Volume III: *Shadow on the Stones,* Rex Collings, 1978, Hill & Wang, 1979; *Adventures by Leaf Light* (juvenile), Green Tiger Press, 1978; *The Lily and the Bull* (young adult and adult novel), Hill & Wang, 1979; *Child of the Dark Star* (young adult and adult science fiction), Corgi, 1980.

Plays: "The Runaway," British Broadcasting Corp., Overseas Service, 1960; "The Wanting Bird" (for children), first produced in London at Rosendale Junior School, 1963.

Work represented in anthologies, including *Gallery,* Methuen; *Rhyme and Rhythm,* Macmillan; *Reading Aloud,* Macmillan. Contributor of poems and articles to magazines, including *Outposts, Freeway, Brief,* and *British Wheel of Yoga.*

WORK IN PROGRESS: A historical biography, *Etheldreda,* just completed; a juvenile and young adult book on Celtic folklore, *The Faery Twins.*

SIDELIGHTS: "My chief interest is the exploration of ancient civilizations for information about a perennial wisdom that I feel is vital to our civilization, but has all but been forgotten in our exploitation of our planet for material gain.

"I have attended many adult educational courses in astronomy (I am *very* interested in space exploration) and geology. I read widely, but am mainly interested in ancient history, religious and philosophical writings, and science fiction. I do not join organizations but I attend conferences and lectures given by the Wrekin Trust (a charitable foundation for those who are committed to the exploration of their spiritual natures and the development of consciousness). I am hopeful of the *new age* when men will remember they are eternal beings in passage on the earth—each with dignity and responsibility for the whole.

"Although I am intensely interested in the working of intuition and imagination and what we loosely term the 'paranormal,' I am anxious to keep the balancing strength of reason, and a sense of discrimination.

"I was the youngest of five children and spent a great deal of my childhood ill in bed. Encouraged by my mother, I read a great deal. When I was recuperating from various illnesses

(including injuries received by being run over by a car), I spent a great deal of my time in our garden talking to various little people I believed were hidden under the leaves. This experience inspired the series of stories called *Adventures by Leaf Light.* When I wrote *Adventures by Leaf Light* Josie was a little girl permanently crippled in a wheel chair because I wanted, if possible, to help children who were so disabled to enjoy the richness of the world of imagination and to know that they were not alone. The publishers and the illustrators, however, felt that the book would appeal to a wider readership if the little girl was not permanently disabled but just recovering from an illness as I had been.

"As I grew older I found myself writing down stories and poems. I went to university and studied English and philosophy. For a while I did not write 'creatively' because I was too busy working. When I had children of my own I took up writing again, but found that I did not have enough time of my own to devote to it. I was determined to be a novelist.

"After many rejections by publishers I gave up trying to be a novelist.

"And then things really started to happen.

"One day I was in the British Museum looking at a twelfth-century chess set carved in walrus ivory. It fascinated me and I began to wonder how such a sophisticated set of carvings could have been lost and buried on the wild and desolate coast of the Outer Hebrides. I began to write. This story became the children's novel, *The Weapons of the Wolfhound,* and was accepted for publication by Rex Collings.

"In the two years it took to be published I became very ill with angina. I spent some time in hospital and a great deal of time in bed at home. I was not a complete invalid—but not far off.

"In the Summer of '75 we went for a holiday to Scotland and I stood in an ancient Stone Circle at Dyce near Aberdeen while my husband sketched. I was overwhelmed by the atmosphere and a story came very vividly to me, so vividly it felt like memory and not imagination. I started writing it down as soon as we returned to London. In fact, I finished the first of the Stone Circle novels, *The Tall Stones,* in the hospital, writing as fast as I could, thinking that I might not live to finish it. I did finish it, and I wrote two more to complete the trilogy. I was cured of my angina by God's grace through a healer and went on to write many more novels. While my teenage daughter, Rachel, was still at school, I used to write and read to her what I had written when she returned home each evening. If it did not hold her interest I used to throw it away. Sometimes it was her questions about the meaning of life that I answered through the characters in the books.

"With each book I write I feel the subject chooses *me.* That is, I get an overwhelming feeling that I have to write a particular story and when I start all kinds of strange things happen to confirm for me that I am on the right track. If I don't have these 'magical' occurrences I tend to lose interest in the story. For instance, I might write something and then find out *afterwards* through research that what I have written is accurate. I wrote of healing by psychic means *before* I experienced it myself. In the *Temple of the Sun* I used the stone sea urchin as Kyra's talisman *before* I read that a stone sea urchin had been found in the burial mound of a woman of this period and that sea urchins were quite often found in their tombs.

"Everywhere I turn I find what I need just at the moment I need it. Even in dreams the answers I need come to me. It is very strange and very exciting."

HOBBIES AND OTHER INTERESTS: Gardening, pottery and batik making, painting.

FOR MORE INFORMATION SEE: Times Educational Supplement, November 18, 1977.

CAMPION, Nardi Reeder   1917-

PERSONAL: Born June 27, 1917, in Honolulu, Hawaii; daughter of Russell Potter (an Army colonel) and Narcissa (Martin) Reeder; married Thomas Baird Campion (director of Parent Giving, Dartmouth College), 1941; children: Thomas, Tad, Toby, Narcissa, Russell. *Education:* Wellesley College, A.B., 1938. *Religion:* Episcopalian. *Home:* 8 Storrs Rd., Hanover, N.H. 03755. *Agent:* Curtis Brown Ltd., 575 Madison Ave., New York, N.Y. 10022.

CAREER: Newport News (Va.) High School, English teacher, 1940-41. United Negro College Fund, committee member.

Member: Planned Parenthood Association, Wellesley Club (Westchester), Wellesley College Alumnae Association (president, 1976-79).

WRITINGS: (With Marty Maher) *Bringing Up the Brass,* McKay, 1951; (with brother, Red Reeder) *The West Point Story,* Random House, 1956; *Patrick Henry, Firebrand of the American Revolution,* Little, Brown, 1961; *Kit Carson, Pathfinder of the West,* Garrard, 1963; (with Rosamund W. Stanton) *Look to This Day* (biography of Dr. Connie Guion), Little, Brown, 1965; *Casa Means Home,* Holt, 1970; *Ann the Word: The Life of Mother Ann Lee, Founder of the Shakers,* Little, Brown, 1976. Contributor to *Encyclopaedia Britannica* and *World Book;* contributor to *Look, Collier's, Reader's Digest, Sports Illustrated, New York Times* Magazine, *Boston Globe* Magazine. Editor, Sarah Lawrence College *Alumnae Magazine,* 1953.

ADAPATATIONS—Movie: *Bringing Up the Brass* was filmed as "The Long Grey Line," starring Tyrone Power, Columbia Pictures, 1953.

SIDELIGHTS: Campion was born in Honolulu, went to grade school in Kansas, and to high school in the Panama Canal Zone. (She was an "army brat.") She went to Wellesley College because she wanted to go to a place where women were important. "When I was little my mother taught me to stand up in my play pen and shout 'Votes for women!'"

(From the movie "The Long Gray Line," based on the novel *Bringing Up the Brass,* starring Tyrone Power. Released by Columbia Pictures Corp., 1957.)

NARDI REEDER CAMPION

Campion majored in English composition. "I can still feel my great English professor, Miss Manwaring, looking over my shoulder whenever I tried to write." After college she taught English in the Virginia public schools, a venture she remembered vividly that included trying to explain *Ivanhoe* to over-age football players at Newport News High School.

Campion married Thomas Baird Campion whom she met when they were both college seniors. Her husband, an executive at *The New York Times* for twenty-three years, was the director of operations when he decided on a second career in education.

The Campions have five children, four boys and one girl. They have attended Dartmouth, Goucher, Harvard, University of Colorado, University College, Dublin, and Queen's College, Oxford (as a Rhodes Scholar), and can now be identified as an attorney in Idaho; a doctor in Boston; a chiropractor-poet Yogi in Chicago; a musician-farmer in Maine; and a 1979 graduate of Dartmouth College.

As "fugitives from Manhattan," the Campions like to garden, golf, hike and cross-country ski. "Out of the rat race and into the mouse race" is the way they describe their new life in the country of Hanover, N.H.

FOR MORE INFORMATION: Horn Book, August, 1965, February, 1977.

CAPPEL, Constance 1936-
(Constance Montgomery)

PERSONAL: Born June 22, 1936, in Dayton, Ohio; daughter of Adam Denison and Louise (Henry) Cappel; married Raymond A. Montgomery, Jr.; divorced April 1, 1980; children: Raymond A. III, Anson Cappel. *Education:* Sarah Lawrence College, B.A., 1959; Columbia University, M.A., 1961; Union Graduate School, Ph.D. candidate, 1976-79. *Home:* Box 30, Waitsfield, Vt. 05673.

CAREER: Newsweek, New York City, reporter, and editor of company magazine, 1961-62; Fleet Publishing Corp., New York City, associate editor, 1963-64; *Vogue,* New York City, researcher and writer, 1964-66; Waitsfield Summer School, Waitsfield, Vt., founder (with Raymond A. Montgomery, Jr.), and teacher, 1966-69; Pine Manor Junior College, Chestnut Hill, Mass., associate professor, 1968-71; Vermont Crossroads Press, Waitsfield, chief executive officer, 1973—; Goddard College, Plainfield, professor, 1975-79. *Member:* Authors League of America, Writers Guild of America, American Association of University Professors. *Awards, honors:* McDowell Colony fellowship, 1972, 1974.

WRITINGS: Hemingway in Michigan, Fleet, 1966; *Vermont School Bus Ride,* Vermont Crossroads Press, 1974; (with Raymond A. Montgomery, Jr.) *Vermont Farm and the Sun,* Vermont Crossroads Press, 1975; (with R. A. Montgomery, Jr.) *Vermont Roadbuilder,* Vermont Crossroads Press, 1975. Columnist for *Park East,* 1963-65.

WORK IN PROGRESS: A novel; poetry.

HOBBIES AND OTHER INTERESTS: The outdoors.

CONSTANCE CAPPEL

CHANDLER, Caroline A(ugusta)   1906-1979

OBITUARY NOTICE: Born December 7, 1906, in Ford City, Pa.; died of emphysema, December 18, 1979, in Washington, D.C. Pediatrician, educator, and writer. An authority on child mental health and hygiene, Chandler held a number of jobs with the National Institute of Mental Health and with various government agencies. From 1959 to 1961 she was chief of the Office of Mental Health and Child Health in Maryland. At one time she served as an instructor of preventive medicine at Johns Hopkins University. In addition to writing specialized books and articles on medicine, Chandler was the author of several books for the general reader, including *Susie Stuart, M.D.; Dr. Kay Winthrop, Intern;* and *Nursing as a Career. For More Information See: American Men and Women of Science: The Social and Behavioral Sciences,* 12th edition, Bowker, 1973; *Contemporary Authors,* Volume 17-20, revised, Gale, 1976; *Who's Who in America,* 40th edition, Marquis, 1978. *Obituaries: Washington Post,* December 21, 1979; *Contemporary Authors,* Volume 93-96, Gale, 1980.

CLEAVER, Bill

PERSONAL: Born in Seattle, Wash.; married wife, Vera (a writer). *Residence:* Winter Haven, Fla.

CAREER: Author of books for children. *Military service:* U.S. Air Force. *Awards, honors:* Finalist for the National Book Award, Children's Book Category, 1971, for *Grover.*

WRITINGS—All with wife, Vera Cleaver: *Ellen Grae* (illustrated by Ellen Raskin; *Horn Book* Honor List), Lippincott, 1967; *Lady Ellen Grae* (illustrated by E. Raskin), Lippincott, 1968; *Where the Lillies Bloom* (illustrated by Jim Spanfeller; *Horn Book* Honor List), Lippincott, 1969; *Grover* (illustrated by Frederic Marvin), Lippincott, 1970; *The Mimosa Tree,* Lippincott, 1970; *I Would Rather Be a Turnip,* Lippincott, 1971; *The Mock Revolt,* Lippincott, 1971; *Delpha Green and Company,* Lippincott, 1972; *The Whys and Wherefores of Littabelle Lee,* Atheneum, 1973; *Me Too* (ALA Notable Book), Lippincott, 1973; *Dust of the Earth,* Lippincott, 1975; *Trial Valley,* Lippincott, 1977; *Queen of Hearts,* Lippincott, 1978; *A Little Destiny,* Lothrop, 1979.

Contributor of stories to *McCall's* and *Woman's Day* magazines.

SIDELIGHTS: "Ideally the writer of fiction comes to the task of doing so with an understanding of what fiction is. For me it is not so much the said but the unsaid. It is that which holds incident and character together, the questing voices that whisper, 'What is it? Why is it? Where are we going? What's on the other side?'

"The question of why I write is put to me often but in all my years at this art or craft or madness or whatever it is I have not yet been able to translate the why of it into a distinct description. I can suppose that it is an inherent energy that pushes me toward some kind of self-validation. I say 'inherent' because I believe that only the mechanics of creative writing may be taught. As a very young child I knew that I was going to be a writer. Also, in that way children know things without being told or shown, I knew that I was going to have to be my own teacher. I have been my own teacher. I am a graduate of the public libraries of the United States of America.

"I like the peace of my daily performance of brooding and poring and study and I revel in the attempts to set to page that which goes beyond the presentation of mere human behaviour. All of this digging and pushing and grinding and examination is not a bid for immortality. It is to put to work that which was given me to use for a while." [John Rowe Townsend, *A Sounding of Storytellers,* Lippincott, 1971.[1]]

When asked how Cleaver and his wife work as an author team, he responded: ". . . We have a close friend with whom we lunch several times a month. He tells us that he has trouble recognizing us when we are not together. He is serious. We have been married that long. We are joint and so all of our endeavours and opinions are joint. This is not a hedge, you understand. That is simply the way it is."[1]

Cleaver's works are included in the Kerlan Collection at the University of Minnesota.

Deep within a dry glen edged around with wild blackberry bramble we found, that morning, a patch of Virginia snakeroot. ■ (From *Where the Lilies Bloom* by Vera and Bill Cleaver. Illustrated by Jim Spanfeller.)

BILL CLEAVER

"Most appealing in [*Where the Lilies Bloom*]," commented a *New York Times* critic, "is the sense of earnestness and determination in the central character and narrator, Mary Call Luther. . . . This is a story of good people, with real natures, living under conditions of hardship, in poverty, in the midst of bereavement, maintaining their independence, wit, and dignity. . . . Only now and then does the natural simplicity of the narrator become noticeably literary. Most of the time she speaks as effortlessly as Huck Finn, another orphan. . . ." *National Observer* wrote that, "Authors Vera and Bill Cleaver had everything going for them in this story of Mary Call's struggle to keep her promise . . . but [they] blow the lot by failing to leave their own sophistication outside when they enter [her] primitive world. . . ." *Saturday Review* described it as ". . . taut in structure and written with flair, flavor, and wry humor."

Horn Book called *Grover* "a sad but not a somber story, in which there is humor to counterbalance sorrow, and action as well as introspection. The language is strong and rich in imagery; the narrative is absorbing. A profoundly wise and real tale." "That children's books are richer by the Cleavers, there is no doubt," a *New York Times* critic wrote. "Their characters are whole grain, their imagery absorbing, with such as 'rain-colored eyes' and 'soup-warm water.' Still *Grover* comes as something of a disappointment after *Where the Lilies Bloom* . . . for it lacks the same poignancy."

FOR MORE INFORMATION SEE: Horn Book, October, 1969, April, 1970, October, 1970, April, 1971, October, 1971, June, 1973, December, 1975, June, 1979, October, 1979; *New York Times Book Review,* May 2, 1971; *Publishers Weekly,* April 16, 1973, March 18, 1974; Doris de Montreville & Elizabeth D. Crawford, editors, *Fourth Book of Junior Authors & Illustrators,* H. W. Wilson, 1978.

CLEAVER, Vera

PERSONAL: Born in Virgil, S.D., married Bill Cleaver (an author). *Residence:* Winter Haven, Fla.

CAREER: Author of books for children with husband, Bill Cleaver. *Awards, honors:* Finalist for the National Book Award, Children's Book Category, 1971, for *Grover.*

WRITINGS—All with husband, Bill Cleaver, except as noted: (Sole author) *The Nurse's Dilemma,* Avalon Books, 1966; *Ellen Grae* (illustrated by Ellen Raskin; *Horn Book* Honor List), Lippincott, 1967; *Lady Ellen Grae* (illustrated by Raskin), Lippincott, 1968; *Where the Lilies Bloom* (illustrated by Jim Spanfeller; *Horn Book* Honor List), Lippincott, 1969; *Grover* (illustrated by Frederic Marvin), Lippincott, 1970; *The Mimosa Tree,* Lippincott, 1970; *I Would Rather Be a Turnip,* Lippincott, 1971; *The Mock Revolt,* Lippincott, 1971; *Delpha Green and Company,* Lippincott, 1972; *The Whys and Wherefores of Littabelle Lee,* Atheneum, 1973; *Me Too* (ALA Notable Book), Lippincott, 1973; *Dust of the Earth,* Lippincott, 1975; *Trial Valley,* Lippincott, 1977; *Queen of Hearts,* Lippincott, 1978; *A Little Destiny,* Lothrop, 1979.

Contributor of stories to *McCall's* and *Woman's Day* magazines.

SIDELIGHTS: "A good book presents to its readers a variety of gifts. Its greatest and most compelling speaks in a familiar voice: 'But this is I, this person described on these pages. I have suffered this same pain, this same aloneness, this worry and anxiety. I have known happiness like this and I

VERA CLEAVER

The chair had gone berserk. It danced away from the wall and ran over to the dresser and whacked it. Mortally wounded, the mirror attached to its top, fell out of its frame. ■ (From *Lady Ellen Grae* by Vera and Bill Cleaver. Illustrated by Ellen Raskin.)

have suffered this same despair. How is it the writer of this book knows me? We have not met.'

"The answer to this lies in that quality which all serious writers seem to possess. People like you pass the doors of these creators every day. They observe you, they talk with you, they listen. Their interest in you is piercing and sympathetic which is not to imply that you are their pawns. This is appropriate and indispensable. There is a sense of urgency about this too, for writers, blessed with their gifts for narrative, are allowed only for a while the use of them. Your role in the life of a writer supplies vitality, importance and integrity.

"I am not sure how, in the very young and untrained and unencouraged, a love for books comes about. There is something mysterious and very splendid about this. The books are silent until what is inside them is discovered. Then it is like seeing a light in a dark place.

"I do not remember the first time I saw a plane or first viewed television. I do remember my first book. I held it, I opened it, I began to read and, even though a child, I felt myself in the presence of excellence. I knew relief. I had found a friend, a forever companion. With me it was that way then and it

is that way now." [Vera and Bill Cleaver, *American Bicentennial Reading,* Children's Book Council, 1975.]

Cleaver's works are included in the Kerlan Collection at the University of Minnesota.

Commenting on *Ellen Grae, Library Journal* said, "The writing is excellent and its combination of comedy, near-tragedy, and suspense are rare in juvenile fiction. The ending is tantalizing, and ambiguous adult values are penetrated as the unforgettable Ellen prys the lid off the platitude about honesty being the best policy. That question, the book, and its heroine are worth talking about." The sequel to *Ellen Grae, Lady Ellen Grae,* caused *Library Journal* to write that, "The Cleavers have squandered their considerable writing talents on a sequel that subverts the essence of the excellent *Ellen Grae.* . . . [They] write well—but they either didn't realize what they created the first time or don't see how they've devalued Ellen Grae in attempting to trot her out again." On the other hand, a *Young Reader's Review* critic wrote that "the writing is unusually direct and girls will appreciate Ellen Grae's feelings. It is a funnier book than the first one and will probably have a wider audience."

I Would Rather Be a Turnip was reviewed by a *Horn Book* critic, who wrote, "The events are vividly told, often hilariously and sometimes a bit melodramatically. . . . [It is] the story of an Ellen Graelike character whose conflicts are fought out as much with herself as with her environment." *Saturday Review* said, "The characters are memorable, the dialogue is both amusing and provocative, and the situation (save for an obtrusive avoidance of the word 'bastard' or its equivalent) is treated with honesty and dignity."

FOR MORE INFORMATION SEE: Horn Book, October, 1969, April, 1970, October, 1970, April, 1971, October, 1971, June, 1973, December, 1975, June, 1979, October, 1979; *New York Times Book Review* May 2, 1971; *Publishers Weekly,* April 16, 1973, March 18, 1974; Doris de Montreville & Elizabeth D. Crawford, editors, *Fourth Book of Junior Authors & Illustrators,* H. W. Wilson, 1978.

COLLIER, Ethel   1903-

PERSONAL: Born July 24, 1903, in Toledo, Ohio; daughter of Henry Eberhard (an artist and artisan) and Pauline (Hoffman) Kuhlman; married Joseph Collier, November 9, 1929; children: Rachel (Mrs Heinrich Bosch). *Education:* University of Toledo, student, 1921-23; University of Michigan, B.A., 1928. *Politics:* Independent. *Residence:* Chagrin Falls, Ohio.

CAREER: Toledo News-Bee, Toledo, Ohio, reporter, 1923-25 and 1930-33; *Toledo Times,* Toledo, reporter, 1928-33. *Member:* Authors Guild of Authors League of America. *Awards, honors:* First prize from the National League of American Pen Women, for *The Gypsy Tree.*

WRITINGS—For children: *I Know a Farm,* William R. Scott, 1960; *The Birthday Tree,* William R. Scott, 1961; *Who Goes There in My Garden?,* William R. Scott, 1963; *The Gypsy Tree,* William R. Scott, 1966; *Hundreds and Hundreds of Strawberries,* William R. Scott, 1969.

At home, I put my seeds away and I waited.

Some days it snowed.

(From *Who Goes There In My Garden?* by Ethel Collier. Illustrated by Honoré Guilbeau.)

ETHEL COLLIER

WORK IN PROGRESS: Children's fiction; an adult story.

SIDELIGHTS: "It was adult fiction I had in mind from age seven, when I saw a woman attacking an indoor cobweb and its spider, and broke morosely into prose. Over the years, though, it was children who came bobbing up from under the lines. Thus, a newspaper series on local women notables turned out happily to be childhood memories, with nice old pictures to match.

"As our daughter grew up I took notes, notes on her; drifted into a nursery school job; and with no formal training, sought and took a job teaching kindergarten for one year. Later it was a real sorrow to find that house-mothering at a child detention center would take more hours than I had.

"Still, it was adults I was trying to write for. A literary agent or two returned my manuscripts, saying 'stories about children are awfully hard to sell' (and magazine editors backed them up) and how about young love or domestic tangles? No!

"My supplementary first readers came about from the distress of a sister. For years she had taught reading with success, even to non-English-speaking Mexican migrant workers' children. When suddenly the teaching emphasis was shifted from phonics to sight reading, many first grade teachers despaired.

"Surely, I thought, a child's small nature encounters with their large wonders could interest and thus help a young child in reading, if recounted in a small vocabulary, well-managed. When my first two of these landed happily together at William

R. Scott, Inc., just as I became a grandmother, it made a five star year.

"*The Gypsy Tree,* for older children, later gave me the leeway in language that I enjoy, as well as some stars and a first prize in a National League of American Pen Women contest.

"All my books have at least a scrap of actuality. My haymow and the find of a new-laid egg in it are child memories; seeing a child step on an earthworm sparked another first reader; and the gypsy harness hook is so real I could take you to it.

"My husband has a gift for the fresh thought and the well written piece, as shown by a wallfull of his own Newspaper Guild awards. He is fun to be with, and we share our major lifetime interest."

CONSTANT, Alberta Wilson

PERSONAL: Born in Dalhart, Tex.; daughter of Albert Edwardes Wilson and Marie (Fite) Wilson (Mrs. W. C. Erwin); married Edwin B(aird) Constant (a purchasing agent), May 9, 1931; children: Anne Louise (Mrs. William Henszey Ewing), John Edwin. *Education:* Oklahoma City University, A.B., 1930; University of Oklahoma, writing courses, 1940-41. *Politics:* Democrat. *Religion:* Methodist. *Home:* 1841 Vassar Ave., Independence, Mo. 64052.

CAREER: Phi Eta National Sorority, educational director, 1938-50; poetry editor, *Veteran's Voices,* hospitalized veterans writing project of Women in Communications, Inc., 1958-70; Jackson County Historical Society, Mo., director of archives, 1960-61, board of directors. *Member:* Society of Midland Authors, Women in Communications, Inc., Friends of Missouri Town 1855, Friends of the Library (University of Missouri at Kansas City branch), Friends of Art (Nelson Gallery, Kansas City). *Awards, honors:* First prize, short story, Midwestern Writers' Conference, Chicago, 1950; *Does Anybody Care About Lou Emma Miller?* was included in the Library of Congress list of best children's books, 1979.

WRITINGS—All published by Crowell: *Oklahoma Run* (People's Book Club selection and Readers' Book Club selection), 1955; *Miss Charity Comes to Stay,* 1959; *Willie and the Wildcat Well,* 1962; *Those Miller Girls,* 1965; *The Motoring Millers,* 1969; *Paintbox on the Frontier: The Life and Times of George Caleb Bingham,* 1974; *Does Anybody Care About Lou Emma Miller?,* 1979. Author of narrative text for Symphony No. 8, "Oklahoma," by Jack Frederick Kilpatrick, commissioned to commemorate the fiftieth anniversary of Oklahoma statehood, 1957. Contributor of articles and short stories to popular magazines, anthologies, and textbooks.

WORK IN PROGRESS: A novel based on an incident in the history of the American west.

SIDELIGHTS: "I was born in Texas, lived in Tennessee, came to Oklahoma with my family when I was eight years old and lived there until I was married some years when my husband was transferred to Missouri where we live now. This makes me very much a typical American, I think.

(From *Does Anybody Care About Lou Emma Miller?* by Alberta Wilson Constant. Jacket illustrated by Gail Owens.)

ALBERTA WILSON CONSTANT

"In my life in Tennessee I was reared by women . . . my mother, my aunt, and my grandmother. All the men in our family had died and though it probably made me one-sided in my growth, I always felt loved and cared for, and was especially given, by all three of these wonderful women, a strong sense of *family,* of belonging. My mother remarried and our stepfather brought us to a small town in central Oklahoma. I truly believe that life in a town of 500 is one of the best things that can happen to a writer . . . you see life very close up. I was lonesome for our Tennessee home and I spent a lot of time roaming around the pasture back of our house. I climbed trees (every book I ever wrote has a 'climbing' episode in it) and safely up in the tree I would talk to myself, dramatize my loneliness, and generally spin off stories of which I was the central character. I suppose I was doing what psychiatrists now get large fees for doing.

"Father always encouraged me to write and when I was sixteen he sent to a small magazine published in Oklahoma City a poem I had written. I did not know he had sent the poem and the day he brought home the magazine with *my poem in print,* is one of the decisive days of my life. From that time on I never wanted to do anything but be a writer. I have had other jobs, but all of them led me right back to writing. At first I worked on short stories and then articles. I wrote some plays used by my college, Oklahoma City University, and a couple of them were included in a textbook of drama. I was a long time getting to a book, but when I did, it began with a little girl up in a tree talking to herself. . . .

"Writing has been my business for more than forty years. It is a joy and a misery; a pleasure and a problem; it is hard work and rewards and I wouldn't trade it for any job I've ever heard of."

HOBBIES AND OTHER INTERESTS: Family and friends, reading, cooking, and local history.

COTTLER, Joseph 1899-

PERSONAL: Born October 26, 1899, in Russia; son of David (a mechanic) and Gertrude (Meltzer) Cottler; married Elizabeth Steinbrook, December 27, 1927 (deceased); married Harriet Barr, 1976. *Education:* University of Pennsylvania, B.S., 1921. *Politics:* Nonpartisan. *Religion:* Jewish. *Home:* Mill Rd., Elkins Park, Pa. 19117.

CAREER: Teacher and counselor in Philadelphia, Pa. 1922-58. *Military service:* U.S. Navy, 1918.

WRITINGS—Juvenile books: (With Haym Jaffe) *Heroes of Civilization,* Little, Brown, 1931, revised edition, 1969; (with Jaffe) *Mapmakers,* Little, Brown, 1933; (with Harold Brecht) *Careers Ahead,* Little, Brown, 1934; *Champions of Democracy,* Little, Brown, 1935; *Man with Wings,* Little, Brown, 1942; *Alfred Wallace,* Little, Brown, 1966; (with Jaffe) *More Heroes of Civilization,* Little, Brown, 1969. Contributor of articles, and of reviews on recordings to journals.

SIDELIGHTS: "In the aftermath of World War I with its senseless carnage, the nations were confronted by the life-or-death problem of how to eliminate war as a way of settling international disputes. The political solution they came up with was a League of Nations. But then, as now, no nation was ready to surrender its ultimate power to international authority. Tragic as that may be, it cannot be denied that the field of battle does foster supreme moral values: personal courage, comradeship and a sense of common destiny, a readiness to sacrifice for the common good.

JOSEPH COTTLER

"Recognizing that without those values we are but clods, the philosopher William James had once spoken of the need to find a moral equivalent of war, and prompted by his suggestion, my friend Haym Jaffe and I conceived our *Heroes of Civilization,* biographical sketches of people engaged in a courageous struggle on behalf, not of one nation, but of all mankind; a battle in which nobody loses and everybody stands to win. We pitched the book to the teen-ager, considering that the adult was hopeless to change.

"After almost half a century the book is still alive, but the moral equivalent not yet accepted. Nonetheless I continue to believe that living models of the idea should be presented to our youth. My several books have that purpose."

Cottler has played the violin professionally and continues to play with chamber music groups. He has lived for extended periods in Europe and Mexico.

CRANE, Royston Campbell 1901-1977 (Roy Crane)

OBITUARY NOTICE: Born November 22, 1901, in Abilene, Tex.; died July 7, 1977, in Orlando, Fla. Cartoonist. Royston Campbell Crane was a pioneer cartoonist, responsible for the innovation of adventure comic strips. In 1924, a time when comedy was the prevalent feature of the cartoon pages, Crane introduced "Wash Tubbs," the swashbuckling story of Washington Tubbs II. Roy Crane also created the "Captain Easy" series, and "Buz Sawyer," the popular strip that has recounted the adventures of Navy pilot Buz Sawyer since 1943. The National Cartoonists Society honored Royston Crane with the Reuben award in 1950, and the Best Story Strip award in 1966. *For More Information See: Editor and Publisher,* April 28, 1951; *Who's Who in America,* 38th edition, Marquis, 1974; *Who's Who in American Art 1978,* Bowker, 1978. *Obituaries: New York Times,* July 12, 1977; *Time,* July 18, 1977; *Contemporary Authors,* Volume 89-92, Gale, 1980.

CRAVEN, Thomas 1889-1969

PERSONAL: Born January 6, 1889, in Salina, Kan.; died February 27, 1969; son of Richard Price and Virgina (Bates) Craven; married Aileen St. John-Brenon (a writer), August 25, 1923; children: Richard Craven. *Education:* Kansas Wesleyan University, B.A., 1908; later studied art in Paris. *Politics:* Independent Democrat.

CAREER: Began as a reporter for a Denver newspaper, 1910; later worked as a night clerk for the Santa Fe Railroad, Las Vegas, Nev., and as a teacher of Latin and Greek at various schools throughout the United States; University of San Juan, San Juan, P.R., instructor, 1913-14; became professional author, critic, lecturer following World War I. *Military service:* Served in the U.S. Navy, 1918; became seaman second class.

WRITINGS: Paint (fiction), Harcourt, 1923; *Men of Art,* Simon & Schuster, 1931, revised edition, 1940; *Modern Art: The Men, the Movements, the Meaning,* Simon & Schuster, 1934, reprinted, Scholarly Press, 1976; (editor) *The Treasury of American Prints,* Simon & Schuster, 1939; *Thomas Hart*

THOMAS CRAVEN

Benton: A Descriptive Catalog, Associated American Artists, 1939; *A Treasure of Art Masterpieces, from the Renaissance to the Present Day,* Simon & Schuster, 1939, new and revised edition, 1958, reissued, 1977; (editor, with Florence and Sydney Weiss) *Cartoon Cavalcade,* Simon & Schuster, 1943; *The Story of Painting, from Cave Pictures to Modern Art,* Simon & Schuster, 1943; *Famous Artists and Their Models,* Pocket Books, 1949, reissued, Washington Square Press, 1962; *The Pocket Book of Greek Art,* Pocket Books, 1950; *The Rainbow Book of Art,* World Publishing, 1956.

SIDELIGHTS: Prior to World War I, Craven lived in Greenwich Village where he roomed with the artist Thomas Hart Benton. It was Benton who most likely shaped Craven's preferences for American regional art and reinforced his growing dislike for "art for art's sake." After the War, Craven began to vent his strong opinions about art in print, establishing himself as a critic, author, and lecturer.

Through his articles in such magazines as *Saturday Evening Post, Newsweek, Good Housekeeping, Nation,* and *New Republic,* Craven sought to make art accessible to all people. Craven was never afraid to express his opinions, and members of the art world either praised him for his directness or decried him as dogmatic and narrow-minded. But while he was sometimes considered offensive, most members of the art world conceded that he managed to stir healthy controversy and enthusiasm.

Because of Craven's straightforward journalistic style, his books have often been recommended for young people and the general reader uninitiated in art. Craven has been credited with introducing art to those who may have never otherwise become interested.

FOR MORE INFORMATION SEE: Forum, January, 1936; *New York Times,* December 14, 1939; *Saturday Review of Literature,* September 30, 1939; *New York Herald Tribune,* December 3, 1943; *Newsweek,* December 20, 1943.

Obituaries: *Current Biography Yearbook,* 1970; *New York Times,* March 1, 1969; *Newsweek,* March 10, 1969.

CRUIKSHANK, George   1792-1878

PERSONAL: Born September 27, 1792, in London, England; died February 1, 1878, in London, England; buried in St. Paul's Cathedral; son of Isaac Cruikshank (a caricaturist); younger brother of Isaac Robert Cruikshank (a caricaturist). *Education:* Cruikshank received little schooling and no formal art training; he learned to make illustrations and caricatures while helping in his father's studio as a child. *Politics:* Outspoken supporter of the temperance movement. *Home:* London.

CAREER: Caricaturist and illustrator. At a very early age, Cruikshank exhibited artistic talent and began to assist his father with lithographs, engravings, designs for valentines, and other illustrations; he earned his first commission at the age of twelve with an etching for a lottery ticket, 1804; began his career as a caricaturist with his cartoons for *The Scourge,* a satirical magazine which appeared 1811-16; continued to produce satirical cartoons which appeared in most of the popular periodicals throughout his career; working until the age of 83, Cruikshank contributed illustrations to more than 200 books in association with many of the leading authors of the time, most notably, Charles Dickens, Sir Walter Scott, Henry Fielding, and the Grimm brothers; he also illustrated innumerable pamphlets, political tracts, comic almanacs, and chapbooks. *Awards, honors:* Cruikshank's oil painting, "Worship of Bacchus; or, The Drinking Customs of Society," was purchased by popular subscription and presented to the National Gallery in London.

ILLUSTRATOR—Works of interest to young people: Jacob Ludwig Carl and Wilhelm Carl Grimm, *German Popular Stories,* C. Baldwyn, 1823; *Mornings at Bow Street,* [London], 1824; Louis C. A. de Chamisso de Boncourt, *Peter Schlemihl* (translated by Sir John Bowring), [London], 1824; Miguel de Cervantes Saavedra, *The Life and Exploits of Don Quixote de la Mancha* (translated by Charles Jarvis), Jones, 1828; John Payne Collier, *Punch and Judy,* S. Prowett, 1828, new edition, B. Blom, 1971; Daniel Defoe, *The Life and Surprising Adventures of Robinson Crusoe,* J. Major, 1831; Sir John Bowring, *Minor Morals for Young People,* Whittaker & Co.,

GEORGE CRUIKSHANK

1834-39; Washington Irving, *The Beauties of Washington Irving,* T. Tegg & Son, 1835; *The Comic Almanac,* [London], 1835-53, reissued, Barnes, 1963; Charles Dickens, *Sketches by "Boz" Illustrative of Every-day Life and Every-day People,* three volumes, J. Macrone, 1836-37; Charles Dickens, *Oliver Twist; or, The Parish Boy's Progress,* R. Bentley, 1838, reissued, Heron Books, 1970; Harriet Beecher Stowe, *Uncle Tom's Cabin,* [London], 1852; *George Cruikshank's Fairy Library,* three volumes, D. Bogue, 1853-54, also published as *The Cruikshank Fairy-Book,* Putnam, 1911, reissued, 1970; Robert Hunt, *Popular Romances of West England; or, The Drolls, Traditions, and Superstitions of Old Cornwall,* two volumes, [London], 1865; J.L.C. and W. C. Grimm, *Grimm's Goblins,* Ticknor & Fields, 1867; Juliana H. Ewing, *The Brownies and Other Tales,* [London], 1870; J. H. Ewing, *Lob Lie-by-the-Fire,* [London], 1874; John Bunyan, *Pilgrim's Progress,* H. Frowde, 1903; J.L.C. and W. C. Grimm, *Grimm's Folk Tales* (translated by Eleanor Quarrie), The Folio Society, 1965.

Single works: *Illustrations of Time,* [London], 1827; *Sunday in London,* E. Wilson, 1833; *Volume One of My Sketch Book,* [London], 1834; *The Bachelor's Own Book,* D. Bogue, 1844; *The Bottle,* Wiley & Putman, 1847; *The Drunkard's Children,* D. Bogue, 1848; *The Betting Book,* W. and F. G. Cash, 1852; *The House That Jack Built,* W. Tweedie, 1853; F. E. Smedley, editor, *George Cruikshank's Magazine,* [London], 1854; *A Discovery Concerning Ghosts: With a Rap at the "Spirit Rappers,"* F. Arnold, 1863 [second edition with additions, Routledge, Warne, 1864].

(From *George Cruikshank's Omnibus.* Jacket design by the author.)

Other works illustrated by Cruikshank: James Caulfield, *Portraits, Memoirs, and Characters of Remarkable Persons,* four volumes, H. R. Young & T. H. Whitely, 1819; David Carey, *Life in Paris,* J. Fairburn, 1822; E. Berens, *Christmas Stories,* J. Parker, 1823; Victor Hugo, *Hans of Iceland,* [London], 1825; George Clinton, *Memoirs of the Life and Writings of Lord Byron,* J. Robins & Co., 1825; *The Universal Songster, or Museum of Mirth,* three volumes, [London], 1825-26; W. F. von Kosewitz, *Eccentric Tales from the German,* [London], 1827; John Collier, *Tim Bobbin's Lancashire Dialect, and Poems,* Hurst, Chance, 1828; William B. Rhodes, *Bombastia Furioso* (one-act burlesque), [London], 1830; Sir Walter Scott, *Letters on Demonology and Witchcraft Addressed to J. G. Lockart,* [London], 1830; Christopher Anstey, *The New Bath Guide,* Hurst, Chance, 1830; John Yonge Akerman, *Tales of Other Days,* [London], 1830; William Clarke, *Three Courses and a Dessert,* Vizetelly, Branston, 1830; Henry Fielding, *Tom Thumb,* [London], 1830.

Ferdinand Franck, *An Autobiographical Sketch of the Youthful Days of a Musical Student,* R. Ackerman, 1831; Tobias

G. Smollett, *The Expedition of Humphry Clinker,* Cochrane & Pickersgill, 1831; H. Fielding, *The History of Amelia,* [London], 1831; H. Fielding, *The History of Tom Jones,* J. Cochrane & Co., 1831; William H. Merle, *Odds and Ends,* [London], 1831; T. L. Pettigrew, *Lucien Greville,* [London], 1833; George Mogridge, *Mirth and Morality,* T. Tegg & Son, 1834; D. Defoe, *A Journal of the Plague Year; or, Memorials of the Great Pestilence in London, in 1665,* T. Tegg & Son, 1835; M. H. Barker, *Tough Yarns: A Series of Naval Tales and Sketches to Please All Hands,* [London], 1835; William H. Ainsworth, *Rookwood,* J. Macrone, 1836; M. H. Barker, *Land and Sea Tales,* [London], 1836; Henry David Inglis, *Rambles in the Footsteps of Don Quixote,* [London], 1837; Joseph Grimaldi, *Memoirs of Joseph Grimaldi* (edited by C. Dickens), two volumes, [London], 1838 [a new edition edited by Richard Findlater, Stein & Day, 1968]; W. H. Ainsworth, *Jack Sheppard,* R. Bentley, 1839; W. M. Thackery and C. Dickens, *The Loving Ballad of Lord Bateman,* C. Tilt, 1839, reissued, Dent, 1969.

(With John Leech and John Tenniel) R. H. Barham, *The Ingoldsby Legends,* R. Bentley, 1840-47; W. H. Ainsworth, *The Tower of London,* R. Bentley, 1840; Charles Dibdin, *Songs of the Late Charles Dibdin,* J. Murray, 1841; C. Dibdin, *Songs, Naval and National,* J. Murray, 1841; W. H. Ainsworth, *The Miser's Daughter,* Cunningham & Mortimer, 1842; W. H. Ainsworth, *Ainsworth's Magazine: A Miscellany of Romance, General Literature and Art,* [London], 1842-54; W. H. Ainsworth, *Windsor Castle,* H. Colburn, 1843, reissued, Chivers, 1974; W. H. Ainsworth, *Modern Chivalry,* [London], 1843; Arthur O'Leary, *Arthur O'Leary, His Wanderings and Ponderings in Many Lands,* William Maginn, *John Manesty, the Liverpool Merchant,* J. Mortimer, 1844; (with H. K. Browne) George Raymond, *Memoirs of R. W. Elliston, Comedian, 1774 to 1810,* [London], 1844-45; H. M. Barker, *The Old Sailor's Jolly Boat,* [London], 1844; W. H. Ainsworth, *Saint James's; or, The Court of Queen Anne,* J. Mortimer, 1844; Catherine Gore, *The Snow Storm: A Christmas Story,* Fisher, Son & Co., 1845; H. Fielding, *The Works of Henry Fielding,* H. G. Bohn, 1845; Augustus and Henry Mayhew, *The Good Genius That Turned Everything into Gold,* [London], 1847; A. and H. Mayhew, *The Greatest Plague of Life,* [London], 1847; Giovanni B. Basile, *The Pentamerone; or, The Story of Stories,* D. Bogue, 1848; A. and H. Mayhew, *Whom to Marry and How to Get Married,* [London], 1848; Angus Bethune Reach, *Clement Lorimer; or, The Book with the Iron Clasps,* [London], 1849; Mary V. C. Clarke, *Kit Bam's Adventures; or, The Yarns of the Old Mariner,* Grant & Griffith, 1849; (with Kenny Meadows) A. and H. Mayhew, *The Magic of Kindness,* [London], 1849.

Francis E. Smedley, *Frank Fairlegh; or, Scenes from the Life of a Private Pupil,* [London], 1850; C. Dibdin, *Under the Patronage of the Lords of the Admiralty,* Harrison & Son, 1850; *1851; or, The Adventures of Mr. and Mrs. Sandboys,* Stringer & Townsend, 1851; Edward G. Flight, *The Horse Shoe; or, The True Legend of St. Dunstan and the Devil,* [London], 1852; C. W. Hoskyns, *Talpha; or, The Chronicles of a Clay Farm,* [London], 1852; Robert Southey, *The Life of Nelson,* J. Murray, 1853; (with William M'Connell) Alfred W. Cole, *Lorimer Littlegood Esq., A Young Gentleman Who Wished to See Society,* J. Blackwood, 1858; Stenelaus and Amylda, *A Christmas Legend for Children of a Larger Growth,* [London], 1858; Dudley Costello, *Holidays with Hobgoblins and Talk of Strange Things,* J. C. Hotten, 1860; Richard Frankum, *The Bee and the Wasp,* [London], 1861; J. G. Lockhart, *The History of Napoleon Bonaparte,* [London], 1867; Baron Munchausen, *The Travels and Surprising Adventures of Baron Munchausen,* [London], 1867;

John B. Gough, *Autobiography and Personal Recollections of J. B. Gough*, Bill & Co., 1869; William Augustus Fraser, *Coila's Whispers, by the Knight of Morar*, W. Blackwood & Sons, 1869; Frederick D. Planche, *Guess Me*, [London], 1872; Charles Gilbert, *Endless Mirth and Amusement*, [London], 1874; Sir W. Scott, *The Waverly Novels*, G. Routledge & Sons, 1875-76; Mary C. Rowsell, *The Pedlar and His Dog*, Blackie & Son, 1885.

Collections or Reproductions: William Hone, *Hone's Popular Political Tracts*, W. Hone, 1825; *Illustrations of Smollett, Fielding, and Goldsmith*, C. Tilt, 1832; *Cruikshankiana*, T. M'Lean, 1835; *Mayhew's Great Exhibition of 1851*, D. Bogue, 1851; *Eighty-two Illustrations on Steel, Stone, and Wood*, W. Tegg, 1870; *George Cruikshank's Omnibus*, Bell & Daldy, 1870; *Scraps and Sketches*, [London], 1882; *Gallery of Comicalities*, C. Hindley, 1891; *The Cruikshankian Momus*, J. C. Nimmo, 1892; *Drawings by George Cruikshank, Collected by Him to Illustrate an Intended Autobiography*, Chatto & Windus, 1895; *A Handbook for Posterity; or, Recollections of "Twiddle Twaddle,"* W. T. Spencer, 1896; *Four Hundred Humorous Illustrations*, Simpkin, Marshall, 1900; *Cruikshank's Water Colours*, A. & C. Black, 1903; *Pictures by George Cruikshank*, Gowans & Gray, 1909.

ADAPTATIONS: H. P. Grattan, "The Bottle" (a poem based on Cruikshank's designs), T. Watts, 1848; Talbot Watts, "The Drunkard's Children" (a poem based on Cruikshank's designs), T. Watts, 1849; Thomas P. Taylor, "The Bottle" (drama based on Cruikshank's designs in two acts), [London], 1850; "The Bottle" (motion picture), Ideal Film Service, Inc., 1915.

SIDELIGHTS: **September 27, 1792.** Born on Duke Street, Bloomsbury, London. Father worked in London as a caricaturist, illustrator and engraver. "I was cradled in caricature." [John Wardroper, *The Caricatures of George Cruikshank*, Godine, 1978.[1]]

1800. With his older brother, assisted his father as an engraver. "... My father, Isaac Cruikshank, was a designer and etcher, and engraver, and a first-rate water-colour draughtsman. My brother, Isaac Robert, was a very clever miniature and portrait painter, and was also a designer and etcher, and your humble servant likewise a designer and etcher.

"When I was a mere boy, my dear father kindly allowed me to *play* at *etching* on some of his copper plates, little bits of shadows, or little figures in the background, and to assist him a *little* as I grew older, and he used to assist *me* in putting in hands and faces. And when my dear brother Robert (who in his latter days omitted the Isaac) left off portrait painting, and took almost entirely to designing and etching, I assisted him at first to a great extent in some of his drawings on wood and his etchings; and all this mixture of head and hand work has led to a considerable amount of confusion, so that dealers or printsellers and collectors have been puzzled to decide which were the productions of the 'I. CK.,' the 'I. R. CK.' (or 'R. CK.'), and the 'G. CK.'; and this will not create much surprise when I tell you that I have myself, in some cases, had a difficulty in deciding in respect to early *handwork*, done some sixty odd years back, particularly when my drawings, made on wood-blocks for common purposes, were hastily executed (according to price) by the engraver. Many of my first productions, such as halfpenny lottery pictures and books for little children, can never be known or seen, having, of course, been destroyed long ago by the dear little ones

(From *The Life and Surprising Adventures of Robinson Crusoe* by Daniel Defoe. Illustrated by George Cruikshank.)

who had them to play with." [Blanchard Jerrold, *The Life of George Cruikshank*, Volume I, Chatto & Windus, 1882.[2]]

1803. Although immersed in artistic endeavors, Cruikshank was also interested in the theater and held youthful ambitions for a military career. "Great Britain at this time might well be compared to the state of a beehive when its inmates have been disturbed by accident or an intruder. . . . Every town was, in fact, a sort of garrison; in one place you might hear the 'tattoo' of some youth learning to beat the drum; at another place some march or national air being practised upon the fife, and every morning at five o'clock the bugle-horn was sounded through the streets, to call the volunteers to a two hours' drill from six to eight, and the same again in the evening; and then you heard the pop, pop, pop, of the single musket, or the heavy sound of the volley, or distant thunder of the artillery; and then sometimes you heard the 'Park' and the 'Tower,' guns firing to celebrate some advantage gained over the enemy. . . .

"I was but a boy—a little boy at that time—but I had a sharp critical eye for all those military movements, and used to be much amused at the occasional blunders of the 'awkward squads'; and as I often had the opportunity of witnessing the regulars 'exercise,' I judged of and compared the evolutions of 'my father's regiment' by this standard; and I remember feeling considerable pride and pleasure when I saw the 'Loyal

St. Giles's and St. George's Bloomsbury Volunteers' wheel out of the old gate of 'Montague House' (then the British Museum, and the site of the present building), to march to Hyde Park to be reviewed. . . .

"Not only did the men . . . form themselves into regiments of volunteers, but the boys of that day did so likewise, and my brother . . . who was my elder by three years, formed one of these juvenile regiments, and appointed *himself* the colonel. We had our drum and fife, our 'colours,' presented by our mammas and sisters, who also assisted in making our accoutrements. We also procured small 'gun-stocks,' into which we fixed mop-sticks for barrels, kindly polished by 'Betty' with a *tinge* of blacklead, to make 'em look like *real* barrels.

"The boys watched their fathers 'drill'; and 'as the old cock crows the young one learns,' so we children followed in the steps of our papas, and we were ready for inspection quite as soon as our elders, and could march in good order, to have *our* 'Field-day,' from Bloomsbury Church to the fields, where Russell and Tavistock Squares now stand. This account of my 'playing at soldiers' may appear to be rather trifling and nonsensical, but just see what it has done for me. Why, by my learning the manual exercise with this mop-stick gun, when a boy, and at the same time learning how to 'march,' 'counter-march,' and to 'mark time,' to 'wheel' and to 'face,' etc., IT HAS MADE ME—AYE, ME, G. C., FIT

(From *Sketches by Boz: Illustrative of Every-day Life, and Every-day People* by Charles Dickens. Etching by George Cruikshank.)

AND ABLE TO HANDLE A MUSKET OR A RIFLE, AND FALL INTO THE RANKS OF AN INFANTRY REGIMENT AT A MOMENT'S NOTICE. I make this assertion with confidence; for when as a young man I joined the rifle company, I found that I required *no drilling;* the only additional knowledge necessary was to understand the 'calls' of the bugle and whistle, which, with the rifles, are used instead of the '*word* of command' when skirmishing; and I can say, having previously learned to prime, and load, and fire, and hit a mark, that I was a tolerable rifleman one week after I had entered."[2]

1805. As a teenager, Cruikshank worked as a designer, as an illustrator of songs, and as a delineator of any current event which excited public attention.

1811. Father died. Assumed responsibility for his mother and four-year-old sister. Abandoned his theatrical ambitions and pursued his more lucrative career in engraving, illustration and caricature. ". . . [I] thought of becoming an assistant scene painter at one of the London theatres and then working [my] way on the stage as an actor, having evinced considerable dramatic ability—amongst [my] youthful associates—both in comedy & tragedy—and always performing the part of scene painter to these juvenile companies. In order to get a proper and respectable introduction—[I] applied to a friend of [my] late father—Mr James Whittle—of the firm of Whittle & Laurie—publisher—to introduce [me] to Mr Raymond—the then manager of Drury Lane Theatre. Mr Whittle told

Jack gets the Golden Hen, away from the Giant.

(From *The Cruikshank Fairy-Book.* Illustrated by George Cruikshank.)

(From *Grimm's Fairy Tales* by the Brothers Grimm. Illustrated by George Cruikshank.)

[me] to paint a scene upon a piece of mill board to show to Mr Raymond—this was imposing an unexpected task—for which . . . [I] had neither the inclination nor the spare time to execute . . . being then fully occupied in making drawings on wood for children's books—and so this little scene was never painted—and so our artist neither became a scene painter nor an actor.''[1]

1813. Caricature output to London periodicals depicting London low life rapidly increased. Convinced his brother to join him in his studio at Dorset Street. ''. . . There was, in the neighbourhood in which I resided, a low public-house; it has since degenerated into a gin-palace. It was frequented by coal-heavers only; and it stood in Wilderness Lane (I like to be particular), between Primrose Hill and Dorset Street, Salisbury Square, Fleet Street. To this house of inelegant resort (the sign was startling, the 'Lion in the Wood'), which I regularly passed in my way to and from the Temple, my attention was one night especially attracted by the sounds of a fiddle, together with other indications of festivity; when, glancing towards the tap-room window, I could plainly discern a small bust of Shakespeare placed over the chimney-piece, with a short pipe stuck in its mouth. This was not clothing the palpable and the familiar with golden exhalations from the dawn, but it was reducing the glorius and immortal beauty of Apollo himself to a level with the commonplace and vulgar. Yet there was something not to be quarrelled with in the association of ideas to which that object led. It struck me to be the perfection of the human picturesque. It was a palpable meeting of the Sublime and the Ridiculous; the world of Intellect and Poetry seemed thrown open to the meanest capacity; extremes had met; the highest and the lowest had united in harmonious fellowship.

I thought of what the great poet had himself been, of the parts that he had played, and the wonders he had wrought within a stone's throw of that very spot; and feeling that even he might have well wished to be there, the pleased spectator of that lower world, it was impossible not to recognise the fitness of the pipe. It was only the pipe that would have become the mouth of a poet in that extraordinary scene, and without it, he himself would have wanted majesty and the right to be present. I fancied that Sir Walter Raleigh might have filled it for him. And *what* a scene was that to preside over and contemplate! What a picture of life was there! It was *all* life! In simple words, I saw, on approaching the window, and peeping between the short red curtains, a swarm of jolly coal-heavers! Coal-heavers all, save a few of the fairer and softer sex—the wives of some of them—all enjoying the hour with an intensity not to be disputed, and in a manner singularly characteristic of the tastes and propensities of aristocratic and fashionable society; that is to say, they were 'dancing and taking refreshments.' They only did what their 'betters' were doing elsewhere. The living Shakespeare, had he been, indeed, in the presence, would but have seen a common humanity working out its objects, and have felt that the *omega,* though the last in the alphabet, has an astonishing sympathy with the *alpha* that stands first.

Cruikshank, portrait by Daniel Maclise.

(From *Oliver Twist; or The Parish Boy's Progress* by Charles Dickens. Illustrated by George Cruikshank.)

(From *Uncle Tom's Cabin* by Harriet Beecher Stowe. Wood engraving by George Cruikshank.)

"This incident, I may be permitted to say, led me to study the characters of that particular class of society, and laid the foundation of scenes afterwards published. The locality and the characters were different, the spirit was the same. Was I, therefore . . . the companion of dustmen, hodmen, coal-heavers, and scavangers? . . . It would be just as fair to assume that Morland was the companion of pigs, that Liston was the associate of louts and footmen, or that Fielding lived in fraternal intimacy with Jonathan Wild."[2]

1815. Worked for radical bookseller, William Hone.

1818-1819. Illustrated Hone's anti-government pamphlet, *The Political House that Jack Built,* which was an immediate success.

Also created what years later Cruikshank considered his most important design—the sketches for the *Bank Restriction Barometer.* "About the year 1817 or 1818 there were one-pound Bank of England notes in circulation, and, unfortunately, there were forged one-pound bank notes in circulation also; and the punishment for passing these forged notes was in some cases transportation for life, and in others DEATH.

"At that time I resided in Dorset Street, Salisbury Square, Fleet Street, and had occasion to go early one morning to a house near the Bank of England; and in returnng home between eight and nine o'clock, down Ludgate Hill, and seeing a number of persons looking up the Old Bailey, I looked that way myself, and saw several human beings hanging on the gibbet opposite Newgate prison, and, to my horror,

two of these were women; and, upon inquiring what these women had been hung for, was informed that it was for passing forged one-pound notes. The fact that a poor woman could be put to death for such a minor offence had a great effect upon me—and I at that moment determined, if possible, to put a stop to this shocking destruction of life for merely obtaining a few shillings by fraud; and well knowing the habits of the low class of society in London, I felt quite sure that in very many cases the rascals who forged the notes induced these poor ignorant women to go into the gin-shops to 'get something to drink,' and thus *pass* the notes, and hand them the change.

"My residence was a short distance from Ludgate Hill (Dorset Street); and after witnessing this tragic scene I went home, and in ten minutes designed and made a sketch of '*Bank-note not to be imitated.*' About half an hour after this was done, William Hone came into my room, and saw the sketch lying upon my table; he was much struck with it, and said, 'What are you going to do with this, George?'

"'To publish it,' I replied. Then he said, 'Will you let me have it?' To his request I consented, made an etching of it, and it was published. Mr. Hone then resided on Ludgate Hill, not many yards from the spot where I had seen the people hanging on the gibbet; and when it appeared in his shop windows, it created a great sensation, and the people gathered round his house in such numbers that the Lord Mayor had to send the City police (of that day) to disperse the CROWD. The Bank directors held a meeting immediately upon the subject, and AFTER THAT they issued *no more*

(From *Robinson Crusoe* by Daniel Defoe. Wood engraving by George Cruikshank.)

one-pound notes, and so there was *no more hanging for passing* FORGED *one-pound notes;* not only that, but ultimately no hanging, even for forgery. AFTER THIS Sir Robert Peel got a Bill passed in Parliament for the 'Resumption of cash payments.' AFTER THIS he revised the Penal Code, and AFTER THAT *there was not any more hanging or punishment of* DEATH *for minor offences.*

"In a work that I am preparing for publication [1875] I intend to give a copy of 'The Bank Note,' as I consider it the most important design and etching that I ever made in my life for it has saved the lives of thousands of my fellow-creatures; and for having been able to do this Christian act I am indeed most sincerely thankful. . . ."[2]

The political illustrations that Cruikshank created for Hone were extremely popular and did much for political reform, although it has been proven that Cruikshank's "Bank Note" sketches did not cease the withdrawal of Bank of England one-pound notes or the death penalty for such offense, as Cruikshank implied.

1824. Married first wife, Mary Ann.

1825. Popularity and output of illustrations were at its peak. Commissioned to illustrate Milton's *Paradise Lost,* but the edition never was published—to his great disappointment.

1835. Illustrated the *Comic Almanac,* which he continued to do for nineteen years.

1838. Illustrated Dicken's *Oliver Twist.* "When *Bentley's Miscellany* was first started, it was arranged that Mr. Charles Dickens should write a serial in it, and which was to be

illustrated by me; and in a conversation with him as to what the subject should be for the first serial, I suggested to Mr. Dickens that he should write the life of a London boy, and strongly advised him to do this, assuring him with all the characters, which my large experience of London life would enable me to do.

"My idea was to raise a boy from a most humble position up to a high and respectable one—in fact, to illustrate one of those cases of common occurrence where men of humble origin, by natural ability, industry, honest and honourable conduct, raise themselves to first-class positions in society. As I wished particularly to bring the habits and manners of the thieves of London before the public . . . I suggested that the poor boy should fall among thieves, but that his honesty and natural good disposition should enable him to pass through this ordeal without contamination; and after I had fully described the full-grown thieves (the *Bill Sykeses*) and their female companions, also the young thieves (the *Artful Dodgers*) and the receivers of stolen goods, Mr. Dickens agreed to act on my suggestion, and the work was commenced, but we differed as to what sort of boy the hero should be. Mr. Dickens wanted rather a queer kind of chap; and, although this was contrary to my original idea, I complied with his request, feeling that it would not be right to dictate too much to the writer of the story, and then appeared 'Oliver Asking for More'; but it so happened just about this time that an inquiry was being made in the parish of St. James's, Westminster, as to the cause of the death of some of the workhouse children who had been 'farmed out.' I called the attention of Mr. Dickens to this inquiry, and said that if he took up this matter, his doing so might help to save many a poor child from injury and death; and I earnestly

"I will give you three days," said he, **"and if at the end of that time you cannot tell my name, you must give up the child to me."** ■ (From "Rumpelstiltskin" in *Grimm's Fairy Tales* by the Brothers Grimm. Illustrated by George Cruikshank.)

begged of him to let me make Oliver a nice pretty little boy; and if we so represented him, the public—and particularly the ladies—would be sure to take a great interest in him, and the work would then be a certain success. Mr. Dickens agreed to that request, and I need not add here that my prophecy was fulfilled; and if any one will take the trouble to look at my representations of 'Oliver,' they will see that the appearance of the boy is altered after the two first illustrations, and, by a reference to the records of St. James's parish, and to the date of the publication of the *Miscellany,* they will see that both the dates tally, and therefore support my statement.''[2]

Cruikshank maintained that his designs were the result of consultations with Dickens, but his biographer, Blanchard Jerrold asserted that he drew from the actual proofs of the manuscript *after* Dickens had created them.

1839. Dickens passed the editorship of *Bentley's Miscellany* to Harrison Ainsworth—Cruikshank and Dickens' collaboration ended, although the two remained friends for several years. On the completion of *Jack Sheppard* and the *Tower of London,* however, Cruikshank quarrelled with Mr. Bentley. ''To *Oliver Twist* and *Jack Sheppard* I devoted my best

exertions; but, so far from effecting a monopoly of my labours, the publisher in question (Mr. Bentley) has not, for a twelvemonth past, had from me more than a single plate for his monthly *Miscellany,* nor will he ever have more than that single plate per month, nor shall I ever illustrate any other work that he may publish.''[2]

1840. Illustrated Ainsworth's *The Tower of London,* which was a great success. Ainsworth described their relationship during this collaboration: ''While writing the *Tower of London* . . . I used to spend a day with the artist at the beginning of each month in the tower itself; and since every facility was afforded us by the authorities, we left no part of the old fortress unexplored. To these visits I look back with the greatest pleasure, and feel that I could not have had a more agreeable companion than the then genial George Cruikshank.''[2]

1841. Began his own magazine, the *Omnibus,* which was unsuccessful. ''. . . After I had been going with my *Omnibus* for something less than twelve months, to my utter astonishment, my friend [Thomas J.] Pettigrew called upon me one day with a message from Mr. W. Harrison Ainsworth, to this effect . . . that he was about to start a monthly mag-

Drawing by Cruikshank of himself and Harrison Ainsworth at work. ■ (From *Ainsworth's* magazine, Volume 1, 1842.)

azine, and that if I would join him, and drive my 'Omnibus' into his magazine, he would take all the risk and responsibilty upon himself, and make such arrangements as would compensate me liberally. . . . My *Omnibus*, in some respects, did merge into *Ainsworth's Magazine*; but upon again joining with Mr. Ainsworth, I announced that the *Omnibus* would henceforth appear as an *annual*.''[2]

1847. First wife, Mary Ann, confined to a sanitarium for tuberculosis. Cruikshank took the pledge of alcoholic abstinence and became an advocate of the Temperance Movement. Prior to this vow, Cruikshank had a reputation for enjoying tavern life. ''I am ashamed to say that for many years I went on following the ordinary custom of drinking, till I fell into pecuniary difficulties. I had some money at a banker's; he fell into difficulties, took to drinking brandy-and-water, and ended by blowing out his brains. I lost my money, and in my distress applied to friends who aided me for a time, but they themselves fell into difficulties, and I was forced to extricate myself by the most extraordinary exertions. In this strait I thought, The best thing I can do is take to water; but still I went on for some time before I quite weaned myself from my own drinking habits. I went to take luncheon with my friend Dickens (who, I am sorry to say, is not a teetotaler); he asked me to take wine, but I told him I had taken to water, for, in my opinion, a man had better take a glass of prussic acid than fall into the other habit of taking brandy-and-water; and I am happy to say that Charles Dickens quite agreed with me, that a man had better wipe himself out at once, than extinguish himself by degrees by the soul-degrading and body-destroying enemy.'' [Blanchard Jerrold, *The Life of George Cruikshank*, Volume II, Chatto & Windus, 1882.[3]]

Cruikshank, about 1840.

1849. First wife died. ''When I left off drinking wine altogether, and became a total abstainer, I became a healthier and stronger man, more capable of meeting the heavy responsibilities that were upon me, and for the following two years I had my life renewed, and all the elasticity of my schoolboy days came back to me. Domestic afflictions then came upon me, ending in death [of wife], and my spirits and health were crushed down. In this extremity I applied to my medical adviser. He said, 'Medicine is of no use to you; you must drink wine again.' I refused, and my medical friend called in some others of his profession; he told me they had had a consultation, the result being that all of them agreed it was necessary I should drink wine to restore my sinking constitution. I replied, 'Doctor, I'll take your physic, but not your wine. Let me try everything else first, and only when there is no other chance give me wine, because I feel there is a great principle at stake in this matter.' I have said, and I believe, wine is unnecessary, even as a medicine, and I do not wish to do a single act which would tend to weaken or destroy the weight and force of that conviction. And here I stand. I have not tasted the vile and destroying enemy, and I am almost restored to health, without haved risked the violation of my principles. I call this a triumph. . . .''[3]

1850. Married second wife.

1853. Having had no formal education, Cruikshank enrolled in the Royal Academy for a brief time. Began to paint in oils.

1860. Began his oil painting, the ''Triumph of Bacchus,'' an exhaustive study. ''This painting, which has not in reality had more than twelve months' work upon the canvas, I had, nevertheless, in hand for eighteen months. The title I give

it is 'THE WORSHIP OF BACCHUS: OR, THE DRINKING CUSTOMS OF SOCIETY'; and it is intended to show how universally the intoxicating drinks are used upon every occasion in life, from the CRADLE to the GRAVE.''[3]

May, 1863. Public exhibition of works, in which the ''Triumph of Bacchus'' was a focal point, failed to draw the anticipated crowds. Cruikshank's biographer, Blanchard Jerrold, recalled the effect this had upon the aging artist. ''I remember seeing him standing in his exhibition room. It was empty. There was a wild, anxious look in his face, when he greeted me. While we talked, he glanced once or twice at the door, when he heard any sound in that direction. Were they coming at last, the tardy, laggard public for whom he had been bravely toiling so many years? Here was his last mighty labour against the wall, and all the world had been told that it was there. His trusty friend Thackeray had hailed it in the *Times*. A great committee of creditable men had combined to usher it with pomp into the world. All who loved and honoured and admired him had spoken words of encouragement. Yet it was near noon, and only a solitary visitor had wandered into the room. Thackeray might well say, 'How little do we think of the extraordinary powers of this man, and how ungrateful we are to him!' ''[3]

1875. Continued to illustrate books and to work indefatigably for the Temperance Movement. ''I believe that by nature, and from the profession that I formerly belonged to, that of a caricaturist, I have as keen a sense of the ridiculous as most men. I can see clearly what is ridiculous in others. I am so sensitive myself, that I am quite alive to ever situation,

George Cruikshank, self-portrait.

and would not willingly place myself in a ridiculous one; and, I must confess, that if to be a teetotaler was to be a milksop, if it was to be a namby-pamby fellow, or a man making a fool of himself or of others, then indeed I would not be one—certainly not; but if, on the contrary, to be a teetotaler is to be a man that values himself, and tries by every means in his power to benefit others; if to be a teetotaler is to be a man who tries to save the thoughtless from destruction; if to be a teetotaler is to be a man who does battle with false theories and bad customs, then I am one. . . . I only wish that I could say . . . that I had never taken a glass of spirits in my life; I wish that I had acted upon the principles of total abstinence only thirty years ago; for if I had, I am convinced that at this time I should have been much better, both in body and mind. . . .''[3]

February 1, 1878. Died at his home in Hampstead Road in London. Buried at St. Paul's.

FOR MORE INFORMATION SEE: Blanchard Jerrold, *The Life of George Cruikshank,* Volumes I and II, Chatto & Windus, 1882; Ruari McLean, *George Cruikshank: His Life and Work as a Book Illustrator,* Pellegrini & Cudahy, 1948; Albert M. Cohn, *George Cruikshank,* Hacker, 1970; William Bates, *George Cruikshank: The Artist, the Humorist, the Man, with Some Account of His Brother,* Schramm, 1972; Michael Katanka and Edgell Rickword, *Gillray and Cruikshank,* Shire Publishing, 1973; Robert L. Patten, *George Cruikshank: A Revaluation,* Princeton University Library, 1974; John Wardropper, *The Caricatures of George Cruikshank,* Gordon Fraser Gallery, 1977; Michael Wynn Jones, *George Cruikshank,* Macmillan, 1978; Hilary and Mary Evans, *The Life and Art of George Cruikshank,* S. G. Phillips, 1978; H. and M. Evans, *Man Who Drew the Drunkard's Daughter,* Muller, 1978; John Wardroper, *The Caricatures of George Cruikshank,* Godine, 1978.

DANA, Barbara 1940-

PERSONAL: Born December 28, 1940, in New York, N.Y.; daughter of Richard (a writer, director, teacher) and Mildred (Ferry; an actress, teacher) Dana; married Alan Arkin (an actor), June 16, 1964; children: Adam, Matthew, Anthony. *Education:* Quintano's School for Young Professionals, high school diploma.

CAREER: Author and stage and television actress. Broadway appearances include roles in "Who's Afraid of Virginia Woolf?," "Where's Daddy?," "Room Service," and "Enter Laughing"; on television has appeared in "As the World Turns," "New York Television Theatre," "N.E.T. Playhouse," "The Fugitive," "June Moon," "The Effect of Gamma Rays," "Sesame Street," "ABC Movie of the Week," and others; films include "The In-Laws," "P.J.," "Fire Sale," and "Popi."

WRITINGS: Spencer and His Friends (juvenile), Atheneum, 1966; *Rutgers and the Water-Snouts,* Harper, 1969; *Crazy Eights,* Harper, 1978. Also author of screenplay, "Chu Chu and the Philly Flash," a Melvin Simon production starring Carol Burnett and Alan Arkin, 1981.

WORK IN PROGRESS: Two young adult novels; two screenplays.

SIDELIGHTS: "I always loved writing, but when I was growing up I never thought of writing as a career. I wanted to be an actress, or a cowgirl. I decided on being an actress and began working professionally while I was still in high school. I continued writing for the fun of it, short stories

BARBARA DANA

The sun was bright, the air was cold, and the searching party was on its way. ■ (From *Rutgers and the Water-Snouts* by Barbara Dana. Illustrated by Fred Brenner.)

mostly. I wanted to write like James Thurber. When I was in my early twenties my husband saw some short stories I had written in high school and suggested I try writing for children. I did try and found that I loved it. The spark of creativity and imagination is still very much alive in children. They are wonderful people to share one's feelings and ideas with. I hope in writing for children, to give them joy and also to say to them, be true to yourselves, to that creative fire that lives inside you. Be daring, don't copy the old ways just for the sake of convenience. You have something very special to give.

"I live in Westchester with my husband and our three sons, Adam, Matthew and Tony. I enjoy most being with my family, writing, acting, singing, playing the recorder and horseback riding. I also have a horse of my own—a cowgirl at last."

DANAHER, Kevin   1913-
(Caoimhin O. Danachair)

PERSONAL: Born January 30, 1913, in Limerick, Ireland; son of William (a schoolteacher) and Maighread (O'Ryan) Danaher; married Anna Mary Ryan (a high school teacher); children: Donal Maolmhuire, Sean Laoiseach. *Education:* University College, Dublin, B.A., 1936, Higher Diploma in Education, 1937, M.A., 1945, D.Litt. 1974; additional graduate study at University of Berlin, 1937-38, University of Leipzig, 1938-39. *Office:* Department of Irish Folklore, University College, Dublin, Ireland.

CAREER: Department of Foreign Affairs, Ireland, editor of *Life and Culture* series, 1965—. University College, National University of Ireland, Dublin, university lecturer in folklore, 1971—. Has lectured in Britain, Germany, Sweden, Denmark, Belgium, Austria, Hungary, Canada, and the United States, as well as in Ireland. *Military service:* Irish Army, Artillery, 1940-45; became captain. *Member:* Military History Society of Ireland (president, 1978).

WRITINGS: In Ireland Long Ago, Mercier, 1962; (editor with J. G. Simms) *The Danish Force in Ireland, 1691-1692,* Irish Manuscripts Commission, 1963; *Gentle Places and Simple Things,* Mercier, 1964; *Irish Country People,* Mercier, 1966; *Folktales of the Irish Countryside* (Irish full edition),

...And when the child was born, God bless the mark! Wasn't it a little girl with a pig's head. ■ (From *Folktales of the Irish Countryside* by Kevin Danaher. Illustrated by Harold Berson.)

KEVIN DANAHER

Mercier, 1967, (young readers edition), David White, 1970; *The Pleasant Land of Ireland,* Mercier, 1970; *The Year in Ireland,* Mercier, 1972; *Ireland's Vernacular Architecture,* Mercier, 1975; *A Bibliography of Irish Ethnology and Folk Tradition,* Mercier, 1978. Contributor of about ninety articles to learned journals. Editor, *Irish Sword,* 1960-71.

SIDELIGHTS: Danaher speaks German and Swedish fluently, as well as English and Gaelic; he reads French, Norwegian, Danish, Dutch, Spanish, Portuguese, and Italian.

DEFOE, Daniel 1660(?)-1731

PERSONAL: Original surname, Foe, was changed about 1703; born about 1660, in St. Giles, London, England; died April 26, 1731, in Moorfields, London, England; buried in Bunhill Fields; son of James Foe (a butcher and candlemaker); married Mary Tuffley, January, 1684; children: seven. *Education:* Studied for the Presbyterian ministry at Morton's Academy in Stoke Newington, and at a Dissenting College in Newington.

CAREER: Novelist, journalist, and pamphleteer. Before becoming a political writer, Defoe engaged in various businesses, working as a hosier, a merchant-adventurer to Spain and Portugal, and a brickmaker. Joined the uprising under the Duke of Monmouth, 1685, entering London in 1688 triumphantly with William of Orange (William III), under whom Defoe held many minor offices and became a trusted confidant. From 1689-1731, he was a pamphleteer under four sovereigns, and an accountant in the Glass-Duty Office, 1695.

Several of his pamphlets caused misunderstandings, and he was accused of libel and treason, which resulted in fines, imprisonment, and pillorying in 1703, and 1712-13. Despite, this, Defoe was sent to Scotland as a secret agent for Robert Harley to aid in Union negotiations, 1703. He edited *The Review,* 1704-13, and later was assistant editor of *Mist's Journal.*

WRITINGS—Novels: *Robinson Crusoe,* W. Taylor, 1719 (originally published in three separate editions entitled, *The Life and Surprizing Adventures of Robinson Crusoe, of York, Mariner; The Further Adventures of Robinson Crusoe;* and *Serious Reflections during the Life and Surprising Adventures of Robinson Crusoe*), reissued, Norton, 1975 [other editions illustrated by Thomas Stothard, J. Stockdale, 1790; George Cruikshank, J. Major, 1831; Charles S. Keene, Burns, 1847; J. J. Grandville (pseudonym of Jean-Ignace Isidore Gérard), D. Appleton, 1853; John E. Millais, Macmillan,

...Had any one in England met such a man as I was, it must either have frightened him, or raised a great deal of laughter; and as I frequently stood still to look at myself, I could not but smile at the notion of my travelling through Yorkshire with such as equipage and in such a dress. ■ (From *Robinson Crusoe* by Daniel Defoe. Illustrated by J.D. Watson.)

1860; George H. Thomas, Cassell, 1864; John D. Watson, Routledge, 1864; Thomas Nast, Hurd & Houghton, 1868; Ernest H. Griset, Hotten, 1869; Gordon F. Browne, Blackie, 1885; Jack Butler Yeats, Dent, 1895, reprinted AMS Press, 1974; Walter S. Paget, Cassell, 1896; Louis and Frederick Rhead, R. H. Russell, 1900, reissued University Microfilms, 1966; Charles E. Brock and D. L. Monroe, with an introduction by Edward Everett Hale, D. C. Heath, 1902; J. Ayton Symington, Dent, 1905, reissued, Dutton, 1966; E. Boyd Smith, Houghton, 1909; Elenore P. Abbott, G. W. Jacobs, 1913; N. C. Wyeth, Cosmopolitan Book Corp., 1920; Edward A. Wilson, Limited Editions, 1930; Fritz Kredel, Doubleday, Doran, 1945; Robert Ball, Lippincott, 1948; adaptations for children include an edition edited by Edward L. Thorndike and illustrated by Henry C. Pitz, Appleton-Century, 1936; an edition edited by Josette Frank and illustrated by Jay Hyde Barnum, Random House, 1952; an edition illustrated by Lyle Justis, Winston, 1953; an edition adapted by Anne Terry White and illustrated by Feodor Rojankovsky, Golden Press, 1960; an edition illustrated by Federico Castellon, Macmillan, 1962; an edition edited by Frank L. Beals, Naylor, 1965; an edition edited by Angus Ross, Penguin, 1965; an edition revised and abridged by Robert Lasson, Fearon, 1968; and an edition edited by Kathleen Lines and illustrated by Edward Ardizzone, Nonesuch Press, 1968].

Memoirs of a Cavalier; or, A Military Journal of the Wars in Germany, and the Wars in England, from 1632-1648, A.

DANIEL DEFOE

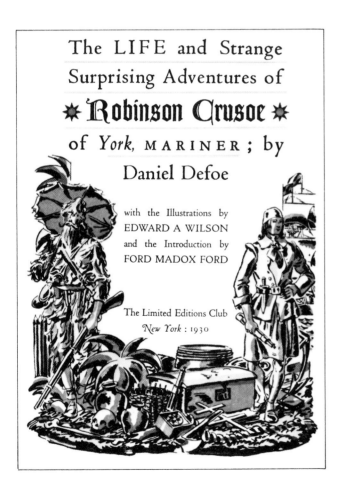

Title page by Edward A. Wilson. ■ (From *The Life and Strange Surprising Adventures of Robinson Crusoe* by Daniel Defoe.)

Bell, 1720, reprinted (with illustrations from J. B. Yeats), AMS Press, 1974; *The Life, Adventures, and Pyracies of the Famous Captain Singleton,* J. Brotherton, 1720, reprinted (with illustrations from Yeats), AMS Press, 1974; *The Fortunes and Misfortunes of the Famous Moll Flanders,* W. Chetwood & T. Edling, 1722, reprinted (with illustrations from Yeats), 1974 [other editions illustrated by Alexander King, Hogarth Press, 1931; Martin Travers, Small, Maynard, 1936; Reginald Marsh, Heritage Press, 1942; Nigel Lambourne, Folio Society, 1954; John Dugan, A. Barker, 1957; John Alan Maxwell, Washington Square Press, 1962; Charles Mozley, Zodiac Press, 1962]; *A Journal of the Plague Year,* E. Nutt, 1722, reprinted (with illustrations from J. B. Yeats), AMS Press, 1974 [other editions illustrated by Edward Wedlake Brayley, T. Tegg, 1839; Leslie Atkinson, Falcon Press, 1957; Peter Pendrey, Folio Society, 1960; Domenico Gnoli, Limited Editions, 1968]; *The History and Remarkable Life of the Truly Honourable Colonel Jacque, Commonly Call'd Colonel Jack,* J. Brotherton, 1723, reprinted (with illustrations from Yeats), AMS Press, 1974; *The Unfortunate Mistress,* T. Warner, 1924, reprinted (with illustrations from Yeats), AMS Press, 1974 [other editions include an edition with an introduction by Willa Cather, A. Knopf, 1924; and an edition illustrated by J. A. Maxwell, Grosset & Dunlap, 1932]; *The Memoirs of an English Officer,* E. Symon, 1728 (later published as *Memoirs of Captain George Carleton*), reissued, Gollancz, 1970.

ROBINSON CRUSOE, oil on canvas, 36"x 25". From Robinson Crusoe by Daniel Defoe, jacket illustration. Harper & Brothers, 1921.

(From *Robinson Crusoe* by Daniel Defoe. Jacket illustrated by Frank Schoonover.)

Poems: *A New Discovery of an Old Intreague*, [London], 1691; *The True-Born Englishman*, [London], 1700; *The Pacificator*, J. Nutt, 1700; *Reformation of Manners*, [London], 1702; *The Mock Mourners*, [London], 1702; *More Reformation: A Satyr upon Himself*, [London], 1703; *A Hymn to Victory*, J. Nutt, 1704; *The Dyet of Poland: A Satyr*, [London], 1705; *The Vision*, B. Bragg, 1706; *Caledonia: A Poem in Honour of Scotland, and the Scots Nation*, [Edinburgh], 1706; *Jure Divino: A Satyr*, [London], 1706; *A Hymn to the Pillory*, [London], 1708; *The Meditations of Daniel Defoe*, printed from the text of a handwritten notebook dated 1681, Cummington Press, 1946, reprinted, Folcroft, 1970.

Other: *An Essay upon Projects*, [London], 1697, reprinted, Scolar Press, 1969; *The Shortest-Way with Dissenters; or, Proposals for the Establishment of the Church*, [London], 1702; *The Storm; or, A Collection of the Most Remarkable Casualties and Disasters Which Happen'd in the Late Dreadful Tempest, both by Sea and Land*, G. Sawbridge, 1704; *More Short-Ways with the Dissenters*, [London], 1704; *An Essay on the Regulation of the Press*, [London], 1704, reis-

"HE STOOD LIKE A MAN TURNED TO STONE"

He stood like a man turned to stone. ■ (From *The Children's Robinson Crusoe* by Edith L. Elias. Illustrated by Stephen Reid.)

sued, B. Blackwell, 1948; *Giving Alms, No Charity*, [London], 1704, reprinted, Johnson Reprint, 1970; *The Consolidator; or, Memoirs of Sundry Transactions from the World in the Moon*, B. Bragg, 1705, reprinted, Garland Publishing, 1972; *A True Relation of the Apparition of One Mrs. Veal, the Next Day after Her Death* (short story), B. Bragg, 1706, reissued, University of California Press, 1965; *The History of the Union of Great Britain*, [Edinburgh], 1709; *Atalantis Major* (a political satire), [Edinburgh], 1711, reissued, University of Illinois Press, 1973; *A Short Narrative of the Life and Actions of His Grace John D. of Marlborough*, J. Baker, 1711, reprinted, University of California Press, 1974; *An Appeal to Honour and Justice tho' It Be of His Worst Enemies* (autobiography), J. Baker, 1715.

The Family Instructor, E. Matthews, 1715-18, reprinted, Bell & Howell, 1967; *A Vindication of the Press; or, An Essay on the Usefulness of Writing, of Criticism, and the Qualifications of Authors*, [London], 1718, reprinted, Garland Publishing, 1972; *The Dumb Philosopher; or, Great Britain's Wonder*, T. Bickerton, 1719; *The History of the Life and Adventures of Mr. Duncan Campbell*, reprinted (with illustrations from J. B. Yeats), AMS Press, 1974; *The King of*

THE PRINT OF A MAN'S NAKED FOOT ON THE SHORE

From *The Life and Strange Surprising Adventures of Robinson Crusoe* by Daniel Defoe. Illustrated by E. Boyd Smith.

...Our voyage was a full two hundred miles, in a poor, sorry sloop, with all our treasure,... ■ (From *The Fortunes and Misfortunes of the Famous Moll Flanders* by Daniel Defoe. Illustrated by Reginald Marsh.)

Pirates: Being an Account of the Famous Enterprises of Captain Avery, the Mock King of Madagascar, A. Bettesworth, 1720, reprinted (with illustrations from Yeats), AMS Press, 1974; *Due Preparations for the Plague, as Well as for Soul as Body,* E. Matthews, 1722, reprinted (with illustrations from Yeats), AMS Press, 1974; *A New Voyage Round the World, by a Course Never Sailed Before,* A. Bettesworth & W. Mears, 1724, reprinted (with illustrations from Yeats), AMS Press, 1974; *A Narrative of All the Robberies, Escapes, etc., of John Sheppard,* J. Applebee, 1724.

A Tour through the Whole Island of Great Britain, G. Strahan, 1724-27, reprinted, Garland Publishing, 1975; *A True and Genuine Account of the Life and Actions of the Late Jonathan Wild,* J. Applebee, 1725; *An Account of the Conduct and Proceedings of the Late John Gow, alias Smith,* J. Applebee, 1725, reprinted, B. Franklin, 1970; *The Complete English Tradesman,* C. Rivington, 1725-27, reprinted, B. Franklin, 1970; *The Political History of the Devil, as Well Ancient as Modern,* T. Warner, 1726, reprinted, Rowman & Littlefield, 1972; *The Four Voyages of Captain George Roberts,* A. Bettesworth, 1726, reprinted, Garland Publishing, 1972; *An Essay on the History and Reality of Apparitions,* A. Millar, 1727, reprinted, AMS Press, 1973; *A Treatise concerning the Use and Abuse of the Marriage Bed,* T. Warner, 1727, reissued as *Conjugal Lewdness; or, Matrimonial Whoredom,* Scolar Press, 1970; *A Plan of English Commerce,* C. Rivington, 1728, reprinted, Kelley, 1967; *Street-Robberies Consider'd: The Reason of Their Being so Frequent, with Probable Means to Prevent 'Em,* J. Roberts, 1728, reissued, Carolingian Press, 1973; *The Compleat English Gentleman,* D. Nutt, 1890, reprinted, Folcroft, 1972.

Selections: *Defoe,* edited by John Masefield, G. Bell, 1909; *The Best of Defoe's Review,* edited by William L. Payne, Columbia University Press, 1951, reprinted, Books for Libraries, 1970; *Selections from the Prose of Daniel Defoe,* edited by Roger Manvell, Falcon Press, 1953; *Selections from Defoe,* edited by Manvell, Blackie, 1966; *Selected Poetry*

and Prose of Daniel Defoe, edited by Michael F. Shugrue, Holt, 1968; *Robinson Crusoe, and Other Writings,* edited by James Sutherland, Houghton, 1968; *A Defoe Anthology: Writings on Politics, Economics, and History,* edited by Laura Ann Goldsmith Curtis, Rugers University Press, 1974.

Collections: *The Novels and Miscellaneous Works of Daniel Defoe,* 20 volumes, D. A. Talboys, 1840-41, reprinted, AMS Press, 1973; *The Works of Daniel Defoe* (includes a memoir of his life and writings by William Hazlitt), J. Clements, 1840-43; *The Works of Daniel Defoe,* edited by John S. Keltie, W. P. Nimmo, 1872; *The Earlier Life and the Chief Earlier Works of Daniel Defoe,* edited by Henry Morley, Routledge, 1889, reissued, B. Franklin, 1970; *The Works of Daniel Defoe,* 16 volumes, G. D. Sproul, 1903-04; *The Shakespeare Head Edition of the Novels and Selected Writings of Daniel Defoe,* 14 volumes, B. Blackwell, 1927-28, reprinted, Rowman & Littlefield, 1974; *Defoe's Review* (facsimile edition of *The Review,* 1704-1713), Columbia University Press, 1938, reprinted, AMS Press, 1965; *Letters of Daniel Defoe,* edited by George Harris Healey, Oxford University Press, 1955.

Also author of numerous essays of social and political commentary.

ADAPTATIONS—Movies and filmstrips: ''Robinson Crusoe'' (motion pictures), Henry W. Savage, Inc., 1916, Universal Film, 1917, Gaumont Co., 1927, Guaranteed Pictures, 1936; ''Robinson Crusoe'' (filmstrips), Eye Gate House, 1946, Young America Films (with a teaching guide), 1957,

(From the puppet production of "Robinson Crusoe." Marionettes by Tony Sarg.)

...I observed a place where there had been a fire made, and a circle dug in the earth, like a
cockpit, where it is supposed the savage wretches had sat down to their inhuman feastings....
■ (From *Robinson Crusoe* by Daniel Defoe. Illustrated by N.C. Wyeth.)

Carmen Educational Associates, 1966, Jam Handy School Service (with captions), 1968, Brunswick Productions, 1971; "Adventures of Robinson Crusoe" (motion pictures), Universal Film (series of 18), 1922, United Artists, 1954; "Mr. Robinson Crusoe" (motion picture), starring Douglas Fairbanks, United Artists, 1932; "Robinson Crusoe on Mars" (motion picture), starring Paul Mantee and Adam West, Paramount Pictures, 1964; "The Amorous Adventures of Moll Flanders" (motion picture), starring Kim Novak and Angela Lansbury, 1965; "Favorite Children's Books: Robinson Crusoe" (filmstrip; with a phonodisc and user's guide), Coronet Instructional Films, 1969; "Highlights from Robinson Crusoe" (filmstrip; with a phonodisc or phonotape), Encyclopaedia Britannica Educational Corp., 1973.

Plays: R.B.B. Sheridan, *Robinson Crusoe; or, Harlequin Friday,* T. Becket, 1781; Issac Pocock, *Robinson Crusoe; or, The Bold Buccaniers* (two-act drama), Hodgson, 1822; F. Fortescue, *Robinson Crusoe; or, The Island of Juan Fernandez* (operatic drama), [Boston], 1822; J. F. Macardle and F. W. Green, *Robinson Crusoe,* Daily Post & Journal Offices, 1878; Francis C. Burnand, *The Real Adventures of Robinson*

Crusoe (burlesque), Bradbury, Agnew, 1893; Margaret Carter, *Robinson Crusoe* (two-act pantomime), Samuel French, 1949.

SIDELIGHTS: **September 30, 1660**(?). Born in London, son of James Foe. "The care, tenderness, love, and benignity of a true parent, cannot be returned; tis not of a kind that can ascend. It may descend, and be paid to posterity." [John R. Moore, *Daniel Defoe, Citizen of the Modern World,* University of Chicago Press, 1958.[1]]

1662. Family left the Church of England to become Presbyterians.

1666. Witnessed the Great Fire of London. "I remember very well what I saw with a sad heart, though I was but young; I mean the Fire of London. That all endeavors having been fruitlessly used to abate the fire, the people gave it over, and despairing citizens looked on and saw the devastation of their dwellings, with a kind of stupidity caused by amazement. If any people, still forward for the public good, made any attempts, the water they cast upon it made it rage with

(From the movie "Lt. Robin Crusoe, USN," starring Dick Van Dyke. Copyright © 1966 by Walt Disney Productions.)

the more fury and boil like a pot; till scorched with the flames from every side, and tired with the fruitless labor, they gave over, as others had done before them . . . and the whole City was laid in ashes.''[1]

1671-1679. Education prepared him to enter the Presbyterian ministry, a vocational idea he later abandoned. ''. . . I myself, then but a boy, worked like a horse, till I wrote out the whole Pentateuch, and then was so tired I was willing to run the risk of the rest.'' [James Sutherland, *Defoe,* Lippincott, 1938.[2]]

''. . . Those gentlemen who reproach my learning to applaud their own, shall have it proved that I have more learning . . . because I have more manners. . . . I easily acknowledge myself blockhead enough to have lost the fluency of expression in the Latin, and so far trade has been a prejudice to me; and yet I think I owe this justice to my ancient father . . . in whose behalf I freely testify, that if I am a blockhead, it was nobody's fault but my own, he having spared nothing in my education. . . .'' [Walter Wilson, *The Life and Times of Daniel Defoe,* Volume I, Hurst, Chance & Co., 1830.[3]]

1683. Established as a merchant, probably in the hosiery trade. ''A Wit turned Tradesman! What an incongruous part of Nature is there brought together, consisting of direct contraries! . . .''[2]

1684. Married Mary Tuffley. ''I have often thought, 'tis the foolishest thing in the world for a man and his wife to quarrel, especially about trifles—when they know they must come together at night.

''How little is regarded of that one essential and absolutely necessary part of the composition, called love, without which the matrimonial estate is, I think, hardly lawful, I am sure it is not rational, and, I think, can never be happy.''[1]

1685. Briefly involved in Monmouth's Rebellion.

1685-1692. Worked as merchant dealing in hosiery, wine, and tobacco; travelled extensively in England and Europe. ''. . . Nothing is more common than for the tradesman, when he once finds himself grown rich, to have his head full of great designs, and new undertakings. He finds his cash flow

(From the movie "The Amorous Adventures of Moll Flanders," starring Kim Novak, Lilli Palmer and Angela Lansbury. Produced by Paramount Pictures, 1965.)

in upon him, and perhaps he is fuller of money than his trade calls for; and as he scarce knows how to employ more stock in it than he does, his ears are the sooner open to any project or proposal that offers itself; and I must add, that this is the most critical time with him in all his life; if ever he is in danger of ruin, 'tis just then. . . . If any man should be so ill-natured as to tell me that I speak too feelingly upon this part of the subject, though it may not be the kindest thing he could have said to a poor author, yet it may not be the worse for the argument. An old sailor that has split upon a sunk rock, and has lost his ship, is not the worst man to make a pilot of for that coast; on the contrary, he is in particular able to guide those that come after him to shun the dangers of that unhappy place.''[2]

1688. Published his first political tract. Joined the forces of William of Orange advancing on London.

1692. Declared bankruptcy. "If I were to run through the infinite mazes of a bankrupt, before he came to the crisis; what shifts, what turnings, and windings in trade, to support his dying credit; what buying of one, to raise money to pay another; what discounting of bills, pledgings and pawnings; what selling to loss for present supply; what strange and unaccountable methods, to buoy up sinking credit!

"What agonies of mind, does the distressed tradesman go through, I appeal to those gentlemen, that have gone through the labyrinths, and entangled in the toil of failing credit, have struggled themselves out of breath, and at last like a deer, hunted down, are driven to stand at bay with the world!''[1]

"If I am asked why honest tradesmen are ruined, and undesigning men come to destruction, the answer is short: knaves run away with their money; knaves break first, and pull honest men down with them.''[3]

1697. Following financial misfortunes, turned to writing with *An Essay Upon Projects.* "The scholar, got into misfortune, is good for just nothing but to scribble for bread. The English tradesman is a kind of Phoenix, who often rises out of his own ashes, and makes the ruin of his fortunes to be a firm foundation to build his recovery.''[1]

1697-1701. Served as agent for King William III in England and Scotland. ". . . If I should say I had the honour to know some things from his majesty, and to transact some things for his majesty, that he would not have trusted his lordship with, perhaps there may be more truth than modesty in it; and if I should say, also, these honours done me, helped to make me that mean thing some people since think fit to represent me, perhaps it should be very true also." [Walter Wilson, *The Life and Times of Daniel Defoe,* Volume II, Hurst, Chance & Co., 1830.[4]]

1701. Wrote "The True-Born Englishman," the most widely sold poem in English literature up to that time. It was a defense of William and his Dutch friends. "During this time there came out a vile abhorred pamphlet, in very ill verse, written by one Mr. Tutchin, and called 'The Foreigners,' in which the author . . . fell personally upon the king himself, and then upon the Dutch nation; and after having reproached his majesty with crimes that his worst enemy could not think of without horror, he sums up all in the odious name of FOREIGNER.

"This filled me with a kind of rage against the book, and gave birth to a trifle, which I could never hope should have met with so general an acceptation as it did; I mean 'The True-Born Englishman.' How this poem was the occasion of my being known to his majesty; how I was afterwards received by him; how employed; and how, above my capacity of deserving, rewarded, is no part of the present case, and is only mentioned here, as I take all occasions to do, for the expressing the honor I ever preserved for the immortal and glorious memory of that greatest and best of princes, and whom it was my honor and advantage to call master, as well as sovereign; whose goodness to me I never forgot, neither can forget; and whose memory I never patiently heard abused, nor ever can do so; and who, had he lived, would never have suffered me to be treated as I have been in the world.''[1]

1703. Arrested for his satire, *The Shortest Way,* and condemned to stand in the pillory for two days. Imprisonment led to the failure of his brick and tile factory. "My Lord, a body unfit to bear the hardships of prison and a mind impatient of confinement have been the only reasons of withdrawing myself. And, my Lord, the cries of a numerous ruined family, the prospect of a long banishment from my native country, and the hopes of her Majesty's mercy move me to throw myself at her Majesty's feet and to intreat your Lordship's intercession.

"Gaol, pillories and such like, with which I have been so much threatened, have convinced me I want passive courage, and I shall never for the future think myself injured if I am called a coward.''[2]

"All my prospects were built on a manufacture I had erected in Essex, all the late King's bounty to me was expended there. I employed a hundred poor families at work, and it began to pay me very well. I generally made six hundred pounds profit per annum. I began to live, took a good house, bought me a coach and horses a second time, I paid large debts gradually, small ones wholly, and many a creditor after composition whom I found poor and decayed, I sent for and paid the remainder to, though actually discharged.

"But I was ruined *the shortest way.*''[1]

1703-1714. Acted as secret agent, travelling widely in England and Scotland. "I have, within these twenty years past, traveled, I think I may say, to every nook and corner of that part of the island called England, either upon public affairs, when I had the honor to serve his late Majesty King William of Glorious (though forgotten) Memory—or upon my private affairs; I have been in every county, one excepted, and in every considerable town in every county, with very few exceptions. I have not, I hope, been an idle spectator or a careless unobserving passenger in any place; and I believe I can give some account of my travels if need were.''[1]

"I have my spies and my pensioners in every place, and I confess 'tis the easiest thing in the world to hire people here to betray their friends. I have spies in the Commission, in the Parliament, and in the Assembly, and under pretence of writing my history I have everything told me.''[2]

1704. Edited *The Review.* "I am told a very strange piece of news of the *Review* lately, namely, that it does not please every body. I never set up for a degree of understanding above other people, but, without vanity, I hope I may say, I never merited to be thought so much a coxcomb as to expect it would. If I write instructive truth, I am sure to please wise men; and I have been always unconcerned for the opinion of the rest.

(From the movie "The Adventures of Robinson Crusoe," starring Dan O'Herlihy. Released by United Artists Corp., 1953.)

"I have studied to inform and to direct the world, and what have I had for my labour? Profit, the press would not allow; and therein I am not deceived, for I expected none. But good manners and good language, I thought I might expect, because I gave no other; and it is but just to treat mankind as they would be treated. But neither has this been paid me, in debt to custom and civility. How often have my ears, my hands, and my head been to be pulled off? Impotent bullies; that, attacked by truth and their vices stormed, fill the air with rhodomontades and indecencies, but never shewed their face to the resentment truth had a just cause to entertain for them! I have passed through clouds of clamour, cavil, raillery and objection: and have this satisfaction, that truth being the design, *finis coronat*, I am never forward to value my own performances; but I cannot but own myself infinitely pleased, and more than satisfied, that wise men read this paper with pleasure, own the just observations in it, and voted it useful."[4]

1713-1714. Arrested three times for debt and alleged treasonable political pamphlets.

"No man has tasted differing fortunes more,
And thirteen times I have been rich and poor."

[Walter Wilson, *The Life and Times of Daniel Defoe,* Volume III, Hurst, Chance & Co., 1830.[5]]

1715. Wrote *An Appeal to Honour and Justice,* an autobiographical justification for his conduct under Tory Ministries; continued as a political writer, now for the Whigs.

1719. Completed the first part of *Robinson Crusoe,* his earliest novel. "The adventures of Robinson Crusoe are one whole scene of real life of eight and twenty years, spent in the most wandering, desolate and afflicting circumstances that ever a man went through, and in which I have lived so long a life of wonders, in continual storms; fought with the worst kind of savages and man-eaters, by unaccountable surprising incidents; fed by miracles greater than that of ravens; suffered all manner of violences and oppressions, injurious reproaches, contempt of men, attacks of devils, corrections from heaven, and oppositions on earth; have had innumerable ups and downs in matters of fortune; been in worse slavery than Turkish; escaped by an exquisite management, as that in the story of Xury and the boat at Sallee; been taken up at sea in distress; raised again and depressed again, and that oftener perhaps in one man's life than ever

The judges sat grave and mute, gave me an easy hearing, and time to say all that I would, but, saying neither yes nor no to it, pronounced the sentence of death upon me,... ■ (From *Moll Flanders* by Daniel Defoe. Illustrated by Reginald Marsh.)

was known before; shipwrecked often, though more by land than by sea; in a word, there's not a circumstance in the imaginary story, but has its just allusion to a real story, and chimes part for part, and step for step, with the inimitable life of Robinson Crusoe.''[5]

1721. His son, Benjamin, who had been employed to write against his father and the government, was arrested.

April 24, 1731. Died ''of a lethargy'' in Moorfields. ''The body is not made for wonders, and when I hint that denying yourself needful and regular hours of rest will disorder the best constitution in the world, I speak by my own immediate experience, who having despised sleep, hours, and rules, have broken in upon a perfectly established health, which no distresses, disasters, jails, or melancholy could ever hurt before.''[1]

FOR MORE INFORMATION SEE: George Chalmers, *Life of Daniel Defoe,* J. Stockdale, 1790, reprinted, Garland Pub-

lishing, 1970; William Chadwick, *Life and Times of Daniel Defoe,* J. R. Smith, 1859, reprinted, B. Franklin, 1969; William Lee, editor, *Daniel Defoe: His Life and Recently Discovered Writing Extending from 1716-1729,* Hotten, 1869, reprinted, B. Franklin, 1969; William Minto, *Daniel Defoe,* Harper, 1887, reprinted, R. West, 1973; Henry Morley, editor, *Earlier Life and the Chief Earlier Works of Daniel Defoe,* Routledge, 1889, reprinted, B. Franklin, 1970; Wilfred Whitten, *Daniel Defoe,* Small, Maynard, 1900, reprinted, Folcroft, 1973; Albinia L. Wherry, *Daniel Defoe,* G. Bell, 1905, reprinted, Folcroft, 1973; William P. Trent, *Daniel Defoe: How to Know Him,* Bobbs-Merrill, 1916, reprinted, Folcroft, 1973; Watson Nicholson, *Historical Sources of Defoe's Journal of the Plague Year,* Stratford, 1919, reprinted, R. West, 1973.

Arthur W. Secord, *Studies in the Narrative Method of Defoe,* University of Illinois Press, 1924, reprinted, Russell, 1963; Paul Dottin, *Life and Strange and Surprising Adventures of Daniel Defoe,* Macauley, 1929, reprinted, Folcroft, 1973; John R. Moore, *Defoe in the Pillory, and Other Studies,*

Indiana University Press, 1939, reprinted, Octagon Books, 1973; Isidore Abramowitz, editor, *Great Prisoners: The First Anthology of Literature Written in Prison*, Dutton, 1946; Bruce W. McCullough, *Representative English Novelists: Defoe to Conrad*, Harper, 1946; William L. Payne, *Mr. Review: Daniel Defoe as Author of The Review*, Kings Crown Press, 1947; James R. Sutherland, *Defoe*, Methuen, 1950, reprinted, Barnes & Noble, 1971; William Freeman, *Incredible Defoe*, Jenkins, 1950, reprinted, R. West, 1973; Francis Watson, *Daniel Defoe*, Longmans, Green, 1952, reprinted, Kennikat, 1969; L. Girdler, "Defoe's Education at Newington Green Academy," *Studies in Philology*, October, 1953; Brian Fitzgerald, *Daniel Defoe: A Study in Conflict*, Secker & Warburg, 1954, reprinted, R. West, 1973.

George H. Healey, editor, *Letters of Daniel Defoe*, Oxford University Press, 1955; Ian Watt, *The Rise of the Novel: Studies in Defoe, Richardson, and Fielding*, University of California Press, 1957; J. R. Moore, *Daniel Defoe: Citizen of the Modern World*, University of Chicago Press, 1958; H. Swados, "Robinson Crusoe: The Man Alone," *Antioch Review*, Spring, 1958; Adam J. Shirren, *Daniel Defoe in Stoke Newington*, Stoke Newington Public Library, 1960; J. R. Moore, *Checklist of the Writings of Daniel Defoe*, Indiana University Press, 1960, reprinted, Shoe String Press, 1971; Maximillian E. Novak, *Defoe and the Nature of Man*, Oxford University Press, 1963; James Joyce, *Daniel Defoe*, State University of New York at Buffalo Press, 1964; James T. Boulton, editor, *Daniel Defoe*, Schocken Books, 1965; George A. Starr, *Defoe and Spiritual Autobiography*, Princeton University Press, 1965, reprinted, Gordian Press, 1971.

J. Paul Hunter, *The Reluctant Pilgrim: Defoe's Emblematic Method and Quest for Form in Robinson Crusoe*, Johns Hopkins University Press, 1966; James Poling, *Men Who Saved Robinson Crusoe: The Strange Surprizing Adventures of the Original Robinson Crusoe and His Most Remarkable Rescuer*, Norton, 1967; Rodney M. Baine, *Daniel Defoe and the Supernatural*, University of Georgia Press, 1968; Michael Shinagel, *Daniel Defoe and Middle-Class Gentility*, Harvard University Press, 1968; J. R. Sutherland, *Daniel Defoe: A Critical Study*, Houghton, 1971; G. A. Starr, *Defoe and Casuistry*, Princeton University Press, 1971; Pat Rogers, editor, *Defoe: The Critical Heritage*, Routledge & Kegan Paul, 1972; John J. Richetti, *Defoe's Narratives: Situations and Structures*, Oxford University Press, 1975; Everett Zimmerman, *Defoe and the Novel*, University of California Press, 1975; E. Anthony James, *Daniel Defoe's Many Voices: A Rhetorical Study of Prose Style and Literary Method*, Humanities, 1976; P. Earle, *The World of Defoe*, Atheneum, 1977.

For children: Elizabeth Rider Montgomery, *Story behind Great Books*, McBride, 1946; John Cournos and H.S.N.K. Cournos, *Famous British Novelists*, Dodd, 1952; Walter E. Allen, *Six Great Novelists*, Hamilton, 1955; William Keal, *Great Spy Stories*, Purnell, 1968; Dorothy J. Stirland, *First Book of Great Writers*, Cassell, 1959.

I know well that only the rarest kind of best in anything can be good enough for the young.

                —Walter de la Mare

LESTER DEL REY

DEL REY, Lester 1915-
(Philip St. John, Erik Van Lhin, Kenneth Wright)

PERSONAL: Full name is Ramon Felipe San Juan Mario Silvo Enrico Alvarez-del Rey; born June 2, 1915, in Clydesdale, Minnesota; son of a carpenter. *Education:* Received a certificate of completion of high school, 1931, but did not formally graduate; attended George Washington University, 1931-33. *Home:* Red Bank, N.J.

CAREER: Author. *Awards, honors:* Boy's Club of America Science Fiction Award, 1953, for *Marooned on Mars;* a short story, *Helen O'Loy*, was selected by the Science Fiction Writers of America for their Hall of Fame volume of the best stories ever published in the field.

WRITINGS—Science fiction: "...And Some Were Human," Prime Press, 1949; *Marooned on Mars*, J. C. Winston, 1952, reissued, Holt, 1962; (under pseudonym Philip St. John) *Rocket Jockey*, J. C. Winston, 1952; *Attack from Atlantis*, J. C. Winston, 1953; (under pseudonym Erik Van Lhin) *Battle on Mercury*, J. C. Winston, 1953; (under pseudonym Kenneth Wright) *The Mysterious Planet*, J. C. Winston, 1953; *Step to the Stars*, J. C. Winston, 1954, reissued, Holt, 1965; (under pseudonym Philip St. John) *Rockets to Nowhere*, J. C. Winston, 1954; (under pseudonym Philip St. John) *Rocket Pilot*, Hutchinson, 1955; *Mission to the Moon*, J. C. Winston, 1956; *Nerves*, Ballantine, 1956, reissued, 1976; (under pseudonym Erik Van Lhin) *Police Your Planet*, Avalon Books, 1956, reissued, Ballantine, 1975; *The Cave of Spears* (illustrated by Frank Nicholas), Knopf, 1957; *Robots and Changelings: Eleven Science Fiction Stories*, Ballantine, 1957; *Day of the Giants*, Avalon Books, 1959, reissued, Airmont, 1964.

Still, it appears that a suit could be designed which would not require that most of it be inflated at all.
■ (From *Rockets Through Space* by Lester del Rey. Illustrated by James Heugh.)

Moon of Mutiny, Holt, 1961, reissued, New American Library, 1969; *Outpost of Jupiter,* Holt, 1963; *Two Complete Novels: The Sky Is Falling* [and] *Badge of Infamy,* Galaxy Publishing, 1963; *The Runaway Robot,* Westminster, 1964; *Mortals and Monsters: Twelve Science Fiction Stories,* Ballantine, 1965; *The Scheme of Things,* Belmont Books, 1966; *Seige Perilous,* Lancer Books, 1966, reissued as *The Man without a Planet,* 1969; *The Infinite Worlds of Maybe,* Holt, 1966; *Tunnel Through Time,* Westminster, 1966, reissued, Scholastic Book Services, 1970; *Rocket from Infinity,* Holt, 1966; *Prisoners of Space,* Westminster, 1968; *Pstalemate* (ALA Best Young Adult Book), Putnam, 1971; *Gods and Golems: Five Short Novels of Science Fiction,* Ballantine, 1973.

Other: *It's Your Atomic Age,* Abelard Press, 1951; *A Pirate Flag for Monterey: The Story of the Sack of Monterey* (illustrated by Donald E. Cooke), J. C. Winston, 1952; *Rockets through Space: The Story of Man's Preparations to Explore the Universe* (illustrated by James Heugh), J. C. Winston 1957, revised edition, 1960; *Space Flight: The Coming Exploration of the Universe* (illustrated by John Polgreen), Golden Press, 1959; *The Mysterious Earth,* Chilton, 1960; *Rocks and What They Tell Us* (illustrated by Pru Herric), Whitman, 1961; *The Mysterious Sea,* Chilton, 1961; *The Eleventh Commandment: A Novel of a Church and Its World,* Regency Books, 1962, reissued, Ballantine, 1976; *The Mysterious Sky,* Chilton, 1964; *Early Del Rey,* Doubleday, 1975.

Editor: *The Year after Tomorrow: An Anthology of Science Fiction Stories,* J. C. Winston, 1954; *Best Science Fiction Stories of the Year,* Dutton, 1972; *Best Science Fiction Stories of the Year: Second Annual Collection,* Dutton, 1973; *Best Science Fiction Stories of the Year: Third Annual Collection,* Dutton, 1974; *Best Science Fiction Stories of the Year: Fourth Annual Collection,* Dutton, 1975; *Fantastic Science Fiction Art, 1926-1954,* Ballantine, 1975; *Best Science Fiction Stories of the Year: Fifth Annual Collection,* Dutton, 1976.

General editor, ''Library of Science Fiction'' series, Garland Publishing.

SIDELIGHTS: Del Rey was born in Clydesdale, Minnesota. His mother died while he was an infant and he was raised by his father and older sister. After high school del Rey moved to Washington, D. C. where he held odd jobs while attending Georgetown University for two years.

At an early age del Rey began writing and selling verses to magazines, but soon relinquished poetry for science fiction stories. A friendly dare resulted in his first published short story, ''The Faithful.'' This first success launched his career as a writer.

As an editor and writer of science fiction, del Rey has pursued an interest in this field throughout his career. ''I have chosen to write of such victories and problems of life and intelligence, whether I placed those attributes in a human being or in a form drawn from future possibility or mythology. And in place of the conflict between man and invading races, I have been interested in the difficult problem of cooperation between different forms of life. There has always been trouble enough in the mere business of living and living together, and I can feel no need for artificially introduced villainies. . . .

''I wrote the stories because I enjoyed writing them, and the fact that I could receive payment for doing what I would have done in any event only added to my pleasure. I never had any other reasons behind my creation of them, and I cannot see why any other reason is necessary. . . .'' [Lester del Rey, introduction to ''. . .And Some Were Human,'' Prime Press, 1949.[1]]

FOR MORE INFORMATION SEE: Science Digest, October, 1951; Doris de Montreville and Donna Hill, editors, *Third Book of Junior Authors,* H. W. Wilson, 1972, *Top of the News,* April, 1973.

Go forth, my little book! pursue thy way!
Go forth, and please the gentle and the good.
               —William Wordsworth

Eat no green apples or you'll droop,
Be careful not to get the croup,
Avoid the chicken-pox and such,
And don't fall out of windows much.
               —Edward Anthony

(From *The Organized Week* by Tom Eaton. Illustrated by the author.)

EATON, Tom 1940-

PERSONAL: Born March 2, 1940, in Wichita, Kan.; son of Newton A. (an engineer) and Betty (Cooper) Eaton; married Shara Pinkley, June 24, 1967. *Education:* University of Kansas, B.F.A., 1962. *Home and office:* 911 W. 100th St., Kansas City, Mo. 64114.

CAREER: Hallmark Cards, Inc., Kansas City, Mo., artist and writer in contemporary cards department, 1962-66; Scholastic Magazines, Inc., New York, N.Y., art editor and cartoonist, 1966-68; free-lance artist, writer, and cartoonist, 1968—. *Military service:* U.S. Army, Medical Field Service School, 1963-65.

WRITINGS—Self-illustrated; all published by Scholastic Book Services, except where noted: *Chicken-Fried Fudge and Other Cartoon Delights,* 1971; *Flap,* Delacorte, 1972; *Captain Ecology, Pollution Fighter,* 1974; *Otis G. Firefly's Phantasmagoric Almanac,* 1974; *Popnut,* 1976; *Tom Eaton's Book of Marvels,* 1976; *The Organized Week,* 1976; *Holiday Greeting Cards,* 1977; *Rufus Crustbuster and the Earth Patrol,* Saturday Evening Post Co., 1978; *Super Valentines to Cut and Color,* 1980.

Illustrator—All published by Scholastic Book Services, except where noted: *Laugh Your Head Off!,* 1967; Peggy Hudson, *Words to the Wise,* 1967; Irwin Silber, editor, *Folksong Festival,* 1967; Richard L. Penney, *The Penguins Are Coming,* Harper, 1969; William J. Cromie, *Steven and the Green Turtle,* Harper, 1970; W. Harmon Wilson and Roman F. Wormke, *Life on Paradise Island,* Scott, Foresman, 1970; Z. S. da Silva, *Nuestro Mundo,* Macmillan, 1970; Richard R. Ricciutti, *An Animal for Alan,* Harper, 1971; Robyn Supraner, *A Sea Parade,* Nutmeg, 1971; Robyn Supraner, *Surprises!,* Nutmeg, 1971; *The Big Time Book,* Mulberry, 1971; Donna Pape, *Leo the Lion Looks for Books,* Garrard, 1972; Lavinia Dobler, *It's Your World: Don't Pollute It!,* 1972;

Richart T. Scott, *Pen the Red Hen,* Reader's Digest, 1972; Gerald Mosler, *Puzzle Fun,* 1973; Donna Pape, *Count on, Leo Lion,* Garrard, 1973; Donna Pape, *The Sleep-Leaping Kangaroo,* Garrard, 1973; B. and L. Delaney, *The Daily Laugh,* 1973; John McInnes, *Have You Ever Seen a Monster?,* Garrard, 1974; John McInnes, *Leo Lion Paints It Red,* Garrard, 1974; Jim Razzi, *Mad Mad Puzzle Parade,* 1974.

Donna Pape and Jeanette Grote, *Pack of Puzzles,* 1975; Jim Razzi, *Pirate Puzzles,* 1975; Leonore Klein, *Mazes & Mysteries,* 1975; Emily Hearn, *T.V. Kangaroo,* Garrard, 1975; The Mossessons, *The Perfect Put-Down,* 1975; B. and L. Delaney, *The Laugh Journal,* 1975; Donna Pape, *Puzzle Panic,* 1976; M. Gerrard and John McInnes, *Hickory Hollow ABC,* T. Nelson (Canada), 1977; Howard Goldsmith, *What Makes a Grumble Smile?,* Garrard, 1977; Nancy L. Robison, *Where Did My Little Fox Go?,* Garrard, 1977; B. and L. Delaney, *The Beastly Gazette,* 1977; Dick Hyman, *Crazy Laws,* 1978; J. Robinson, *Language I,* 1978; J. Robinson, *Language II,* 1978; L. Eisenberg and K. Hall, *Chicken Jokes and Puzzles,* 1978; Donna Pape, *Where Is My Little Joey?,* Garrard, 1978; J. M. Blanchard, *More See-Saw Crossword Puzzles,* 1978; K. Markoe and L. Phillips, *Super Puzzlemix,* 1979.

Illustrator of workbooks—All published by Scholastic Book Services, except where noted: Lawrence Charry, *Across and Down,* 1967; Charry and Herber, *Word Puzzles and Mysteries,* 1967; Beryl Goldsweig, *Countdown,* 1969; Scholastic editors, *SCOPE Visuals 4,* 1969; Beryl Goldweig, *Sprint,* 1970; *Panorama,* Houghton, 1971, revised edition, 1974; Scholastic editors, *SCOPE Visuals II,* 1972. Contributor of cartoons to *Playboy, Look, Saturday Evening Post,* and *Teen.*

WORK IN PROGRESS: Three novels for children; two adult novels.

TOM EATON

SIDELIGHTS: "As a child my interests jelled early—science, the future, fantasy and cartoons—and I wrote and drew for the amusement of myself and my classmates. As I grew older it dawned on me that I was expected to buy my own groceries and gasoline, and I began exchanging my talent for money, that is, working. Luckily people were willing to pay me to do the things I liked, and basically my life has changed little since about age twelve, except that I now eat less candy and have more homework.

"I have loved cartoons and comic strips all my life, and spent much of my early childhood (as opposed to my later childhood, i.e., now) sprawled on the floor reading the funnies which overflowed the local newspaper like a cornucopia. Little did I realize that that flowering orchard would wither to the dry weedpatch it is today. However, being a thrifty child, I began saving much of that treasure, and today have a basementful of old Sunday funnies that would drive many a wife to despair. Fortunately my own wife, besides being beautiful and a talented artist herself, is tolerant of my various fits of foolishness and understands when I disappear down there for days at a time.

"My own cartoon books, written for teenagers, have met with some success, five of them having sold a total of over a million copies, and the sixth having sold a total of twelve copies. Actually I tend to write and draw for myself, and am always pleasantly surprised when someone else likes it, too. Humor is such an individual product that it is impossible to describe how it originates, and is best enjoyed, not analyzed.

"As a free-lance artist and writer, I work in a studio in my home, and rely on self-discipline to keep me at the drawing board until a job is done. However, one advantage to this is that my schedule can be flexible, and I can, therefore, enjoy a day off now and then, especially when the Internal Revenue Service man is due to come by.

"Contrary to vicious rumor, my dogs do not help me with either the writing or the art on my books. They have their own contacts and work for different publishers entirely."

HOBBIES AND OTHER INTERESTS: Science fiction, science, travel (Europe and Scandinavia).

EDELMAN, Lily (Judith) 1915-

PERSONAL: Born September 2, 1915, in San Francisco, Calif.; daughter of Morris and Rachel (Margolis) Podvidz; married Nathan Edelman, May 30, 1936; children: Jean Louise (deceased). *Education:* Hunter College (now Hunter College of the City University of New York), B.A., 1936; Columbia University, M.A., 1938, diploma in adult education from Teachers College, 1954. *Religion:* Jewish. *Home:* 560 Riverside Dr., New York, N.Y. 10027. *Office:* 823 United Nations Plaza, New York, N.Y. 10017.

LILY EDELMAN

Grandma handed each child a cluster of grapes and a little box of raisins as special Sukkoth treats. ■(From *The Sukkah and the Big Wind* by Lily Edelman. Illustrated by Leonard Kessler.)

CAREER: East & West Association, New York City, education director, 1941-50; U.S. State Department, New York City, free-lance writer and editor, 1950-52; National Academy for Adult Jewish Studies, New York City, executive secretary, 1953-57; B'nai B'rith, Washington, D.C., editorial associate, 1957-61, director of commission of adult education and national program director for the mass-membership organization, 1961–77, director of lecture bureau, 1977—. *Member:* B'nai B'rith Women, Adult Education Association, Maryland Association of Adult Education (board member), National Council on Adult Jewish Education, Jewish Book Council, Phi Beta Kappa.

WRITINGS: Mexican Mural Painters and Their Influence in the United States, Service Bureau for Intercultural Education, 1938; *Music in China and Japan: Classroom Material,* Service Bureau for Intercultural Education, 1940; *Japan in Story and Pictures* (juvenile), Harcourt, 1953; *Hawaii,*

U.S.A., Nelson, 1954; *The Sukkah and the Big Wind* (juvenile), United Synagogue Books, 1956; *Israel: New People in an Old Land,* Nelson, 1958, revised edition, 1969, also published as *Modern Israel,* Wilshire, 1969.

(Editor) *Jewish Heritage Reader,* Taplinger, 1965; *Study Guide for Jewish Heritage Reader,* B'nai B'rith Adult Education, 1965; (editor) *Face to Face: A Primer in Dialogue,* B'nai B'rith Adult Education, 1967; (compiler with Goldie Adler) Morris Adler, *May I Have a Word with You?,* Crown, 1967; (translator from the French with the author) Elie Wiesel, *A Beggar in Jerusalem,* Random House, 1970; (translator from the French with author) Elie Wiesel, *One Generation After,* Random House, 1970. Editor of "Jewish Heritage Classic Series." Editor, *Jewish Heritage Review, Anti–Defamation League Bulletin,* and *Face to Face: An Interreligious Quarterly.*

ELLISON, Lucile Watkins 1907(?)-1979

OBITUARY NOTICE: Born about 1907, in Pennington, Ala.; died of cancer, December 20, 1979, in Washington, D.C. Associate executive and author. Ellison spent thirty-three years with the National Education Association, serving her last nine years there as executive secretary of the citizenship committee. After learning in 1974 that she had terminal cancer, Ellison began to write children's books based on her own childhood experiences. The first book, *Butter on Both Sides,* was published in 1979. *Obituaries: Washington Post,* December 17, 1979, December 22, 1979; *Contemporary Authors,* Volume 93-96, Gale, 1980.

FABRE, Jean Henri (Casimir) 1823-1915

PERSONAL: Born December 21, 1823, in Saint-Léons, France; died October 11, 1915, in Serignan, France; son of peasants; married twice; children: eight. *Education:* Attended Normal School in Vaucluse, and in Rodez; Ph.D., University of Paris. *Home:* Serignan, France.

CAREER: Entomologist, naturalist, professor, and author. Professor of mathematics and physics at the Universities of Corsica and Avignon. *Member:* French Academy of Sciences, Royal Academy (Sweden). *Awards, honors:* Received the Cross of the Legion of Honor, and was presented at the French court.

*WRITINGS—*For children: *The Story-Book of Science* (translation from the French by F. C. Bicknell), Century, 1917; *The Story Book of Birds and Beasts* (translation from the French), Hodder & Stoughton, 1919; *The Secret of Everyday Things* (translation from the French by F. C. Bicknell), Century, 1920; *The Wonder Book of Science* (translation from the French), Hodder & Stoughton, 1921; *Animal Life in Field and Garden* (translation from the French by F. C. Bicknell), Century, 1921; *The Story Book of the Fields* (translation from the French), Hodder & Stoughton, 1921; *The Wonder Book of Chemistry* (translation from the French by F. C. Bicknell), Century, 1922; *La Science de l'Oncle Paul,* C. Delagrave, 1926; *Curiosities of Science* (translation from the French by Percy F. Bicknell), 1927.

Souvenirs Entomologiques, 10 volumes (includes *Nouveaux Souvenirs Entomologiques*), C. Delagrave, 1879-1907, translation by Alexander Teixeira de Mattos published as *The Works of J. H. Fabre,* Hodder & Stoughton, 1912; excerpts from the above English translation published separately— *The Life and Love of the Insect,* A. & C. Black, 1911; *The Life of the Spider,* Hodder & Stoughton, 1912, reprinted, Horizon Press, 1971; *The Life of the Fly,* Dodd, Mead, 1913; *The Mason-Bees,* Dodd, Mead, 1914; *Bramble-Bees and Others,* Dodd, Mead, 1915; *The Hunting Wasps,* Dodd, Mead, 1915; *The Life of the Caterpillar,* Dodd, Mead, 1916; *The Life of the Grasshopper,* Dodd, Mead, 1917; *The Sacred Beetle, and Others,* Dodd, Mead, 1918; *The Glow-Worm and Other Beetles,* Dodd, Mead, 1919; *The Mason-Wasps,* Dodd, Mead, 1919; *More Hunting Wasps,* Dodd, Mead, 1921; (retold by Mrs. Rodolph Stawell) *Fabre's Book of Insects* (illustrated by Edward J. Detmold), Dodd, Mead, 1921; *More Beetles,* Dodd, Mead, 1922; *The Life of the Weevil,* Dodd, Mead, 1922; *The Life of the Scorpion,* Dodd, Mead, 1923.

Social Life in the Insect World (translation from the French by Bernard Miall), T. F. Unwin, 1912, Century, 1914, reprinted, Gale, 1974; *Les Ravageurs,* C. Delagrave, 1912, B. J. Sanborn, 1923, translation by J. E. Michell published as *The Spoilers,* Hodder & Stoughton, 1927; *Les Merveilles de l'Instinct chez les Insectes,* C. Delagrave, 1913, translation by A. Teixeira de Mattos and B. Miall published as *The Wonders of Instinct,* Century, 1918; *Les Auxiliaires: Recits sur les Animaux Utiles a l'Agriculture,* [Paris], 1913, translation by B. Miall published as *Farm Friends and Foes: Talks about the Creatures Useful to Agriculture,* T. F. Unwin, 1925; *Le Ciel,* [Paris], 1913, translation by E. E. Fournier d'Albe published as *The Heavens,* Lippincott, 1925; *Our Humble Helpers* (translation of *Les Serviteurs* by Florence C. Bicknell), Century, 1918; *Field, Forest, and Farm* (translation from the French by F. C. Bicknell), Century, 1919; *Le Monde Merveilleux des Insectes,* C. Delagrave, 1921, translation by Percy F. Bicknell published as *Marvels of the Insect World* (illustrated by Robert Gibbings), Appleton-Century, 1938; *This Earth of Ours* (translation of *La Terre* by P. F. Bicknell), Century, 1923; *The Wonder Book of Plant Life* (translation from the French by B. Miall), Lippincott, 1924, reissued, 1973; *Chimie Agricole* (title means "Agricultural Chemistry"), C. Delagrave, 1925; *Here and There in Popular Science* (translation from the French by P. F. Bicknell), Century, 1926.

Selections: *The Insect World of J. Henri Fabre* (translation from the French), Dodd, Mead, 1949, reissued, Fawcett, 1964.

SIDELIGHTS: **December 21, 1823.** Born at Saint-Léons, France. First of two children born to Antoine Fabre and Victoire Salgues. Due to family's poor financial situation, Fabre was entrusted to the care of his grandparents. "I have . . . precise information regarding my grandparents on the father's side, for their green old age allowed me to know them both. They were people of the soil, whose quarrel with the alphabet was so great that they had never opened a book in their lives; and they kept a lean farm on the cold granite ridge of the Rouergue table-land. . . .

"Padded with a perpetual layer of cow-dung, in which I sank to my knees, broken up with shimmering puddles of dark-brown liquid manure, the farm-yard also boasted a numerous population. Here the lambs skipped, the geese trumpeted, the fowls scratched the ground and the sow grunted with her swarm of little pigs hanging to her dugs.

". . . How dumbfounded [grandfather] would have been to learn that, in the remote future, one of his family would become enamoured of those insignificant animals to which he had never vouchsafed a glance in his life! Had he guessed that that lunatic was myself, the scapegrace seated at the table by his side, what a smack I should have caught in the neck, what a wrathful look!

"The idea of wasting one's time with that nonsense!' he would have thundered. [Jean Henri Fabre, *The Life of the Fly,* Dodd, 1913.[1]]

From early childhood Fabre possessed a passion for the natural sciences. "I owe a great deal to you, dear grandmother: it was in your lap that I found consolation for my first sorrows. You have handed down to me, perhaps, a little of your physical vigour, a little of your love of work; but certainly you were no more accountable than grandfather for my passion for insects."[1]

1830-1833. Parents recalled Fabre to Saint-Léons to begin his education. "I am back in the village, in my father's house. I am now seven years old; and it is high time that I went to school. Nothing could have turned out better: the master is my godfather. What shall I call the room in which I was to become acquainted with the alphabet? It would be difficult to find the exact word, because the room served for every purpose. It was at once a school, a kitchen, a bedroom, a dining-room and, at times, a chicken-house and a piggery. Palatial schools were not dreamt of in those days; any wretched hovel was thought good enough.

"What was read at my school? At most, in French, a few selections from sacred history. Latin recurred oftener, to teach us to sing vespers properly. The more advanced pupils tried to decipher manuscript, a deed of sale, the hieroglyphics of some scrivener.

"And history, geography? No one ever heard of them. What difference did it make to us whether the earth was round or square! In either case, it was just as hard to make it bring forth anything.

"And grammar? The master troubled his head very little about that; and we still less. We should have been greatly

JEAN HENRI FABRE

surprised by the novelty and the forbidding look of such words in the grammatical jargon as substantive, indicative and subjunctive. Accuracy of language, whether of speech or writing, must be learnt by practice. And none of us was troubled by scruples in this respect. What was the use of all these subtleties, when, on coming out of school, a lad simply went back to his flock of sheep!

"And arithmetic? Yes, we did a little of this, but not under that learned name. We called it sums. To put down rows of figures, not too long, add them and subtract them one from the other was more or less familiar work. . . . I was able to enjoy the school-window only at rare intervals, when the master left his little table; the other was at my disposal as often as I liked. I spent long hours there, sitting on a little fixed window-seat.

"The view was magnificent. I could see the ends of the earth, that is to say, the hills that blocked the horizon, all but a misty gap through which the brook with the crayfish flowed under the alders and willows. High up on the sky-line, a few wind-battered oaks bristled on the ridges; and beyond there lay nothing but the unknown, laden with mystery."[1]

Fabre's parents had hoped to raise some money by breeding ducks; and, to Fabre's delight, made him their "duck-heardsman." During his declining years, Fabre reflected fondly of his days around that first duck pond. "Many another have I come upon since that distant time, ponds very much richer and, moreover, explored with the ripened eye of experience. Enthusiastically I searched them with the net, stirred up their mud, ransacked their trailing weeds. None in my memories comes up to the first, magnified in its delights and mortifications by the marvellous perspective of the years."[1]

Front view of Fabre's house.

The Praying Mantis. ■(From *Fabre's Book of Insects,* retold by Mrs. Rodolph Stawell. Illustrated by Edward J. Detmold.)

1833. Family moved to Rodez. "I come to the time when I was ten years old and at Rodez College. My functions as a serving-boy in the chapel entitled me to free instruction as a day-boarder. There were four of us in white surplices and red skull-caps and cassocks. I was the youngest of the party and did little more than walk on. I counted as a unit; and that was about all, for I was never certain when to ring the bell or move the missal. I was all of a tremble when we gathered two on this side and two on that, with genuflexions, in the middle of the sanctuary, to intone the *Domine, salvum fac regem* at the end of mass. Let me make a confession: tongue-tied with shyness, I used to leave it to the others.

"Nevertheless, I was well thought of, for, in the school, I cut a good figure in composition and translation. In that classical atmosphere, there was talk of Procas, King of Alba, and of his two sons, Numitor and Amulius. . . .

"Had they talked to me about the man in the moon, I could not have been more startled. I made up for it with my animals, which I was far from forgetting amid this phantasmagoria of heroes and demigods. While honouring the exploits of Cadmus and Cynoegirus, I hardly ever failed, on Sundays and Thursdays, to go and see if the cowslip or the yellow daffodil was making its appearance in the meadows, if the Linnet was hatching on the juniper-bushes, if the Cockchafers were plopping down from the wind-shaken poplars. Thus was the sacred spark kept aglow, ever brighter than before.

"By easy stages, I came to Virgil and was very much smitten with Meliboeus, Corydon, Menalcas, Damoetas and the rest of them. The scandals of the ancient shepherds fortunately passed unnoticed; and within the frame in which the characters moved were exquisite details concerning the Bee, the Cicada, the Turtle-dove, the Crow, the Nanny-goat and the golden broom. A veritable delight were these stories of the fields, sung in sonorous verse; and the Latin poet left a lasting impression on my classical recollections.

"As a boy, I was always an ardent reader; but the niceties of a well-balanced style hardly interested me: I did not understand them. A good deal later, when close upon fifteen, I began vaguely to see that words have a physiognomy of their own. Some pleased me better than others by the distinctness of their meaning and the resonance of their rhythm; they produced a clearer image in my mind; after their fashion, they gave me a picture of the object described. Coloured by its adjective and vivified by its verb, the name became a living reality: what it said I saw. And thus, gradually, was the magic of words revealed to me, when the chances of my undirected reading placed a few easy standard pages in my way."[1]

1839. Family economics grew desperate. "Then, suddenly, good-bye to my studies, good-bye to Tityrus and Menalcas. Ill-luck is swooping down on us, relentlessly. Hunger threatens us at home. And now, boy, put your trust in God; run about and earn your pen-n'orth of potatoes as best you can. Life is about to become a hideous inferno. . . .

"Amid this lamentable chaos, my love for the insect ought to have gone under. Not at all. It would have survived the raft of the *Medusa*. I still remember a certain Pine Cockchafer met for the first time. The plumes on her antennae, her pretty pattern of white spots on a dark-brown ground were as a ray of sunshine in the gloomy wretchedness of the day."[1]

1841. Entered a competitive examination for a bursary at the École Normale Primaire of Avignon. " . . . Good fortune, which never abandons the brave, brought me to the primary normal school at Vaucluse, where I was assured food: dried chestnuts and chick-peas. The principal, a man of broad views, soon came to trust his new assistant. He left me practically a free hand, so long as I satisfied the school curriculum, which was very modest in those days. Possessing a smattering of Latin and grammar, I was a little ahead of my fellow-pupils. I took advantage of this to get some order into my vague knowledge of plants and animals. While a dictation-lesson was being corrected around me, with generous assistance from the dictionary, I would examine, in the recesses of my desk, the oleander's fruit, the snap-dragon's seed-vessel, the Wasp's sting and the Ground-beetle's wing-case.

"With this foretaste of natural science, picked up haphazard and by stealth, I left school more deeply in love than ever with insects and flowers. And yet I had to give it all up. That wider education, which would have to be my source of live-

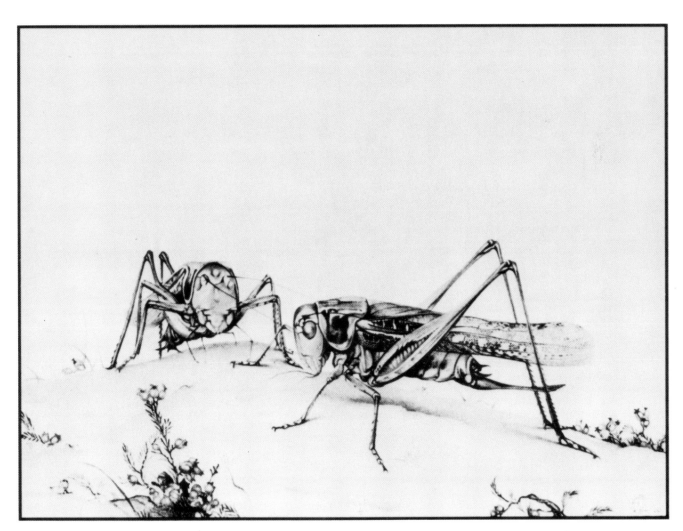

(From *Fabre's Book of Insects,* retold by Mrs. Rodolph Stawell. Illustrated by Edward J. Detmold.)

(From *Fabre's Book of Insects*, retold by Mrs. Rodolph Stawell. Illustrated by Edward J. Detmold.)

The Field Cricket. ■(From *Fabre's Book of Insects*, retold by Mrs. Rodolph Stawell. Illustrated by Edward J. Detmold.)

lihood in the future, demanded this imperiously. What was I to take in hand to raise me above the primary school, whose staff could barely earn their bread in those days? Natural history could not bring me anywhere. The educational system of the time kept it at a distance, as unworthy of association with Latin and Greek. Mathematics remained, with its very simple equipment: a blackboard, a bit of chalk and a few books.''[1]

1842. Won a bursary for a position as a primary teacher in the College of Carpentras.

October 30, 1844. Married Marie Villard.

January, 1853. Assumed the vacant post of professor of physics and chemistry at the College of Ajaccio in Corsica.

1853. A severe attack of malaria contacted in Corsica resulted in Fabre's eventual transfer to the lycée of Avignon as professor of physics and chemistry. ''New lights burst forth: I received a sort of mental revelation. So there was more in science than the arranging of pretty Beetles in a cork box and giving them names and classifying them; there was something much finer: a close and loving study of insect life, the examination of the structure and especially the faculties of each species. I read of a magnificent instance of this, glowing with excitement as I did so. Some time after, aided by those lucky circumstances which he who seeks them eagerly is always able to find, I myself published an entomological article, a supplement to Léon Dufour's. This first work of mine won honourable mention from the Institute of France, and was awarded a prize for experimental physiology. But soon I received a far more welcome recompense, in the shape of a most eulogistic and encouraging letter from the very man who had inspired me. From his home in the Landes the revered master sent me a warm expression of his enthusiasm and urged me to go on with my studies. Even now, at that sacred recollection, my old eyes fill with happy tears. O fair days of illusion, of faith in the future, where are you now?'' [Augustin Fabre, *The Life of Jean Henri Fabre*, Dodd, 1921.[2]]

1859. Cited by Charles Darwin in his ''Origin of Species.'' ''Since Darwin bestowed upon me the title of 'incomparable observer,' the epithet has often come back to me, from this side and from that, without yet understanding what particular merit I have shown. It seems to me so natural, so much within everybody's scope, so absorbing to interest one's self in everything that swarms around us! . . . .''[1]

1873. Curatorship of the Requien Museum was taken from Fabre. ''With less ceremony than would have been used in discharging a hall-boy entrusted with the handling of broom and feather duster.'' [Percy F. Bicknell, *The Human Side of Fabre*, Century Co., 1923.[3]]

1862-1901. Wrote over forty volumes on such subjects as math and physics as well as natural history—designed primarily as textbooks for the young. Gave free lectures in the Abbey of Saint-Martial and was given charge of The Requien Museum. ''What matters in learning is not to be taught, but to wake up.'' [Eleanor Doorly, *The Insect Man*, Dufour Editions, Inc., 1951.[4]]

1878. Son, Jules, died. The first volume of *Souvenirs Entomologiques* was dedicated to him. ''TO MY SON JULES.— Beloved child, my zealous collaborator in the study of insects, my perspicacious assistant in the study of plants, it was for your sake that I began this volume; I have continued it for the sake of your memory, and I shall continue it in the

bitterness of my mourning. Ah! how hateful is death when it reaps the flower in all the radiance of its blossoming! Your mother and your sisters bring to your tomb wreaths gathered in the rustic flower-bed that you delighted in. To these wreaths, faded by a day's sunshine, I add this book, which, I hope, will have a to-morrow. It seems to me that it thus prolongs our common studies, fortified as I am by my indomitable faith in a reawakening in the Beyond.''[2]

Jules' death affected Fabre's own health. ''After a hard winter, when the snow had lain on the ground for a fortnight, I wanted once more to look into the matter of my Halicti. I was in bed with pneumonia and to all appearances at the point of death. I had little or no pain, thank God, but extreme difficulty in living. With the little lucidity left to me, being able to do no other sort of observing, I observed myself dying; I watched with a certain interest the gradual falling to pieces of my poor machinery. Were it not for the terror of leaving my family, who were still young, I would gladly have departed. The after-life must have so many higher and fairer truths to teach us.

''My hour had not yet come. When the little lamps of thought began to emerge, all flickering, from the dusk of unconsciousness, I wished to take leave of the Hymenoptera, my fondest joy, and first of all of my neighbour, the Halictus. My son Emile took the spade and went and dug the frozen ground. Not a male was found, of course; but there were plenty of females, numbed with the cold in their cells.

''A few were brought for me to see, and roused from their torpor by the warmth of the room, they began to wander about my bed, where I followed them vaguely with my failing eyes.'' [2] Fabre recovered.

1879. Retired to Serignan which Fabre called ''the great museum of the fields.'' ''This is what I wished for, *hoc erat in votis:* a bit of land, oh, not so very large, but fenced in, to avoid the drawbacks of a public way; an abandoned, barren, sun-scorched bit of land, favoured by thistles and by Wasps and Bees. Here, without distant expeditions that take up my time, without tiring rambles that strain my nerves, I could contrive my plans of attack, lay my ambushes, and watch their effects at every hour of the day. *Hoc erat in votis.* Yes, this was my wish, my dream, always cherished, always vanishing into the mists of the future.''[2] Here Fabre displayed yet another talent—creating beautiful watercolor paintings of ''his botanical joys''—mushrooms. Wife died shortly after move to Serignan.

1883. Married second wife.

July 11, 1887. Elected a corresponding member of the Académie des Sciences.

From 1894. Popularity of books for school children declined. ''Despite all my efforts here I am more anxious than ever about the future, two more of my books are about to disappear, a prelude to total shipwreck. . . . I begin to despair.'' [Dr. Georges V. Legros, *Fabre, Poet of Science*, Century Co., 1913.[5]]

1903. At the age of eighty, Fabre confessed. ''The more I go forward, the more clearly I see that I have struck my pick into an inexhaustible vein, well worthy of being exploited.

''As though I had a long future before me, I continue indefatigably my researches into the lives of these little creatures. ''The outer world scarcely tempts me at all; surrounded by my little family, it is enough for me to go into the woods from time to time, to listen to the fluting of the blackbirds. The very idea of the town disgusts me. Henceforth it would be impossible for me to live in the little cage of a citizen, Here I am, run wild, and I shall be so till the end."[5]

"Away with repose! For him who would spend his life properly there is nothing like work—so long as the machine will operate."[2]

1908. In precarious financial situation, Fabre decided to sell to a museum his water-color plates of fungi. "I have never thought of profiting by my humble fungoid water-colours . . . . Fate will perhaps decide otherwise.

". . . Until latterly I had lived modestly on the product of my school-books. To-day the weathercock has turned to another quarter, and my books no longer sell. So here I am, more than ever in the grip of that terrible problem of daily bread. . . ."[2]

April 3, 1910. Admirers honored Fabre with a celebration of his jubilee.

1912. Second wife died.

October 11, 1915. Died in Serignan, Vaucluse, France. "An exquisitely sweet link binds us to our native soil; we are like the plant that has to be torn away from the spot where it put out its first roots. Poor though it be, I should love to see my own village again; I should like to leave my bones there."[2]

FOR MORE INFORMATION SEE: Georges V. Legros, *La Vie de J. H. Fabre, Naturaliste,* C. Delagrave, 1913, translation by B. Miall published as *Fabre: Poet of Science,* Century, 1913, reprinted, Horizon Press, 1971; Edith F. Wyatt, *Great Companions,* Appleton-Century, 1917; Augustin Fabre, *The Life of Jean Henri Fabre, the Entomologist* (translation from the French by B. Miall), Dodd, Mead, 1921; Mrs. D. B. Hammond, "Fabre, Poet of Science," in her *Stories of Scientific Discovery,* Macmillan, 1923; Percy F. Bicknell, *The Human Side of Fabre,* Century Co., 1923; A. Gilbert, "Uncommon Thrills from Common Things," in his *Over Famous Thresholds,* Appleton-Century, 1931; John A. Thomson, *Great Biologists,* Methuen, 1932; Donald C. Peattie, "Fabre and the Epic Commonplace," in his *Green Laurels,* Simon & Schuster, 1936; E. W. Teale, "Fabre: The Explorer Who Stayed Home," *Coronet,* February, 1951; Eleanor Doorly, *The Insect Man,* Dufour Editions, Inc., 1951; D. C. Peattie, *Lives of Destiny,* Houghton, 1954; Gilbert Highet, *Talents and Geniuses,* Oxford University Press, 1957; A. Porges, "Darwin and Fabre: A Sidelight," *School Science and Mathematics,* November, 1961; Margaret Lane, *Purely for Pleasure,* Knopf, 1967.

For children: Hallie E. Rives and G. E. Forbush, *John Book,* Beechhurst Press, 1947; Stanley J, Kunitz and Howard Haycraft, editors, *Junior Book of Authors,* second revised edition, H. W. Wilson, 1951; Lorus J. Milne and M.J.G. Milne, *Famous Naturalists,* Dodd, Mead, 1952; J. Compton, "Jean Henri Fabre: Explorer of the Insect World," in *Children's Book of Famous Lives,* edited by Eric Cuthie, Odhams, 1958; Richard S. R. Fitter, *Six Great Naturalists,* Hamilton, 1959; Patrick Pringle, *101 Great Lives,* Ward, Lock, 1963; Arthur L. Mann and Charles Vivian, *Famous Biologists,* Museum Press, 1963.

Movies: "Fabre: The Genius of the Insects" (60 minutes; sound, color), Canadian Broadcasting Corp., 1972.

FARB, Peter 1929-1980

OBITUARY NOTICE—See sketch in SATA Volume 12: Born July 25, 1929, in New York, N.Y.; died of leukemia, April 8, 1980, in Boston, Mass. Naturalist, linguist, anthropologist, and author. Farb wrote a number of highly popular books on the natural and human sciences. For Time, Inc. he wrote books on a variety of topics in the natural science realm, including *The Forest, The Insects,* and *Ecology.* In 1963, *Face of America: The Natural History of a Continent* was published, with a young reader's edition appearing in 1964. This book exemplifies the broad popularity of Farb's approach to science. It was a Book-of-the-Month Club selection, won a Notable Book Citation from the American Library Association, and President Kennedy presented a copy of it to the heads of one hundred foreign governments. In 1964 Farb was heralded by then-Secretary of the Interior Stewart Udall as "one of the finest conservation spokesmen of our period." *For More Information See: The Author's and Writer's Who's Who,* 6th edition, Burke's Peerage, 1971; *Who's Who in the East,* 14th edition, Marquis, 1973; *Who's Who in the World,* 2nd edition, Marquis, 1973; *Who's Who in America,* 38th edition, Marquis, 1974; *Contemporary Authors,* Volume 13-16, revised, Gale, 1975. *Obituaries: Contemporary Authors,* Volume 97-100, Gale, 1980; *New York Times,* April 9, 1980; *Chicago Tribune,* April 10, 1980; *AB Bookman's Weekly,* April 21, 1980; *Publishers Weekly,* May 6, 1980.

FINK, William B(ertrand) 1916-

PERSONAL: Born May 11, 1916, in Yonkers, N.Y.; son of Perley C. (a realtor) and Agnes (Heuchele) Fink; married Esther Cheney (director of Head Start), April 16, 1941; children: William B., Jr., Marilyn C. *Education:* Wesleyan University, B.A., 1937; Columbia University, M.A., 1939, Ph.D., 1950. *Politics:* Democrat. *Religion:* Presbyterian. *Home:* Main St., Laurens, N.Y. 13796. *Office:* Department of History, State University of New York, Oneonta, N.Y. 13820.

CAREER: High school social studies teacher in New York, 1937-38, in Maryland, 1939-42; State University College, Albany, N.Y., instructor in Campus School, 1946-49; Columbia University, New York, N.Y., instructor in history, 1949-51; State University College, Oneonta, N.Y., professor of history, 1953—, head of social science department, 1960-70, head of social science education department, 1970—. Fulbright lecturer in Philippines, 1961-62. *Military service:* U.S. Naval Reserve, 1942-46; became lieutenant. *Member:* American Historical Association, Organization of American Historians, National Council for the Social Studies, Association of State and Local History, New York State Historical Association, New York State Council for the Social Studies, Phi Beta Kappa.

WRITINGS: (With David Ellis and James Frost) *New York: The Empire State,* Prentice-Hall, 1961; (with Frost, Ellis, and Ralph Brown) *A History of the United States,* Follett, 1968; *Getting to Know the Hudson,* Coward, 1970; *Getting to Know New York State,* Coward, 1971.

WORK IN PROGRESS: A teenage biography of Harry Truman; a collection of documents of New York history, 1984.

...Washington Irving, wrote a popular story entitled "The Legend of Sleepy Hollow," which took place near Tarrytown. It was about a schoolmaster named Ichabod Crane and a headless horseman who chased him one night. ■(From *Getting to Know New York State* by William B. Fink. Illustrated by Don Almquist.)

FLORY, Jane Trescott 1917-

PERSONAL: Born June 29, 1917, in Wilkesbarre, Pa.; daughter of Leroy Charles (an engineer) and Hazel (Nixon) Trescott; married Arthur Louis Flory (an artist and college instructor), September 29, 1941 (died in 1972); married Barnett R. Freedman, July 8, 1980; children: (first marriage) Cynthia Jane, Christine Kate, Erika Susan. *Education:* Philadelphia Museum School of Industrial Art (now Philadelphia College of Art), diploma, 1939. *Home:* 1814 Beech Ave., Melrose Park, Philadelphia, Pa. 19126.

CAREER: Free-lance writer and illustrator of children's books, 1939—; Philadelphia College of Art, Philadelphia, Pa., director of evening division, 1958-74.

WRITINGS—Juveniles; all self-illustrated, except as indicated: *Snooty, the Pig Who Was Proud,* Whitman Publishing, 1944; *How Many?,* Holt, 1944; *What Am I?* Domesday, 1945; *The Wide Awake Angel,* Grosset, 1945; (illustrator) Laura Harris, *Away We Go,* Garden City Books, 1945; *The Hide-Away Ducklings,* Grosset, 1946; (with husband, Arthur Flory) *The Cow in the Kitchen,* Lothrop, 1946; *Fanny Forgot,* Whitman Publishing, 1946; *Once Upon a Windy Day,* Whitman Publishing, 1947; *Toys,* Whitman Publishing, 1948; *The Powder Puff Bunny Book,* Capitol Publishing Co., 1948; *The Lazy Lion,* Whitman Publishing, 1949; *Timothy, the Little Brown Bear,* Rand McNally, 1949; *ABC,* Whitman Publishing, 1949.

Farmer John, Whitman Publishing, 1950; *Mr. Snitzel's Cookies,* Rand McNally, 1950; *The Too-Little Fire Engine,* Wonder Books, 1950; *The Pop-up Runaway Train,* Avon, 1951; *Count the Animals,* Loew, 1952; *Surprise in the Barn,* Whitman Publishing, 1955; *Jeremy's ABC Book,* Behrman, 1957; *Peddler's Summer,* Houghton, 1960; *A Tune for the Towpath,* Houghton, 1962; *One Hundred and Eight Bells,* Houghton, 1963; *Clancy's Glorious Fourth,* Houghton, 1964; *Mist on the Mountain,* Houghton, 1966; *Faraway Dream,* Houghton, 1968.

Ramshackle Roost, (illustrated by Carolyn Croll), Houghton, 1972; *The Liberation of Clementine Tipton,* Houghton, 1974; *We'll Have a Friend for Lunch* (illustrated by Carolyn Croll), Houghton, 1974; *The Golden Venture,* Houghton, 1976; *The Unexpected Grandchildren* (illustrated by Carolyn Croll), Houghton, 1977; *It Was a Pretty Good Year,* Houghton, 1977; *The Lost and Found Princess,* Houghton, 1979; *The Bear on the Doorstep,* Houghton, 1980.

WORK IN PROGRESS: A spy story for younger readers, and another historical book.

SIDELIGHTS: "I was sure I wanted to make books from the moment I knew they existed. From the very first my scribblings and pictures were always folded into books, with a pin or a few stitches in the back to make a book spine.

"When I went to art school it was with the intention of learning to do one thing—illustrate for children. I had a lot of encouragement for my writing efforts, but no formal training. It was all self-taught. I learned from years of reading, and trial-and-error (with a lot of errors.) But soon after I graduated from art school I sold my first magazine story, and from then on I never stopped.

"All my work was self-illustrated until recently, when I began to do an occasional book with illustrator Carolyn Croll."

JANE TRESCOTT FLORY

"I grew up in a small town, Woodbury, New Jersey, and had an uneventful but very happy, busy childhood that has furnished me with material for years. My mother and father were both good story tellers. The tales of their farm childhoods, and the family stories that go back several generations to pioneer days, fed my active imagination.

"History fascinates me, and I am never happier than when I am working on a book with a well-researched historical background. Specific historic personnages are not my concern, but I do feel a need to provide a living, breathing atmosphere in which my fictional characters can move freely.

"My three daughters, now grown, have been an endless inspiration for me. From the very first they have been editors, critics, models and cheering section for whatever I write or draw, and now I have grandchildren coming along to help me.

"Next to writing and drawing, gardening is my continuing passion, along with weaving and quiltmaking. Housework comes in a very poor last."

FOR MORE INFORMATION SEE: Horn Book, June, 1964, August, 1972, December, 1974, October, 1976; *Young Reader's Review,* May, 1966.

Barney was ten years old, and ten was just the right age to appreciate the joys of Reed Street—the sounds, the sights, the smells. ■ (From *It Was a Pretty Good Year* by Jane Flory. Illustrated by the author.)

Let nothing which is disgraceful to be spoken of, or to be seen, approach this place, where a child is.

—Juvenal

MICHAEL FOONER

FOONER, Michael

PERSONAL: Born in London, England; married; children: two. *Education:* Earned B.Sc. from City College (now of the City University of New York), and M.A. from University of Wisconsin—Madison. *Residence:* New York, N.Y.

CAREER: Employed as an economist in Washington, D.C.; reporter for *U.S. News & World Report;* member of sociology faculty of Hunter College of the City University of New York, New York City; professor of criminology at New York Institute for Advanced Studies; faculty member of New School for Social Research, New York City. Visiting professor at University of London; lecturer at colleges and universities. Consultant to Presidential commissions, police agencies, and business corporations. *Member:* American Association for the Advancement of Sciences (fellow).

WRITINGS: Interpol: The Inside Story of the International Crime-Fighting Organization, Regnery, 1973; *Inside Interpol: Combatting World Crime Through Science and International Police Cooperation* (for young people), Coward, 1975; *Women in Policing: Fighting Crime Around the World* (for young people), Coward, 1976; *Smuggling Drugs: The Worldwide Connection,* Coward, 1977; *Blue Domino,* Putnam, 1978.

Film scripts: "The Family Man," "The League of Red-Head Women."

Author of material for television and radio. Contributor to scientific journals, law and police journals, and popular mag-azines, including *Penthouse, Saturday Review, Argosy, Nation,* and *Family Circle,* and to newspapers.

WORK IN PROGRESS: A suspense series, describing contemporary international conspiracies concerned with drugs, forgery, financial fraud, and white slavery; historical novel of Spain in the Middle Ages.

SIDELIGHTS: Fooner began writing on crime, drugs, police, international crooks and sleuthing more than ten years ago, first in professional and scientific journals, then in general interest magazines and books. He has written film adaptations of books and has produced television shorts and radio spots—all on crime. He lectures at universities around the country, and serves as consultant to police and corporations on crime prevention.

While visiting in Rome some years ago, Fooner was introduced to the noted international detective, Dr. Giuseppe Dosi. "I learned later that he had once been the Italian delegate to Interpol, and that he had been the one to propose the name 'Interpol.' At that time my response was exactly the same as I was myself to hear over and over: "What's Interpol?'

"Many people had the idea it was some sort of a mystery show on television. In actuality, Interpol is a real-life organization operating to fight crime and criminals around the world. The United States became a member in 1938. The organization does its work quietly, without fanfare, and al-

The women pictured here are regular police officers on patrol in downtown Hong Kong. ■(From *Women in Policing* by Michael Fooner. Photograph courtesy of Hong Kong Government Information.)

ways lets local police take credit for accomplishments. Naturally, I was curious about it. I had been a news reporter and in those days I was making a national study of crime in the United States. I obtained an invitation to visit Interpol's headquarters and was permitted to observe some of their ingenious methods for dealing with the complexities of international criminal activities. After that I visited Interpol bureaus in various countries. In 1973 I wrote the first book published in America on the subject.''

FORBERG, Ati 1925-

PERSONAL: Born December 19, 1925, in Germany; daughter of Walter Gropius (the architect and head of the Bauhaus, 1919-28); married Charles Forberg (an architect); children: two daughters. *Education:* Attended the Chicago Institute of Design and Black Mountain College, where she was a pupil of Josef Albers. *Home:* Brooklyn Heights, N.Y.

CAREER: Illustrator, artist, and editor.

WRITINGS: The Very Special Baby: A Christmas Story (illustrated by Carol Woodard), Fortress Press, 1969.

Illustrator: Charlotte Bronte, *Jane Eyre*, Macmillan, 1962; Wendy Sanford and George Mendoza, *The Puma and the Pearl*, Walker, 1962; (and editor) *On a Grass-Green Horn: Old Scotch and English Ballads*, Atheneum, 1965; Edgar Allan Poe, *Tales*, Whitman, 1965; Doris H. Lund, *Attic of*

Month after month dragged by as she waited for her trial to begin. From the slit of a window in her cell she saw leaves change from green to gold. ■ (From *Jeanne D'Arc* by Aileen Fisher. Illustrated by Ati Forberg.)

the Wind, Parents Magazine Press, 1966; Doris Orgel, *Cindy's Snowdrops*, Knopf, 1966; D. Orgel, *Cindy's Sad and Happy Tree*, Knopf, 1967; Dorothy Levenson, *The Magic Carousel*, Parents Magazine Press, 1967; Aileen Fisher, *Easter*, Crowell, 1968; Frances Brailsford, *In the Space of a Wink*, Follett, 1969; George Mendoza, *The Starfish Trilogy*, Funk & Wagnalls, 1969; Lawrence F. Lowery and Albert B. Carr, *Quiet as a Butterfly*, Holt, 1969.

Ruth J. Adams, *Fidelia*, Lothrop, Lee, 1970; Aileen L. Fisher, *Jeanne d'Arc*, Crowell, 1970; Barbara Schiller, *Erec and Enid*, Dutton, 1970; Florence P. Heide, *The Key*, Atheneum, 1971; Chloe Lederer, *Down the Hill of the Sea*, Lothrop, Lee, 1971; Sarah F. Tomaino, *Persephone, Bringer of Spring*, Crowell, 1971; Pauline P. Meek, *God Speaks to Me*, John Knox Press, 1972; Doris Van Liew Foster, *Feather in the Wind: The Story of a Hurricane*, Lothrop, Lee, 1972; Yoshiko Uchida, *Samurai of Gold Hill*, Scribner, 1972; G. Mendoza, *Poem for Putting to Sea*, Hawthorne, 1972; Barbara K. Walker, *The Ifrit and the Magic Gifts*, Follett, 1972; Ann McGovern, *If You Lived with the Circus*, Four Winds, 1972; A. L. Fisher, *"You Don't Look Like Your Mother,"* Said the Robin to the Fawn, Bowmar, 1973; Lyon S. De Camp, compiler, *Tales Beyond Time: From Fantasy to Science Fiction*, Lothrop, Lee, 1973; Anne N. Baldwin, *A Friend in the Park*, Four Winds, 1973; Nancy C. Smith, *Josie's Handful of Quietness*, Abingdon, 1975; Edna Barth, *Cupid and Psyche: A Love Story Retold*, Seabury Press, 1976; Helen

ATI FORBERG

Cresswell, *A Game of Catch,* Macmillan, 1977; Robbin Fleisher, *Quilts in the Attic,* Macmillan, 1978; Carol Fenner, *The Skates of Uncle Richard,* Random, 1978; Barbara S. Hazen, *The Me I See,* Abingdon, 1978.

SIDELIGHTS: Ati Forberg spent her childhood in Germany. The most important part of her education was the time spent at Black Mountain College, where she studied under the well-known abstractionist, Josef Albers. She claims that the Chicago Institute of Design influenced much of her approach to design. Her career started out to be very diverse. As a free-lance artist, she had done various projects in advertising, display, graphics, and book jackets. Now, however, she is exclusively illustrating children's books. She works in a variety of media, most often in black and white, or full color.

Mrs. Forberg collected 18 familiar Scottish and English ballads in a book called *On a Grass-Green Horn: Old Scotch and English Ballads.* A *Horn Book* critic commented, "In eighteen ballads—chosen for their drama, cadence, and imagery—romantic figures act out their tales of love or treachery. Lairds, knights, and soldiers parade; mermaids, queens, and fairies weave their spells. Luring the reader are the illustrations, shaded swirls veiling mysterious forms. Through imaginative presentation in format and sensitive interpretation in drawings, the modern child will be caught by the magic of familiar old ballads." *Book Week* added, "Ati Forberg . . . has decorated the book beautifully, with swirling, eerie drawings that might have been made behind the green hill. Some of the ballads are printed in rust type, others in black; all are inviting. The old ballads have immense power to stir the heart. . . . [They] can be found in larger anthologies, but a small and excellent sampling of ballads, tragic, comic, mysterious, and handsomely mounted like this one, is a valuable contribution."

Forberg's works are included in the Kerlan Collection at the University of Minnesota.

FOR MORE INFORMATION SEE: Horn Book, June, 1977; Lee Kingman and others, compilers, *Illustrators of Children's Books, 1957-1966,* Horn Book, 1968. Doris de Montreville and Elizabeth D. Crawford, editors, *Fourth Book of Junior Authors and Illustrators,* H. W. Wilson, 1978.

FOWLES, John 1926-

PERSONAL: Born March 31, 1926, in Essex, England; son of Robert John and Gladys (Richards) Fowles; married Elizabeth Whitton, April 2, 1954. *Education:* Oxford University, B.A. (honors in French), 1950. *Residence:* Dorset, England. *Agent:* Anthony Shield Associates, 2/3 Morwell St., London WC1B 3AR.

CAREER: Once taught in France and in Greece; was head of English department at a London college; now full-time writer. *Military service:* Royal Marines; became lieutenant.

WRITINGS: The Collector, Little, Brown, 1963; *The Aristos: A Self Portrait in Ideas,* Little, Brown, 1964, revised edition, 1970; *The Magus* (Literary Guild selection), Little, Brown, 1966, revised edition, 1978; (contributor) *Afterwards: Novelists on Their Novels,* Harper, 1969; *The French Lieutenant's Woman,* Little, Brown, 1969; *Poems,* Ecco, 1973; *The Ebony Tower,* Little, Brown, 1974; *Shipwreck,* Little, Brown,

JOHN FOWLES

1974; (translator) *Cinderella,* Little, Brown, 1976; *Islands,* Little, Brown, 1977; *Daniel Martin,* Little, Brown, 1977; *The Tree,* Little, Brown, 1979.

ADAPTATIONS—Movies: "The Collector," (motion picture), Columbia Pictures, 1965; "The Magus," (motion picture), Twentieth Century-Fox, 1968; "The French Lieutenant's Woman," United Artists.

SIDELIGHTS: Fowles is renowned as the author of several highly successful adult works—*The French Lieutenant's Woman, The Magus,* and *The Ebony Tower,* among others. His first book for children, however, met with less success. The critical reaction may be summed up in Ann Martin's mixed review in the *Times Literary Supplement.* She found Fowles' adaption of Perrault's classic *Cinderella* ". . . a colloquial, easy translation . . . which may delight some while enraging those who prefer a more stylish rendering." Martin was less pleased with the illustration: "The whole effect is unfortunately undermined by the artist's inclination to glamorize, so that hero, heroine and ugly sisters alike have large Disneyesque eyes which make the pictures far too sugary for the text."

HOBBIES AND OTHER INTERESTS: Nature and isolation.

FOR MORE INFORMATION SEE: New York Times Book Review, January 28, 1963, July 28, 1963, January 9, 1966;

Times Literary Supplement, May 17, 1963; *New Statesman,* June 21, 1963, July 2, 1965; *Saturday Review,* July 27, 1963; *New York Herald Tribune Book Review,* July 28, 1963; *Publishers Weekly,* September 30, 1963; Roy Newquist, editor, *Counterpoint,* Rand McNally, 1964; *Time,* November 20, 1964, January 14, 1966; *Library Journal,* January 15, 1965; *Harper's,* July, 1968; *Sports Illustrated,* December, 1970; William J. Palmer, *The Fiction of John Fowles,* University of Missouri, 1974; *Times Literary Supplement,* December 6, 1974; Peter Wolfe, *John Fowles, Magus and Moralist,* Bucknell, 1976, revised edition, 1979; Barry N. Olshen, *John Fowles,* Ungar, 1978.

FRANKENBERG, Robert 1911-

PERSONAL: Born March 19, 1911, in Mount Vernon, N.Y.; son of Edward J. (a sign painter) and Edwina (Lafevre Jacquin) Frankenberg; married Celestine James Gilligan (a research librarian), April 4, 1959. *Education:* Studied at the Art Students League, New York, N.Y. *Religion:* Christian. *Home:* 601 E. 20th St., New York, N.Y. 10010. *Agent:* Hans Fybel, 648 Kelton, Los Angeles, Calif.

CAREER: Free-lance illustrator and painter. Jenter Exhibits, New York and New Jersey, artist and designer, 1933-40; School of Visual Art, New York, N.Y., instructor, 1947—, head of the drawing department, 1958-67. *Exhibitions:* Six one-man shows of drawings and watercolors in New York, N.Y., 1950-71. Works are in the permanent collections of St. Patrick Cathedral, New York, N.Y., and the War Museum, Washington, D.C. *Military service:* U.S. Army, medical regiment, 1941-42, Army Signal Corp, 1942-45. *Awards, honors:* National winner for film strips "Jews in America," 1954 and "Einstein," 1956, National Jewish Council of Audio-visual Aids; First merit award for teaching, Alumni Association, School of Visual Arts.

ILLUSTRATOR: Mark Twain, *Tom Sawyer,* Dodd, 1945; Allen Bosworth, *Sancho of the Long, Long Horns,* Doubleday, 1947; John Cecil Holm, *McGarrety and the Pidgeons,* Holt, 1948; Edward Hungerford, *Escape to Danger,* Follett, 1949; Richard H. Dana, *Two Years Before the Mast* (Junior Literary Guild selection), Doubleday, 1949; Clara I. Judson, *Abe Lincoln,* Follett, 1950; Edward Hungerford, *Forbidden Island,* Follett, 1950; Glenn Batch, *Indian Fur,* Crowell, 1951; Janette Lowry, *Margaret,* Lippincott, 1951; Alden Stevens, *Lion Boys,* White Brothers, Lippincott, 1951; Clara I. Judson, *George Washington,* Follett, 1951; Francis X. Weiser, *The Christmas Book,* Harcourt, 1952; Clara I. Judson, *Thomas Jefferson: Champion of the People* (ALA Notable Children's Book), Follett, 1952; Evelyn Lampman, *Tree Wagon,* Doubleday, 1953; Pamela Brown, *Family Troupe,* Harcourt, 1953; Glenn Batch, *Indian Saddle-Up,* Crowell, 1953; Francis X. Weiser, *The Easter Book,* Harcourt, 1954; Mildred Lawrence, *Dreamboats for Trudy,* Harcourt, 1954; Clara I. Judson, *The Mighty Soo,* Follett, 1955; Dorothy Phillips, *Big Enough Boat,* Follett, 1956; Earl Miers, *Mark Twain on the Mississippi,* World, 1957; Clara I. Judson, *Benjamin Franklin,* Follett, 1957; Rutherford Montgomery, *The Silver Hills,* World, 1958; Noel Streatfeild, *Queen Victoria,* Random House, 1958; Harold Lamb, *Chief of the Cossacks,* Random House, 1959; Bruce Grant, *Cyclone,* World, 1959.

E. Ormondroyd, *The Tale of Alan,* Follett, 1960; Robert Louis Stevenson, *Treasure Island,* Doubleday, 1960; Ruth

ROBERT FRANKENBERG

Fox Hume, *Florence Nightingale,* Random House, 1960; Bruce Grant, *Zachary,* World, 1960; Jonathan Daniels, *Robert E. Lee,* Houghton, 1960; Ruth Fox Hume, *Great Men of Medicine,* Random House, 1961; Nan Agle, *Makon and the Dauphin,* Scribner, 1961; Farley Mowat, *Owls in the Family* (Junior Literary Guild selection; ALA Notable Children's Book), Little, Brown, 1961; Regina Kelly, *Abigail Adams,* Houghton, 1962; Helen Miller, *The Lucky Laceys,* Doubleday, 1962; Alma Reck, *All Aboard for Tin Cup,* Scribner, 1962; Mimi C. Levy, *Whaleboat Warriors,* Viking, 1963; Kay Hill, *Glooscap and His Magic: Legends of the Wabanaki Indians,* Dodd, 1963; László Hámori, *Adventure in Bangkok,* Harcourt, 1964; Ruth Sawyer, *Daddles,* Little, Brown, 1964; Kathryn Hitte, *The Brave and the Free,* American Book Co., 1964; Grace Brett, *Tom Paine,* Follett, 1965; Eleanor B. Heady, *Jambo, Sungura,* Norton, 1965; Alan Jenkins, *Wild Swans at Suvanto,* Norton, 1965; Janet Bartosiak, *A Dog for Ramon,* Dial, 1966; Eva Evans, *Skookum,* Houghton, 1966; James Playsted Wood, *Boston,* Seabury, 1967; Patricia Beatty, *The Lady from Black Hawk,* McGraw, 1967; Ruth Park, *Ten Cent Island,* Doubleday, 1968; Elizabeth Coatsworth, *American Adventures: 1620-1945,* Macmillan, 1968; George Sheer, *Cherokee Animal Tales,* Holiday House, 1968; Jane and Paul Annixter, *Ahmeek,* Holiday House, 1968; Michael Turner, *King Bear,* Golden Press, 1968; Stephen Meader, *The Cape May Packet,* Harcourt, 1969.

Patricia Martin, *Indians: The First Americans,* Parents' Magazine Press, 1970; Patricia Martin, *Eskimos,* Parents' Magazine Press, 1970; Selma Williams, *Fifty-five Fathers,* Dodd, 1970; Lee Bennett Hopkins, *Zoo: A Book of Poems,* Crown, 1971; Patricia Martin, *Chicanos,* Parents' Magazine Press,

(From *Glooscap and His Magic: Legends of the Wabanaki Indians* by Kay Hill. Illustrated by Robert Frankenberg.)

1971; Sid Fleischman, *McBroom's Ghost,* Grosset, 1971; Eleanor Heady, *The Soil That Feeds Us,* Parents' Magazine Press, 1972; *Here Comes Parren,* World, 1972; Solveig Russell, *Everyday Wonders: Ideas of the Past That We Use Today,* Parents' Magazine Press, 1973. Work has appeared in *Fortune, Saturday Evening Post, Medical Journal, Look, Woman's Day, Boys' Life, Esquire, Colliers, Good Housekeeping, Life, Time, Pagent, SAGA, Reader's Digest,* and has also illustrated many textbooks.

SIDELIGHTS: "As a child I was always a poor student but fascinated by books. As I look back over the years, perhaps the most significant point of my development as an illustrator was a gift of one very special book when I was eight or nine years old. This book, *Two Little Savages,* by Ernest Thompson Seton, was full of fascinating information about the outdoors, Indians, and animal lore. Over the years I have collected all of his books, some first editions.

"Although I do not consider myself an animal artist, I have hundreds of drawings of them in sketchbooks, sketched from life and included them in my illustrations whenever possible. (I have taught life drawing at the School of Visual Arts since its founding over thirty years ago.)

"Outside of art and the pure love of good drawing, books, just books are my greatest love. I read and have read books on almost any subject. Research is of great importance to any artist and especially for an illustrator who needs background information, and observation of life through sketching gives your work a sense of 'this is how it is,' a rightness, a believability.

"I've done a good deal of backpacking and camping in the United States and always the sketchbook went along waiting to be filled with ideas for the oils and watercolors I do in my studio.

"My wife and I have made many trips to Europe to see the great museums, the fascinating cities, the countrysides, and the people, sketching as we travelled—browsing in almost every bookstore we came across. Besides collecting books, I have what I think is another unique if modest hobby— lithographed paper and cardboard toy soldiers. These are difficult to come by as all date before the early part of this century. English guardsmen, Zouaves, Napoleonic and Civil War soldiers, Indians and Western cavalrymen all come out of their boxes and stand slightly askew on their little wooden stands each Christmas season—but then, a children's book illustrator should never really grow up.

''My first job was with Jenter Exhibits as artist and designer. I was associated with artists and designers from the Bauhaus which influenced my work, and my designs for murals, stage sets, and dioramas were incorporated into the exhibits for the Pennsylvania Building, North Carolina Building, the Chase Brass and Copper, and the Alcoa Aluminum exhibits for the 1939 New York World's Fair.

''My work depends on good drawing and design and a search for movement and life so I do not have a built-in technique but one that changes with the ideas I am trying to portray at a given time.''

Frankenberg's works are included in the Kerlan Collection at the University of Minnesota and in the Acquisitions Special Collections at the University of Oregon.

FOR MORE INFORMATION SEE: B. M. Miller, and others, compilers, *Illustrators of Children's Books, 1946-56*, Horn Book, 1958; Lee Kingman, and others, compilers, *Illustrators of Children's Books: 1957-1966*, Horn Book, 1968; Nick Melgin, *On-the-Spot Drawing*, Watson-Guptill, 1969; Martha E. Ward and Dorothy A. Marquardt, *Illustrators of Books for Young People*, Scarecrow, 1975; *Who's Who in American Art*, 1978–79.

FREED, Alvyn M. 1913-

PERSONAL: Born June 19, 1913, in Philadelphia, Pa.; son of Jesse (a merchant) and Amy (Jacobs) Freed; married Margaret DeHaan (a teacher and writer), May 22, 1947; children: Lawrence Douglas, Jesse Mark. *Education:* Temple University, B.S., 1938, M.A., 1948; University of Texas, Austin, Ph.D., 1955; also studied at University of California,

ALVYN M. FREED

Long hair can be beautiful, or it can be a mess.
■ (From *T.A. for Teens (And Other Important People)* by Alvyn M. Freed. Illustrated by Regina Faul-Jansen.)

Miami University, and Claremont College. *Home:* 1129 Commons Dr., Sacramento, Calif. 95825. *Office:* Jalmar Press, 6501 Elvas Ave., Sacramento, Calif. 95819.

CAREER: Physical education teacher in public schools in Philadelphia, Pa., 1940-49; school psychologist in Ventura, Calif., 1949-52: RAND Corp., Santa Monica, Calif., human factors scientist, 1955-57; System Development Corp., Santa Monica, Human factors scientist, 1957-61; Aerojet-General Corp., Sacramento, Calif., employed in quality and reliability division, 1961-64; San Juan Unified School District, Sacramento, school psychologist, 1961-64; private practice in Sacramento, 1967—; Jalmar Press, Inc., Sacramento, president and owner, 1973—. Lecturer, University of California, Riverside, 1956-59, Sacramento State College (now California State University, Sacramento), 1961-63. *Military service:* U.S. Army Air Force. 1940-46; became sergeant. *Member:* International Transactional Analysis Association, American Psychological Association, American Society for Clinical Hypnosis, California Psychological Association, Sacramento Psychological Association, Sacramento Academy for Professional and Clinical Hypnosis (founding member; first president). *Awards, honors:* Cindy Award from Industrial Film Producers Association, 1963, for film, ''Power of the Individual.''

WRITINGS: TA for Kids (and Grown Ups Too), Jalmar Press, 1971, third revision, 1978; *TA for Tots (and Other Prinzes)*, Jalmar Press, 1973; *TA for Teens (and Other Important People)*, Jalmar Press, 1976; *TA for Tots Coloring Book*, Jalmar Press, 1976; (with Herb Michelson), *Please Keep on $moking*, Jalmar Press, 1980; *TA for Tots*, Volume II, Jalmar Press,

1980. Wrote screenplay for film, "Power of the Individual," produced by Aerojet-General Corp., 1962. Contributor to journals.

ADAPTATIONS: Audio-visual packages: "Tot Pac," adapted from *TA for Tots*, "Kid Pac," based on *TA for Kids*, "Parent Pac."

SIDELIGHTS: "I have always enjoyed writing. I edited a newspaper while in the Air Force and have written columns for newspapers, professional papers and journals and articles for scientific journals before I wrote my first book, *TA for Kids (and Grown Ups, Too).*

"As a teacher and psychologist, I have been interested in people, their feelings and their relationships to each other. When I was introduced to Transactional Analysis by Dr. Thomas Harris, I found a way to help people of all ages to better understand themselves and others. By writing for very young people *(TA for Tots)* I hope to help prevent some of the problems which so many of us face as we grow up. One beautiful thing about TA is that it says you can change when you want to and you don't have to repeat or regret the mistakes of the past."

GAGLIARDO, Ruth Garver   1895(?)-1980

OBITUARY NOTICE: Born about 1895, in Hastings, Neb.; died January 5, 1980, in Wichita, Kan. Librarian, educator, book reviewer. Early in her career, Gagliardo was on the staff of the *Emporia Gazette*, where her book review column was one of the first to review books for children. From 1942-1966 she was the director of library services for the Kansas State Teachers Association. As a natural outgrowth of her work in children's literature, Gagliardo founded, in 1952, the William Allen White Children's Book Award, and was the originator of the children's Traveling Book Exhibit, which became a prototype for subsequent book fairs in others states. For children, Gagliardo edited *Let's Read Aloud. For More Information See: Publishers Weekly*, October 30, 1948; *Authors of Books for Young People*, 2nd edition, Scarecrow, 1971. *Obituaries: Publishers Weekly*, February 8, 1980; *School Library Journal*, February, 1980.

GERSON, Noel B(ertram)   1914-
(Ann Marie Burgess, Michael Burgess,
Samuel Edwards, Paul Lewis, Leon
Phillips, Carter A. Vaughan)

PERSONAL: Born November 6, 1914, in Chicago, Ill.; son of Samuel Philip and Rosa Anna (Noel) Gerson; married Cynthia Ann Vautier; married second wife, Marilyn Allen Hammond; children: (first marriage) Noel Anne Gerson Brennan; stepchildren: Michele, Margot, Paul. *Education:* University of Chicago, A.B., 1934, M.A., 1935. *Address:* 63 Pratt Ave., Clinton, Conn. 06413.

CAREER: Chicago *Herald-Examiner*, Chicago, Ill., reporter and rewrite man, 1931-36; radio station WGN, Chicago, Ill., executive, 1936-41; radio and television scriptwriter for national networks, 1936-51; author. Goodspeed Opera House Foundation, Haddam, Conn. (president); Connecticut Advocates of Arts, member of board of directors. *Military ser-*

vice: U.S. Army, Military Intelligence, World War II. *Member:* Centro Studi e Scambi Internazionali (Rome, Italy), P.E.N., Authors Guild, American Academy of Political and Social Sciences, American Historical Association, Mississippi Valley Historical Association, Phi Beta Kappa, Kappa Alpha, Linguanea Club (Jamaica, W.I.), Players Club (New York City).

WRITINGS—For children: *Nathan Hale: Espionage Agent*, Doubleday, 1960; *Rock of Freedom: The Story of the Plymouth Colony* (illustrated by Barry Martin), Messner, 1964; *The Last Wilderness: The Saga of America's Mountain Men* (illustrated by B. Martin), 1966; *Mr. Madison's War: 1812, The Second War for Independence* (illustrated by B. Martin), Messner, 1966; *Survival: Jamestown; First English Colony in America* (illustrated by B. Martin), Messner, 1967; *Passage to the West: The Great Voyages of Henry Hudson* (illustrated by B. Martin), Messner, 1968; *James Monroe: Hero of American Diplomacy* (illustrated by Tommy Upshur), Prentice-Hall, 1969; *Free and Independent: The Confederation of the United States*, Thomas Nelson, 1970.

Fiction; all published by Doubleday, except as noted: *Savage Gentleman*, 1950; *The Mohawk Ladder*, 1951; *The Cumberland Rifles*, 1952; *The Golden Eagle*, 1953; *The Impostor*, 1954; *The Forest Lord: A Romantic Adventure of 18th Century Charleston*, 1955; *The Highwayman*, 1955; *That Egyptian Woman*, 1956; *The Conqueror's Wife*, 1957; *Daughter of Eve*, 1958; *The Emperor's Ladies*, 1959; *The Yankee from Tennessee*, 1960; *The Hittite*, 1961; *The Land Is Bright*, 1961; *The Trojan*, 1962; *The Golden Lyre*, 1963; (under pseudonym Michael Burgess) *Mister*, New Authors Ltd., 1964; *Old Hickory*, 1964; *The Slender Reed: A Biographical Novel of James Knox Polk*, 1965; *Yankee Doodle Dandy: A Biographical Novel of John Hancock*, 1965; *Give Me Liberty: A Novel of Patrick Henry*, 1966; *I'll Storm Hell: A Biographical Novel of 'Mad Anthony' Wayne*, 1967; *The Swamp Fox: Francis Marion*, 1967, reissued, Mockingbird Books, 1975; *Jefferson Square: A Novel*, M. Evans, 1968; *Sam Houston: A Biographical Novel*, 1968; *The Golden Ghetto: A Novel*, M. Evans, 1969; *P.J., My Friend*, 1969.

Clear for Action!, 1970; *The Crusader: A Novel on the Life of Margaret Sanger*, Little, Brown, 1970; *Mirror, Mirror*, Morrow, 1970; *TR*, 1970; *Warhead*, 1970; *Island in the Wind: A Novel*, 1971; *Talk Show*, Morrow, 1971; *Double Vision: A Novel*, 1972; *The Sunday Heroes*, Morrow, 1972; *Temptation to Steal: A Novel*, 1972; *State Trooper*, 1973; *All That Glitters*, 1975 (published in England under pseudonym Samuel Edwards, Heineman, 1976); *Neptune*, Dodd, 1976; *Special Agent*, Dutton, 1976; *Liner: A Novel about a Great Ship*, 1977.

Nonfiction: (Under pseudonym Ann Marie and Michael Burgess) *Neither Sin nor Shame*, Belmont Books, 1961; (under pseudonym Ann Marie and Michael Burgess) *The Girl Market*, Monarch Books, 1963; *Belgium* (young adult), Macmillan, 1964; *Kit Carson: Folk Hero and Man*, Doubleday, 1964; (with Louis P. Saxe) *Sex and the Mature Man*, Gilbert Press, 1964, reissued, Simon & Schuster, 1970; *Food*, Doubleday, 1965; (with Ellen F. Birchall) *Sex and the Adult Woman*, Gilbert Press, 1965; *Light-Horse Harry: A Biography of Washington's Great Cavalryman*, Doubleday, 1966, reissued, Mockingbird Books, 1974; *The Anthem*, M. Evans, 1967; *Franklin: America's "Lost State"* (young adult), Macmillan, 1968; *The Edict of Nantes* (illustrated by Bob Pepper), Grosset, 1969; *Because I Loved Him: The Life and Loves of Lillie Langtry*, Morrow, 1971 (published in England as

Lillie Langtry: A Biography, R. Hale, 1972); *The Prodical Genius: The Life and Times of Honoré de Balzac,* Doubleday, 1972; *Daughters of Earth and Water: A Biography of Mary Wollstonecraft Shelley,* Morrow, 1973; *The Velvet Glove: A Life of Dolly Madison* (young adult), Thomas Nelson, 1975; *Harriet Beecher Stowe: A Biography,* Praeger, 1976; *Sad Swashbuckler: The Life of William Walker* (young adult), Thomas Nelson, 1976; *Statue in Search of a Pedestal: A Biography of the Marquis de Lafayette,* Dodd, 1976; *Trelawny's World: A Biography of Edward John Trelawny,* Doubleday, 1977; *The Trial of Andrew Johnson* (young adult), Thomas Nelson, 1977.

Under pseudonym Samuel Edwards: *The Scimitar,* Farrar, Straus, 1955; *The King's Messenger,* Farrar, Straus, 1956; *The Naked Maja,* McGraw, 1959; *The Queen's Husband,* McGraw, 1960; *The White Plume,* Morrow, 1961; *Master of Castile,* Morrow, 1962; *Daughter of Gascony,* Macrae, 1963; *55 Days at Peking: A Novel* (based on the screenplay by Philip Yordan and Bernard Gordon), Bantam, 1963; *The Magnificent Adventures of Alexander Mackenzie,* Redman, 1965; *Barbary General: The Life of William H. Eaton,* Prentice-Hall, 1968; *Theodora: A Novel,* Prentice-Hall, 1969; *The Divine Mistress,* McKay, 1970; *George Sand: A Biography of the First Modern, Liberated Woman,* McKay, 1973 (published in England under author's name, R. Hale, 1974); *Victor Hugo: A Tumultuous Life,* McKay, 1971, reissued as *Victor Hugo: A Biography,* New American Library, 1975; *The Double Lives of Francisco de Goya,* Grosset, 1973; *Peter Paul Rubens: A Biography of a Giant,* McKay, 1973; *The Exploiters,* Praeger, 1974; *Rebel! A Biography of Tom Paine,* Praeger, 1974; *The Caves of Guernica: A Novel,* Praeger, 1975; *The Vidocq Dossier: The Story of the World's First Detective,* Houghton, 1977.

Under pseudonym Paul Lewis: *The Nelson Touch,* Holt, 1960; *The Gentle Fury,* Holt, 1961; *Queen of Caprice: A Biography of Kristina of Sweden,* Holt, 1962; *Lady of France: A Biography of Gabrielle d'Estrees,* Funk, 1964 (published in England under pseudonym Samuel Edwards, Redman, 1964); *Queen of the Plaza: A Biography of Adah Issacs Menken,* Funk, 1964 (published in England under pseudonym Samuel Edwards, Redman, 1965); *The Great Rogue: A Biography of Captain John Smith,* McKay, 1966; *Yankee Admiral: A Biography of David Dixon Porter,* McKay, 1968; *The Grand Incendiary: A Biography of Samuel Adams,* Dial, 1973; *The Man Who Lost America: A Biography of Gentleman Johnny Burgoyne,* Dial, 1973.

Under pseudonym Leon Phillips: *When the Wind Blows,* Farrar, Straus, 1956; *Split Bamboo,* Doubleday, 1966; (for children) *The Fantastic Breed: Americans in King George's War,* Doubleday, 1968; *First Lady of America: A Romanticized Biography of Pocahontas,* Westover, 1973.

Under pseudonym Carter A. Vaughan; all published by Doubleday: *The Devil's Bride,* 1956; *The Invincibles,* 1958; *The Charlatan,* 1959; *The Wilderness,* 1959; *The Yankee Brig,* 1960; *Scoundrel's Brigade,* 1962; *The Yankee Rascals,* 1963; *Dragon Cove,* 1964; *Roanoke Warrior,* 1965; *Fortress Fury,* 1966; *The Silver Saber,* 1967; *The River Devils,* 1968; *The Seneca Hostage,* 1969.

SIDELIGHTS: Before devoting his time solely to creating fiction and nonfiction books, Gerson wrote numerous scripts for radio and television and articles for magazines. For the past three decades, however, he has devoted himself to writing books for adults and young people. His books include

When P.J. joined our family at the age of three months I told him I had paid $98 for him at the pet store on Lexington Avenue. Since he was only a kitten at the time, and therefore knew relatively little about matters of high finance, I am inclined to think he took my word. ■(From *P.J., My Friend* by Noel B. Gerson. Illustrated by Patricia Coombs.)

fiction, biography, historical fiction, and biographical fiction and have been translated into seventeen languages. ''. . .The first principle in the application of fiction techniques to nonfiction writing lies in the choice of subject. If the subject is sufficiently dramatic, the book will *read* like fiction, even though the author adheres, *as he must,* to the facts of the story he is telling.

''The rules of what-not-to-do in applying fiction techniques to nonfiction writing are even more important than a list of what-to-do. Above all:

''1. Never fictionalize (or falsify, if you please) factual data for the sake of storytelling. Your reputation depends on your accuracy.

''2. Similarly, never invent situations. Always stay within the strictly defined boundaries of what actually happened to your subject. Tell the story of his life in pungent, dramatic terms, if you wish, but don't stray from truth.

''3. Unless you find actual dialogue you can verify—as in the correspondence of a reliable, contemporary, preferably a principal in your book—never invent it. Don't give in, under any circumstances, to the temptation to write this-is-what-they-might-have-said dialogue, or even this-is-what-they must-have-said. The moment you veer into this type of writing, you are no longer doing nonfiction but fictionalized biography. If you prefer the latter, write accordingly, but be sure you label your work a biographical novel.

''Research is the core of nonfiction writing. . . . But you must teach yourself to slash away the irrelevant, and even the semi-relevant. A reader can drown in the trivial details, so you must winnow, sift, eliminate, using only those details that contribute to an overall mosaic pattern, that are significant in the elucidation of character, motivation and action. Too often, the amateur or semi-professional is so proud of

NOEL B. GERSON

his research that he wants to utilize every last snippet to prove how thorough and industrious he has been. . . .

"All of us who write for a living know the pain of discarding research material that can't be appropriately fitted into the tightly-knit fabric of a story, be it fiction or nonfiction. What it must be is *taut,* if the writer hopes to retain his reader's attention. . . .

". . .I deplore any tendency on the part of a writer to use sharply different techniques as he moves from one type of writing to the other. The fundamentals are the same: a book of nonfiction, like a novel, must be well written and must tell a significant story in clear terms, and be dramatically presented. A novel is entirely the product of the author's imagination, while the other is based on the bedrock of fact, but both rely on the literacy, taste, wit and sense of the dramatic in the man or woman who sits staring at that damnable typewriter keyboard.

"Besides, who dares to say that the factual can't be presented to the reader in imaginative, even poetic terms? Who dares to claim that a book of nonfiction must read like a seed catalog or telephone directory?" [Noel Bertram Gerson, "Fiction Techniques in Nonfiction Writing," *The Writer,* December, 1971.[1]]

Gerson combined fact and fiction in his novels, which frequently received mixed reviews from literary critics who either praised or questioned the credibility of the book's historical aspects. Gerson's first historical novel, *Savage Gentleman,* was set in the eighteenth century during the French and Indian wars. A critic for the *Chicago Sunday Tribune* noted, "*Savage Gentleman* has the merit of restraint and spare writing, tho not at the expense of color or action. Its movement is rapid and steady, and no reader will find the novel dragging at any time. Mr. Gerson's historical research seems to have been adequate, and he has indeed re-created a little known period of American history. . . ."

In reviewing Gerson's novel, *Mohawk Ladder,* a critic for the *Saturday Review of Literature* wrote, "Mr. Gerson's kind is the tale with action, plenty of it, a fast-moving plot with enough intricacies to baffle us agreeably, a sympathetic hero, a villainous villain, and somewhat perfunctory characterization." In reviewing the same book a reviewer for the *New York Herald Tribune* commented, "The narrative may not be history, but it is certainly a lusty package of entertainment."

Gerson used the Mexican War as a backdrop for his book *The Golden Eagle.* "Seldom does a historical adventure novel combine the elements of authenticity, readability and suspense as convincingly as does *The Golden Eagle,*" observed a critic for the *Springfield Republican.* A reviewer for the *New York Times* noted, "The Mexican War has figured too seldom in historical fiction; Mr. Gerson's novel rouses that somewhat torpid conflict from its long siesta and puts zip and vinegar in it."

In *The Highwayman* Gerson told a tale based upon America's colonial lifestyle in 1745. "The author displays, as in earlier books, a writing style that depends for suspense on the devices of posing threats which are never quite fulfilled, [and] raising impossibilities that are always overcome. . . . The result is that *The Highwayman* builds up to an exciting tale, mellerdrammerish in tone. It provides pleasant, light entertainment for a quiet evening. . . . But it carries little conviction that here is life as it may have been lived at a crucial period in history," wrote a reviewer for the *Chicago Sunday Tribune.* In contrast a critic for the *San Francisco Chronicle* noted, "The author takes his history seriously enough to insist on accuracy of detail, and he has skill enough to create believable people who speak in a most plausible way."

Gerson wove a fictitious tale about the lives of William the Conqueror and his consort, Matilda, in *The Conqueror's Wife.* A *Kirkus* reviewer observed, "It is a vivid picture of the times, but one stumbles now and again over Gerson's interpretation and exposition of the emotions and the thinking of the times in terms that might be placed in any modern age. Of sturdy fabric, however, the characters and the story stand the test." A critic for the *Saturday Review* commented, "Like all Gerson's historical fiction, this is competent and convincing reportage on boudoir and battlefield encounters."

Daughter of Earth and Water is one of Gerson's later novels. "[The book] is an objective and entertaining life story of one of literature's most intriguing and little-known figures," noted a critic for the *Christian Science Monitor.* While a reviewer for the *New York Times* noted, ". . . [Gerson] writes a well-paced script with a good, clean sentence. With a cast of characters like Percy Bysshe Shelley, Lord Byron, Trelawny, Leigh Hunt and Frankenstein, Mary Shelley and the reader deserve more substance."

In reviewing Gerson's most recent book, *The Trial of Andrew Johnson,* a *Booklist* critic wrote, "A prolific author of books for both adults and young people concentrates this time on Andrew Johnson, 17th president of the U.S. . . . An adulatory portrait, but readable and illuminating."

HOBBIES AND OTHER INTERESTS: Gardening and swimming.

FOR MORE INFORMATION SEE: Chicago Sunday Tribune, June 11, 1950; *Saturday Review of Literature,* July 7, 1951; *New York Herald Tribune Book Review,* July 8, 1951; *New York Times,* June 14, 1953; *Springfield Republican,* August 9, 1953; *Chicago Sunday Tribune,* November 20, 1955; *San Francisco Chronicle,* December 11, 1955; *Kirkus,* March 15, 1957; *Saturday Review,* July 6, 1957; *The Writer,* August, 1970, December, 1971, July, 1978; *Christian Science Monitor,* January 31, 1973; *New York Times Book Review,* February 11, 1973; *Booklist,* May 1, 1977.

GILGE, Jeanette 1924-

PERSONAL: Surname is pronounced with two hard "g"s; born March 31, 1924, in Phillips, Wis.; daughter of Edward and Emma (Meier) Kudrna; married Kenneth Gilge, September 26, 1942; children: Donna (Mrs. Ron Childress), Kent, Karl, Dean; (foster children) Janice (Mrs. Paul Stevko), Dennis. *Education:* Attended Triton College, 1971-74. *Religion:* Christian. *Home:* 1010 North Seventh Ave., Maywood, Ill. 60153.

CAREER: Writer. Lecturer; Christian broadcasting volunteer worker. *Member:* Children's Reading Round Table (Chicago), Off Campus Writers (Winnetka, Ill.), Penhandlers. *Awards, honors:* Triton Summer Writer's Workshop award, 1974; David C. Cook juvenile award, 1975, for *City-Kid Farmer.*

WRITINGS: Never Miss a Sunset (adult), David Cook, 1975; *City-Kid Farmer* (juvenile), David Cook, 1975; *Growing Up Summer,* David Cook, 1976.

WORK IN PROGRESS: A non-fiction book tentatively titled *This New Life,* concerning her commitment to Christ; *Look To The Sunset,* a book on aging.

SIDELIGHTS: "Little did I know, as I rode past a certain farm on the school bus day after day, that I would one day write about it in my books *(City-Kid Farmer* and *Growing-Up Summer).* I swam in the lake, 'Stone Lake' is its real name, in the summer and skated on it in the winter. We had a toboggan slide like the one I wrote about, too.

"'Mark' is a fictional character but I used many of my son Dean's experiences—including getting drunk at the school picnic. Dean is twenty-one now, works as a herdsman on a large Wisconsin farm, and doesn't drink. He and his new bride are much like Jeff and Lou Ann.

"The characters in *Never Miss a Sunset* are real people. 'Baby' Roy (Meier) still lives in that house and enjoys greeting the many visitors who come to see his museum 'Meier's Yesterday House,' and the locale of 'Sunset.' (It is located about twenty miles west of Tomahawk, Wisconsin, off highway 86 on county trunk YY.)

"I have received many letters asking what happened to the people in 'Sunset.' Briefly; Ellen did marry Henry, they had seven children and lived in the neighborhood all their lives. Ellen died before the book was published, but she helped fill in many details. 'Papa' died of cancer in 1919 (at age 59) while 'little' Eddie was in the army in France. Eddie became a rural mail carrier and had fourteen children. 'Mama' did have more children; Emma, my mother, Carl and Henry. My mother died when I was six weeks old and 'Mama,' my

JEANETTE GILGE

grandmother, reared me. I grew up in that house, which now had the kitchen addition, I sat on that oven door, fished and played in the river and walked its banks many hours as my grandmother told about many of the incidents I wrote about. We'd pick violets in the spring and we'd pull the high grass away from the rose bushes that marked the little grave.

"My closest friends were my cousins, Ruby, Al's daughter, Grace and Myrtle, Ellen's daughters. I spent much time alone and still like to be alone at times. I wish every child could have quiet hours alone, a river to play in, tall grass to run through, time to think, time to plan, time to question and time to listen to the answers."

HOBBIES AND OTHER INTERESTS: Nature and the out-of-doors, reading, hiking, bicycle riding.

Come away, O human child!
To the waters and the wild
With a faery, hand in hand,
For the world's more full of weeping than you can understand.

                             —William Butler Yeats

MARGERY JEAN GILL

GILL, Margery Jean   1925-

PERSONAL: Born April 5, 1925, in Coatbridge, Scotland; married in 1946; children: two daughters. *Education:* Attended Harrow School of Art; graduated from Royal College of Art, England, 1951. *Home:* England.

CAREER: Illustrator. Began drawing as a child; turned to illustrating books as a means of working while remaining at home; has also taught art.

ILLUSTRATOR: Anita Hewett, *A Honey Mouse, and Other Stories,* John Lane, 1957; Rene Guillot, *The Blue Day* (translation from the French by Gwen Marsh), Bodley Head, 1958, Abelard, 1959; Margaret Kornitzer, *Mr. Fairweather and His Family,* Bodley Head, 1960; A. Hewett, *The Tale of the Turnip,* Bodley Head, 1961, McGraw, 1961; Walter J. De La Mare, editor, *Tom Tiddler's Ground: A Book of Poetry for Children,* Bodley Head, 1961, Knopf, 1962; Ruth Mabel Arthur, *Dragon Summer,* Hutchinson, 1962, Atheneum, 1963; Barbara Bingley, *The Story of Tit-Be and His Friend Mouffette,* Abelard, 1962; Paul-Jacques Bonson, *The Gold Cross of Santa Anna* (translation from the French by Thelma Niklaus), University of London Press, 1962, published in America as *Pursuit in the French Alps,* Lothrop, 1963; William Mayne, *The Last Bus,* Hamish Hamilton, 1962; Andrew Lang, *Fifty Favourite Fairy Tales,* edited by Kathleen Lines, Nonesuch, 1963, F. Watts, 1964; Jose Maria Sanchez-Silva, *The Boy and the Whale,* Bodley Head, 1963, McGraw, 1964; M. Jean Craig, *What Did You Dream?,* Abelard, 1964; Eleanor Graham, editor, *A Thread of Gold,* Bodley Head, 1964, Books for Libraries, 1969; William Mayne, *A Day Without Wind,* Dutton, 1964.

Lucy Maria Boston, *The Castle of Yew,* Harcourt, 1965; Susan Cooper, *Over Sea, Under Stone,* J. Cape, 1965, Harcourt, 1966; Rosalie Kingsmill Fry, *The Castle Family,* Dent, 1965, Dutton, 1966; R. K. Fry, *September Island,* Dent, 1965, Dutton, 1965; Elisabeth Beresford, *The Hidden Mill,* Benn, 1965, Meredith Press, 1967; Edward Thomas, *Four and Twenty Blackbirds,* Bodley Head, 1965, published in America as *The Complete Fairy Tales of Edward Thomas,* F. Watts, 1966; Peter Vansittart, *The Dark Tower: Tales from the Past,* Macdonald & Co., 1965, Crowell, 1969; R. M. Arthur, *A Candle in Her Room,* Atheneum, 1966; Susan Coolidge (pseudonym of Sarah Chauncey Woolsey), *What Katy Did,* Rylee, 1966; W. Mayne, *The Old Zion,* Hamish Hamilton, 1966, Dutton, 1967; Norah Montgomerie, editor, *This Little Pig Went to Market,* Bodley Head, 1966; Marjorie A. Sindall, *Three Cheers for Charlie,* Oliver & Boyd, 1966, Criterion, 1968; R. M. Arthur, *Requiem for a Princess* (Junior Literary Guild selection), Atheneum, 1967; E. Beresford, *Looking for a Friend,* Benn, 1967; R. M. Arthur, *Portrait of Margarita,* Atheneum, 1968; Barbara Ker Wilson, editor, *Australian Kaleidoscope,* Collins, 1968, Meredith Press, 1969; R. M.

I went and sat by the window holding the medallion to the light, turning it this way and that, polishing it with my handkerchief, hardly able to believe my astonishing luck in finding it. ■ (From *Requiem for a Princess* by Ruth M. Arthur. Illustrated by Margery Gill.)

Arthur, *The Whistling Boy*, Atheneum, 1969; Christina Georgina Rossetti, *Doves and Pomegranates: Poems for Young Readers*, edited by David Powell, Bodley Head, 1969, Macmillan, 1971.

R. M. Arthur, *The Saracen Lamp*, Atheneum, 1970; S. Cooper, *Dawn of Fear* (ALA Notable Book), Harcourt, 1970; Joseph Jacobs, *English Fairy Tales*, Penguin, 1970; R. M. Arthur, *The Little Dark Thorn*, Atheneum, 1971; A. Lang, *Selection from Andrew Lang's Fairy Tales*, edited by Alice Dickinson, F. Watts, 1971; V. Corinne Renshaw, *Thalassine*, Warne, 1971; Jakob Ludwig Karl Grimm, *Briar Rose: The Story of the Sleeping Beauty*, Walck, 1972; R. M. Arthur, *The Autumn People*, Atheneum, 1973; R. M. Arthur, *After Candlemas*, Atheneum, 1974; R. M. Arthur, *On The Wasteland*, Atheneum, 1975; Helen Cresswell, *Butterfly Chase*, Penguin, 1975; Joseph Jacobs, *Jack and the Beanstalk*, Walck, 1975; R. M. Arthur, *An Old Magic*, Atheneum, 1977; A. Lang, *The Rainbow Fairy Book: A Selection of Outstanding Fairy Tales from the Color Fairy Books*, edited by Kathleen Lines, Schocken, 1977.

SIDELIGHTS: Born **April 5, 1925** in Coatbridge, Scotland, Gill writes: "I have been drawing for as long as I can remember and was pretty set in my ways by the time I was four years old." [Lee Kingman, editor, *Illustrators of Children's Books: 1957-1966*, Horn Book, 1968.[1]]

After the birth of her two daughters, Gill turned to illustration as a means of working while remaining at home. "[My daughters] make me feel like Grandma Moses only less successful. The need to earn, yet remain at home, turned me to illustration. I did one or two books between 1947 and 1952, but I didn't really get going until about 1954. So far as materials and techniques are concerned, I've done more black-and-white drawing for reproduction in line than anything else. I have done a certain amount of full color work, but hope to do a great deal more in the next year or so."[1]

"To me drawing is a compulsion, like biting one's nails. The only time I don't draw is when I am on holiday; only then can I relax.

"My favourite books are anthologies. I can interpret each story or poem differently and the challenge is in liking them together. I was intrigued when I was drawing for Edward Thomas' *Four and Twenty Blackbirds*, for I cannot believe that he wrote those stories seriously. I have the feeling that he was irritated by the sayings and that his stories were a form of attack on them, and I illustrated them in a similar frame of mind. It is a set of drawings that I like." [Judy Taylor, "Introducing Illustrators: Margery Gill," *The Junior Bookshelf*, October, 1966.[2]]

A children's editor offers the following opinion of Gill's work: "Her work is distinguished by a total lack of sentimentality: it is strong, full of character, absolutely down to earth, yet illuminated by a special kind of warmth and tenderness. Her drawing is completely honest—you feel as you look at her children that this is the way children *are,* they are flesh and blood, with hopes and fears, sudden terrors and simple joys. She has been criticised on the grounds that her children look 'too solemn,' but surely this is all part of her realism? The average facial expression in repose *is* reflective, not perpetually split by a meaningless grin. Look at the drawings on pages 23, 41 and 67 of *This Little Pig Went to Market* (Norah Montgomerie). Where is the solemnity here? These are real children enjoying real moments, and one's response to them

is immediate. Again, look at the illustration on page 139 of *The Gentle Heritage* (Frances E. Crompton). What other artist could illustrate so poignant an incident with such insight? Her imaginative approach to traditional tales can be seen in the Nonesuch Cygnet edition of *Fifty Favourite Fairy Tales* by Andrew Lang, which is superbly illustrated. The essence of Margery Gill's art is humanity. She knows what makes people tick and she has a rare gift for communicating this in her work."[2]

FOR MORE INFORMATION SEE: Judy Taylor, "Introducing Illustrators: Margery Gill," *The Junior Bookshelf*, October, 1966; Lee Kingman, editor, *Illustrators of Children's Books: 1957-1966*, Horn Book, 1968; *Horn Book*, October, 1975.

GILMORE, Iris   1900-

PERSONAL: Born September 4, 1900, near Cairo, Ill.; daughter of C.W.B. Pavey (a merchant); married Harold Gilmore (a director of religious education; died 1975); children: Diane, Ross. *Education:* Schuster-Martin School of Drama, B.A., 1921; University of Denver, M.A., 1944. *Religion:* Methodist. *Home:* 1638 Clermont St., Denver, Colo. 80220.

CAREER: Writer. KOA-Radio (now National Broadcasting Corp. [NBC-Radio]), Denver, Colo., radio actress and drama director, 1924-30; Gilmore worked for ten years as co-director of the Children's Theatre in Denver and spent another ten years as a professor of speech and English at the University of Denver. *Member:* American Association of University Women, Children's Writers Club, Colorado Authors' League, Denver Women's Club. *Awards, honors:* Boy's Life-Dodd, Mead Prize (shared with Marian Talmadge), 1956, for *Pony Express Boy;* nine Top Hand awards from Colorado Authors' League for best books.

WRITINGS—All with Marian Talmadge; all juvenile, unless otherwise indicated: *Pony Express Boy*, Dodd, 1956; *Wings of Tomorrow: The Adventure of a Cadet at the Air Force Academy*, Dodd, 1958; *Wings for Peace: A Story of Cadet Frank Barton of the Air Force Academy*, Dodd, 1959; *Colorado Hi-Ways and By-Ways: Picturesque Trails and Tours* (travel), Monitor Publications, 1959, 3rd edition published as *Colorado Hi-Ways and By-Ways: A Comprehensive Guide to Picturesque Trails and Tours*, Pruett, 1976; *This Is the Air Force Academy*, Dodd, 1961; *Let's Go to the United States Air Force Academy*, Putnam, 1962; *Let's Go to a Truck Terminal*, Putnam, 1964; *NORAD: The North American Air Defense Command*, Dodd, 1967; *Six Great Horse Rides*, Putnam, 1968; *Emma Edmonds: Nurse and Spy*, Putnam, 1970; *Barney Ford, Black Baron*, Dodd, 1973.

WORK IN PROGRESS: Research on her descendant, Benjamin West, for a biography.

SIDELIGHTS: "My childhood was Elysian in that fairy land of magnolia trees and flowering hillsides in the Delta area of the Ohio and Mississippi rivers in southern Illinois. Strawberry farming was the main industry and I watched the hundreds of 'barefoot black pickers' come shuffling up the roadway from Kentucky and Tennessee to live in the shanties during 'the season.'

"I was endowed with a vivid imagination and everything was a story book unfolding before me. My report cards emphasized this overly dramatic imagination, and 'make-believe' world as contrasted to my disinterest in mathematics and science. My ministerial grandparents were shocked beyond belief at the strange little girl who was play-acting from the age of three straight through until now. After graduation from drama school I came to Denver, remembering the years with favorite teachers, including Robert Frost, Mrs. Joyce Kilmer, and Tyrone Power, Sr. I tried out for a part at the new, wonderful radio station in Denver and became one of the first radio actresses in the United States. This started a glamorous and exciting career in radio acting.

"I became very involved in the world of youth with my late husband, Harold, in our mountain camp, Geneva Glen, in Indian Hills, Colorado. Because of my busy time with my children, my collaborator, the late Marian Talmadge, had more flexibility with her time and more energy than I, and did much more digging, researching and detailed work. Our last book, *Barney Ford, Black Baron,* offers me a dream: the increasing interest on the part of producers for a film of that wonderful man. He was a slave who escaped by underground railroad to the gold rush of Colorado, became a most affluent person in financial and political circles locally and nationally, and kept Colorado from statehood for ten years until they permitted the blacks to vote.

IRIS GILMORE

"I have a new novel for teenagers, about the Cajun-Louisiana country called *Bon Patriots of the Bayou* which is presently being considered by a publishers."

Emma Edmonds disguised herself as a man and served during the Civil War as soldier, "male" nurse, and spy.
■(From *Emma Edmonds: Nurse and Spy* by Marian Talmadge and Iris Gilmore. Illustrated by Lee J. Ames.)

GLES, Margaret Breitmaier   1940-

PERSONAL: Born December 7, 1940, in New York, N.Y.; daughter of Gottlob (a contractor) and Elisabeth (Linder) Breitmaier; married Carlos R. Gles (an architect), November 26, 1969. *Education:* Cazenovia College, A.A.S., 1960; attended Hunter College of the City University of New York, 1969-70; George Mason Univeristy, B.S., 1973; University of Virginia, further study in reading and learning disabilities. *Home:* 2813 East West Highway, Chevy Chase, Md. 20015.

CAREER: B. Altman & Co., New York, N.Y., assistant buyer, 1960-63; Wallachs, New York, N.Y., assistant to men's clothing manager and buyer, 1963-64; Roaman's Mail Order, Inc., New York, N.Y., administrative assistant to general manager, 1964-65; *Chemical Week,* New York, N.Y., advertising service manager and production manager of "Buyers Guide," 1965-69; substitute teacher of kindergarten and elementary school in Virginia, 1973-74; full-time elementary school teacher in Sterling, Va., 1974—.

WRITINGS: Come and Play Hide and Seek, Garrard, 1975. Correspondent, *Commentary,* 1969-70.

Let's look in here. ■ (From *Come Play Hide and Seek* by Margaret Gles. Illustrated by Lou Cunette.)

SIDELIGHTS: "I feel it is extremely important for children to be exposed to varied literature which is easy and enjoyable for them to read. This not only helps them to read better but increases their literary interest as they mature."

HOBBIES AND OTHER INTERESTS: Knitting, needlepoint (designs her own), music, theatre and cooking.

GOETZ, Delia   1898-

PERSONAL: Born in June, 1898, near Wesley, Iowa; daughter of Joseph (a farmer) and Elizabeth (Matern) Goetz. Education: Graduated from Iowa State Teachers' College, 1922.

CAREER: Author, translator, and teacher. Has taught in many places, including Panama, Cuba, and Guatemala, as well as Minot Teacher's College in North Dakota. Translator at the Guatemalan Embassy in Washington, D.C.; later worked for the Foreign Policy Association and, during World War II, for the Pan American Union and the U.S. Office of Education; staff member of the U.S. Office of Education, Division of International Educational Relations, beginning 1946.

WRITINGS: The Good Neighbors: The Story of the Two Americas (illustrated by Juan Oliver), Foreign Policy Association, 1939; *Neighbors to the South,* Harcourt, 1941, revised edition, 1956; *Letters from Guatemala* (illustrated by Katharine Knight), D. C. Heath, 1941; *Panchita, a Little Girl of Guatemala* (illustrated by Charlotte A. Chase), Harcourt, 1941; *The Incas,* [Washington, D.C.], 1942; *Teamwork in the Americas* (illustrated by Aline Appel), Foreign Policy As-

sociation, 1943; *Half a Hemisphere: The Story of Latin America* (illustrated by Chase), Harcourt, 1943; *The Dragon and the Eagle: America Looks at China* (illustrated by Thomas Handforth), Foreign Policy Association, 1944; *Russia and America: Old Friends-New Neighbors* (illustrated by Louis Slobodkin), Foreign Policy Association, 1945; *The Burro of Barnegat Road* (illustrated by Hilda Van Stockum), Harcourt, 1945.

Education in Panama, Office of Education, Federal Security Agency, 1948; *Other Young Americans: Latin America's Young People,* Morrow, 1948; *Education in Venezuela,* Office of Education, Federal Security Agency, 1948; *World Understanding Begins With Children,* Office of Education, Federal Security Agency, 1949; *The Hidden Burro* (illustrated by Dorothy B. Morse), Morrow, 1949; *Let's Read about South America,* Fideler, 1950; *Deserts* (illustrated by Louis Darling), Morrow, 1956; *Tropical Rain Forests* (illustrated by Darling), Morrow, 1957; *South America,* Fideler, 1958; *The Arctic Tundra* (illustrated by Darling), Morrow, 1958; *At Home Around the World,* Ginn, 1958, reissued, 1965; *Grasslands* (illustrated by Darling), Morrow, 1959.

At Home in Our Land, Ginn, 1961; *Swamps* (illustrated by L. Darling), Morrow, 1961; *Mountains* (illustrated by Darling), Morrow, 1962; *Islands of the Ocean* (illustrated by Darling), Morrow, 1964; (translator with Adrian Recinos) *The Annals of Cakchiquels,* University of Oklahoma Press, 1967; *Rivers* (illustrated by John Kaufman), Morrow, 1969; *State Capital Cities,* Morrow, 1971; *Lakes* (illustrated by Lydia Rosier), Morrow, 1973; *Valleys* (illustrated by Leslie Morrill), Morrow, 1976. Also author of pamphlets for the Pan American Union and the Foreign Policy Association.

After a hard rain water runs in the gutters of some streets. Place an obstacle that stops the flow in the stream. Immediately the water backs up behind the obstacle and makes a small pool. On a much larger scale a lake may form in the same way. ■ (From *Lakes* by Delia Goetz. Illustrated by Lydia Rosier.)

SIDELIGHTS: Goetz's career has taken her throughout Central and South America. Many of the author's earlier works have been based on her personal knowledge about the culture and people of the Latin American countries. A Horn Book critic reviewing Goetz's Panchita: A Little Girl of Guatemala, wrote, "Details about the ancient art [of pottery making] . . . accompany the gentle story which introduces a little girl with real personality and charm. . . ."

A book dealing with life in other areas of the world is Islands of the Oceans. "Unusual examples of island plants and animals and of the people of isolated islands . . . are described in particularly interesting chapters. . . ," noted a reviewer for Horn Book.

One of Goetz's more recent books, Rivers, was described by a Library Journal reviewer as "A straightforward, knowledgeable exposition . . . of basic facts about rivers. The materials on life and ecology along the riverbank, and on the development and effects of pollution are particularly timely. . . ."

FOR MORE INFORMATION SEE: Current Biography, H. W. Wilson, 1949.

GRIMM, Jacob Ludwig Karl   1785-1863
and
GRIMM, Wilhelm Karl   1786-1859

PERSONAL: Sons of a lawyer. Both born in Hanau, Hesse-Cassel, Germany; Jacob born January 4, 1785; died September 20, 1863, in Berlin, Germany; buried in Berlin next to Wilhelm. Wilhelm born February 24, 1786; died December 16, 1859, in Berlin; married Dorothea Wild, May 15, 1825. Education: Both attended the University of Marburg, and qualified as lawyers. Home: Berlin, Germany.

CAREER: Literary scholars, philologists, collectors and writers of folk tales. Jacob was employed in the Minister of War's Office in Cassel, and later became librarian to the King of Westphalia, auditor to his council of state, 1808, and secretary to the Ambassador of the Elector of Hesse at Paris, 1814. Wilhelm was employed for many years as an assistant librarian at the University of Göttingen. Both brothers were appointed professors of German literature and librarians at the University of Göttingen, 1830-37. Because of his political views, Wilhelm was dismissed from his office. The King of Prussia secured teaching positions for both brothers at the University of Berlin, 1840.

Awards, honors: The Fisherman and His Wife (illustrated by Madeleine Gekiere) was among the New York Times Choice of Best Illustrated Children's Books of the Year, 1957; The Seven Ravens (illustrated by Felix Hoffmann) received the Book World Children's Spring Book Festival Award, 1963; The Wren and the Bear was selected for the American Institute of Graphic Arts Children's Book Show, 1971-72.

WRITINGS—Collected fairy tales: Kinder und Hausmärchen, three volumes, [Berlin], 1812-22, first English translation, by Edgar Taylor, published as German Popular Tales, two volumes (illustrated by George Cruikshank), [London], 1823-26, reprinted Scolar Press (Menston, England), 1971, new translation by Ralph Manheim, published as Grimm's Tales for Young and Old: The Complete Stories, Doubleday, 1977.

Other collected editions in English translation appear in numerous and variously-titled editions, including the following: The Fairy Ring (translated by John Edward Taylor; illustrated by Richard Doyle), J. Murray, 1846; Household Stories, two volumes (illustrated by Edward Henry Wehnert), Addey, 1853 [other editions include those illustrated by Walter Crane (translated by Lucy Crane), Macmillan, 1882, reissued, McGraw, 1966; Johannes Troyer, Macmillan, 1954; Grimm's Goblins (illustrated by Phiz, pseudonym of Hablot Knight Brown), S. Vickers, 1861; Grimm's Household Tales, two volumes (translated and edited by Margaret Hunt), H. G. Bohn, 1884, reissued, Singing Tree Press, 1968 other edition illustrated by Robert Anning Bell, Dutton, 1901; Fairy Tales from Grimm (illustrated by Gordon Browne), Wells, Gardner, 1895; Fairy Tales (illustrated by E. Stuart Hardy and others), Nister, 1898 [other editions include those illustrated by Arthur Rackham (translated by Alice "Mrs. Edgar" Lucas), Freemantle, 1900; Lancelot Speed, Pearson, 1904; Hope Dunlap, Rand McNally, 1913; Floyd Hildebrand, Peter Pauper Press, 1941; Fritz Wegner, Blackie, 1959; Lucille Corcos, Heritage Press, 1962; Ulrik Schramm, Walck, 1962].

Grimm's Fairy Tales (illustrated by Helen Stratton), Blackie & Son, 1905 [other editions illustrated by Charles Robinson, Jerrold, 1910; Millicent Sowerby, F. A. Stokes, 1910; Charles Folkard, A. & C. Black, 1911; John Robert Monsell, Cassell, 1913; Noel Pocock, Hodder & Stoughton, 1913; Monro S. Orr, Harrap, 1914; Louis Rhead, Harper, 1917; Elenore Abbott, Scribner, 1920; Ruth Moorwood and Harry Rountree, Thomas Nelson, 1932; Fritz Kredel, Stackpole, 1937; Josef Scharl, Pantheon, 1944; Helen Sewell and Madeleine Gekiere, Oxford University Press, 1954; Leonard Weisgard, Junior Deluxe Editions, 1954; Shirley Hughes, Hutchinson Educational, 1960; Jiri Trnka, P. Hamlyn, 1961; Janusz Grabianski, Duell, Sloan, 1962; Arthur Rackham, Viking, 1973].

Favourite Tales from Jakob and Wilhelm Grimm (illustrated by Thomas Heath Robinson), Collins, 1908; Stories from Grimm (edited by Amy Stedman; illustrated by H. Rountree), Dutton, circa 1908; Grimm's Animal Stories (translated by L. Crane; illustrated by John Rae), Duffield, 1909; Tales from Grimm (translated and illustrated by Wanda Gág), Coward-McCann, 1936; Three Gay Tales from Grimm (translated and illustrated by W. Gág), Coward-McCann, 1943; The Complete Grimm's Fairy Tales (edited by James Stern; illustrated by J. Scharl), Pantheon, 1944, reissued, 1976; Household Tales (illustrated by Mervyn Peake), Eyre & Spottiswoode, 1946, revised edition, Methuen, 1973; More Tales from Grimm (translated and illustrated by W. Gág), Coward-McCann, 1947; Favorite Fairy Tales Told in Germany (edited by Virginia Haviland; illustrated by Susanne Suba), Little, Brown, 1959; Stories That Never Grow Old, Random House, 1966; About Wise Men and Simpletons: Twelve Tales from Grimm (translated by Elizabeth Shub; illustrated by Nonny Hogrogian), Macmillan, 1971.

Single tales published separately or as title stories of collections: Clever Hans (illustrated by John Lawson), De La Rue, 1883; The Magic Mirror, and Other Stories (translated by Ella Boldey; illustrated by Richard Andre), McLoughlin, 1890; The Shepherd's Dream (translated by Mary A. Sprague; illustrated by Rose Mueller Sprague), L. Prang, 1893; The House in the Wood, and Other Old Fairy Stories (illustrated by L. Leslie Brooke), F. Warne, 1910, reissued, 1962; The Ogre with the Three Golden Hairs, and Other Stories (illustrated by Susan B. Pearse), F. A. Stokes, 1915, also published as The Giant with Three Golden Hairs (illustrated by Gustaf

WILHELM AND JACOB GRIMM

So he did his work seven years in hell, did not wash, comb, or trim himself or cut his hair or nails, or wash the water out of his eyes, and the seven years seemed so short to him that he thought he had only been half a year. ■ (From "The Devil's Sooty Brother" in *The Complete Grimm's Fairy Tales* by the Brothers Grimm. Illustrated by Josef Scharl.)

Tenggren), Simon & Schuster, 1955; *Little Brother and Little Sister, and Other Tales* (illustrated by A. Rackham), Dodd, 1917; *Hansel and Gretel, and Other Tales* (translated by A. Lucas; illustrated by A. Rackham), Dutton, 1920 [other editions illustrated by Kay Nielsen, Hodder & Stoughton, 1925; Warren Chappell, Knopf, 1944; Henry C. Pitz, Limited Editions Club, 1952; Eloise Wilkin, Simon & Schuster, 1954; Arnold Lobel, Delacorte, 1971; Tadasu Izawa and Shigemi Hijikata, Grosset, 1971; Celine Leopold, Walck, 1971], also published as *Nibble, Nibble, Mousekin: A Tale of Hansel and Gretel* (edited and illustrated by Joan Walsh Anglund), Harcourt, 1962.

Snowdrop and Other Tales ("Schneewitchen"; illustrated by A. Rackham), Constable, 1920, also published as *Snow White, and Other Stories* (illustrated by Wuanita Smith and Edward Shenton), G. W. Jacobs, 1922 [other editions illus-

(From *Household Stories* from the collection of the Brothers Grimm by Lucy Crane. Illustrated by Walter Crane.)

trated by Walt Disney Studio, McKay, 1937; W. Gág, Cow-ard-McCann, 1938; Nancy Ekholm Burkert, Farrar, Straus, 1972; F. Wegner, Walck, 1973; another edition translated by Paul Heins, illustrated by Trina Schart Hyman, Little, Brown, 1974]; *The Golden Bird, and Other Stories* ("Der Goldene Vogel"; illustrated by W. Smith and E. Shenton), G. W. Jacobs, 1922 [another edition translated by Richard Sadler, illustrated by Lilo Fromm, Doubleday, 1970]; *The Enchanted Fawn* (illustrated by Robert A. Graef), Mc-Loughlin, 1942; *Adventure of Chanticleer and Partlet* (illustrated by Hans E. Fischer), Cassell, 1947; *The Golden Goose* ("Die Goldene Gans"; illustrated by Arnold E. Bare), Houghton, 1947.

The Traveling Musicians ("Die Bremer Stadtmusikanten"; illustrated by H. E. Fischer), Cassell, 1948 [another edition edited by Edith Lowe; illustrated by Dolli Tingle, Follett, 1965], also published as *The Musicians of Bremen* (illustrated by J. P. Miller), Simon & Schuster, 1954 [another edition illustrated by Svend Otto, Larousse, 1974]; also published as *The Four Musicians* (illustrated by Tony Palazzo), Doubleday, 1962, and as *The Bremen Town Musicians* (illustrated by Paul Galdone), McGraw, 1968; *The Fisherman and His Wife* ("Vom Fischer und Seiner Frau"; illustrated by M. Gekiere), Pantheon, 1957 [other editions illustrated by Margot Zemach, Norton, 1966; Katria Brandt, Follett, 1970]; *The Good-for-Nothings* (illustrated by H. E. Fischer), Harcourt, 1957; *The Wolf and the Seven Little Kids* ("Der Wolf und die Sieben Jungen Geislein"; illustrated by Felix Hoffmann), Oxford University Press, 1958 [another edition illustrated by Jose Correas, World Publishing, 1965]; *The Sleeping Beauty* ("Dornröschen"; translated by Peter Collier, illustrated by

(From *Grimm's Fairy Tales* by the Brothers Grimm. Illustrated by Frank Schoonover.)

In her rage she seized Rapunzel's beautiful hair, twisted it twice round her left hand, snatched up a pair of shears and cut off the plaits, which fell to the ground. ■ (From "Rapunzel" in *Grimm's Fairy Tales*, translated by Mrs. Edgar Lucas. Illustrated by Arthur Rackham.)

F. Hoffmann), Oxford University Press, 1959, Harcourt, 1960 [another edition illustrated by Wayne Brown, Childrens Press, 1969], also published as *Briar Rose:The Story of the Sleeping Beauty* (illustrated by Margery Gill), Walck, 1972.

Rapunzel (translated by Katya Sheppard; illustrated by F. Hoffmann), Oxford University Press, 1960, Harcourt, 1961 [another edition translated by James Dobson, illustrated by Bernadette Watts, Dobson, 1975]; *The Seven Ravens* (illustrated by F. Hoffmann), Harcourt, 1963; *The Elves and the Shoemaker* ("Die Wichtelmänner"; illustrated by Manning de Villeneuve Lee), Rand McNally, 1959 [other editions illustrated by Adrienne Adams, Scribner, 1960; T. Izawa and S. Hijikata, Grosset, 1971; Richard Hefter, Small World Enterprises, 1973; Brinton Turkle, Four Winds Press, 1975], also published as *The Secret Shoemakers, and Other Stories* (edited by James Reeves; illustrated by Edward Ardizzone), Abelard, 1966; *The Frog King, and Other Tales* ("Der Frosch-König"; illustrated by Sheila Greenwald), New American Library, 1964, also published as *The Frog Prince*

(illustrated by P. Galdone), McGraw, 1974 [another edition illustrated by James Marshall, Four Winds Press, 1974]; *Snow White and Rose Red* ("Schneeweisschen und Rosenroth"; translated by Wayne Andrews; illustrated by A. Adams), Scribner, 1964 [another edition illustrated by Barbara Cooney, Delacorte, 1966].

The Brave Little Tailor ("Tapfere Schneiderlein"; edited by Edith Lowe; illustrated by D. Tingle), Follett, 1965, also published as *The Valiant Little Tailor* (illustrated by Anne Maria Jauss), Harvey House, 1967; *Lucky Hans* ("Hans im Glck"; edited by Evalyn Kinkead; illustrated by Emile Probst), McGraw, 1966, also published as *Hans in Luck* (illustrated by F. Hoffmann), Atheneum, 1975; *The Old Goose Woman* (edited by Eve Rouke; illustrated by Pablo Ramirez), World Publishing, 1966; *The Twelve Dancing Princesses* (translated by E. Shub; illustrated by Uri Shulevitz), Scribner, 1966; *The Cold Flame* (edited by J. Reeves; illustrated by Charles Keeping), Hamish Hamilton, 1967, Meredith Press, 1969; *The Four Clever Brothers* (illustrated by F.

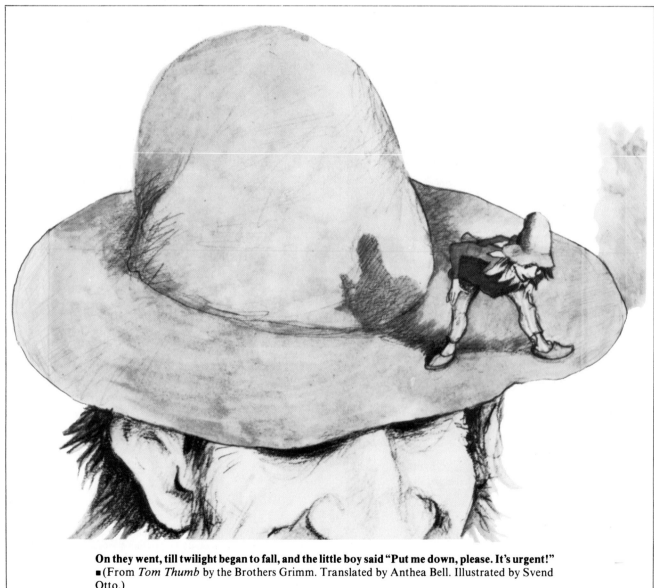

On they went, till twilight began to fall, and the little boy said "Put me down, please. It's urgent!"
■ (From *Tom Thumb* by the Brothers Grimm. Translated by Anthea Bell. Illustrated by Svend Otto.)

She kept ever going on and on until she came to the end of the world. ■ (From "The Seven Ravens" in *Fairy Tales of the Brothers Grimm,* translated by Mrs. Edgar Lucas. Illustrated by Arthur Rackham.)

Hoffmann), Harcourt, 1967; *Rumpelstiltskin* (illustrated by Jacqueline Ayer), Harcourt, 1967 [other editions illustrated by William Stobbs, Walck, 1971; Edward Gorey, Four Winds Press, 1974].

Jorinda and Joringel (illustrated by Adrienne Adams), Scribner, 1968 [another edition illustrated by Bernadette Watts, World Publishing, 1970]; *The Horse, the Fox, and the Lion* ("Der Fuchs und das Pferd"; edited and illustrated by P. Galdone), Seabury, 1963; *King Thrushbeard* ("König Drosselbart"; edited and illustrated by Kurt Werth), Viking, 1968

[another edition illustrated by F. Hoffmann, Harcourt, 1970], also published as *King Grisly-Beard* (translated by E. Taylor; illustrated by Maurice Sendak), Farrar, Straus, 1973; *Little Red Riding Hood* (illustrated by Harriet Pincus), Harcourt, 1968 [another edition illustrated by B. Watts, World Publishing, 1969]; *The Hedgehog and the Hare* ("Der Hase und der Igel"; edited and illustrated by Wendy Watson), World Publishing, 1969; *Mother Carey* ("Frau Hölle"; translated by R. Sadler; illustrated by Regine Grube-Heinecke), Sadler, 1969, also published as *Mother Holly* (edited and illustrated by B. Watts), Crowell, 1972.

She found...ripe strawberries poking up dark red out of the snow. ■ (From *Grimm's Fairy Tales* by the Brothers Grimm. Illustrated by Charles Folkard.)

Six Companions Find Their Fortune ("Sechese Kommen Durch die Ganze Welt"; translated by K. Sheppard; illustrated by L. Fromm), Macdonald, 1970, Doubleday, 1971; *How the Moon Began* (edited by J. Reeves; illustrated by E. Ardizzone), Abelard, 1971; *The Wren and the Bear* ("Der Zaunkönig und der bï"; translated by Alexander Nesbitt; illustrated by Ilse Buchert), Third & Elm Press, 1971; *Punch and the Magic Fish* (edited by Emanuele Luzzati), Pantheon, 1972 [another edition edited by Gwen Marsh, Dent, 1972]; *Clever Kate* (edited by E. Shub; illustrated by Anita Lobel), Macmillan, 1973; *The Forbidden Forest, and Other Stories* (illustrated by Raymond Briggs), Heinemann, 1973; *The Juniper Tree, and Other Tales* (edited by Lore Segal and M. Sendak; translated by L. Segal and R. Jarrell; illustrated by M. Sendak), Farrar, Straus, 1973; *Tom Thumb* ("Der Daumling"; illustrated by F. Hoffmann), Atheneum, 1973; *Thorn Rose* (illustrated by Errol Le Cain), Faber, 1975.

Nonfiction: (Editors) *Altdeutsche Wälder,* Thurneissen (Cassel), 1813-16; (translators) *Lieder der Alten Edda,* Halle (Berlin), 1815; *Deutsche Sagen* ("German Legends"), [Berlin], 1816-18; *Deutsches Wöterbuch* ("German Dictionary"), S. Hirzel (Leipzig), 1854-1919.

By Jacob Grimm: *Geschichte der Deutschen Sprache,* two volumes, [Leipzig], 1818; *Deutsche Grammatik* ("German Grammar"), four volumes, Dieterich (Göttingen), 1822-37; *Deutsche Rechtsalter-theumer,* Dieterich, 1828, (editor) *Silva de Romances Viejos,* Schmidl (Vienna), 1831; *Reinhart Fuchs,* Reimer (Berlin), 1834; *Deutsche Mythologie,* [Göttingen], 1935, translation by James Steven Stallybrass published as *Teutonic Mythology,* G. Bell, 1882-88, reissued, Dover, 1966; (editor) *Weisthuemer Gesammelt,* Dieterich, 1840-78; (editor) *Lateinische Gedichte,* Dieterich, 1848; *Über den Ursprung der Sprache,* F. Duemmler (Berlin), 1852; *Über den Personenwechsel in der Rede,* F. Duemmler, 1856; *John Mitchell Kemble and Jakob Grimm: A Correspondence, 1832-1852,* edited and translated from the German by Raymond A. Wiley, Brill (Leiden), 1971.

By Wilhelm Grimm: (Translator from the Danish) *Altdänische Heldenlieder, Balladen und Märchen,* Mohr & Zimmer (Heidelberg), 1811, translation published as *Old Danish Ballads,* Hope, 1856; (translator) *Drei Altschottische Lieder,* Mohr & Zimmer, 1813; *Über Deutsche Runen,* [Göttingen], 1821; *Die Deutsche Heldensage,* Dieterich, 1829; *Kleinere Schriften,* edited by Gustav Hinrichs, F. Duemmler, 1881-87.

They lifted her up and looked to see whether any poison was to be found, unlaced her dress, combed her hair, washed her with wine and water, but it was no use; their dear child was dead. ■ (From "Snowdrop" in *Fairy Tales of the Brothers Grimm,* translated by Mrs. Edgar Lucas. Illustrated by Arthur Rackham.)

ADAPTATIONS—Movies and filmstrips; all based on *Snow White and the Seven Dwarfs*: ''Snow White'' (motion pictures), Famous Players Film Co., 1916, Universal Film, 1917; ''Snow White and the Seven Dwarfs'' (motion pictures), Walt Disney Productions, 1938, Sterling Films, featuring the Salzburg marionettes, 1951; ''Snow White and the Three Stooges'' (motion picture), starring Carol Heiss and the Three Stooges, Twentieth Century-Fox, 1961; The Dwarf's Dilemma (motion picture; excerpts from the 1938 Walt Disney film), Walt Disney Home Movies, 1968; Snow White and the Seven Dwarfs (filmstrips), Society for Visual Education, 1953, Encyclopaedia Britannica Films (color, with filmstrip facts), 1957, Eye Gate House (color, with a teacher's manual), 1961; ''The Story of Snow White'' (filmstrip; color, with a phonodisc and a teacher's guide), Encyclopaedia Britannica Films, 1965, rereleased, 1974; ''Snow White and the Seven Dwarfs'' (filmstrips), Universal Education and Visual Arts (color, with a phonodisc and a student participation guide), 1969, Walt Disney Educational Materials Co. (color, available in both sound and captioned versions, with a teacher's guide), 1970; ''Snow White'' (filmstrip; color, with a phonodisc and teacher's guide), Viewlex, 1972.

''Rumpelstiltskin'' (motion pictures), Coronet Instructional Films (11 minutes, sound, color, with a teacher's guide), 1949, Sterling Films (featuring the Salzburg marionettes; 15 minutes, sound, black & white), 1951, Encyclopaedia Britannica Films (eight minutes; sound, black & white), 1952 rereleased, 1969, Sterling Educational Films (10 minutes; sound, color, with a study guide), 1963, McGraw-Hill (17 minutes; sound, color), 1966; ''The Tale of Rumpelstiltskin'' (motion picture; 21 minutes, sound, color, with a teacher's guide), Encyclopaedia Britannica Educational Corp., 1974; ''Rumpelstiltskin'' (filmstrips), Stillfilm, 1949, Curriculum Films (color, with a teacher's manual), 1951, revised, 1957, McGraw-Hill (color, with a phonodisc), 1960, Eye Gate House (color, with a phonodisc and a teacher's guide), 1961, Society for Visual Education (color, with a phonodisc and

Snow White was not worried. She stood before the woman, and permitted herself to be laced up with new ribbons;... ■ (From *Snow White* by the Brothers Grimm. Illustrated by Trina Schart Hyman.)

a teacher's guide), 1966, Spoken Arts (color, with a phonodisc, teaching guide, script, and work sheet), 1967, Encyclopaedia Britannica Educational Corp. (color, with a phonodisc), 1969, Cooper Films and Records (color, with a phonodisc and a teacher's guide), 1969, Universal Education and Visual Arts (color, with a teacher's guide; released in two parts, with one set of captioned drawings for reading and one set without captions to encourage story telling), 1969, Troll Associates (black & white), 1970.

''Little Red Riding Hood'' (motion pictures), Encyclopaedia Britannica Films (10 minutes, sound, color, with a teacher's guide), 1950, Bailey Films (10 minutes, sound, color), 1951, Sterling Films (featuring the Salzburg marionettes; 15 minutes, sound, black & white), 1951, Walter Lantz Productions (sound, color), 1953; ''Red Riding Hood'' (filmstrip), Stillfilm, 1949; ''Grimm Brothers' Favorites: Little Red Riding Hood'' (filmstrip; color, with a phonodisc and a user's guide), 1970; ''The Sleeping Beauty'' (motion pictures), Coronet Films (13 minutes, sound, color), 1950, Sterling Films (featuring the Salzburg marionettes; 15 minutes, sound, black & white), 1951, March of Time (15 minutes, sound, black & white), 1952, Walt Disney Productions, 1958; ''The Prince and the Dragon'' (motion picture; excerpts from the 1958

She pushed poor Grethel towards the oven, and said: "Creep in and see if it is properly heated, and then we will put the bread in." ■ (From "Hansel and Grethel" in *Grimm's Fairy Tales,* translated by Mrs. Edgar Lucas. Illustrated by Arthur Rackham.)

Walt Disney film), Walt Disney Home Movies, 1968; "Sleeping Beauty" (motion picture; seven minutes, sound, color, with a teacher's guide), Encyclopaedia Britannica Educational Corp., 1969; "Sleeping Beauty" (filmstrip), Universal Education and Visual Arts (color, with a teacher's guide; released in two parts, with one set of captioned drawings for reading and one set without captions to encourage reading), 1969, Cooper Films and Records (color, with a phonodisc and a teacher's guide), 1969; "Sleeping Beauty and the Prince" (filmstrip; color, with a phonodisc), Encyclopaedia Britannica Educational Corp., 1969.

"Hansel and Gretel" (motion pictures), Austin Productions (59 minutes, sound, color), 1951, Sterling Films (featuring the Salzburg marionettes; 15 minutes, sound, black & white), 1951, Cathedral Films (11 minutes, sound, color), 1952, Bailey Films (11 minutes, sound, color), 1954, RKO Radio Pictures (78 minutes, sound, color), 1954, McGraw-Hill (17 minutes, sound, color), 1966; "Hansel and Gretel" (filmstrips), Young America Films (color, with a teacher's guide), 1947, Stillfilm, 1949, Jam Handy Organization, 1953, Audio-Visual Guide, 1954, McGraw-Hill (color, with a phonodisc), 1960, Educational Audio Visual (color, with a teacher's notes and script), 1964, Museum Extension Service (color, with a teacher's manual; released in two parts, with one set drawings for reading and one set without captions to encourage story telling), 1965, Coronet Instructional Films (color, with a user's guide; available in both sound and captioned versions), 1968, Encyclopaedia Britannica Films (color, with a phonodisc), 1969, Metropolitan Opera Guild (color, with script), 1969, Doubleday Multimedia (color, with a phonotape and script and teacher's guide), 1972.

"Puss in Boots" (motion picture; 15 minutes, sound, black & white; featuring the Salzburg marionettes), Sterling Films, 1951; "Puss in Boots" (filmstrips), Stillfilm, 1949, Curriculum Films (color, with a teacher's manual), 1951; "The Wolf and the Seven Little Kids" (filmstrips), Jam Handy Organization, 1954, BFA Educational Media (color, available with phonotape or phonodisc), 1972; "The Wolf and the Kids" (filmstrip; color, with a user's guide; available in both sound

and captioned versions), Coronet Instructional Films, 1968; "Rapunzel" (motion pictures), Trident Films (29 minutes, color, sound), 1954, Bailey Films (11 minutes, color, sound), 1955; "Rapunzel" (filmstrips), Stillfilm, 1949, Jam Handy Organization, 1954, Eye Gate House (color, with a teacher's manual), 1961, Troll Associates, 1970, BFA Educational Media (color, available with phonotape or phonodisc), 1972, Imperial Film (color, available with phonotape or phonodisc), 1973; "Snow White and Rose Red" (motion picture; 29 minutes, sound, color), Trident Films, 1954; "Snow White and Rose Red" (filmstrips), Eye Gate House (color, with a teacher's manual), 1961, Encyclopaedia Britannica Educational Corp. (color, with a phonodisc), 1969, Urban Media Materials (color, available with phonotape or phonodisc, with a teacher's guide and duplicating masters), 1973; "Spindle, Shuttle, and Needle" (filmstrip), Jam Handy Organization, 1954.

All based on *The Bremen Town Musicians*—"The Town Musicians" (motion picture; nine minutes, color), Brandon Films, 1956; "The Musicians in the Woods" (motion picture; 14 minutes, sound, color), Coronet Instructional Films, 1962; "Bremen Town Musicians" (motion picture; 15 minutes, sound, color), Films Incorporated, 1972; "Traveling Musicians: A Grimm's Fairy Tale" (filmstrip; color, wtih a teacher's guide), Film Strip-of-the-Month Clubs, 1962; "The Four Musicians" (filmstrip; color, with phonodisc and teacher's guide), Society for Visual Education, 1966; "The Band in the Forest" (filmstrip; color, available in both sound and captioned versions, with a user's guide), Coronet Instructional Films, 1968; "The Musicians of Bremen" (filmstrip; color, with a phonodisc and a teacher's guide), Cooper Films and Records, 1969; "The Four Animal Musicians" (filmstrip; color, with a teacher's manual), Educational Projections Corp., 1972; "The Bremen Town Musicians" (filmstrip; color, available with phonotape or phonodisc), Encyclopaedia Britannica Educational Corp., 1973.

"Tom Thumb" (motion picture), starring Russ Tamblyn and Peter Sellers, Metro-Goldwyn-Mayer, 1958; "The Magic Fountain" (motion picture), starring Cedric Hardwicke and

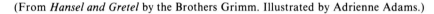

(From *Hansel and Gretel* by the Brothers Grimm. Illustrated by Adrienne Adams.)

Jacob Grimm, 1817. Pencil drawing by Ludwig Emil Grimm.

Hans Conried, Classic World Films, 1961; "The Shoemaker and the Elves" (motion picture; 14 minutes, sound, color), Coronet Instructional Films, 1962; "The Elves and the Shoemaker" (motion picture; 27 minutes, sound, color), International Film Bureau, 1967; "The Shoemaker and the Elves" (motion picture; 14 minutes, sound, color), Films Incorporated, 1972; "The Shoemaker and the Elves" (filmstrip), Jam Handy Organization, 1954; "The Elves and the Shoemaker" (filmstrip; color, with a phonodisc and a teacher's guide), Society for Visual Education, 1965; "Shoemaker and the Elves" (filmstrip), Educational Record Sales, 1967; "The Elves and the Shoemaker" (filmstrips), Coronet Instructional Films (color, with a phonodisc, available in both sound and captioned versions), 1968, Cooper Films and Slides (color, with a phonodisc and a teacher's guide), 1969, Universal Education and Visual Arts (color, with a teacher's guide; released in two parts, with one set of captioned drawings for reading and one set without captions to encourage story telling), 1969, Encyclopaedia Britannica Educational Corp. (color, with a phonodisc), 1969, Troll Associates, 1970; "The Shoemaker and the Elves" (filmstrips), Urban Media Materials (color, available with phonotape or phonodisc, and with teacher's guide and duplicating masters), 1973, Miller-

Brody Productions (color, available with phonotape or phonodisc, with teacher's notes), 1974.

"Sweetheart Roland" (motion picture; nine minutes, sound, color), John M. Raymond, 1965; "The Golden Goose" (filmstrips), Eye Gate House (color, with a phonodisc and a teacher's manual), 1966, Spoken Arts (color, with a phonodisc and teaching guide, script, and work sheet), 1967, Jam Handy Organization, 1967, Scott Education Division (color, available with phonotape or phonodisc, and with a teacher's guide), 1971; "Twelve Dancing Princesses" (motion picture; 12 minutes, animated), Columbia University Press, Center for Mass Communication, 1968; "Clever Gretel" (filmstrip; color, with a phonodisc and a teacher's guide), Cooper Films and Records, 1969; "The Frog Prince" (motion picture; seven minutes, sound color), Encyclopaedia Britannica Educational Corp., 1969; "The Frog Prince" (filmstrips), Jam Handy Organization, 1954, Eye Gate House (color, with a teacher's manual), 1961, Spoken Arts (color, with a phonodisc, and a teaching guide, script, and work sheet), 1967, Universal Education and Visual Arts (color, with a teacher's guide; released in two parts, with one set of captioned drawings for reading and one set without captions to encourage story telling), 1969, Imperial Film Co. (color, available with phonotape or phonodisc), 1973.

"The Fisherman and His Wife" (motion picture; 29 minutes, sound, color), Weston Woods Studios, 1970; "The Golden

The King, however, had a lion which was a wondrous animal, for he knew all hidden and secret things.
■ (From *Household Tales* by the Brothers Grimm. Illustrated by Mervyn Peake.)

Fish'' (filmstrip; color, available with phonotape or phonodisc), adaptation of *The Fisherman and His Wife,* Viewlex, 1972; ''The Fisherman and His Wife'' (filmstrip; color, available with phonotape or phonodisc, and with teacher's guide and duplicating masters), Urban Media Materials, 1973; ''Ballad of the Bleeding Heart'' (motion picture; 26 minutes, sound, color), adaptation of *Jorinda and Joringel,* Appleton Films, 1971; ''Jorinda and Joringel'' (filmstrip), Troll Associates, 1970; ''The Three Golden Hairs'' (filmstrip; color, available with phonotape or phonodisc), BFA Educational Media, 1972; ''The Hare and the Hedgehog'' (filmstrip; color, available with phonotape or phonodisc), BFA Educational Media, 1972.

''The Brave Little Tailor'' (motion picture; 28 minutes, sound, color), Indiana University Audio-Visual Center, 1973; ''Seven at a Blow'' (filmstrip), adaptation of *The Brave Little Tailor,* Stillfilm, 1949; ''The Table, the Donkey, and the Wonderful Stick'' (filmstrip; color, available with phonotape or phonodisc), adaptation of *The Brave Little Tailor,* BFA Educational Media, 1972; ''The Valiant Tailor'' (filmstrip; color, available with phonotape or phonodisc), adaptation of *The Brave Little Tailor,* Imperial Film Co., 1973; ''The Master Thief'' (motion picture; 15 minutes, sound, color, featuring animated puppets), Indiana University Audio-Visual Center, 1973. ''The Four Servants'' (filmstrip; color, available with phonotape or phonodisc, and with a teacher's guide and reading script), Society for Visual Education, 1974; ''The Golden Buttons'' (filmstrip; color, available with phonotape or phonodisc, and with a teacher's guide and reading script), adaptation of *Frederick and Catherine,* Society for Visual Education, 1974; ''King Grisly-Beard'' (filmstrip;

Wilhelm Grimm, 1822. Pencil drawing by Ludwig Emil Grimm.

color, available wth phonotape or phonodisc, and with a teacher's guide and reading script), Society for Visual Education, 1974; ''The Water of Life'' (filmstrip; color, available with phonotape or phonodisc, and with a teacher's guide and reading script), Society Visual Education, 1974; ''Donkey-Lettuce'' (filmstrip; color, available with phonotape or phonodisc, and with a teacher's guide and reading script), Society for Visual Education, 1974; ''The Goose-Girl'' (filmstrip; color, available with phonotape or phonodisc, and with a teacher's guide and reading script), Society for Visual Education, 1974.

All based on *Cinderella*—''The Slipper and the Rose'' (motion picture), starring Richard Chamberlain, Universal Pictures, 1976; ''Cinderella'' (filmstrips), Viewlex (color, available with phonotape or phonodisc, with a teacher's guide), 1972, Imperial Film Co. (color, available with phonotape or phonodisc), 1973, Aids Audiovisual Instructional Devices (color, available with phonotape or phonodisc, with a teacher's guide), 1973; ''Cinderella; or, The Little Glass Slipper'' (filmstrip; color, available with phonotape or phonodisc, and with a teacher's guide and duplicating masters), Urban Media Materials, 1973.

Operas: Engelbert Humperdinck (1854-1921), ''Hansel und Gretel,'' first performed in Weimar, Germany, at the Court Theatre, December 23, 1893; E. Humperdinck, ''Die Sieben Geislein'' (''The Seven Little Kids''), first performed in Berlin, Germany, at the Schiller Theatre, December 19, 1895.

Plays: Alfred Scott-Gatty, *The Goose Girl* (a musical play), Boosey, 1896; Louis Davis, *The Goose at the Well* (a musical

And soon came a gale of wind, and carried away Curdken's hat, while the girl went on combing and curling her hair. ■ (From *Grimm's Fairy Tales* by the Brothers Grimm. Illustrated by George Cruikshank.)

(From the movie "Tom Thumb," starring Russ Tamblyn. Released by Metro-Goldwyn-Mayer Pictures, 1958.)

(From the movie "Snow White and the Three Stooges," based on the fairy tale *Snow White and the Seven Dwarfs.* Released by Twentieth Century-Fox Film Corp., 1961.)

(From the animated movie "Snow White and the Seven Dwarfs." Copyright 1938 by Walt Disney Productions, Ltd.)

(From the animated movie "Snow White and the Seven Dwarfs." Copyright 1938 by Walt Disney Productions, Ltd.)

play; songs by Dollie Radford), E. Mathews, 1906; Ethel Sidgwick, *Two Plays for Schools: The Three Golden Hairs, The Robber Bridegroom,* Sidgwick & Jackson, 1922; Jessie B. White, *Snow White and the Seven Dwarfs,* S. French, 1925; Eleanor Bowman, *Snow White and Rose Red* (three-scene), S. French, 1934; Rosalind Vallance, *The Two Brothers* (four-scene), E. Mathews & Marrot, 1937; G. Olwen M. Jones, *Hansel and Gretel* (two-act), S. French, 1939; Kitty

(From *Snow-White and the Seven Dwarfs* by the Brothers Grimm. Jacket illustrated by Nancy Ekholm Burkert.)

They lost no time in getting to the table, finding their favourite food and gobbling as much as they could eat. ■ (From *The Musicians of Bremen*. Illustrated by Svend Otto.)

Laverty, *The Enchanted Mirror*, adaptation of *Snow White and the Seven Dwarfs*, F. Warne, 1946; K. Laverty, *The Spell-Bound Princess*, adaptation of *The Golden Goose*, F. Warne, 1946; Lillian D. Masters and Robert Masters, *Hansel and Gretel* (three-act), S. French, 1949; Joe Grenzeback, *Song Ho for a Prince* (a musical play; music by Haakon Bergh; adaptation of *Sleeping Beauty*,) Coach House Press, 1951; Albert L. Wells, *The Sleeping Beauty* (three-scene), F. Warne, 1951; Eva Chadwick, *The Forest Witch*, adaptation of *Hansel and Gretel*, W. Paxton, 1953; Arthur Winckless, *The Golden Goose* (one-act), Leonard's Plays, 1955.

Charlotte B. Chorpenning, *Hansel and Gretel*, Coach House Press, 1956; Marian Jonson, *Snow White and the Seven Dwarfs* (a musical play), Coach House Press, 1957; Wilfred Harvey, *Master Luck*, Southwold Press, 1958; Margery Evernden, *Rumpelstiltskin*, Coach House Press, 1959; Miriam Adams, *Rumpelstiltskin*, Oxford University Press, 1959; Aurand Harris, *The Brave Little Tailor*, Children's Theatre Press, 1961; Nicholas S. Gray, *The Stone Cage*, adaptation of *Rapunzel*, Dobson, 1963.

Television: "Cinderella," music by Richard Rodgers and lyrics by Oscar Hammerstein, starring Lesley Ann Warren, Ginger Rogers, and Walter Pidgeon, first shown on CBS, February 22, 1966; "Mr. Magoo's Little Snow White," originally shown in two parts on NBC, January 2 and 9, 1965, later released as part of "Mr. Magoo's Holiday Festival," Maron Films, 1970; "Once upon a Brothers Grimm," lyrics by Sammy Cahn and music by Mitch Leigh, starring Dean Jones and Paul Sand, first shown on CBS, November 23, 1977.

SIDELIGHTS: **January 4, 1785.** Jacob Grimm born in Hanau, Hesse-Cassel, Germany.

February 24, 1786. Wilhelm Grimm born in Hanau. The Grimm brothers were two of nine children, six of whom survived infancy. They had a happy childhood; spending much time with their Grandfather Zimmer and with their father's widowed sister, Aunt Schlemmer. It was Aunt Schlemmer who told the boys their first Bible stories and taught them to read and write from one book. ". . . Its covers were made of wood, with painted pictures, on one side was a cornet, painted red, on the other children blowing bubbles, and some allegorical figures. From a fan our aunt had made herself an ivory pointer which was used also as a bookmark after lessons. Usually she took a pin, to be able to point more finely, and eventually all letters looked pierced. . . ." [Ruth Michaelis-Jena, *The Brothers Grimm*, Praeger, 1970.[1]]

1791. Father was made a judge and the family settled happily in Steinau which became their true childhood home—a magical place for children. There were gates, towers, rambling stairways and passages in the houses, and yards and alleys around them that made exciting playgrounds. There were woods and fields and hills to be explored. They showed an early interest in collecting and drawing plants, feathers, stones and marbles and there was much trading with other boys.

The Grimm brothers led a happy life, warm and secure, with parents who were very loving, but strict, sternly Protestant, and devoted to duty. But this was not to last. On **January 10, 1796,** Jacob wrote to Grandfather Zimmer: ". . . Our dear father is very weak . . . and this is not surprising, as during

A hedge of thorns sprang up round the palace and grew higher and higher, so that it was lost to sight. ■ (From *Thorn Rose* by the Brothers Grimm. Illustrated by Errol le Cain.)

the last few days he has been bled five times, and three large blisters were raised on his chest. With violent stinging pains at every breath, and having had nothing but medicine and drinks for a week, he is completely exhausted, while worry about us has also increased his suffering."[1]

On that same day their father died of pneumonia at the age of forty-four. There now began a hard struggle for their mother who had to bring up six children by herself. Aunt Schlemmer also died that year. Her place was taken by their maternal aunt, Henrietta Zimmer. Their mother gladly accepted Aunt Zimmer's offer to take care of Jacob and Wilhelm, now thirteen and twelve.

The Grimm brothers moved to Cassel and enrolled in school. Unfortunately, their previous schooling was so inadequate that Jacob was placed in the lowest class and Wilhelm had to get private tutoring before entering high school. Although this was a great disappointment, their family continually counselled and encouraged them.

Grandfather Zimmer wrote: "... I cannot repeat often enough that you must remember your goal, the reason for

being where you are. This means diligence during lessons and away from them, so that you may lay the foundations for your future good, do yourselves credit, and give pleasure to your mother, to me and the whole family. Therefore, keep away from company which might lead you into temptations, but associate with sensible men from whom, you can profit, and above all fear the Lord, which is the beginning of all wisdom. It will give your old grandfather great pleasure at all times to have good news from you. . . ."[1]

Mother wrote to Wilhelm: "... I remind you, my son, to be diligent, particularly at home. You must do without many pleasures just now. Do not look for company of other young lads around, or you will become too distracted, and also be a nuisance to your good landlord. Wilhelm, do use this heaven-sent opportunity, and remember that, if it pleased the Lord, to call me or your good aunt, everything would be finished at once, and you would be forced to do something else. Also, remember how you and your brother have advantages, not granted to your brothers and sister on whom not the same amount of money can be spent. You must not compare yourself to other young people of your age who may go out and enjoy themselves. Perhaps they still have both their parents. But you have no longer a father, and that counts for a lot. Jacob can help you with anything you do not know

They saw that the cottage was made of bread and cakes. ■ (From *Hansel and Gretel and Other Stories* by the Brothers Grimm. Illustrated by Kay Nielsen.)

(From the movie version of Humperdinck's opera "Hansel and Gretel." Released by RKO
Radio Pictures Inc., 1954.)

(From an early theatre production of "Snow White and the Seven Dwarfs.")

Although they found many of the lectures dull and the professors uninspiring, there was one professor for whom the Grimms had the greatest admiration: Friedrich Karl von Savigny. He was a brilliant professor who had a doctor's degree and was a lecturer in law. Savigny took a special interest in the Grimms and taught them scientific method, the advantages of the historical approach, and introduced them to his particular circle of friends and gave them access to his library where they spent much of their time. It was in his library that Jacob came across the old German, romantic poems. He immediately became hooked on the language and the literature of the German past. Wilhelm soon also became addicted to the older German literature. Wilhelm wrote: "... The ardour with which the studies of Old German were pursued, helped to overcome the spiritual depression of those days. Without doubt, world events and the need to retire into the peace of research, contributed to the re-discovery of this long-forgotten literature; but not only did we seek some consolation in the past, it was natural, too, for us to hope that the course we were taking, would add something towards the return of better days. . . ."[1]

1805. Jacob went to Paris with Savigny to help him on research for a proposed history of Roman law. Paris was a great experience for Jacob and the library a treasure house of rare books and manuscripts on German language and literature.

The brothers' separation increased their love for each other and they vowed never to separate again. Jacob wrote: "... We do not want to separate ever, and if at any time one of us shoud be sent away, the other must give notice at once. We are so used to being together that the mere thought of separation grieves me deeply. . . ."[1]

Although the brothers were qualified to be lawyers, the thought of legal careers became less and less attractive. They

(From the television special "Hansel and Gretel," starring Red Buttons. Presented on NBC television, April 27, 1958.)

longed for positions where they would have much leisure time to continue their researches into older German literature. Jacob wrote: "It is high time that these old traditions were collected and rescued before they perish like dew in the hot sun or fire in a stream, and fall silent for ever in the unrest of our days." [Muriel E. Hammond, *Jacob and Wilhelm Grimm: The Fairy-Tale Brothers,* Dennis Dobson, 1968.[2]]

1806. Jacob became a clerk in the Hessian War office for a short time.

May 27, 1808. Mother died. Jacob, at twenty-three, became head of the household. He obtained a position as librarian to King Jerome which carried a good salary and gave plenty of leisure time for his private study.

Wilhelm who had often been ill, became increasingly so. "... After my mother's death the poor state of my health became increasingly worse; to the shortness of breath which made climbing even a few steps a terrible burden, and constant fierce pains in my chest, there was now added a heart condition. The pain which I could only compare to the sensation of a fiery arrow being shot through my heart from time to time, left me with a constant feeling of anxiety. Sometimes I experienced violent palpitations, appearing suddenly without obvious cause, and ending the same way. Several times this state lasted, uninterrupted, for twenty hours, leading to extreme exhaustion; a feeling of imminent death seemed not

(From the animated movie "Seven Ravens," produced by Learning Corporation of America, 1971.)

"Husband," said the wife, **"go, at once. I want to be king."** ■ (From *About Wise Men and Simpletons* by the Brothers Grimm. Etching by Nonny Hogrogian.)

Little by little, material collected on the brothers' desks. They became the center of a group of young people, all anxious to help. From their next-door neighbor's nanny, they collected *Snow White, Little Red Riding Hood,* and *The Sleeping Beauty.*

The brothers asked for authentic material only. They wanted local tales, legends, traditions; especially tales told to children. They wanted them taken down faithfully with nothing added and nothing left out for they were mainly interested in documenting a history of German literature. Jacob wrote in a letter to Arnim: ". . . Since your visit here our collection has grown considerably, always from oral tradition, and I believe it will make a rich and delightful book. Every day I see more clearly what an important part these ancient tales play in the evolution of literature. If we overestimate their influence, let people reduce our statements by a little. Enough will remain to make up for the injustice these tales have suffered by being overlooked for so long. . . ."[1]

1812. First volume of *Nursery and Household Tales* published. Although it was mildly received by critics, children loved it. It encouraged collectors of tales everywhere and soon the brothers planned a second volume.

They were fortunate to meet a peasant woman who told them some twenty new tales. Wilhelm wrote in the preface to the second volume: ". . . It was one of those lucky chances through which we made the acquaintance of a peasant woman from the village of Zwehrn, near Cassel. From her we got a good number of the genuinely Hessian tales, published in this volume, as well as some supplements to our first volume. This woman, still vigorous, and not much over fifty, is called Viehmann. She has a strong and pleasant face, and a clear sharp look in her eyes. In her youth she must have been beautiful. She retains these old tales firmly in her mind, a

unjustified. Many a sleepless night I sat upright, without moving, waiting for the dawn to provide some comfort. . . . It is incredible how much one can endure physically for years, without losing the joy of life. The feeling of youth may have helped; I was not completely cast down by my illness, and when things were bearable, I continued working, even with pleasure. . . ."[1]

About this time, the Grimm brothers met the poet Clemens Breutano, the brother-in-law of Savigny, who first kindled the brothers' interest in fairy tales. Breutano was preparing a book of folk songs with Achim von Arnim which would create for him the famous, *The Boy's Magic Horn.* The brothers collaborated with them on the second and third volumes of that work.

The Grimms kept searching for tales, especially those passed along orally. They received two fairy tales recorded from fisherman by the painter Phillip Otto Runge. One was *The Fisherman and HIs Wife,* a tale of a fisherman and his greedy wife; the other, *The Juniper Tree,* a tragic story of a child who, slaughtered by his mother and eaten by his father, comes back as a singing bird to take revenge. Runge had written down the stories just as they had been told and his method set an example for the brothers.

"The more I think of it," said he to himself, **"the better the bargain seems; first I get the roast goose; then the fat; that will last a whole year for bread and dripping; and lastly the beautiful white feathers which I can stuff my pillow with; how comfortably I shall sleep upon it, and how pleased my mother will be!"** ■ (From *Fairy Tales* by the Brothers Grimm. Illustrated by Jean O'Neill.)

At two o'clock the raven came, drawn by
her four white horses.

(From *Grimm's Fairy Tales* by the Brothers Grimm.   Illustrated by Fritz Kredel.)

gift, as she says, not possessed by everyone, as some cannot keep anything in their heads at all. She recounts her stories thoughtfully, accurately, with uncommon vividness and evident delight, first quite easily, but then, if required, over again, slowly, so that with some practice one can take them down. In this way much has been left exactly as it was told, and its genuine ring will be unmistakable. those who believe that, as a rule, tradition is easily tampered with, that there is carelessness in preservation, and that therefore tales cannot possibly survive in the same form for long, should hear how exact this woman is in the telling of a story, anxious to keep it right. In repetition she never changes anything, and should she make a mistake, she will immediately correct it while still talking. . . .''[1]

1816. First volume of *Deutsche Sagen* legends collected from oral and written sources, was published. The brothers expressed their joy of collecting in the introduction: ''. . . The

business of collecting, when one sets about it in earnest, soon repays the trouble, and is nearest to that innocent pleasure of childhood when it suddenly chances in moss and bushes upon a little bird, brooding on its nest. With oral traditions, too, there is a gentle lifting of the leaves and a careful bending aside of the branches, . . . to catch a stolen glance into the strange realm of nature which modestly nestles in itself, smelling of leaves, meadow-grass and newly fallen rain. . . .''[1]

1819. Jacob published the first volume of *Deutsche Grammatik,* a study of the German language and its historical development. Jacob thought such a study was necessay in order to understand German literature.

May 15, 1825. Wilhelm married Dorothea Wild. ''. . . I have never ceased to thank God for the blessing and happiness of this marriage. I had known my wife ever since she was a child, and my mother had loved her like one of her own,

Then she went up to the bed and drew back the curtains. There lay her grandmother with her cap pulled over her eyes, so that she looked very odd. ■ (From *Little Red Riding Hood* by the Brothers Grimm. Illustrated by Harriet Pincus.)

"Heavens!" thought he, "when will it have done growing?" ■ (From "The Nose-Tree" in
Household Tales by the Brothers Grimm. Illustrated by Mervyn Peake.)

without ever guessing that one day she would be . . . [my
wife]."[1]

The couple had five children, one of whom died his first year.
Jacob lived with Wilhelm and Dorothea and was like a second
father to the children.

1830. Both accepted an invitation to become professors and
librarians at the University of Göttingen. Jacob wrote:
". . . We shall leave Cassel and Hessian service. It would
have been better for our advancement and our future, if we
had done this ten years earlier. However, may God bless this
belated, but well considered decision, forced on us in every
kind of way. . . . The state of Hanover has now appointed
us to Göttingen. I am to be professor in ordinary and librarian,
and Wilhelm librarian. This allows us to continue our way
of life together; without that we should not have considered
the matter. I am to get a thousand, and Wilhelm five hundred

thalers, apart from what we can earn by lecturing. We shall
both have more work, at least to begin with. . . ."[1]

1840. In recognition of the brothers' work on German language and literature, the King of Prussia invited them to
move to Berlin where they would be able to continue their
work on a German dictionary in security, with all the re-
sources of the Prussian captial at their disposal. Jacob wrote:
". . . Our lives are past their zenith. All we can wish for is
to devote the rest of our days to completing our work concerning the language and history of our beloved country. The
king's generosity will allow us the carefree leisure needed
for such a task. . . ."[1]

1841. Wilhelm wrote: ". . . Our personal position is as happy
as we can wish. We are completely free, with the possibility
of academic work. Gratefully aware of this, we intend to live
as quietly as possible, and hope we will succeed. Life in

general is just what I had expected it to be. People are courteous, obliging and friendly, but I could not truthfully say that I have found many to gladden my heart. . . ."[1]

1843. The brothers began lecturing on German language, literature and religious beliefs at the University of Berlin.

The Grimms lived together quietly and harmoniously. Of course, their fame attracted many visitors. A writer, Julius Rodenberg, described an evening spent at the Grimms: ". . . From the moment I arrived, I felt warm and comfortable, more than I had ever done since I came here. The *Professorin* is a dear lady, an honest Hessian character, and unpretentious, the most amiable hostess one could wish for. . . . Wilhelm came in first, a man with a quietly-contented face, with blue eyes and long grey hair. He looks more a man of feeling than an intellectual. The mildness of his ways is attractive, and he does not intimidate through intellectual superiority. Quite different, Jacob, who came in after him. He immediately induces a little nervousness. The liveliness of his eyes is fascinating and compelling, but when his en-

dearing smile lights up his features, and the hasty intenseness of his manners changes to loveable sprightliness, any uneasiness one may have experienced, turns to quite an exceptional feeling of attraction . . . one must love him in the same way one has loved as a child his *Household Tales*."[1]

December 16, 1859. Wilhelm died at the age of seventy-three in Berlin.

Jacob talked about the closeness the brothers shared throughout their lives: ". . . We shared one bed and one small room. We sat working at the same table, later, in our student days, there were two beds and two tables in one and the same room. Later again, we had two desks, still in the same room, and up to the very end, we worked in two rooms next to each other, always under one roof. . . ."[1]

September 20, 1863. Jacob died in Berlin at the age of seventy-eight.

The frog feasted heartily, but every morsel seemed to stick in her throat. ▪ (From *The Frog Prince* by the Brothers Grimm. Illustrated by Paul Galdone.)

...When the feast began, the three women entered in strange apparel, and the bride said, "Welcome, dear aunts." ■ (From "The Three Spinners" in *Grimm's Fairy Tales* by the Brothers Grimm. Illustrated by Jiří Trnka.)

FOR MORE INFORMATION SEE: (For children) Elizabeth R. Montgomery, *Story behind Great Stories*, McBride, 1947; T. Roscoe, "Home of Grimm's Fairy Tales," *Contemporary Review*, October, 1948; C. E. Hammil, "Once upon a Time," *Grade Teacher*, November, 1953; Rene Wellek, "Brothers Grimm," in his *History of Modern Criticism: 1750-1950*, Volume 2, Yale University Press, 1955; E. Bowen, "Enchanted Centenary of the Brothers Grimm," *New York Times Magazine*, September 8, 1963; H. R. Meisels, "Grimm Tale," *Wilson Library Bulletin*, October, 1964; G. Kent, "Happily Ever After with the Brothers Grimm," *Readers Digest*, January, 1965; T. Benfey, "Jacob Ludwig Karl Grimm," in *Portraits of Linguists*, edited by Thomas A. Sebeok, Indiana University Press, 1966; Stanley J. Kunitz and Vineta Colby, editors, *European Authors*, H. W. Wilson, 1967; Brian Doyle, editor, *Who's Who of Children's Literature*, Schocken Books, 1968; (for children) Laura Benét, *Famous Storytellers for Young People*, Dodd, 1968; (for children) Muriel E. Hammond, *Jacob and Wilhelm Grimm: The Fairy-Tale Brothers*, Dobson, 1968; Ruth Michaelis-Jena, *Brothers Grimm*, Praeger, 1970; Murray B. Peppard, *Paths through the Forest: A Biography of the Brothers Grimm*, Holt, 1971; Anne Sexton, *Transformations*, Houghton, 1972; Wystan H. Auden, "Grimm and Andersen," in *Forewords and Afterwords*, Random House, 1973.

Movies: "The Wonderful World of the Brothers Grimm," starring Laurence Harvey, Yvette Mimieux, Barbara Eden, Walter Slezak, and Russ Tamblyn, Metro-Goldwyn-Mayer, 1962.

EARL A. GROLLMAN

GROLLMAN, Earl A.   1925-

PERSONAL: Born July 4, 1925, in Baltimore, Md.; son of Gerson S. (a bookseller) and Dora (Steinbach) Grollman; married Netta Levinson, August 14, 1949; children: David, Sharon, Jonathan. *Education:* University of Cincinnati, B.A., 1947; Hebrew Union College-Jewish Institute of Religion, Cincinnati, Ohio, M.H.L., 1950; Boston University, graduate study at School of Theology and School of Legal Medicine. *Home:* 79 Country Club Lane, Belmont, Mass. 02178. *Office;* Beth El Temple Center, 2 Concord Ave., Belmont, Mass. 02178.

CAREER: Temple Israel, Boston, Mass., assistant rabbi, 1950-51; Beth El Temple Center, Belmont, Mass., rabbi, 1951—. Chairman of United Rabbinical Chaplaincy Commission; past president of Massachusetts Board of Rabbis. Chairman of Massachusetts Ecumenical Council on Health and Morality; member of Governor's Council on Action for Mental Health and Massachusetts Committee for the Aged; social action chairman of Belmont Religious Council. *Awards, honors:* D.D. from Portia Law School, 1964, and Hebrew Union College-Jewish Institute of Religion, 1975.

WRITINGS—All published by Beacon Press, except as noted: *Judaism in Sigmund Freud's World,* Appleton, 1965; (editor and contributor) *Rabbinical Counseling,* Bloch Publishing, 1966; (editor and contributor) *Explaining Death to*

Children, 1967; (editor and contributor) *Explaining Divorce to Children,* 1969; *Suicide: Prevention, Intervention, Post-vention,* edited by Clyde and Barbara Dodder, 1971; *Talking About Death: A Dialogue Between Parent and Child,* 1972, new edition, 1976; *Concerning Death: A Practical Guide for the Living,* 1974; *Talking about Divorce: A Dialogue Between Parent and Child,* 1975; *Living—When a Loved One Has Died,* 1977; *Living Through Your Divorce,* 1978; *Caring For Your Aged Parents,* 1978. Contributor to *Psychiatric Opinion, American Imago, Pastoral Psychology,* and other periodicals.

SIDELIGHTS: "Usually I write a book not when I have answers but a question to which I cannot properly respond. It usually arises from my own experiences as a clergy person when I feel particularly inept. I remember walking into a home when my closest friend died and the children asked me what to do. I realized then that I didn't have any answers, and that began my quest in the field of explaining death to children.

"Divorce is sometimes even more painful for young people. There is no closure as in a funeral. So I began writing for children so they might understand their own legitimate feelings and emotions.

"Suicide is becoming more frequent among our youth, and I wrote my book so I could better understand the subject as well as my young audience.

"In the course of a year I speak before dozens and dozens of schools, for children and youth of all ages. I must admit that I learn more from them than they do from me. But they have challenged me in the field of crisis intervention and that is the thrust of my work."

HALTER, Jon C(harles)   1941-

PERSONAL: Born November 24, 1941, in Hamilton, Ohio; son of Samuel L. (a purchasing agent) and Helen (an artist; maiden name, Olds) Halter; married Corina Garcia, February 14, 1968; children: Jon Julian, Helen Margaret. *Education:* Syracuse University, B.A., 1964, M.A., 1966. *Religion:* Presbyterian. *Home:* 1249 Monterrey, Apt. #176, Euless, Tex. 76039. *Office: Boys' Life Magazine,* P.O. Box 61030, Ft. Worth Airport, Dallas, Tex. 75261.

CAREER: Peace Corps volunteer in Venezuela, assigned to Venezuelan Scout Association, 1966-68; McGraw-Hill (publishers), New York, N.Y., assistant editor of *National Petroleum News,* 1968-72; *Boys' Life* (magazine), North Brunswick, N.J., associate editor, 1972—. *Member:* Society of Professional Journalists, Sigma Delta Chi.

WRITINGS—Juvenile: *Bill Bradley: One to Remember,* Putnam, 1974; *Reggie Jackson: All Star in Right,* Putnam, 1975; *Top Secret Projects of World War II,* Messner, 1978; *Their Backs to the Wall,* Messner, 1980.

WORK IN PROGRESS: A nonfiction book on the Great Depression and a historical novel on the Latin American war of independence, both for young readers; a book on Latin American baseball stars.

JON C. HALTER

SIDELIGHTS: ''The five major interests of my professional life are journalism, history, sports and athletics, the Scout movement, and Latin America. Growing up in Oxford, Ohio, as the sons of a former high school coach and college athlete, my older brother and I were constantly exposed to sports on all levels. The seasons of our lives were not spring, summer, winter, fall, but rather baseball, football, and basketball. We published our own newspaper on my brother's printing press and I turned out sports columns on my own until I was in high school. By then I knew that I wanted to be (and was suited to be) a journalist more than anything else.

''My Peace Corps assignment led to my interest in Latin America, an area about which I was totally ignorant until then. While in the Peace Corps, I met and married my wife, who is Venezuelan. That event has only helped to perpetuate my interest in the people and history of that area of the world.''

'Tis the good reader that makes the book.
—Ralph Waldo Emerson

HARRIS, Lorle K(empe) 1912-

PERSONAL: Born January 9, 1912, in Hackensack, N.J.; daughter of Adolf (a research chemist) and Irma (Kortum) Kempe; married Herbert Burton Harris (a businessman and writer), July 26, 1935 (died, 1978); children: Herbert Kempe, Frank Werner. *Education:* Mount Holyoke College, B.A., 1933; University of Denver, M.A., 1963. *Home:* 639 18th St., Boulder, Colo. 80302.

CAREER: Writer. Owner of bookstore in Boulder, Colo., 1954-62; University of Colorado, Boulder, librarian, 1963-70; director of Basin Land & Livestock Co., Greybull, Wyo., 1970—. Board member, Boulder Council for International Visitors, 1970-75, and Friends of the Library, University of Colorado, 1975—. *Member:* Society for Children's Book Writers, Boulder Writers' Club, Soroptimist International (president of Boulder branch, 1961-62). *Awards, honors:* Biography of a Whooping Crane was named one of the best science books for children for 1977, by the National Science Teachers Association and the Children's Book Council.

WRITINGS: Biography of a Whooping Crane, Putnam, 1977; *Biography of a River Otter,* Putnam, 1979; *Biography of a Mountain Gorilla,* Putnam, 1981.

SIDELIGHTS: ''My interest in nature dates from early childhood. My father frequently brought home small creatures and plants from the woods near the factory where he worked as a research chemist.

''Raising two boys, taking an active part in school affairs, and sharing my husband's interest in Western history, kept me well occupied. My husband enjoyed the light verse I wrote occasionally to accompany a gift or mark a special

LORLE K. HARRIS

She kept the cubs paddling about in deep water for almost fifteen minutes before she let them go ashore.
■ (From *Biography of a River Otter* by Lorle Harris. Illustrated by Ruth Kirschner.)

occasion. He urged me to write for children, but he had more confidence in my ability than I.

"When my husband's health required a drier climate, we moved to Boulder, Colorado, where we opened a bookstore. Most of our trade was with schools and libraries and I really became involved in children's books as I helped librarians make their selections. When my husband's health broke down again we were forced to give up our book business. He retired, but I wasn't ready for that yet, so I went to library school. I was a librarian at the University of Colorado for seven years.

"In the meantime my husband discovered that he received a great deal of relief from his asthma and hay fever at sea. Whenever possible, we boarded freighters to escape the peak of the ragweed season. We've sailed as far north as Iceland and Alaska, west to Japan and Taiwan, and east to the Canary Islands, the Mediterranean and Europe."

HOBBIES AND OTHER INTERESTS: "I swim and walk regularly and garden spasmodically. I enjoy watching the birds at my feeder, the squirrels in my yard, and my dog, Chico. I also travel whenever I can and have recently taken up photography."

> That place that does contain
> My books, the best companion, is to me
> A glorious court where hourly I converse
> With the old sages and philosophers.
> —John Fletcher and Francis Beaumont

> A house full of books, and a garden of flowers.
> —Andrew Lang

HARTMAN, Louis F(rancis)   1901-1970

PERSONAL: Born January 17, 1901, in New York, N.Y.; died August 22, 1970, in Washington, D.C.; son of Louis Francis and Josephine (Grennan) Hartman. *Education:* Studied at St. Mary's College, North East, Pa., 1915-21, Mount St. Alphonsus Seminary, Esopus, N.Y., 1922-28, and Catholic University of America, 1929; Pontifical Biblical Institute, Rome, Italy, Licentiate in Sacred Scripture, 1932, Licentiate in Oriental Languages, 1934. *Politics:* Independent. *Home:* Holy Redeemer College, 3112 Seventh St. N.E., Washington, D.C. 20017. *Office:* Semitic Department, Catholic University of America, Washington, D.C. 20017.

CAREER: Entered Congregation of the Most Holy Redeemer (Redemptorists), 1922, and was ordained priest, 1927; Mount St. Alphonsus Seminary, Esopus, N.Y., professor of Sacred Scripture, 1932-34, 1936-48; Catholic Biblical Association of America, Washington, D.C., executive secretary, 1948—; Catholic University of America, Washington, D.C., assistant professor, 1950-53, associate professor, 1953-62, professor of Semitics, 1962—. American School of Oriental Research

The work continued, though as it progressed there were other difficulties. The only time Jon could safely work was in the hours he should have been sleeping.
■ (From *The Monstrous Leathern Man* by Lou Hartman. Illustrated by Paul Sagsoorian.)

in Jerusalem, annual professor, 1959-60. *Member:* Society of Biblical Literature, American Oriental Society. *Awards, honors:* Citation from St. Bonaventure University, 1958, for outstanding contributions to Catholic biblical scholarship.

WRITINGS—For children: (With Betty Morrow) *Jewish Holidays,* Garrard, 1967; *The Monstrous Leathern Man* (illustrated by Paul Sagsoorian), Atheneum, 1970.

Other writings: (Co-editor and contributor) *Commentary on the New Testament,* Sadlier, 1942; (contributor) *A Monument to Saint Jerome: Essays on Some Aspects of His Life, Works and Influence,* edited by F.X. Murphy, Sheed, 1952; (co-editor) "Confraternity Version of the Bible," St. Anthony, Volume I; *Genesis to Ruth,* 1952, Volume II: *Job to Sirach,* 1955, Volume IV: *Isaiah to Malachi,* 1961; (editor) *Lives of the Saints,* Crawley, Volume II, 1962; (translator and adapter) *Encyclopedic Dictionary of the Bible* (based on A. van den Borne's *Bijbels Woordenboek),* McGraw, 1963; (translator) *The Imitation of Christ,* Crawley, 1964; (contributor) *Background to Morality,* edited by J. P. Lerhinan, Desclee, 1964. Staff editor, *The New Catholic Encyclopedia.* Author with A. Leo Oppenheim of a book-length supplement to *Journal of the American Oriental Society,* "On Beer and Brewing Techniques in Ancient Mesopotamia," 1950; contributor of occasional articles and about forty reviews to *Catholic Biblical Quarterly* and other journals.

SIDELIGHTS: Competent in Latin, Greek, German, French, Dutch, Spanish, Italian, Akkadian, Ugaritic, Sumerian, Syriac, Hebrew, Aramaic.

HOBBIES AND OTHER INTERESTS: Bird watching.

FOR MORE INFORMATION SEE: Catholic Biblical Quarterly, Volume 29, 1967.

NANCY WALLACE HENDERSON

HECHT, George J(oseph)   1895-1980

OBITUARY NOTICE: Born November 1, 1895, in New York, N.Y.; died April 23, 1980, in New York, N.Y. Publisher. Hecht was the founder and publisher of *Parents' Magazine,* the foundation of a publishing empire that included *Humpty Dumpty* magazine, *Children's Digest, Baby Care,* and the largest book wholesaler in the United States, Baker & Taylor. He also owned the New York toy store F.A.O. Schwarz from 1963 to 1970 and expanded its operation to sixteen branches. In the late 1950's, Hecht established a book club division within his magazine empire, which was spawned by his recognition of the value of reading for children. The Read-Aloud and Easy Reading Program is one part of this division, with over 10-million children claiming membership since its beginning. Hecht, who had financed family-planning programs in India and Bangladesh, was a vigorous campaigner for child-welfare programs and population control. *For More Information See: Current Biography,* Wilson, 1947; *Who's Who in World Jewry,* Pitman, 1972; *Who's Who in America,* 41st edition, Marquis, 1980. *Obituaries: Current Biography,* Wilson, June, 1980; *New York Times,* April 24, 1980; *Washington Post,* April 26, 1980; *Newsweek,* May 5, 1980; *Publishers Weekly,* May 9, 1980.

HENDERSON, Nancy Wallace   1916-

PERSONAL: Born July 21, 1916, in Wilmington, N.C.; daughter of Oliver Terrell (a real estate developer) and Mary (Borden) Wallace; married William Henderson, August 9, 1942 (deceased); children: William McCranor, Nicholas Charles. *Education:* Mary Baldwin College, B.A., 1936; Columbia University, M.A. (education and social work), 1938; University of North Carolina, M.A. (dramatic art), 1952. *Home and office:* 13 Bank St., Apt. 3R, New York, N.Y. 10014.

CAREER: Greenwich House, New York City, social group worker, 1939-40, social group worker and administrator, 1941-42; writer, 1946—; secretary in New York City, 1963-70. Teacher at workshops and camps; member of extension faculty at University of North Carolina. *Member:* Authors Guild of Authors League of America, Dramatists Guild, Appalachian Mountain Club. *Awards, honors:* First prizes from University of North Carolina, 1950, University of Wisconsin, Madison, 1951, and Dramatists Alliance, 1952, all for "Lo the Angels."

WRITINGS—For children: *The Scots Helped Build America,* Messner, 1969; (with Jane Dewey) *Circle of Life: The Miccosukee Indian Way,* Messner, 1974; *Janet Climbs* (novel), Concordia, 1978. Contributor to newspapers.

Published plays: *Walk Together: Five Plays on Human Rights* (juvenile; contains "Get on Board, Little Children," a one-act, first produced in New York City at Ralph Bunche School,

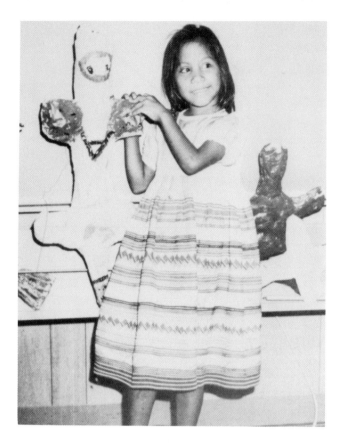

Sculpture in papier-mâché suggests some of the Everglades' animals. ■ (From *Circle of Life: The Miccosukee Indian Way* by Nancy Henderson and Jane Dewey. Photograph by David Pickens.)

May 3, 1971), Messner, 1972; *Medusa of Forty-Seventh Street* (one-act for adults; first produced in New York City at Old Reliable Theatre Tavern, December 6, 1967), Samuel French, 1973; *Celebrate America: A Baker's Dozen of Plays* (juvenile; contains thirteen short one-acts for each month in the year, and a spare: "Soul Force," "Hail the Lucky Year," "Legend for Our Time," "John Muir, Earth-Planet Universe," "Honor the Brave," "Casey at the Bat" [adaptation], "Moonlife 2069," "Come to the Fair," "Little Turtle," "The Land We Love," "M.D. in Petticoats," "Keeping Christmas Merry" [adaptation] and "Popcorn Whoppers," Messner, 1978. Also author of the following published plays: *Look Behind the Mask* (one-act; first produced by WRDU-TV, November, 1972); *The Pledge* (one-act; first produced at St. Luke's Parish School, New York City, November, 1971); *Harvest for Lola* (one-act); *Automa* (one-act).

Work represented in an anthology: "Speed, Bonnie Boat" (one-act for adults; first produced in Chapel Hill, N.C., at the University of North Carolina, January 25, 1952), in *Plays for Players*, Row, Peterson & Co., 1957.

Unpublished plays: "Lo the Angels" (three-act), first produced in Chapel Hill, N.C., by the Carolina Playmakers, at the University of North Carolina, March 8, 1951; "Monochrome" (one-act), first produced in New York City, at Old Reliable Theatre Tavern, February 26, 1968; "Hot Pink Blues" (two-act), first produced in Chester, N.J., at Black River Playhouse, September 17, 1971; (with Charlotte Kraft)

"Feel Free" (two-act), first produced in New York City, as an Equity Showcase, Gene Frankel Theatre, October 28, 1976.

WORK IN PROGRESS: A novel about a mother-and-son trip to Death Valley entitled, "You've Got to be Crazy to Go to Death Valley in June;" "96-A," a two-act play.

SIDELIGHTS: "I am forever concerned with the struggles of human beings to achieve freedom, to become themselves, on both an individual and a collective level. This seems to lead inevitably to stories of conflict and struggles to escape life's traps.

"I majored in English literature in college and went to New York to study social work. There I met my husband, a Scotsman, who died in World War II. He and I lived and worked at Greenwich House, an interesting settlement house in Greenwich Village.

"Somewhere along the way I switched from social work to writing, moved to Chapel Hill, N.C., and enrolled in the graduate department of dramatic art at University of North Carolina. I have done some acting, a great deal of directing at the university and community theatres. I've also done a good bit of teaching of creative writing in workshops and worked with children's drama groups.

"In New York I joined the Appalachian Mountain Club, a group that hikes, camps, engages in all kinds of sports, and is open to people of all ages and degrees of skill. It is a most relaxed and relaxing organization, a godsend for people like me, single, who don't know how or don't want to camp or hike alone. Through them I've learned almost all I know about outdoor living and activities. I went on one of their hiking trips to huts in the White Mountains of New Hampshire; the one Janet took in my book *Janet Climbs*. The story was my own, but the week of hiking provided the framework and ideas about people living and traveling together in some of this country's most difficult and exciting wilderness, as well as ideas about a young girl's self-discovery through learning the meaning of friendship.

"Although I have done some nonfiction, I am basically a fiction writer of fairly realistic stories with romantic overtones. I like to put characters in situations of adventure and danger, while maintaining their real life connections. I am fascinated with heightened language, poetic images, fantasy, but approach all this with much trepidation, for it is not in any way easy for me to handle in terms of an authentic style."

Dear little child, this little book
   Is less a primer than a key
To sunder gates where wonder waits
   Your "Open Sesame!"

—Rupert Hughes

Come, my best friends, my books, and lead me on.
—Abraham Cowley

HOBAN, Lillian 1925-

PERSONAL: Born May 18, 1925, in Philadelphia, Penn.; married Russell Hoban (an author and artist), January 31, 1944; children: Phoebe, Abrom, Esme, Julia. *Education:* Attended Philadelphia Museum School of Art, 1942-44, and the Hanya Holm School of Dance. *Residence:* Wilton, Conn.

CAREER: Illustrator of books for children. Has also worked in a slenderizing salon, and as a modern dance instructor in New York and Connecticut. *Awards, honors:* Christopher Award, Children's Book Category, 1971, for *Emmett Otter's Jug-Band Christmas* (written by Russell Hoban).

WRITINGS: (With husband, Russell Hoban) *London Men and English Men,* Harper, 1962; (with R. Hoban) *Some Snow Said Hello,* Harper, 1963; (with R. Hoban) *Save My Place,* Norton, 1967; (with R. Hoban) *Charlie the Tramp,* Scholastic Book Services, 1970; *Arthur's Christmas Cookies* (self-illustrated), Harper, 1972; *The Sugar Snow Spring* (self-illustrated), Harper, 1973; *Arthur's Honey Bear* (self-illustrated), Harper, 1974; *Arthur's Pen Pal* (self-illustrated), Harper, 1976; *Stick-in-the-Mud Turtle* (self-illustrated), Greenwillow Books, 1977; *I Met a Traveler,* Harper, 1977; *Mr. Pig and Sonny Too,* Harper, 1977; *Arthur's Prize Reader* (self-illustrated), Harper, 1978; *Turtle Spring,* Greenwillow Books, 1978.

Illustrator: Russell Hoban, *Herman the Loser,* Harper, 1961; R. Hoban, *The Sorely Trying Day,* Harper, 1964; R. Hoban, *Nothing to Do,* Harper, 1964; R. Hoban, *Bread and Jam for Frances,* Harper, 1964; R. Hoban, *Baby Sister for Frances,* Harper, 1964, reissued, 1976; Robert P. Smith, *When I Am Big,* Harper, 1965; R. Hoban, *What Happened When Jack and Daisy Tried to Fool with the Tooth Fairies,* Four Winds, 1965; R. Hoban, *The Story of Hester Mouse Who Became a Writer,* Norton, 1965; R. Hoban, *Tom and the Two Handles,* Harper, 1965; Felice Holman, *Victoria's Castle,* Norton,

Gloria said her wish inside her head and blew out all the candles at once. ▪ (From *A Birthday for Frances* by Russell Hoban. Illustrated by Lillian Hoban.)

1966; Carl Memling, *A Gift-Bear for the King,* Dutton, 1966; Mitchell F. Jayne, *The Forest in the Wind,* Bobbs-Merrill, 1966; R. Hoban, *The Little Brute Family,* Macmillan, 1966, reissued, 1972; R. Hoban, *Charlie the Tramp,* Four Winds, 1966; R. Hoban, *Goodnight,* Norton, 1966; R. Hoban, *Henry and the Monstrous Din,* Harper, 1966; Miriam Cohen, *Will I Have a Friend?,* Macmillan, 1967; R. Hoban, *Mouse and His Child,* Harper, 1967; R. Hoban, *The Stone Doll of Sister Brute,* Macmillan, 1968; R. Hoban, *A Birthday for Frances,* Harper, 1968, reissued, 1976; R. Hoban, *Ugly Bird,* Macmillan, 1969; Jan Wahl, *A Wolf of My Own,* Macmillan, 1969; R. Hoban, *Harvey's Hideout,* Parents Magazine Press, 1969; R. Hoban, *The Mole Family's Christmas,* Parents Magazine Press, 1969; R. Hoban, *Best Friends for Frances,* Harper, 1969, reissued, 1976; Aileen T. Fisher, *In One Door and Out the Other: A Book of Poems,* Crowell, 1969.

R. Hoban, *A Bargain for Frances,* Harper, 1970, reissued, 1978; Alma M. Whitney, *Just Awful,* Addison-Wesley, 1971; Ellen Parsons, *Rainy Day Together,* Harper, 1971; Meinder De Jong, *Easter Cat,* Macmillan, 1971; R. Hoban, *Emmett Otter's Jug-Band Christmas,* Parents Magazine Press, 1971, reissued, 1978; M. Cohen, *Best Friends,* Macmillan, 1971, reissued, 1973; R. Hoban, *Egg Thoughts, and Other Frances Songs,* Harper, 1972; M. Cohen, *The New Teacher,* Macmillan, 1972; Marjorie W. Sharmat, *Sophie and Gussie,* Macmillan, 1973; M. Cohen, *Tough Jim,* Macmillan, 1974; William Cole, *What's Good for a Three-Year-Old?,* Holt, 1974; Crescent Dragonwagon, *Strawberry Dress Escape,* Scribner, 1975; Janet Schulman, *The Big Hello,* Greenwillow Books, 1976; Diane Wolkstein, *Squirrel's Song,* Knopf, 1976; Marjorie W. Sharmat, *I Don't Care,* Macmillan, 1977; M. Cohen, *When Will I Read,* Greenwillow Books, 1977; M. Cohen, *Bee My Valentine,* Greenwillow Books, 1978; Theresa Zagone, *No Nap for Me,* Dutton, 1978. Also editor of *Here Come Raccoons* for Harper.

ADAPTATIONS—Filmstrips: "Frances Series," distributed by BFA Educational Media; "Will I Have a Friend," Macmillan, 1974.

The oldest girl turtle braided daisies and violets into her jump rope.
▪ (From *Stick-in-the-Mud Turtle* by Lillian Hoban. Illustrated by the author.)

LILLIAN HOBAN

SIDELIGHTS: Hoban always wanted to be an illustrator, but gave it up for a while after her marriage in order to study dance professionally. After the birth of her third child, she began illustrating her husband's books for children, as well as the writings of other authors, and eventually wrote and illustrated her own books. Hoban finds drawing completely satisfying and cozy. She usually works in black and white or in two colors. The illustrations for *Bread and Jam for Frances* and several others have been done in pencil. She also uses a pen and ink wash.

FOR MORE INFORMATION SEE: Lee Kingman and others, compiler, *Illustrators of Children's Books: 1957-1966*, Horn Book, 1968; Doris de Montreville and Donna Hill, editors, *Third Book of Junior Authors*, H. W. Wilson, 1972; *Horn Book*, December, 1972, June, 1973, August, 1974, August, 1976.

HOBAN, Tana

PERSONAL: Born in Philadelphia, Pa.; daughter of Russian parents; married Edward Gallob; children: a daughter, Meila. *Education:* Graduated from Moore College of Art.

CAREER: Children's author and illustrator, photographer, artist. Painted in Europe as a recipient of the John Frederick Lewis Fellowship; free-lance artist, doing advertising and magazine illustration, Philadelphia; later became a professional photographer; taught photography and graphics at the University of Pennsylvania, 1966-1969; with her husband,

Edward Gallob, has been partner-owner of the Hoban-Gallob studio, Philadelphia, since 1946. Tana Hoban's photographs are in the permanent collection of the Museum of Modern Art, and have appeared in such magazines as *Life*, *Look*, *McCall's* and *Harper's Bazaar*. *Awards, honors: Look Again!* was a *New York Times* Choice of Best Illustrated Children's Books of the Year, 1971, and a Children's Book Showcase Title, 1972; *Count and See* was a Children's Book Showcase Title, 1973; *Circles, Triangles, and Squares* was a runner-up in the Fourth Annual Children's Science Competition, 1975.

WRITINGS—All for children; all self-illustrated: *Shapes and Things*, Macmillan, 1970; *Look Again!*, (ALA Notable Book), Macmillan, 1971; *Count and See*, Macmillan, 1972; *Push, Pull, Empty, Full: A Book of Opposites*, Macmillan, 1972, reissued, Collier, 1976; *Over, Under and Through, and Other Spatial Concepts*, Macmillan, 1973; *Where Is It?*, Macmillan, 1974; *Circles, Triangles, and Squares*, Macmillan, 1974; *Dig, Drill, Dump, Fill* (Junior Literary Guild selection), Greenwillow, 1975; *Big Ones, Little Ones*, Greenwillow, 1976; *Is It Red? Is It Yellow? Is It Blue?*, Greenwillow, 1978.

Other: *How to Photograph Your Child*, Crown, 1955.

Illustrator: Edna Bennett, *Photographing Youth*, Amphoto, 1961; Edith Baer, *The Wonder of Hands*, Parents' Magazine Press, 1970.

SIDELIGHTS: Tana Hoban began her career in the field of painting and sketching, and when she turned her hand to photography after the birth of her daughter, the early influence left its imprint on her photographs. Having always been interested in child development, children became a main subject and focus for her, which eventually led her to design and write books for them. Her basic purpose is to take note of the ordinary objects of the world with a fresh eye and share her discoveries of new sight with children. She tries to give them something to reach for.

Critics have praised her approach to her books, the *Saturday Review* remarking about *Shapes and Things*, ''This has no words, tells no story; yet it is a book through which a small child may wish to browse, alone or with a friend to share the pleasure of recognizing simple things by their shapes. . . . The objects, white on black, are almost wholly in silhouette, although there are hints of shadow. Some of the pages are almost blunt: a single apple. Some are arranged in patterns on a theme: tools, sewing things, kitchen utensils. Very attractive, useful for discussion, good for stirring perceptual acuteness.''

And a *New York Times Book Review* feels that, '''Black-and-white photography' is too limiting a term when applied to Miss Hoban's art, for her searching camera picks up every nuance, from the pale gray of a dandelion whisp to the intense black of a sunflower's shadow on a hot day.''

FOR MORE INFORMATION SEE: Saturday Review, November 14, 1970; *New York Times Book Review,* May 2, 1971; Doris de Montreville and Elizabeth D. Crawford, editors, *Fourth Book of Junior Authors and Illustrators,* H. W. Wilson, 1978.

(From *Big Ones, Little Ones* by Tana Hoban. Photograph by the author.)

TANA HOBAN

HOLYER, Erna Maria 1925-
(Ernie Holyer)

PERSONAL: Born March 15, 1925, in Weilheim, Germany; came to United States in 1956, naturalized citizen; daughter of Mathias (a hotel, theater, and farm owner) and Anna (Goldhofer) Schretter; married Friedrich Rupp, May 27, 1943; married second husband, Gene Wallace Holyer (president, Holyer Construction Co.), August 24, 1957. *Education:* San Jose Junior College, A.A., 1964; attended San Mateo College, San Jose State University, and University of Santa Cruz, 1965-74. *Home:* 1314 Rimrock Dr., San Jose, Calif. 95120.

CAREER: Free-lance writer, mainly for children; painter, with several one-woman shows. Teacher of creative writing in San Jose adult education program. *Member:* California Writers Club.

WRITINGS—Juveniles under pseudonym Ernie Holyer: *Rescue at Sunrise, and Other Stories,* Review & Herald, 1965; *Steve's Night of Silence, and Other Stories,* Review & Herald, 1966; *A Cow for Hansel,* Review & Herald, 1967; *At the Forest's Edge,* Southern Publishing, 1969; *Song of Courage,* Southern Publishing, 1970; *Lone Brown Gull, and Other Stories,* Review & Herald, 1971; *Shoes for Daniel,* Southern Publishing, 1974; *Sigi's Fire Helmet,* Pacific Press Publishing Association, 1974; *The Southern Sea Otter,* Steck, 1975. Also contributor to *Und Wieder Scheint die Sonne* (three volume anthology), edited by G. Tobler, Advent Verlag (Zurich). Contributor of several book-length serials and 200 short stories and articles to magazines.

WORK IN PROGRESS: Reservoir Road, a junior novel about Mexican-American migrants; *Elisha Brooks,* a biography of a backwoods boy who became a leading educator; *Marine Mammals and Other; North American Mammals;* a book about suicide prevention in the young; Egyptian subjects; translation (German to English) of a book on a history of Faust films; various animal stories for possible picture books.

SIDELIGHTS: "I was born in a magical town. It was a place where stories were made. The railroad brought people from all directions. I'd dangle over the station's banister and watch travelers hurry to and from the trains. Where did they come from? Where were they going? Why did some look happy? Why did others frown? And what was in those suitcases they lugged around? I wondered about such things.

"Going home to my parents' place, called 'Gasthof zur Post,' a kind of hotel, I often followed travelers who had alighted. At the 'Post' people went in and out. Day and night, guests arrived and departed. Some guests wore colorful garb. Some spoke foreign languages, or hard-to-understand dialects. Some came from as far as Russia and China. Some brought pet poodles, canaries, squirrels. One guest even brought a big, fat bear that had to be locked up.

"Travelers carried with them joys and problems. They told their stories to strangers in the restaurant, or spilled them in the kitchen to my mother. It made for fine listening.

"Weekends, mother sat in the box office inside the movie theater and held me on her lap. My older sister was supposed to baby-sit with me, but she ran off with friends her own age. When people were through buying tickets, the theater got dark and I watched the action on the linen screen. Characters, dialogue, settings, moods, and plots became part of me.

"On circus days, I rubbed shoulders with exotic folks. How could I forget the African sword swallower? Or the quiet man who made his brown bear dance? Or the children who walked the high wire? Or the beautiful white stallions who pranced in waltz time? I could watch the goings on in the open tent from my second story window.

"On market days, the merry-go-round spun me around the square. Straddling a charging horse or haughty swan, listening to the loud organ music, I saw high-gabled houses whiz around me.

"Puppet theaters involved me in Kasperle's funny and energetic jokes. Marionette theaters staged dramas of damsels and knights and made me cry.

"The old 'Kren' woman came once a year. She carried a wicker basket filled with long, black horseradish roots, on sturdy shoulders and her skirt swept the floor. The grooved face between the tightly bound bandana made her appear like a creature from the forest. Mama said the 'Kren' woman had walked all the way from Franconia (wherever that was).

"Not all people were transients though. The chimney sweep lived in town. He carried a ladder, assorted brushes, and an iron ball on a sturdy chain. The sooty fellow did his stuff mostly on the roof. His picture was on New Year's cards the postman brought late in December. Chimney sweeps were supposed to bring good luck.

"The Schuhplattler group met in the side room once a week. Under the ceiling, the boys slapped their cheeks, leather shorts, and shoe soles. The girls whirled around the boys, red skirts and white underskirts flying. On May day, the group performed under the brand new Maypole. Townfolk cheered as the wooden platform shook under the dancers' shoes. Gutsy fellows climbed the swaying Maypole, plucked pretzels from the swinging wreath, and tossed them to youngsters on the ground to fight over. You can read more about these happenings in my book *A Cow for Hansel.*

"On special evenings, a lady played the harp in the restaurant, or men played the zither, and everybody sang melancholy folk songs. Music and words drifted up to my room and broke my heart.

"In the apartments (my parents rented out) lived friends my own age. My friends were poor. They did different things, such as collecting snails for money, so the family could buy food and clothes. Their mothers were gentle women who cradled babies, knitted, or crocheted.

"When things got dull, I directed plays. I had kittens and cats for actors. 'Peter, the Rat Catcher' always bounded off before finishing his part. He was a true villain. 'Mietzy, the Leading Lady,' usually tired of being groomed and dressed. Even the kittens tumbled away when a cute little mouse swished along the baseboard. Left without a cast, I had to carry on with dolls.

"Mornings, Hans hitched the horse to the postal wagon, which then clattered over cobble stones to the rear exit. At the post office, he loaded packages into the back and onto the rack atop the wagon. Hans then mounted the high seat and headed for the villages. My father was the town's official 'Posthalter,' and my birth records duly proclaim me as '*Posthalter's* daughter.'

"Once, I was allowed to ride beside Hans. I felt every bit as proud as he looked. In his blue, gold-buttoned uniform, and the tall plume on his hat, Hans definitely deserved his title of 'postilion,' Nearing a village, Hans sounded his brass horn, announcing our arrival. Village children greeted us with jubilant cries, 'The mail is coming!'

"The ride proved a highlight of my childhood. Mama had bought me a patent leather purse for the occasion. It was yellow like the postal wagon and all the mailboxes in Bavaria.

"I remember wondering what life was like in a village. I found that out, at age thirteen, when my family left the magical town of Weilheim and moved to our farmhouse in the Alpine foothills.

"People were different in the village. They baked their own bread and grew their own grain. They watched the weather, milked cows, and worked outdoors. Children worked along with grown-ups in barn and field. They had little time for play or making friends. Now *I* was the stranger.

"Reading would have helped me over this difficult time, but we no longer received the weeklies that used to hang in the 'Gasthof.' Book stores were far away and there wasn't any money for books anyway. I searched the house for moldy books and read them in a secret corner.

"I was growing, and my sister and I discovered that we both were teenagers. At last, we had something in common! We

ERNA MARIA HOLYER

became best friends. We did things together and she made up for the childhood world I'd lost. In winter, we watched deer that came to eat the hay papa put outside the kitchen window. We snuggled under feather bolsters and listened to bells that chimed in the frosty morning air. In spring, we discovered a bristling hedgehog under the lilac bush. In summer, we swam in clear mountain lakes. Or we sat at the forest's edge, high above the patchwork of fields, and admired the snow-capped Alps. Among tinkling cowbells, we talked about the wonderful things the future would bring us.

"One fateful autumn day, we came down with scarlet fever. I recovered, but my sister did not. Her death was the biggest loss of my life. I couldn't cry, the horror was too great.

"How could people leave behind that which is inside of them? I thought of that day and night, even while her still body lay in the open coffin in the house. I thought of great artists—composers, painters, writers. They lived on through their creative work. Because they cared to leave the best in them behind, we still enjoy their operas, paintings, books, and plays.

"I started to write. Fairy tales at first, then short stories and chapters of a book. My head buzzed with stories, people, backgrounds. I was eighteen, and I was going to be a writer. Wherever I would live, I'd make my own stories and create my own magical place and share it with others."

The Standard University Library carries a special "Erna Holyer Collection" in its Special Collections Department.

FOR MORE INFORMATION SEE: San Jose Mercury, December 1, 1965, September 5, 1969, June 12, 1974; *Standard Register Leader,* December 2, 1966; *Santa Clara Journal,* June 14, 1967; *Sunnyvale Standard,* June 12, 1968; *Weilheimer Tagblatt,* August 25, 1969, June 29/30, 1974, December 8, 1978, January 10, 1980; *California Today,* April 2, 1972; *Valley Journal,* May 29, 1974; *San Jose News,* June 11, 1974; *San Jose Mercury-News Sunday,* June 16, 1974; *San Jose Sun,* June 4, 1975, January 16, 1980; *PHP International,* May, 1975; *Family Happiness TV Schedule,* November 15-21, 1975; *Sun* Magazine, January 19, 1977; "Beauty from Ashes," television documentary on writer and painter Erna Holyer, produced by Patricia Griffin, aired on Channel 32 (San Francisco), December 22, 1979.

HOSFORD, Dorothy (Grant) 1900-1952

PERSONAL: Born in 1900, in Pittsburgh, Pa.; died June 28, 1952, in London, England; buried in London; married Raymond F. Hosford (a hospital administrator), 1924; children: Frederick Duff and Hugh Malcolm (twins). *Education:* Graduated from Margaret Morrison School of Carnegie Institute of Technology, 1923. *Home:* Bradford, Pa.

CAREER: Author of books for children. Held various secretarial positions including secretary of the extension service of Pennsylvania State University. Served as secretary of the Carnegie Library School from 1924 to 1929. Began writing career, 1929.

*WRITINGS—*For children: *Sons of the Volsungs* (adapted from *Sigurd the Volsung* by William Morris; illustrated by

DOROTHY HOSFORD

. . . As he rode he sang the song of Greyfell, the horse that Odin gave, who swam through the sweeping river and back through the toppling wave. ■ (From *Sons of the Volsungs,* adapted by Dorothy G. Hosford from *Sigurd the Volsung* by William Morris. Illustrated by Frank Dobias.)

Frank Dobias), Macmillan, 1923; *By His Own Might: The Battles of Beowulf* (illustrated by Laszlo Matulay), Holt, 1947; *Thunder of the Gods* (illustrated by Claire and George Louden), Holt, 1952, reissued, 1967.

SIDELIGHTS: In an article, "Our Northern Heritage," Hosford evaluated the virtues of the Norse Sagas in children's literature. "Now do these qualities of the Norse stories . . . have value and meaning for children? I think they do, if not in quite the terms that they have meaning for us as adults. Children may not appreciate them with just the same kind of awareness, but they do respond to them. A child may not recognize the technique of good narrative, but no one responds more quickly than a child to a good story well told, nor grows more quickly restive with a story weak and halting in its narration. Simplicity and directness of telling, un-impeded action, make a strong appeal. And a child is, or can be, sensitive to beauty of language. I think we all agree that children often enjoy the sound of words even before they comprehend their meaning.

"The qualities of the hero in *Beowulf* and in the Norse sagas—certainly these have meaning for children. Perhaps they have a special value for the children of today, so besieged by the cheap, shallow superman of the comics and radio. A diet of the comics and radio may not matter too much, if the child has other fare as well. But it makes me feel a little sad when that is all he knows of heroes and adventure. I should like him also to know the hero of the saga. This is not a hero who always triumphs; he is often one defeated in action, but always undaunted in spirit. He is a man of integrity and loyalty as well as courage; and kindliness and courtesy (in spite of a primitive background of violence) are among his attributes.... Children do identify themselves with their heroes, and I think the hero of the saga offers a more sound and creative identification than the trite and spurious hero of the comics.

"The Norse stories have also humor, and a great deal of sound, earthy wisdom about life. And in these days when we try to teach our children the true meaning of democracy, what procedure could be more democratic than the settling of grievances at the Icelandic Althing?

"The qualities of this type of material, of all legends and hero tales and myths, are elusive; not to be easily named or labeled; not to be pigeonholed. They partake of the quality of poetry and are therefore to be experienced rather than analyzed. The child has need of the supernatural, of exten-sions beyond everyday reality, and he finds this realm of wonders in these tales. Though they mingle fact with legend, they possess 'essential verity.' It is this inner truth which gives them their individuality and power. Perhaps they are not for all children, but it is a great loss if they are not within reach of the children who have the capacity for their enjoy-ment. No other kind of reading quite duplicates them, or can quite substitute for them, or can give quite the same quality of experience as the epics and legends . . . which have them-selves grown from man's vision of what man can be, from the core of greatness in the human soul.

"One encounters, of course, many problems in making such material readable for young people. There is the necessity of reconciling the differences in a story as it may appear in various sources and of choosing that best suited to one's purpose. The material is often complex and involved, but usually at the heart of a story is a simplicity and directness. Then there is the choice of making a close or a free re-telling of the particular story chosen. It is probably a matter of personal temperament that I have preferred, in the work I have done, to make as close a retelling as possible. For one thing, I have hoped that when children met the story again as adults they would feel at home with it and recognize it as an old friend.

"I do not write easily, but with a good deal of labor and much re-writing. My method has been to make first of all the closest possible transcription of a story and to work gradually away from that toward the finished re-telling, always, of course, with constant reference to the original. The problem is to give one's narrative pace and movement, and one's characters depth and reality, always within the limitations

imposed by the original version of the story. And one tries as well, in so far as it can be done at all, to preserve that intangible something which we call the atmosphere or quality of a story. I have found it useful not only to know well the story I am adapting, but to know more about its history and background and the life of the times than one may actually make use of in the re-telling. I also make it a point, while I am working, not to read other adaptations for children of the same material, so that I will not be influenced or confused by the methods or approach of others—nor discouraged by their excellence. As a final test I always read aloud what I have written, read it aloud many times, for the ear will detect rough spots that the eye will overlook. That, briefly, is the way I go about the re-telling of an old story.

Hosford, as a final note, addressed herself to the role of the librarian. "I should like . . . to say just a word about the role of the children's librarian in making this kind of material known to children. This is a time, I think, when a sense of futility often overwhelms us, no matter what our particular place in life or what the work in which we are engaged. The problems of the world are so desperate and so vast and we have grown so acutely aware of them; the pressures of mod-ern life give so little time for pause or reflection, that it is small wonder the individual so often feels frustrated and defeated, and as though his particular endeavors were of little account. Yet, in this confused and difficult world, yours is a work I should be glad to be doing. It is among the creative and positive and significant occupations. I do not say this as a speaker offering easy compliments to his audience, but from a feeling of profound conviction. Nor do I underestimate the difficulties and discouragements of your task: the inertia, indifference, the practical problems of lack of time, lack of adequate staff, etc.—I suppose you could multiply them in-definitely. Yet in this important business of bringing children and good books together, the children's librarian has a very special place. You can reach the child in a way that the schools cannot. I know that there is group and class work, but he also comes to you in a spontaneous relationship and as an individual. He comes to you for something that he wants—what he wants may be often something mediocre—but still you have your chance. And you have, in these in-dividual relationships, an opportunity to give some special attention to the needs of the superior child, so often neglected or thwarted in the exigencies of mass education, our insist-ence upon conformity, and our standardizations. Remember Emerson's 'we read as superior beings,' and give the child who has a capacity for the unusual a chance to follow his own bent in his own way. You can do that better than anyone else.

"It is through you that the imaginative literature of the past, and of the present, will continue to find readers. The hero tales, the material which we have been discussing today, is only one of many kinds of such literature. The important thing is that the child learns to enjoy—and the first emphasis, of course, must be on pleasure and enjoyment in the reading, without which there is no value—that the child learns to enjoy some of the kind of reading that opens the mind, and the heart, to new horizons, and that contributes to the re-sources of the spirit." [Dorothy Hosford, "Our Northern Heritage," in *Horn Book,* September, 1947.]

FOR MORE INFORMATION SEE: Horn Book, September, 1947; Muriel Fuller, editor, *More Junior Authors,* H. W. Wilson, 1963. Obituaries—*Publishers Weekly,* July 26, 1952; *Horn Book,* February, 1953.

Hand knitting and crochet seem to be growing as hobbies almost as fast as machine-knitting has grown. ■ (From *Warm as Wool, Cool as Cotton* by Carter Houck. Illustrated by Nancy Winslow Parker.)

HOUCK, Carter   1924-

PERSONAL: Born May 2, 1924, in Washington, D.C.; daughter of David Thomas (a farmer) and Eliza (Mason) Greene; married Louis Talmadge Houck, February 3, 1945 (divorced, December, 1965); children: Linda Page, Carl Thomas. *Education:* Attended College of William and Mary, 1941-43, University of Connecticut, 1962-65, and Hunter College of the City University of New York, 1965-68. *Politics:* Independent. *Religion:* Episcopalian. *Home:* 16 West 16th St., Apt. 12DS, New York, N.Y. 10011.

CAREER: Singer Sewing Co., teacher, 1943-44; Butterick Co., pattern maker, 1944-45; *Fort Worth Star-Telegram,* Fort Worth, Tex., author of column "Sewing," 1950-51; *Parents' Magazine,* New York, New York, author of column "Sewing," 1962-72; *Lady's Circle,* New York City, editor of *Needlework,* 1971-78, and *Patchwork,* 1971—. Part-owner of Rag Doll (fabric shop), 1968-74. *Member:* New York Embroiderers Guild, Appalachian Mountain Club (vice-chairman of executive committee).

WRITINGS: (With Joanne Schreiber) *Betty Crocker's Good and Easy Sewing Book for You and Your Family,* Universal Publishing, 1972; *Warm as Wool, Cool as Cotton: Natural Fibers and Fabrics and How to Work with Them* (illustrated by Nancy Parker), Seabury, 1975; (with Myron Miller) *American Quilts and How to Make Them,* Scribner, 1975; (with Myron Miller) *The Big Bag Book,* Scribner, 1977. Contributor to magazines, including *Appalachia, Trail Walker,* and *Action Vacations.*

WORK IN PROGRESS: A book on white-work embroidery, for Dover; a book on boat designs for three types of simple embroidery, with Myron Miller, for Scribner.

SIDELIGHTS: "As a small child growing up on a farm a mile from the highway in the Virginia Piedmont, I had to do a good deal of making my own fun. The Depression struck farming in that area an almost deadly blow when I was five years old, which meant that new cars, movies, coats that weren't hand-me-downs from wealthy city cousins, and a lot of other things I never missed, were unknown to me. What I did have was a horse, a whole menagerie of pets, including occasional wild ones that boarded for a while, and a great deal of delightful neglect. That sort of neglect enabled me to climb trees and swing from the branches, use the tools in my father's workshop, sew on my mother's treadle machine, and sometimes play wild imaginative games with my brother. I still hold conversations with cats, dogs, horses, or any other animals that will hold still for long enough to listen.

"I lived with an assortment of very different relatives, mostly in cities. One uncle had an exquisite townhouse in Washington, D.C., which is now a parking lot. One aunt lived on the Main Line of Philadelphia, complete with swimming pool and tennis court, cottage at the shore, and two bratty children. One aunt was the penurious widow of a minister. She counted the grains of sugar on the cereal, the drops of water in the shower, and all of my sins.

"As life has a habit of doing, all things came full circle, and the little girl who'd used the treadle machine as a rainy-day toy headed straight for design school and the Big City.

"I have never lost the habit of writing down descriptions of things I see, places I go, emotions that I cannot share easily. I carry a camera now when I travel, but I find that words paint a clearer picture for me. I see many things around me in terms of needlework designs, and I want to share these things that are a pleasure to me with anyone who will listen. Teaching small groups isn't enough—I can reach a much larger audience by writing. I do, however, like the contact and feedback of teaching workshops.

"When anyone comes to me and asks about being a writer or designer and about working free-lance, I suggest that being used to being alone and keeping oneself amused are helpful character traits. Being creative alone is only possible if being alone is comfortable and even fun."

HUME, Ruth Fox   1922-1980

OBITUARY NOTICE: Born in 1922 in New York, N.Y.; died of cancer, March 1, 1980. Educator and author. Hume taught chemistry at Dunbarton College and Latin at Catholic University before beginning her career as an author. Collaborating with Anne Fahrenkopf under the pseudonym Alexander Irving, she began by writing mysteries for Dodd, Mead & Co., including *Deadline*, *Bitter Ending*, and *Symphony in Two Time*. A former student of medicine, she next turned to the field of medical history and wrote a number of books for Random House, including *Milestones of Medicine*, and *Great Women of Medicine*. She also collaborated with her husband, music critic Paul Hume, on biographies of Ignace Paderewski and John McCormack. Her other books for children include *Our Lady Came to Fatima* and *St. Margaret Mary, Apostle of the Sacred Heart*. *For More Information See: Authors of Books for Young People*, 2nd edition, Scarecrow, 1971. *Obituaries: Washington Post*, March 3, 1980; *Contemporary Authors*, Volume 97-100, Gale, 1980.

HUNT, Morton   1920-

PERSONAL: Born February 20, 1920, in Philadelphia, Pa.; married Lois Marcus (now a singer under name Lois Hunt), August 10, 1946 (divorced, 1965); married Bernice Kohn (children's book author and editor), 1971; children: Jeffrey. *Education:* Temple University, A.B., 1941; University of Pennsylvania, graduate study, 1941, 1946. *Politics:* Democrat. *Home:* RFD 2, Box 118, Bedford, N.Y. 10506.

CAREER: Look, New York, N.Y., researcher, staff writer, 1946-47; *Science Illustrated*, New York, N.Y., associate editor, 1947-49; free-lance writer, 1949—. *New Yorker*, contract writer, mainly of "Profiles," 1958-72. University of Denver, lecturer, summer of 1958. *Military service:* U.S. Army Air Force, pilot, 1942-46; became first lieutenant; awarded Air Medal with two Oak Leaf Clusters. *Member:* American Society of Journalists and Authors (president, 1955). *Awards, honors:* Has won numerous awards, including the George

Westinghouse Award of American Association for Advancement of Science, for best science article of the year, 1952.

WRITINGS—Juveniles: *The Young Person's Guide to Love*, Farrar, Straus, 1975; *Gay: What You Should Know About Homosexuality*, Farrar, Straus, 1977; *What Is a Man? What Is a Woman?*, Farrar, Straus, 1979.

Other writings: *The Natural History of Love*, Knopf, 1959; *Mental Hospital*, Pyramid, 1962; *Her Infinite Variety: The American Woman as Lover, Mate and Rival*, Harper, 1962; (with Rena Corman and Lois Ormont) *The Talking Cure: A Practical Guide to Psychoanalysis*, Harper, 1964; *The Thinking Animal*, Little, Brown, 1964; *The Inland Sea*, Doubleday, 1965; *The World of the Formerly Married*, McGraw, 1966; *The Affair*, New American Library, 1969; *The Mugging*, Atheneum, 1972; (with Bernice Hunt) *Prime Time*, Stein and Day, 1975; (with Bernice Hunt) *The Divorce Experience*, McGraw, 1977. Contributor of about four hundred articles, many of them in the field of psychology and psychiatry, to periodicals, including *Harper's*, *Saturday Evening Post*, *Redbook*, *Horizon*, and *Cosmopolitan*.

SIDELIGHTS: Speaks French and German.

HOBBIES AND OTHER INTERESTS: Sailing, swimming, gardening.

JOHNSON, Lois W(alfrid)   1936-

PERSONAL: Born November 23, 1936, in Starbuck, Minn.; daughter of A. B. (a clergyman) and Lydia (Christiansen) Walfrid; married Roy A. Johnson (an elementary school teacher), June 26, 1959; children: Gail, Jeffrey, Kevin. *Education:* Gustavus Adolphus College, B.A. (magna cum laude), 1958; University of Oklahoma, graduate study, 1968-72; Luther-Northwestern Seminaries, special student, 1976—. *Politics:* Independent. *Religion:* Lutheran. *Home:* 8117 35th Ave. N., Minneapolis, Minn. 55427.

CAREER: High school English teacher in Wayzata, Minn., 1958-59, and lay reader in Edina, Minn., 1962-63, 1964-65; free-lance writer, and speaker, 1971—. Has taught at *Decision* Magazine School of Christian Writing in Minneapolis, 1973-77, 1979-80, and their Canadian School, Toronto, 1976, Midwest Writer's Conference, 1974-75, 1978, Wartburg Seminary Writer's Conference, 1977, Brite Christian Writer's Conference, 1980; editorial associate, *Writer's Digest* School (correspondence school), 1974-77. *Member:* Society of Children's Book Writers, Minnesota Guild of Christian Writers (vice-president, 1970-71; president, 1971-72), Authors Guild, Authors League of America, Iota Delta Gamma. *Awards, honors:* Dwight L. Moody Award for excellence in Christian literature, from *Decision* Magazine School of Christian Writing, 1969, for short story "Spaces in the Heart."

WRITINGS—Juvenile: *Just a Minute, Lord* (prayers for girls), Augsburg, 1973; *Aaron's Christmas Donkey* (picture book), Augsburg, 1974; *Hello, God! Prayers for Small Children* (picture book), Augsburg, 1975; *You're My Best Friend, Lord* (for girls), Augsburg, 1976.

Adult: *Gift in My Arms: Thoughts for New Mothers*, Augsburg, 1977; *Either Way, I Win: A Guide to Growth in the Power of Prayer*, Augsburg, 1979; *Song for Silent Moments: Prayers for Daily Living*, Augsburg, 1980.

Work has been anthologized in *Complete Christmas Programs,* Volume IV, edited by Grace Ramquist, Zondervan, 1972; *Children of Light* (juvenile), edited by Wilson G. Egbert, Augsburg, 1973; a short story was included as part of a chapter in *Jesus Stood by Us,* by Helen Reagan Smith, Broadman, 1970; *Family Prayers,* edited by Ron and Lyn Klug, Augsburg, 1979.

Lyrics for hymns: "Father, Lead Us to Your Table," Augsburg, 1974; "Come to Us, Living Spirit," Augsburg, 1975.

Contributor of about sixty articles, poems, stories, and reviews to religious and general magazines, including *Decision, Scope, Christian Herald, Moody Monthly, A.D., Tech, Lutheran Standard,* and *Newstime.*

WORK IN PROGRESS: Two children's books; an adult book.

SIDELIGHTS: "In my book, *Either Way, I Win,* I describe my decision to become a writer, for it had special meaning in connection with the diagnosis of my cancer in 1977.

"I remember well the spring in which I was nine and a half years old. It was my task to clean leaves out of the barberry bushes in front of our home. The thorns pricked my fingers,and I poked along, moving slowly, finally sitting down on the sidewalk warmed by spring sunshine. As I sat there, our church bell began to toll. I knew someone had died; automatically I counted. long tolls rang on and on, filling the countryside.

"89, 90, 91, I counted. Then they stopped. Ninety-one years old. What a long time for someone to live, I thought. I wonder what that person left behind? And then, What will I leave behind?

"In that Moment, with the spring sunlight warm upon my back, I decided I wanted to write. If I could possibly write a book, I wanted to let people know how I felt about things. To my nine-year-old mind, that meant telling how I felt about Jesus Christ." [Lois Walfrid Johnson, *Either Way, I Win,* Augsburg, 1979.[1]]

Slowpoke answered by nudging Aaron's cap. ■ (From *Aaron's Christmas Donkey* by Lois Walfrid Johnson. Illustrated by Jim Roberts.)

LOIS W. JOHNSON

"To break into writing I needed a willingness to attempt new forms, even when I didn't know if I could succeed. I began by writing articles and stories for adults. Then one of Augsburg's editors told me they needed material for pre-teens. 'I don't know if I can write for that age level,' I responded. 'But I'd like to try.' Those efforts became my first book, *Just a Minute, Lord.*

"I keep regular weekday hours for my writing. I do much of my thinking while performing routine tasks such as washing dishes, so that I have an idea of what I want to say when I actually sit down. Each of my books has involved some sort of learning process in my personal life and in my development as a writer. Out of my need for inspiration in my work, I learned the creativity available through prayer and the guidance of the Holy Spirit.

"I take special delight in the writing I do for juveniles and the children themselves make it that way. My husband has taught in elementary schools since 1958 and is my favorite resource person when I wonder about age-level characteristics, likes and dislikes. Whenever I research, I also talk as much as possible with the kind of person to whom a book is directed. *You're My Best Friend, Lord* grew out of discussions with twelve and thirteen year-olds in a class I taught. *Hello, God!* originally had a different title, but when I read the book to neighborhood children, I realized they didn't understand what I was saying. I changed the title, as well as parts of the book, because of comments made by four and five-year olds."

HOBBIES AND OTHER INTERESTS: Biking, swimming, water and cross-country skiing, music, playing piano and flute, traveling, photography, reading.

JONES, Helen L.   1904(?)-1973

OBITUARY NOTICE: Born about 1904, in Billerica, Mass.; died January 6, 1973. Editor, publishing executive. A graduate of Wellesley College, Helen L. Jones began her publishing career, about 1926, as an assistant to the first proofreader at Riverside Press. She soon found a clerical position in the textbook department of Little, Brown & Company. Her career gradually but steadily progressed, and by 1950, she had become the associate editor of Little, Brown's newly revived children's book program. Two years later she was promoted to editor, supervising and coordinating the publication of children's books under three imprints—Little, Brown, the Atlantic Monthly Press, and Duell, Sloan and Pearce. Helen Jones retired from the publishing industry in 1969, but she remained active in the children's book field as a member of the Women's National Book Association as well as president and director of the Children's Book Council. In 1971, she served as a juror for the National Book Award for Children's Literature. She shared some of her insights into the publication and illustration of children's books in *Robert Lawson, Illustrator,* published by Little, Brown in 1972. *For More Information See : Publishers Weekly,* October 22, 1955. *Obituaries: Publishers Weekly,* January 22, 1973.

JOSEPH, Joseph M(aron)   1903-1979

PERSONAL: Born August 1, 1903, in Philadelphia, Pa.; died May 22, 1979, in New York, N.Y.; son of Elias Farras (a merchant) and Hesna (Rohanna) Joseph; married Doris Hagens (a secretary), July 3, 1937; children: Peter Maron, Helene Farras. *Education:* Shippensburg State College, B.S. in Education, 1931; University of Pennsylvania, M.S. in Education. *Religion:* Presbyterian. *Home:* 202 West 23rd St., Chester, Pa. *Office:* Administration Bldg., Chester School District, 17th & Melrose Ave., Chester, Pa.

CAREER: Public schools, Chester, Pa., science teacher, 1931-46, junior high school principal, 1946-59, director, secondary curriculum, 1959-70. Camp Sunshine, Delaware County, Pa., member, president, 1943-70, became president emeritus; superintendent of Sunday school, Christian Education Committee, 1944-54; Chester Civil Service Commission, president, 1953; Delaware Valley Science Fair, Philadelphia, Pa., charter member. *Member:* National Science Teachers Association, National Education Association, Association for Supervision and Curriculum Development, Pennsylvania State Science Teachers Association (past president), Association of Secondary School Principals, American Association for the Advancement of Science, Rittenhouse Astronomical Society (Philadelphia), Pennsylvania Opera Company (board of directors), National Retired Teachers Association, Studebaker Drivers Club. *Awards, honors:* Distinguished Citizen of the Year, Chester American Legion Post 190, 1948.

WRITINGS: (With William H. Barton) *Starcraft,* McGraw, 1938, revised, 1946; (with Sarah Lee Lippincott) *Point to the Stars,* McGraw, 1963, 1977. Contributor to professional jour-

JOSEPH M. JOSEPH

nals. Earth and space department editor, *The Pennsylvania Science Teacher.*

SIDELIGHTS: Interested in mentally gifted students, preventive aspects of juvenile delinquency, radio astronomy, judging science fairs, developing home "open-air" observatories in yards and gardens, implementing theory that "anthropology precedes psychology" as a learning approach, promoting theory that "perception" should precede coordinates in constellation identification and location. Enjoyed the symphony, and lieder and operatic music.

FOR MORE INFORMATION SEE—Obituaries: *Delaware County Daily Times,* May 24, 1979, May 25, 1979.

KAPLAN, Bess 1927-

PERSONAL: Born July 1, 1927, in Winnipeg, Manitoba, Canada; daughter of Jacob (a butcher) and Rachel (Dicktor) Olin; married Phil Kaplan, February 11, 1951 (died August 12, 1976); children: Gerry, Allan, Elaine, Sheldon. *Education:* Attended junior high school in Winnipeg, Manitoba. *Religion:* Jewish. *Home and office:* 9 O'Meara St., Winnipeg, Manitoba, Canada R2W 3Z1.

CAREER: Factory worker, 1943-51; writer, 1959—. *Member:* Canadian Authors Association (Winnipeg president, 1969-71), Penhandlers (president, 1973), B'nai B'rith. *Awards, honors:* Centennial award from Winnipeg branch of the Canadian Authors Association, 1969, for story "Rainy Day";

award, 1972, for article, "The Magic of Fiction"; Kathleen Strange Memorial Award from Winnipeg branch of the Canadian Authors Association, 1973; grant from Manitoba Arts Council, 1977.

WRITINGS: Corner Store (novel), Queenston House, 1976, published as *The Empty Chair,* Harper, 1977; *Malke, Malke,* (novel), Queenston House, 1977. Author of "The Better Years," a weekly humor column in *Winnipeg Free Press,* 1959-64. Contributor of articles and stories to Canadian magazines and newspapers, including *Chatelaine* and *Montrealer.* Editor of *Jewish Post,* 1973, 1974, and 1975.

WORK IN PROGRESS: Some Call Me God, a novel.

SIDELIGHTS: "I have always wanted to be a writer—since the illuminating moment I discovered that those squiggly little marks actually had meaning. I remember it as a flash in my mind. I devoured every book in sight from the age of six onward. Probably, *Little Women* was a great influence on me when I first read it and I decided I too would write books someday. But first I tried my hand at short stories; really awful ones by today's standards, very romantic, soppy ones that deserved oblivion. However, at the time (in my early teens) I was sure they were beautiful and sent them out to various magazines, positive of acceptance. The heartache of psoriasis has nothing on the heartbreak of the silent rejection slip, as I discovered very soon. I wrote them all out in my best penmanship, too. The beasts!

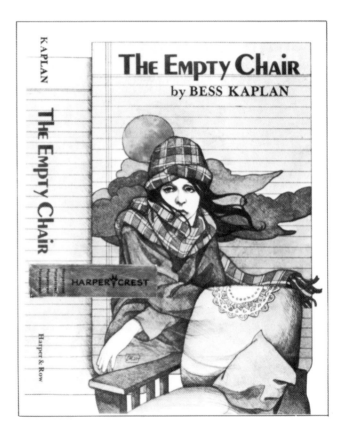

Sometimes something can happen that changes everything in your whole life. ■(From *The Empty Chair* by Bess Kaplan. Jacket illustrated by Charles Mikolaycak.)

BESS KAPLAN

"I wrote my first two novels in long hand, a veritable out-pouring of words, but they came later, much later. First, I dropped out of school to get a job in a biscuit factory. Oh, how excited I was ! On my sixteenth birthday, I landed my first job! I picked hot biscuits off trays that came steaming out of the huge ovens below. It takes a certain skill to keep from blistering your fingertips. After a week, the blisters were gone. I worked there almost a year, then automation kicked fifty girls right out of work.

"I did a variety of things. Ground glass edges for frost shields for cars, learned to sew overalls, pajamas, parkas and many, many things in four or five different sewing factories. Then one magical July day I met Phil. We married six months later, had children and I began to get stirrings of restlessness. I needed a creative outlet to give me relief from diapers and formulas.

"I began to paint, and then to write and for awhile I wasn't sure which was more important. But there's no doubt now that writing is my main activity. It has given my life all its meaning and purpose, especially after I lost my husband after twenty-five years and six months of fitting my life around him and my four children. The utter devastation death wreaks on the one who's left is hard to write about. Books have been written by widows about widowhood, but I would rather write about life.

"I think all my books celebrate life. I'd like to hope; I do hope, that people reading my novels get a lift. My characters are Jewish because I understand the Jewish soul, but I believe that we all have the same needs, the same problems, the same feelings about the world around us. So if I'm writing about a young Jewish artist—it's only because I have been involved in that world and so I know it best. But it could just as easily be an Irish young woman, or Italian, maybe. We have to show that which we know best. This is what I try to do.

"I started writing *Corner Store* when the Winnipeg *Free Press*, the major newspaper in Winnipeg, decided five years of my weekly column was quite long enough. At the time, it was shattering. Free-lance markets were drying up all over Canada and the U.S. Over the years I had built up a following of readers and yet—to do that to me! It turned out to be the best thing that could have happened. Now I started that novel (which Harper and Row call *The Empty Chair*) although I had no idea at all about my subject. It seemed to be there, around me, and when I sat down at the kitchen table after everyone had gone to work and school and picked up my pen and opened the writing pad, the words marched through my head. Of course it went through five drafts before I was satisfied with it, but my subject had been hanging around, waiting for me to begin, and my only problem was remembering to stop in time to prepare meals.

"My life is serene now. Although I still mother whoever is home to be mothered, my main concerns are writing, or doing things in connection with writing. I have judged the young writers' short story contest here in Manitoba since I first set it up in 1971. I write letters to promising young writers. I speak about the writing craft in schools and creative writing classes and I also write."

HOBBIES AND OTHER INTERESTS: Oil painting, travel (including Israel).

FOR MORE INFORMATION SEE: Winnipeg Tribune, December 13, 1975, June 23, 1976; *Winnipeg Guide,* March 9, 1977; *Regina Leader-Post,* June 15, 1977; *Winnipeg Free Press,* July 22, 1977; *Star-Phoenix,* August 5, 1977; *Canadian Jewish News,* December 16, 1977; *Horn Book,* June, 1978.

KENNEDY, (Jerome) Richard 1932-

PERSONAL: Born December 23, 1932, in Jefferson City, Mo.; son of Donald and Mary Louise (O'Keefe) Kennedy; married Lillian Nance, 1960; children: Joseph Troy, Matthew Cook. *Education:* Portland State University, B.S., 1958; Oregon State University, graduate study, 1964-65. *Home:* 415 West Olive, Newport, Ore. 97365.

CAREER: Writer. Worked as a fifth grade teacher in Harrisburg, Oregon and in Dayton, Oregon, 1968-69. *Military service:* U. S. Air Force, 1951-54. *Awards, honors:* Pacific Northwest Bookseller's Award for *The Blue Stone* and *The Porcelain Man,* 1976.

WRITINGS: The Parrot and the Thief (illustrated by Marcia Sewall), Atlantic-Little, Brown, 1974; *The Contests at Cowlick* (illustrated by March Simont), Atlantic-Little, Brown, 1975; *The Porcelain Man* (illustrated by Marcia Sewall), Atlantic-Little, Brown, 1976; *Come Again in the Spring,*

...Death had lost the wager and must leave Old Hark to live until spring, for his father's words on seeing his newborn son had been "Open the window! Let the birds sing!" ■ (From *Come Again in the Spring* by Richard Kennedy. Illustrated by Marcia Sewall.)

Harper (illustrated by Marcia Sewall), 1976; *The Blue Stone* (ALA Notable Book; illustrated by Ronald Himler), Holiday House, 1976; *Oliver Hyde's Dishcloth Concert* (illustrated by Robert A. Parker), Atlantic-Little, Brown, 1977; *The Dark Princess* (ALA Notable Book; illustrated by Donna Diamond), Holiday House, 1978; *The Rise and Fall of Ben Gizzard* (illustrated by Marcia Sewall), Atlantic-Little, Brown, 1978; *The Mouse God,* Atlantic-Little, Brown, 1979; *Delta Baby and Two Sea Songs* (illustrated by Lydia Dabcovich and Charles Mikolaycak), Addison-Wesley, 1979; *The Lost Kingdom of Karnica* (illustrated by Uri Shulevitz), Sierra Club/Scribner, 1979; *The Leprechaun's Story* (illustrated by Maria Sewall), Dutton, 1979; *Inside My Feet: The Story of A Giant* (illustrated by Ronald Himler), Harper, 1979; *Crazy in Love,* Dutton, 1980.

FOR MORE INFORMATION SEE: Horn Book, February, April, and June, 1977.

KING, Frank O.   1883-1969

OBITUARY NOTICE: Born April 9, 1883, in Cashton, Wis.; died June 23, 1969. Artist and creator of cartoon strips. King drew for the *Minneapolis Times, Chicago Examiner,* the *Chicago Tribune,* and for the Chicago Tribune-New York News Syndicate. His "Bobby Make Believe" and "The Rectangle" comic strips appeared before he began his popular "Gasoline Alley" strip in 1918. He was recognized by the National Cartoonists Society as the best strip cartoonist, in 1957, and as cartoonist of the year, in 1958. His book titles include *Skeezix and Uncle Walt, Skeezix at the Circus,* and *Skeezix Out West. For More Information See: Coronet,* February, 1949; *Editor and Publisher,* May 13, 1950; *Coronet,* June, 1954; *Who Was Who in America,* 5th edition, Marquis, 1973. *Obituaries: New York Times,* June 25, 1969; *Time,* July 4, 1969; *Newsweek,* July 7, 1969; *Contemporary Authors,* Volume 89-92, Gale, 1980.

KOLBA, Tamara
(St. Tamara)

PERSONAL: Born in Byelorussia; emigrated to the U.S. in 1950; married Alexander Kolba (government worker), February 22, 1958. *Education:* Western College, Oxford, Ohio, B.A., 1954; Columbia University, M.F.A., 1956; attended Art Students League, New York, N.Y. and Institute of Fine Arts, N.Y.U. *Home and office:* 235 Hockhockson Rd., Tinton Falls, N.J. 07724.

CAREER: Free-lance artist. *Exhibitions*—One man shows: Aenle Gallery, New York, N.Y., 1956; Western College, Oxford, Ohio, 1956; Avanti Gallery, New York, N.Y., 1968; Fine Arts Museum, Asbury Park, N.J., 1973; Free Public Library of Woodbridge, Woodbridge, N.J., 1975; Guild of Creative Art, Shrewsbury, N.J., 1975, 1977; Little Silver Borough Hall, Little Silver, N.J., 1977.

Group shows: Lever House, New York, N.Y.; Byelorussian Institute of Arts and Sciences, New York, N.Y., National Arts Club, New York, N.Y.; New Hampshire Graphics Annual; Sculptors and Gravers Society, Washington, D.C.; United Nations, New York, N.Y.; Miniature Art Society of New Jersey; George Walter Smith Museum, Springfield, Mass.; Davidson National Print and Drawing Competition, Davidson, N.C.; Couturier Gallerie, Stamford, Conn.; National Academy of Design, New York, N.Y.; Audubon Artists at the National Academy, New York, N.Y.; Norwalk Museum, South Norwalk, Conn.; New York Public Library; UNICEF Exhibit.

Traveling exhibits: Hunterdon Arts Center, traveling through New Jersey museums and colleges; Catharine Lorillard Wolf Art Club, traveling in the greater New York City metropolitan area; The Herron School of Art, Indianapolis, Ind., Young Printmakers Show, traveling nationwide for two years. Permanent collections: Columbia University, New York, N.Y.; New York Public Library, New York, N.Y.; Fine Arts Museum, Asbury Park, N.J.; UNICEF Collection, United Nations, New York, N.Y.; California College, San Francisco, Calif.; The Free Public Library of Woodbridge, Woodbridge, N.J.; The Print Club of Albany, Albany, N.Y.; and in many private collections in the U.S., Canada, Europe and South America.

MEMBER: Byelorussian Institute of Art and Sciences, Byelorussian Art Club, Metropolitan Museum and Art Center, Hunterdon Art Center, Printmaking Council of New Jersey, Catharine Lorillard Wolfe Art Club, The Print Club of Albany, Guild of Creative Art. *Awards, honors:* Second prize, 1971, honorable mention, 1975, Ida Becker Fund for Graphic Award, 1978, CLWAC, National Arts Club; gold medal, CLWAC, National Academy, 1971; third prize, 1973, 1974, second place, 1974, first prize, 1976, Monmouth Arts Gallery; honorable mention, Art Center of the Oranges, 1973; honorable mention, 1973, Best Traditional Award, 1974, Fall Arts Fete; library award, judges choice, Dubois, Wyo., 1974; graphics award, Oklahoma Museum, 1975, 1976; Purchase Prize, Print Club of Albany, 1975; International Women's Year Award, 1976; second place, and most outstanding wildlife miniature, Ada V. Wester Award, Laluz, N.M., 1978; *Save That Raccoon!* was named Outstanding Science Book for Children, 1976; Purchase Award, Valley City, N.D.; Martin T. Hannon Memorial Award from Salmagundi Club, New York, N.Y. for "Taos Pueblo" drawing, 1980; Merit Award, Springfield Art League, Springfield, Mass. for "Pa-

TAMARA KOLBA

lessie" #2 drawing, 1980; Merit Award, New York, N.Y. for "... And They Were Left Behind...," 1980.

WRITINGS—Self-illustrated: *Asian Crafts,* Lion Press, 1970; *Chickaree, a Red Squirrel,* Harcourt, 1980.

Illustrator: Barbara A. Steiner, *Biography of a Polar Bear,* Putnam, 1972; Eugenia Alston, *Come Visit a Prairie Dog Town,* Harcourt, 1976; Russell Freedman, *Animal Games,* Holiday House, 1976; Gloria D. Miklowitz, *Save That Raccoon!,* Harcourt, 1978.

WORK IN PROGRESS: Translations of Byelorussian folktales; two mystery detective stories; research on family history; a series, "Taos Pueblo" in oil, drawings, lithographs and etchings.

SIDELIGHTS: "I use mostly pen & ink (Rapidograph with #000) but also use washes (ink diluted with water). This line technique is very close to the effect my etchings create. My main concern is nature and animals. I am working on the whole line of animal etchings done in drypoint, sizes 3"x3" or 4"x4". I always start my animals with the eye and if I feel it 'looks' at me than I proceed with my etching or illustration."

FOR MORE INFORMATION SEE: Asbury Park Press (N.J.), March 13, 1977; Zina Stankievic, *Let's Get Acquainted with an Artist,* Byelarus, 1977.

KUNHARDT, Dorothy Meserve 1901(?)-1979

OBITUARY NOTICE: Born about 1901; died December 23, 1979, in Beverly, Mass. Author and illustrator. Kunhardt was the author and illustrator of numerous children's books, including *Pat the Bunny,* first published in 1940 and still listed as a bestseller on the list of children's classics. She also collaborated with her son, Philip B. Kunhardt, Jr., on *Twenty Days,* a book about the period of national mourning that followed President Abraham Lincoln's assassination, and *Matthew Brady and His World.* Her other books included the popular ''tiny'' series—*Tiny Animals Stories* and *Tiny Nonsense Stories*—and such juveniles as *The Telephone Book, Junket Is Nice, Lucky Mrs. Ticklefeather,* and *Feed the Animals. For More Information See: American Picturebooks from Noah's Ark to the Beast Within,* Macmillan, 1976; *Obituaries: New York Times,* December 25, 1979; *Contemporary Authors,* Volume 93-96, Gale, 1980; *Publishers Weekly,* January 18, 1980.

LAWSON, Marion Tubbs 1896-

PERSONAL: Born August 8, 1896, in Elkhorn, Wis.; daughter of Henry H. (a civil engineer) and Helen Marion (Andrus) Tubbs; married Philip C. Lawson (a salesman), December 6, 1927. *Education:* Carroll College, Waukesha, Wis., A.B., 1919. *Politics:* Republican. *Religion:* Protestant. *Home:* 160 Cabrini Blvd., New York, N.Y. 10033.

CAREER: Worked in Milwaukee, Wis., for printing and publishing companies and an investment house, 1919-27. *Member:* American Association of University Women.

WRITINGS: Solomon Juneau, Voyageur, Crowell, 1960; *Proud Warrior: The Story of Black Hawk,* Hawthorn, 1968; *Maggie Flying Bird,* Morrow, 1974. Contributor of articles

(From *Maggie Flying Bird* by Marion Lawson. Illustrated by Miriam Schottland.)

to *National Business Woman, Wisconsin Magazine of History,* of short stories to literary magazines.

SIDELIGHTS: ''My interest in Indians began at the age of ten when our family lived in Montana. Our home base was Wisconsin but my father was a civil engineer. When railroads were extending their lines rather than abandoning them, he was the engineer in charge of a division of the last long extension of the Chicago, Milwaukee and St. Paul railroad. In summers when my brother and I were out of school we followed my father to the railroad jobs. One of our happiest summers was spent in a railroad camp in Wyoming 8,000 feet up, running over the foothills of the Rockies in red waists and overalls to make us more visible and comfortable. A psychopathic landlady soured our stay in the Dakotas.

''The Montana job lasted two years. We lived in a little house in Forsyth, with my father's engineering party camping in a tent in our backyard. Two of my schoolmates were half-Indian girls, daughters of the agent of the Indian reservation and his Indian wife. The girl's grandmother often sat on the side porch and we whispered about her being a real 'blanket Indian.'

''At times Indians came in from the reservation to beg. One day a man and two women came to our back door, and stood there silently—waiting. My mother's kind heart exploded in generosity at their bedraggled appearance. Ragged clothes, broken, ill-fitting shoes, one of the women wearing a bedspread for a blanket.

''Mother invited them into the house, seated them at the table and fed them everything left over from our own dinner. Milk that tasted of sagebrush, and beef stew. She had cooked generously as it was intended to serve the family for two days. It didn't. They ate it all, the best meal they had had for some time I imagine. My mother was a very good cook which came from her New England ancestry. My brother and I stood bug-eyed, curious and ill-mannered, but very interested and indignant that they had to be so poor.

''The older woman's eyes were sore and mattery. Before she let them go Mother mixed up a boric acid solution, found clean cloth and gently bathed the old woman's eyes. Then she sent them off with the younger woman carrying a bottle of the eye wash, clean cloth and earnest instructions to see that it was used.

''So it began and in later years my writing career quite naturally turned to Indians. For years I have been collecting books on Indian history, contemporary Indian art, pictures, rugs, pots, baskets, silver jewelry.

''Since I never had any children I have not attempted to write for small people—just for the young in mind and body, and heart, whatever their age; and left it to editors to assign the age group. I've found that adults as well as young enjoy my books.

''By the time I had learned to write professionally my kind of novels were out of style. I've had an unusually happy marriage with a wonderful husband so my life experience had not equipped me for the sexy modern novel popular in today's market. Hence, quite naturally I have turned to history and Indians. It seems to work and I've enjoyed the research and the writing.''

HOBBIES AND OTHER INTERESTS: Contemporary American Indian art, antiques, bird watching.

Lee, Manning de V(illeneuve)   1894-1980

OBITUARY NOTICE: Born March 15, 1894, in Summerville, S.C.; died March 31, 1980, in Chestnut Hill, Pa. Artist and illustrator. Lee trained for his craft at the Pennsylvania Academy of Fine Arts in Philadelphia, but his studies were interrupted by field artillery service in Mexico and later in France during World War I. His paintings can be found in a number of private collections and public collections including the U.S. Mint in Philadelphia, Cranbrook Academy in Birmingham, Mich., the U.S. Naval Academy in Annapolis, Md., and the Presidential Palace in Monrovia, Liberia. Specializing in historical subjects, Lee illustrated more than 200 books including *Kidnapped* by Robert Louis Stevenson, *Historic Ships* and *Historic Railroads* by Rupert S. Holland, and *George Washington: First President* by Elsie Ball. *For More Information See:* Muriel Fuller, *More Junior Authors,* Wilson, 1963; *Who's Who in America,* 40th edition, Marquis, 1978; *Who's Who in American Art, 1978,* Bowker, 1978. *Obituaries: Publishers Weekly,* May 30, 1980.

LESSER, Margaret   1899(?)-1979

OBITUARY NOTICE: Born about 1899; died November 21, 1979, in New York, N.Y. Editor. Lesser was a children's book editor at Doubleday for thirty years. In that capacity, she worked on several award-winning books, including Thomas Handforth's *Mei Li,* Leonard Weisgard's *The Little Island,* and *Abraham Lincoln* by Ingri and Edgar Parin d'Aulaire, all winners of the Caldecott Medal, as well as Marguerite de Angeli's *Door in the Wall,* a Newbery Medal winner. In addition to her duties as editor, Lesser was a two-term president of the Children's Book Council, and served as a consultant to the Junior Literary Guild in her later years. *Obituaries: Publishers Weekly,* December 24, 1979; *Contemporary Authors,* Volume 93-96, Gale, 1980.

LIEBLICH, Irene   1923-

PERSONAL: Born April 20, 1923, in Zamosc, Poland; daughter of Leon (a secretary) and Anna Wechter; married Jakob Lieblich (a businessman), July 21, 1946; children: Mahli, Nathan. *Education:* Attended Gimnazjun, Zamosc, Poland. *Residence:* Brooklyn, N.Y.

CAREER: Artist. *Exhibitions:* Artists Equity, New York, N.Y.; neighborhood galleries and in Canada and Israel. *Member:* Artists Equity Association.

ILLUSTRATOR: Isaac Bashevis Singer, *A Tale of Three Wishes,* Farrar, 1976.

WORK IN PROGRESS: Illustrations for eight Hanukkah stories written by Singer, to be published by Farrar.

SIDELIGHTS: "Through my work I want to project to the children all over the world the nobility and the eternal endurance of the Jewish spirit."

FOR MORE INFORMATION SEE: Publishers Weekly, February 23, 1976; *Flatbush Life,* March 26, 1979.

(From *A Tale of Three Wishes* by Isaac Bashevis Singer. Illustrated by Irene Lieblich.)

IRENE LIEBLICH

(From *The Collecting Book* by Ellen and Lewis Liman.)

LIMAN, Ellen (Fogelson)   1936-

PERSONAL: Born January 4, 1936, in New York, N.Y.; married Arthur Liman (an attorney), September 20, 1959; children: Lewis, Emily, Douglas. *Education:* Barnard College, B.A., 1957. *Home:* 1 East 87th St., New York, N.Y. 10028. *Agent:* Julian Bach, Jr., 747 Third Ave., New York, N.Y. 10017.

CAREER: Writer. Member of board of governors of International Center of Photography.

WRITINGS: The Money Saver's Guide to Decorating, Macmillan, 1971; *Decorating Your Country Place,* Coward, 1973; (with Carol Panter) *Decorating Your Room: A Do it Yourself Guide,* F. Watts, 1974; *The Spacemaker Book,* Viking, 1977; (with son, Lewis Liman) *The Collecting Book,* Penguin, 1980.

SIDELIGHTS: "*The Collecting Book,* my latest project, is for children (as well as adults) and was in fact written in part by a grown-up (almost) child, my son Lewis, age eighteen. He's been a collector of political memorabilia since kindergarten and it was his hobby that led to the conception of this book and our subsequent collaboration. A survey of popular collectibles—everything from butterflies to buttons to beer cans—*The Collecting Book* includes, in its 312 pages, large format, interviews with experts, celebrities and others; tips on buying, selling, displaying and care of collections; lists of clubs, hundreds of publications to send away for (many free) and is illustrated with over 700 photographs."

LIPINSKY de ORLOV, Lino S.   1908-

PERSONAL: Born January 14, 1908 in Rome, Italy; became an American citizen, 1945; son of Siegmund (an artist) and Elinita K. (Burgess) Lipinsky de Orlov; married Leah S. Penner, October 1, 1943; children: Lino, Lucian. *Education:* Attended Lipinsky Art School, Rome; British Academy of Arts, Rome, 1922-25; Reale Accademia Di Belle Arti, Rome, graduate, 1935. *Home:* John Jay Homestead, Katonah, N.Y. 10536 and Via Margutta 33, Rome, Italy 00187.

CAREER: Artist, painter, etcher and illustrator. The Garibaldi and Meucci Memorial Museum, Rosebank, Staten Island, N.Y., director, curator, 1956—; Seventh Regiment Armory, New York, N.Y., Annual Winter Antiques Show, director, 1957-60; Museum of the City of New York, New York, N.Y., curator of exhibitions, 1959-67; John Jay Homestead, New York State Historic Site, Katonah, N.Y., director, curator of history, 1967—; Philipse Manor Hall, New York State Historic Site, Yonkers, N.Y., director, curator of history, 1975—; art and history consultant to Italian Embassy, Washington, D.C., and Consulate General of Italy, New York, N.Y.; consultant to Bedford Historical Society, Bedford Court House Restoration and History Museum, Southeast Museum, Brewster, N.Y. and North Salem Historical Society, North Salem, N.Y. Art Admission Committee Huntington Hartford Foundation, Pacific Palisades, Calif., member, 1962-65.

EXHIBITIONS—Group Shows: Los Angeles Museum, 1927, 1928, 1932; Mills College, San Francisco, Calif., 1932; Art Institute of Chicago, 1934, 1941, 1950; The Society of American Etchers, New York, N.Y., 1942, 1943, 1945, 1946, 1953; The Library of Congress, Washington, D.C., 1942, 1943, 1949, 1950, 1953; Grand Central Art Galleries, New York, N.Y., 1942; The National Academy of Design, 1943, 1944, 1946, 1947, 1948, 1949; The Cleveland Museum of Art,

1943; The Detroit Institute of Arts, 1943; Albany Institute of History and Art, 1945, 1947; Thomas Moran Memorial Gallery at Guild Hall, East Hampton, N.Y., 1946, 1948; Audubon Artists, New York, N.Y., 1946, 1950, 1951; Metropolitan Opera House, New York, N.Y., 1946; The Kosciuszko Foundation, New York, N.Y., 1948, 1949; Carnegie Institute, Pittsburgh, Pa., 1949, 1950, Ridgefield, Conn., 1975; Albright Art Gallery, Buffalo, N.Y., 1949; Memorial Art Gallery, Rochester, N.Y., 1953; Oklahoma School of Architecture and Applied Art, Stillwater, Okla., 1953; Columbia University Avery Architectural Library, New York, N.Y., 1955; Museum of the City of New York, 1955; St. Matthews Art Fair, Bedford, N.Y., 1973.

One-man shows: Symphony Hall, Boston, Mass., 1941; Vose Galleries, Boston, Mass., 1941; Junior League Gallery, Boston, Mass., 1942; St. Paul Guild Gallery, New York, N.Y., 1945; Knoedler Art Galleries, New York, N.Y., 1945; Cosmos Club, Washington, D.C., 1955; Smithsonian Institution, United States National Museum, Washington, D.C., 1955. He also participated in exhibitions throughout many foreign countries.

Permanent collections: Archdiocese of New York, New York, N.Y.; Library of Congress, Washington, D.C.; Severance Hall, Cleveland, Ohio; New York Public Library, New York, N.Y.; Metropolitan Museum of Art, New York, N.Y.; Cranbrook Art Museum, Bloomfield Hills, Mich.; Detroit Institute of Art, Detroit, Mich.; Vassar College, Poughkeepsie, N.Y.; New York Public Library, New York, N.Y.; Florida State University Library, Tallahassee, Fla.; Yale University Library, New Haven, Conn.; Museum of the City of New York, Theatre Collection, New York, N.Y.; works are also in many permanent collections throughout Europe.

Military service: Officers training course, 52nd Infantry Regiment Alpi, Spoleto, Italy, 1936, Lieutenant in Second Regiment Grenadiers of Sardinia in Rome. U.S. Army, World War II, Intelligence Division, Sixth Service Command.

MEMBER: Audubon Artists, Chicago Society of Etchers, Society of American Graphic Artists, United Scenic Artists, American Association of Museums, Comitato Nazionale Per Le Onoranze a Giovanni da Verrazzano (vice-president), Gruppo Romano Incisori Artisti, Gruppo Artisti di Via Margutta, International Platform Association, Bedford Farmers' Club, Washington Irving Council and Westchester Putnam Council, Boy Scouts of America, Paternoster Corner Gallery, New York State Association of Museums, Hammond Museum, The Katonah Gallery, Knights of Mark Twain, Bedford Historical Society, New York State Employee's Association, America-Italy Society, National Society of Literature and the Arts, Bicentennial Committee (Yorktown, N.Y.), Tricentennial Committee (Bedford, N.Y.).

AWARDS, HONORS: Silver Medal of the Ministero dell' Educazione Nazionale, Rome, 1931; Diplome d'Honneur,

(From *The Ghost of Peg-Leg Peter, and Other Stories of Old New York* by M.A. Jagendorf. Illustrated by Lino S. Lipinsky.)

Exposition Internationale, Budapest, 1936; Gold Medal, Diplome de Grand Prix, and Diplome d'Honneur, Exposition Internationale, Paris, 1937; Purchase prize, 1941, honorable mention, 1950, The Chicago Society of Etchers; John Taylor Arms Prize, The Society of American Etchers, 1942; Joseph Pennell Prize, The Library of Congress, 1942; Hal H. Smith Purchase prize, Detroit Institute of Art, 1943; honorable mention, Guild Hall, 1946; Purchase prize, popular vote award, and first honorable mention, The Kosciuszko Foundation, 1948; made an Officer Order of Merit Republic of Italy, by President Giovanni Gronchi, 1958; gold medal and certificate of merit, The National Historical Society, Order Sons of Italy in America, 1961; L. L. Huttleston Staff Award, State of New York, Council of Parks and Recreation, 1974; Historic Tomahawk award, Westchester Historical Society, 1979.

WRITINGS: *Pocket Anatomy for Artists,* International House, 1947; (contributor) Margaret Scherer, *The Marvels of Ancient Rome,* Phaidon Press, 1955; *Giovanni da Verrazzano, the Discoverer of New York Bay 1524,* Cultural Division of the Italian Embassy and the Museum of the City of New York, 1958; (contributor) Preston R. Bassett, *A History of Long Island Maps,* Volume VII, Journal of Long Island History, 1967; (contributor) Lawrence C. Wroth, *The Voyages of Giovanni da Verrazzano, 1524-1528,* Yale University Press, 1970; *Jay Genealogy,* Friends of John Jay Homestead, Inc., Newsletters, 1979.

Illustrator: *Incisori Contemporanei,* Fratelli Buratti Editori [Italy], 1930; *Fine Prints of the Year,* Halton & Co., 1936, 1937; George Fielding Eliot, *The Strength We Need* (bookjacket), Viking, 1946; *American Prize Prints of the 20th Century,* American Artists Group, 1949; Stephen Mizwa, *Frederic Chopin,* Macmillan, 1949; George Santayanna, *My Host the World* (bookjacket and title page), Scribner, 1953; Will Oursler, *N.Y., N.Y.* (cover), Coward, 1954; Olivia Coolidge, *Roman People,* Houghton, 1959; W. M. Williamson, *Henry Hudson, Discoverer of the Hudson River, 1609,* Museum of the City of New York, 1959; W. M. Williamson, *Adriaen Block, Navigator, Fur Trader, Explorer, New York's First Shipbuilder,* Museum of the City of New York, 1959; Jacques Habert, *La Vie et les Voyages de Jean de Verrazane,* Le Cercle du Livre de France [Canada], 1964; Anita Daniel, *Sehnsucht nach der Ferne,* Birkhäuser Verlag [Switzerland], 1965; M. A. Jagendorf, *The Ghost of Peg-Leg Peter: And Other Stories of Old New York,* Vanguard, 1965; Norman Henfrey, *Selected Critical Writings of George Santayana,* Cambridge University Press, 1968. Work has also appeared in *The Atlantic Monthly, The Polish Revue,* and *La Revue Moderne des Arts et de la Vie* [Paris].

SIDELIGHTS: "The first olfactory sensations I experienced in my life were those of turpentine, linseed oil, and the fragrance of varnishes. My father, following a family tradition set by his ancestors from Warsaw in Poland, was an artist, painter, and etcher. He was the recipient of the Prix de Rome twice and was sent to Rome to complete his art studies. There he settled permanently, got married, raised a family, and died in 1940 after a life dedicated exclusively to his work. He won recognition and fame as an etcher and painter and a teacher in the art academy he founded in 1900.

"Thus, I was born and raised in Via Margutta, the street in Rome that had acquired a special flair, impressed upon it by

LINO S. LIPINSKY de ORLOV

several generations of its exceptional occupants: composers, painters, sculptors, writers, and poets. They were all working in great anonymity, hidden away in their studios scattered along the inclines of the Pincio Hill, which flanks the eastern side of that street. Here also were the open shops of the most skillful artisans, casters of statues, furniture carvers, framers, restorers, leather toolers, and the most refined and expert fakers of art in all forms.

"These surroundings cast me into the overall mold, and I followed in my father's footsteps in the creative field. He taught me first to observe and understand nature in order to be able to draw it. I was trained in a variety of techniques: painting in various media, graphic arts, and printing. My father believed in good craftsmanship, and that no matter what one's project was going to be, the basic foundation of a good drawing had to come first.

"Our summers were spent in Terrancina and on the Island of Capri. Early, often before sunrise, my father and I set out for the mountains with our equipment and easels. The warm hours were spent in the cool studio at home, and, following an abundant lunch and the traditional afternoon siesta, we went out again to paint and draw until dusk. While walking home in the dark, there was the Bay of Naples to contemplate, the sight of distant Naples with all its lights, and Mt. Vesuvius with its continuous display of fireworks.

"I won early recognition for my landscape etchings, engraved bookplates, and illustrations, and received official invitations to participate in Europe's international exhibitions. Then came the awards, prizes, diplomas, and medals, but none of these could take the place of the pleasurable sensations of toiling away at one's projects and mulling over resolutions to intricate artistic problems.

"I have been active in many aspects of the art world all my life. Since 1940, I have made my home in the United States, where I have been well received by my contemporaries. I have drawn portraits of children and adults, illustrated books, decorated churches, and created a museum. I became a scene designer, a director of exhibits for museums, and for the past thirteen years, the curator of a State historic house located in the most beautiful surroundings.

"Looking back, it all began with collecting pencil stubs and scraps of paper from my father's pupils; later, irritating teachers in school by 'scribbling' during boring sessions. I have been illustrating my personal diaries and my letters to friends. I have drawn from mountain tops and inside the crater of a live volcano. My art helped me brighten the tediousness of military life. My booklet on the 16th century navigator-explorer Verrazzano was instrumental in having the suspension bridge over New York Bay named for him.

"In progress is a publication on the descendants of John Jay, a Founding Father, first Chief Justice of the United States, and an illustrated autobiography to include bits of historic backgrounds of artists' lives in Italy from the 16th century onward.

"An artist's life is, of course, not always a bed of roses. During bumpy periods I found solace in re-reading the lines written into my diary by Vincenzo Gemito, the renowned Italian sculptor: 'Carry on faithfully through all suffering and hardship up to the moment when the Almighty Creator will recognize you as the selected one upon whom He had bestowed the special gift of creativity, the greatest gift of all.'"

FOR MORE INFORMATION SEE: Lee Kingman and others, compilers, *Illustrators of Children's Books: 1957-1966,* Horn Book, 1968.

LIPPINCOTT, Sarah Lee 1920-

PERSONAL: Born October 26, 1920, in Philadelphia, Pa.; daughter of George E. and Sarah (Evans) Lippincott; married Dave Garroway. *Education:* University of Pennsylvania, B.A., 1942; Swarthmore College, M.A., 1950. *Office:* Sproul Observatory, Swarthmore College, Swarthmore, Pa.

CAREER: Swarthmore College, Swarthmore, Pa., research associate at Sproul Observatory, 1951-72, lecturer, 1960—, director, 1972—, professor of astronomy, 1977—. Fulbright fellow at Paris Observatory, Meudeon, France, 1953-54; member of French Solar Eclipse Expedition to Oland, Sweden, and researcher at Pic du Midi Observatory in French Pyrenees, 1954; summer researcher at High Altitude Observatory, Sunspot, N.M., 1955; participant in General Assembly of Astronomical Union, Moscow, 1958, in North Atlantic Treaty Organization-sponsored course in problems on galactic structure, Netherlands, 1960, and in visiting professors in astronomy program of American Astronomical Society, 1961—. *Member:* International Astronomical Union, American Astronomical Society, Rittenhouse Astronomical Society, Commission 26 (president, 1973-76), Societé de Bienfaisance de Philadelphie (board), Sigma Xi (president of Swarthmore chapter, 1959-60), Kappa Kappa Gamma. *Awards, honors:* D.Sc. from Villanova University, 1973; Distinguished Daughter of Pennyslvania; Kappa Kappa Gamma Achievement Award.

SARAH LEE LIPPINCOTT

WRITINGS: (With Joseph M. Joseph) *Point to the Stars,* McGraw, 1963, 2nd edition, 1972; (with Laurence Lafore) *Philadelphia: The Unexpected City,* Doubleday, 1965. Contributor of scientific research papers to journals in United States, Canada, France, and Netherlands, and popular articles to magazines.

SIDELIGHTS: "A fascination for the sparkling night sky gripped me early in life and has never subsided. I am one of the fortunate ones who has been able to combine and mesh an avocation with a vocation. Astronomy can be enjoyed on all levels; perhaps that is one of the reasons there are so many amateur astronomers. In writing, lecturing, or just talking about astronomy, it is natural for me to show enthusiasm, integrity and imagination when describing the beauties of the night sky or when dealing with a difficult equation man has formulated to express in the purest manner the intricacies of what appears to be true millions of light years away. Besides observing the universe far beyond the earth, I enjoy observing the handiwork of man as well as of God close by. This has also led to photography and recognition as a professional with the portrayal of man and the monuments he has built."

LLOYD, Errol 1943-

PERSONAL: Born April 19, 1943, in Jamaica; son of W. A. (a civil servant) and Joyce (Lucille) Lloyd; married Joan-Ann Ingrid Maynard (an actress), July 9, 1977; children: Asana Leah. *Education:* Council of Legal Education, Barrister at Law, 1974. *Religion:* Christian. *Home:* 27A Chalk Farm Rd., London NW1 8AG, England.

Then he proudly wheeled his new red bike in through the front door. ■ (From *Shawn's Red Bike* by Petronella Breinburg. Illustrated by Errol Lloyd.)

ERROL LLOYD

CAREER: Artist and illustrator. Camden Arts Centre, London, England, tutor, 1975-77; Keskidee Arts Centre, London, England, resident artist, 1978. *Exhibitions:* West Indian Students Centre, London, 1966, 1968; University of Kent, 1968; Commonwealth Institute Gallery, 1971; Keskidee Arts Centre Gallery, London, 1975, 1977; Jamaican High Commission, 1978; Warehouse Gallery, 1978; Action Space, 1979; Caribbean Gallery, 1979. *Member:* Middle Temple Inns of Court, Rainbow Art Group. *Awards, honors:* Runner-up for Kate Greenaway Medal for *My Brother Shawn*, 1973.

WRITINGS—Self-illustrated: *Nina at Carnival,* Bodley Head, 1977.

Illustrator: Petronella Breinburg, *My Brother Shawn,* Bodley Head, 1973; Petronella Breinburg, *Doctor Shawn,* Bodley Head, 1974, T. Y. Crowell, 1975; Petronella Breinburg, *Shawn Goes to School,* T. Y. Crowell, 1974; Petronella Breinburg, *Shawn's Red Bike,* T. Y. Crowell, 1976.

SIDELIGHTS: "The relatively recent presence of West Indians in Britain has created a social and educational need for books reflecting our special cultural needs and besides, I enjoy creating for children generally."

FOR MORE INFORMATION SEE: Guardian Newspaper, 1974; Lee Kingman, and others, compilers, *Illustrators of Children's Books: 1967-1976,* Horn Book, 1978; *Children's Book Bulletin,* June, 1979.

(From *Jonathan* by Margaret Lovett. Jacket illustrated by Harry Carter.)

LOVETT, Margaret (Rose)   1915-

PERSONAL: Born August 30, 1915, in Buenos Aires, Argentina; daughter of William (a businessman) and Effie (Evans) Lovett. *Education:* St. Hugh's College, Oxford, B.A. (second class honors), 1936. *Politics:* "liberal (small 'l')." *Religion:* Church of England. *Home:* 61 Wootton, Boar's Hill, Oxford OX1 5HP, England.

CAREER: Teacher of history in a preparatory school in Hampton, England, 1956-66; Hephaistos School (for physically handicapped boys), Reading, England, teacher of history, 1966—.

WRITINGS—All for children: *Adventure for Fivepence,* Faber, 1945; *Family Pie,* Faber, 1947; *No Other Children,* Faber, 1949; *Sir Halmanac and the Crimson Star,* Faber, 1965; *The Great and Terrible Quest,* Holt, 1967; *Jonathan,* Dutton, 1972.

WORK IN PROGRESS: A history of the Hephaistos School, with its founder, Dorothy Woolley.

SIDELIGHTS: "Although like many authors I have told stories to myself for as long as I can remember, I rarely write these stories down, and if I do they are not successful. I suppose this is because they are too self-indulgent, being designed to meet my own emotional needs rather than communicate with others. The six books I have had published have all been written because an idea has popped into my head which seemed to me an amusing or interesting one, or on two occasions because there seemed to me a gap in the reading matter available to a particular group or on a particular subject, and the idea or incident would fit well into that gap. Once at least, with *The Great and Terrible Quest,* the germ of the book was a dream, in which two people, a man and a boy, together with a little dog, were trying to climb a steep hillside with a very important purpose and with a very rigid time limit. By the time I woke up I had forgotten what the purpose was and why there was a time limit, so the book was the result of working out a possible solution to these problems.

"I never have a whole book clear in my mind when I start to write. To the preliminary idea or incident I add some characters, and the ending is usually quite clear in my mind, but it sometimes takes me a long time to find a satisfactory beginning, and the details and incidents or characters add themselves on as I write. I imagine my subconscious takes a hand, as I am often astonished how something I wrote quite casually at the beginning turns out to have been an integral and important part of the working out of plot or relationships.

MARGARET LOVETT

"I would hate my books to be regarded as preaching or allegories, but I have very firm moral beliefs, and one reason why I write for children is to communicate these to them, who these days seem to me to have so little firm foundation for their lives. As well as this, it is a sad but true fact that only in books meant for children do publishers seem to accept fairly simple and clear delineations of basic virtues and values. I also have an old fashioned prejudice in favor of plots, adventures and definite beginnings and endings which in novel adult fiction are only to be found in detective stories and thrillers—and not always in them."

FOR MORE INFORMATION SEE: Horn Book, October, 1967.

LUTTRELL, Guy L. 1938-

PERSONAL: Born March 3, 1938, in Chicago, Ill.; son of Aubrey and Marie Luttrell; married Patricia Libbert, August 15, 1959; children: Greg, Lori. *Education:* Vander Cook College of Music, B.Mus.Ed., 1959; Arizona State University, M.A., 1962. *Home:* 6343 Noble Ave. N., Brooklyn Center, Minn. 55429. *Office:* School District #14, Fridley, Minn.

CAREER: Band and choir director at public schools in Swayzee, Ind., 1959-60; band and orchestra director at public schools in Lompoc, Calif., 1961-68; orchestra director at public school in Elmhurst, Ill., 1968-70; North Hennepin Community College, Brooklyn Park, Minn., director of band, orchestra, and choir, 1970-73; School District #14, Fridley,

Minn., orchestra director, 1974—. Orchestra director for School District #16, Spring Lake Park, Minn.

WRITINGS: The Instruments of Music (juvenile), Thomas Nelson, 1977. Contributor to music journals, *Highlights for Children,* and newspapers.

WORK IN PROGRESS: Touring the Capitols (tentative title), on state capitol buildings.

SIDELIGHTS: "My life has been continually centered around music and teaching, both socially and professionally, and my family shares this enjoyment. My wife plays piano, my son is a cellist, my daughter plays the flute, and, of course, we all sing. My own musical education began with guitar lessons in fifth grade. From there I progressed to string bass and French horn, both of which I have played professionally.

"Younger students have a real interest in music and its instruments, and this interest often leads them to learning to play. Unfortunately, they seldom learn anything else about their own—and other—instruments. In my writing *The Instruments of Music* I've tried to flesh this out, to broaden their appreciation and increase their enjoyment of music."

HOBBIES AND OTHER INTERESTS: Travel, flying (licensed private pilot).

GUY L. LUTTRELL

MacINNES, Helen 1907-
(Helen Highet)

PERSONAL: Born 1907, in Glasgow, Scotland; came to U.S., 1937, naturalized, 1951; daughter of Donald and Jessica (McDiarmid) MacInnes; married Gilbert Highet (a professor and an author), 1932 (died January, 1978); children: Gilbert Keith. *Education:* Glasgow University, M.A., 1928; University College, London, Diploma in Librarianship, 1931. *Religion:* Presbyterian. *Home:* 15 Jefferys Lane, East Hampton, N.Y. 11937.

CAREER: Acted with Oxford University Dramatic Society and with the Experimental Theatre, both Oxford, England; with Gilbert Highet, translated several German books into English, 1932-38; novelist, 1941—.

WRITINGS—Novels; under name, Helen MacInnes: *Above Suspicion*, Little, Brown, 1941; *Assignment in Brittany*, Little, Brown, 1942; *While Still We Live*, Little, Brown, 1944 (published in England under title, *The Unconquerable*, Harrap, 1944); *Horizon*, Harrap, 1945, Little, Brown, 1946; *Friends and Lovers*, Little, Brown, 1947; *Rest and Be Thankful*, Little, Brown, 1949; *Neither Five Nor Three*, Harcourt, 1951; *I and My True Love*, Harcourt, 1953; *Pray for a Brave Heart*, Harcourt, 1955; *North from Rome*, Harcourt, 1958; *Decision at Delphi*, Harcourt, 1960; *Venetian Affair*, Harcourt, 1963; *Home Is the Hunter* (play), Harcourt, 1964; *Double Image* (Book-of-the-Month Club alternate), Harcourt, 1966; *The Salzburg Connection*, Harcourt, 1968; *Message from Málaga*, Harcourt, 1971; *The Snare of the Hunter*, Harcourt, 1976; *Agent in Place*, Harcourt, 1976; *Prelude to Terror*, Harcourt, 1978.

Omnibus volumes: *Assignment: Suspense* (includes *Above Suspicion, Horizon,* and *Assignment in Brittany*), Harcourt, 1961.

Under name, Helen Highet; translator with husband, Gilbert Highet: Otto Kiefer, *Sexual Life in Ancient Rome*, Routledge & Kegan Paul, 1934, Dutton, 1935; Gustav Mayer, *Friedrich Engles*, Chapman & Hall, 1935.

ADAPTATIONS—Movies: "Above Suspicion" (motion picture), Metro-Goldwyn-Mayer, 1943; "Assignment in Brittany" (motion picture), Metro-Goldwyn-Mayer, 1943; "Venetian Affair" (motion picture), Metro-Goldwyn-Mayer, 1966.

SIDELIGHTS: "I'm continually interested in the question of how an ordinary guy of intelligence and guts resists oppression. I'm against totalitarians in general—national or religious, extremists of the right or left. If I can be labeled anything, I am a Jeffersonian Democrat. I used to read George Orwell a lot—he was also from Scotland. And Rebecca West is another mentor of mine—she's a very courageous woman. Both wrote as strong anti-totalitarians. My basic characters have a certain decency and honesty. They still believe in standards of human conduct, and they rise to the occasion without fear, whether they're Europeans or Americans." [Herbert Mitgang, "Behind the Best Sellers," *New York Times Book Review,* December 17, 1978.]

MacInnes' suspense novels have often been cited as among the best in the genre. Robert Phelps wrote: "An exceptional suspense story is always a matter of how it's told, of the fine art of unravelling. . .and no one in the business today knows and practices its secrets with more finesse than Helen

HELEN MacINNES

MacInnes." Not only does she excel in plotting a thriller, her novels are based firmly on extensive research and news analysis ("I have never. . .been intimidated by research," she told Roy Newquist), and nearly always incorporate a philosophical or moral argument. In an interview with Harry Gilroy of the *New York Times,* MacInnes said that she was "thoroughly familiar with places that figure in her books. She gets ideas for plots from factual stories. . . .Technical details about espionage she has taken from evidence accumulated by the Federal Bureau of Investigation." She told Newquist: "Underlying everything is the fact that I'm interested in international politics, in analyzing news, to read newspapers both on and between the lines, to deduct and add, to utilize memory." In an interview with Harvey Breit she added: "I never know quite when a book starts. . . .I don't worry about it too much. I don't believe in forcing the pace. I take it when I can, sort of seize the moment."

C. E. Kilpatrick's review of *Decision at Delphi* can be cited as exemplary of critical reaction toward MacInnes' work: "It is uncanny how this MacInnes woman can feed you vital information little by little so that nerves tingle and suspense swallows up the reader. High accomplishment from a real master of the genre."

HOBBIES AND OTHER INTERESTS: The American west and travel.

FOR MORE INFORMATION SEE: Harvey Breit, *The Writer Observed,* World, 1956; *Kirkus,* August 15, 1960; *Library Journal,* September 15, 1960, December 15, 1964; *New York Herald Tribune Books,* October 30, 1960; Roy Newquist, *Counterpoint,* Rand McNally, 1964; *New York Times,* January 8, 1966; *Writer's Yearbook* (interview), Writer's Digest, 1967; *New York Times Book Review,* December 17, 1978.

MARK, Jan 1943-

PERSONAL: Born June 22, 1943, in Welwyn, England; daughter of Colin Denis and Marjorie Brisland; married Neil Mark (a computer operator), March 1, 1969; children: Isobel, Alexander. *Education:* Canterbury College of Art, N.D.D., 1965. *Politics:* Labour. *Religion:* None. *Home:* 10 Sydney St., Ingham, Norfolk NR12 9TQ, England. *Agent:* Murray Pollinger, 4 Garrick St., London WC2E 9BH, England.

CAREER: Southfields School, Gravesend, England, teacher of art and English, 1965-71; free-lance writer, 1974—. *Awards, honors:* Penguin/*Guardian* Award, 1975, and Carnegie Medal by The Library Association, 1976, both for *Thunder and Lightnings*.

WRITINGS: Thunder and Lightnings, Kestrel, 1976, Crowell, 1979; *Under the Autumn Garden,* Kestrel, 1977, Crowell, 1979; *The Ennead,* Crowell, 1978; *Divide and Rule,* Kestrel, 1979, Crowell, 1980; *The Short Voyage of the Albert Ross,* Granada, 1980; *Nothing to be Afraid Of,* Kestrel, 1980; *Hairs in the Palm of the Hand,* Kestrel, 1981. Contributor of stories and articles to magazines and anthologies.

SIDELIGHTS: "Although I did not go to school until I was nearly eight I learned to read when I was three and to write when I was four. My educational career comprised fourteen glorious years of state-subsidized reading time. I cannot recall doing very much else, certainly not learning, since I reckoned, along with one of my fictional characters that anything I wanted to know would stick. I do not write specifically for children, any more than I write for adults. I tend rather to write about children; the vocabulary and ambiance of a book derive from the age and preoccupations of its central characters, since my main aim always is to write about people. I am not engaged as a writer by victims and innocents. A character must be the author of his own misfortune and he is likely to be venal, amoral or downright corrupt. He is not likely to prosper thereby, however, since he is stimulated by

Isaac danced in the dust and the dust danced with him.
■ (From *The Ennead* by Jan Mark. Jacket illustrated by Kinuko Craft.)

a flourishing and invariably misplaced faith in his own faulty perceptions. *The Ennead* was constructed upon the premise that an underdog need not be a sympathetic character, and that only lack of opportunity prevents him from changing places with his oppressor. If there are any villains in my books they are the opportunists who have been successful."

FOR MORE INFORMATION SEE: Guardian, July 17, 1975; *Publishers Weekly,* December 11, 1978; *Horn Book,* June, 1979.

JAN MARK

MATTE, (Encarnacion) L'Enc 1936-

PERSONAL: Born March 5, 1936, in Reus, Tarragona, Spain; daughter of Jose and Encarnacion (Redo) Marine; married Lorenzo Matte (a certified public accountant), May 21, 1955; children: Margarita Helena and Andres Javier (deceased). *Education:* Attended Instituto Nacional de Reus, Spain, for seven years and Colegio Maria Cortina, Spain, for seven years. *Religion:* Lutheran. *Home:* 1809 Maryland Ave., S., St. Louis Park, Minn. 55426. *Office:* Lerner Publications, 241 First Ave., N., Minneapolis, Minn. 55401.

CAREER: Illustrator. Lerner Publications Co., Minneapolis, Minn., illustrator and keyliner, 1973—. *Member:* Graphics Now.

ILLUSTRATOR: Anabel Dean, *Bats, the Night Fliers,* Lerner, 1974; Naida Dickson, *The Biography of a Honeybee,*

Lerner, 1974; O. Nelson, *The Girl Who Owned a City*, Lerner, 1975; Annabel Dean, *Strange Partners: The Story of Symbiosis*, Lerner, 1976; Annabel Dean, *Plants That Eat Insects: A Look at Carnivorous Plants*, Lerner, 1977. Work has also appeared in *Motorcross Motorcycle Racing, Motorcycles on the Move, Bicycles on Parade* and *Bicycling Is for Me*.

SIDELIGHTS: "From the time I was a young child I enjoyed drawing. My first teacher was my father. When I was only seven years old, however, I began at the Art Institute under the tutorship of some of Spain's finest artists, among them Fuste and Bidiella.

"When I was fourteen years old, my family and I moved to Chile, South America. It was then that I enjoyed the experience of showing my art to the public. I was invited to participate in an art show in Santiago, featuring many artists from throughout the world.

"That introduction provided me opportunities to produce art work on commission. It also encouraged me to continue studying until I felt that I could take my place among the professionals in the art field.

"In 1973 my family moved to Minneapolis, Minnesota. While we were still settling, I was invited to show my art at the Minnesota International Center. That exclusive display marked a new beginning in a new country for me.

"Since I moved to this country, I have been working for Lerner Publications Company as a book illustrator and keyliner. I also free-lance upon request.

"Critics have commented favorably about my style in India Ink, especially those showing realistic subjects.

"By working at Lerner Publications Company, I became very skillful as a keyliner and experienced with the Brown

L'ENC MATTE

Commodore 20" x 24" camera, shooting Kodak PMT's, making colored proofs using 3M negative acting color key material, making dylux proofs, reversals, and duplicates using contacting and duplicating films. I also have knowledge and practical experience on litho stripping techniques. At present I am a full-time litho stripping trainee and will receive my certificate as an expert litho stripper in three years."

(From *The Girl Who Owned a City* by O.T. Nelson. Illustrated by L'Enc Matte.)

McMILLAN, Bruce   1947-

PERSONAL: Born May 10, 1947, in Boston, Mass.; son of Frank H., Jr. and Virginia M. W. McMillan; married V. Therese Loughran; children: Brett Brownrigg. *Education:* University of Maine, B.S., 1969. *Home address:* Old County Rd., Shapleigh, Me. 04076.

CAREER: Maine Public Broadcasting Network, Orono, director and photographer, 1969, producer-director, 1970-73; caretaker of McGee Island, Me., 1973-75; photographer and writer, 1975—.

WRITINGS—All with own photographs: *Finest Kind O'Day: Lobstering in Maine* (juvenile), Lippincott, 1977; *The Alphabet Symphony* (juvenile picture book), Greenwillow Books, 1977; *The Remarkable Riderless Runaway Tricycle* (juvenile), Houghton, 1978; *Punography* (adult photography), Penguin, 1978; *Apples, How They Grow*, Houghton, 1979; *Punography Too*, Penguin, 1980; *Making Sneakers*, Houghton, 1980. Contributor to *Down East, Life, US*, and *Yankee*.

WORK IN PROGRESS: Books for children and adults, with his own photographs.

SIDELIGHTS: "I'm pretty enthusiastic about what I do—photographing and writing books for children and adults—and I hope my enthusiasm's contagious.

"I'm a photographer who also writes. Photography has been a part of me since my youth, something that has been an ongoing learning experience with no formal training. I worked at my writing for two years when we moved to an island off the Maine coast to become the sole year-round inhabitants. When we were ready to come ashore I decided to work in children's books, noting the lack of photography in them.

"My children's book ideas come from my surroundings and experiences. My first book (done before we left the island), was about lobstering because I had done a bit of lobstering. I like music and wanted to share with children the way I see things visually so I photographed *The Alphabet Symphony.* I grew up around Kennebunkport, Maine and its famous dump so I rescued a tricycle from the dump and did *The Remarkable Riderless Runaway Tricycle.* One year I planted three apple trees. I really got interested in them, and three years later I had sixty trees planted and *Apples, How They Grow* published. There was a sneaker factory in the next town, and that led to *Making Sneakers.*

"My humorous streak has come through in the form of visual puns, *Punography,* which never seems to end, hence the sequel, *Punography Too.* The photographs are all of local people and places, but seen with a touch of humor. The humorous streak also comes out when I speak to groups of adults or children, always bringing along my alter ego, my tricycle from that book. I identify with my tricycle that perseveres, no matter what, to get where it's going in *The Re-*

(From *The Alphabet Symphony: An ABC Book* by Bruce McMillan. Photograph by the author.)

markable Riderless Runaway Tricycle. You might even call that book my autobiography.

"I was especially pleased when the Children's Book Council asked me, a photographer, to do one of the streamers for the 1980 National Children's Book Week. I'm an advocate of more photography, and different uses of it, in children's books.

"I have a lot of fun doing what I'm doing and enjoy sharing my fun with the books or speaking (informally) with the children or the adults."

FOR MORE INFORMATION SEE: Horn Book, December, 1977, June, 1978.

There is no frigate like a book to take us lands away,
Nor any coursers like a page of prancing poetry.
—Emily Dickinson

BRUCE McMILLAN

McNICKLE, (William) D'Arcy 1904-1977

OBITUARY NOTICE: Born January 18, 1904, in St. Ignatius, Mont.; died December, 1977. Educator, administrator, and writer. Beginning in 1936, McNickle held several posts in Washington, D.C., with the Bureau of Indian Affairs, where he last served as director of tribal relations. In 1952 he left that post to direct American Indian Development, Inc., in Boulder, Colo. His books deal mostly with Indian affairs and include *The Indian Tribes of the United States: Ethnic and Cultural Survival* and *Indian Man: A Life of Oliver La Farge.* His book for young people also runs in the same vein, *They Came Here First: The Epic of the American Indian.* His last book, a novel—*Wind from an Enemy Sky*—was published posthumously. McNickle was the recipient of a Guggenheim fellowship, 1963-64. *For More Information See: American Men and Women of Science: The Social and Behavioral Sciences,* 12th edition, Bowker, 1973; *World Literature Today,* Spring, 1979. *Obituaries: Contemporary Authors,* Volume 85-88, Gale, 1980.

MELCHER, Frederic Gershom 1879-1963

OBITUARY NOTICE: Born April 12, 1879, in Malden, Mass.; died March 9, 1963, in Montclair, N.J. Publisher and editor for over half a century. A bookseller in Boston and Indianapolis for twenty-three years, Melcher became co-editor of *Publishers Weekly* in 1918, and chairman of R. R. Bowker & Co. in 1958. With Franklin K. Mathiews, the Boy Scouts' chief librarian, Melcher developed Children's Book Week in 1919, a week still observed by libraries, bookshops, and schools across the nation. He also established the John Newbery Medal in 1921, awarded annually for the most distinguished contribution to American literature for children, and in 1937, the Caldecott Medal, for the best American picture book for children. Melcher was involved in numerous civic and trade organizations, and indeed was a founding member of the National Book Committee. Various honors were bestowed on him, and they include everything from honorary doctorates to the establishment of a scholarship in his name by the Children's Librarians' Association. *For More Information See: Current Biography,* Wilson, 1945; *Who Was Who in America,* 4th edition, Marquis, 1968; *Dictionary of American Library Biography,* Libraries Unlimited, 1978. *Obituaries: Current Biography,* Wilson, 1963; *New York Times,* March 11, 1963; *Publishers Weekly,* March 18, 1963; *Saturday Review,* March 30, 1963; *Library Journal,* April 1, 1963; *Wilson Library Bulletin,* April, 1963; *Horn Book,* June, 1963.

MICALE, Albert 1913-

PERSONAL: Surname pronounced Mi-cah-lee; born December 8, 1913, in Punxytawney, Pa.; son of Albert (a miner and construction worker) and Concetta (Formica) Micale; married Anne Geisinger (an agent and print producer of Micale's work), September 5, 1936; children: Concetta (Mrs. Rolf Schwarting). *Education:* Pratt Institute of Fine and Applied Arts, Brooklyn, N.Y., 1933-36. *Religion:* Catholic. *Home and studio:* 7574 N. Mockingbird Lane, Paradise Valley, Ariz. 85253. *Agent:* Anne Micale, 7574 N. Mockingbird Lane, Paradise Valley, Ariz. 85253.

(From *Climb to the Top* by Matthew Kostka. Illustrated by Albert Micale.)

CAREER: Free-lance illustrator, 1936-75; painter and sculptor, 1970—. *Exhibitions*—Group shows: Kennedy Gallery, New York, N.Y., 1968, 1973; Arcade Art Gallery, Santa Barbara, Calif., 1969; Jamison Gallery, Sante Fe, N.M., 1969, 1972; O'Brien's Art Emporium, Scottsdale, Ariz., 1970, 1971; Buck Saunders Gallery, Scottsdale, Ariz., 1970, 1975; Main Trail Galleries, Scottsdale, Ariz., 1971, 1972; Desert Southwest Art Gallery, Palm Springs, Calif., 1971, 1973; Hampton Gallery, Scottsdale, Ariz., 1974, 1975; Mountain Oyster's Club Western Art Show, Tucson, Ariz., 1974-79; Dagres Gallery, Phoenix, Ariz., 1975; Wyoming's Cody County Invitational Art Show, Cody, Wyo., 1975-77; Nebraskaland Days Art Show, North Platte, Neb., 1975-76; Robert E. Peters Gallery, Scottsdale, Ariz., 1975, 1977; Art Colony, Scottsdale, Ariz., 1976, 1979; Colorado's Western Heritage Foundation and Art Fair, Littleton, Colo., 1976-79; Estate Gallery, Scottsdale, Ariz., 1977; Thackeray Gallery, San Diego, Calif., 1977; Cross Gallery, Fort Worth, Tex., 1978; Sanders Gallery, Tucson, Ariz., 1979. One man shows: Lincoln Thrift Presidential Club, Phoenix, Ariz., 1975; Robert E. Peters Gallery, Scottsdale, Ariz., 1976. Two of Micale's paintings are owned by the Riveredge Foundation Museum in Calgary, Alberta, Canada; bronze sculpture "Apache Hunter" was on loan through the State Department to the

ALBERT MICALE

U.S. Embassy in Oslo, Norway, 1976-79. *Member:* Western Art Associates, Phoenix Museum. *Awards, honors: Let's Go on a Space Shuttle* was named Outstanding Science Book for Children, 1976, by the National Science Teacher's Association.

ILLUSTRATOR: Norah Smaridge, *Hands of Mercy,* Benziger, 1960; Frank Kolaris, *The Long Trail,* Benziger, 1960; Ferris Weddle, *Blazing Mountain,* Watts, 1961; Sidney Offit, *Cadet Quarterback,* Young Readers Press, 1961; Helen Lynch, *Hackamore,* Duell, Sloan and Pearce, 1961; Naomi Buchheimer, *Let's Go Down the Mississippi with LaSalle,* Putnam, 1962; Matthew Kostka, *Climb to the Top,* Doubleday, 1962; Robert Ashley, *Stolen Train: The Story of the Andrews Raiders,* Scholastic Book Service, 1962; Jean L. Latham, *Medals for Morse,* Scholastic Book Service, 1962; *Living God's Law* (textbook), Benziger, 1962; Rutherford Montgomery, *The Capture of West Wind* (Junior Literary Guild selection), Duell, Sloan and Pearce, 1962; Jane and Paul Annixter, *Trouble at Paint Rock,* Golden Press, 1962; Belle Coates, *The Sign of the Open Hand,* Scribner, 1962; Harry Walker, *How to Bat,* McGraw, 1963; Bernard Rosenfield, *Let's Go to Build the First Transcontinental Railroad,* Putnam, 1963; Kirk Polking, *Let's Go with Lewis and Clark,* Putnam, 1963; Henry Castor, *First Book of the Spanish-American West,* Watts, 1963; K. Polking, *Let's Go on the Half Moon with Henry Hudson,* Putnam, 1964; Marian Talmadge and Iris Gilmore, *Let's Go to a Truck Terminal,* Putnam, 1964; John Clarke, *High School Dropout,* Doubleday, 1964, reprinted 1970; H. Castor, *First Book of the War with Mexico,* Watts, 1964; Michael Chester, *Let's Go to the Moon,*

Putnam, 1965, revised edition, 1973; Newlin B. Wildes, *The Best Summer,* Rand McNally, 1965; Newlin B. Wildes, *The Horse That Had Everything,* Rand McNally, 1965; Judith M. Spiegelman, *With Washington at Valley Forge,* Putnam, 1967; M. Chester, *Let's Go to Stop Air Pollution,* Putnam, 1968; Barbara Williams, *I Know a Bank Teller,* Putnam, 1968; M. Chester, *Let's Go to Stop Water Pollution,* Putnam, 1969; Margo McWilliams and Patricia Reisdorf, *Let's Go to Build a Highway,* Putnam, 1971; M. Chester, *Let's Go on a Space Shuttle,* Putnam, 1975.

Illustrator of dailies for "Captain Yank" strip, McNaught Syndicate, 1941-44; "Roy Rogers Western Adventure" strip, Western Publishing, 1943-56; other miscellaneous strips, 1941-58. Has also illustrated many textbooks, advertisements, and work has appeared in *Street and Smith, Popular Magazine, Western Horseman, Coronet, Scholastic Magazine, Outdoor Arizona,* and numerous other magazines and newspapers.

SIDELIGHTS: "I consider myself fortunate that I had the opportunity to be an illustrator. Even as a boy, my artistic leanings were to draw story-telling pictures of high adventure and men and animals in action, in sports and the great outdoors.

"My family moved to Niagara Falls from Pennsylvania when I was about two-and-half years of age. The Niagara Frontier is an area rich in history and Indian lore, and offered many opportunities for a young boy to explore along the upper and lower Niagara River and Lake Ontario, both on the American and Canadian sides.

"As a boy, I played ice hockey and baseball with the Indian boys from the nearby Tuscarora Indian Reservation. Every year Indians would have great powwows and come from miles around, including Canada, to rendezvous in Niagara Falls, N.Y.

"LaSalle Creek was a favorite spot for boys to fish for bull heads and swim. This is where the explorer LaSalle built the 'Griffon' which set sail to explore the Great Lakes and never was seen or heard from again.

"I remember when fire engines were pulled by magnificent looking dappled grey horses, and one bitter cold winter's day, when the streets were covered with ice, one fire wagon didn't make the turn. Horses, men, and equipment were scattered all over the street and front yards around us.

"I recall my father, his eyes shining with pride, telling me of the days when he had been in the Italian Light Cavalry. I could picture the action of the galloping horses, the colorful uniforms, the dust swirling under the bright Italian sun, and I could picture his description of the acrobatic riding required in the Light Cavalry.

"I listened to stories recounted by adults of their experiences and adventures encountered in their work, their hunting or travels. I am and was a prodigious reader of stories of adventure, the American West, in both fiction and non-fiction. I have a great interest in physical anthropology, (the theory of man's evolution). I am fond of all animals and have made a study of their habits and sketch them from life whenever possible. I have a great interest in the universe and space. All the above, I believe, was invaluable to me, as at a very early age drawing was my way of expressing myself. I was aware, early in life, of the great drama of men and events in history, and the magic of artistic creation came naturally to me.

"I always knew I wanted to be an artist. My words to a young aspiring artist are: 'All the arts are very demanding. Unless you have a burning desire to be an artist, choose another profession or trade.'

"In traveling around the country, I have crossed the great trails, such as Lewis and Clark Trail, Chisholm, Camino Real, Santa Fe, Butterfield Stage, Mormon Trail, Coronado's Route. I illustrated a story for *Coronet* Magazine (March, 1961) of eight famous Western trails. My wife and I have camped in the High Sierras of California, the Rocky Mountains, Adirondack Mountains, and the Appalachian Mountains.

"I particularly enjoy illustrating books, as the artist is given more freedom to work in his style, and particularly, I like to work in line (pen and ink and pencil) but I like to work in all media.

"Since moving to Arizona in 1970, I have devoted my art to depicting the West and it's people and animals in oils, water colors, drawings and recently, in bronze sculpture."

FOR MORE INFORMATION SEE: Phoenix Gazette, August 10, 1974, March 6, 1976; *Arizona Living,* May 9, 1975; *Outdoor Arizona,* October, 1975; *Southwest Art,* December, 1975; *Enterprise* (Carefree, Ariz.), March, 1976; *Scottsdale Progress Weekend,* June 18, 1976; *The Arizona Horseman,* May, 1977.

ALICE P. MILLER

MILLER, Alice P(atricia McCarthy)

PERSONAL: Born in Lynn, Mass.; daughter of William Henry and Julia (McCarthy) McCarthy; married Warren Hudson Miller (an insurance executive), April 3, 1942; children: Nancy, Jacqueline. *Education:* Hunter College (now Hunter College of the City University of New York), A.B.; New School for Social Research, M.S.S.; Columbia University, M.A., 1963. *Home:* 216 West Victoria St., Santa Barbara, Calif. 93101.

CAREER: Former editor and staff writer for various publications, and substitute teacher in high schools; New York City Community College, Brooklyn, N.Y., instructor in communication arts and skills, 1960-61; Pratt Institute, Brooklyn, instructor in psychology, 1961-65; Julliard School of Music (now Juilliard School), New York City, instructor in sociology and psychology, 1965-66; Harper & Row, New York City, free-lance writer, 1969—; instructor in sociology, Helene Fuld School of Nursing, 1973; instructor in creative writing, Riverdale Community Center, 1977—. Founding trustee, Levittown Public Library, 1950-52. *Member:* Society of Children's Book Writers, Authors Guild, Phi Beta Kappa. *Awards, honors:* Indiana University writing fellowship, 1958; merit award, *Woman's Day* Bicentennial Essay Contest, 1976.

But Mr. Dooley knew what boys and girls like. He always gave the children something extra for their money. ■ (From *The Little Store on the Corner* by Alice P. Miller. Illustrated by Lisl Weil.)

WRITINGS: The Heart of Camp Whippoorwill (young people), Lippincott, 1960; *Make Way for Peggy O'Brien* (young people), Lippincott, 1961; *The Little Store on the Corner* (young people), Abelard, 1961; *In Cold Red Ink: How Term Papers Are Graded and Why* (adult), Allwyn, 1968; *It Happened in 1918* (adult), Allwyn, 1968; *A Kennedy Chronology* (adult), Allwyn, 1968; (with husband, Warren H. Miller) *Who Shares Your Birthday?* (adult), Allwyn, 1970; (with W. H. Miller) *The 1910-1919 Decade* (adult), Allwyn, 1972; *Edmund Burke: A Biography* (young adult), Allwyn, 1976; *Edmund Burke and His World* (adult), Devon-Adair, 1979; *The Mouse Family's Blueberry Pie* (young people), Dandelion Press, 1980. Writer for Dave Garroway's "Today" television show, National Broadcasting Co., 1952-53. Contributor to magazines and anthologies.

SIDELIGHTS: "I'm interested in current movements to eliminate prejudice from books for the young but not uncritical about some of the methods being used to eradicate such prejudice. We need greater representation of the various minority groups among those who decide which manuscripts shall be published and which published books shall be purchased by school and public library systems. We need greater encouragement of writing talent among persons from many backgrounds."

PARK, W(illiam) B(ryan)   1936-
(Bill Park)

PERSONAL: Born June 12, 1936, in Sanford, Fla.; son of Charles Lanier, Sr. (a physician) and Geneva (Whitehead) Park; married Eva Kratzert (director of a child care center), December 28, 1961; children: William Bryan II, Robert Christopher, Anne-Marie. *Education:* University of Florida, B.A., 1959; graduate study at School of Visual Arts, New York, N.Y., 1961-62, and Rollins College, 1967, 1977. *Politics:* Democrat. *Religion:* Presbyterian. *Office:* Park-Art Studio, 110 Park Ave. S., Winter Park, Fla. 32789.

CAREER: McGraw-Hill Book Co., New York City, staff artist, 1960-61; Tucker Wayne Advertising, Atlanta, Ga., assistant art director, 1961-63; Park-Art Studio (free-lance service for advertisers and agencies), Orlando, Fla., owner and manager, 1963-75; Park-Art Studio, Winter Park, Fla., owner and manager, 1975—. Exhibitions of art work include "The Artist as a Journalist," for Time, Inc., in New York City, 1977; a feature in *Communication Arts,* 1978; one-man show at the University of Central Florida, November, 1979. *Military service:* U.S. Army Reserve, 1959-67. *Member:* Authors Guild of Authors League of America, Society of Illustrators.

WRITINGS: The Pig in the Floppy Black Hat (self-illustrated juvenile), Putnam, 1973; *Jonathan's Friends* (self-illustrated juvenile), Putnam, 1977.

W. B. PARK

After supper Michael was busy as usual, showing Jonathan how to do things his way. ▪ (From *Jonathan's Friends* by W.B. Park. Illustrated by the author.)

Illustrator: Robert Newton Peck, *King of Kazoo,* Knopf, 1976; Robert Newton Peck, *Basket Case,* Doubleday, 1979. Contributor of articles, stories, and illustrations (including cover illustrations) to national magazines and newspapers, including *Travel and Leisure, Publishers Weekly, Saturday Review, Flying, Intellectual Digest, Fortune, Sports Illustrated, Harper's, Look, Holiday, New York Times,* and *St. Petersburg Times.*

WORK IN PROGRESS: Charlie-Bob's Fan, for Harcourt; *You Think You're Sick?,* for Warne; *Circus Acts,* for Putnam.

SIDELIGHTS: "I've always had a great love of fantasy—always told a lot of stories even before I had children of my own. It's hard to decide now whether to call myself an artist or a writer." [Jim Allen, "Bill Park: The Author of 'Jonathan's Friends' Has a Few Other Tricks Up His Paint Brush," *Winter Park–Maitland Sun Herald,* October 6, 1977.[1]]

"The world has become an abysmally serious place. The hard-eyed realists have taken over, casting the romantics and

poets and dreamers into outer darkness. Machine-like, the realists click and whir through life, expertly cutting up the wild flowers of fun and fantasy, and leaving a perfectly trimmed, barren, golf green of a lawn.

"I don't want to live on a golf green. I want to wander through the wild flowers and uncut grasses and unswept leaves and yes, weeds, too. Weeds can be beautiful.

"Childhood is full of wild flowers and weeds, and the realists especially want to cut those. If they can create a golf green out of childhood, they can count on a veritable assembly line of little realists, brittle and hard-eyed as they are, marching up into adulthood.

"So they sweep the children's books of fun and innocence from the shelves, and replace them with serious books about anger and truth and success and justice, and as soon as they can, they reduce Santa Claus and E. Bunny and all the other fantasies of childhood to jokes. They do this by 'enlightening' children.

"To step on those first fragile, intoxicating dreams and hopes, and click on the searing light of the 'real world' is not only unnecessary; it is destructive. Fantasy is the stretching of young wings; clip those wings and they may never grow back.

"A child's belief in the fantasies of childhood need never be broken. Parents who nurture and share these things with their children reap breathtaking treasures. If the believing is defended and encouraged in the face of a world of cynics, young and old, it will gradually mature into a higher intellectual and, indeed, spiritual understanding. And then it will be discovered that the fantasies *are* real, and that the reality is in the love and fun and hope of them.

"I refuse to let the realists cancel childhood. My book, *Jonathan's Friends*, is a celebration of faith, and the importance of holding onto it."

FOR MORE INFORMATION SEE: Floridian, February 27, 1972; *Winter Park-Maitland Sun Herald*, October 6, 1977; *Orlando Sentinel Star*, October 11, 1977; *Communication Arts*, Volume XIX, number 6, 1978.

PATENT, Dorothy Hinshaw 1940-

PERSONAL: Born April 30, 1940, in Rochester, Minn.; daughter of Horton Corwin (a physician) and Dorothy (Youmans) Hinshaw; married Gregory Joseph Patent (a professor of zoology), March 21, 1964; children: David Gregory, Jason Daniel. *Education:* Stanford University, B.A., 1962; University of California, Berkeley, M.A., 1965, Ph.D., 1968; also studied at University of Washington, Friday Harbor, 1965-67. *Home:* 5445 Skyway Dr., Missoula, Mont. 59801.

DOROTHY HINSHAW PATENT

CAREER: Sinai Hospital, Detroit, Mich., post-doctoral fellow, 1968-69; Stazione Zoologica, Naples, Italy, post-doctoral researcher, 1970-71; University of Montana, Missoula, faculty affiliate in department of zoology, 1975—, acting assistant professor, 1977. Member of board of directors of Missoula Farmers' Market. *Member:* American Association for the Advancement of Science, American Institute of Biological Sciences, Society for Children's Book Writers. *Awards, honors:* National Science Teachers Association named the following as outstanding science trade books: *Weasel, Otters, Skunks and Their Family*, 1973, *How Insects Communicate*, 1975, *Plants and Insects Together*, 1976, *The World of Worms*, 1978, *Animal and Plant Mimicry*, 1978, *Beetles and How They Live*, 1978, *Butterflies and Moths: How They Function*, 1979, *Sizes and Shapes in Nature—What They Mean*, 1979, *Racoons, Coatimundis and Their Family*, 1979; *Evolution Goes on Every Day* was named a Golden Kite Honor Book, 1977, by the Society of Children's Book Writers.

WRITINGS—For children; all published by Holiday House: *Weasels, Otters, Skunks and Their Family*, 1973; *Microscopic Animals and Plants*, 1974; *Frogs, Toads, Salamanders and How They Reproduce*, 1975; *How Insects Communicate*, 1975; *Fish and How They Reproduce*, 1976; *Plants and Insects Together*, 1976; *Reptiles and How They Reproduce*, 1977; *Evolution Goes on Every Day*, 1977; *The World of Worms*, 1978; *Animal and Plant Mimicry*, 1978; (with Paul C. Schroeder) *Beetles and How They Live*, 1978; *Butterflies and Moths: How they Function*, 1979; *Sizes and Shapes in Nature—What They Mean*, 1979; *Raccoons, Coatimundis and Their Family*, 1979; *Bears of the World*, 1980; *Bacteria: How They Affect Other Living Things*, 1980; *The Lives of Spiders*, 1980.

WORK IN PROGRESS—All for Holiday House: A book on hunting animals and their prey; a book on the horse family for ages ten and older; a book on horses and horse breeds for ages seven to nine. Also a book on racquetball for youngsters, with Donna Diefenback Egnew; a book on garden crop vegetables as living things, with Dianne Bilderback; an international cookbook with husband, Greg Patent.

SIDELIGHTS: "Ever since I was a child I have been interested in living things. In Minnesota, we lived near woods, meadows, and ponds, so I was able to observe many different and interesting plants and animals. My brother and I caught tadpoles each year and tried to raise them, usually with little success, and we would capture toads and turtles to keep as pets. In California, too, I lived near the woods and took long walks with my dog, which we both enjoyed very much. I collected butterflies and raised tropical fish, snakes, and frogs, and generally drove my mother crazy with all my pets. Both she and my father, who is a trained zoologist as well as a doctor, encouraged my strange interests. They even let me show my lizards to their party guests. Whenever I became involved in a new biological hobby, I would read everything I could find about it. Unfortunately, in those days there were very few biological science books for kids, so I had to make do with 'grownup' books.

"I always enjoyed telling other people the exciting things I had learned about the living world, and folks often told me I explained things so well I should become a writer. When my family and I moved from Naples to North Carolina, I had no job and decided I would like to write biology books for kids. I felt, and still do feel, that scientists have an obligation to explain their work so that nonscientists can understand

The social arrangements of a muskrat colony are quite complicated, and the weakest animals are driven away from the best muskrat areas.... ■ (From *Weasels, Otters, Skunks and Their Family* by Dorothy Hinshaw Patent. Illustrated by Matthew Kalmenoff.)

it. My first efforts were not very successful, but in 1972, right after we had moved to Missoula, Ed Lindemann from Holiday House wrote asking me to try my hand at a book on the weasel family. Ever since then, I have been writing books for Holiday and enjoying it greatly. Writing gives me the flexibility to spend time learning more about the exciting world of living things while telling other people about it. No matter how many books I write, I always have enough new ideas in my head to last several more years.''

HOBBIES AND OTHER INTERESTS: Gardening, cooking, international folk dancing, travel (Europe, especially Yugoslavia, Greece, and Italy).

FOR MORE INFORMATION SEE: Horn Book, October, 1973, April, 1978, October, 1979, February, 1980; *San Rafael Independent-Journal,* January 26, 1974.

I heard Harry gasp in back of me where he'd skied up, then the old man turned away and came back in a couple of seconds with a mask over the lower part of his face, a black cloth thing that covered everything but his eyes. ▪ (From *The Foxman* by Gary Paulsen. Jacket cover drawing by Richard Cuffari.)

PAULSEN, Gary 1939-

PERSONAL: Born May 17, 1939, in Minneapolis, Minn.; son of Oscar and Eunice Paulsen; married second wife, Ruth Ellen Wright (an artist), May 5, 1971; children: James Wright. *Education:* Attended Bemidji College, 1957-58; and University of Colorado, 1976. *Politics:* "As Solzhenitsyn has said, 'If we limit ourselves to political structures we are not artists.'" *Religion:* "I believe in spiritual progress." *Home and office address:* Box 123, Elbert, Colo. 80106. *Agent:* Ray Peekner Literary Agency, 2625 North 36th St., Milwaukee, Wis. 53210.

CAREER: Has worked variously as a teacher, electronics field engineer, soldier, actor, director, farmer, rancher, truck driver, trapper, professional archer, migrant farm worker, singer, and sailor; now a full-time writer. *Military service:* U.S. Army, 1959-62; became sergeant. *Awards, honors:* Central Missouri Award for Children's Literature, 1976.

WRITINGS—Juvenile books: *Mr. Tucket,* Funk & Wagnalls, 1968; (with Dan Theis) *The Man Who Climbed the Mountains,* Raintree, 1976; *The Small Ones,* Raintree, 1976; *The Grass Eaters,* Raintree, 1976; *Dribbling, Shooting, and Scoring Sometimes,* Raintree, 1976; *Hitting, Pitching, and Running Maybe,* Raintree, 1976; *Tackling, Running, and Kicking—Now and Again,* Raintree, 1977; *Riding, Roping, and*

Bulldogging—Almost, Raintree, 1977; *The Golden Stick,* Raintree, 1977; *Careers in an Airport,* Raintree, 1977; *The CB Radio Caper,* Raintree, 1977; *The Curse of the Cobra,* Raintree, 1977; *The Golden Stick,* Raintree, 1977; *Running, Jumping, and Throwing—If You Can,* Raintree, 1978; *Forehanding and Backhanding—If You're Lucky,* Raintree, 1978.

Novels: *The Implosion Effect,* Major Books, 1976; *The Death Specialists,* Major Books, 1976; *Winterkill,* Thomas Nelson, 1977; *The Foxman,* Thomas Nelson, 1977; *Tiltawhirl John,* Thomas Nelson, 1977; *C.B. Jockey,* Major Books, 1977; *The Day the White Deer Died,* Thomas Nelson, 1978; *Hope and a Hatchet,* Thomas Nelson, 1978; *Downhill, Hotdogging & Cross-Country—If the Snow Isn't Sticky,* Raintree, 1979; *Facing Off, Checking & Goaltending—Perhaps,* Raintree, 1979; *Going Very Fast in a Circle—If You Don't Run Out of Gas,* Raintree, 1979; *Launching, Floating High & Landing—If Your Pilot Light Doesn't Go Out,* Raintree, 1979; *Pummeling, Falling & Getting Up—Sometimes,* Raintree, 1979; *Track, Enduro & Motorcross—Unless You Fall Over,* Raintree, 1979.

Nonfiction: *The Special War,* Sirkay, 1966; *Some Birds Don't Fly,* Rand McNally, 1969; *The Building a New, Buying an Old, Remodeling a Used Comprehensive Home and Shelter Book,* Prentice-Hall, 1976; *Farm: A History and Celebration of the American Farmer,* Prentice-Hall, 1977; *Hiking and Backpacking,* Simon & Schuster, 1978; *Canoeing and Kayaking,* Simon & Schuster, in press; *Home Repair Book,*

GARY PAULSEN

Structures Publishing, in press; *Farm Machines,* Raintree, in press.

Plays: "Communications" (one-act), first produced in New Mexico at a local group theatre, 1974; "Together-Apart" (one-act), first produced in Denver at Changing Scene Theatre, 1976.

Also author of *Meteor, The Sweeper,* and more than two hundred short stories and articles.

WORK IN PROGRESS: "Currently working on the great American novel. Period."

SIDELIGHTS: "I write because it's all I can do. Every time I've tried to do something else I cannot, and have to come back to writing, though often I hate it—hate it and love it. It's much like being a slave, I suppose, and in slavery there is a kind of freedom that I find in writing: a perverse thing. I'm not 'motivated,' as you put it. Nor am I particularly driven. I write because it's all there is."

PERL, Susan 1922-

PERSONAL: Born September 8, 1922, in Vienna, Austria; daughter of Norbert (an accountant) and Marie (Bargl) Perlman. *Education:* Attended state and art schools in Vienna, Austria. *Politics:* Democrat. *Religion:* "Metaphysic, New Thought." *Residence:* New York, N.Y.

Health and energy are important; bulk and extra weight are not. ■ (From *Sparrows Don't Drop Candy Wrappers* by Margaret Gabel. Illustrated by Susan Perl.)

SUSAN PERL

CAREER: Advertising artist, and book and magazine illustrator. *Member:* Save a Cat Club, Greenwich Village Humane Society, Friends of Animals. *Awards, honors:* New York Art Directors Show awards; Palma d'Oro Award (for international cartoonists), Italy, 1965.

ILLUSTRATOR: Irmengarde Eberle, *The Favorite Place* (Junior Literary Guild selection) Watts, 1957; A. A. Milne, *Once on a Time,* New York Graphic Society, circa 1962; Hubert I. Bermont, *Psychoanalysis Is a Great Big Help!,* Stein & Day, 1963; Clement Moore, *The Night Before Christmas,* Dell, 1963; Sara Murphey, *Bing-Bang Pig,* Follett, 1964; Ruth S. Radlauer, *Stein, the Great Retriever,* Bobbs-Merrill, 1964; Ralph Underwood, *Tell Me Another Joke,* Grosset, 1964; Norah Smaridge, *Watch Out!,* Abingdon, 1965; E. H. MacPherson, *The Wonderful Whistle,* Putnam, 1965.

Johanna Johnston, *The Story of the Barber of Seville,* Putnam, 1966; Bill Adler, editor, *Letters to Smokey the Bear,* Wonder Books, 1966; Norah Smaridge, *What a Silly Thing to Do,* Abingdon, 1967; Alice T. Gilbreath, *Beginning-to-Read Riddles and Jokes,* Follett, 1967; John Greenway, *Don't Talk to My Horse,* Silver Burdett, 1968; Harold S. Longman, *What's Behind the Word,* Coward, 1968; Herb Valen, *The Boy Who Could Enter Paintings,* Little, Brown, 1968; William Wise, *Sir Howard the Coward,* Putnam, 1968; Beth Goff, *Where Is Daddy?: The Story of a Divorce,* Beacon Press, 1969; Dan Greenburg, *Jumbo the Boy and Arnold the Elephant,* Bobbs-Merrill, 1969; Susanne Kirtland, *Easy Answers to Hard Questions,* Grosset, 1969; Patrick McGivern, *The Ultimate Auto,* Putnam, 1969; Lilian Moore, *Too Many Bozos,* Western, 1969.

Barbara Klimowicz, *The Word-Birds of Davy McFifer,* Abingdon, 1970; Margaret Gabel, *Sparrows Don't Drop Candy Wrappers,* Dodd, 1971; Betty F. Horvath, *Small Paul and the Bully of Morgan Court,* Ginn, 1971; Marguerita Rudolph, *Sharp and Shiny,* McGraw, 1971; Solveig P. Russell, *Motherly Smith and Brother Bimbo,* Abingdon, 1971; Martha L. Moffett, *A Flower Pot Is Not a Hat,* Dutton, 1972; Norah Smaridge, *You Know Better Than That,* Abingdon, 1973; Joel Rothman, *I Can Be Anything You Can Be,* Scroll, 1973; Patrick Mayers, *Lost Bear, Found Bear,* A. Whitman, 1973; Leslie McGuire, *You: How Your Body Works,* Platt, 1974; Paul Showers, *The Moon Walker,* Doubleday, 1975; Paul Showers, *A Book of Scary Things,* Doubleday, 1977; Leslie McGuire, *Susan Perl's Human Body Book,* Platt, 1977; Peter Robinson, *Susan Perl's Color Wheel,* Platt, 1978.

Creator of television commercial cartoons, "The Health-Tex Kids."

Author and illustrator of *The Sex Life of the American Female,* Stein & Day, 1964.

ADAPTATIONS—Filmstrip: "I Can Be Anything You Can Be," distributed by Doubleday Multimedia.

HOBBIES AND OTHER INTERESTS: Children, animals (has five cats), travel, religion, metaphysics, and psychology.

FOR MORE INFORMATION SEE: Lee Kingman and others, compilers, *Illustrators of Children's Books: 1957-1966,* Horn Book, 1968.

PIKE, E(dgar) Royston 1896-

PERSONAL: Born April 9, 1896, in Enfield, Middlesex, England; married Winifred Bower, June 4, 1921. *Education:* Attended Enfield Grammar School. *Religion:* "Liberal thinker." *Home:* 14 Hinchley Dr., Esher, Surrey KT10 0BZ, England.

CAREER: Amalgamated Press Inc., London, England, associate editor, encyclopedia department, 1932-44; Hutchinson & Co. Ltd. (publishers), London, editor-in-chief, 1944-48; *World Digest,* editor, 1950-60; free-lance writer, 1961—. Esher Urban District Council, member, 1934-68, former chairman. *Military service:* British Army, Machine Gun Corps, 1914-19; became second lieutenant.

WRITINGS: Political Parties and Policies, Pitman, 1924, 3rd edition, revised, 1948. *The Story of the Crusades: A Popular Account*, C.A. Watts, 1927; *Temple Bells; or, The Faiths of Many Lands*, C.A. Watts, 1930; *Slayers of Superstition*, C.A. Watts, 1931, Kennikat, 1970.

Ethics of the Great Religions, C.A. Watts, 1948; *Round the Year with the World's Religions*, C.A. Watts, H. Schuman, 1951; *Encyclopaedia of Religion and Religions*, Allen & Unwin, 1951, Meridian, 1958; (editor of English edition and author of preface) Eva Ingersoll, editor, *The Life and Letters of Robert Ingersoll*, C.A. Watts, 1952; *Jehovah's Witnesses: Who They Are and What They Do*, Philosophical Library, 1954.

Finding Out About the Babylonians, Muller, 1961, Sportshelf, 1965; *Ancient Persia*, Weidenfeld & Nicolson, 1961; *Ancient India*, Weidenfeld & Nicolson, 1961; *Mohammed: Founder of the Religion of Islam*, Weidenfeld & Nicolson, 1962, Roy, 1964, 2nd edition published as *Mohammed: Prophet of the Religion of Islam*, Weidenfeld & Nicolson, 1968, Praeger, 1969; *Lands of the Bible*, Weidenfeld & Nicolson, 1962, Sportshelf, 1966; *The True Book About Charles Darwin*, Muller, 1962; *Finding Out About the Minoans*, Muller, 1962; *Finding Out About the Assyrians*, Muller, 1963, Sportshelf, 1965; *Pioneers of Social Change*, Barrie & Rockliff, 1963; *Finding Out About the Etruscans*, Muller, 1964; *Adam Smith: Founder of the Science of Economics*, Weidenfeld & Nicolson, 1965, Hawthorn, 1966; *Love in Ancient Rome*, Muller, 1965, Humanities, 1966; (with Walter Hugh Jordan) *Finding Out About the Aztecs*, Muller, 1965; *Hard Times: Human Documents of the Industrial Revolution*, Praeger, 1966 (published in England as *Human Documents of the Industrial Revolution in Britain*, Allen & Unwin, 1966); *Republican Rome*, John Day, 1966; *The World's Strangest Customs*, Odhams, 1966, published in America as *The Strange Ways of Man: Rites and Ritual and Incredible Origins*, Hart Publishing, 1967; *Golden Times: Human Documents of the Victorian Age*, Praeger, 1967 (published in England as *Human Documents of the Victorian Golden Age, 1850-1875*, Allen & Unwin, 1967), Schocken, 1972; (editor) Anthony Bird, *Gottlieb Daimler, Inventor of the Motor Engine*, Dufour, 1968; *Britain's Prime Ministers: From Walpole to Wilson*, Odhams, 1968, Transatlantic, 1970; *Human Documents of the Age of the Forsytes*, Allen & Unwin, 1969, published in America as *Busy Times: Human Documents of the Age of the Forsytes*, Praeger, 1970.

Human Documents of the Lloyd George Era, St. Martin's, 1972; *Human Documents of Adam Smith's Time*, Allen & Unwin, 1974. Editor, "Exploring the Past" series, Muller, "Pathfinder Biographies" series, Weidenfeld & Nicolson, 1962—, and "Creators of the Modern World," Arthur Barker, 1964—.

SIDELIGHTS: Pike's books have appeared in French, Portuguese, and Mexican editions.

FOR MORE INFORMATION SEE: Times Literary Supplement, March 2, 1967, August 31, 1967; *Observer Review*, August 6, 1967; *Best Sellers*, April 1, 1969; *Library Journal*, May 18, 1970, October 7, 1970.

JACK PRELUTSKY

PRELUTSKY, Jack

PERSONAL: Born in New York City. *Education:* Attended Hunter College (now of the City University of New York). *Residence:* Seattle, Washington.

CAREER: Singer, actor, poet and translator.

WRITINGS: (Translator) Rudolf Neumann, *The Bad Bear*, Macmillan, 1967; *The Mountain Bounder*, Macmillan, 1967; *A Gopher in the Garden, and Other Animal Poems* (illustrated by Robert Leydenfrost), Macmillan, 1967; (translator) *No End of Nonsense: Humorous Verses* (illustrated by Wilfried Blecher), Macmillan, 1968; *Lazy Blackbird, and Other Verses* (illustrated by Janosch), Macmillan, 1969; *Three Saxon Nobles, and Other Verses* (illustrated by Eva Johanna Rubin), Macmillan, 1969.

The Terrible Tiger (illustrated by Arnold Lobel), Macmillan, 1970; *Toucans Two, and Other Poems* (illustrated by Jose Aruego), Macmillan, 1970 (published in England as *Zoo Doings, and Other Poems*, Hamilton, 1971); *Circus* (illustrated by Arnold Lobel), Macmillan, 1974, reissued, 1978;

**Tonight they have
their party,...**
■ (From *It's Halloween* by Jack Prelutsky. Illustrated by Marylin Hafner.)

The Pack Rat's Day and Other Poems (illustrated by Margaret Bloy Graham), Macmillan, 1974; *Nightmares: Poems to Trouble Your Sleep* (illustrated by Arnold Lobel), Greenwillow Books, 1976; *It's Halloween* (illustrated by Marylin Hafner), Greenwillow Books, 1977; *The Snopp on the Sidewalk and Other Poems* (illustrated by Byron Barton), Greenwillow Books, 1977; *The Mean Old Mean Hyena* (illustrated by Arnold Lobel), Greenwillow Books, 1978; *The Queen of Eene* (Junior Literary Guild selection; illustrated by Victor Chess), Greenwillow Books, 1978.

SIDELIGHTS: Prelutsky was born in New York City, where he graduated from the High School of Music and Art. He has studied voice at various music schools and has sung with summer opera companies in Boston and in the state of Washington, where he lives.

Besides being a singer and actor, Prelutsky has worked at such diversified jobs as a photographer, day laborer, carpenter, clerk, bookseller, taxi driver, moving man, waiter, dishwasher, lecturer, and door-to-door salesman.

A friend who liked Prelutsky's drawings of imaginary animals and nonsense verses convinced him to seek a publisher. His first book was published in 1967 and since then he has published many books of children's verse and has translated books of verse from German. He claims that all of his characters contain parts of people he knows and parts of himself.

The critics seem to agree that Jack Prelutsky has a delightful manner of presenting nonsense in rhymed, rhythmic verse designed to appeal to children. According to *Horn Book,* "The author can be counted on for easy, original nonsense, offered with an unerring rhythm and freshness of diction." Or, as a reviewer for *Young Readers' Review* has stated, "Mr. Prelutsky writes clever, funny poems with definite child appeal and a lovely use of words. These verses bring to mind poems by Shel Silverstein, Ian Serraillier, John Ciardi, Eve Merriam—the best of contemporary poets of nonsense for children."

Prelutsky's works are included in the Kerlan Collection at the University of Minnesota.

HOBBIES AND OTHER INTERESTS: Music, book collecting, making wooden toys, metal and kinetic sculpture, collecting model frogs, inventing word and board games, reading, making collages, playing tennis, and bicycle riding.

FOR MORE INFORMATION SEE: Young Reader's Review, November, 1967; *Christian Science Monitor,* November 6, 1969, May 1, 1974; *Horn Book,* August, 1970, April, 1971, August, 1974, December, 1974, October, 1976, October, 1977, June, 1978.

PRICE, Garrett   1896-1979

OBITUARY NOTICE: Born in 1896 in Bucyrus, Kan.; died April 8, 1979, in Norwalk, Conn. Illustrator and cartoonist best known for his cover work for *New Yorker* and *Colliers.* Price's drawings were featured in the collection *Drawing Room Only* and in various editions of *The New Yorker Anniversary Album.* His work, which was said to reflect a gentle humor, graced children's books as well. He did the illustrations for Polly Burroughs' *The Honey Boat,* a Junior Literary Guild selection, for several of Mary Nash's "Mrs. Coverlet" books, and for *No Magic, Thank You,* a book by Elizabeth Johnson. *For More Information See: Illustrators of Children's Books: 1957-1966,* Horn Book, 1968; *Illustrators of Books for Young People,* 2nd edition, Scarecrow, 1975. *Obituaries: New York Times,* April 10, 1979; *Washington Post,* April 11, 1979; *Contemporary Authors,* Volume 85-88, Gale, 1980.

QUINN, Elisabeth   1881-1962
(Dale Adams, Vernon Quinn, Capini Vequin)

PERSONAL: Born January 5, 1881, in Waldorf, Md.; died March 21, 1962; daughter of William Thomas (a Methodist minister) and Elisabeth (Peck) Quinn. *Education:* Attended Peabody College, University of Nashville, 1897-98. *Politics:* Democrat. *Religion:* Methodist.

CAREER: Author and editor. Frederick A. Stokes Company, New York, N.Y., editor, 1905-18, 1922-41. *Member:* Daughters of the American Revolution, Daughters of the Confederacy, Women's Overseas Service League of New York.

WRITINGS—All under pseudonym Vernon Quinn, except where indicated; all published by Lippincott: (With Rose O'Neill) *The Kewpie Primer* (juvenile), 1916; (editor) *The Wonder Book of Fairy Tales* (juvenile), 1917; (editor) *The Spanish Fairy Book* (juvenile), 1918; *Beautiful America,* 1923; (editor) *Big Beasts and Little Beasts* (juvenile), 1924; (editor) *Stories for Six-Year-Olds* (juvenile), 1924; *Beautiful Canada,* 1925.

(Under pseudonym Capini Vequin) *Hand Up! A Book on Palmistry* (juvenile), 1928; *The Exciting Adventures of Captain John Smith* (juvenile), 1928; *War Paint and Powder Horn: History of the Santa Fe Trail* (juvenile), 1928; *The March of Iron Men: History of the Crusades* (juvenile), 1930; *Picture Map Geography of the United States* (juvenile), 1931,

ELISABETH QUINN

revised edition, 1959; *Picture Map Geography of the World* (juvenile), 1932; (under pseudonym Dale Adams) *Card Games for Children* (juvenile), 1933; *Picture Story of Franklin D. Roosevelt* (juvenile), 1934.

Seeds: The Legends Thereof, 1936; *Leaves: The Legends Thereof,* 1937; *Roots: The Legends Thereof,* 1938; *Stories and Legends of Garden Flowers,* 1939; *Shrubs in the Garden,* 1940; *Picture Map Geography of South America* (juvenile), 1941, revised edition, 1966; *Vegetables in the Garden: The Legends Thereof,* 1942; *Picture Map Geography of Mexico, Central America and the West Indies* (juvenile), 1943, revised edition, 1965; *Picture Map Geography of Canada and Alaska* (juvenile), 1944, revised edition, 1960; *Picture Map Geography of the Pacific Islands* (juvenile), 1945, revised edition, 1964.

Picture Map Geography of Asia (juvenile), 1946, revised edition, 1963; *Pageant of the Seven Seas* (juvenile), 1948; *Picture Map Geography of Africa* (juvenile), revised edition, 1964. Also author (under pseudonym Dale Adams) *Fun with Cards* (juvenile).

SIDELIGHTS: Davis Quinn, Quinn's nephew writes: "In 1918 she resigned from Stokes Company to join the Young

Women's Christian Association Expeditionary forces in Europe where she served until 1922.

"Miss Quinn was widely travelled: Seventeen countries of Europe, northern Africa and extensively in North and South America.

"After college she taught school for one year in a log cabin school in Cloyd's Mountain, Va. She came to New York early in the century and joined Frederick A. Stokes and Company as a proofreader but quickly moved up to editorial work and for many years was Stokes' senior editor.

"She knew General Pershing from World War I and edited his classic two-volume work, *My Experiences in the World War.*

"Miss Quinn was fluent in French and Spanish and translated several books from these languages into English. She also did ghost writing.

"Her interests were American Indians, early American history, and plants, especially wild flowers. She lived most of her life in New York City but had an experiemental farm in Dutchess County for research on botanical subjects; the last years of her life she had retired to this farm where she had transplanted and grown most of the wild flowers indigenous to New York State."

FOR MORE INFORMATION SEE: Horn Book, Volume XXIII, January-December, 1947; *American Authors and Books, 1640 to the Present Day,* Crown, 1972.

Ransome as a young boy.

RANSOME, Arthur (Michell)   1884-1967

PERSONAL: Born January 18, 1884, in Leeds, Yorkshire, England; died June 3, 1967 in England; son of Cyril Ransome (a college history professor); married Ivy Constance Walker, 1909 (marriage dissolved); married Eugenia Shelepin, 1924; children: (first marriage) Tabitha. *Education:* Educated at Rugby School. *Home:* Suffolk, England.

CAREER: Writer, critic, and journalist. Began writing around the age of seven; worked in a publisher's office until his late teens; traveled to Russia to learn the language and study their folklore, 1913; became a war correspondent in Russia for English newspapers during the first World War and the Russian Revolution; beginning 1921, he sailed his own boat in the Baltic, and later visited China, Egypt, and the Sudan; ill-health ended his sailing days, but started his career in writing books for children at the age of forty-five. *Awards, honors:* Awarded the first Carnegie Medal, 1936, for *Pigeon Post;* honorary Litt.D., University of Leeds, 1952; Commander of the Order of the British Empire, 1953; *The Fool of the World and the Flying Ship,* illustrated by Uri Shulevitz, received the Caldecott Medal, 1969; honorary M.A., University of Durham.

WRITINGS—For children: *Nature Books for Children,* Anthony Treherne, 1906; *Old Peter's Russian Tales* (illustrated by Dmitri Mitrokhin), F. A. Stokes, 1917, new edition, Puffin, 1974 (excerpt published separately—*The Fool of the World and the Flying Ship,* [ALA Notable Book; *Horn Book* Honor List] Farrar, Straus, 1968); *Aladdin and His Wonderful Lamp in Rhyme* (illustrated by Mackenzie), Nisbet, 1920; *Swallows and Amazons,* J. Cape, 1930, 2nd edition (illustrated by Clif-

ford Webb), 1931, new edition (illustrated by the author), Penguin, 1968, American edition (illustrated by Helene Carter), Lippincott, 1931, reissued, 1958; *Swallowdale* (illustrated by C. Webb), J. Cape, 1931, new edition, Penguin, 1968, American edition (illustrated by H. Carter), Lippincott, 1932; *Peter Duck* (self-illustrated), J. Cape, 1932, American edition (additional illustrations by H. Carter), Lippincott, 1933; *Winter Holiday,* J. Cape, 1933, new edition, 1961, American edition (illustrated by H. Carter), Lippncott, 1934; *Coot Club,* J. Cape, 1934, American edition (illustrated by the author and H. Carter), Lippincott, 1935.

Pigeon Post, J. Cape, 1936, reissued, 1956, American edition (illustrated by Mary E. Shepard), Lippincott, 1937; *We Didn't Mean to Go to Sea* (self-illustrated), J. Cape, 1937, reissued, 1965, American edition, Macmillan, 1938; *Secret Water* (self-illustrated), J. Cape, 1939, Macmillan, 1940; *The Big Six* (self-illustrated), J. Cape, 1940, Macmillan, 1941; *Missee Lee* (self-illustrated), J. Cape, 1941, Macmillan, 1942; *The Picts and the Martyrs; or, Not Welcome at All* (self-illustrated), Macmillan, 1943; *Great Northern?,* J. Cape, 1947, reissued, 1966, American edition, Macmillan, 1948.

Nonfiction: *Bohemia in London* (illustrated by Fred Taylor), Dodd, 1907; *A History of Story-Telling: Studies in the Development of Narrative* (illustrated by J. Gavin), T. C. & E. C. Jack, 1909, reprinted, Folcroft, 1972; *Edgar Allan Poe: A Critical Study,* M. Secker, 1910, reprinted, Haskell House, 1972; *Oscar Wilde: A Critical Study,* M. Secker, 1912, reprinted, Folcroft, 1972; *Portraits and Speculations,* Macmillan, 1913, reprinted, Folcroft, 1972; *Russia in 1919,* B. W. Huebsch, 1919 (published in England as *Six Weeks in Russia in 1919,* Allen & Unwin, 1919); *The Crisis in Russia,* B. W. Huebsch, 1921; *"Racundra's" First Cruise,* B. W. Huebsch, 1923, reissued, Hart-Davis, 1958; *The Chinese Puzzle,* Allen

& Unwin, 1927; *Rod and Line: With Aksakow on Fishing,* J. Cape, 1929; *Mainly about Fishing,* Black, 1959.

Other: *The Souls of the Streets, and Other Little Papers,* Brown, Langham, 1904; *The Stone Lady: Ten Little Papers and Two Mad Stories,* Brown, Langham, 1905; *The Imp and the Elf and the Ogre,* Nisbet, 1910; *The Hoofmarks of the Faun,* Martin Secker, 1911; *The Elixir of Life,* Methuen, 1915; *The Soldier and Death,* B. W. Huebsch, 1922.

Editor: *The World's Story Tellers,* T. C. & E. C. Jack, 1908; *The Book of Friendship,* T. C. & E. C. Jack, 1909; *The Book of Love,* T. C. & E. C. Jack, 1910; John MacGregor, *The Voyage Alone in the Yawl Rob Roy,* Hart-Davis, 1954.

Also translator of a work by Yury N. Libedinsky published as *A Week,* Allen & Unwin, 1923.

SIDELIGHTS: "I was born on **January 18, 1884,** in Leeds, where my father was Professor of History. . . .

". . . My father thought that he saw in me signs of the ir-responsibility, carelessness and flibber-tigibbet inability to stick to anything for long. . . . I cannot but recognise now that I gave him plenty of cause so to think. I was for ever after some new thing and, much worse, for ever planning that it should be the occupation of a lifetime. I spent every penny I had on coloured paper, made spills in dozens and grosses and formed a one-man company that should make spills for all Leeds, for all Yorkshire, for all the world, and put the match-factories out of business. In this my father saw at once a foreshadowing of something like my grandfather's disastrous venture as a manufacturing chemist. It seemed to him (and indeed was) a miserable, mercenary ambition, and in the small boy of six or seven he saw already the man who threw away in exchange for empty husks the prospect, open before him, of a useful scientific career. When I had glutted the spill-market and loaded his own mantelpiece and those of his friends who, not seeing the dread implications of my activities, annoyed him by paying pennies for my merchan-dise, spills were forgotten and I was practising day in day out the simpler conjuring tricks that were to lead me to the prideful moments of a professional magician who, before vast audiences, should produce rabbits out of a hat (for the mo-ment I was content to produce white mice). My father was still more disheartened. His hopes rose a little when I showed a deep interest in caterpillars and found and identified some of the rarer hawkmoths, but fell again on learning that I proposed to breed them on a gigantic scale and sell them sordidly to collectors. . . .

"I cannot remember learning to read, but my father gave me on my fourth birthday a copy of *Robinson Crusoe* as a reward for having myself read it from end to end. Thereafter I read voraciously and very fast, though I have always been able to forget what I have read, retaining, however, a sort of geographical memory that would send me quickly to the right page in the right book to find something I had half-forgotten but wished to remember. . . .

"Whenever we were not out of doors we were reading or listening to my mother reading aloud. Fortunately for us my mother enjoyed this and read extremely well. For one thing, she would never read aloud to us a book that she did not enjoy reading to herself. This simple rule, which should be observed by all mothers who read aloud (and I am sorry for the children of mothers who do not), saved us from a deal of rubbish. Any book worth reading by children is also worth reading by grown-up persons. . . ." [Arthur Ransome, *The Autobiography of Arthur Ransome,* edited by Rupert Hart-Davis, Jonathan Cape, 1976.[1]]

Of his early schooldays Ransome noted that: "The school was the Old College at Windermere to which, in preparation for the great public schools, went many of the young sons of the lake country families. . . . Some were the sons of rich men. Others, such as myself, were not. A few of the sons of the rich, who went fishing in Norway with the headmaster in their holidays, were naturally on a different footing from the rest of us. I was the only small boy with an academic father whose books were beginning to find their way through the schools and universities. Much was expected of me, and expected in vain. It may have been a good school for boys. It was not so for me. Work here was not learning but merely the anxious avoidance of punishment. I do not suppose I really knew less when I left that school than when I first went there. A worse thing had happened. I had lost the power of eager learning for its own sake, and was not to recover it until, many years later, with school behind me and earning my living, I set about educating myself. . . .

"I was extremely miserable at that school. . . . and was so lonely that on the one occasion when I heard a kind word there, as the headmaster's wife, passing me on the stairs, patted my head and said 'Cheer up, old man,' I was speech-less with surprise and had to run to the water-closet to hide the tears I knew to be ridiculous. My parents had no suspicion that all was not well. Once a week we were given time to write a letter home. For this we sat at our desk, with a master sitting at his or walking round to see that we were writing legibly. My letters, whether read or not, were in danger of inspection. They nearly always echoed the approved sen-tence, 'I am very happy,' and usually went on with gossip about white mice or with news of walks to vantage-points on Orrest Head or on the road to Troutbeck from which I had been able to see, in the distance, the hills that I had seen from Nibthwaite. Small boys are reticent and resilient and, not knowing the world, are ready to make the best of it. When parents receive letters from their sons beginning 'I am very happy' they must not be too sure that their sons are living in Elysium.

"In later life I have had many friends but I had none at the Old College. One reason for this was that I cut a contemptible figure at all games. I have never been very good at games, though I have enormously enjoyed them. But until my first terms at Rugby had been made miserable in the same way it was not discovered that I was so short-sighted as to be almost blind to detail unless very near. I have never been able without spectacles to see the eyes of a man talking to me except as vague blurs. Such eyesight is no hindrance to the enjoyment of landscape, nor yet to reading and the de-tailed examination of things near by. But, to take one ex-ample, to be unable to see your opponent's eye in a fight is to be absolutely at his mercy. Our headmaster was a muscular Christian. He had been a good boxer himself and loved noth-ing better than to pick a brace of small boys, fit them with boxing gloves and teach them the elements of self-defence. When I was thus set to battle, it meant merely that I was continually battered in the face, blow after blow coming which I could not foresee or counter in any way. I could do nothing but stand up to be battered.

"No great damage can be done by a small boy wearing boxing gloves but there is something dreadful in not being able even to try to parry blows of which you know nothing until they

ARTHUR RANSOME, 1949

land one after another on your eyes and nose. I saw no worse when my eyes were bunged up and used to welcome the bleeding of my nose because as the blood poured down, my turn at fighting came to an end, so that I could use a hand-kerchief and save my clothes. The headmaster called me a coward. The other boys jeered at me and knowing my utter inability to retaliate used to attack me at any odd moment just for fun. It was the same at football, when I seldom saw the ball until it landed in my face. It was worst of all at cricket, a game which, once these early horrors were for-gotten, has given me a great deal of pleasure. Obviously, if a boy cannot see a ball, he cannot hit it. He cannot catch it, nor is he likely even to stop it unless by painful accident. The headmaster, disgusted at my fielding failures, set himself to cure me. He made me stand while he threw a cricket ball at me again and again, other boys laughing at my frantic efforts, jeering when the ball hit me, fielding it themselves and throwing it back to my tormentor to try me with it again. He meant well, I have no doubt, and did not for a moment suspect that he was throwing cricket balls at a blind boy. I nearly went off my head and next day ran away from school.

"It was not a very good example of running away. I did not run away romantically, to join a ship and go to sea. I did not run to seek a refuge among friends, for I had none within reach. I did not try to go home, or even to my dear great-aunt for, much as I loved her, I knew very well that in the matter of running away not even she would be on my side. I merely ran away, without any thought of destination. I ran away over the Kirkstone Pass, taking the turn to the right off the Windermere-Ambleside road, trudging blindly through the Troutbeck valley, climbing up and up the steep, winding road and at last, very tired, passing at the summit of the pass the Traveller's Rest, no rest for me, the old inn that claims to be the highest in England, and so on and down the other side between the enormous hills into country I had never seen.

"My only idea was to keep going. Tired right out, I was still trudging like a machine when my running away was brought to an end by the sight of a coach climbing up towards the pass from Ullswater. Hitherto, at sight or sound of other people, I had slipped off the road and hidden till they went by. Here there was no bracken in which to hide, no trees, and I was too tired to do anything but keep on walking. The coach moving slowly up the steep came to meet me. A shout came from the red-coated driver on the box-seat. It was my friend Red Coat Robinson. He asked me where I was away to and I could not tell him because I did not know. 'Tha'd better climb oop here, lad,' he said, making room for me beside him, and I had not the strength to refuse. My running away was over and I came back to Windermere on the box-seat of the Ullswater coach. I cannot remember my coming back to the Old College. I do remember, however, that I suffered no punishment. . . .

"My next and last attempt to win a scholarship was at Rugby, where there were particular reasons why I wished to do well. My father's old schoolfellow, Robert Whitelaw, was a house-master there and, partly on his advice, my father had resigned from his chair at Leeds so as to be nearer London and free for political work. He was only forty-six, was making a con-siderable income from his history-books which were used in schools all over the world, was writing political articles, was to have been temporarily a sixth-form tutor at Rugby and was eagerly looking forward to a political career. He refused to recognise that even the amputation of his leg had failed to save him. He had already moved to Rugby when his illness suddenly grew much worse and when I came there to sit for the scholarship he was laying in bed desperately ill. I went into his room to see him and knew how much he hoped that I would win it.

"There were a hundred and two competitors for the nine or ten scholarships and we sat for the examination in New Big School. I stayed not with my father and mother but in White-law's house, where I met for the first time Ted Scott and his elder brother John, who was very kind to both Ted and me. More than twenty years later we three were to be closely associated on the *Manchester Guardian*. Next day a list of the first hundred competitors was pinned up on the door of

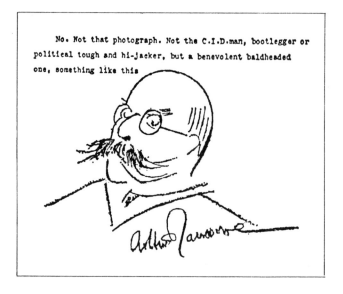

Self-caricature of Ransome.

There they were, on solid ground at last, after so many days and nights of rolling and pitching at sea, and yet for a minute or two they found it much harder to balance themselves on the island beach than on the swaying decks of the Wild Cat. ■ (From *Peter Duck* by Arthur Ransome. Illustrated by the author.)

the school, the scholarship winners at the top of the list. Having a modest (and rightly so) estimate of my learning and having learnt by this time that no matter how well I might know a subject I always did badly under examination, I began reading that list at the bottom, where I expected to see my name. It was not there. By the time I had come half way up the list and had not found it, an incredulous hope began to dawn. Could I, after all have done better than I feared? I read on, higher and higher, name after name, until, in growing excitement, I had reached those names beside which were printed the scholarships that had been awarded to their owners. Hardly able to breathe I read on until I came to the very top of the list and knew the dreadful truth. I had not won a scholarship. I was not even in the first hundred but was either No. 101 or No. 102, one of the pair protected by a merciful anonymity from knowing who was last of all.

"I went miserably back to Windermere and there, a few weeks later, the headmaster's wife came to me in the dormitory over the gateway in the old square tower that used to rock in high winds. She sat down on my bed and told me that I should not see my father again. He was dead and I lay and wept with my head under the bedclothes. I have been learning ever since how much I lost in him. He had been disappointed in me, but I have often thought what friends we could have been had he not died so young. There were years after his death during which I took no interest in sport

of any kind and indeed had not a day to spare from reading and writing and the walking that served both, but later my ancestors began to have their way with me, and by the time I was thirty fishing had become what it has remained, one of the passions of my life. It has been a delight to me to fish the waters he fished, because he fished them.

"At school, forgetful, absent-minded though not exactly idle because though I neglected my work it was always because I was busy with something else, I progressed so slowly and showed so little promise that it was small wonder my unwavering conviction that I was going to be a writer seemed as absurd to my masters (with the exception of Rouse) as to my contemporaries who were, one and all, my betters, even, now that I was no longer in Rouse's form, in English composition. The thing was ridiculous and I remember a junior master coming to my study and asking, 'What is all this about you wanting to write? What are you doing about it?' 'Reading the classics,' said I in self-defense. He looked at the book lying open on my table. It happened to be *Pickwick Papers.* 'Classics! Faugh.' said he in disgust and went out. It was perhaps an unlucky choice. But no matter. I had been reading since I was four years old and for my age I had read a very great deal. One term we had worked, slab by slab, so many lines to a lesson, through a book of *The Faerie Queene* and I had gone plunging on by myself to the neglect of other things. I had read a good deal of Shakespeare, a good deal

"Shoo," said Mrs. Dixon. "Shoo," and the geese went off to the other end of the yard. "Just you say 'shoo' to them and make as if you'd give them what for if they didn't shift; and they'll not trouble you." ■ (From *Swallowdale* by Arthur Ransome. Illustrated by Helene Carter.)

of Carlyle, a lot of Stevenson, and every book of folk tales I had been able to get hold of. My Greek grammar was hopeless but I was taking great delight in the limpid Greek of the New Testament. In the school library I rushed eagerly through one book of exploration after another. At home I had my father's library on which to draw and joined my brother and sisters to listen to my mother's reading aloud. I suppose I was learning something all the time but I had nothing to show for it and had not the sense to keep my ambitions to myself. When asked what I was going to be I always gave the same answer, and always it raised a laugh from those who knew my position in the school and cost me endless ragging, besides discomfort at home.

"I left Rugby from the Lower Fifth. We spent the summer holidays that year at Scarborough. I worked very hard to make ready for matriculation at Leeds and to everybody's astonishment, my own most of all, I passed in the first division, thanks I believe to doing well in precisely those subjects that had least importance for one who was supposed to be setting out on a scientific career.

"Going to the Yorkshire College at Leeds (it did not become an independent university till after I had left) meant that for the first time in my life I was not conscious of a surrounding

atmosphere of doubt or disapproval. This emancipation was immediate. . . .

"The decisive moment found me in the College library. I had gone there from the laboratory to consult a book on mensuration or magnetism, and happening on some shelves where the books were classified not by their subjects but by the names of their authors I saw two tall brown volumes with richly gilt lettering and decoration on their backs: J. W. Mackail's *Life of William Morris*. I began dipping into one of them, sat down with it and never went back to the laboratory that day. I read entranced of the lives of the young Morris and his friends, of lives in which nothing seemed to matter except the making of lovely things and the making of a world to match them. I took the books home with me, walking on air, across Woodhouse Moor, in a thick Leeds fog, and had read them through before I went to bed. No second-best choice would satisfy me now. Nothing would change my mind. Nothing should stop me. From that moment, I suppose, my fate was decided, and any chance I had ever had of a smooth career in academic or applied science was gone for ever. For days after that I moved in a dream reading that book again and again.

". . . I could excuse the collapse of my resolve to please my mother by becoming a scientist only by showing that, by going some other way, I should even sooner cease to be a burden on my family."[1]

1903. "For the better part of two terms things dragged on so. I was working as hard as I have ever worked, but not at science. I was writing and reading, reading and writing, and my landlady exclaimed at the frequency with which she had to empty my waste-paper basket. With extreme lack of practical sense my choice of form was that least likely to bring a financial reward. I had a passion for William Hazlitt and, to balance my admiration for his athletic discursive prose, had never lost my childhood's passion for fairy stories. I wanted to write essays. I wanted to write tales for children. . . ."[1]

1907. Took up residence in Paris. "I sent a drawing of my studio to my mother and also a sketch of the whole building and she ponted out at once that if anybody were to upset a stove in any of the studios the whole place would flare up like a match-box. Was there a fire-escape? There was not, but I agreed to calm her fears by making one. I went out to look for a stout rope that would reach from the top of the building to the bottom. After looking at several ropes in a neighbouring shop and rejecting them, I found one that seemed strong enough and threw an end of it over a beam and swung on it to see if it would bear my weight. The *patronne* from behind her desk watched this performance with a face increasingly grave. She left her desk, waved aside the man who was serving me, and spoke seriously in my ear. 'No, no, Monsieur,' she said, 'you are young and life is still sweet.' I reassured her and went out of the shop with the big coil of rope over my shoulder. Back in my studio I had to try it. I fastened one end of it round my box-mattress, wedged so that it could not shift and paid the rope out of the window. I had been a little mean and it did not quite reach the ground. Still, it did not look much too short and I climbed out of the window and began to go down. My fire-escape, meant to save life, very nearly took me to my death. I went slowly down the rope, passing as I went the glass fronts of the lower studios. At that time Paris was suffering from an epidemic of robberies with violence, and the sudden appearance of a man on a rope outside his studio on the fifth floor shocked a French artist at his work. I had reached the floor below his when a window opened above me and he leaned out, voluble and hostile. '*Au secours!*' he yelled. '*Les Apaches! Les Apaches!*' I could do nothing but continue my descent. And then that lunatic, no doubt thinking that he was virtuously defeating a marauder, grabbed my rope and began trying to shake me off it. I became the bob of a pendulum that was beginning to swing. There was a crash of glass and then another. Hand over fist I went down to tinkling music, in a shower of glass. I had six feet to drop at the bottom and a lot of glass to pay for. But my mother, on hearing that I had now an efficient fire-escape, was at peace. I thought it better not to tell her how it had been tested."[1]

March 13, 1909. Married Ivy Walker. "I was able to sublet my flat, and we set up house at Stoner Hill Top, Petersfield. . . . I was already a month or so late with my *History of Story-Telling*, which was due . . . on March 31, so that I had little time for anything but work. I had hoped that, once I had removed [Ivy] by marriage from the fantastic atmosphere of her home life, ordinary life would be possible for her. It never was. We had not been married more than a few weeks when she told me she had learned that her cousin and two other of her former suitors had met and discussed a plan for her abduction and detention in a lighthouse bought for that purpose by the cousin. She asked me to buy a revolver. I noted in my diary that I felt justified in doing so 'in case any of this melodrama should take a practical shape' and that 'in case of any future trouble' I had 'taken the precaution to write down here my only reason for such an action.' To this note I later added another 'Have not yet bought the revolver, 29 Nov. 1909.' I never did buy one. I had by that time become accustomed to a life in which from one day to the next I never knew what new form melodrama would take. Nothing could be too extravagant. Nor could I ever take any plain statement at its face value. I did not think she was to blame for all this. Brought up in a house where her father and mother competed for her affection, and accused each other of every kind of horror and depravity, she had had no chance of growing up a normal human being. Her father said of her mother, 'She is like a blow-fly depositing—is it five million or only five hundred thousand?—poisonous germs wherever she sets her foot.' Her mother was ready to say as much of her father and to go further in horrible particularisation. With this nightmarish family background of mutual hate what could be expected?

"Much of the winter of **1909-10** we spent in lodgings at Peak's Farm, near Semley in Wiltshire, where besides the reviews and other small things, I worked on Poe, did some translations from Daudet and sent more of the storytellers to press. In March we moved to lodgings in Bournemouth, where my daughter Tabitha was born on May 9. My wife had insisted that I should be in the room while my daughter was being born but, just before the delivery was complete, her doctor had the humanity to send me to his own house for a bottle he pretended to have forgotten. He too, poor man, had been given a place in the general fantasia. It had been explained to me that my mother-in-law had been allowed to suppose that he was in love with her while he was in fact in love with her daughter—and so on, and so on."[1] The marriage dissolved.

1924. Married Eugenia Shelepin whom he had met during his years in Russia, where he traveled to learn the language, study their folklore and eventually serve as a war correspondent.

He sailed past the staithe and the boat-houses till he came to a little old house with a roof thatched with reeds, and a golden bream swimming merrily into the wind high above one of the gables. ▪ (From *Coot Club* by Arthur Ransome. Illustrated by the author and Helene Carter.)

Old Peter's Russian Tales, a collection of twenty-one stories that Russian peasants tell their children was the result of his sojourn to Russia. In his note to the first edition, Ransome said: "I think there must be more fairy stories told in Russia than anywhere else in the world. In this book are a few of those I like best. I have taken my own way with them more or less, writing them mostly from memory." [Hugh Shelley, "Arthur Ransome," *Three Bodley Head Monographs,* edited by Kathleen Lewis, The Bodley Head, 1960.[2]]

1930. At age 45, Ransome achieved his greatest success with the publication of *Swallows and Amazons.* The story concerned real children, who were likeable and understandable, and who did things every child likes to do. It was based in part on Ransome's childhood memories of the holidays spent at Lake Windermere. *New Statesman* said, "The outward aspect of the book will please the grown-up eye and may raise an expectation that the children in it are psychologically studied for adult reading. But the child-reader wll be delighted to find nothing so uninteresting to him as child-psychology, and the things that do interest him treated on a real and serious plane. The ideal reader should certainly be not too

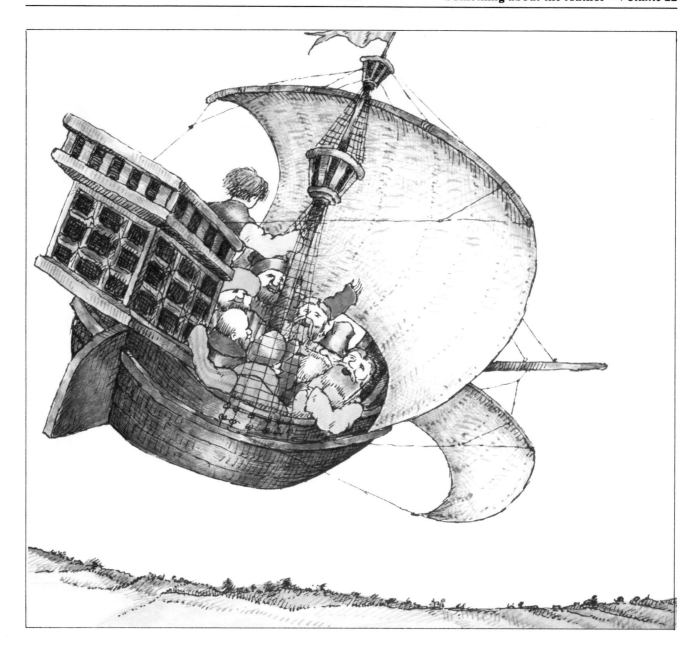

...And away they all sail together, singing like to burst their lungs. ■ (From *The Fool of the World and the Flying Ship,* retold by Arthur Ransome. Picture by Uri Shulevitz.)

old tor make-believe about a miniature desert-island.'' *Spectator* added, ''One of the great charms of the book is its extreme reasonableness. Mr. Ransome is as thoughtful of detail as Defoe: he tells how tents were made, how pike . . . were scaled, how meals were cooked and leading lights set above the tiny harbour. . . .''

1931. *Swallowdale,* the sequel to *Swallows and Amazons,* was reviewed by a *New York Times* critic who said, ''Like its predecessor, *Swallows and Amazons,* meets the test of a good book for children, for it can be read with pleasure by adults as well as boys and girls. The book is full of adventure, not artificial excitement, but the kind that a child who has not been too much interfered with will find for himself anywhere, though, in this instance, an island for camping, a sail boat, and a sympathetic and sensible mother furnish an ideal starting point for imaginative play.''

1932. *Peter Duck* published. *Peter Duck* has been a favorite among older readers. The *New York Times* said of it, ''Mr. Ransome is one of those rare authors who can write for children and about children at the same time. . . . His fine prose style is a delight. The illustrations add to the interest of the book.'' *Saturday Review* commented, ''The story contains all the ingredients necessary to make it not only eminently readable, but also thrilling enough to satisfy the most exacting of tastes. What more could anyone demand than a book about the sea together with a buried treasure in the Caribbean Islands, pirates, storms, sharks, a waterspout, and a happy ending.''

1936. *Pigeon Post* was the first book to win the now famous Carnegie Medal. ''You write not *for* children but for yourself, and if, by good fortune, children enjoy what you enjoy, why then you are a writer of children's books. . . . No special credit to you, but simply thumping good luck."[2]

1946. After the war the Ransomes spent half of each year in a riverside flat in London and the other half on board a yacht on the South Coast, and later in an old farmhouse in the Lake Country. After a fall in 1958 which resulted in severe illness, Ransome never fully regained good health. Boats and the water, both of which he loved dearly, come into all of his books.

June 3, 1967. Died in England. ". . . Writing is the one profession in which one can have one's cake and eat it, and it seems to me that in writing books for boys and girls I have the best of growing-up years over again and the best of being old as well." [*Publishers Weekly,* October 27, 1945.[3]]

HOBBIES AND OTHER INTERESTS: Fishing, sailing, fairy stories.

The only living thing to be seen was John, who had raced across a hundred yards or so of open ground to climb a ridge of grey rock. He was signalling to them to come on.

"Not a sign of him," said John, when the rest of the prospectors joined him. ■ (From *Pigeon Post* by Arthur Ransome. Illustrated by Mary E. Shepard.)

FOR MORE INFORMATION SEE: Junior Book of Authors, edited by Stanley Kunitz and Howard Haycraft, H. W. Wilson, 1934; *Horn Book* Magazine, January-December, 1948; Roger Lancelyn Green, *Teller of Tales,* new enlarged edition, Ward, 1953; Hugh Shelley, *Arthur Ransome,* Bodley Head, 1960, reissued with *Rudyard Kipling [and] Walter de la Mare,* 1968; Brian Doyle, editor, *Who's Who of Children's Literature,* Schocken Books, 1968; Margery Fisher, *Who's Who in Children's Books,* Holt, 1975; Arthur Ransome, *The Autobiography of Arthur Ransome,* edited by Rupert Hart-Davis, Jonathan Cape, 1976. Obituaries—*New York Times,* June 6, 1967; *Publishers Weekly,* June 26, 1967.

Childhood shows the man as morning does the day.
—John Milton

RAWLS, (Woodrow) Wilson 1913-

PERSONAL: Born September 24, 1913, in Scraper, Okla.; son of Minzy O. and Winnie (Hatfield) Rawls; married Sophie Ann Styczinski (budget analyst for Atomic Energy; retired, 1972), August 23, 1958. *Education:* Attended schools in Oklahoma. *Religion:* Presbyterian. *Home:* Route 2, Box 73, Cornell, Wis. 54732.

CAREER: Became itinerant carpenter in teens and worked for an oil company on a construction job in Mexico and in South America; also worked on the Alcan Highway in Alaska, on five of the major dam jobs in the United States, in West Coast shipyards, for the Navy in Oregon, for a lumber company in British Columbia. Full-time writer, 1959—. Visited with and lectured to students in elementary and secondary schools, colleges and universities throughout the West, and, since 1975, in the East as well. Banquet and convention speaker for state, national, and international educational associations. *Member:* Authors Guild, Authors League of America, International Platform Association, Idaho PTA (lifetime honorary member). *Awards, honors: Where the Red Fern Grows* selected for the "Gold Star List," 1962, by the Syracuse Library, and received the Evansville Book Award, 1979; *Summer of the Monkeys* received the Sequoyah Children's Book Award, and the William Allen White Children's Book Award, 1979, and the Golden Archer Award, 1980.

WRITINGS: Where the Red Fern Grows (Literary Guild selection), Doubleday, 1961; *Summer of the Monkeys,* Doubleday, 1976.

ADAPTATIONS—Movies: "Where the Red Fern Grows" (motion picture), Doty-Dayton Productions, 1974.

WORK IN PROGRESS: Third novel (also a dog story), tentatively titled *The Story of Shep.*

SIDELIGHTS: "I spent the first few years of my life on a farm in north-eastern Oklahoma. There were no schools in that part of the country. My mother taught us to read and write. Later a school was built and my sisters and I were able to attend for two or three months every summer. After we moved to Tahlequah, I attended a regular school for the first time but didn't finish the eighth grade because the depression hit the country and we moved to Muskogee.

WILSON RAWLS

"Long before we moved from the farm, I learned the joy of reading. On winter evenings, Mama would read stories from books that Grandma bought for us. After Mama finished reading the stories, each of us had to read a page or two aloud every night until we went through the book again.

"For a long time, I couldn't get interested in those stories. I called them 'girl stories.' I was beginning to think that's all there were—stories like 'Little Red Riding Hood,' 'Little Red Hen,' 'Chicken Little,' and 'The Three Little Pigs.' One day Mama brought home a book that changed my life. It was a story about a man and a dog—Jack London's *Call of the Wild*.

"After we finished reading the book, Mama gave it to me. It was my first real treasure and I carried it with me wherever I went. I read it every chance I got. One day while I was working in the fields, I got the idea that I would like to write a book like *Call of the Wild*.

"This was quite an ambitious dream for me. I didn't have an education, and my parents were too poor to buy paper and pencils for me. When I talked it over with my father, he said, 'Son, a man can do anything he sets out to do, if he doesn't give up.' I've never forgotten his words.

"When speaking in the schools, I tell the youngsters to keep reaching out for whatever goals they set for themselves. As long as they are honest and truthful and don't hurt anyone along the way, they will have help in reaching their goal. I know I did.

"With my desire to write known only to me, I spent years working as a carpenter and doing odd jobs wherever I could find them. I kept writing on every spare piece of paper I could get. I stored my writings in an old trunk at my mother's home.

"Just before I got married, I opened the trunk, took out my writings, and burned them—including manuscripts of five full-length novels. One of them was *Where the Red Fern Grows,* a novel I had written years before. After we were married, my wife talked me into rewriting one of the novels. I picked *Where the Red Fern Grows* because it was based on my boyhood life. It was first serialized in the *Saturday Evening Post* under the title 'Hounds of Youth,' then published in hard cover by Doubleday, and later ran in two newspapers.

"I love to fish and hunt. During the summer, you will find me fishing every chance I get. My days of wandering from job to job are over. On the day I married, I took off my vagabond shoes and set them in a corner. I know they'll be there forever.

"Children are always asking me what advice I can give them on trying to be a writer. I always tell them: 'Do a lot of reading. Read and study creative writing. Do not wait to start writing. You are never too young to start. Do not worry about grammar and punctuation on your first draft. The important thing is to get your story down on paper. Your first work will probably need a lot of rewriting. You can worry about grammar and punctuation then. Remember, the more you write and rewrite, the better you will get. And most important of all, do not get discouraged. If you keep trying and don't give up, you will make it some day. The road can be rough, but the day you see your work in print will make it all worth it. Best of luck!'"

Rawl's novel, *Summer of the Monkeys,* has been translated into German and French.

FOR MORE INFORMATION SEE: Library Journal, February, 1961; *Desert News,* February 16, 1974; *The Post-Register,* March 17, 1974; *The Herald-Republic,* March 24, 1974; *The Salt Lake Tribune,* April 7, 1974; *Milwaukee Journal,* June 25, 1978; *The Courier-Sentinel,* January 25, 1979, January 3, 1980; *Leader -Telegram,* June 21, 1979; *Lebo Enterprise,* November 14, 1979; ''Hilites,'' January 12, 1980.

My castle has a lot of doors;
Each one is numbered too.
No matter which you open first,
Two pages wait on you.

—L.J. Bridgman

RAYNER, Mary 1933-

PERSONAL: Born December 30, 1933, in Mandalay, Burma; daughter of A. H. and Yoma Grigson; married E. H. Rayner, 1960; children: Sarah, William, Benjamin. *Education:* University of St. Andrews, M.A. (second class honors), 1954. *Residence:* Richmond, Surrey, England. *Address:* c/o Macmillan London Ltd., 4 Little Essex St., London W.C.2, England.

CAREER: Worked in various London publishing houses, 1956-62; free-lance book illustrator and writer, 1972—. *Member:* Association of Illustrators, Society of Authors. *Awards, honors: Mr. and Mrs. Pig's Evening Out* and *Garth Pig and the Icecream Lady* were named in the *Horn Book* Honor List for 1977 and 1978, respectively.

WRITINGS—Self-illustrated: *The Witchfinder* (juvenile), Morrow, 1976; *Mr. and Mrs. Pig's Evening Out* (juvenile), Atheneum, 1976; *Garth Pig and the Icecream Lady* (juvenile), Atheneum, 1978.

Illustrator: Daphne Ghose, *Harry,* Lutterworth, 1973; Stella Nowell, *The White Rabbit,* Lutterworth, 1975; Griselda Gif-

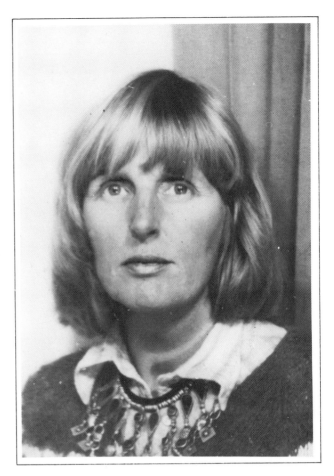

MARY RAYNER

ford, *Because of Blunder,* Gollancz, 1977; Griselda Gifford, *Cass the Brave,* Gollancz, 1978; Partap Sharma, *Dog Detective Ranjha,* Macmillan, 1978.

Work represented in anthologies: *Allsorts Six,* edited by Ann Thwaite, Methuen, 1974; *Allsorts Seven,* edited by Ann Thwaite, Methuen, 1975; *Young Winters' Tales Seven,* edited by M. R. Hodgkin, Macmillan, 1976. Has also contributed short stories to *Cricket* Magazine.

WORK IN PROGRESS: The Rain Cloud, a picture book to be published by Atheneum; illustrating *The Boggart,* a story by Emma Tennant, to be published by Granada Publishing.

SIDELIGHTS: "The pig stories began as stories invented for my children and, although they have now grown beyond picture books, their comments and criticisms are a great help to me still."

FOR MORE INFORMATION SEE: Horn Book, October, 1976, June, 1977.

Then she snatched him up and carried him off downstairs. He made such a snorting and a squealing that all his brothers and sisters sat bolt upright in bed. ■ (From *Mr. and Mrs. Pig's Evening Out* by Mary Rayner. Illustrated by the author.)

Lynne Reid Banks, portrait by June Mendoza.

REID BANKS, Lynne   1929-

PERSONAL: Born July 31, 1929, in London, England; daughter of James (a doctor) and Muriel (an actress; maiden name Marsh) Reid Banks; married Chaim Stephenson (a sculptor), 1965; children: Adiel, Gillon, Omri. *Education:* Attended Queen's Secretarial College, London, 1945-46, Italia Conte Stage School, 1946, and Royal Academy of Dramatic Art, 1947-49. *Politics:* "Just right of center in Britain; quite far left in Israel." *Religion:* "Practising Atheist." *Residence:* London, England. *Agent:* Bolt & Watson, 8-12 Old Queen St., London S.W.1., England.

CAREER: Actress, 1949-54; free-lance journalist, 1954-55; Independent Television, London, television news reporter, 1955-57, television news scriptwriter, 1958-62; Kibbutz Yasur and Mossad Na' aman, Galilee, high school English teacher, 1963-71; writer of adult and children's books, 1971—. *Awards, honors:* Yorkshire Arts Literary Award for *Dark Quartet: The Story of the Brontes,* 1977.

WRITINGS—Adults: *The L-Shaped Room,* Simon & Schuster, 1961; *House of Hope,* Simon & Schuster, 1962; *Children at the Gate,* Simon & Schuster, 1968; *Backward Shadow,* Simon & Schuster, 1970; *Two Is Lonely,* Simon & Schuster, 1974; *Dark Quartet: The Story of the Brontes,* Delacorte, 1977; *Path to the Silent Country: Charlotte Bronte's Years of Fame,* Delacorte, 1977.

Juveniles: *The Adventures of King Midas,* Dent, 1976; *The Farthest-Away Mountain,* Doubleday, 1977; *I, Houdini: The Autobiography of a Self-Educated Hamster,* Dent, 1979; *The Indian in the Cupboard,* Doubleday, in press.

Young Adults: *One More River,* Simon & Schuster, 1972; *Sarah and After, Five Women Who Founded a Nation,* Doubleday, 1977; *My Darling Villain,* Harper, 1977; *Letters to My Israeli Sons: The Story of Jewish Survival,* Frederick Watt, in press. Author of "The Gift," a three-act play produced in London, 1965, and of other stage, radio, and television plays. Contributor to magazines and newspapers, including *McCall's, Cornhill,* and *Ladies' Home Journal.*

WORK IN PROGRESS: The Writing on the Wall, for young adults; a modern novel for adults, an oral history of Israel's War of Independence.

SIDELIGHTS: "I was the only child of highly contrasted and interesting parents. My father was a Scottish doctor who'd been born in India; my mother was a gifted actress, once a star of the London stage, and she'd been born in Dublin and lived through the Easter Rebellion, about which—among many other fascinating subjects—she told me exciting stories. Because of those she told me about her stage career, there was never a doubt in my mind that I would become an actress, and I began my 'career' at school. Drama and English were the only subjects I cared about or in which I was any good. I was definitely a 'C' student in everything else.

"For some odd reason my parents sent me to a Catholic convent in the country when I was nine and I spent two strange years there, just before World War II. The location was quite beautiful and, as war approached and strict school routines slackened, the girl-pupils were given a lot of freedom to play in the bluebell woods: we formed a secret society called 'The League of the Deadly Nightshade' whose chief function was to waylay soldiers from the nearby camp and make them recite or otherwise pay a forfeit—the nuns would have had fits, though it was all entirely innocent and enormous fun. I always adored secret societies. When war came, and I was evacuated to the Canadian Prairies with my mother and my cousin, Christopher, I helped form another [secret society]—I think we had to sign declarations in blood for that one, and undergo terrifying initiations.

"My life in Canada during my 'formative years' (of course, all the years of childhood are formative) had a profound effect on my future. Cut off from my country and her ordeals by bombing and fear and shortages, I lived in a paradise of ease and plenty, even though we were (so my mother tells me) very hard up when we went to live alone on 'the wrong side of the tracks' on a very small allowance given to us by my great-uncle Arthur, himself poor; while my mother went through a protracted private hell of anxiety, loneliness and cheese-paring, my cousin and I lived a normal, carefree life, scarcely giving a thought to what was happening in Britain. It would have been very different without my mother; many evacuees endured appalling trials; but with her near me, I was perfectly content, and became as nearly as I could, a real Canadian.

"When the war ended in 1945 we returned to London—wartorn, war-weary London, to find our relations looking haggard and much, much more than five years older—my father's hair had turned white, and it was very difficult to re-establish our family. I now think our going to Canada was a great mistake, but who could foresee at the time that Hitler would not invade? The impression made on me by my gradually

...And now in it came, poking about to see if anyone was in there. Dakin crept backward, staying out of its reach. ■ (From *The Farthest-Away Mountain* by Lynne Reid Banks. Illustrated by Victor Ambrus.)

coming to realise what my family and my country had been through was profound. But perhaps the core and symbol of these revelations was my discovery, at the age of sixteen, of what the Nazis had done to the Jews of Europe.

"In my book, *Letters to My Israeli Sons,* I've tried to describe how the ghastly post-war revelations have affected my whole life by turning my attention to the Jews and their problems. My obsession with the subject eventually led, indirectly, to my marriage to a Jew—an English-born Israeli—and my living, for nearly nine years, in a kibbutz in the Galilee. These were perhaps the happiest, though not the most productive in a literary sense, years of my life. All the careers I had had before—acting, at which I had failed; writing, at which I had succeeded; even my brief and unwilling periods as a secretary, and my training as a singer, came in useful when I was launched willy-nilly on a new job—that of teaching English to kibbutz children. In the kibbutz my three sons were born to me in my late thirties, and I learned that to be an Atheist is not merely to have no religion, but to be a believer in no God and in the potential of human beings. I also learnt what true socialism is, by living it; I also learnt that, like so many other 'isms,' it only works for the few.

"In 1971, I and my family returned to London. My husband and I had come to realise that if we remained in the kibbutz we would never be real, full-time, working writer and sculptor—for that, you have to be financially dependent upon your work, you need the 'goad of necessity' behind you. Since then we have worked full-time on our 'arts,' and struggled at the same time to be something other than very mediocre parents to our growing boys.

"We now live in a large house with a huge garden (for London) in a rather ropy district of West London. It's always in chaos, but at least we have space to move and each boy his own room. We delight in our big lawn and demanding, but very satisfying, vegetable garden. How long we will 'rest' here before taking off on a new venture, heaven knows—we never seem to settle anywhere for longer than a few years.

"My attitude to my writing is very mixed. I regard it as the hardest, loneliest work in the world, and except for those very rare moments when it 'takes off,' I get no satisfaction out of it until it is done. But there is no doubt that, while other forms of writing (such as plays) give more immediate excitement and stimulation because you see their effect on others, and because you get to work with others, still there is nothing to beat holding your own book in your hands and looking through it and knowing that there are people all over the place reading it and perhaps—one hopes—enjoying it. Plays 'fade away,' but books can go on forever. Somehow the memory of those that have struck deep into people's minds can go on and on, too. Nothing delights me more than to have a stranger say, 'Oh, I did love your book! I keep thinking about it.' Not that *that* happens often, but when it does . . . !

"Writing for young people is a much pleasanter, and easier, thing than writing for adults. My mother has a theory that all the ages we have ever been are still shut up inside us. There is the three-year-old you, the ten-year-old you, the teenage you . . . all of which you can 'tap' for feelings and information if you can just keep in touch with them. All the child-me's have been brought out for exercise since I began writing for different age-groups. I especially enjoy writing sort of wish-fullfillment tales for younger children—I'm doing one at the moment about a plastic Indian who comes to life, a very real and troublesome life—he's no toy, but a real Indian from another time. I always test out my work on my own children, though they don't always like what others like—my most successful children's books have not been the ones they like best (but then my most successful adult books were not the ones my mother liked best either). In the end one has to write what one wants to write, or what one is commissioned to write, and hope for the best. You can't win 'em all."

FOR MORE INFORMATION SEE: Times Literary Supplement, March 25, 1977; *Horn Book,* August, 1977, October, 1977.

Books are keys to wisdom's treasure;
Books are gates to lands of pleasure;
Books are paths that upward lead;
Books are friends. Come let us read.

—Emilie Poulsson

JAMES RICE

RICE, James   1934-

PERSONAL: Born February 10, 1934, in Coleman, Tex.; son of James W. (a railroad worker) and Mary (Jennings) Rice; married Martha Oustad (a secretary/editor), June 4, 1954; children: Zel, Maria, Lyn, Patti, Jason. *Education:* University of Texas, B.F.A., 1959; Howard Payne College, M.Ed., 1960. *Residence:* Shamrock, Tex. *Agent:* Ann Elmo Agency, Inc., 60 E. 42nd St., New York, N.Y. 10017.

CAREER: Teacher of art and music in public schools of Kingsville, Tex., Hampton, Va., and the Canal Zone, 1959-

64; Southeastern Louisiana University, Hammond, assistant professor of art, 1964-66; Louisiana State University, Baton Rouge, assistant professor of art, 1967-68; Southeastern Louisiana University, assistant professor of art, 1969-75; Shamrock High School, Shamrock, Tex., band director, 1979—. Author and illustrator, 1973—. *Military service:* U.S. Army, 1955-56.

WRITINGS—Self-illustrated books for children, except as noted: *Gaston the Green-Nosed Alligator*, Pelican, 1974; *Lyn and the Fuzzy*, Pelican, 1975; *Gaston the Green-Nosed Alligator Coloring Book*, Pelican, 1976; *Cajun Alphabet*, Pelican, 1976; *Gaston Goes to Mardi Gras*, Pelican, 1977; *Gaston Goes to Texas*, Pelican, 1978; *Prairie Christmas*, Shoal Creek, 1978; *Cowboy Alphabet*, Shoal Creek, 1978; *Cajun Calendar*, Pelican, in press; *Gaston Lays an Offshore Pipeline*, Pelican, in press; *Texas: Night Before Christmas*, Pelican, in press; *Nashville 98* (adult), Moore, in press; (with Howard Jacobs) *Cajun Folk Tales*, Moore, in press.

Illustrator: Howard Jacobs, editor, *Cajun Night Before Christmas*, Pelican, 1973; Annie F. Johnson, editor, *The Little Colonel*, Pelican, 1974; Alice Durio, *Cajun Columbus*, Pelican, 1975; *A Cajun Night Before Christmas Coloring Book*, Pelican, 1976.

WORK IN PROGRESS: Gaston Goes Offshore, Texas Alphabet, and two adult novels, *Goodbye Nashville* and *Badman*.

HOBBIES AND OTHER INTERESTS: Reading, chess, playing piano and woodwinds, motorcycling, painting and sculpture.

**Now you know your ABC's,
As every Cajun should,...**
■(From *Cajun Alphabet* by James Rice. Illustrated by the author.)

RIDLON, Marci 1942-
(Marci McGill; Marci Carafoli)

PERSONAL: Born July 27, 1942 in Chicago, Ill.; daughter of John and Henrietta (Wilfinger) Ridlon; married second husband, Edward P. McGill, December 15, 1979. *Education:* Attended MacMurray College. *Politics:* Independent. *Religion:* None. *Residence:* New York, N.Y.

CAREER: Follett Publishing Co., Chicago, Ill., editor of children's books, 1964-77; Random House, New York, N.Y., editor of children's books, 1977-79; Doubleday & Co., Inc., New York, N.Y., editorial director of books for young readers, 1979—.

WRITINGS—Under name Marci Ridlon; all published by Follett, except as indicated: *Kittens and More Kittens*, 1967; *That Was Summer* (poems for children), 1969; *A Frog Sandwich*, 1973; *Lightning Strikes Twice*, Fisher Price, 1979; *Grandma and Grandpa's Grand Opening*, Fisher Price, 1980; *Uncle Filbert Saves the Day*, Fisher Price, 1980.

Under name Marci Carafoli; all published by Follett: (With John Carafoli) *Look Who's Cooking*, 1974; *The Strange Hotel*, 1975.

SIDELIGHTS: "My parents were avid readers and my mother was especially talented at reading stories to me. Before I went to school, she would always allow me two hours of story-telling time a day and I loved it. I grew up loving books and wanting to be part of their creation in whatever way I could."

HOBBIES AND OTHER INTERESTS: Playing alto recorder, sailing, yoga, astrology, Chinese cooking.

FOR MORE INFORMATION SEE: Library Journal, July, 1969.

RUKEYSER, Muriel 1913-1980

OBITUARY NOTICE: Born December 15, 1913, in New York, N.Y.; died February 12, 1980, in New York, N.Y. Social activist, teacher, poet, biographer, screenwriter, novelist, dramatist, translator, and author of children's books. Rukeyser united her personal and political interests in her poetry. While covering the Scottsboro trial in 1932 for the *Student Review*, she was detained briefly because she had been observed talking with some black journalists. This experience is recorded in one of her early poems, "The Trial." Rukeyser's voice of protest was to be heard again in the succeeding years. During the Spanish civil war she lobbied for the cause of the Spanish loyalists. An early advocate of women's rights, in her later years she protested the Vietnamese War and expressed concern about the persecution of the Kurds in Iran. Counted among her volumes of verse are *Theory of Flight, Soul and Body of John Brown, The Green Wave,* and *The Gates. The Collected Poems of Muriel Rukeyser* was published in 1979. Rukeyser was the recipient of the Shelley Memorial Award and the Copernicus Award. Although she won wide acclaim as a poet of social protest, she also ventured successfully into other genres. She translated the work of such authors as Octavio Paz and Bertold Brecht, wrote a biography of Wendell Willkie, and produced several children's books, including *I Go Out* and *Bubbles.*

For More Information See: Current Biography, Wilson, 1943; *Contemporary Authors,* Volume 7-8, revised, Gale, 1969; *Contemporary Poets,* 2nd edition, St. Martin's, 1975; *Biography News,* Volume II, Gale, 1975; *Who's Who in America,* 40th edition, Marquis, 1978; *The Writers Directory, 1980-82,* St. Martin's, 1979; *Ms.,* January, 1979. *Obituaries: Contemporary Authors,* Volume 93-96, Gale, 1980; *New York Times,* February 13, 1980; *Chicago Tribune,* February 15, 1980; *Newsweek,* February 25, 1980; *Time,* February 25, 1980.

RUTGERS van der LOEFF, An(na) Basenau 1910-
(Rutger Bas)

PERSONAL: Born March 15, 1910, in Amsterdam, The Netherlands; daughter of Jacob F. (a doctor of medicine) and Nora (Goemans) Basenau; married Michael Rutgers van der Loeff (a doctor of philosophy and an electrical engineer), September 18, 1934; children: Paul, Frits and Romee (twins, boy and girl; Romee is now Mrs. R. J. Velthuys), Lucy. *Education:* Barlaeus Gymnasium, Amsterdam, graduated, 1929; studied classical languages at University of Amsterdam, two years. *Home:* "Pax," Patrijslaan 3, Huizen-N.H., The Netherlands. *Agent:* Robert Harben, 3 Church Vale, London N.2 9PD, England.

CAREER: Writer and translator. *Member:* Dutch Association of Writers, P.E.N. *Awards, honors:* Prijs voor het Beste Kinderboek (Dutch prize for the best children's book), 1955, for *Lawines razen;* second Dutch prize, Atlantic competition, 1958, for *Je bent te goed, Giacomo;* honor book award, *New York Herald Tribune* Children's Spring Book Festival, 1958, *New York Times Book Review* "One Hundred Outstanding Books" list, 1958, and Junior Book Award, Boys' Clubs of America, 1959, all for *Avalanche;* first prize for best information book, German governmental competition for juvenile novels, 1959, for *Amerika;* first prize for literary work in the sphere of travel, 1961, for *Gideons reizen;* Austrian governmental prize, 1966, for *Mens of Wolf?;* prize for the entirety of her juveniles from the Dutch government, 1968; received the Gold Medal of Verona, Italy, 1971, for *Mens of Wolf?;* made a knight in the Order of Orange (Nassau), 1976; honored by Delta Kappa Gamma Society (international) for distinguished service to education in the Netherlands, 1976; Lista d'Onore in Padua, Italy, 1976, for *De Reus van Pech-zonderend;* first prize in the German governmental competition for juvenile novels, 1977, for *Ik ben Fedde.*

WRITINGS—All Dutch editions published by Ploegsma, unless otherwise indicated: *Van een dorp, een jongen en een orgel* (title means "A Village, a Boy, and an Organ"), 1946; *Zweden, droom em werkelijkheid* (title means "Sweden, Dream and Reality"), 1948; *De Kinderkaravaan,* 1949, 14th edition, 1980, translation by Roy Edwards published in England as *Children on the Oregon Trail,* University of London Press, 1961, published in America as *Oregon at Last!,* Morrow, 1962; *Wij Amsterdammers wat doen we met onze kinderen in de vacanties?,* 1950; *Amerika: Pioniers en hun kleinzoons,* R. van Goor, 1951, 3rd edition published as *Amerikaans avontuur,* 1966; *Anna Menander,* R. van Goor, 1951; *Mens of Wolf?* (title means "Man or Wolf?"), 1951, 7th edition, E. Querido, 1964; *Rossy, dat krantenkind,* 1952, translation by Edward Fitzgerald published as *Rossy, This Newspaper Child,* University of London Press, 1964; *Vader, de kinderen en ik* (title means "Father, the Children, and I"), Strengholt,

AN BASENAU RUTGERS van der LOEFF

Polar Night, Brockhampton, 1968; *De Elfstedentocht*, De Bezige Fij, 1965, translation by Henrietta Anthony published as *Great Day in Holland: The Skating Race*, Abelard, 1965; *Alles om een Speelplats* (title means "Everything for a Playground"), Wolters-Noordhoff, 1965; *Als je zou durven* (title means "If You had the Courage"), 1965; *Lieverdjes en Ijzervreters* (title means "Darlings and Fire-eaters"), Wolters-Noordhoff, 1966; *Vriend of vijand* (title means "Friend or Enemy"), Wolters-Noordhoff, 1966; *August en Roosje* (title means "August and Roosje"), Wolters-Noordhoff, 1967; *Vlas spoor in Waterland* (title means "Wrong Track in Waterland"), 1967; *Het uur der Scapinezen* (title means "The Hour of the Scapino Ballet"), 1968; *Met open oogen* (title means "With Open Eyes"), Samson, 1968; *Donald,* E. Querido, 1969.

Wrak onder water (title means "Wreck Under Water"), 1970; *Gerwoon in het ongewone* (title means "Common in the Uncommon"), 1971; *Ik ben Fedde* (title means "I Am Fedde"), 1972; (under pseudonym Rutger Bas) *De reus van Pech-zonder-end* (title means "The Giant of Trouble-Without-end"), 1974; *Het Kerstuverhaal,* 1975; (under pseudonym Rutger Bas) *De dubbel bodem van Pech-zonder-end*

1953; *Voor een kans op geluk* (title means "In Pursuit of Happiness"), 1953; *Het Verhaal van de hond Max,* 1953; *Lawines razen,* 1954, 13th edition, 1977, translation by Dora Round published as *Avalanche!,* University of London Press, 1957, Morrow, 1958; *Jimmy en Ricky,* 1955; *Het licht in je ogen* (title means "The Light in Your Eyes"), Arbeiderspers, 1956; *Konijne-Japie* (title means "Rabbit-Jack"), 1957; *Ze verdrinken ons dorp,* 1957, translation by Roy Edwards published as *They're Drowning Our Village,* University of London Press, 1959, Watts, 1960; *Je bent te goed, Giacomo* (title means "You Are Too Good, Giacomo"), 1957; *Het verloren kofferje* (title means "The Lost Handbag"), 1958; *Dat zijn M–brigadiers* (title means "The Milk Brigade"), 1959.

Gideons reizen (title means "The Voyages of Gideon"), 1960; *Het wilde land* [*en*] *Iedersland,* Samson, 1961, translation by Elizabeth Meijer published as *Everybody's Land,* University of London Press, 1964; *Vlucht, Wassilis, vlucht!,* 1962, translation by George Mocniak published as *Vassilis on the Run,* University of London Press, 1965, Follett, 1969; *Het Witte huis in hetgroen,* Samson, 1962; *Alleen Tegen alles* (title means "Alone Against All"), 1962; *Kinderen van 1813,* (title means "Children of 1813") Wolters-Noordhoff, 1963; *Steffos en zijn paaslam,* Samson, 1963, translation by Elizabeth Meijer published as *Steffos and His Easter Lamb,* Brockhampton, 1969; *Bevrijdingsspel 1813,* Wolters-Noordhoff, 1963; *Een vlinder achterna* (title means "The Chase for the Butterfly"), 1964; *Vlucht uit de Poolnacht,* Samson, 1964, translation by Marieke Clarke published as *Flight from the*

The schoolmaster and his son had the same quiet walk and the same sturdy legs. "There go the two best ski-runners in the village," said Old John. ■ (From *Avalanche!* by A. Rutgers van der Loeff. Illustrated by Gustave Schrotter.)

(title means "The False Bottom of Trouble-Without-end"), 1975; (under pseudonym Rutger Bas) *Het goud van Pech-zonder-end* (title means "The Gold of Trouble-Without-end"), 1976; (self-illustrated) *Myn Tuin, Klein erfgoed* (title means "My Garden, Small Patrimony"), 1977. Translator of about sixty books into Dutch from Scandinavian languages, English, German, and French.

SIDELIGHTS: **March 15, 1910.** Born in Amsterdam; eldest of three children. "We lived on the Keizergracht (Emperor Canal). That's where I was born and lived till I was a grownup. My youth on that Amsterdam canal has left its mark on me. My room was in the front; thus, my nose was always in the trees—the big elms and, underneath, on the dark waters the boats with their small deck-houses and their tiny curtains which hid the poverty and cramped quarters within; the wash on the lines, the worn-out clothes and inside, the small pot-belly stove. We sometimes brought [these people] soup and clothing, milk and eggs when yet another child was born."

Attended local schools and graduated from a gymnasium (a college preparatory school). Rutgers van der Loeff's father was a bacteriologist who used the fourth floor of their Keizergracht home as his office. For Rutgers van der Loeff, his laboratory yielded magic, magnetic powers. "Four times a day the long walk to and from school along the canal; first with my nursemaid and later, alone, with brothers and friends. [I remember] the canal with the many front steps and dark cellars here and there, the push carts, the bridges, the boats, the snow and ice in the winter, [and] the fallen leaves in autumn. In every season the sounds were different. I remember in the late summer, when it was time to return to school, the voices of the street vendors and the horns of the taxis had a very special quality, perhaps because of the heavy canopy of elm leaves. It was especially noticeable on the first day back in the city. On that day we always had beefsteak and sandwiches and apricot jam—steady fare. The following morning [we were] on our way to buy new notebooks, pencils, and pens. I always enjoyed myself endlessly. But I understood even then—if in a limited degree—how terribly privileged I was. Not only materially. We saw much, we did much, we had many opportunities. Both parents stimulated us (each in his own way) toward adventure and activities. Only much later I began to see that it was unusual for a girl to go to a gymnasium and to continue studying afterwards.

"We children were given everything by both our parents of which love and respect were the most important. But between them they had an especially difficult time. They both had very strong personalities, like two horses each wanting to go the opposite way. But to this very day I am thankful that because of us they stayed together. . . . As a child one seems to be able to live many lives at once. I did, at least. And I believe, in a way, it all bore fruit and later gave meaning to my work, where I must act the part of different characters. . . .

"[I studied] Latin and Greek, but after the death of my father I gave some lessons and translated from Norwegian, Swedish and Danish. From this I learned a tremendous amount. It was through my mother that I got into this work. She was, in the beginning of the century, an emancipated, working woman. Her sisters also had careers; one had studied in Paris and taught literature, the other restored antique porcelain. My mother completed studies at a Swedish institute for physical therapy. . . . Much later, after a relatively late marriage

and we children were somewhat grown, she wanted to 'work' again. My father thought it was nonsense. So she began translating Swedish books. She collected stories and through her I 'rolled' into the book world at an opportune moment."

1934. Married her childhood friend, Michael Rutgers van der Loeff, and the couple had four children. "My husband and I have always allowed each other plenty of freedom. My husband went mountain climbing; I travelled for my work, and the children were in summer camps. These were international camps . . . [and] very well organized. Not only my children, but I, too, learned a lot from them." In two school booklets, *Friend or Enemy,* I've described some of that camp life."

1949. Publication of her first book launched her career. "One day a publisher (Mr. Brinkman van Ploegsma) thought I would be able to write and gave me an assignment to do a book about Sweden. I thought: Who knows how a cow catches a hare? Let me give it a try. It worked! I found the work uplifting. After that [I got] a contract to do a youth book based on historical happenings of pioneer children in the North American wilderness. Yes, that was really the beginning of something which would never let go of me.

"Everyone working with children's books must know what he's doing. You have to realize you're manipulating with an important tool—an instrument not only for playing a fine role in giving children pleasure, but with which you build an entire world for the reading child in which he presently lives. Therefore, you must handle the instrument subtly; no doling out of lessons, no forcing down the throat, etc. Present them only with facts that are worth something. Not just a lollipop licked down to the stick and then thrown away. It happens all too often that the children are left with empty hands. Sad."

A grandmother, Rutgers van der Loeff continues today to write books, especially books for youngsters. "I want to be deeply interested in my subject and make everything I can out of it. I want to let [the children] live in worlds they do not know, far away and close to home. To stand in another man's shoes; better yet, to crawl into the other's skin—that's the kind of game I want to play with them. By discovering others they'll discover the world and, after all, themselves too."

The author's works have been translated into many different languages, including Finnish, Indonesian, Hebrew, Japanese, Portuguese, and Czech.

HOBBIES AND OTHER INTERESTS: Gardening, handicrafts, cycling, traveling, and painting.

Child! do not throw this book about;
Refrain from the unholy pleasure
Of cutting all the pictures out!
Preserve it as your chiefest treasure.

—Hilaire Belloc

JOHN RYAN

RYAN, John (Gerald Christopher) 1921-

PERSONAL: Born March 4, 1921, in Edinburgh, Scotland; son of Andrew and Ruth (van Millingon) Ryan; married Priscilla Ann Blomfield, January 1, 1950; children: Marianne, Christopher, Isabel. *Education:* Attended school in England. *Home and office:* 12 Airlie Gardens, London W8, England.

CAREER: Artist, illustrator, and maker of films for children. *Military service:* British Army, 1941-45.

WRITINGS—All self-illustrated; all for children; all published by Bodley Head except as indicated: *Captain Pugwash,* 1955; *Pugwash Aloft,* 1957; *Pugwash and the Ghost Ship,* 1962, S. G. Phillips, 1968; *Pugwash in the Pacific,* S. G. Phillips, 1973; *Dodo's Delight* (picture book), Deutsch, 1977, Fontana, 1979; *Doodle's Homework* (picture book), Deutsch, 1978. Author and producer of films for BBC-Television: "Captain Pugwash" series, 1958-68; "Mary Mungo and Midge," 1969; Sir Prancelot," 1972.

WORK IN PROGRESS: Six children's picture books for Hamlyn on the subject of Noah's Ark.

SIDELIGHTS: "I am more of an artist than a writer. The latter I find hard work, but drawing and painting is usually sheer pleasure. I've lived all my life on *ideas*. . .for stories, films etc. . .and have, as someone put it, just enough talent to put a line round the ideas. I work for children (apart from a weekly cartoon for the English *Catholic Herald),* presum-

ably because I am happiest in that field. Whatever the reason, I never write or draw *down* to children, but simply give them whatever entertains or amuses *me,* with no holds barred, excepting needless violence, obscenity, etc. It's a peaceful life if an uncertain one, and I hope to carry on until I drop."

SANCHEZ, Sonia 1934-

PERSONAL: Born September 9, 1934, in Birmingham, Ala.; daughter of Wilson L. and Lena (Jones) Driver; children: Anita, Morani, Mungu. *Education:* Hunter College (now Hunter College of the City University of New York), B.A., 1955. *Politics:* "Blackness." *Home:* 407 West Chelten Ave., Philadelphia, Pa. 19144.

CAREER: Staff member, Downtown Community School, San Francisco, Calif., 1965-67; San Francisco State College (now University), San Francisco, instructor, 1966-68; University of Pittsburgh, Pittsburgh, Pa., assistant professor, 1969-70; Rutgers University, New Brunswick, N.J., assistant professor, 1970-71; Manhattan Community College of the City University of New York, New York, N.Y., assistant professor of Black literature and creative writing, 1971-73; adjunct professor, City College of the City University of New York, 1972; associate professor, Amherst College, Amherst, 1972-75. *Awards, honors:* P.E.N. Writing Award, 1969; National Insitute of Arts and Letters grant, 1970; Ph.D., Wilberforce University.

WRITINGS: Homecoming (poetry), Broadside Press, 1969; *We a BaddDDD People* (poetry), Broadside Press, 1970; *It's a New Day: Poems for Young Brothas and Sistuhs,* Broadside Press, 1971; (editor) *Three Hundred and Sixty Degrees of Blackness Comin' at You* (poems), 5x Publishing Co., 1971; *Love Poems,* Third Press, 1973; *A Blues Book for Blue Magical Women* (poems), Broadside Press, 1973; *The Adventures of Fat Head and Square Head* (juvenile), Third Press, 1973; (editor) *We Be Word Sorcerers: 25 Stories by Black Americans* (anthology), Bantam, 1973; *The Afternoon of Small Head, Fat Head and Square Head* (juvenile), Third Press, 1974; *A Blues Book for Blue Black Magical Woman,* Broadside Press, 1974; *Love Poems,* Third Press, 1974; *The Adventures of Fat Head, Small Head, and Square Head,* Third Press, 1974; *I've Been a Woman: New and Selected Poems,* Black Scholar Press, 1978; *A Sound Investment and Other Stories,* Third World Press, 1979.

Contributor of poetry to numerous anthologies, including *Potero Negro* ("Black Power"), edited by Roberto Giammanco, Giu. Laterza & Figli, 1968; *BlackFire,* edited by LeRoi Jones and Roy Neal, Morrow, 1968; *For Malcolm: Poems on the Life and Death of Malcolm X,* edited by Dudley Randall and Margaret G. Burroughs, Broadside Press, 1968; *The Writing on the Wall: One Hundred Eight American Poems of Protest,* edited by Walter Lowenfels, Doubleday, 1969; *In a Time of Revolution: Poems from Our Third World,* edited by Lowenfels, Random House, 1970; *Soulscript,* edited by June M. Jordan, Doubleday, 1970; *Broadside Treasury,* edited by Gwendolyn Brooks, Broadside Press, 1971; *Black Poets,* edited by Dudley Randall, Bantam, 1971; *We Speak as Liberators: Young Black Poets,* edited by Orde Coombs, Dodd, 1971; *Cavalcade,* edited by A. Davis and S. Redding, Houghton, 1971; *Making It New,* edited by J. Chace and W. Chace, Canfield Press, 1973; *We Become New: Poems by Contemporary American Women,* edited by Lucille Iverson and Kathryn Ruby, Bantam, 1975; *Sports in Liter-*

SONIA SANCHEZ

ature, edited by Henry B. Chapin, McKay, 1976; *Understanding Poetry*, edited by Brooks and Warren, Holt, 1976. Poems also included in *Night Comes Softly* and *Black and Loud.*

Plays: "The Bronx Is Next," first produced in New York at Theatre Black, October 3, 1970; "Sister Son/ji," first produced with "Cop and Blow" and "Players Inn" by Neil Harris and "Gettin' It Together" by Richard Wesley as "Black Visions," Off-Broadway at New York Shakespeare Festival Public Theatre, 1972 (included in *New Plays from Black Theatre*). Also author of plays, "Dirty Hearts," 1972, "Malcolm/Man Don't Live Here No More," 1972, and "Uh Huh, But How Do It Free Us," 1973. Contributor to periodicals, including *Black Scholar, Journal of Black Poetry, Negro Digest*, and *Nickel Review.*

FOR MORE INFORMATION SEE: Black World, June, 1971; *Newsweek*, April 17, 1972; *Time*, May 1, 1972; *Black Creation*, fall, 1973; *Contemporary Literary Criticism*, Volume 5, Gale, 1976.

SCHONE, Virginia

PERSONAL: Born in McAlester, Okla.; daughter of William (a minister) and Lillie I. (Howe) Schone; married Dan Levin (a stage and television director). *Education:* Columbia University, B.A. (with honors), 1972; Bank Street College of Education, M.S., 1975. *Office:* 262 Central Park W., Apt. 7-C, New York, N.Y. 10024.

CAREER: CBS-TV, New York, N.Y., producer and writer of "Vanity Fair," 1950-55; NBC-Radio, New York, N.Y., writer of "Weekday," starring Mike Wallace and others, 1955-56; Young & Rubicam, Inc., New York, N.Y., senior advertising copywriter, 1956-60; elementary and remedial reading teacher, New York, N.Y., 1973—. Helped to create "Sesame Street," named it, wrote scripts, and presented photographic essays. Member of board of trustees of All Souls School (preschool and kindergarten), 1976-79. *Awards, honors:* Emmy Award for Outstanding Achievement in Children's Television Programming, from Academy of Television Arts and Sciences, 1970, for work on "Sesame Street."

WRITINGS: Penny Tales (juvenile stories), Parents' Magazine Press, 1977. Author of five filmstrips. Consultant and writer of six elementary readers for Random House. Contributor to *Co-Ed* and *Mademoiselle.*

WORK IN PROGRESS: Two humorous novels for children; easy-to-read books.

SIDELIGHTS: "I love humor. I am particularly interested in finding new ways to look at things—this includes new forms of communication."

VIRGINIA SCHONE

But there are lots of tennis courts looking for tennis players. ■(From *Jenny and the Tennis Nut* by Janet Schulman. Illustrated by Marylin Hafner.)

SCHULMAN, Janet 1933-

PERSONAL: Born September 16, 1933, in Pittsburgh, Pa.; daughter of Albert C. (in insurance) and Edith (Spielman) Schuetz; married L. M. Schulman (a writer and editor). children: Nicole. *Education:* Antioch College, B.A., 1956. *Residence:* New York, N.Y. *Office:* Random House, 201 E. 50th St., New York, N.Y., 10022.

CAREER: Writer. Macmillan Publishing Co., Inc., New York City, vice-president and juvenile marketing manager, 1961-74; Random House, Inc., New York City, director of library marketing, 1978—. Member of board of directors of Children's Book Council; member of publishing industry committees; consultant to juvenile publishers. *Member:* American Library Association.

WRITINGS—Juveniles; all published by Greenwillow, except as noted: *The Big Hello,* 1976; *Jack the Bum and the Halloween Handout,* 1977; *Jack the Bum and the Haunted House,* 1977; *Jenny and the Tennis Nut* (Junior Literary Guild selection), 1978; *Jack the Bum and the UFO,* 1978; *Camp*

Kee Wee's Secret Weapon, 1979; *The Great Big Dummy,* 1979; (adaptor), *The Nutcracker,* Dutton, 1979. Author of abridgements of literary works, including C. S. Lewis's *Chronicles of Narnia* and nineteenth-century literary classics, for Caedmon Records.

SIDELIGHTS: "I was the 'baby' of the family and always felt the outsider. During World War II my older brother was in the Air Force, my other brother was in the Navy, my sister was a secretary at U.S. Steel, and I was in elementary school. My role in the war effort was in buying war stamps with my ten-cents-a-week allowance and, as a Junior Commando, collecting scrap iron, tin cans, and newspaper for recycling. At some point I quite sensibly ceased trying to compete with my glamorous brothers and sister and began creating a world of my own, mainly through books, drawing, and making up stories. They thought I was strange, perhaps a bit daft, as I sat huddled under a tent blanket construction in the corner of the living room, talking to myself. But what I was really doing was creating little story/plays, in which I played all roles. Many of them were about a child who miraculously saved her family when the father lost his job or had to go to war.

"I was very much a child of the Great Depression, when my mother literally counted pennies to put food on the table for us, and the World War II era, both of which helped me keep a wary eye on reality. I think it shows in the kinds of stories I write for children today. Though none of them are set in those periods, I try to show children operating not in a vacuum but surrounded by circumstances of reality which do affect their lives. In *The Big Hello* a little girl moves to California because her father has gone there to find a new job. In *Camp KeeWee's Secret Weapon* Jill has to go to summer camp because her mother has just gotten a job and Jill is too young to stay home alone during the day. In *Jenny and the Tennis Nut* Jenny's father wants to see Jenny take up tennis enthusiastically because tennis is his game.

"Growing up in a large family also exposes one to a certain amount of teasing, and I think I learned at an early age that a sense of humor and a sharp wit are good defenses against a lot of things. I am always happy when a child says my books are funny because you can't trick children: they know when something is funny and when it isn't.

"Another thing that makes me happy is hearing a reviewer call my books non-sexist. I would hate to set out to write a non-sexist book—it would be awfully dull—but if some of my books just happen to be non-sexist, among other things, it must be because I grew up believing that I did not have to live a certain way because I was a girl, and I have pretty much followed that all my life. Nowadays many girls are doing just that. I wish they had been around when I was growing up!

"My daughter, Nicole, has also helped me as a writer. I doubt if I would have written the kinds of stories I write if I had not started just at the time Nicole was in the first grade. I wanted to write stories for her, stories she could read and would like. None of my stories are based directly on anything that has happened in our family, but all of them have grown or been inspired by my daily life with Nicole. And she is my most severe critic! She is the one who gives me encouragement but also criticism (much of it very sound) before I even take the manuscript to my editor, who helps me make my books even better."

HOBBIES AND OTHER INTERESTS: Tennis.

FOR MORE INFORMATION SEE: Publishers Weekly, February 23, 1976, February 28, 1977; *Horn Book,* August, 1977.

SHIEFMAN, Vicky

PERSONAL: Born in Detroit, Mich.; daughter of Saul (in public relations) and Emma (a teacher; maiden name, Goldman) Shiefman. *Education:* University of Chicago, B.A., 1964; New York University, M.A., 1973. *Politics:* Democrat. *Religion:* Jewish. *Residence:* New York, N.Y. *Agent:* Carole Abel, 160 W. 87th St., New York, N.Y. 10024.

CAREER: Board of Education, New York, N.Y., teacher of pre-kindergarten through second grade classes, 1968—. *Member:* United Federation of Teachers, Society of Children's Book Writers, Authors Guild of Authors League of America, Nu Pi Sigma.

WRITINGS: Mindy (juvenile), Macmillan, 1974; *M is for Move,* Dutton, 1981. Contributor of articles on education to

Nana, Mademoiselle, Moderator, and *University of Chicago Maroon.*

WORK IN PROGRESS: Goodbye to the Trees; Decisions; To Get to the Other Side.

SIDELIGHTS: "I grew up in a close Jewish family. One aunt, uncle, and cousins lived a few blocks away in one direction and another aunt, uncle, and cousins lived blocks away in another direction. My grandparents or other cousins lived upstairs. Besides the traditional, my home was full of new ideas (in education, psychology, social thought, religion, art) discussed by my parents and their friends. I was so young when I first attended an art exhibit by Paul Klee that I thought I could do as well and said so. I remember lots of music from classical through jazz and lots of books including Margaret Wise Brown, Ludwig Bemelmans, and the 'Babar' books. My parents loved children's literature. It was a very rich atmosphere and since I was the oldest granddaughter, one of the first three children at the private, progressive school, and the first of my parents' friends' children, I was in a favored position. Sometimes this was fun. Other times, I felt overwhelmed. I liked to retreat into my own private world of stories.

Mindy felt so good in her dream. She could feel the red skirt she wore over her jeans twirling round and round. She could feel the air whoosh by as she moved. ■(From *Mindy* by Vicky Shiefman. Illustrated by Lisl Weil.)

VICKY SHIEFMAN

"I wrote my first book—pictures and the names of my extended family—at seven or eight. A few months later, I drew and wrote a story that you put in a box and moved for Purim, the holiday celebrating the book of Esther. About the same age, I lay in bed imagining what I wanted to be when I grew up; my decision: an adventurer and writer."

STAFFORD, Jean   1915-1979

OBITUARY NOTICE: Born July 1, 1915, in Covina, Calif.; died March 26, 1979, in White Plains, N.Y. Novelist and author of short stories. Long admired for her literary craftmanship and her deft characterization, Stafford had written three novels and several short story collections when she received the 1970 Pulitzer Prize in fiction for her *Collected Stories.* Her works commonly featured women and children as protagonists who battled alienation and isolation in their imprisoned worlds. Among her best-known writings are two of her novels, *Boston Adventure* and *The Mountain Lion,* and her 1953 short story collection, *Children Are Bored on Sunday.* She also wrote juvenile books—*Elephi: The Cat with the High I.Q.* and *The Lion and the Carpenter and Other Tales from the Arabian Nights Retold*—and a book based on interviews with the mother of Lee Harvey Oswald, *A Mother in History.* Stafford was the recipient of several grants and fellowships, including two Guggenheim fellowships, and

her short story "In the Zoo" won the O. Henry Memorial Award for the best short story of 1955. She was married three times to writers: poet Robert Lowell, Oliver Jensen, and *New Yorker* critic A. J. Liebling. *For More Information See: Current Biography,* Wilson, 1951; *Contemporary Authors,* Volume 1-4, revised, Gale 1967; *Encyclopedia of World Literature in the Twentieth Century,* updated edition, Ungar, 1967; *The Reader's Adviser: A Layman's Guide to Literature,* Volume I: *The Best in American Fiction, Poetry, Essays, Literary Biography, and Reference,* 12th edition, Bowker, 1974; *Contemporary Novelists,* 2nd edition, St. Martin's, 1976; *Who's Who in Twentieth Century Literature,* Holt, 1976; *Who's Who in America,* 40th edition, Marquis, 1978. *Obituaries: Current Biography,* Wilson, 1979; *Chicago Tribune,* March 29, 1979; *Washington Post,* March 29, 1979; *Time,* April 9, 1979; *Newsweek,* April 9, 1979; *Publishers Weekly,* April 9, 1979; *AB Bookman's Weekly,* April 16, 1979; *Contemporary Authors,* Volume 85-88, Gale, 1980.

STUBLEY, Trevor (Hugh)   1932-

PERSONAL: Born November 27, 1932, in Leeds, England; son of Frank (a window cleaner) and Marie (a mill worker; maiden name Ellis) Stubley; married Valerie Ann Churm (an

TREVOR STUBLEY

"Sometimes the river is angry, and sometimes it is kind," said Sita.

"We are part of the river," said the boy. "We cannot live without it." ■ (From *Angry River* by Ruskin Bond. Illustrated by Trevor Stubley.)

art teacher), August 7, 1963; children: Adam, Justin, Gabriel, Nathan. *Education:* Attended Leeds College of Art, 1949-51; Edinburgh College of Art, D.A., 1953, post diploma scholar, 1954, Andrew Grant travelling scholar, 1955. *Home and studio:* The Hart Holes Studios, Greenfield Road, Holmfith near Huddersfield HD7 2XQ, England.

CAREER: Children's book illustrator. Huddersfield School of Art, assistant lecturer, 1957-59. Chairman of Kirklees Art Action Group. *Exhibitions:* Many one-man and group exhibitions in the United Kingdom; mixed exhibitions in Bologna, Bratislava and Wichita Falls, Kansas. *Military service:* Royal Army Educational Corps, sergeant, 1955-57. *Member:* Royal Society of Portrait Painters, Society of Industrial Artists and Designers, Association of Illustrators, The Pastel Society, The Midland Group of Artists, Kirkless Art Action Group. *Awards, honors:* The William Hoffmann Wood Gold Medal, 1953, for painting; Yorkshire television fine art (fellow), 1980.

ILLUSTRATOR: Jenny Seed, *Kulumi the Brave: A Zulu Tale,* World, 1970; Jenny Seed, *Vengeance of the Zulu King,* Pantheon, 1971; Nicholas Tucker, *Mother Goose Lost,*

Crowell, 1971; Prudence Andrew, *Dog,* Nelson, 1973; Mary L. Clifford, *Bisha of Burundi,* Crowell, 1973; Ruskin Bond, *Angry River,* Puffin, 1974; Ruskin Bond, *The Blue Umbrella,* Hamish Hamilton, 1974; Nicholas Fisk, *Little Green Spaceman,* Heinemann, 1974; Hans-Eric Hellburg, *Maria,* Methuen, 1974; Michael Hardcastle, *Free Kick,* Methuen, 1974; Nicholas Tucker, editor, *Mother Goose Abroad: Nursery Rhymes,* Hamish Hamilton, 1974, Crowell, 1975; Ursula Synge, *Audun and the Bear,* Bodley Head, 1975; David Rees, *Storm Surge,* Lutterworth, 1975; Gordon Boshell, *Captain Cobwebb and the Crustaks,* Macdonald & Jane's, 1975; Marie Burg, *Salt and Gold,* Blackie, 1976; Aidan Chambers, *Funny Folk: A Book of Comic Tales,* Heinemann, 1977; Frank Walker, *Vipers and Co.,* Macmillan [London], 1977; Dick Cate, *Never Is a Long, Long Time,* Nelson, 1977; *Tony's Special Place,* Bodley Head, 1977; T. H. White, *The Book of Merlyn,* Texas Press, 1977; Michael Hardcastle, *The Saturday Horse,* Methuen, 1978; Alan T. Dale, *Portrait of Jesus,* Oxford, 1979.

WORK IN PROGRESS: Illustrating more books.

SIDELIGHTS: "A painter by instinct and training, I fell into book illustration when I decided that teaching was not my forte! I still find thinking as an illustrator difficult, but, it is a very acceptable way of making ends meet."

FOR MORE INFORMATION SEE: Yorkshire Life magazine, November, 1976; *Growing Point,* November, 1976; Lee Kingman and others, compilers, *Illustrators of Children's Books: 1967-1976,* Horn Book, 1978.

SWAN, Susan 1944-

PERSONAL: Born September 13, 1944, in Coral Gables, Fla.; daughter of Arnold H. (a plastics designer) and Regis (deGlanville) Swan. *Education:* Florida State University, B.A., 1966, M.F.A., 1968. *Home and office:* 8 Belden Place, Westport, Conn. 06880.

CAREER: Illustrator. *Member:* Graphic Artists Guild, Westport Artists (secretary, 1974, president, 1975). *Awards, honors:* Citation for Merit from 15th Exhibition of Society of Illustrators.

ILLUSTRATOR: Ruth B. Gross (reteller), *The Mouse's Wedding,* Scholastic Book Services, 1972; Claire Merrill, *A Seed Is a Promise,* Scholastic Book Services, 1973; Lee Vinson, *The Early American Song Book,* Ridge Press, 1974; Eleanor B. Heady, *Plants on the Go: A Book About Reproduction and Seed Dispersal,* Parents' Magazine Press, 1975; Jane Thayer, *I Don't Believe in Elves,* Morrow, 1975; *The Pop-up Book of Trains,* Random House, 1976; Mary Francis Shura, *Chester,* Dodd, 1980; Mary Elting and Ann Goodman, *Dinosaur Mysteries,* Platt & Munk, in press; Barbara S. Hozen, *Pets on Parade* (tentative title), C. R. Gibson, in press. Illustrator of numerous textbooks.

SIDELIGHTS: "The mediums I use are watercolor, dyes, colored pencil, and paper sculpture."

FOR MORE INFORMATION SEE: North Light, September-October, 1976.

There goes the circus train!

(From *The Pop-Up Book of Trains,* paper engineering by Ib Penick. Illustrated by Susan Swan.)

SYLVESTER, Natalie G(abry) 1922-

PERSONAL: Born September 30, 1922, in Newark, N.J.; daughter of L. S. and Natalie (Mackay) Gabry; married Dr. Ralph K. Sylvester (an educator, now retired) September 21, 1943; children: Lewis S. *Education:* Attended Ventura College, 1956-57. *Religion:* Christian Scientist. *Home and office:* 939 Hartford St., Cambria, Calif. 93428. *Agent:* Ann Elmo Agency, Inc., 60 East 42nd St., New York, N.Y. 10017.

CAREER: Author and illustrator. American Optical Co., New York, N.Y., secretary, 1940-41; American Optical Co., Newark, N.J., secretary, 1942-43; Galamander Shop, Vinalhaven Island, Me., manager and designer, 1960-61; writer and illustrator, 1967—.

WRITINGS—All self-illustrated: *The Home Cooking Cookbook,* Grosset, 1972; *The Home Baking Cookbook,* Grosset, 1973; *Summer on Cleo's Island* (juvenile), Farrar, 1977; *Lions in the Castle* (story and coloring book for children), California State Parks Foundation, 1979. Has also designed bookmark for the Children's Book Council, 1979.

WORK IN PROGRESS—All self-illustrated: Two children's books in rhyme; a cookbook on dates; a craft book; three coloring books for children: *Castles in the Castle, Animals That Are in the Castle,* and *Animals That Aren't in the Castle*.

SIDELIGHTS: "My early years were spent in Newark, N.J., as a middle child, never getting the attention I craved—spending hours alone in my attic 'studio' making doll clothes, drawing, and reading. The very first recognition I received for my artistic endeavors was when I let my drawings 'float' down through the crawl hole onto my unsuspecting family, thereby receiving the attention I needed and sometimes praise for my drawings as well.

"I entered some drawings of ballet dancers in an art contest and won first prize. Later, in eighth grade, I entered a painting in the oils category and won a scholarship—Saturday morning art classes at the Newark Art Club. No one seemed aware that I hadn't used oil paints. What I used was printer's ink, brought to me by my father, scrapings from printing presses at a local shop. My canvas was a piece of oilcloth, underside out, tacked to a frame which my dad made from kindling. Having grown up during the Depression, I never had 'proper' art supplies. I worked with charcoal, secured from Girl Scout campfires, bits of blackboard chalk from a friendly teacher, brown wrapping paper donated by a clerk in the corner grocery store, and one small box of pastels.

"I was fortunate to be able to attend a high school which offered courses in commercial and fine arts.

"As the years progressed I married, had a son, moved from coast to coast. I enrolled in art classes, took up handweaving, designed and sewed my own clothes, refurbished and sold houses, cooked and painted, until the day I realized our son was going off to college, and my life had to change.

The dory was still there. ■ (From *Summer on Cleo's Island* by Natalie G. Sylvester. Illustrated by the author.)

NATALIE G. SYLVESTER

"At the time, we were living in northern Maine, where winter and confined isolation go hand in hand and the freedom of spring seems a promise and nothing more. It was then that I started writing—to fill the coming void in my life. I gathered together our families' favorite recipes and hand-lettered a cookbook for our son, which I intended to bind and give to him when he married. Each page was illustrated with drawings of antiques and things meaningful to him. Before long a friend saw it and suggested that it be sent to a publisher. So I embarked on a new career.

"I wrote *Summer on Cleo's Island* after living on Vinalhaven Island off the coast of Maine. The book is a reminder of the quietly eventful days when Cleo and our family roamed the storm-strewn beaches. It is also an attempt to record a few of the fascinating things we saw there. My intent was to share this rich experience and to create a desire in my readers to go-have-a-look, too.

"Now my husband, our two cats (Cleo and Tomas), and I live in a small peasant-like cottage overlooking the Pacific Ocean. Our son has been given the cookbook and is living in a cabin in the redwoods. I create beach stone mosaics, design and make jewelry from bones I find on the beaches, and am employed as a tour guide at Hearst Castle.

"When I was in guide training, I observed that our biggest problems were with the children, because there was nothing to interest them on the tour. 'Why not?' I asked myself. I had become fascinated with the hundreds of animals carved out of wood, marble, cast in concrete, and molded from metal. I concluded that there was much of interest to children, if they could be made aware of it. So I wrote a series of story-coloring books about the castle. Now I am designing needlepoint canvases of the animals, some of which I hope can be worked by children."

HOBBIES AND OTHER INTERESTS: Collecting antique cooking utensils.

FOR MORE INFORMATION SEE: Christian Science Monitor, May 7, 1971; *Santa Monica Evening Outlook,* July 3, 1971; *Los Angeles Times,* December 7, 1972; *Cambrian,* June 27, 1974, August 12, 1976, June 11, 1979, September 1, 1979; *Phoenix Gazette,* March 19, 1975; *Scottsdale Daily Progress,* July 9, 1975; *Morro Bay Sun Bulletin,* January 24, 1976, February 26, 1976, July 14, 1977; *Publishers Weekly,* February 28, 1977.

TABER, Gladys (Bagg)   1899-1980

OBITUARY NOTICE: Born April 2, 1899, in Colorado Springs, Colo.; died March 11, 1980, in Hyannis, Mass. Poet, columnist, and author of children's stories and more than fifty books. Taber wrote columns for the *Ladies' Home Journal* and *Family Circle.* Her best-known works are nonfiction books describing New England country living, especially the "Stillmeadow" journals series. Her books for children include *Daisy and Dobbin, First Book of Dogs,* and *First Book of Cats. Still Cove Journal,* Taber's latest work, will be published posthumously. *For More Information See: Current Biography,* Wilson, 1952; *Contemporary Authors,* Volume 5-8, revised, Gale, 1969; *Foremost Women in Communications,* Bowker, 1970; *The Author's and Writer's Who's Who,* 6th edition, Burke's Peerage, 1971; *Who's Who of American Women,* 8th edition, Marquis, 1973; *Who's Who in America,* 40th edition, Marquis, 1978; *The Writers Directory, 1980-82,* St. Martin's, 1980. *Obituaries: New York Times,* March 12, 1980; *Chicago Tribune,* March 14, 1980; *AB Bookman's Weekly,* April 14, 1980; *Publishers Weekly,* April 25, 1980.

TAYLOR, Herb(ert Norman, Jr.)   1942-

PERSONAL: Born June 11, 1942, in Brooklyn, N.Y.; son of Herbert Norman (a clerk) and Jennie (a clerk; maiden name, Palasciano) Taylor. *Education:* New York City Community College, A.A., 1973; further study at City College of the City University of New York. *Office:* The Photographic Book Co., 11 Broadway, New York, N.Y. 10004.

CAREER: Clerk for technical publishers in New York City, 1960-64; free-lance writer and photographer in New York City and San Diego, Calif., 1968-71; Editorial Photocolor Archives, New York City, writer and photographer, 1971-74; American Photographic Book Publishing Co. (Amphoto), Garden City, N.Y., in acquisitions, planning, and management, 1974-80; project editor for *Encyclopedia of Practical Photography,* 1977-78. *Military service:* U.S. Air Force, 1964-68. *Awards, honors: The Lobster* was selected as one of the best science books for children by the New York

Academy of Science, 1975; *Encyclopedia of Practical Photography* was selected by the Society for Technical Communication as the best book in their 1979 competition.

WRITINGS—With own photographs: *The Lobster: Its Life Cycle* (juvenile), Sterling, 1975; *Underwater with the Nikonos and Nikon Systems,* Amphoto, 1976.

Contributor to magazines and newspapers, including the *New York Times, National Observer, Reader's Digest, National Fisherman, Skin Diver* and *Oceans*. His work has also appeared in numerous textbooks.

WORK IN PROGRESS: A "catalog" of diving equipment and activities for sport divers, to be published by Lippincott in 1981.

SIDELIGHTS: Taylor began taking underwater photographs after becoming a certified diver in 1961. He has conducted research on aquaculture and marine ecosystems.

THOLLANDER, Earl   1922-

PERSONAL: Born April 13, 1922, in Kingsburg, Calif.; married Janet Behr, May 31, 1947; children: Kristie, Wesley. *Education:* University of California, B.A., 1944; attended The Art Institute, The Academy of Art, and The Art League of California. *Home:* House in the Woods, Murray Hill, Calistoga, Calif. 94515.

CAREER: Free-lance illustrator, painter, and author. San Francisco *Examiner,* Calif., 1949-56; Landphere Associates, San Francisco, Calif., illustrator, 1956-58. *Exhibitions:* DeYoung Museum, San Francisco, Calif.; San Francisco Museum of Art, Calif.; Los Angeles County Museum, Calif.; 12 Adler Place, San Francisco, Calif.; Lucien LeBaudt Gallery, San Francisco, Calif.; Oakland Art Gallery; Crocker Art Gallery, Sacramento, Calif.; Fresno Art Center, Calif.; Marin Art Gallery; Feingarten Galleries, Chicago and San Francisco; Richmond Art Gallery; Bolles Gallery, San Fran-

Until he was ten years old, he felt the scorching earth under his bare feet. He knew the sting of hot dust on his brown skin. ■ (From *Cesar Chavez* by Ruth Franchere. Illustrated by Earl Thollander.)

EARL THOLLANDER

cisco; Nevada Art Gallery, Reno; Brunn Gallery, San Francisco; Room at the Top Gallery, Palo Alto, Calif.; Galerie Du Roi, Burlingame; San Marco Gallery, San Rafael; Depot Gallery, Napa Valley; Larsen Gallery, Yakima, Wash.; Boise Art Gallery, Idaho; Vintage 1870, Napa; San Francisco Art Festival; Jack London Square, Oakland, Calif.; Avenida Art Festival; has also exhibited at many colleges throughout the United States. *Military service:* U.S. Navy, 1944-47. *Awards, honors: Ramon Makes a Trade* was named one of the "100 Best Children's Books," 1959, *Sunset Cook Book,* 1960, and *Delights & Prejudices,* 1965, were named one of the "Fifty Books of the Year," by American Institute of Graphic Artists; Tastemaker's Award for *1000 Recipe Chinese Cookbook,* 1967.

WRITINGS—All self-illustrated: *Back Roads of California,* Sunset Books, 1970; *Back Roads of New England,* Clarkson N. Potter, 1974; *Barns of California,* California Historical Society, 1974; *Back Roads of Arizona,* Northland Press, 1978; *Back Roads of Oregon,* Clarkson N. Potter, 1979; *Back Roads of Texas,* Northland Press, 1980.

Illustrator: Barbara Ritchie, *Ramon Makes a Trade,* Parnassus, 1959; The Sunset Editorial Staff, *Sunset Cook Book,* Lane Book Co., 1960; Beverly Cleary, *Hullabaloo ABC,* Parnassus, 1960; Patricia M. Martin, *No, No Rosina,* Putnam, 1964; James Beard, *Delight & Prejudices,* Atheneum, 1964; Barbara Ritchie, *To Catch a Mongoose,* Parnassus, 1964; Florence Rowland, *The Singing Leaf,* Putnam, 1965; Patricia M. Martin, *Jump, Frog, Jump,* Putnam, 1965; Vera C. Mullins, *Kala and the Sea Bird,* Golden Gate, 1966; Vivian L. Thompson, *Keola's Hawaiian Donkey,* Golden Gate, 1966; Patricia M. Martin, *Mrs. Crumble and Fire House #7,* Putnam, 1966; Gloria B. Miller, *1000 Recipe Chinese Cookbook,* Atheneum, 1966; Daniel Chu and Samuel Chu, *Passage to the Golden Gate: A History of the Chinese in America to 1910,* Doubleday, 1967; Edwin P. Hoyt, *The Jewel Hunters,* Little, Brown, 1967; Rudyard Kipling, *The Jungle Book,* Fearon, 1967; Myra B. Brown, *Where's Jeremy,* Golden Gate, 1968; James W. Hackett, *Bug Haiku,* Japan Publications, 1968; Virginia F. Voight, *Little Brown Bat,* Putnam, 1969; Florence W. Rowland, *School for Julio,* Putnam, 1969; John Tebbel and Ramon R. Ruiz, *South by Southwest: The Mexican-American and His Heritage,* Doubleday, 1969; Patricia M. Martin, *The Dog and the Boat Boy,* Putnam, 1969; Laura N. Baker, *Wild Peninsula: The Story of Point Reyes National Seashore,* Atheneum, 1969; Vivian L. Thompson, *Maui-Full-of-Tricks: A Legend of Old Hawaii,* Golden Gate, 1970; Ruth Franchere, *Cesar Chavez,* Crowell, 1970; Vivian L. Thompson, *Aukele the Fearless: A Legend of Old Hawaii,* Golden Gate, 1972; Gloria D. Miklowitz, *Sad Song, Happy Song,* Putnam, 1973; Aileen Paul, *50 States Cookbook,* Doubleday, 1976; Daisy Kouzel, *The Cuckoo's Reward: El Premio Del Cuco,* Doubleday, 1977.

WORK IN PROGRESS: Back Roads of Washington, a travel book for Clarkson N. Potter.

SIDELIGHTS: "I was born in Kingsburg, California, on April 13, 1922, of second generation Swedish heritage. Educated in the San Francisco public schools, I began studies in art at City College in 1939. Later on I was an art student at the University of California receiving a B.A. degree in 1944. Trained at Columbia University, New York, I served two years aboard a landing ship as a naval officer during World War II. The ship navigated chiefly among the Philippines after making the long voyage from the Canal Zone, Society Islands, New Hebrides and New Guinea. Four invasions were participated in, the most dramatic being the massive landings at Lingayen Gulf, Luzon. A year was spent carrying cargo to and from various Philippine Islands before sailing on to Okinawa, Korea, Shanghai, Guam, Hawaii and San Francisco. I sketched and painted often during my tour of duty.

"I returned to civilian life attending classes at The Art Institute, The Academy of Art and The Art League of California. In 1947 I was married. The family increased to four with the birth of two children. For seven years, from 1949, I was employed as an artist by The San Francisco *Examiner.* This was followed by two years work as an illustrator with Landphere Associates in San Francisco.

"In 1955 I made a sketching trip to Mexico for three weeks visiting Mexico City, Cuernavaca, San Miguel de Allende, Guanajuato, Guadalajara, Tequila, Uruapan, Paracho, Patzcuaro, Morelia, Oaxaca and Acapulco. The drawings were used as research for paintings as well as for book illustrations.

"I made a two week drawing and painting trip in 1956 to the Hawaiian Islands. In 1959, now a free-lance artist, I went to draw for three months in Denmark, Norway, Sweden, Finland, U.S.S.R., Rumania, Yugoslavia, Italy and Czechoslovakia.

"Two years later I traveled up and down the west coast of the United States and to the island of San Marcos, Baja California, making paintings for Kaiser Company of Oakland. Later in 1961 I traveled five weeks in the Orient sketching for American President Lines. I visited Tokyo, Yokohama, Kyoto, Osaka and Kobe in Japan, Hong Kong, Manila and the Mountain Province of Luzon, Philippines, Saigon, South Vietnam, Singapore, Kuala Lumpur and Penang in Malaya, Bangkok, Thailand and Hawaii.

"Early in 1962 I traveled and sketched in Guaymas and Alamos, Sonora, Mexico. In August of the same year I went to Martinique sketching for a children's book. The Caribbean journey also gave me stops at Antiqua, St. Thomas, Puerto Rico and Haiti. Immediately following this I proceeded to New York, and by boat, to Paris. I, and five other people, drove two small Volkswagens through France, Italy, Sicily, Tunisia, Libya, Egypt, Lebanon, Syria, Turkey, Greece and Switzerland. All through the three month drive I had been adding to my collection of drawings.

"In 1964 I spent two weeks sketching and painting on Molokai, Maui, Hawaii and Kauai in the Hawaiian Islands. Three years hence I participated in the United States Air Force art program observing and sketching in Saigon, Cam Ranh Bay, Pleiku and Danang, South Vietnam.

"I sketched, too, in Thailand at Bangkok and Tak Li. In Japan I made drawings in Tokyo, Matsuyama City and Hiroshima. I traveled 20,000 miles in 1970 sketching and writing for a book about the backroads of California.

"Illustrating and writing a book about barns of California took me traveling about the state again in the Fall of 1972. In the Spring of 1973 I was traveling, sketching and writing a book about back roads in New England. For three weeks in the Fall of 1974 I took a group of artists to the wine country of France, directing our travels and giving instruction in drawing.

"Since 1975 I have led three more sketching trips to Europe, Spain, Portugal, Italy and Germany and twice have been art instructor on the Cruise-Cargo ship, *Santa Magdalena* (Delta Steamship Lines) on two month voyages around South America.

"I have designed a U.S. postage stamp, done paintings for a John Denver television special (March, 1977) and many editorial and commercial assignments in addition to having exhibits of my paintings.

"Otherwise life is quietly lived on a twenty acre hilly ranch adjacent to the lovely wine country of the Napa Valley, California."

Earl Thollander's works are included in the Kerlan Collection at the University of Minnesota.

FOR MORE INFORMATION SEE: American Artist, April, 1954, March, 1960; *CA Magazine,* November, 1959, September-October, 1962; Adrian Wilson, *The Design of Books,* Rheinhold, 1967; Lee Kingman and others, compilers, *Illustrators of Children's Books: 1957-1966,* Horn Book, 1968; Diana Klemin, *The Illustrated Book,* Clarkson N. Potter, 1970; Martha E. Ward and Dorothy A. Marquardt, *Illustrators of Books for Young People,* Scarecrow Press, 1975.

TORBERT, Floyd James 1922-

PERSONAL: Born February 7, 1922, in Jacksonville, Fla.; son of James Knox and Gertrude (Voss) Torbert; married Margaret Fryer (deceased); children: Bruce (deceased). *Education:* Attended Philadelphia College of Art, four years. *Religion:* Baptist. *Home and studio:* 73 Chapel Road, New Hope, Pa. 18938.

CAREER: Free-lance illustrator of magazine illustrations, covers, and caricatures, also books, comic books, daily and weekly syndicated cartoons for newspapers, all types of advertising art; presently working on portraits and fine arts,

He did not see that Bill Smith was looking up at the ball and tearing from his position behind the plate.
■ (From *Fifth Inning Fade-Out* by C. Paul Jackson. Illustrated by Floyd James Torbert.)

FLOYD JAMES TORBERT

and as an art teacher. *Exhibitions:* Several one-man shows in Pennsylvania and New Jersey. *Military service:* U.S. Air Corps, special services, sergeant, created art work for *Daily Okinawan*, 1942-45. *Member:* New Hope Art League (president, 1974-79), Doylestown Art League, Hunterdon Art Center.

WRITINGS—Self-illustrated; all published by Hastings House: *Policemen the World Over*, 1965; *Postmen the World Over*, 1966; *Firefighters the World Over*, 1967; *Park Rangers & Game Wardens the World Over*, 1968.

Illustrator—All published by Hastings House except where indicated: *Connie Mack's Baseball Book*, Knopf, 1950; Ada Claire Barby, *Brave Venture*, Winston, 1951; Joseph H. Gage, *The Beckoning Hills*, Winston, 1951; Mark Twain, *Tom Sawyer*, Winston, 1952; Shepherd Knapp, *Rope 'Em Cowboy*, Knapp, 1954; Robert Ashley, *Rebel Raiders*, Winston, 1956; C. Paul Jackson, *Tommy: Soap Box Derby Cham-*

pion, 1963; Helen D. Francis, *Martha Norton: Operation U.S.A.*, 1963; Anne Molloy, *Mystery of the Pilgrim Trading Post*, 1964; C. Paul Jackson, *Super Modified Driver*, 1964; Donald E. Cooke, *Presidents in Uniform*, 1969; Dorothy Shuttlesworth, *The Tower of London: Grim & Glamorous*, 1970; C. Paul Jackson, *Fifth Inning Fade-Out*, 1972.

WORK IN PROGRESS: To be an Artist (tentative title).

SIDELIGHTS: "I work in all media, at present, oils. Love animals and people, therefore, I prefer painting and illustrating them. Also like sports of all kinds. Have traveled extensively.

"I was strongly influenced by Henry Pitz and Thorton Oakley as teachers. Norman Rockwell was my idol."

FOR MORE INFORMATION SEE: Daily Intellegencia, January 30, 1979.

TRIVETT, Daphne (Harwood) 1940-

PERSONAL: Born July 7, 1940, in Boston, Mass.; daughter of Reed and Faith Harwood; married John Venner Trivett, April 27, 1968; children: Joslyn, Erica and Lesley. *Education:* Sarah Lawrence College, B.A., 1962; University of Chicago, M.A.T., 1966. *Home:* 1975 Kings Ave., West Vancouver, British Columbia, Canada V7V 2B6.

CAREER: Elementary school teacher in Weston, Conn., 1962-63; University of Chicago, Chicago, Ill., teacher and mathematics specialist at Laboratory Schools, 1964-67; teacher at elementary schools in Vancouver, British Columbia, 1968-70; North Vancouver Night School, North Vancouver, British Columbia, teacher of quilting and English, 1975-79; writer, 1979—.

WRITINGS—For children: *Shadow Geometry*, Crowell, 1974; *Time for Clocks*, Crowell, 1979.

WORK IN PROGRESS—For children: *Mirror Play; Stop, I Love It; The Multiplication Table: A New Study*.

SIDELIGHTS: "I am interested in creative mathematics for children. As children can do creative writing (and society smiles), I wish to encourage in children and adults a relaxed, indulgent attitude toward creative work in mathematics, secure in the knowledge that the creative work will in the end lead to greater proficiency and fewer bad feelings toward the subject.

"My master's degree was in geometry for second graders and my work in mirrors and shadows is an extension of that interest.

"Geometry and mathematics in general have played an active part in my enjoyment of and creative work in dance, quilt-making, music, clowning, nature study, drawing, and language learning. As a writer, I hope to increase children's sense of their own power. As a teacher, I hope to bring more interdisciplinary work into classrooms."

FOR MORE INFORMATION SEE: Horn Book, April, 1975.

(From *The Duke's Children* by Anthony Trollope. Illustrated by Charles Mozley.)

TROLLOPE, Anthony 1815-1882

PERSONAL: Born April 24, 1815, in London, England; died December 6, 1882, in Harting, Sussex, England; son of Thomas Anthony (a barrister) and Frances (an author) Trollope; brother of writer, Thomas Adolphus Trollope; married Rose Heseltine, 1844. *Education:* Educated at Harrow School and Winchester College (secondary schools). *Politics:* Liberal.

CAREER: Author. Entered the British postal service as a clerk, 1834, became deputy postal surveyor in Ireland, 1841-59, retired, 1867; ran unsuccessfully as a Liberal candidate for Parliament, 1868; assisted in founding the *Fortnightly Review,* 1865; editor of *St. Paul's Magazine,* 1867-70.

WRITINGS—"The Chronicles of Barsetshire" series: *The Warden,* [London], 1855, reissued, Dutton, 1972 [other editions illustrated by Edward Ardizzone, Oxford University Press, 1952; Fritz Kredel, Limited Editions Club, 1956]; *Barchester Towers,* three volumes, [London], 1857, reissued, Heron Books, 1969 [other editions illustrated by Donald McKay, Doubleday, 1945; E. Ardizzone, Oxford University Press, 1953; F. Kredel, Limited Editions Club, 1958]; *Doctor Thorne,* Harper, 1858, reissued, Pan Books, 1968; *Framley Parsonage* (illustrated by John Everett Millais), three volumes, Smith, Elder, 1861, reissued, Dutton, 1972; *The Small House at Allington* (illustrated by J. E. Millais), two volumes, [London], 1864, reissued, Dutton, 1972; *The Last Chronicle of Barset* (illustrated by George H. Thomas), Smith, Elder, 1867, reissued, Heron Books, 1969.

Political novels: *Can You Forgive Her?* (illustrated by Hablot Knight Browne), [London], 1864, reissued, Penguin, 1975 [another edition illustrated by Lynton Lamb, Oxford University Press, 1948]; *Phineas Finn: The Irish Member,* Harper, 1868, reissued, Penguin, 1975 [another edition illustrated by J. E. Millais, (London), 1869]; *The Eustace Diamonds,* Harper, 1872, new edition, edited by Stephen Gill and John Sutherland, Penguin, 1975; *Phineas Redux,* Harper, 1874, reissued, Oxford University Press, 1973; *The Prime Minister,* Chapman & Hall, 1876, reissued, Oxford University Press, 1973; *The Duke's Children,* Chapman & Hall, 1880, new edition illustrated by Charles Mozley, Oxford University Press, 1973; the above political novels were published together as *The Palliser Novels,* Oxford University Press, 1975.

Other novels: *The Macdermots of Ballycloran,* three volumes. T. C. Newby, 1847; *The Kellys and the O'Kellys,* three volumes, H. Colburn, 1848, reissued, Oxford University Press, 1975; *La Vendée; An Historical Romance,* three volumes, [London], 1850; *The Three Clerks,* three volumes, [London], 1858, reissued, Oxford University Press, 1975; *The Bertrams,* Harper, 1859; *Castle Richmond,* three volumes, Chapman & Hall, 1860; *The Struggles of Brown, Jones and Robinson* (originally published in *Cornhill Magazine,* 1861-62), [London], 1870; *Orley Farm* (illustrated by J. E. Millais), Chapman & Hall, 1862, reissued, Oxford University Press, 1963; *Rachel Ray,* two volumes, Chapman & Hall, 1863, reissued, Knopf, 1952; *Miss Mackenzie,* Chapman & Hall, 1865; *The Belton Estate,* three volumes, Chapman & Hall, 1866, reissued, Oxford University Press, 1958; *Nina Balatka: The Story of a Maiden of Prague,* two volumes, W. Blackwood, 1867; *Linda Tressel* (originally published in *Blackwood's Magazine,* 1867-68), [London], 1868; the latter two books were reissued together as *Nina Balatka* [and] *Linda Tressel,* Oxford University Press, 1946; *The Claverings* (illustrated by M. Ellen Edwards), Smith, Elder, 1867, reis-

Anthony Trollope, portrait by S. Lawrence.

sued, Oxford University Press, 1975; *He Knew He Was Right* (illustrated by Marcus Stone), Strahan, 1869, reissued, Oxford University Press, 1975.

The Vicar of Bullhampton, Harper, 1870, reissued, Oxford University Press, 1975; *Sir Harry Hotspur of Humblethwaite* (originally published in *Macmillan's Magazine,* 1870), Harper, 1871; *Ralph the Heir,* Hurst & Blackett, 1871; *The Golden Lion of Granpere,* Harper, 1872, reissued, Oxford University Press, 1946; *Harry Heathcote of Gangoil: A Tale of Australian Bush Life* (originally published in *Graphic,* 1873), Low, Marston, 1874, reissued, Angus & Robertson, 1963; *Lady Anna* (originally published in *Fortnightly Review,* 1873-74), Chapman & Hall, 1874; *The Way We Live Now,* Harper, 1875, reissued, Bobbs-Merrill, 1974; *The American Senator,* Harper, 1877, reissued, Oxford University Press, 1962; *Is He Popenjoy?* (originally published in *All the Year Round,* 1877-78), Harper, 1878, reissued, Oxford University Press, 1965; *An Eye for an Eye* (originally published in *Whitehall Review,* 1878-79), [London], 1879, reissued, Blond Educational, 1967; *John Caldigate* (originally published in *Blackwood's Magazine,* 1878-79), Harper, 1879, reissued, Zodiac Press, 1972; *Cousin Henry,* two volumes, Chapman & Hall, 1879.

Dr. Wortle's School (originally published in *Blackwood's Magazine,* 1880), Chapman & Hall, 1881, reissued, Oxford University Press, 1960; *Ayala's Angel,* three volumes, Chapman & Hall, 1881, reissued, Oxford University Press, 1960; *The Fixed Period* (originally published in *Blackwood's Magazine,* 1881-82), W. Blackwood, 1882; *Marian Fay* (originally published in *Graphic,* 1881-82), Chapman & Hall, 1882; *Kept in the Dark,* two volumes, Chatto & Windus, 1882; *The Two Heroines of Plumplington* (originally published in *Good*

"Young man," said the voice, **"if you want to catch rheumatism, that's the way to do it. Why, it's young Eames, isn't it?"** ■ (From *The Small House at Allington* by Anthony Trollope. Illustrated by Sir John E. Millais.)

Cheer, 1882), G. Munro, 1882, new edition, illustrated by Lynton Lamb, Oxford University Press, 1954; *Mr. Scarborough's Family*, J. W. Lovell, 1883, reissued, Oxford University Press, 1973; *The Land Leaguers: A Story of Irish Life in the Present Time* (originally published in *Life*, 1882-83), G. Munro, 1883; *An Old Man's Love*, J.W. Lovell, 1884.

Short stories: *Tales of All Countries*, Chapman & Hall, 1861-63; *Lotta Schmidt and Other Stories*, [London], 1867; *An Editor's Tales* (originally published in *St. Paul's Magazine*, 1869-70), [London], 1870; *Christmas at Thompson Hall* (originally published in *Graphics*, 1876), Harper, 1877; *The Lady of Launay*, Harper, 1878; *Why Frau Frohmann Raised Her Prices, and Other Stories*, W. Isbister, 1882 [another edition published as *Frau Frohmann, and Other Stories*, Chatto & Windus, 1882]; *Alice Dugdale, and Other Stories*, B. Tauchnitz [Leipzig], 1883; *La Mere Bauche, and Other Stories*, G. Munro, 1884; *The Parson's Daughter and Other Stories*, edited by John Hampden, Folio Society, 1949; *The Spotted Dog and Other Stories*, Pan Books, 1950; *Mary Gresley, and Other Stories*, edited by J. Hampden, Folcroft, 1974 [the title story was originally published with an edition of *An Editor's Tales*, (London), 1871].

Nonfiction: *The West Indies and the Spanish Main*, [London], 1859, reissued, International Scholarly Book Service, 1968; *North America*, two volumes, Chapman & Hall, 1862, reissued, Penguin, 1968; *Hunting Sketches*, Chapman & Hall, 1865, reissued, Arno, 1967 [another edition illustrated by Lionel Edwards, Day, 1953]; *Traveling Sketches* (originally published in *Pall Mall Gazette*, 1865-66), Chapman & Hall, 1866; *Clergymen of the Church of England* (originally published in *Pall Mall Gazette*, 1865-66), [London], 1866, reprinted, Humanities, 1974; (editor) *British Sports and Pastimes*, Virtue & Yarston, 1868; *The Commentaries of Caesar*, W. Blackwood, 1870; *Australia and New Zealand*, Chapman & Hall, 1873, reissued, Dawsons, 1968; *South Africa*, two volumes, Chapman & Hall, 1878, reissued, Verry, 1973; *Thackeray*, Harper, 1879, reprinted, Gale, 1968; *The Life of Cicero*, Chapman & Hall, 1880; *Lord Palmerston*, W. Isbister, 1881; *An Autobiography*, Harper, 1883, reissued, Collins, 1962.

Letters: *The Tireless Traveler: Twenty Letters to the "Liverpool Mercury,"* edited by Bradford Allen Booth, University of California Press, 1941; *Letters*, edited by B. A. Booth, Oxford University Press, 1951; *Trollope's Letters to the*

He was a thin man over fifty years of age, very full of scorn and wrath, impatient of a fool, and thinking most men to be fools; afraid of nothing on earth. ■ (From *The Eustace Diamonds* by Anthony Trollope. Illustrated by Kenneth Riley.)

"Examiner," edited by H. Garlinghouse King, Princeton University Library, 1965.

Also author of the play, *Did He Steal It?* (three-act comedy), [London], 1869, reissued, Princeton University Library, 1952.

Collections and selections: *The Shakespeare Head Edition of the Works of Anthony Trollope,* edited by Michael Sadleir, Basil Blackwell, 1929; *Four Lectures,* edited by Morris L. Parrish, Constable, 1938, reprinted, Folcroft, 1969; *The Trollope Reader,* edited by Esther Cloudman Dunn and Marion E. Dodd, Oxford University Press, 1947; *The Oxford Trollope,* edited by M. Sadleir and Frederick Page, Oxford University Press, 1948; *The Bedside Barsetshire,* edited by Lance O. Tingay, Faber, 1949.

ADAPTATIONS—Plays: Thomas Job, *Barchester Towers: A Victorian Comedy* (three-act), Dramatists Play Service, 1938; Vera Wheatley, *Scandal at Barchester,* [London], 1946; John Draper, *Barchester Towers: A Comedy,* [London], 1953; Harold Simpson, *Mrs. Proudie Militant [and] Mrs. Proudie Triumphant* (two one-act comedies), Samuel French, 1955.

BILL GAZY–HIS BLOT

(From *The Warden* by Anthony Trollope. Illustrated by F.C. Tilney.)

"The Pallisers," starring Susan Hampshire, was produced for television as a weekly series of twenty-two programs presented on the Public Broadcasting Network in 1977.

SIDELIGHTS: **April 24, 1815.** "I was born. . .in Keppel Street, Russell Square; and while a baby, was carried down to Harrow, where my father had built a house on a large farm which, in an evil hour, he took on a long lease from Lord Northwick. That farm was the grave of all my father's hopes, ambition, and prosperity, the cause of my mother's sufferings, and of those of her children, and perhaps the director of her destiny and of ours. My father had been a Wykamist and a fellow of New College, and Winchester was the destination of my brothers and myself; but as he had friends among the masters at Harrow, and as the school offered an education almost gratuitous to children living in the parish, he, with a certain aptitude to do things differently from others, which accompanied him throughout his life, determined to use that august seminary as a 't'other school' for Winchester, and sent three of us there, one after the other, at the age of seven. . . .

"Then I was sent to a private school at Sunbury, kept by Arthur Drury. This, I think, must have been done in ac-

"HE IS OF THAT SORT THAT THEY MAKE THE ANGELS OF," SAID THE VERGER.

(From *Framley Parsonage* by Anthony Trollope. Illustrated by J.E. Millais.)

cordance with the advice of Henry Drury, who was my tutor at Harrow School, and my father's friend, and who may probably have expressed an opinion that my juvenile career was not proceeding in a satisfactory manner at Harrow. To Sunbury I went, and during the two years that I was there, though I never had any pocket-money, and seldom had much in the way of clothes, I lived more nearly on terms of equality with other boys than at any period during my very prolonged school-days. Even here, I was always in disgrace. I remember well how, on an occasion, four boys were selected as having been the perpetrators of some nameless horror. What it was, to this day I cannot even guess; but I was one of the four, innocent as a baby, but adjudged to have been the guiltiest of the guilty. We each had to write out a sermon, and my sermon was the longest of the four. During the whole of one term-time we were helped last at every meal. We were not allowed to visit the playground till the sermon was finished. Mine was only done a day or two before the holidays. Mrs. Drury, when she saw us, shook her head with pitying horror.

"There were ever so many other punishments accumulated on our heads. It broke my heart, knowing myself to be innocent, and suffering also under the almost equally painful feeling that the other three—no doubt wicked boys—were the curled darlings of the school, who would never have selected me to share their wickedness with them. I contrived to learn, from words that fell from Mr. Drury, that he had condemned me because, I having come from a public school, might be supposed to be the leader of wickedness! On the first day of the next term he whispered to me half a word that perhaps he had been wrong. With all a stupid boy's slowness, I said nothing; and he had not the courage to carry reparation further. All that was fifty years ago, and it burns me now as though it were yesterday. What lily-livered curs those boys must have been not to have told the truth!—at any rate as far as I was concerned. I remember their names well, and almost wish to write them here.

"When I was twelve there came the vacancy at Winchester College which I was destined to fill. My two elder brothers had gone there, and the younger had been taken away, being already supposed to have lost his chance of New College. It had been one of the great ambitions of my father's life that his three sons, who lived to go to Winchester, should all become fellows of New College. But that suffering man was never destined to have an ambition gratified. We all lost the prize which he struggled with infinite labour to put within our reach. My eldest brother all but achieved it, and afterwards went to Oxford, taking three exhibitions from the school, though he lost the great glory of a Wykamist. He has since made himself well known to the public as a writer in connection with all Italian subjects. He is still living as I now write. But my other brother died early.

"While I was at Winchester my father's affairs went from bad to worse. He gave up his practice at the bar, and, unfortunate that he was, took another farm. It is odd that a man should conceive,—and in this case a highly educated and a very clever man,—that farming should be a business in which he might make money without any special education or apprenticeship. Perhaps of all trades it is the one in which an accurate knowledge of what things should be done, and the best manner of doing them, is most necessary. And it is one also for success in which a sufficient capital is indispensible. He had no knowledge, and, when he took this second farm, no capital. This was the last step preparatory to his final ruin.

"Soon after I had been sent to Winchester, my mother went to America, taking with her my brother Henry and my two sisters, who were then no more than children. This was, I think, in 1827. I have no clear knowledge of her object, or of my father's; but I believe that he had an idea that money might be made by sending goods,—little goods, such as pincushions, pepper-boxes, and pocket-knives,—out to the still unfurnished States; and that she conceived that an opening might be made for my brother Henry by erecting some bazaar or extended shop in one of the Western cities. Whence the money came I do not know, but the pocket-knives and the pepper-boxes were bought, and the bazaar was built. I have seen it since in the town of Cincinnati,—a sorry building! But I have been told that in those days it was an imposing edifice. My mother went first, with my sisters and second brother. Then my father followed them, taking my elder brother before he went to Oxford. But there was an interval of some year and a half during which he and I were at Winchester together.

"Over a period of forty years, since I began my manhood at a desk in the Post Office, I and my brother, Thomas Adolphus, have been fast friends. There have been hot words between us, for perfect friendship bears and allows hot words. Few brothers have had more of brotherhood. But in those schooldays he was, of all my foes, the worst. In accordance with the practice of the college, which submits, or did then submit, much of the tuition of the younger boys to the elder, he was my tutor; and in his capacity of teacher and ruler, he had studied the theories of Draco. I remember well how he professed to exact obedience after the manner of that lawgiver. Hang a little boy for stealing apples, he used to say, and other little boys will not steal apples. The doctrine was already exploded elsewhere, but he stuck to it with conservative energy. The result was that, as a part of his daily exercise, he thrashed me with a big stick. That such thrashings should have been possible at a school as a continual part of one's daily life, seems to me to argue a very ill condition of school discipline.

"After a while my brother left Winchester and accompanied my father to America. Then another and a different horror fell to my fate. My college bills had not been paid, and the school tradesmen who administered to the wants of the boys were told not to extend their credit to me. Boots, waistcoats, and pocket-handkerchiefs, which, with some slight superveillance, were at the command of other scholars, were closed luxuries to me. My schoolfellows of course knew that it was so, and I became a Pariah. It is the nature of boys to be cruel. I have sometimes doubted whether among each other they do usually suffer much, one from the other's cruelty; but I suffered horribly! I could make no stand against it. I had no friend to whom I could pour out my sorrows. I was big, and awkward, and ugly, and, I have no doubt, skulked about in a most unattractive manner. Of course I was ill-dressed and dirty. But, ah! how well I remember all the agonies of my young heart; how I considered whether I should always be alone; whether I could not find my way up to the top of that college tower, and from thence put an end to everything?

"And a worse thing came than the stoppage of the supplies from the shopkeepers. Every boy had a shilling a week pocket-money, which we called battels, and which was advanced to us out of the pocket of the second master. On one awful day the second master announced to me that my battels would be stopped. He told me the reason,—the battels for the last half-year had not been repaid; and he urged his own unwillingness to advance the money. The loss of a shilling a week would not have been much,—even though pocket-money from other sources never reached me,—but that the other boys all knew it! Every now and again, perhaps three

(From the twenty-two part BBC series "The Pallisers," based on six novels by Anthony Trollope, published together as *The Palliser Novels*, starring Susan Hampshire. Presented on PBS television, 1977.)

or four times in a half-year, these weekly shillings were given to certain servants of the college, in payment, it may be presumed, for some extra services. And now, when it came to the turn of any servant, he received sixty-nine shillings instead of seventy, and the cause of the defalcation was explained to him. I never saw one of those servants without feeling that I had picked his pocket.

"When I had been at Winchester something over three years, my father returned to England and took me away. Whether this was done because of the expense, or because my chance of New College was supposed to have passed away, I do not know. As a fact, I should, I believe, have gained the prize, as there occurred in my year an exceptional number of vacancies. But it would have secured me nothing, as there would have been no funds for my maintenance at the University till I should have entered in upon the fruition of the founder's endowment, and my career at Oxford must have been unfortunate.

"When I left Winchester, I had three more years of school before me, having as yet endured nine. My father at this time having left my mother and sisters with my younger brother in America, took himself to live at a wretched tumble-down farmhouse on the second farm he had hired! And I was taken there with him. It was nearly three miles from Harrow, at Harrow Weald, but in the parish; and from this house I was again sent to that as a day-boarder. Let those who know what is the usual appearance and what the usual appurtenances of a boy at such a school, consider what must have been my condition among them, with a daily walk of twelve miles through the lanes, added to the other little troubles and labours of a school life!

"After [father's] death my mother moved to England, and took and furnished a small house at Hadley, near Barnet. I was then a clerk in the London Post Office. . . .

"When I had been nearly seven years in the Secretary's office of the Post Office, always hating my position there, and yet always fearing that I should be dismissed from it, there came a way of escape. There had latterly been created in the service a new body of officers called surveyors' clerks. There were at that time seven surveyors in England, two in Scotland, and three in Ireland. To each of these officers a clerk had been lately attached, whose duty it was to travel about the country under the surveyor's orders. There had been much doubt among the young men in the office whether

The doctor was at her elbow to the last;—and all her boxes, and trunks seemed to extricate themselves from the general mass with a readiness which is certainly not experienced by ordinary passengers. ■ (From *Ralph the Heir* by Anthony Trollope. Illustrated by F.A. Fraser.)

they should or should not apply for these places. The emoluments were good and the work alluring; but there was at first supposed to be something derogatory in the position. There was a rumour that the first surveyor who got a clerk sent the clerk out to fetch his beer; and that another had called upon his clerk to send the linen to the wash. There was, however, a conviction that nothing could be worse than the berth of a surveyor's clerk in Ireland. The clerks were all appointed, however. To me it had not occurred to ask for anything, nor would anything have been given me. But after a while there came a report from the far west of Ireland that the man sent there was absurdly incapable. It was probably thought then that none but a man absurdly incapable would go on such a mission to the west of Ireland. When the report reached the London office I was the first to read it. I was at that time in dire trouble, having debts on my head and quarrels with our Secretary-Colonel, and a full conviction that my life was taking me downwards to the lowest pits. So I went to the Colonel boldly, and volunteered for Ireland if he would send me. He was glad to be so rid of me, and I went. This happened in August 1841, when I was twenty-six years old. My salary in Ireland was to be but £100 a year; but I was to receive fifteen shillings a day for every day that I was away from home, and six-pence for every mile that I travelled. The same allowances were made in England; but at that time travelling in Ireland was done at half the English prices. My income in Ireland, after paying my expenses,

became at once £400. This was the first good fortune of my life.

"It was altogether a very jolly life that I led in Ireland. I was always moving about, and soon found myself to be in pecuniary circumstances which were opulent in comparison with those of my past life. The Irish people did not murder me, nor did they even break my head. I soon found them to be good-humoured, clever—the working classes very much more intelligent than those of England—economical, and hospitable. We hear much of their spendthrift nature; but extravagance is not the nature of an Irishman. He will count the shillings in a pound much more accurately than an Englishman, and will with much more certainty get twelve pennyworth from each. But they are perverse, irrational, and but little bound by the love of truth. I lived for many years among them—not finally leaving the country until 1859, and I had the means of studying their character.

"...At Kingstown, the watering-place near Dublin, I met Rose Heseltine, the lady who has since become my wife. The engagement took place when I had been just one year in Ireland; but there was still a delay of two years before we could be married. She had no fortune, nor had I any income beyond that which came from the Post Office; and there were still a few debts, which would have been paid off no doubt sooner, but for that purchase of a horse. When I had been nearly three years in Ireland we were married on the 11th of June 1844;—and perhaps I ought to name that happy day as the commencement of my better life, rather than the day on which I first landed in Ireland. . . .

"My marriage was like the marriage of other people, and of no special interest to anyone except my wife and me. It took place at Rotherham in Yorkshire, where her father was the manager of a bank. We were not very rich, having about £400 a year on which to live. Many people would say that we were two fools to encounter such poverty together. I can only reply that since that day I have never been without money in my pocket, and that I soon acquired the means of paying what I owed. Nevertheless, more than twelve years had to pass over our heads before I received any payment for any literary work which afforded us an appreciable increase to our income.

"Immediately after our marriage, I left the west of Ireland and the hunting surveyor, and joined another in the south. It was a better district, and I was enabled to live at Clonmel, a town of some importance, instead of at Banagher, which is little more than a village. I had not felt myself to be comfortable in my old residence as a married man. On my arrival there as a bachelor I had been received most kindly, but when I brought my English wife I fancied that there was a feeling that I had behaved badly to Ireland generally. When a young man has been received hospitably in an Irish circle, I will not say that it is expected of him that he should marry some young lady in that society;—but it certainly is expected of him that he shall not marry any young lady out of it. I had given offence, and I was made to feel it." [Anthony Trollope, *An Autobiography*, Oxford University Press, 1923.[1]]

Trollope expounded on the method he employed in writing. ". . . I have always prepared a dairy, divided into weeks, and carried on for the period which I have allowed myself for the completion of the work. In this I have entered, day by day, the number of pages I have written, so that if at any time I have slipped into idleness for a day or two, the record of that idleness has been there, staring me in the face, and demanding of me increased labour, so that the deficiency might be supplied. According to the circumstances of the time,—whether my other business might be then heavy or light, or whether the book which I was writing was or was not wanted with speed,—I have allotted myself so many pages a week. The average number has been about 40. It has been placed as low as 20, and has risen to 112. And as a page is an ambiguous term, my page has been made to contain 250 words; and as words, if not watched, will have a tendency to struggle, I have had every word counted as I went. In the bargains I have made with publishers I have,—not, of course, with their knowledge, but in my own mind,—undertaken always to supply them with so many words, and I have never put a book out of hand short of the number by a single word. I may also say that the excess has been very small. I have prided myself on completing my work exactly within the proposed dimensions. But I have prided myself especially in completing it within the proposed time,—and I have always done so. There has ever been the record before me, and a week passed with an insufficient number of pages has been a blister to my eye, and a month so disgraced would have been a sorrow to my heart.

"I have been told that such appliances are beneath the notice of a man of genius. I have never fancied myself to be a man of genius, but had I been so I think I might well have subjected myself to these trammels. Nothing surely is so potent as a law that may not be disobeyed. It has the force of the waterdop that hollows the sone. A small daily task, if it be really daily, will beat the labours of a spasmodic Hercules."[1]

October 9, 1867. Resigned from the Post Office to edit *St. Paul's Magazine.* "And so my connection was dissolved with the department to which I had applied the thirty-three best years of my life;—I must not say devoted, because devotion implies an entire surrender, and I certainly had found time for other occupations. It is however absolutely true that during all those years I had thought very much more about the Post Office than I had of my literary work, and had given to it a more unflagging attention. Up to this time I had never been angry, never felt myself injured or unappreciated in that my literary efforts were slighted. But I had suffered very much bitterness on that score in reference to the Post Office; and I had suffered not only on my own personal behalf, but also and more bitterly when I could not procure to be done the things which I thought ought to be done for the benefit of others. . . ."[1]

December 6, 1882. Died in Harting, Sussex, England. "Now I stretch out my hand, and from the further shore I bid adieu to all who have cared to read any among the many words that I have written."[1]

FOR MORE INFORMATION SEE: Anthony Trollope, *An Autobiography,* Harper, 1883, reissued, Collins, 1962; Thomas Hay Sweet Escott, *Anthony Trollope: His Public Service, Private Friends, and Literary Originals,* John Lane, 1913, reprinted, Kennikat, 1967; Michael Sadleir, *Trollope: Commentary,* Constable, 1927, reissued, Octagon, 1975; Hugh Walpole, *Anthony Trollope,* Macmillan, 1928, reissued, Folcroft, 1973; Beatrice Curtis Brown, *Anthony Trollope,* Swallow Press, 1950, reissued, Arthur Barker, 1969; A. Trollope, *Letters,* edited by Bradford Allen Booth, Oxford University Press, 1951; Anthony O. Cockshut, *Anthony Trollope: A Critical Study,* Collins, 1955, reissued, New York University Press, 1968; Rafael Helling, *Century of Trollope Criticism,* Helsingsfors, 1956, reprinted, Kennikat, 1967; B.A. Booth, *Anthony Trollope: Aspects of His Life and Art,* Indiana University Press, 1958; (for children) Howard Jones, *Men of Letters,* G. Gell, 1959.

A. Trollope, *Trollope's Letters to the "Examiner,"* edited by H. Garlinghouse King, Princeton University Library, 1965; Robert M. Polhemus, *The Changing World of Anthony Trollope,* University of California Press, 1968; Peter David Edwards, *Anthony Trollope,* Humanities, 1969; Donald A. Smalley, editor, *Trollope: The Critical Heritage,* Barnes & Noble, 1969; Ruth ApRoberts, *Moral Trollope,* Ohio University Press, 1971; Alice Fredman, *Anthony Trollope,* Columbia University Press, 1971; James Pope-Hennessy, *Anthony Trollope,* Little, Brown, 1971; David Skilton, *Anthony Trollope and His Contemporaries,* St. Martin's, 1972; Michael Hardwick, *A Guide to Anthony Trollope,* Scribner, 1974; Charles Percy Snow, *Trollope: His Life and Art,* Scribner, 1975.

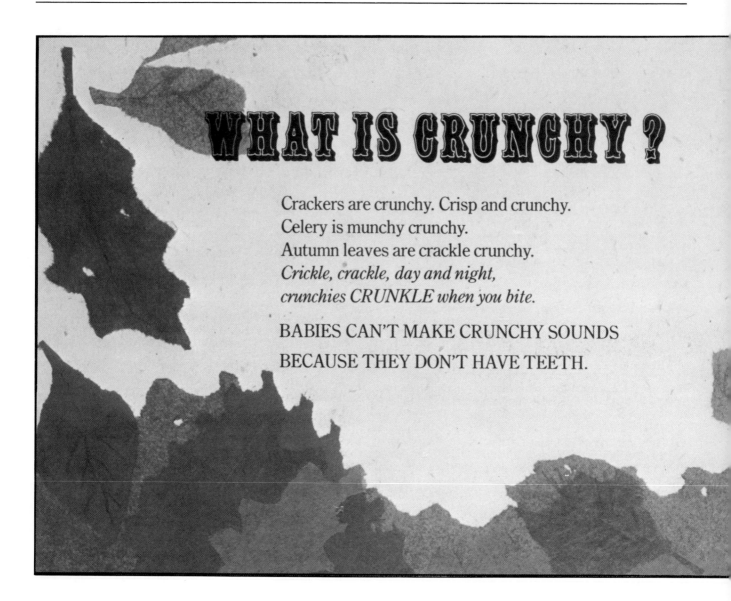

(From *Giggly-Wiggly, Snickety-Snick* by Robyn Supraner. Illustrated by Stan Tusan.)

TUSAN, Stan   1936-

PERSONAL: Born August 6, 1936, in Fresno, Calif.; son of Leo and Anna (Dalalian) Tusan; married Barbara Gould, August 15, 1969; children: Cary, Ali. *Education:* Fresno City College, Calif., A.A., 1956; Art Instruction School, Minneapolis, Minn., diploma in correspondence course, 1958; Chouinard Art Institute, Los Angeles, Calif., B.F.A., 1960. *Home and office:* Walnut Creek, Calif. 94598.

CAREER: Free-lance writer and artist. UPA Animated Film Studio, Los Angeles, Calif., storyboard artist, 1960; N. W. Ayer Ad Agency, Chicago, Ill., art director, 1962-63; *Children's Digest* Magazine, New York, N.Y., art director, 1970-75.

WRITINGS—Self-illustrated: *Write-A-Letter Book,* Grosset, 1971.

Illustrator: Christopher Davis, *Sad Adam—Glad Adam,* Crowell, 1966; Barbro Lindgren, *Hilding's Summer,* Macmillan, 1967; Ann Wainwright, *Girls & Boys Easy-To-Cook Book,* edited by Barbara Zeitz, Grosset, 1967; Barbara Zeitz, *Make-A-Sweet Cookbook,* Grosset, 1969; Robyn Supraner, *Giggly-Wiggly, Snickety-Snick,* Parents' Magazine Press, 1978; Joan Eckstein and Joyce Gleit, *Fun with Making Things,* Avon, 1979. Author and illustrator of works for Hallmark cards, educational books and materials, and magazines.

SIDELIGHTS: "Working with or for children is a most satisfying pleasure. The usual research involved with each different assignment is an enlightening sidelight. I have found that one can never grow 'too young!'"

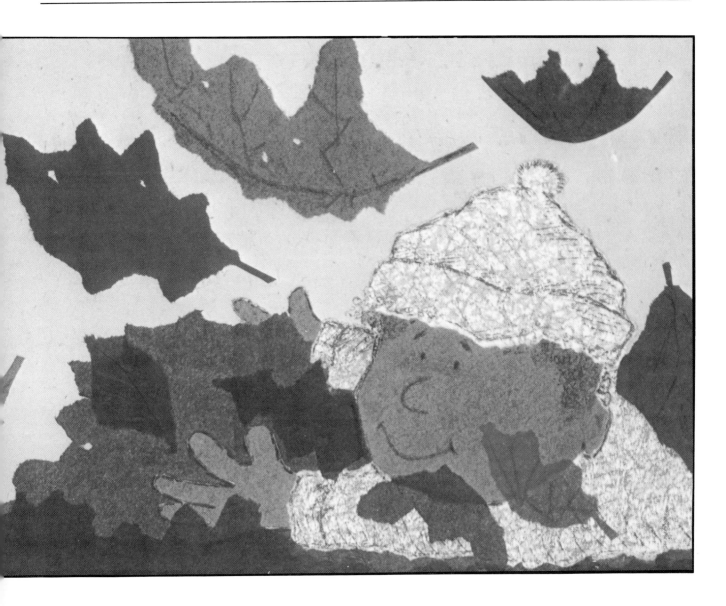

WILLIAMS, Ferelith Eccles 1920-
(Eccles)

PERSONAL: Born August 12, 1920, in Oxford, England; daughter of C. A. Eccles (a schoolmaster) and Hermòne à Beckett (Terrell) Williams. *Education:* Attended Central School of Arts and Crafts, London, England, 1945-47. *Home:* Flat 8, 65/67 Longridge Rd., London SW5, England.

CAREER: Free-lance illustrator. Design Research Unit, London, England, junior designer, 1947; Colman Prentis & Varley, London, England, designer, 1947-48; Kemsley Newspapers, London, England, illustrator, 1948-51; Associated Newspapers, London, England, illustrator, 1951-53; Brighton Polytechnic, Brighton, England, instructor, 1964-71; Leicester Polytechnic, Leicester, England, instructor, 1971-73. *Exhibitions:* A.I.A. Gallery, London; London Group, Nash House. *Military service:* Red Cross ambulance driver, 1940-45. *Member:* Society of Industrial Artists and Designers, Association of Illustrators.

WRITINGS—All self-illustrated: *Dame Wiggins of Lee,* World's Work, 1975; *One Old Oxford Ox,* World's Work, 1976; *The Oxford Ox's Alphabet,* World's Work, 1977; *The Oxford Ox's Calendar,* World's Work, 1980.

Illustrator: John Pudney, *The Hartwarp Light Railway,* Hamish Hamilton, 1962; John Pudney, *The Hartwarp Dump,* Hamish Hamilton, 1962; John Pudney, *The Hartwarp Circus,* Hamish Hamilton, 1963; John Pudney, *The Hartwarp Balloon,* Hamish Hamilton, 1963; John Pudney, *The Hartwarp Bakehouse,* Hamish Hamilton, 1964; Susan Hale, *Painters Mate,* Methuen, 1964; Susan Hale, *Mystery Boxes,* Methuen, 1965; John Pudney, *The Hartwarp Jets,* Hamish Hamilton, 1967; Denise Hill, *Helicopter Children,* Methuen, 1967; Phyllis Arkle, *Magic at Midnight,* Brockhampton, 1967, Funk & Wagnells, 1968; Phyllis Arkle, *The Village Dinosaur,* Brockhampton, 1968; Phylis Arkle, *Two Village Dinosaurs,* Brockhampton, 1969.

P. W. Cordin, *Number in Mathematics,* Books 1 and 2, Macmillan, 1970; Joan Cass, *The Witch of Witchery Wood,* Brockhampton, 1973; Pamela Oldfield, *The Halloween Pumpkin,* Brockhampton, 1974, Children's, 1976; Joan Cass, *The Witch and the Naughty Princesses,* Brockhampton, 1976; A. J. McCallen, *Listen,* Collins, 1976; Keith Snow, *I*

(From *The Oxford Ox's Alphabet* by Ferelith Eccles Williams. Illustrated by the author.)

Am a Squirrel, World's Work, 1978; Keith Snow, *I Am a Fox,* World's Work, 1978; Keith Snow, *I Am a Hedgehog,* World's Work, 1979; Keith Snow, *I Am a Badger,* World's Work, 1979; A. J. McCallen, *Praise,* Collins, 1979. Illustrator of reading series "One Two Three and Away," by Sheila McCullagh, includes forty titles, published by Hart-Davis, 1964-79. Work has appeared in *Homes and Gardens* and many other magazines.

SIDELIGHTS: "I was born and brought up in Oxford where my father was headmaster of a boys' boarding school. The school had extensive grounds, a small farm and fields running down to the River Cherwell. It was a good place to grow up and I used to wander around the fields for hours and swim in the river whenever possible. I went to school in Oxford and then to a convent school at Wantage in Berkshire. I was never fond of school and left, thankfully, at sixteen to go to art school in Oxford.

"After a year, war having broken out, I drove an ambulance for the Oxford A.R.P. (Air Raid Precautions) and then for the British Red Cross stations at Army camps and areodromes all over the country. After the Normandy invasion we met planes flying wounded directly from the battlefields in Europe. During this boring and uncomfortable period I used to draw whenever possible and once won a Russian/British poster competition for building a British hospital in Stalingrad.

"The war over, I went to the Central School of Art in London leaving in 1947 to take a couple of jobs first in exhibition designing and then in advertising. Hearing that the *Daily Graphic,* a London daily newspaper required an illustrator, I joined them in 1949. This was my first venture into illustration, until then I had been more concerned with typography and general designing. On the paper I did layouts for the feature pages and any drawings that were needed, always in a mad rush to catch the evening deadline. After three years the paper was sold to another press which changed its name to the *Daily Sketch* and the pace became hotter. At the end of another two years I felt like a one man factory turning out five pages a day and several drawings always with one eye on the clock.

"I decided to get out and try free-lancing as an illustrator. At this time (1955) there was a great deal of illustration in advertising and most of my work was in this field working for J. Walter Thompson and many other agencies. At the same time I started to work for several magazines including *Homes and Gardens* for whom I have worked regularly until the present day. As advertising fashions changed, I gradually moved into publishing and started to illustrate more children's books. Today most of my work is in this field. About 1962 I started to illustrate a series of readers for schools written by Sheila McCullagh and published by Hart-Davis with an overall title of 'One Two Three and Away.' These have proven very successful. There are now forty titles in the series and I am still illustrating new ones. They are written around three or four families of children living in a particular village and over the years I have come to know the characters so well they have almost taken on a reality of their own.

"In the sixties there was an expansion of art and design education in this country and a need for experienced professionals to bring their practical knowledge to the students. I thought this would be an interesting experience and spent the next seven years teaching one day a week at Brighton Polytechnic and for a further two years at Leicester Polytechnic. I enjoyed teaching, found the students stimulating and the work an interesting contrast to full-time illustrating.

"After many years of illustrating other people's books I decided the time had come to illustrate my own and in 1975 illustrated *Dame Wiggins of Lee* for World's Work followed in 1976 by *One Old Oxford Ox* and in 1977 by *The Oxford Ox's Alphabet*. Since then I have illustrated four animal books with a zoologist, Dr. Keith Snow. I have also recently illustrated the Bible and a version of the psalms. These together with the animal books have given me a wider scope and interests and a chance to experiment in several different directions.

"Usually I like to illustrate stories where I can have some fun and make people laugh. The more ridiculous the situation the more I enjoy it. It is always exciting and sometimes surprising to see what emerges on the page."

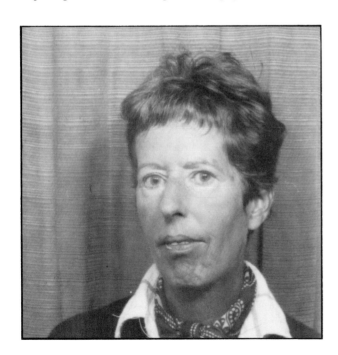

FERELITH ECCLES WILLIAMS

JOHN WILSON

WILSON, John   1922-

PERSONAL: Born April 14, 1922, in Boston, Mass.; son of Reginald and Violet (Caesar) Wilson; married Julia Kowitch (a teacher), June 25, 1950; children: Rebecca, Roy, Erica. *Education:* School of the Museum of Fine Arts, graduated, 1944; Tufts University, B.S., 1947; attended Fernand Léger's School, Paris, 1949, Instiute Politecnico, Mexico City, 1952, Esmeralda School of Art, Mexico City, 1952, and Escuela de las Artes del Libro, Mexico City, 1954-55. *Residence:* Brookline, Mass.

CAREER: Artist, illustrator and teacher. Boris Mirski School of Modern Art, Boston, Mass., instructor, 1945-47; School of the Museum of Fine Arts, Boston, Mass., instructor, 1950; Pratt Institute, Brooklyn, N.Y., instructor in anatomy, 1958; New York Board of Education, New York, N.Y., high school teacher, 1959-64; Boston University, Boston, Mass., professor, 1964——. Elma Lewis School of Fine Arts, Inc., Boston, Mass., board member, 1970-75.

EXHIBITIONS—One-man shows: Boris Mirski Art Gallery, Boston, Mass., 1946; Art Wood Gallery, Boston, Mass., 1954; Joseph Grooper Gallery, Cambridge, Mass., 1967; Sim-

BY JULIA WILSON
ILLUSTRATED BY JOHN WILSON
Thomas Y. Crowell Company New York

BECKY

(From *Becky* by Julia Wilson. Illustrated by John Wilson.)

mons College, Boston, Mass., 1968; School of the Museum of Fine Arts, Boston, Mass., 1970; American International College, Springfield, Mass., 1971; Embassy of Guyana, Washington, D.C., 1973.

Group shows: Smith College, Northampton, Mass., 1941, 1976; Wellesley College, Wellesley, Mass., 1943; Institute of Modern Art, Boston, Mass., 1943-45; Carnegie Institute Annual, 1944-46; Boris Mirski Art Gallery, Boston, Mass., 1944-46; Library of Congress, Washington, D.C., 1945-46, 1953; Addison Gallery of American Art, 1946; Pepsi-Cola Annual, 1946; Museum of Modern Art, New York, N.Y., 1949, 1954; Metropolitan Museum of Art, New York, N.Y., 1950; Society of American Etchers, Gravers, Lithographers, and Woodcutters, Inc., New York, N.Y., 1952, 1953, 1955; Cincinnati Museum, Cincinnati, Ohio, 1953; Exchange Exhibit of American Prints, Italy, 1956; National Academy of Design, New York, N.Y., 1956, 1966, 1975; Brooklyn Museum, Brooklyn, N.Y., 1958, 1977; Tenth Annual South Shore Art Festival, 1965; Rose Art Museum, Boston, Mass., 1969; Detroit Institute of Arts, Detroit, Mich., 1969-70; Museum of Fine Arts, Boston, Mass., 1970, 1973, 1975, 1977; Boston University School of Fine and Applied Arts, Boston, Mass., 1971; Mews Gallery, Lexington, Mass., 1973; High Museum of Art, Atlanta, Ga., 1973, 1976; Brockton Arts Center, Brockton, Mass., 1973; Museum· of the National Center of Afro-American Artists, Boston, Mass., 1974; Pratt Institute Graphic Center (traveling exhibit), 1974; Boston

Visual Artist's Union Gallery, Boston, Mass., 1974; Boston University, Boston, Mass., 1974; Southern Illinois University, Carbondale, Ill., 1975; Philadelphia Museum of Art, Philadelphia, Pa., 1976; Fitchberg Art Museum, Fitchberg, Mass., 1976; Los Angeles County Museum, Los Angeles, Calif., 1976; Museum of Fine Arts, Dallas, Tex., 1977; University of Massachusetts, Amherst, Mass., 1977.

Traveling exhibits: Bibliotheque National, Paris, France, 1951; Muses des Beaux-Arts, Rouen, France, 1952; Dijon, France, 1953; Lyons, France, 1954.

Permanent collections: Boston Public Library; Museum of Fine Arts, Boston, Mass.; Smith College Museum of Art, Northampton, Mass.; Museum of Modern Art, New York, N.Y.; Atlanta University; Carnegie Institute; Bezalel Museum, Jerusalem; Florence Heller School of Social Work, Brandeis University, Waltham, Mass.; Howard University, Washington, D.C.; Tufts University, Medford, Mass.; Department of Fine Arts, French government; Rose Art Museum, Brandeis University; First National Bank, Boston, Mass.; Mugar Library Collection, Boston University; Fitchburg Art Museum, Fitchberg, Mass. *Member:* Boston Visual Artists Union.

AWARDS, HONORS: First National Art Exhibit, Atlanta University's John Hope Award; Second National Art Exhibit, first prize for painting, third prize for prints; Third

National Art Exhibit, first prize for Best Portrait or Figure Painting; National Art Exhibit, third prize for prints, 1951, first prize for prints, 1952, first prize for prints and first prize for watercolor, 1954, first prize for Best Portrait or Figure Painting, 1955, second prize for watercolor and first prize for prints, 1957, first prize for prints, 1965, second prize for prints, 1966, first prize for prints, 1969; $500 award and $250 popular prize, Annual Pepsi-Cola Exhibit, 1945; James William Paige traveling fellowship for study in Europe, School of the Museum of Fine Arts, 1946; John May Whitney fellowship for study in Mexico, 1950-51; International Institute of Education Exchange-Student Fellowship for study in Mexico, 1952; Best Lithograph Award, First National Print Exhibit, Silvermine Guild, Conn., 1956; purchase prize, Hunterdon Art Center Annual Print Exhibit, N.J, 1958; Best Cover Design from the International Federation of Periodical Press, Paris, France, 1964; merit citation, Society of Illustrators National Exhibit, 1964; Fellowship for Sculpture, Massachusetts Arts and Humanities Foundation, Inc., 1976.

ILLUSTRATOR: Jean Craighead George, *Spring Comes to the Ocean* (ALA Notable Book), Crowell, 1965; Julia Wilson, *Becky*, Crowell, 1967; Joan Lexau, *Striped Ice Cream*, Lippincott, 1968; Arnold Adoff, *Malcolm X*, Crowell, 1970.

SIDELIGHTS: "I got into illustrating for two reasons: First, to make money to help support me in producing my own personal art work in the form of paintings and limited edition prints.

"Secondly, because of treasured boyhood memories of books I would pore over in the library of the Roxbury Boy's Club in Boston. They seemed to be teeming with drawings that brought the stories alive. They fascinated and amazed me with the magical illusions that the artists created.

"I get a great deal of satisfaction from feeling that my book illustrations are being shared in such an intimate, one-to-one relationship by thousands of young people."

WORK IN PROGRESS: Drawings and sculpture for an exhibit.

FOR MORE INFORMATION SEE: Oliver Willis Willis, *New Worlds of Reading,* Harcourt, 1959; Cedric Dover, *American Negro Art,* Graphic Society, 1960; Lee Bennett Hopkins, *Books Are by People,* Citation Press, 1969; *Boston University Journal,* Vol. XVII, Winter, 1969, Vol. XX, 1972; June Jordan, *Who Look at Me,* Crowell, 1969; *Boston Sunday Globe,* September 5, 1971; Elton Fax, *17 Black Artists,* Dodd, 1971; *Daily News* (Springfield, Mass.), April 7, 1971; *The Instructor* Magazine, April, 1973; Unger Johnson, *Land of Progress,* Ginn, 1974; Robert Blackburn, *Impressions: Our World,* Volume I, Printmaking Workshop, 1974; Perry London, *Beginning Psychology,* Dorsey Press, 1975; Martha E. Ward and Dorothy A. Marquardt, *Illustrators of Books for Young People,* Scarecrow, 1975; *The Mass Review,* Autumn, 1977; *Reader's Digest,* June, 1978.

Youth and white paper take any impression.
— **Proverb**

WODEHOUSE, P(elham) G(renville) 1881-1975
(P. Brooke-Haven, Pelham Grenville, J. Plum, C. P. West, J. Walker Williams, Basil Windham)

PERSONAL: Surname is pronounced *Wood*-house; born October 15, 1881, in Guildford, Surrey, England; died February 14, 1975, in Southampton, N.Y.; became U.S. citizen, 1955; son of Henry Ernest (a civil servant and judge) and Eleanor (Deane) Wodehouse; married Ethel Rowley, September 30, 1914; children: Leonora (stepdaughter; deceased). *Education:* Attended Dulwich College, 1894-1900. *Home:* Basket Neck Lane, Remsenburg, Long Island, N.Y.

CAREER: Worked as bank clerk in England, 1901-03; writer of "By the Way" column for *London Globe,* 1903-09; writer, under various pseudonyms, and drama critic for *Vanity Fair,* 1915-19; novelist and playwright. *Member:* Dramatists Guild, Old Alleynian Association (New York; president), Coffee House (New York). *Awards, honors:* Litt.D., Oxford University, 1939; Knight Commander of the Order of the British Empire, 1975.

WRITINGS—Juvenile fiction: *The Pothunters* (serialized in *The Public School Magazine,* 1901), A. & C. Black, 1902, reissued, International Scholastic Book Service, 1977; *A Prefect's Uncle,* A. & C. Black, 1903, reissued, International Scholastic Book Service, 1977; *Tales of St. Austin's,* A. & C. Black, 1903, reissued, International Scholastic Book Service, 1977; *The Gold Bat* (serialized in the boys' magazine *The Captain,* 1903-04), A. & C. Black, 1904, reissued, International Scholastic Book Service, 1977; *The Head of Kay's* (serialized in *The Captain,* 1904), A. & C. Black, 1905, reissued, International Scholastic Book Service, 1977; "Tales of Wrykyn," published in *The Captain,* 1905; *The White Feather* (serialized in *The Captain,* 1905-06), A. & C. Black, 1907, reissued, International Scholastic Book Service, 1977; (with William Townsend, under pseudonym Basil Windham) "The Luck Stone," (serialized in the boys' paper *Chums,* 1908-09); *Mike: A Public School Story* (serialized in *The Captain* in two parts as "Jackson Junior" and "The Lost Lambs," 1907-08), A. & C. Black, 1909, revised edition published in two volumes as *Mike at Wrykyn* and *Mike and Psmith,* Jenkins, 1953, reissued, Meredith Press, 1968 (*Mike and Psmith* also published as *Enter Psmith,* Macmillan, 1935); *Psmith in the City* (serialized in *The Captain* as "The New Fold," 1908-09), A. & C. Black, 1910, reissued Penguin, 1970; *The Little Nugget* (serialized in *The Captain* as "The Eighteen-Carat Kid," 1912-13), Methuen, 1913, W. J. Watt, 1914, reissued, Barrie & Jenkins, 1972; *Psmith, Journalist* (serialized in *The Captain,* 1909-10), A. & C. Black, 1915, reissued, Penguin, 1970; *Leave It to Psmith,* Jenkins, 1923, Doran, 1924, reissued, Random House, 1975, also published in *Nothing but Wodehouse* [see below].

Adult fiction: *Love Among the Chickens: A Story of the Haps and Mishaps on an English Chicken Farm,* G. Newnes, 1906, Circle Publishing, 1909, revised edition, Jenkins, 1921, reissued, British Book Center, 1963; (with H. W. Westbrook) *Not George Washington,* Cassell, 1907; (with Westbrook) *The Glove by the Way Book: A Literary Quick-Lunch for People Who Have Only Got Five Minutes to Spare,* Globe, 1908; *The Swoop!; or, How Clarence Saved England: A Tale of the Great Invasion,* Alston Rivers, 1909; *The Intrusion of Jimmy,* W. J. Watt & Co., 1910 (published in England as *A Gentleman of Leisure,* Alston Rivers, 1910, reissued, British Book Center, 1962); *The Prince and Betty,* W. J. Watt, 1912;

The Man Upstairs, and Other Stories, Methuen, 1914, reissued with a new preface by Wodehouse, Barrie & Jenkins, 1971; *Something New,* Appleton, 1915, reissued, Ballantine, 1977 (published in England as *Something Fresh,* Methuen, 1915, reissued, Jenkins, 1969); *The Man with Two Left Feet, and Other Stories,* Methuen, 1917, reissued, Barrie & Jenkins, 1971; *Uneasy Money,* Appleton, 1916, reissued, Jenkins, 1969; *Piccadilly Jim,* Dodd, 1917, reissued, Penguin, 1969; *My Man Jeeves,* G. Newnes, 1919, reissued as *Carry on, Jeeves!,* Jenkins, 1925, Doran, 1927, reissued, Penguin, 1975, also published with *Right Ho, Jeeves* [see below]; *A Damsel in Distress,* 1919, reissued, British Book Center, 1956; *Their Mutual Child,* Boni & Liveright, 1919 (published in England as *The Coming of Bill,* Jenkins, 1920).

The Little Warrior, Doran, 1920 (published in England as *Jill the Reckless,* Jenkins, 1921, reissued, British Book Center, 1958); *The Indiscretions of Archie,* Doran, 1921, reissued, Jenkins, 1965; *The Clicking of Cuthbert,* Jenkins, 1922, reissued, British Book Center, 1956, published in America as *Golf without Tears,* Doran, 1924, also published in *Wodehouse on Golf* [see below]; *Three Men and a Maid,* Doran, 1922 (published in England as *The Girl on the Boat,* Jenkins, 1922, reissued, Pan Books, 1968); *The Adventures of Sally,* Jenkins, 1922, reissued, Barrie & Jenkins, 1973, published in America as *Mostly Sally,* Doran, 1923; *Jeeves,* Doran, 1923 (published in England as *The Inimitable Jeeves,* Jenkins, 1923, reissued, Penguin, 1975); *Ukridge,* Jenkins, 1924, reissued, Barrie & Jenkins, 1976, published in America as *He Rather Enjoyed It,* Doran, 1925; *Bill the Conqueror: His Invasion of England in the Springtime,* Doran, 1924, reissued, British Book Center, 1975; *Sam in the Suburbs,* Doran, 1925 (published in England as *Sam the Sudden,* Methuen, 1925, reissued, Barrie & Jenkins, 1972).

The Heart of a Goof, Jenkins, 1926, published in America as *Divots,* Doran, 1927 (includes "The Heart of a Goof," reprinted separately, Penguin, 1972, "High Stakes," "Keeping in with Vosper," "Chester Forgets Himself," "The Magic Plus Fours," "The Awakening of Rollo Podmarch," "Rodney Fails to Qualify," "Jane Gets Off the Fairway," and "The Purification of Rodney Spelvin"); *The Small Bachelor* (based on his play, "Oh! Lady, Lady!"), Doran, 1927, reissued, Ballantine, 1977; *Meet Mr. Mulliner,* Jenkins, 1927, Doubleday, Doran, 1928, reissued, Ballantine, 1977; *Money for Nothing,* Doubleday, Doran, 1928, reissued, British Book Center, 1959; *Mr. Mulliner Speaking,* Jenkins, 1929, reissued, British Book Center, 1975 (includes "The Reverent Wooing of Archibald," "The Man Who Gave Up Smoking," "The Story of Cedric," "The Ordeal of Osbert Mulliner," "Unpleasantness at Bludleigh Court," "Those in Peril on the Tee," "Something Squishy," "The Awful Gladness of the Mater," and "The Passing of Ambrose"); *Fish Preferred,* Doubleday, Doran, 1929, reissued, Simon & Schuster, 1969 (published in England as *Summer Lightning,* Jenkins, 1929, reissued, British Book Center, 1964; also published under the first title in *The Week-end Wodehouse* [see below]).

Very Good, Jeeves, Doubleday, Doran, 1930, reissued, Penguin, 1975; *Big Money,* Doubleday, Doran, 1931, reissued, British Book Center, 1965; *If I Were You,* Doubleday, Doran, 1931, reissued, British Book Center, 1958; *Doctor Sally,* Methuen, 1932, reissued, T. Nelson, 1966; *Hot Water,* Doubleday, Doran, 1932, reissued, British Book Center, 1956; *Louder and Funnier* (essays), Faber, 1932, reissued, British Book Center, 1963; *Mulliner Nights,* Doubleday, Doran, 1933, reissued, Random House, 1975; *Heavy Weather,* Little, Brown, 1933, reissued, Penguin, 1966; *Thank You, Jeeves!,*

Little, Brown, 1934, reissued, British Book Center, 1956; *Brinkley Manor: A Novel about Jeeves* (originally published as a serial in *Saturday Evening Post,* under title, "Right Ho, Jeeves"), Little, Brown, 1934 (published in England as *Right Ho, Jeeves,* Jenkins, 1934, reissued, Penguin, 1975; also published with *Carry On, Jeeves* [see above]; (editor) *A Century of Humor,* Hutchinson, 1934; *Blandings Castle* (short stories), Doubleday, Doran, 1935, reissued, British Book Center, 1957 (published in England as *Blandings Castle and Elsewhere,* Jenkins, 1935); *Trouble Down at Tudsleigh,* International Magazine Co., 1935, also published in *The Best of Wodehouse* [see below]; *The Luck of the Bodkins,* Jenkins, 1935, Little, Brown, 1936, reissued, Penguin, 1975.

Young Men in Spats, Doubleday, Doran, 1936, reissued, British Book Center, 1957; *Laughing Gas,* Doubleday, Doran, 1936, reissued, Ballantine, 1977; (contributor) Peter Wait, editor, *Stories by Modern Masters: P. G. Wodehouse, George A. Birmingham, Arnold Bennett, H. C. Bailey, Ernest Bramah, A. A. Milne,* Methuen, 1936; *The Crime Wave at Blandings,* Doubleday, Doran, 1937 (published in England as *Lord Emsworth and Others,* Jenkins, 1937, reissued, Penguin, 1975; also published under the first title in *The Best of Wodehouse* [see below]); *Summer Moonshine,* Doubleday, Doran, 1937, reissued, Penguin, 1972; *The Code of the Woosters,* Doubleday, Doran, 1938, reissued, Random House, 1975; *Uncle Fred in the Springtime,* Doubleday, Doran, 1939, reissued, Penguin, 1976.

Eggs, Beans, and Crumpets, Doubleday, Doran, 1940, reissued, Penguin, 1976; *Quick Service,* Doubleday, Doran, 1940, reissued, British Book Center, 1960; *Dudley Is Back to Normal,* Doubleday, Doran, 1940; *Joy in the Morning,* Doubleday, 1946, reissued, Barrie & Jenkins, 1974; *Full Moon,* Doubleday, 1947, reissued, Ballantine, 1977; *Spring Fever,* Doubleday, 1948, reissued, Penguin, 1969; *Uncle Dynamite,* Jenkins, 1948, reissued, Penguin, 1966; *The Mating Season,* Didier, 1949.

Nothing Serious (short stories), Jenkins, 1950, Doubleday, 1951, reissued, British Book Center, 1964; *The Old Reliable,* Doubleday, 1951, reissued, Pan Books, 1968; *Angel Cake* (based on George S. Kaufman's play, "The Butter and Egg Man"), Doubleday, 1952 (published in England as *Barmy in Wonderland,* Jenkins, 1952); *Pigs Have Wings,* Doubleday, 1952, reissued, Ballantine, 1977; (compiler with Scott Meredith, and author of introduction) *The Week-end Book of Humour,* Washburn, 1952, reprinted, Books for Libraries, 1971, also published as *The Best of Modern Humor,* Metcalf Associates, 1952, reissued as *P. G. Wodehouse Selects the Best of Humor,* Grosset, 1965; *Ring for Jeeves,* Jenkins, 1953, new edition, 1963, published in America as *The Return of Jeeves,* Simon & Schuster, 1954; *Performing Flea: A Self-Portrait in Letters,* Jenkins, 1953, published in America as *Author! Author!,* Simon & Schuster, 1962; (with Guy Bolton) *Bring On the Girls!: The Improbable Story of Our Life in Musical Comedy, with Pictures to Prove It,* Simon & Schuster, 1953; *Jeeves and the Feudal Spirit,* Jenkins, 1954, reissued, British Book Center, 1962; *Bertie Wooster Sees It Through,* Simon & Schuster, 1955.

America, I Like You, Simon & Schuster, 1956; *French Leave,* Jenkins, 1956, Simon & Schuster, 1959, reissued, Barrie & Jenkins, 1974; *The Butler Did It* (originally published in short form in *Collier's* under title, "Something Fishy"), Simon & Schuster, 1957 (published in England as *Something Fishy,* Jenkins, 1957); *Over Seventy: An Autobiography with Digressions,* Jenkins, 1957; *Cocktail Time,* Simon & Schuster, 1958; *Selected Stories* (with an introduction by John W. Aldridge),

Modern Library, 1958; *A Few Quick Ones* (short stories), Simon & Schuster, 1959.

How Right You Are, Jeeves, Simon & Schuster, 1960 (published in England as *Jeeves in the Offing,* Jenkins, 1960); *Ice in the Bedroom,* Simon & Schuster, 1961; *Service with a Smile,* Simon & Schuster, 1961, reissued, Penguin, 1975; *Stiff Upper Lip, Jeeves,* Simon & Schuster, 1963, reissued, Penguin, 1975; *Biffen's Millions,* Simon & Schuster, 1964 (published in England as *Frozen Assets,* Jenkins, 1964); *The Brinkmanship of Galahad Threepwood: A Blandings Castle Novel,* Simon & Schuster, 1965 (published in England as *Galahad at Blandings,* Jenkins, 1965); *Plum Pie,* Jenkins, 1966, Simon & Schuster, 1967 (includes "Jeeves and the Greasy Bird," "Sleepy Time," "Sticky Wicket at Blandings," "Ukridge Starts a Bank Account," "Bingo Bans the Bomb," "Stylish Stouts," "George and Alfred," "A Good Cigar Is a Smoke," and "Life with Freddie"); (editor with S. Meredith, and author of introduction) *A Carnival of Modern Humor,* Delacorte, 1967; *Company for Henry,* Jenkins, 1967; *Do Butlers Burgle Banks?,* Simon & Schuster, 1968; *A Pelican at Blandings,* Jenkins, 1969.

The Girl in Blue, Barrie & Jenkins, 1970, Simon & Schuster, 1971; *No Nudes Is Good Nudes,* Simon & Schuster, 1970; *Jeeves and the Tie That Binds,* Simon & Schuster, 1971; *Much Obliged, Jeeves,* Barrie & Jenkins, 1971; *Pearls, Girls, and Monty Bodkin,* Barrie & Jenkins, 1972; *The Plot That Thickened,* Simon & Schuster, 1973; *Bachelors Anonymous,* Barrie & Jenkins, 1973, Simon & Schuster, 1974; *Aunts Aren't Gentlemen: A Jeeves and Bertie Story,* Barrie & Jenkins, 1974, published in America as *The Cat-Nappers: A Jeeves and Bertie Story,* G. K. Hall, 1975; *Sunset at Blandings,* Simon & Schuster, 1978.

Omnibus volumes: *Jeeves Omnibus,* Jenkins, 1931; *Nothing but Wodehouse,* edited by Ogden Nash, Doubleday, Doran, 1932 (includes selections from *Jeeves; Very Good, Jeeves; He Rather Enjoyed It; Meet Mr. Mulliner; Mr. Mulliner Speaking;* and the complete novel, *Leave It to Psmith*); *P. G. Wodehouse* (anthology of selections from writings), edited by E. V. Knox, Methuen, 1934; *Mulliner Omnibus,* Jenkins, 1935, new and enlarged edition published as *The World of Mr. Mulliner,* Barrie & Jenkins, 1972, Taplinger, 1974; *The Week-end Wodehouse,* Doubleday, Doran, 1939, new edition, Jenkins, 1951 (includes Part 1: "Mulliner Stories," Part 2: "Jeeves Stories," Part 3: "Drones and Others," and Part 4: "Fish Preferred"); *Wodehouse on Golf,* Doubleday, Doran, 1940, new edition published as *The Golf Omnibus,* Barrie & Jenkins, 1973, Simon & Schuster, 1974 (includes "Divots," "Golf without Tears," "The Medicine Girl," There's Always Golf," "The Letter of the Law," and "Archibald's Benefit"); *The Best of Wodehouse,* selected and introduced by Scott Meredith, Pocket Books, 1949 (includes "Jeeves and the Yuletide Spirit," "Trouble Down at Tudsleigh," "Good-bye to Butlers," "Strychnine in the Soup," "The Level Business Head," "The Crime Wave at Blandings," "Sonny Boy," "The Letter of the Law," "Tried in the Furnace," and "Freddie, Oofy, and the Beef Trust"); *The Most of P. G. Wodehouse,* Simon & Schuster, 1960; *The World of Jeeves,* Jenkins, 1967, reissued, Manor Books, 1976; *Right Ho, Jeeves [and] Carry On Jeeves,* Heron Books, 1970; *The World of Psmith,* Barrie & Jenkins, 1974; *The World of Blandings,* Barrie & Jenkins, 1976.

Plays: (With John Stapleton) "A Gentleman of Leisure" (comedy), first produced on Broadway at Playhouse Theatre, August 24, 1911; (with Stapleton) "A Thief for the Night,"

P. G. WODEHOUSE

first produced on Broadway at Playhouse Theatre, 1913; (with H. W. Westbrook) "Brother Alfred," first produced in West End at Savoy Theatre, 1913; *The Play's the Thing* (three-act drama; adapted from Ferenc Molnar's *Spiel im Schloss;* first produced on Broadway at Henry Miller's Theatre, November 3, 1926), Brentano's, 1927; (with Valerie Wyngate) "Her Cardboard Lover" (adapted from play by Jacques Deval), first produced in New York at Empire Theatre, March 21, 1927; *Good Morning, Bill* (three-act comedy; based on the Hungarian of Ladislaus Fodor; first produced in London at Duke of York's Theatre, November 28, 1927), Methuen, 1928; (with Ian Hay) *A Damsel in Distress* (three-act comedy; first produced Off-Broadway at New Theatre, August 13, 1928), Samuel French, 1930; (with Hay) *Baa, Baa, Black Sheep* (three-act comedy; first produced Off-Broadway at New Theatre, April 22, 1929), Samuel French, 1930; *Candle-light* (three-act drama; adapted from "Kleine Komodie" by Siegfried Geyer; first produced in New York at Empire Theatre, September 30, 1929), Samuel French, 1934; (with Hay) *Leave It to Psmith* (three-act comedy; first produced in London at Shaftesbury Theatre, September 29, 1930), Samuel French, 1932; (with Guy Bolton) "If I Were You" (three-act comedy), 1931, first produced in London under title "Who's Who" at Duke of York's Theatre, September 20, 1934; "The Inside Stand" (three-act farce), first produced in London at Saville Theatre, November 20, 1935; (with Bolton) "Don't Listen Ladies" (two-act comedy; adapted from the play "N'ecoutez pas, mesdames," by Sacha Guitry), first produced on Broadway at Booth Theatre, December 28, 1948; (with Bolton) *Come On, Jeeves* (three-act comedy), Evans Brothers, 1956.

Collaborator on musicals: (With others) "The Gay Gordons," first produced in London at Aldwych Theatre, 1913; (with C. H. Bovill and F. Tours) "Nuts and Wine," first produced in London at Empire Theatre, 1914; (with E. Kalman, Guy Bolton, and H. Reynolds) "Miss Springtime," first produced in New York at New Amsterdam Theatre, September 25, 1916; (with Bolton) "Ringtime," 1917; (author of book and lyrics with Bolton) "Have a Heart," music by Jerome Kern, first produced in New York at Liberty Theatre, January 11, 1917; (author of book and lyrics with Bolton) "Oh, Boy," first produced in New York at Princess Theatre, February 20, 1917, produced in London as "Oh, Joy," 1919; (author of book and lyrics with Bolton) "Leave It to Jane" (musical version of George Ade's "The College Widow"), music by Kern, first produced in Albany, N.Y., July, 1917, produced on Broadway at Longacre Theatre, August 28, 1917; (author of book and lyrics with Bolton) "The Riviera Girl," music by Emmerlich Klaman, first produced in New York at New Amsterdam Theatre, September 24, 1917; (author of book and lyrics with Bolton) "Miss 1917," music by Victor Herbert and Kern, first produced Off-Broadway at Century Theatre, November 5, 1917; (author of book and lyrics with Bolton) "Oh! Lady, Lady!," music by Kern, first produced in New York at Princess Theatre, February 1, 1918; (with Bolton) "See You Later," first produced in Baltimore at Academy of Music, April 15, 1918; (author of book and lyrics with Bolton) "The Girl Behind the Gun" (based on play "Madame et son filleul," by Hennequin and Weber), music by Ivan Caryll, first produced in New York at New Amsterdam Theatre, September 16, 1918, produced in London as "Kissing Time" at Winter Garden Theatre, 1918; (author of book and lyrics with Bolton) "Oh My Dear," music by Louis Hirsch, first produced in New York at Princess Theatre, November 27, 1918, produced in Toronto as "Ask Dad," 1918; (with Bolton and Armand Veesey) "The Rose of China," first produced in New York at Lyric Theatre, November 25, 1919.

(Author of lyrics with Clifford Grey) "Sally," music by Jerome Kern, first produced in New York by Flo Ziegfeld, 1920; (author of book and lyrics with Fred Thompson) "The Golden Moth," music by Ivor Novello, first produced in London at Adelphi Theatre, October 5, 1921; (author of book and lyrics with George Grossmith) "The Cabaret Girl," music by Kern, first produced in London at Winter Garden Theatre, 1922; (author of book and lyrics with Grossmith) "The Beauty Prize," music by Kern, first produced in London at Aldwych Theatre, September 5, 1923; (author of book and lyrics with Bolton) "Sitting Pretty," music by Kern, first produced in New York at Fulton Theatre, April 8, 1924; (adapter with Laurie Wylie) *Hearts and Diamonds* (light opera; adapted from *The Orloy* by Bruno Granichstaedten and Ernest Marischka; first produced in London at Strand Theatre, June 1, 1926), English lyrics by Graham John, Keith Prowse & Co., 1926; (author of book with Bolton) "Oh Kay!," lyrics by Ira Gershwin, music by George Gershwin, first produced on Broadway at Imperial Theatre, November 8, 1926; (author of book and lyrics with Bolton) "The Nightingale," music by Veesey, first produced on Broadway at Al Jolson's Theatre, January 3, 1927; (author of lyrics with Ira Gershwin) "Rosalie," book by Bolton and Bill McGuire, music by George Gershwin and Sigmund Romberg, first produced in New York at New Amsterdam Theatre, January 10, 1928; (author of book with George Grossmith, author of lyrics with Grey) *The Three Musketeers* (based on the novel by Alexandre Dumas; first produced in New York at Lyric Theatre, March 13, 1928), music by Rudolph Friml, Harms Inc., 1937; (author of book with Bolton, Howard Lindsay, and Russel Crouse) *Anything Goes* (first produced on Broadway at Alvin

Theatre, November 21, 1934), music and lyrics by Cole Porter, Samuel French, 1936. Also author of lyrics for song, "Bill" (for which Oscar Hammerstein wrote the music), originally written for "Oh! Lady, Lady!" but cut and later used for "Showboat," first produced on Broadway at Ziegfeld Theatre, December 27, 1927.

Films: (Author of screenplay with others) "A Damsel in Distress," RKO, 1920; (author of filmscript) "Rosalie," Metro-Goldwyn-Mayer, 1930. Also author of screenplay, "Three French Girls."

SIDELIGHTS: **October 15, 1881.** Born at One Vale Place, Epson Road, Guilford, Surrey, England; the third of four sons of Eleanor Deane and Henry Ernest Wodehouse. His mother was a talented artist and his father a civil servant stationed in Hong Kong. While the Wodehouse children were educated in England, their parents remained in Hong Kong making parental visits infrequent. For the most part Wodehouse and his brothers lived in boarding schools, shunted from relative to relative during school holidays. "My father was very indulgent to us boys, my mother less so. Having seen practically nothing of her until I was fifteen, I met her as virtually a stranger and it was not easy to establish cordial relations. With my father, on the other hand, I was always on very good terms—though never in any sense very close. In those days, parents tended to live a life apart from their children: or it may be that that was just what happened in our family owing to not having grown up together. Looking back, I can see that I was just passed from hand to hand. It was an odd life with no home to go to, but I have always accepted everything that happens to me in a philosophical spirit; and I can't remember ever having been unhappy in those days. My feeling now is that it was very decent of those aunts to put up three small boys for all those years. We can't have added much entertainment to their lives. The only thing you could say for us is that we never gave any trouble." [David A. Jasen, *P. G. Wodehouse: A Portrait of a Master,* Lippincott, 1974.[1]]

1886. Sent to a dame school in Croydon, Surrey where Wodehouse remained for three years. The school was run by two sisters, Florrie and Cissie Prince. "Croydon in those days was almost in the country, and I remember getting into bad trouble for stealing a turnip out of a field. It was looked on as a major crime. Probably that is what has given me the respect for the law which I have always had. I suppose it was a good bringing up, but it certainly did not tend to make one adventurous. I can't remember having done any other naughty thing the whole of the three years I was there. One other thing I remember is how fond I was of the various maids who went through the Prince home. It may have given me my liking for the domestic-servant class."[1]

1888. Wrote his first story at the age of seven: "About five years ago in a wood there was a Thrush, who built her nest in a Poplar tree. and sang so beautifully that all the worms came up from their holes and the ants laid down their burdens. and the crickets stopped their mirth. and moths settled all in a row to hear her, she sang a song as if she were in heaven—going up higher and higher as she sang.

"At last the song was done and the bird came down panting.

"Thank you said all the creatures. Now my story is ended."[1]

1889. Sent with his brothers to Elizabeth College, Guernsey. "Guernsey in those days was a delightful place full of lovely bays; and as far as I can remember, our movements were never restricted and we were allowed to roam where we liked. My recollections are all of wandering about the island and of the awful steamer trips back to England for the holidays. Paddle-wheel steamers, like on the Mississippi—very small and rolling with every wave. It was hell to go back for the holidays at the end of the winter term.... We would spend our holidays with various aunts, some of whom I liked but one or two of whom were very formidable Victorian women."[1]

May, 1894. Was sent to Dulwich College for six years. "It was what you would call a middle-class school. We were all the sons of reasonably solvent but certainly not wealthy parents, and we all had to earn our living later on. Compared with Eton, Dulwich would be something like an American State University compared with Harvard or Princeton. Bertie Wooster's [a Wodehouse character] parents would never have sent him to Dulwich, but Ukridge [another Wodehouse character] could very well have been there. There were four 'sides' at the school—the Classical, the Modern, the Science and the Engineering. The Classical was by far the largest, although the present headmaster of Dulwich tells me that everybody today goes on the Science side and the Classical side has become very small. Some farseeing parents, knowing that their sons would have to go into business later, put them on the Modern side, where they learned French and German and mathematics; but the average parent chose the Classical, where they learned Latin and Greek, presumably with a vague idea that if all went well they would go to Oxford or Cambridge. In my day, to the ordinary parent, education meant Classics. I went automatically on the Classical side and, as it turned out, it was the best form of education I could have had as a writer. But it certainly was not much help to me when at the end of my school career I joined the Hong Kong and Shanghai Bank, for I was utterly incapable of understanding business."[1]

1895. Father retired from overseas service and returned to England. This was the first time the family had ever been together for a prolonged period.

Autumn, 1896. When the family moved to Stableford in Shropshire, Wodehouse returned as a boarder at Dulwich College.

1898-1900. Enjoyed his schooldays at Dulwich College, where he was a noted athlete, school prefect, and editor of the school paper. "Except for Alec Waugh, I seem to be the only author who enjoyed his schooldays. To me, the years . . . were like heaven. This may have been because we had one of the recognised great headmasters, A. H. Gilkes, who is looked on today as one of England's greatest educators. I came into actual contact with him only in my last two years, but even at that early age I could see how big he was. He was a man with a long white beard who stood six-foot-six in his socks, and he had one of those deep musical voices. I can still remember how he thrilled me when he read us that bit from Carlyle's *Sartor Resartus* which ends 'But I, mine Wether, am above it all.' It was terrific. But he also always scared the pants off me!"[1]

July, 1900. Education at Dulwich ended. "You had a fairly good time at school if you were good at games. I had the greatest luck. I always had a good time there. The fashionable thing is to look back and hate your school, but I loved Dulwich. . . ."

The ecstasy which always came to the vague and woollenheaded peer when in the society of this noble animal was not quite complete.... ■ (From *Full Moon* by P. G. Wodehouse. Illustrated by Paul Galdone.)

September, 1900. Entered the Lombard Street office of the London branch of the Hong Kong and Shanghai Bank. "My father had bought a house in Shropshire in 1900, and what I would have liked to do on leaving school was to dig in there and concentrate on the daily short story: but, placing this idea before my parents, I found them cold toward it. The cross all young writers have to bear is that, while they know they are going to be spectacularly successful some day, they find it impossible to convince their nearest and dearest that they will ever amount to a row of beans. Write in your spare time, parents say, and they pull that old one about literature being a good whatever-it-is, but a bad crutch.

". . . So Commerce got me, and Literature lost out for the time being.

"Looking back, I don't think Literature missed much." [P. G. Wodehouse, *Author! Author!*, Simon & Schuster, 1962.[2]]

November, 1900. First humorous article published in *Tid Bits*.

1901-1902. While employed by the bank, Wodehouse wrote numerous stories with great diligence, but little financial success. "Only two things connected with the banking industry did I really get into my head. One was that from now on all I would be able to afford for lunch would be a roll and butter and a cup of coffee, a discovery which, after the lavish meals of school, shook me to my foundations. The other was that if I was late in getting to the office oftener than three times a month, I would forfeit my Christmas bonus. One of the great sights in the City of London . . . was me rounding into the straight with my coattails flying and my feet going pitter-patter-pat and just making it across the threshold, while thousands cheered. It kept me in splendid condition and gave me a rare appetite for the daily roll and butter.

". . . During my two years in the bank all I got out of my literary efforts was a collection of rejection slips, and what I have always felt about rejection slips is that their glamour soon wears off. When you have seen one, you have seen them all.

"The handicap under which most commencing authors struggle is that they don't know how to write. I was no exception to the rule. Worse bilge than mine may have been submitted to the editors of London in 1901 and 1902, but I should think it very unlikely. I was sorry for myself at the time when the stamped and addressed envelopes came homing back to me, but today my sympathy is for the unfortunate men who had to read my contributions. I can imagine nothing more depressing than being an editor and coming to the office on a rainy morning in February with a nail in one shoe and damp trouser legs and finding oneself confronted with six early Wodehouses—I used to send them out in batches of six—written, to make it more difficult, in longhand.

"I was a quick worker in those days. In the summer of 1901 I contracted mumps and went home to have them in the bosom of my family. I was there three weeks, swelling all the time, and wrote twenty-one short stories, all of which, I regret, editors were compelled to reject owing to lack of space. The editors regretted it too. They said so."[2]

September 9, 1902. Replaced the vacationing assistant editor of the "By the Way" column of *The Globe,* an evening newspaper. In his diary he wrote: "On September 9th, having to choose between *The Globe* and the Bank, I chucked the latter and started out on my wild one as a freelance. This month starts my journalistic career."[1]

September 18, 1902. Became an author when his first book, *The Pothunters,* was published. Resolved never to do any work that was not connected with writing.

August, 1903. Became a full time journalist for *The Globe* and continued writing verses and short stories. ". . . I didn't go out very much. I was working too hard. After *The Globe* in the morning, I'd walk back to my lodgings and more or less start work right away, doing short stories and things. I played a certain amount of cricket and I really never wanted anything to do, I was so keen on my work. However, I was always fond of reading anything that came along."[1]

September, 1903. Second novel about public school life, *A Prefect's Uncle,* was published.

November, 1903. A collection of short stories on public school life, *Tales of St. Austin's,* was published.

Spring, 1904. First trip to America. Upon his return to London he found that the trip had helped him professionally. "After that trip to New York I was someone who counted. The manner of editors changed towards me. Where before it had been 'Throw this man out,' they now said 'Come in, my dear fellow, come in and tell us all about America.' When some intricate aspect of American politics had to be explained to the British public, it was 'Ask Wodehouse. Wodehouse will know.' My income rose like a rocketing pheasant."[2]

September 30, 1914. Married Ethel Rowley in New York City. "When Ethel and I got married, she had seventy-five dollars and I had fifty, and I remember the pang of envy I felt when we fetched up at The Little Church Around the Corner and the clergyman who was going to marry us bounded in and told us he had just made ten thousand bucks on the Stock Exchange. All through the ceremony I could see his eyes sparkling as he thought of it. I had the feeling that his mind wasn't really on his job, but he fixed us up all right, and we took the train to Bellport, Long Island, where we had rented a moth-eaten old shack for twenty-five dollars the first month and twenty after that. The home comforts were fairly slim, but I found it a great place to work and in the intervals of writing articles for *Vanity Fair* was able to finish a novel called *Something New,* which I hoped I might be able to sell to *Mumsey's* or one of the other pulps.

"But I wasn't feeling too good. *Vanity Fair* had only just started, and these new magazines have a nasty way of folding after the seventh issue. If it did suddenly call it a day, I asked myself, Where would I get off? It was a pretty testing period and affected my nervous system quite a good deal, inclining me to jump at sudden noises and to think that I was being followed about by little men with black beards."[2]

Autumn, 1914. Rejected by the English and American armies during World War I. "I was rejected for service because of my eyes. They had been bad as a child and I was kept out of the navy because of them. I tried to enlist again over here when America went to war, but I was rejected once more."[1]

1915. Sold *Something New* to the *Saturday Evening Post* for $3,500. This started a relationship with the *Post* which lasted for twenty-two years. "I was plugging along like this, the wolf still outside the door but sticking around and licking its lips in a meaning manner, when suddenly everything changed. The sun shone out, the United States Marines arrived, and the millennium set in. The *Saturday Evening Post* bought *Something New,* a miracle which absolutely stunned me, as I had never even considered the possibility of a long story by an unknown author having a chance there. Since then I have had three more serials in the *S.E.P.—Uneasy Money, Piccadilly Jim,* and *A Damsel in Distress.* They gave me a raise with each one—$3,500, $5,000, $7,500, and for the *Damsel* $10,000—so that now I can afford an occasional meat meal, not only for self but for wife and resident kitten and bulldog, all of whom can do with a cut off the joint."[2]

1916. Collaborated with Guy Bolton and Jerome Kern on musical Broadway plays.

March, 1918. Moved to Great Neck, Long Island. "We had a house which was nicely situated. It was in the middle of a lot of property owned by the Grace (shipping magnate) family and it wasn't built over at all. In fact, Great Neck was an absolute village when we were there. You know, there was a general store where you bought everything, and they had a wooden railroad station. We were more towards King's Point, at a place called Arrandale Avenue. It was rather a bit outside Great Neck proper. Scott Fitzgerald and his crowd lived about three miles from us. I loved Great Neck in those days."[1]

April, 1920. Moved to England to be nearer to his stepdaughter, Leonora.

December, 1922. Returned to New York. "I've been swamped with work since I got here. We wrote the Ziegfeld musical comedy in two weeks, and it has been lying in a drawer ever since, Ziegfeld being busy with another production. This in spite of the fact that in his cable he said that every moment was precious. You never heard anything like the fuss he made when I told him I couldn't make the Wednesday boat but would sail on the Saturday. He gave me to understand that my loitering would ruin everything.''

''After putting the musical comedy in its drawer, I sat down to finish *Leave It to Psmith* and wrote 40,000 words in three weeks. Since then I have been working with Guy [Bolton] on a show for the Duncan Sisters, music by Irving Berlin. . . .''[2]

1923. *Leave It to Psmith* became Wodehouse's most popular book in England. ''I am not one of those authors to whom mere material gain is everything: and it was not entirely the thought of the box of cigars which the proprietor of the *Saturday Evening Post* had promised me for the serial rights nor the reflection that, if he brought it out as a book, George H. Doran would be practically bound to send me a card next Christmas that induced me to write *Leave it to Psmith*. I was urged to the task principally by the importunity of my daughter Leonora, who, if I may coin a phrase, is my best pal and severest critic. It was the fact that she kept after me like a bloodhound to write another Psmith story that at length induced me to set typewriter to paper.

''Psmith—the p is silent as in pshrimp—was the hero of a book for boys which I wrote in the year 1909 when I was young and slim and had quite a crop of hair. I had always intended some day to write of his after-school life, but never quite got down to it till my golden-haired child, who is the world's worst pest, harried me day by day in every way to such an extent that I saw the thing had to be done. So I did it.''[1]

November, 1923. Worked on his juvenile novel, *Bill the Conqueror: His Invasion of England in the Springtime,* which was published in 1924. ''I am halfway through mapping out a new novel, *Bill the Conqueror,* I'm going on a new system this time, making the scenario very full, putting in atmosphere, dialogue, etc., so that when I come actually to write it the work will be easy. So far I have scenarioed out to about the 40,000-word mark, and it has taken me 13,000 words to do it. I have now reached a point where deep thought is required. I'm not sure I haven't got too much plot, and may have to jettison the best idea in the story. I suppose the secret of writing is to go through your stuff till you come on something you think is particularly good, and then cut it out.''[2]

1924. Bought a fashionable house at 23 Gilbert Street, Grosvenor Square. It was the right address for a successful author but Wodehouse found it difficult to concentrate on his writing there. ''I find it's the hardest job to get at the stuff here. We have damned dinners and lunches which just eat up the time. I find that having a lunch hanging over me kills my morning's works, and dinner isn't much better. I'm at the stage now, if I drop my characters, they go cold.''[1]

Autumn, 1928. When his wife bought a new home for them in London she surprised Wodehouse with a beautifully furnished study. The author, who worked best under the most spartan conditions with his favorite Monarch typewriter, was most disappointed. ''It's rather funny. You know when a cat's going to have kittens you fix up a cozy apartment for her with a warm blanket and all the trimmings, and then she goes and has them in a drafty corner of the cellar lying in the dark on damp stone. Much the same thing has happened with me. Ethel, bless her, was determined that I should have a really good place for my writing, so her first move was to furnish a large room on the first floor as a library—old books round the walls, luxurious chairs, a massive desk, etc.—and, of course, my first move was to go and do all my work in my bedroom on a kitchen table. Did you read a recent story in the *Post* about an author who could never write unless he was in the greatest discomfort? I remember that his masterpiece was turned out in a haunted house with strange groanings going on and doors opening silently without hands. I'm rather like that.''[2]

Spring, 1930. Hired by Metro-Goldwyn-Mayer (M-G-M) for six months at $2,500 a week and a six-month option as a screenwriter. ''. . . Do I like Hollywood? I like the place and the weather and particularly the people. About everybody I know in the Broadway theater is here, plus a large contingent from London, so one has lots of congenial society. Interesting conversationalists in every nook and cranny.

''When the Talkies came in and they had to have dialogue, the studios started handing out contracts right and left to everyone who had ever written a line of it. Only an author of exceptional ability and determination could avoid getting signed up. And if you didn't want to be a writer, they would be just as pleased to take you on as a diction teacher or a voice specialist. With the result that the migration to Hollywood has been like one of those great race movements of the Middle Ages. So though there is a touch of desert island about the place and one feels millions of miles from anywhere, one can always count on meeting half a dozen kindred spirits when one is asked out to dinner.

''It's the work I don't like, if you can call it work. They have this extraordinary idea that if one writer can do a good job, ten will do ten times as good a one.''[2]

Spring, 1931. In a newspaper interview Wodehouse candidly commented on his Hollywood experience: ''They paid me $2,000 a week—$104,000—and I cannot see what they engaged me for. They were extremely nice to me, but I feel as if I have cheated them. You see, I understood I was engaged to write stories for the screen. After all, I have twenty novels, a score of successful plays, and countless magazine stories to my credit. Yet apparently they had the greatest difficulty in finding anything for me to do. Twice during the year they brought completed scenarios of other people's stories to me and asked me to do some dialogue. Fifteen or sixteen people had tinkered with those stories. The dialogue was really quite adequate. All I did was to touch it up here and there.

''Then they set me to work on a story called *Rosalie,* which was to have some musical numbers. It was a pleasant little thing, and I put in three months on it. When it was finished, they thanked me politely and remarked that as musicals didn't seem to be going so well they guessed they would not use it.

''That about sums up what I was called upon to do for my $104,000. Isn't it amazing?''[1] Wodehouse returned to Hollywood five years later under contract with M-G-M.

August, 1934. Bought a house in Le Touquet, France. ''The big item of news is that we have bought a house here. . . . At first I didn't like the place, and then suddenly it began to get me, and it struck both Ethel and me that as regards situation it was the one ideal spot in the world. I can get over to England by boat in a few hours, and by plane, and I am within motoring distance of Cherbourg.''[1]

June, 1936. Received a medallion from the International Mark Twain Society.

1939. Wodehouse's popularity was at its peak in England and America. He was a meticulous writer who was constantly revising. "The absolute cast-iron good rule, I'm sure, in writing a story, is to introduce all your characters as early as possible especially if they are going to play important parts later. I think the success of every novel depends largely on one or two high spots. The thing to do is to say to yourself, 'Which are my big scenes?' and then get every drop of juice out of them. I believe that when one has really got a bit of action going, it can extend as long as you like.

". . . What a problem it is to get a novel started just right. That business of introducing your characters and trying not to have them jostle one another and get in each other's way, and at the same time trying to make the damned thing readable. Particularly when you reflect that an editor probably makes up his mind about a story after reading page one. Guy Bolton says the great thing in writing plays is never let your characters sit down—i.e. keep the characters buzzing about without a pause. He also thinks that it's a mistake to give the audience too much to think about at any one time. In other words, in a play one mustn't try to develop two threads simultaneously, and this applies equally to stories. My besetting sin is a tendency to do all the exposition in one chunk on the first two pages instead of taking my time and spreading it out, and it generally takes me about six shots before I get the first five hundred words right.

". . . I think one has to be ruthless with one's books. I find I have a tendency to write a funny line and then add another, elaborating it where there is no necessity for the second bit. I keep coming on such bits in the thing I'm doing now. I go through the story every day and back them out.

". . . It's a funny thing about writing. If you are a writer by nature, I don't believe you write for money, for fame, or even for publication, but simply for the pleasure of turning out the stuff. Personally, I love rewriting and polishing. Directly I have got something down on paper, however rough it is, I feel the thing is in the bag.''[1]

July, 1940. During the German occupation of Le Touquet, France in World War II, Wodehouse was taken from his home and interned by the Germans. "It is a curious experience, being completely shut off from the outer world, as one is in an internment camp. One lives on potatoes and rumours. One of my friends used to keep a notebook in which he would jot down all the rumours that spread through the corridors, and they made curious readings. To military prisoners, I believe, rumours are known for some reason as 'Blue Pigeons.' We used to call them bedtime stories. They never turned out true, but a rumour a day kept depression away, so they served their purpose. Certainly, whether owing to bedtime stories or simply the feeling that if one was in one was in and it was no use making heavy weather about it, the morale of the men at Tost [a German camp] was wonderful. I never met a more cheerful crowd, and I loved them like brothers.''[1]

June, 1941. Released by the Germans from prison but remained in Berlin for two years. While there he made several broadcasts to America innocently hoping to inform his Eng-

lish friends that he was alive. These broadcasts were misinterpreted by some English reporters as treasonous. When the war was over Wodehouse was rightly exonerated.

1943-1945. Sent by the Germans to Paris with his wife. Continued to write stories. During the war two personal tragedies had occurred; the death of his mother in 1941 and the sudden death of his thirty-nine year old stepdaughter in 1944.

Spring, 1947. After a ten year absence, returned to America. ". . . It's quite a business arriving in New York now. In the old days the only newspaper man one saw was the ship reporter of the N.Y. *Times,* who sauntered up as one was seeing one's stuff through the Customs and asked if one had had a pleasant voyage, but now a whole gang of reporters flock aboard at Quarantine and a steward comes to you and tells you that the gentlemen of the press are in the saloon and request your presence. It's like being summoned before a Senate Committee.''[1]

April, 1948. *The Play's the Thing* opened on Broadway.

February, 1951. Became ill. A suspected brain tumor was at first diagnosed, but further tests revealed nothing. "The score, then, to date is that I am deaf in the left ear, bald, subject to mysterious giddy fits, and practically cockeyed. I suppose the moral of the whole thing is that I have simply got to realise that I am a few months off being seventy. I had been going along as if I were in the forties, eating and drinking everything I wanted to and smoking far too much. I had always looked on myself as a sort of freak whom age could not touch, which was where I made my ruddy error, because I'm really a senile wreck with about one and a half feet in the grave.''[1]

September, 1955. At the age of seventy-four became a naturalized U.S. citizen. "I've lived here for many years now. I just wanted to make it official. It's like being asked to join a very good club.''[1]

1956. *The Butler Did It* (one of Wodehouse's most popular books since World War II) was published.

September 30, 1961. Of his forty-seven-year marriage he remarked: "We are like one person really. After you are happily married for such a long time, you get like that. At the beginning it was wonderful. I think it's not so much doing things together but that you are absolutely at your ease together. There is never a sense of strain or anything. Of course, we are both devoted to animals, which is a terrific bond.''[1]

October 15, 1961. Turned eighty. ". . . Once one has got the knack of it, one comes to enjoy being what Somerset Maugham calls a 'very old party.' Life becomes more tranquil. The hot blood of the late seventies has cooled. Today when I see a sexagenarian—Frank Sullivan, as it might be, or somebody like that—climbing a tree, I smile and say to myself, 'Boys will be boys. When you are my age, child,' I say to myself, 'you will realize that the true pleasures are mental.' I am eighty and may quite easily go to par, and I find I am quite happy just sitting and thinking, or at any rate sitting. I can detach myself from the world. And if there is a better world to detach oneself from than the one functioning as of even date, I have yet to hear of it.

"The great thing about being an octogenarian is that you can legitimately become set in your ways. I have always wanted to do this, but in the old days something was always happening to prevent it. There was never a chance of simply doing the same thing every day and being able to work regular hours without interruption, as I can now. One was perpetually dashing about, leaping from continent to continent, seeing editors, lunching with managers, going on the road with shows, popping off to Hollywood, popping back again, and generally behaving more like the jackrabbit of the prairies than anything human. Today in my quiet rural retreat I do the same things day after day, with no variation. Morning exercises, breakfast, work till noon, watch *Love of Life* on television, lunch, take the dogs to the post office, walk back, more work, cocktails, dinner, and then the quiet evening with a Rex Stout or an Erle Stanley Gardner. Monotonous? Not a bit of it. I love it. The cry goes around Remsenburg [Long Island], 'Wodehouse has found his niche.' And an octogenarian, mind you, is not expected to go to parties. The thought that I shall never have to wear a paper hat again is a very sustaining one."[2] In his late eighties, Wodehouse was still under pressure to produce a book a year.

February 14, 1975. Died at the age of ninety-four in Southampton, N.Y. "I had always supposed that the whole idea of the thing was that others might make the Obituary column but that I was immortal and would go on forever. I see now that I was mistaken, and that I, too, must ere long hand in my dinner pail. I'm not sure I like the new arrangement, but there it is."[2]

FOR MORE INFORMATION SEE: George Orwell, *The Orwell Reader,* Harcourt, 1933; Richard Usborne, *Wodehouse at Work,* Jenkins, 1916, revised edition published as *Wodehouse at Work to the End,* Barrie & Jenkins, 1976; John W. Aldridge, *Time to Murder and Create,* McKay, 1966; Richard Voorhees, *P. G. Wodehouse,* Twayne, 1966; R.B.D. French, *P. G. Wodehouse,* Oliver & Boyd, 1966, Barnes & Noble, 1967; Geoffrey W. Jaggard, *Wooster's World,* Macdonald & Co., 1967; G. W. Jaggard, *Blandings the Blest and the Blue Blood,* Macdonald & Co., 1968; D.A.A. Jasen, *A Bibliography and Reader's Guide to the First Editions of P. G. Wodehouse,* Archon, 1970; H. W. Wind, *The World of P. G. Wodehouse,* Praeger, 1972; Thelma Cazalet-Keir, editor, *Homage to P. G. Wodehouse,* Barrie & Jenkins, 1973; David A. Jasen, *P. G. Wodehouse: A Portrait of a Master,* Mason & Lipscomb, 1974; Gerald Clarke, "P. G. Wodehouse: The Art of Fiction LX," *Paris Review* (Flushing, N.Y.), Winter, 1975, reprinted in *Authors in the News,* Volume 2, Gale, 1976.

Obituaries: *New York Times,* February 15, 1975, February 19, 1975; *Washington Post,* February 16, 1975; *Detroit News,* February 16, 1975; *New Statesman,* February 21, 1975; *Time,* February 24, 1975; *Newsweek,* February 24, 1975; *AB Bookman's Weekly,* March 3, 1975; *National Review,* March 14, 1975; *Current Biography Yearbook,* 1975.

O youth, whose hope is high,
Who dost to Truth aspire,
Whether thou live or die,
O look not back nor tire.

—Robert Bridges

RHODA WOOLDRIDGE

WOOLDRIDGE, Rhoda 1906-

PERSONAL: Born May 25, 1906, in Buckner, Mo.; daughter of James Walter (a farmer) and Georgia (Tucker) Phillips; married Clinton Prather Wooldridge (a dentist), September 13, 1930 (died, 1962); children: Clinton Prather, Jr., Georgia (Mrs. Dennis Reardon). *Education:* Stephens College, graduate, 1926; attended Univeristy of Missouri. *Politics:* Independent (Democrat background). *Religion:* Methodist. *Home:* Route 2, Independence, Mo. 64058. *Agent:* Phil Sadler, C.M.S.U., Department of Education, Warrensburg, Mo. 64093.

CAREER: Writer, 1962—. Farmer on family farm in Independence, Mo.; Fort Osage, Sibley, Mo., historical consultant.

WRITINGS: Hannah's Brave Year, Bobbs, 1964; *That's the Way Joshuway,* Bobbs, 1965, Independence Press, 1977; *Hannah's House,* Independence Press, 1972; *And Oh! How Proudly,* Independence Press, 1972; *Chouteau and the Founding of St. Louis,* Independence Press, 1975.

WORK IN PROGRESS: The Flood of Hannah's Town.

Yes, they were lucky...that is, as lucky as a family without father or mother could be. ■(From *Hannah's House* by Rhoda Wooldridge. Illustrated by Alta Adkins.)

SIDELIGHTS: "I started writing after my husband died in 1962, for need of a family. My children were grown and gone so I created the family of children in *Hannah's Brave Year* and they became my family in that first lonely winter.

"My travels have been limited to taking my daughter around the world and taking my granddaughter to the British Isles."

FOR MORE INFORMATION SEE: Horn Book, February, 1965.

WORMSER, Sophie 1897-

PERSONAL: Born October 21, 1897, in Astoria, N.Y. *Education:* Attended City College of the City University of New York. *Home and office:* 3314 Waverly Dr., Los Angeles, Calif. 90027.

CAREER: Worked as supervisor and organizer for Hearst International Magazines in New York, as secretary in New York City, as residence manager in Morristown, N.J., and as manager at Rockefeller Center. Has taught remedial reading and creative writing, and English to speakers of foreign languages. Has done volunteer work in settlement houses, in hospitals, for the blind, and for political campaigns. *Military service:* U.S. Navy, World War I. *Awards, honors:* Many poetry prizes.

WRITINGS: About Silkworms and Silk, Melmont, 1961; *The Belted Kingfisher,* Anthelion Press, 1976; *A Family of Blue-Winged Teals,* Crescent, 1978. Contributor of about sixty poems and many articles and short stories to magazines, newspapers, and anthologies.

WORK IN PROGRESS: Monkey Baker, Miranda, the Garden Spider, My Brother Juan, A Family Is for Loving, all for Oddo; *Make Me a World* (novel), *America, Land of the Indians* (history), and a nature article, "Death Valley."

SIDELIGHTS: "During our poverty-stricken days at the beginning of the twentieth century I became acquainted with two different environments. Each left an indelible impression on me. Astoria, at that time, was a wilderness. Goats roamed the streets and fields were covered with wild flowers. My mother told me that one day I ran away from home and returned to a cemetery where a relative had been buried to gather violets from a grave. Then came the stark ugliness of tenement living in Harlem where one could hear no bleatings of goats but the roar of the Third Avenue elevated train overhead and the clang of the motorman's signal as he drove the horse-drawn street cars under the elevated structure.

"The cold-water flat in which we lived was rat and vermin infested. In winter the only heat we had was from a kitchen stove when my brothers could collect wood and old newspaper. One hears such glorious stories of pioneer women and their endurance. What about the tenement house women? Many of them lost children during periods of deadly epidemics. My mother and father were fortunate. They raised five children and died before my elder brothers passed away.

"I can't remember who taught me to read but I never remember being without a library card. My oldest brother introduced me to literature which he had discovered for himself. He would sit on the cover of the large kitchen sink, which was also our bathtub on Saturday nights, and read aloud to us. We had no bathroom. There was one toilet room on each floor shared with other tenants. Now when I see the luxuries we have grown accustomed to, I wish my parents were here to share them with us.

"In addition to going to college at night, I researched and wrote and studied subjects not in my curriculum. After I had more time in the evenings I did a great deal of volunteer work. During the second World War I taught English and citizenship to refugees and after the war was over I worked in settlement houses, in children's wards in hospitals, and in public schools teaching remedial reading, language arts, and creative writing."

...he who please children will be remembered with pleasure by men.

—James Boswell

Children—catapults of energy, dynamos of ideas, summer suns of affection, lonesome dark dreamers.

—Louise Seaman Bechtel

But the eagle sprang from his perch, and dragged his "buddy" to safety. ■(From *Old Abe: The Eagle Hero* by Patrick Young. Illustrated by John Kaufmann.)

YOUNG, (Rodney Lee) Patrick (Jr.) 1937-

PERSONAL: Born October 19, 1937, in Ladysmith, Wis.; son of Rodney Lee (a lawyer) and Janice (a medical technologist; maiden name, Wolf) Young; married Leah Ruth Figelman (a reporter), October 8, 1966; children: Justine Rebecca. *Education:* University of Colorado, B.A. (cum laude), 1960. *Home and office:* 16101 Goodman Court, Laurel, Md. 20810. *Agent:* Barbara Lowenstein, 250 West 57th St., New York, N.Y. 10019.

CAREER: United Press International (UPI), Washington, D.C., reporter, 1960-63; *National Observer,* Silver Spring, Md., staff science writer, 1965-77; free-lance writer, 1977-79; Newhouse News Service, national science and medical correspondent, 1980—. Was also a senior writer for the Presidential commission investigating the nuclear accident at Three Mile Island from May to November, 1979. *Military service:* U.S. Navy, 1963-65. *Member:* National Association of Science Writers. *Awards, honors:* Howard W. Blakeslee Award from American Heart Association, 1970; Journalism award from Society of Abdominal Surgeons, 1972; award in physics and astronomy from American Institute of Physics and U.S. Steel Foundation, 1974; Russell Cecil Award from Arthritis Foundation, 1976; James T. Grady Award from American Chemical Society, 1977.

WRITINGS: Old Abe: The Eagle Hero (juvenile; Junior Literary Guild selection), Prentice-Hall, 1965; *Drifting Continents, Shifting Seas: An Introduction to Plate Tectonics* (young adult), Watts, 1976. Contributor to popular magazines, including *Harper's, Saturday Review, Family Circle, Parade, Smithsonian, Good Housekeeping, Popular Science, Omni,* and *Vogue.*

SIDELIGHTS: "I wrote my first two books, *Mutiny on Deck* and *A Camping Trip,* when I was eight. When typed by my father's secretary and bound between the cardboard backs of writing tablets, my efforts ran but a few pages each. I didn't resume an attempt at authorship for a number of years.

"My first book was written at the request of Prentice-Hall, after one of its employees read an article I had written for *The National Observer.* The piece was on an eagle named Old Abe, a mascot of the Eighth Wisconsin Infantry Volunteers during the Civil War. My great grandfather on my mother's side had commanded the company that owned the eagle, and when in college I set out to attempt a magazine piece, I chose Old Abe. I spent my free time in the summer of 1958 researching and writing a 5,000 word article. It sold nowhere. After accummulating a number of rejection slips, I set it aside for several years. Then I rewrote the article, shortening it considerably, and still failed to make a sale. In

PATRICK YOUNG

1964, while serving in the Navy, I made a third attempt. This time an article of 1,200 words sold to *The National Observer*. Prentice-Hall liked the subject, and in 1965 it published *Old Abe: The Eagle Hero* for youngsters five to eight. It became a Junior Literary Guild selection and eventually was published in a paperback edition.

"*Drifting Continents, Shifting Seas* is a book I desperately wanted to write. Among the amazing stories of this century is the revolution within the earth sciences brought about by the theory of plate tectonics. Late in 1974 it struck me that no volume existed that explained this very important concept to young readers and the desire grew very quickly to write one. I quickly wrote a proposal—the outline and introductory chapter were drafted in an intensive effort over a single weekend—and sent it to an editor I knew at Franklin Watts. We signed a contract and I wrote a book that a few of my colleagues in science writing use themselves when they want simple explanations for some of the complex processes involved in the new geology."

ZELLAN, Audrey Penn   1950-

PERSONAL: Born May 4, 1950, in Tacoma Park, Md.; daughter of Harry Joseph (a lawyer and business manager) and Rose (Miller) Penn; married Lester Zellan (a lighting technician), December 19, 1970; children: Garth Lee. *Education:* Attended National Ballet School, 1965-68, University of Maryland, 1967-68, and New York City dance and acting schools, 1968-70. *Politics:* Democrat. *Religion:* Jewish. *Home and office:* 14323 Georgia Ave., #302, Silver Spring, Md. 20906. *Agent:* Mitch Douglas, I.C.M., New York, N.Y.

CAREER: Professional actress in Washington, D.C., and New York, N.Y., on national tours, and in summer stock productions, 1965-70; professional ballet dancer, 1967-75; writer, 1975. Dance coach for Olympic gymnasts and ice skaters, 1973-75. *Member:* Council on Physical Fitness, Arthritis Association. *Awards, honors: Happy Apple Told Me* was presented by the U.S. State Department to School 157 Proletarskya Dicturtura I, Leningrad, Russia as a gift from the children of the United States, 1976, and was awarded the Mid-State Children's Library Selection Award, 1979.

WRITINGS—Juveniles: *Happy Apple Told Me*, Independence Press, 1975.

WORK IN PROGRESS—Juveniles: *Blue Out of Season; Albert and the Pentapus*, for a cartoon special; *No Bones About Driftiss; How to Visit Grandma Becky; Garth and the Giant Bubble;* a mystery of Brookeville, Md., the U.S. capital for one day, entitled *Ghost at Howard Hall; 847 Avenue C*, a mystery; *The Frog from Squoze; The Kissing Hand;* editing *Mystery at Blackbeard's Cave.*

Audrey Zellan and son, Garth.

My job is important and I'm really quite proud. I pick kisses and flick them onto happiness clouds. ■(From *Happy Apple Told Me* by Audrey Penn Zellan. Illustrated by Carolyn Ewing Bowser.)

SIDELIGHTS: "In August of 1975, I collapsed while dancing, ending a twenty-year battle with juvenile rheumatoid arthritis. I remained in bed, unable to walk or work for the next eighteen months. During the time that followed, as I became stronger, I worked with friends and a cassette to finish the book I had already begun and go on to complete four more books. I now wear hand braces, and can walk, so I am back at the typewriter. It is very important for me to write, because it's the only outlet I have left. My aim is to have enough money to support a diagnostic program at Children's Hospital.

"I hope all authors enjoy their research and writing as much as I do. I draw my characters from actors I have met on and off Broadway and have a great deal of fun turning them into animals and 'kiss me' trees. In my mysteries, I do what I ask my characters to do and often get into trouble doing it. But what fun. Imitation is life itself, so why not enjoy it."

FOR MORE INFORMATION SEE: Publishers Weekly, February 24, 1975; *Washington Star,* October 3, 1975.

CUMULATIVE INDEX TO
ILLUSTRATIONS AND AUTHORS

Illustrations Index

(In the following index, the number of the volume in which an illustrator's work appears is given *before* the colon, and the page on which it appears is given *after* the colon. For example, a drawing by Adams, Adrienne appears in Volume 2 on page 6, another drawing by her appears in Volume 3 on page 80, another drawing in Volume 8 on page 1, and another drawing in Volume 15 on page 107.)

YABC

Index citations including this abbreviation refer to listings appearing in *Yesterday's Authors of Books for Children,* also published by the Gale Research Company, which covers authors who died prior to 1960.

Author Index

(In the following index, the number of the volume in which an author's sketch appears is given *before* the colon, and the page on which it appears is given *after* the colon. For example, the sketch of Aardema, Verna, appears in Volume 4 on page 1).

YABC

Index citations including this abbreviation refer to listings appearing in *Yesterday's Authors of Books for Children,* also published by the Gale Research Company, which covers authors who died prior to 1960.

Almedingen, Martha Edith von.
    See Almedingen, E. M., *3:* 9
Allsop, Kenneth, *17:* 13
Almedingen, E. M., *3:* 9
Almquist, Don, *11:* 8
Alsop, Mary O'Hara, *2:* 4
Alter, Robert Edmond, *9:* 8
Altsheler, Joseph A(lexander),
    YABC 1: 20
Alvarez, Joseph A., *18:* 2
Ambrus, Victor G(tozo), *1:* 6
Amerman, Lockhart, *3:* 11
Ames, Evelyn, *13:* 1
Ames, Gerald, *11:* 9
Ames, Lee J., *3:* 11
Ames, Mildred, *22:* 14
Amon, Aline, *9:* 8
Amoss, Berthe, *5:* 4
Anckarsvard, Karin, *6:* 2
Ancona, George, *12:* 10
Andersen, Hans Christian,
    YABC 1: 23
Andersen, Ted. *See* Boyd, Waldo
    T., *18:* 35
Anderson, C(larence) W(illiam),
    11: 9
Anderson, Ella. *See* MacLeod,
    Ellen Jane (Anderson), *14:* 129
Anderson, Eloise Adell, *9:* 9
Anderson, George. *See* Groom,
    Arthur William, *10:* 53
Anderson, J(ohn) R(ichard) L(ane),
    15: 3
Anderson, Joy, *1:* 8
Anderson, (John) Lonzo, *2:* 6
Anderson, Lucia (Lewis), *10:* 4
Anderson, Mary, *7:* 4
Anderson, Norman D(ean), *22:* 15
Andrews, F(rank) Emerson, *22:* 17
Andrews, J(ames) S(ydney), *4:* 7
Andrews, Julie, *7:* 6
Andrews, Roy Chapman, *19:* 1
Angell, Judie, *22:* 18
Angell, Madeline, *18:* 3
Angelo, Valenti, *14:* 7
Angier, Bradford, *12:* 12
Angle, Paul M(cClelland), *20:* 1
    (Obituary)
Anglund, Joan Walsh, *2:* 7
Angrist, Stanley W(olff), *4:* 9
Annett, Cora. *See* Scott, Cora
    Annett, *11:* 207
Annixter, Jane. *See* Sturtzel, Jane
    Levington, *1:* 212
Annixter, Paul. *See* Sturtzel,
    Howard A., *1:* 210
Anno, Mitsumasa, *5:* 6
Anrooy, Frans van. *See* Van
    Anrooy, Francine, *2:* 252
Anthony, C. L. *See* Smith, Dodie,
    4: 194
Anthony, Edward, *21:* 1
Anticaglia, Elizabeth, *12:* 13
Anton, Michael (James), *12:* 13
Appel, Benjamin, *21:* 5 (Obituary)
Appiah, Peggy, *15:* 3

Appleton, Victor [Collective
    pseudonym], *1:* 9
Appleton, Victor II [Collective
    pseudonym], *1:* 9
Apsler, Alfred, *10:* 4
Aquillo, Don. *See* Prince, J(ack)
    H(arvey), *17:* 155
Arbuthnot, May Hill, *2:* 9
Archer, Frank. *See* O'Connor,
    Richard, *21:* 111
Archer, Jules, *4:* 9
Archer, Marion Fuller, *11:* 12
Archibald, Joseph S. *3:* 12
Arden, Barbie. *See* Stoutenburg,
    Adrien, *3:* 217
Ardizzone, Edward, *1:* 10; *21:* 5
    (Obituary)
Arehart-Treichel, Joan, *22:* 18
Arenella, Roy, *14:* 9
Armer, Alberta (Roller), *9:* 11
Armer, Laura Adams, *13:* 2
Armour, Richard, *14:* 10
Armstrong, George D., *10:* 5
Armstrong, Gerry (Breen), *10:* 6
Armstrong, Richard, *11:* 14
Armstrong, William H., *4:* 11
Arnett, Carolyn. *See* Cole, Lois
    Dwight, *10:* 26
Arnold, Elliott, *5:* 7; *22:* 19
    (Obituary)
Arnold, Oren, *4:* 13
Arnoldy, Julie. *See* Bischoff, Julia
    Bristol, *12:* 52
Arnosky, Jim, *22:* 19
Arnott, Kathleen, *20:* 1
Arnov, Boris, Jr., *12:* 14
Arnstein, Helene S(olomon), *12:* 15
Arntson, Herbert E(dward), *12:* 16
Arora, Shirley (Lease), *2:* 10
Arquette, Lois S(teinmetz), *1:* 13
Arrowood, (McKendrick Lee)
    Clinton, *19:* 10
Arthur, Ruth M., *7:* 6
Artis, Vicki Kimmel, *12:* 17
Artzybasheff, Boris (Miklailovich),
    14: 14
Aruego, Ariane. *See* Dewey,
    Ariane, *7:* 63
Aruego, Jose, *6:* 3
Arundel, Honor, *4:* 15
Arundel, Jocelyn. *See* Alexander,
    Jocelyn (Anne) Arundel, *22:* 9
Asbjörnsen, Peter Christen, *15:* 5
Asch, Frank, *5:* 9
Ashabranner, Brent (Kenneth),
    1: 14
Ashe, Geoffrey (Thomas), *17:* 14
Ashey, Bella. *See* Breinburg,
    Petronella, *11:* 36
Ashford, Daisy. *See* Ashford,
    Margaret Mary, *10:* 6
Ashford, Margaret Mary, *10:* 6
Ashley, Elizabeth. *See* Salmon,
    Annie Elizabeth, *13:* 188
Asimov, Isaac, *1:* 15
Asinof, Eliot, *6:* 5

Aston, James. *See* White,
    T(erence) H(anbury), *12:* 229
Atene, Ann. *See* Atene, (Rita)
    Anna, *12:* 18
Atene, (Rita) Anna, *12:* 18
Atkinson, M. E. *See* Frankau,
    Mary Evelyn, *4:* 90
Atkinson, Margaret Fleming, *14:* 15
Atticus. *See* Fleming, Ian
    (Lancaster), *9:* 67
Atwater, Florence (Hasseltine
    Carroll), *16:* 11
Atwater, Montgomery Meigs,
    15: 10
Atwood, Ann, *7:* 8
Aung, (Maung) Htin, *21:* 5
Aung, U. Htin. *See* Aung, (Maung)
    Htin, *21:* 5
Austin, Elizabeth S., *5:* 10
Austin, Margot, *11:* 15
Austin, Oliver L. Jr., *7:* 10
Austin, Tom. *See* Jacobs, Linda C.,
    21: 78
Averill, Esther, *1:* 16
Avery, Al. *See* Montgomery,
    Rutherford, *3:* 134
Avery, Gillian, *7:* 10
Avery, Kay, *5:* 11
Avery, Lynn. *See* Cole, Lois
    Dwight, *10:* 26
Avi. *See* Wortis, Avi, *14:* 269
Ayars, James S(terling), *4:* 17
Ayer, Jacqueline, *13:* 7
Ayer, Margaret, *15:* 11
Aylesworth, Thomas G(ibbons),
    4: 18
Aymar, Brandt, *22:* 21

Baastad, Babbis Friis. *See* Friis-
    Baastad, Babbis, *7:* 95
Babbis, Eleanor. *See* Friis-Baastad,
    Babbis, *7:* 95
Babbitt, Natalie, *6:* 6
Babcock, Dennis Arthur, *22:* 21
Bach, Richard David, *13:* 7
Bachman, Fred, *12:* 19
Bacmeister, Rhoda W(arner), *11:* 18
Bacon, Elizabeth, *3:* 14
Bacon, Margaret Hope, *6:* 7
Bacon, Martha Sherman, *18:* 4
Bacon, Peggy, *2:* 11
Baden-Powell, Robert (Stephenson
    Smyth), *16:* 12
Baerg, Harry J(ohn), *12:* 20
Bagnold, Enid, *1:* 17
Bailey, Alice Cooper, *12:* 22
Bailey, Bernadine Freeman, *14:* 16
Bailey, Carolyn Sherwin, *14:* 18
Bailey, Jane H(orton), *12:* 22
Bailey, Maralyn Collins (Harrison),
    12: 24
Bailey, Matilda. *See* Radford, Ruby
    L., *6:* 186
Bailey, Maurice Charles, *12:* 25

Cooper, John R. [Collective pseudonym], *1:* 68
Cooper, Kay, *11:* 55
Cooper, Lee (Pelham), *5:* 47
Cooper, Susan, *4:* 57
Copeland, Helen, *4:* 57
Coppard, A(lfred) E(dgar), *YABC 1:* 97
Corbett, Scott, *2:* 78
Corbin, William. *See* McGraw, William Corbin, *3:* 124
Corby, Dan. *See* Catherall, Arthur, *3:* 38
Corcoran, Barbara, *3:* 53
Corcos, Lucille, *10:* 27
Cordell, Alexander. *See* Graber, Alexander, *7:* 106
Cormack, M(argaret) Grant, *11:* 56
Cormier, Robert Edmund, *10:* 28
Cornell, J. *See* Cornell, Jeffrey, *11:* 57
Cornell, Jeffrey, *11:* 57
Correy, Lee. *See* Stine, G. Harry, *10:* 161
Corrigan, Barbara, *8:* 36
Cort, M. C. *See* Clifford, Margaret Cort, *1:* 63
Corwin, Judith Hoffman, *10:* 28
Cosgrave, John O'Hara II, *21:* 26 (Obituary)
Coskey, Evelyn, *7:* 55
Cottler, Joseph, *22:* 71
Courlander, Harold, *6:* 51
Cousins, Margaret, *2:* 79
Cowie, Leonard W(allace), *4:* 60
Cowley, Joy, *4:* 60
Cox, Jack. *See* Cox, John Roberts, *9:* 42
Cox, John Roberts, *9:* 42
Coy, Harold, *3:* 53
Craig, John Eland. *See* Chipperfield, Joseph, *2:* 57
Craig, M. Jean, *17:* 45
Craig, Margaret Maze, *9:* 43
Craig, Mary Francis, *6:* 52
Crane, Caroline, *11:* 59
Crane, Roy. *See* Crane, Royston Campbell, *22:* 72 (Obituary)
Crane, Royston Campbell, *22:* 72 (Obituary)
Crane, Stephen (Townley), *YABC 2:* 94
Crane, Walter, *18:* 44
Crane, William D(wight), *1:* 68
Crary, Margaret (Coleman), *9:* 43
Craven, Thomas, *22:* 72
Crawford, Deborah, *6:* 53
Crawford, John E., *3:* 56
Crawford, Phyllis, *3:* 57
Crayder, Dorothy, *7:* 55
Crayder, Teresa. *See* Colman, Hila, *1:* 65
Crayon, Geoffrey. *See* Irving, Washington, *YABC 2:* 164
Crecy, Jeanne. *See* Williams, Jeanne, *5:* 202

Credle, Ellis, *1:* 68
Cresswell, Helen, *1:* 70
Cretan, Gladys (Yessayan), *2:* 82
Crew, Helen (Cecilia) Coale, *YABC 2:* 95
Crichton, (J.) Michael, *9:* 44
Cromie, William J(oseph), *4:* 62
Crompton, Richmal. *See* Lamburn, Richmal Crompton, *5:* 101
Cronbach, Abraham, *11:* 60
Crone, Ruth, *4:* 63
Crosby, Alexander L., *2:* 83
Crosher, G(eoffry) R(obins), *14:* 51
Cross, Wilbur Lucius, III, *2:* 83
Crossley-Holland, Kevin, *5:* 48
Crouch, Marcus, *4:* 63
Crout, George C(lement), *11:* 60
Crowe, Bettina Lum, *6:* 53
Crowell, Pers, *2:* 84
Crowfield, Christopher. *See* Stowe, Harriet (Elizabeth) Beecher, *YABC 1:* 250
Crownfield, Gertrude, *YABC 1:* 103
Crowther, James Gerald, *14:* 52
Cruikshank, George, *22:* 73
Crump, Fred H., Jr., *11:* 62
Crump, J(ames) Irving, *21:* 26 (Obituary)
Cruz, Ray, *6:* 54
Cuffari, Richard, *6:* 55
Cullen, Countee, *18:* 64
Culp, Louanna McNary, *2:* 85
Cummings, Betty Sue, *15:* 51
Cummings, Parke, *2:* 85
Cummins, Maria Susanna, *YABC 1:* 103
Cunliffe, John Arthur, *11:* 62
Cunningham, Captain Frank. *See* Glick, Carl (Cannon), *14:* 72
Cunningham, Dale S(peers), *11:* 63
Cunningham, E. V. *See* Fast, Howard, *7:* 80
Cunningham, Julia W(oolfolk), *1:* 72
Curiae, Amicus. *See* Fuller, Edmund (Maybank), *21:* 45
Curie, Eve, *1:* 73
Curry, Jane L(ouise), *1:* 73
Curry, Peggy Simson, *8:* 37
Curtis, Peter. *See* Lofts, Norah Robinson, *8:* 119
Cushman, Jerome, *2:* 86
Cutchen, Billye Walker, *15:* 51
Cutler, (May) Ebbitt, *9:* 46
Cutler, Samuel. *See* Folsom, Franklin, *5:* 67
Cutt, W(illiam) Towrie, *16:* 67
Cuyler, Stephen. *See* Bates, Barbara S(nedeker), *12:* 34

Dahl, Borghild, *7:* 56
Dahl, Roald, *1:* 74
Dahlstedt, Marden, *8:* 38
Dale, Jack. *See* Holliday, Joseph, *11:* 137

Dalgliesh, Alice, *17:* 47; *21:* 26 (Obituary)
Daly, Jim. *See* Stratemeyer, Edward L., *1:* 208
Daly, Maureen, *2:* 87
D'Amato, Alex, *20:* 24
D'Amato, Janet, *9:* 47
Damrosch, Helen Therese. *See* Tee-Van, Helen Damrosch, *10:* 176
Dana, Barbara, *22:* 84
Danachair, Caoimhin O. *See* Danaher, Kevin, *22:* 85
Danaher, Kevin, *22:* 85
D'Andrea, Kate. *See* Steiner, Barbara A(nnette), *13:* 213
Dangerfield, Balfour. *See* McCloskey, Robert, *2:* 185
Daniel, Anne. *See* Steiner, Barbara A(nnette), *13:* 213
Daniel, Hawthorne, *8:* 39
Daniels, Guy, *11:* 64
Darby, J. N. *See* Govan, Christine Noble, *9:* 80
Darby, Patricia (Paulsen), *14:* 53
Darby, Ray K., *7:* 59
Daringer, Helen Fern, *1:* 75
Darke, Marjorie, *16:* 68
Darling, Lois M., *3:* 57
Darling, Louis, Jr., *3:* 59
Darling, Kathy. *See* Darling, Mary Kathleen, *9:* 48
Darling, Mary Kathleen, *9:* 48
Darrow, Whitney. *See* Darrow, Whitney, Jr., *13:* 24
Darrow, Whitney, Jr., *13:* 24
Daugherty, Charles Michael, *16:* 70
Daugherty, James (Henry), *13:* 26
d'Aulaire, Edgar Parin, *5:* 49
d'Aulaire, Ingri (Maartenson Parin) *5:* 50
Daveluy, Paule Cloutier, *11:* 65
Davenport, Spencer. *See* Stratemeyer, Edward L., *1:* 208
David, Jonathan. *See* Ames, Lee J., *3:* 11
Davidson, Basil, *13:* 30
Davidson, Jessica, *5:* 52
Davidson, Margaret, *5:* 53
Davidson, Marion. *See* Garis, Howard R(oger), *13:* 67
Davidson, Mary R., *9:* 49
Davis, Bette J., *15:* 53
Davis, Burke, *4:* 64
Davis, Christopher, *6:* 57
Davis, Daniel S(heldon), *12:* 68
Davis, Julia, *6:* 58
Davis, Mary L(ee), *9:* 49
Davis, Mary Octavia, *6:* 59
Davis, Paxton, *16:* 71
Davis, Robert, *YABC 1:* 104
Davis, Russell G., *3:* 60
Davis, Verne T., *6:* 60
Dawson, Elmer A. [Collective pseudonym], *1:* 76

Eagar, Frances, *11:* 85
Eager, Edward (McMaken), *17:* 54
Eagle, Mike, *11:* 86
Earle, Olive L., *7:* 75
Earnshaw, Brian, *17:* 57
Eastman, Charles A(lexander),
    YABC *1:* 110
Eastwick, Ivy O., *3:* 64
Eaton, George L. *See* Verral,
    Charles Spain, *11:* 255
Eaton, Tom, *22:* 99
Ebel, Alex, *11:* 88
Eberle, Irmengarde, *2:* 97
Eccles. *See* Williams, Ferelith
    Eccles, *22:* 237
Eckert, Horst, *8:* 47
Edell, Celeste, *12:* 77
Edelman, Lily (Judith), *22:* 100
Edgeworth, Maria, *21:* 33
Edmonds, I(vy) G(ordon), *8:* 48
Edmonds, Walter D(umaux), *1:* 81
Edmund, Sean. *See* Pringle,
    Laurence, *4:* 171
Edsall, Marian S(tickney), *8:* 50
Edwards, Bertram. *See* Edwards,
    Herbert Charles, *12:* 77
Edwards, Bronwen Elizabeth. *See*
    Rose, Wendy, *12:* 180
Edwards, Dorothy, *4:* 73
Edwards, Harvey, *5:* 59
Edwards, Herbert Charles, *12:* 77
Edwards, Jane Campbell, *10:* 34
Edwards, Julie. *See* Andrews,
    Julie, *7:* 6
Edwards, Julie. *See* Stratemeyer,
    Edward L., *1:* 208
Edwards, Monica le Doux Newton,
    12: 78
Edwards, Sally, *7:* 75
Edwards, Samuel. *See* Gerson,
    Noel B(ertram), *22:* 118
Eggenberger, David, *6:* 72
Egielski, Richard, *11:* 89
Egypt, Ophelia Settle, *16:* 88
Ehrlich, Bettina (Bauer), *1:* 82
Eichberg, James Bandman. *See*
    Garfield, James B., *6:* 85
Eichenberg, Fritz, *9:* 53
Eichner, James A., *4:* 73
Eifert, Virginia S(nider), *2:* 99
Einsel, Naiad, *10:* 34
Einsel, Walter, *10:* 37
Eiseman, Alberta, *15:* 102
Eisenberg, Azriel, *12:* 79
Eitzen, Allan, *9:* 57
Eitzen, Ruth (Carper), *9:* 57
Elam, Richard M(ace, Jr.), *9:* 57
Elfman, Blossom, *8:* 51
Elia. *See* Lamb, Charles, *17:* 101
Eliot, Anne. *See* Cole, Lois
    Dwight, *10:* 26
Elisofon, Eliot, *21:* 38 (Obituary)
Elkin, Benjamin, *3:* 65
Elkins, Dov Peretz, *5:* 61
Ellacott, S(amuel) E(rnest), *19:* 117
Elliott, Sarah M(cCarn), *14:* 57

Ellis, Edward S(ylvester),
    YABC *1:* 116
Ellis, Ella Thorp, *7:* 76
Ellis, Harry Bearse, *9:* 58
Ellis, Mel, *7:* 77
Ellison, Lucile Watkins, *22:* 102
    (Obituary)
Ellison, Virginia Howell, *4:* 74
Ellsberg, Edward, *7:* 78
Elspeth. *See* Bragdon, Elspeth,
    6: 30
Elting, Mary, *2:* 100
Elwart, Joan Potter, *2:* 101
Emberley, Barbara A(nne), *8:* 51
Emberley, Ed(ward Randolph),
    8: 52
Embry, Margaret (Jacob), *5:* 61
Emerson, Alice B. [Collective
    pseudonym], *1:* 84
Emery, Anne (McGuigan), *1:* 84
Emrich, Duncan (Black
    Macdonald), *11:* 90
Emslie, M. L. *See* Simpson, Myrtle
    L(illias), *14:* 181
Engdahl, Sylvia Louise, *4:* 75
Engle, Eloise Katherine, *9:* 60
Englebert, Victor, *8:* 54
Enright, Elizabeth, *9:* 61
Epp, Margaret A(gnes), *20:* 38
Epple, Anne Orth, *20:* 40
Epstein, Anne Merrick, *20:* 41
Epstein, Beryl (Williams), *1:* 85
Epstein, Samuel, *1:* 87
Erdman, Loula Grace, *1:* 88
Ericson, Walter. *See* Fast,
    Howard, *7:* 80
Erlich, Lillian (Feldman), *10:* 38
Ervin, Janet Halliday, *4:* 77
Estep, Irene (Compton), *5:* 62
Estes, Eleanor, *7:* 79
Estoril, Jean. *See* Allan, Mabel
    Esther, *5:* 2
Ets, Marie Hall, *2:* 102
Eunson, Dale, *5:* 63
Evans, Katherine (Floyd), *5:* 64
Evans, Mari, *10:* 39
Evans, Mark, *19:* 118
Evans, Patricia Healy. *See*
    Carpenter, Patricia, *11:* 43
Evarts, Hal G. (Jr.), *6:* 72
Evernden, Margery, *5:* 65
Ewen, David, *4:* 78
Ewing, Juliana (Horatia Gatty),
    16: 90
Ewing, Kathryn, *20:* 42
Eyerly, Jeannette Hyde, *4:* 80

Fabe, Maxene, *15:* 103
Faber, Doris, *3:* 67
Faber, Harold, *5:* 65
Fabre, Jean Henri (Casimir),
    22: 102
Facklam, Margery Metz, *20:* 43
Fadiman, Clifton (Paul), *11:* 91

Fair, Sylvia, *13:* 33
Fairfax-Lucy, Brian, *6:* 73
Fairman, Joan A(lexandra), *10:* 41
Faithfull, Gail, *8:* 55
Falconer, James. *See* Kirkup,
    James, *12:* 120
Falkner, Leonard, *12:* 80
Fall, Thomas. *See* Snow, Donald
    Clifford, *16:* 246
Fanning, Leonard M(ulliken), *5:* 65
Faralla, Dana, *9:* 62
Faralla, Dorothy W. *See* Faralla,
    Dana, *9:* 62
Farb, Peter, *12:* 81; *22:* 109
    (Obituary)
Farjeon, (Eve) Annabel, *11:* 93
Farjeon, Eleanor, *2:* 103
Farley, Carol, *4:* 81
Farley, Walter, *2:* 106
Farnham, Burt. *See* Clifford,
    Harold B., *10:* 24
Farquhar, Margaret C(utting),
    13: 35
Farr, Finis (King), *10:* 41
Farrell, Ben. *See* Cebulash, Mel,
    10: 19
Farrington, Benjamin, *20:* 45
    (Obituary)
Farrington, Selwyn Kip, Jr., *20:* 45
Fassler, Joan (Grace), *11:* 94
Fast, Howard, *7:* 80
Fatchen, Max, *20:* 45
Father Xavier. *See* Hurwood,
    Bernhardt J., *12:* 107
Fatio, Louise, *6:* 75
Faulhaber, Martha, *7:* 82
Feagles, Anita MacRae, *9:* 63
Feague, Mildred H., *14:* 59
Fecher, Constance, *7:* 83
Feelings, Muriel (Grey), *16:* 104
Feelings, Thomas, *8:* 55
Feelings, Tom. *See* Feelings,
    Thomas, *8:* 55
Feiffer, Jules, *8:* 57
Feil, Hila, *12:* 81
Feilen, John. *See* May, Julian,
    11: 175
Feldman, Anne (Rodgers), *19:* 121
Fellows, Muriel H., *10:* 41
Felsen, Henry Gregor, *1:* 89
Felton, Harold William, *1:* 90
Felton, Ronald Oliver, *3:* 67
Fenner, Carol, *7:* 84
Fenner, Phyllis R(eid), *1:* 91
Fenten, D. X., *4:* 82
Fenton, Carroll Lane, *5:* 66
Fenton, Edward, *7:* 86
Fenton, Mildred Adams, *21:* 38
Feravolo, Rocco Vincent, *10:* 42
Ferber, Edna, *7:* 87
Ferguson, Bob. *See* Ferguson,
    Robert Bruce, *13:* 35
Ferguson, Robert Bruce, *13:* 35
Fergusson, Erna, *5:* 67
Fermi, Laura, *6:* 78
Fern, Eugene A., *10:* 43

Ferris, Helen Josephine, *21:* 39
Ferris, James Cody [Collective pseudonym], *1:* 92
Fiammenghi, Gioia, *9:* 64
Fiarotta, Noel, *15:* 104
Fiarotta, Phyllis, *15:* 105
Fichter, George S., *7:* 92
Fidler, Kathleen, *3:* 68
Fiedler, Jean, *4:* 83
Field, Edward, *8:* 58
Field, Eugene, *16:* 105
Field, Rachel (Lyman), *15:* 106
Fife, Dale (Odile), *18:* 110
Fighter Pilot, A. *See* Johnston, H(ugh) A(nthony) S(tephen), *14:* 87
Figueroa, Pablo, *9:* 66
Fijan, Carol, *12:* 82
Fillmore, Parker H(oysted), *YABC 1:* 121
Fink, William B(ertrand), *22:* 109
Finkel, George (Irvine), *8:* 59
Finlayson, Ann, *8:* 61
Firmin, Peter, *15:* 113
Fischbach, Julius, *10:* 43
Fisher, Aileen (Lucia), *1:* 92
Fisher, Dorothy Canfield, *YABC 1:* 122
Fisher, John (Oswald Hamilton), *15:* 115
Fisher, Laura Harrison, *5:* 67
Fisher, Leonard Everett, *4:* 84
Fisher, Margery (Turner), *20:* 47
Fitch, Clarke. *See* Sinclair, Upton (Beall), *9:* 168
Fitch, John, IV. *See* Cormier, Robert Edmund, *10:* 28
Fitschen, Dale, *20:* 48
Fitzgerald, Captain Hugh. *See* Baum L(yman) Frank, *18:* 7
Fitzgerald, Edward Earl, *20:* 49
Fitzgerald, F(rancis) A(nthony), *15:* 115
Fitzgerald, John D(ennis), *20:* 50
Fitzhardinge, Joan Margaret, *2:* 107
Fitzhugh, Louise, *1:* 94
Flack, Marjorie, *YABC 2:* 123
Flash Flood. *See* Robinson, Jan M., *6:* 194
Fleischman, (Albert) Sid(ney), *8:* 61
Fleming, Alice Mulcahey, *9:* 67
Fleming, Ian (Lancaster), *9:* 67
Fleming, Thomas J(ames), *8:* 64
Fletcher, Charlie May, *3:* 70
Fletcher, Helen Jill, *13:* 36
Flexner, James Thomas, *9:* 70
Flitner, David P., *7:* 92
Floethe, Louise Lee, *4:* 87
Floethe, Richard, *4:* 89
Flood, Flash. *See* Robinson, Jan M., *6:* 194
Flora, James (Royer), *1:* 95
Florian, Douglas, *19:* 122
Flory, Jane Trescott, *22:* 110
Flynn, Barbara, *9:* 71

Flynn, Jackson. *See* Shirreffs, Gordon D., *11:* 207
Folsom, Franklin (Brewster), *5:* 67
Fooner, Michael, *22:* 112
Forberg, Ati, *22:* 113
Forbes, Esther, *2:* 108
Forbes, Graham B. [Collective pseudonym], *1:* 97
Forbes, Kathryn. *See* McLean, Kathryn (Anderson), *9:* 140
Ford, Albert Lee. *See* Stratemeyer, Edward L., *1:* 208
Ford, Elbur. *See* Hibbert, Eleanor, *2:* 134
Ford, Hildegarde. *See* Morrison, Velma Ford, *21:* 110
Ford, Marcia. *See* Radford, Ruby L., *6:* 186
Foreman, Michael, *2:* 110
Forester, C(ecil) S(cott), *13:* 38
Forman, Brenda, *4:* 90
Forman, James Douglas, *8:* 64
Forrest, Sybil. *See* Markun, Patricia M(aloney), *15:* 189
Forsee, (Frances) Aylesa, *1:* 97
Foster, Doris Van Liew, *10:* 44
Foster, E(lizabeth) C(onnell), *9:* 71
Foster, Elizabeth, *10:* 45
Foster, Elizabeth Vincent, *12:* 82
Foster, F. Blanche, *11:* 95
Foster, Genevieve (Stump), *2:* 111
Foster, John T(homas), *8:* 65
Foster, Laura Louise, *6:* 78
Foster, Margaret Lesser, *21:* 43 (Obituary)
Fourth Brother, The. *See* Aung, (Maung) Htin, *21:* 5
Fowke, Edith (Margaret), *14:* 59
Fowles, John, *22:* 114
Fox, Charles Philip, *12:* 83
Fox, Eleanor. *See* St. John, Wylly Folk, *10:* 132
Fox, Freeman. *See* Hamilton, Charles Harold St. John, *13:* 77
Fox, Lorraine, *11:* 96
Fox, Michael Wilson, *15:* 117
Fox, Paula, *17:* 59
Frances, Miss. *See* Horwich, Frances R., *11:* 142
Franchere, Ruth, *18:* 111
Francis, Dorothy Brenner, *10:* 46
Francis, Pamela (Mary), *11:* 97
Francoise. *See* Seignobosc, Francoise, *21:* 145
Frank, Josette, *10:* 47
Frankau, Mary Evelyn, *4:* 90
Frankel, Bernice, *9:* 72
Frankenberg, Robert, *22:* 115
Franklin, Harold, *13:* 53
Franklin, Steve. *See* Stevens, Franklin, *6:* 206
Franzén, Nils-Olof, *10:* 47
Frasconi, Antonio, *6:* 79
Frazier, Neta Lohnes, *7:* 94
Freed, Alvyn M., *22:* 117
Freedman, Russell (Bruce), *16:* 115

Freeman, Don, *17:* 60
Freeman, Ira M(aximilian), *21:* 43
French, Allen, *YABC 1:* 133
French, Dorothy Kayser, *5:* 69
French, Fiona, *6:* 81
French, Paul. *See* Asimov, Isaac, *1:* 15
Frewer, Glyn, *11:* 98
Frick, C. H. *See* Irwin, Constance Frick, *6:* 119
Frick, Constance. *See* Irwin, Constance Frick, *6:* 119
Friedlander, Joanne K(ohn), *9:* 73
Friedman, Estelle, *7:* 95
Friendlich, Dick. *See* Friendlich, Richard, *11:* 99
Friendlich, Richard J., *11:* 99
Friermood, Elisabeth Hamilton, *5:* 69
Friis, Babbis. *See* Friis-Baastad, Babbis, *7:* 95
Friis-Baastad, Babbis, *7:* 95
Friskey, Margaret Richards, *5:* 72
Fritz, Jean (Guttery), *1:* 98
Froman, Elizabeth Hull, *10:* 49
Froman, Robert (Winslow), *8:* 67
Frost, A(rthur) B(urdett), *19:* 122
Frost, Erica. *See* Supraner, Robyn, *20:* 182
Frost, Lesley, *14:* 61
Frost, Robert (Lee), *14:* 63
Fry, Rosalie, *3:* 71
Fuchs, Erich, *6:* 84
Fujita, Tamao, *7:* 98
Fujiwara, Michiko, *15:* 120
Fuller, Catherine L(euthold), *9:* 73
Fuller, Edmund (Maybank), *21:* 45
Fuller, Iola. *See* McCoy, Iola Fuller, *3:* 120
Fuller, Lois Hamilton, *11:* 99
Funk, Thompson. *See* Funk, Tom, *7:* 98
Funk, Tom, *7:* 98
Funke, Lewis, *11:* 100
Fyleman, Rose, *21:* 46

Gaeddert, Lou Ann (Bigge), *20:* 58
Gág, Wanda (Hazel), *YABC 1:* 135
Gage, Wilson. *See* Steele, Mary Q., *3:* 211
Gagliardo, Ruth Garver, *22:* 118 (Obituary)
Galdone, Paul, *17:* 69
Gallant, Roy (Arthur), *4:* 91
Gallico, Paul, *13:* 53
Galt, Thomas Franklin, Jr., *5:* 72
Galt, Tom. *See* Galt, Thomas Franklin, Jr., *5:* 72
Gamerman, Martha, *15:* 121
Gannett, Ruth Stiles, *3:* 73
Gannon, Robert (Haines), *8:* 68
Gantos, Jack. *See* Gantos, John (Bryan), Jr., *20:* 59
Gantos, John (Bryan), Jr., *20:* 59

Green, Morton, *8:* 71
Green, Norma B(erger), *11:* 120
Green, Phyllis, *20:* 65
Green, Roger (Gilbert) Lancelyn, *2:* 123
Green, Sheila Ellen, *8:* 72
Greenaway, Kate, *YABC 2:* 129
Greenberg, Harvey R., *5:* 77
Greene, Bette, *8:* 73
Greene, Carla, *1:* 108
Greene, Constance C(larke), *11:* 121
Greene, Graham, *20:* 66
Greene, Wade, *11:* 122
Greenfeld, Howard, *19:* 140
Greenfield, Eloise, *19:* 141
Greening, Hamilton. *See* Hamilton, Charles Harold St. John, *13:* 77
Greenleaf, Barbara Kaye, *6:* 95
Greenwald, Sheila. *See* Green, Sheila Ellen, *8:* 72
Gregg, Walter H(arold), *20:* 75
Gregori, Leon, *15:* 129
Grendon, Stephen. *See* Derleth, August (William), *5:* 54
Grenville, Pelham. *See* Wodehouse, P(elham) G(renville), *22:* 241
Gretz, Susanna, *7:* 114
Gretzer, John, *18:* 117
Grey, Jerry, *11:* 123
Grice, Frederick, *6:* 96
Grieder, Walter, *9:* 83
Griese, Arnold A(lfred), *9:* 84
Grifalconi, Ann, *2:* 125
Griffith, Jeannette. *See* Eyerly, Jeanette, *4:* 80
Griffiths, G(ordon) D(ouglas), *20:* 75 (Obituary)
Griffiths, Helen, *5:* 77
Grimm, Jacob Ludwig Karl, *22:* 126
Grimm, Wilhelm Karl, *22:* 126
Grimm, William C(arey), *14:* 75
Grimsley, Gordon. *See* Groom, Arthur William, *10:* 53
Gringhuis, Dirk. *See* Gringhuis, Richard H. *6:* 97
Gringhuis, Richard H., *6:* 97
Grinnell, George Bird, *16:* 121
Gripe, Maria (Kristina), *2:* 126
Grohskopf, Bernice, *7:* 114
Grol, Lini Richards, *9:* 85
Grollman, Earl A., *22:* 152
Groom, Arthur William, *10:* 53
Gross, Sarah Chokla, *9:* 86
Grossman, Robert, *11:* 124
Groth, John, *21:* 53
Gruenberg, Sidonie M(atsner), *2:* 127
Gugliotta, Bobette, *7:* 116
Guillaume, Jeanette G. (Flierl), *8:* 74
Guillot, Rene, *7:* 117
Gunston, Bill. *See* Gunston, William Tudor, *9:* 88
Gunston, William Tudor, *9:* 88

Gunther, John, *2:* 129
Gurko, Leo, *9:* 88
Gurko, Miriam, *9:* 89
Gustafson, Sarah R. *See* Riedman, Sarah R., *1:* 183
Guy, Rosa (Cuthbert), *14:* 77

Haas, Irene, *17:* 76
Habenstreit, Barbara, *5:* 78
Haber, Louis, *12:* 90
Hader, Berta (Hoerner), *16:* 122
Hader, Elmer (Stanley), *16:* 124
Hadley, Franklin. *See* Winterbotham, R(ussell) R(obert), *10:* 198
Hafner, Marylin, *7:* 119
Haggard, H(enry) Rider, *16:* 129
Haggerty, James J(oseph) *5:* 78
Hagon, Priscilla. *See* Allan, Mabel Esther, *5:* 2
Hahn, Emily, *3:* 81
Hahn, Hannelore, *8:* 74
Hahn, James (Sage), *9:* 90
Hahn, (Mona) Lynn, *9:* 91
Haig-Brown, Roderick (Langmere), *12:* 90
Haines, Gail Kay, *11:* 124
Haining, Peter, *14:* 77
Haldane, Roger John, *13:* 75
Hale, Edward Everett, *16:* 143
Hale, Helen. *See* Mulcahy, Lucille Burnett, *12:* 155
Hale, Kathleen, *17:* 78
Hale, Linda, *6:* 99
Hall, Adele, *7:* 120
Hall, Anna Gertrude, *8:* 75
Hall, Elvajean, *6:* 100
Hall, James Norman, *21:* 54
Hall, Jesse. *See* Boesen, Victor, *16:* 53
Hall, Lynn, *2:* 130
Hall, Malcolm, *7:* 121
Hall, Marjory. *See* Yeakley, Marjory Hall, *21:* 207
Hallard, Peter. *See* Catherall, Arthur, *3:* 38
Hallas, Richard. *See* Knight, Eric (Mowbray), *18:* 151
Halliburton, Warren J., *19:* 143
Hallin, Emily Watson, *6:* 101
Hall-Quest, Olga W(ilbourne), *11:* 125
Hallstead, William F(inn) III, *11:* 126
Hallward, Michael, *12:* 91
Halsell, Grace, *13:* 76
Halter, Jon C(harles), *22:* 152
Hamberger, John, *14:* 79
Hamil, Thomas Arthur, *14:* 80
Hamil, Tom. *See* Hamil, Thomas Arthur, *14:* 80
Hamilton, Charles Harold St. John, *13:* 77

Hamilton, Clive. *See* Lewis, C. S., *13:* 129
Hamilton, Dorothy, *12:* 92
Hamilton, Edith, *20:* 75
Hamilton, Robert W. *See* Stratemeyer, Edward L., *1:* 208
Hamilton, Virginia, *4:* 97
Hammer, Richard, *6:* 102
Hammerman, Gay M(orenus), *9:* 92
Hammontree, Marie (Gertrude), *13:* 89
Hampson, (Richard) Denman, *15:* 129
Hamre, Leif, *5:* 79
Hancock, Sibyl, *9:* 92
Hane, Roger, *20:* 79 (Obituary)
Hanff, Helene, *11:* 128
Hanlon, Emily, *15:* 131
Hann, Jacquie, *19:* 144
Hanna, Paul R(obert), *9:* 93
Hano, Arnold, *12:* 93
Hanser, Richard (Frederick), *13:* 90
Hanson, Joan, *8:* 75
Harald, Eric. *See* Boesen, Victor, *16:* 53
Hardwick, Richard Holmes Jr., *12:* 94
Hardy, Alice Dale [Collective pseudonym], *1:* 109
Hardy, David A(ndrews), *9:* 95
Hardy, Stuart. *See* Schisgall, Oscar, *12:* 187
Hark, Mildred. *See* McQueen, Mildred Hark, *12:* 145
Harkaway, Hal. *See* Stratemeyer, Edward L., *1:* 208
Harkins, Philip, *6:* 102
Harlan, Glen. *See* Cebulash, Mel, *10:* 19
Harmelink, Barbara (Mary), *9:* 97
Harmon, Margaret, *20:* 80
Harnan, Terry, *12:* 94
Harnett, Cynthia (Mary), *5:* 79
Harper, Wilhelmina, *4:* 99
Harrington, Lyn, *5:* 80
Harris, Christie, *6:* 103
Harris, Colver. *See* Colver, Anne, *7:* 54
Harris, Dorothy Joan, *13:* 91
Harris, Janet, *4:* 100
Harris, Joel Chandler, *YABC 1:* 154
Harris, Leon A., Jr., *4:* 101
Harris, Lorle K(empe), *22:* 153
Harris, Rosemary (Jeanne), *4:* 101
Harrison, Deloris, *9:* 97
Harrison, Harry, *4:* 102
Hartman, Louis F(rancis), *22:* 154
Hartshorn, Ruth M., *11:* 129
Harwin, Brian. *See* Henderson, LeGrand, *9:* 104
Harwood, Pearl Augusta (Bragdon), *9:* 98
Haskell, Arnold, *6:* 104
Haskins, James, *9:* 100

Jefferies, (John) Richard, *16:* 168
Jeffers, Susan, *17:* 86
Jefferson, Sarah. *See* Farjeon,
  Annabel, *11:* 93
Jeffries, Roderic, *4:* 129
Jenkins, Marie M., *7:* 143
Jenkins, William A(twell), *9:* 115
Jennings, Gary (Gayne), *9:* 115
Jennings, Robert. *See* Hamilton,
  Charles Harold St. John, *13:* 77
Jennings, S. M. *See* Meyer, Jerome
  Sydney, *3:* 129
Jennison, C. S. *See* Starbird, Kaye,
  6: 204
Jennison, Keith Warren, *14:* 86
Jensen, Virginia Allen, *8:* 90
Jewett, Eleanore Myers, *5:* 90
Jewett, Sarah Orne, *15:* 144
Johns, Avery. *See* Cousins,
  Margaret, *2:* 79
Johnson, A. E. [Joint pseudonym]
  See Johnson, Annabell and
  Edgar, *2:* 156, 157
Johnson, Annabell Jones, *2:* 156
Johnson, Charles R., *11:* 146
Johnson, Chuck. *See* Johnson,
  Charles R., *11:* 146
Johnson, Crockett. *See* Leisk,
  David Johnson, *1:* 141
Johnson, Dorothy M., *6:* 123
Johnson, Edgar Raymond, *2:* 157
Johnson, Elizabeth, *7:* 144
Johnson, Eric W(arner), *8:* 91
Johnson, Evelyne, *20:* 95
Johnson, Gaylord, *7:* 146
Johnson, Gerald White, *19:* 166
Johnson, James Ralph, *1:* 126
Johnson, LaVerne B(ravo), *13:* 108
Johnson, Lois S(mith), *6:* 123
Johnson, Lois W(alfrid), *22:* 165
Johnson, of Boone, Benj. F. *See*
  Riley, James Whitcomb,
  17: 159
Johnson, (Walter) Ryerson, *10:* 58
Johnson, Shirley K(ing), *10:* 59
Johnson, Siddie Joe, *20:* 95
  (Obituary)
Johnson, William Weber, *7:* 147
Johnston, Agnes Christine. *See*
  Dazey, Agnes J., *2:* 88
Johnston, H(ugh) A(nthony)
  S(tephen), *14:* 87
Johnston, Johanna, *12:* 115
Johnston, Portia. *See* Takakjian,
  Portia, *15:* 273
Johnston, Tony, *8:* 94
Jones, Adrienne, *7:* 147
Jones, Diana Wynne, *9:* 116
Jones, Elizabeth Orton, *18:* 123
Jones, Evan, *3:* 90
Jones, Gillingham. *See* Hamilton,
  Charles Harold St. John, *13:* 77
Jones, Harold, *14:* 87
Jones, Helen L., *22:* 167 (Obituary)
Jones, Hortense P., *9:* 118
Jones, Mary Alice, *6:* 125

Jones, Weyman, *4:* 130
Jonk, Clarence, *10:* 59
Jordan, Hope (Dahle), *15:* 150
Jordan, June, *4:* 131
Jordan, Mildred, *5:* 91
Jorgenson, Ivar. *See* Silverberg,
  Robert, *13:* 206
Joseph, Joseph M(aron), *22:* 167
Joslin, Sesyle, *2:* 158
Joyce, J(ames) Avery, *11:* 147
Jucker, Sita, *5:* 92
Judd, Frances K. [Collective
  pseudonym], *1:* 127
Jumpp, Hugo. *See* MacPeek,
  Walter G., *4:* 148
Jupo, Frank J., *7:* 148
Juster, Norton, *3:* 91
Justus, May, *1:* 127

Kabdebo, Tamas. *See* Kabdebo,
  Thomas, *10:* 60
Kabdebo, Thomas, *10:* 60
Kakimoto, Kozo, *11:* 147
Kalashnikoff, Nicholas, *16:* 173
Kaler, James Otis, *15:* 151
Kalnay, Francis, *7:* 149
Kamen, Gloria, *9:* 118
Kane, Henry Bugbee, *14:* 91
Kane, Robert W., *18:* 131
Kaplan, Bess, *22:* 168
Kaplan, Irma, *10:* 61
Kaplan, Jean Caryl Korn, *10:* 62
Karen, Ruth, *9:* 120
Kark, Nina Mary, *4:* 132
Karlin, Eugene, *10:* 62
Karp, Naomi J., *16:* 174
Kashiwagi, Isami, *10:* 64
Kästner, Erich, *14:* 91
Katchen, Carole, *9:* 122
Kathryn. *See* Searle, Kathryn
  Adrienne, *10:* 143
Katona, Robert, *21:* 84
Katz, Bobbi, *12:* 116
Katz, Fred, *6:* 126
Katz, William Loren, *13:* 109
Kaufman, Mervyn D., *4:* 133
Kaufmann, Angelika, *15:* 155
Kaufmann, John, *18:* 132
Kaula, Edna Mason, *13:* 110
Kay, Helen. *See* Goldfrank, Helen
  Colodny, *6:* 89
Kay, Mara, *13:* 111
Kaye, Geraldine, *10:* 64
Keane, Bil, *4:* 134
Keating, Bern. *See* Keating, Leo
  Bernard, *10:* 65
Keating, Leo Bernard, *10:* 65
Keats, Ezra Jack, *14:* 99
Keegan, Marcia, *9:* 121
Keen, Martin L., *4:* 135
Keene, Carolyn. *See* Adams,
  Harriet S., *1:* 1
Keeping, Charles (William James),
  9: 123

Keir, Christine. *See* Pullein-
  Thompson, Christine, *3:* 164
Keith, Carlton. *See* Robertson,
  Keith, *1:* 184
Keith, Harold (Verne), *2:* 159
Kelen, Emery, *13:* 114
Keller, B(everly) L(ou), *13:* 115
Keller, Charles, *8:* 94
Keller, Gail Faithfull. *See* Faithfull,
  Gail, *8:* 55
Kellin, Sally Moffet, *9:* 125
Kellogg, Gene. *See* Kellogg, Jean,
  10: 66
Kellogg, Jean, *10:* 66
Kellogg, Steven, *8:* 95
Kellow, Kathleen. *See* Hibbert,
  Eleanor, *2:* 134
Kelly, Eric P(hilbrook),
  YABC 1: 165
Kelly, Ralph. *See* Geis, Darlene,
  7: 101
Kelly, Regina Z., *5:* 94
Kelly, Walt(er Crawford), *18:* 135
Kelsey, Alice Geer, *1:* 129
Kempner, Mary Jean, *10:* 67
Kempton, Jean Welch, *10:* 67
Kendall, Carol (Seeger), *11:* 148
Kendall, Lace. *See* Stoutenburg,
  Adrien, *3:* 217
Kennedy, John Fitzgerald, *11:* 150
Kennedy, Joseph, *14:* 104
Kennedy, (Jerome) Richard,
  22: 169
Kennedy, X. J. *See* Kennedy,
  Joseph, *14:* 104
Kennell, Ruth E., *6:* 127
Kenny, Herbert A(ndrew), *13:* 117
Kent, Margaret, *2:* 161
Kent, Rockwell, *6:* 128
Kent, Sherman, *20:* 96
Kenworthy, Leonard S., *6:* 131
Kenyon, Ley, *6:* 131
Kepes, Juliet A(ppleby), *13:* 118
Kerigan, Florence, *12:* 117
Kerman, Gertrude Lerner, *21:* 85
Kerr, Jessica, *13:* 119
Kerr, M. E. *See* Meaker, Marijane,
  20: 124
Kerry, Frances. *See* Kerigan,
  Florence, *12:* 117
Kerry, Lois. *See* Arquette, Lois S.,
  1: 13
Ker Wilson, Barbara, *20:* 97
Kessler, Leonard P., *14:* 106
Kesteven, G. R. *See* Crosher,
  G(eoffry) R(obins), *14:* 51
Kettelkamp, Larry, *2:* 163
Key, Alexander (Hill), *8:* 98
Khanshendel, Chiron. *See* Rose,
  Wendy, *12:* 180
Kherdian, David, *16:* 175
Kiddell, John, *3:* 93
Kiefer, Irene, *21:* 87
Killilea, Marie (Lyons), *2:* 165
Kilreon, Beth. *See* Walker, Barbara
  K., *4:* 219

Miller, John. *See* Samachson, Joseph, *3:* 182

Miller, Mary Beth, *9:* 145

Milne, A(lan) A(lexander), *YABC 1:* 174

Milne, Lorus J., *5:* 133

Milne, Margery, *5:* 134

Milotte, Alfred G(eorge), *11:* 181

Minarik, Else Holmelund, *15:* 197

Miner, Lewis S., *11:* 183

Minier, Nelson. *See* Stoutenburg, Adrien, *3:* 217

Mintonye, Grace, *4:* 156

Mirsky, Jeannette, *8:* 135

Mirsky, Reba Paeff, *1:* 161

Miskovits, Christine, *10:* 98

Miss Francis. *See* Horwich, Francis R., *11:* 142

Miss Read. *See* Saint, Dora Jessie, *10:* 132

Mitchell, (Sibyl) Elyne (Keith), *10:* 98

Mizumura, Kazue, *18:* 222

Moe, Barbara, *20:* 126

Moffett, Martha (Leatherwood), *8:* 136

Mohn, Viola Kohl, *8:* 138

Mohr, Nicholasa, *8:* 138

Molarsky, Osmond, *16:* 204

Molloy, Paul, *5:* 135

Monjo, F(erdinand) N., *16:* 206

Monroe, Lyle. *See* Heinlein, Robert A(nson), *9:* 102

Montana, Bob, *21:* 110(Obituary)

Montgomery, Constance. *See* Cappell, Constance, *22:* 65

Montgomery, Elizabeth Rider, *3:* 132

Montgomery, L(ucy) M(aud), *YABC 1:* 182

Montgomery, Rutherford George, *3:* 134

Montresor, Beni, *3:* 136

Moody, Ralph Owen, *1:* 162

Moon, Sheila (Elizabeth), *5:* 136

Moore, Anne Carroll, *13:* 158

Moore, Clement Clarke, *18:* 224

Moore, Eva, *20:* 127

Moore, Fenworth. *See* Stratemeyer, Edward L., *1:* 208

Moore, Janet Gaylord, *18:* 236

Moore, John Travers, *12:* 151

Moore, Margaret Rumberger, *12:* 154

Moore, Marianne (Craig), *20:* 128

Moore, Regina. *See* Dunne, Mary Collins, *11:* 83

Moore, Rosalie. *See* Brown, Rosalie (Gertrude) Moore, *9:* 26

Mordvinoff, Nicolas, *17:* 129

More, Caroline. *See* Cone, Molly Lamken, *1:* 66

More, Caroline. *See* Strachan, Margaret Pitcairn, *14:* 193

Morey, Charles. *See* Fletcher, Helen Jill, *13:* 36

Morey, Walt. *3:* 139

Morgan, Jane. *See* Cooper, James Fenimore, *19:* 68

Morgan, Lenore, *8:* 139

Morgan, Shirley, *10:* 99

Morrah, Dave. *See* Morrah, David Wardlaw, Jr., *10:* 100

Morrah, David Wardlaw, Jr., *10:* 100

Morris, Desmond (John), *14:* 146

Morris, Robert A., *7:* 166

Morrison, Gert W. *See* Stratemeyer, Edward L., *1:* 208

Morrison, Lillian, *3:* 140

Morrison, Lucile Phillips, *17:* 134

Morrison, Velma Ford, *21:* 110

Morrison, William. *See* Samachson, Joseph, *3:* 182

Morriss, James E(dward), *8:* 139

Morrow, Betty. *See* Bacon, Elizabeth, *3:* 14

Morse, Carol. *See* Yeakley, Marjory Hall, *21:* 207

Morton, Miriam, *9:* 145

Moscow, Alvin, *3:* 142

Mosel, Arlene, *7:* 167

Moss, Don(ald), *11:* 183

Motz, Lloyd, *20:* 133

Mountfield, David. *See* Grant, Neil, *14:* 75

Mowat, Farley, *3:* 142

Mulcahy, Lucille Burnett, *12:* 155

Muller, Billex. *See* Ellis, Edward S(ylvester), *YABC 1:* 116

Mullins, Edward S(wift), *10:* 101

Mulvihill, William Patrick, *8:* 140

Mun. *See* Leaf, (Wilbur) Munro, *20:* 99

Munari, Bruno, *15:* 199

Munce, Ruth Hill, *12:* 156

Munowitz, Ken, *14:* 149

Munson(-Benson), Tunie, *15:* 201

Munzer, Martha E., *4:* 157

Murphy, Barbara Beasley, *5:* 137

Murphy, E(mmett) Jefferson, *4:* 159

Murphy, Pat. *See* Murphy, E(mmett) Jefferson, *4:* 159

Murphy, Robert (William), *10:* 102

Murray, Marian, *5:* 138

Murray, Michele, *7:* 170

Musgrave, Florence, *3:* 144

Mussey, Virginia T. H. *See* Ellison, Virginia Howell, *4:* 74

Mutz. *See* Kunstler, Morton, *10:* 73

Myers, Bernice, *9:* 146

Myers, Hortense (Powner), *10:* 102

Nash, Linell. *See* Smith, Linell Nash, *2:* 227

Nash, (Fredric) Ogden, *2:* 194

Nast, Elsa Ruth. *See* Watson, Jane Werner, *3:* 244

Nathan, Dorothy (Goldeen), *15:* 202

Nathan, Robert, *6:* 171

Navarra, John Gabriel, *8:* 141

Naylor, Penelope, *10:* 104

Naylor, Phyllis Reynolds, *12:* 156

Nazaroff, Alexander I., *4:* 160

Neal, Harry Edward, *5:* 139

Nee, Kay Bonner, *10:* 104

Needleman, Jacob, *6:* 172

Negri, Rocco, *12:* 157

Neigoff, Anne, *13:* 165

Neigoff, Mike, *13:* 166

Neilson, Frances Fullerton (Jones), *14:* 149

Neimark, Anne E., *4:* 160

Nelson, Esther L., *13:* 167

Nesbit, E(dith), *YABC 1:* 193

Nesbit, Troy. *See* Folsom, Franklin, *5:* 67

Nespojohn, Katherine V., *7:* 170

Ness, Evaline (Michelow), *1:* 165

Neufeld, John, *6:* 173

Neumeyer, Peter F(lorian), *13:* 168

Neurath, Marie (Reidemeister), *1:* 166

Neville, Emily Cheney, *1:* 169

Neville, Mary. *See* Woodrich, Mary Neville, *2:* 274

Nevins, Albert J., *20:* 134

Newberry, Clare Turlay, *1:* 170

Newbery, John, *20:* 135

Newell, Edythe W., *11:* 185

Newlon, Clarke, *6:* 174

Newman, Robert (Howard), *4:* 161

Newman, Shirlee Petkin, *10:* 105

Newton, Suzanne, *5:* 140

Nic Leodhas, Sorche. *See* Alger, Leclaire (Gowans), *15:* 1

Nichols, Cecilia Fawn, *12:* 159

Nichols, (Joanna) Ruth, *15:* 204

Nickelsburg, Janet, *11:* 185

Nickerson, Betty. *See* Nickerson, Elizabeth, *14:* 150

Nickerson, Elizabeth, *14:* 150

Nicol, Ann. *See* Turnbull, Ann (Christine), *18:* 281

Nicolas. *See* Mordvinoff, Nicolas, *17:* 129

Nicolay, Helen, *YABC 1:* 204

Nicole, Christopher Robin, *5:* 141

Nielsen, Kay (Rasmus), *16:* 210

Nielsen, Virginia. *See* McCall, Virginia Nielsen, *13:* 151

Nixon, Joan Lowery, *8:* 143

Nixon, K. *See* Nixon, Kathleen Irene (Blundell), *14:* 152

Nixon, Kathleen Irene (Blundell), *14:* 152

Noble, Iris, *5:* 142

Nodset, Joan M. *See* Lexau, Joan M., *1:* 144

Nolan, Jeannette Covert, *2:* 196

Noonan, Julia, *4:* 163

Norcross, John. *See* Conroy, Jack (Wesley), *19:* 65

Nordstrom, Ursula, *3:* 144

Smith, Mike. *See* Smith, Mary Ellen, *10:* 152

Smith, Nancy Covert, *12:* 204

Smith, Norman F., *5:* 172

Smith, Robert Kimmel, *12:* 205

Smith, Ruth Leslie, *2:* 228

Smith, Sarah Stafford. *See* Smith, Dorothy Stafford, *6:* 201

Smith, Susan Carlton, *12:* 207

Smith, Vian (Crocker), *11:* 213

Smith, William A., *10:* 153

Smith, William Jay, *2:* 229

Smith, Z. Z. *See* Westheimer, David, *14:* 242

Snedeker, Caroline Dale (Parke), *YABC 2:* 296

Sneve, Virginia Driving Hawk, *8:* 193

Sniff, Mr. *See* Abisch, Roslyn Kroop, *9:* 3

Snodgrass, Thomas Jefferson. *See* Clemens, Samuel Langhorne, *YABC 2:* 51

Snow, Donald Clifford, *16:* 246

Snow, Dorothea J(ohnston), *9:* 172

Snyder, Anne, *4:* 195

Snyder, Jerome, *20:* 171 (Obituary)

Snyder, Zilpha Keatley, *1:* 202

Snyderman, Reuven K., *5:* 173

Sobol, Donald J., *1:* 203

Soderlind, Arthur E(dwin), *14:* 183

Softly, Barbara (Frewin), *12:* 209

Sohl, Frederic J(ohn), *10:* 154

Solbert, Romaine G., *2:* 232

Solbert, Ronni. *See* Solbert, Romaine G., *2:* 232

Solonevich, George, *15:* 245

Solot, Mary Lynn, *12:* 210

Sommer, Elyse, *7:* 192

Sommer, Robert, *12:* 211

Sommerfelt, Aimee, *5:* 173

Sonneborn, Ruth, *4:* 196

Sorche, Nic Leodhas. *See* Alger, Leclaire (Gowans), *15:* 1

Sorensen, Virginia, *2:* 233

Sorrentino, Joseph N., *6:* 203

Sortor, June Elizabeth, *12:* 212

Sortor, Toni. *See* Sortor, June Elizabeth, *12:* 212

Soskin, V. H. *See* Ellison, Virginia Howell, *4:* 74

Sotomayor, Antonio, *11:* 214

Soudley, Henry. *See* Wood, James Playsted, *1:* 229

Soule, Gardner (Bosworth), *14:* 183

Soule, Jean Conder, *10:* 154

Southall, Ivan, *3:* 210

Spanfeller, James J(ohn), *19:* 230

Spangenberg, Judith Dunn, *5:* 175

Spar, Jerome, *10:* 156

Sparks, Mary W., *15:* 247

Spaulding, Leonard. *See* Bradbury, Ray, *11:* 29

Speare, Elizabeth George, *5:* 176

Spearing, Judith (Mary Harlow), *9:* 173

Specking, Inez, *11:* 217

Speicher, Helen Ross (Smith), *8:* 194

Spellman, John W(illard), *14:* 186

Spence, Eleanor (Rachel), *21:* 163

Spencer, Ann, *10:* 156

Spencer, Cornelia. *See* Yaukey, Grace S. *5:* 203

Spencer, Elizabeth, *14:* 186

Spencer, William, *9:* 175

Sperry, Armstrong W., *1:* 204

Sperry, Raymond, Jr. [Collective pseudonym], *1:* 205

Spiegelman, Judith M., *5:* 179

Spier, Peter (Edward), *4:* 198

Spilhaus, Athelstan, *13:* 209

Spilka, Arnold, *6:* 203

Spink, Reginald (William), *11:* 217

Spinossimus. *See* White, William, *16:* 276

Spollen, Christopher, *12:* 213

Sprigge, Elizabeth, *10:* 157

Spykman, E(lizabeth) C., *10:* 157

Spyri, Johanna (Heusser), *19:* 232

Squire, Miriam. *See* Sprigge, Elizabeth, *10:* 157

Squires, Phil. *See* Barker, S. Omar, *10:* 8

S-Ringi, Kjell. *See* Ringi, Kjell, *12:* 168

Stadtler, Bea, *17:* 215

Stafford, Jean, *22:* 218 (Obituary)

Stahl, Ben(jamin), *5:* 179

Stamaty, Mark Alan, *12:* 214

Stambler, Irwin, *5:* 181

Stanhope, Eric. *See* Hamilton, Charles Harold St. John, *13:* 77

Stankevich, Boris, *2:* 234

Stanley, Robert. *See* Hamilton, Charles Harold St. John, *13:* 77

Stanstead, John. *See* Groom, Arthur William, *10:* 53

Stapp, Arthur D(onald), *4:* 201

Starbird, Kaye, *6:* 204

Stark, James. *See* Goldston, Robert, *6:* 90

Starkey, Marion L., *13:* 211

Starret, William. *See* McClintock, Marshall, *3:* 119

Staunton, Schuyler. *See* Baum, L(yman) Frank, *18:* 7

Stearns, Monroe (Mather), *5:* 182

Steele, Chester K. *See* Stratemeyer, Edward L., *1:* 208

Steele, Mary Q., *3:* 211

Steele, (Henry) Max(well), *10:* 159

Steele, William O(wen), *1:* 205

Steig, William, *18:* 275

Stein, M(eyer) L(ewis), *6:* 205

Stein, Mini, *2:* 234

Steinbeck, John (Ernst), *9:* 176

Steinberg, Alfred, *9:* 178

Steinberg, Fred J., *4:* 201

Steiner, Barbara A(nnette), *13:* 213

Steiner, Stan(ley), *14:* 187

Stephens, Mary Jo, *8:* 196

Stephens, William M(cLain), *21:* 165

Steptoe, John (Lewis), *8:* 198

Sterling, Dorothy, *1:* 206

Sterling, Helen. *See* Hoke, Helen (L.), *15:* 133

Sterling, Philip, *8:* 198

Stern, Madeleine B(ettina), *14:* 188

Stern, Philip Van Doren, *13:* 215

Stern, Simon, *15:* 248

Sterne, Emma Gelders, *6:* 205

Steurt, Marjorie Rankin, *10:* 159

Stevens, Carla M(cBride), *13:* 217

Stevens, Franklin, *6:* 206

Stevens, Peter. *See* Geis, Darlene, *7:* 101

Stevenson, Anna (M.), *12:* 216

Stevenson, Augusta, *2:* 235

Stevenson, Janet, *8:* 199

Stevenson, Robert Louis, *YABC 2:* 307

Stewart, A(gnes) C(harlotte), *15:* 250

Stewart, Charles. *See* Zurhorst, Charles (Stewart, Jr.), *12:* 240

Stewart, Elizabeth Laing, *6:* 206

Stewart, John (William), *14:* 189

Stewart, George Rippey, *3:* 213

Stewart, Mary (Florence Elinor), *12:* 217

Stewart, Robert Neil, *7:* 192

Stiles, Martha Bennett, *6:* 207

Stillerman, Robbie, *12:* 219

Stine, G(eorge) Harry, *10:* 161

Stinetorf, Louise, *10:* 162

Stirling, Arthur. *See* Sinclair, Upton (Beall), *9:* 168

Stirling, Nora B., *3:* 214

Stirnweis, Shannon, *10:* 163

Stobbs, William, *17:* 216

Stoddard, Edward G., *10:* 164

Stoddard, Hope, *6:* 207

Stoddard, Sandol. *See* Warburg, Sandol Stoddard, *14:* 234

Stoiko, Michael, *14:* 190

Stokes, Cedric. *See* Beardmore, George, *20:* 10

Stokes, Jack (Tilden), *13:* 218

Stolz, Mary (Slattery), *10:* 165

Stone, Alan [Collective pseudonym], *1:* 208. *See also* Svenson, Andrew E., *2:* 238

Stone, D(avid) K(arl), *9:* 179

Stone, Eugenia, *7:* 193

Stone, Gene. *See* Stone, Eugenia, *7:* 193

Stone, Helen V., *6:* 208

Stone, Irving, *3:* 215

Stone, Raymond [Collective pseudonym], *1:* 208

Stone, Richard A. *See* Stratemeyer, Edward L., *1:* 208

Stonehouse, Bernard, *13:* 219

Storch, Anne B. von. *See* von Storch, Anne B., *1:* 221